Religion
and the
Racist Right

Michael Barkun

REVISED EDITION

The University of North Carolina Press | Chapel Hill and London

Religion and the Racist Right

The

Origins

of the

Christian

Identity

Movement

The paper in this book meets
the guidelines for permanence
and durability of the Committee
on Production Guidelines for
Book Longevity of the Council
on Library Resources.

Library of Congress
Cataloging-in-Publication Data
Barkun, Michael.
Religion and the racist right :
the origins of the Christian Identity
movement / Michael Barkun. —
Rev. ed.
p.   cm.
Includes bibliographical references
and index.
ISBN 0-8078-2328-7 (cloth: alk. paper) —
ISBN 0-8078-4638-4 (pbk.: alk. paper)
1. White supremacy movements —
United States — History.   2. Anglo-
Israelism — United States — History.
3. United States — Race relations.
I. Title.
E184.A1B245   1997   96-28347
320.5'6 — dc20   CIP

01 00 99 98 97   5 4 3 2 1

Contents

Preface to the Revised Edition

Although less than three years have passed since this work was first published, a revised edition is already necessary. In the interim, the hermetic subculture of the radical right has lost much of its isolation. Its current notoriety was thrust upon it in April 1995 by the Oklahoma City bombing. At the same time, the rise of the militias and the spread of belief in a New World Order conspiracy have taken the radical right's worldview at least part way into mainstream American politics.

The full text of the original edition appears here unchanged, including the conclusion, chapter 12. I have had no reason to alter my original views concerning Identity's importance and its capacity for rapid transformation. However, the bombing and the sudden national awareness of the radical right make the inclusion of a new concluding chapter imperative. The new material in chapter 13, "Epilogue: Oklahoma City and the Rise of the Militias," extends the themes discussed in the first edition by taking the story up to mid-1996. The first half of the 1990s saw not only the Oklahoma City bombing but also a surge of paramilitary organizing, a rising fear of New World Order plots, and an obsessive concern for movement martyrs, including those who died at Waco, Texas.

In hindsight, the original text survived these events remarkably well. However, subsequent research has shed new light on three earlier points that are worth noting here. In chapter 4, I suggested but was unable to document the existence of early links between Christian Identity and American neo-Nazis. A forthcoming biography of George Lincoln Rockwell by Frederick J. Simonelli will amply describe the connection. Research underway in Canada suggests that it will soon be possible to identify the pseudonymous author of the apocalyptic novel *When?* discussed in chapters 4, 7, and 8. Finally, chapter 10 minimized the likelihood that Reconstructionist theology had influenced Identity. However, Jeffrey Kaplan has drawn my attention to the recent impact of Reconstructionist ideas on Dan Gayman and other Identity figures.

Preliminary versions of some of the ideas in chapter 13 were first presented in 1995 at the annual meeting of the American Academy of Religion and at a conference on racism and violence sponsored by the Harry Frank Guggenheim Foundation. I am grateful to those who responded to these presentations. I am also appreciative of the many individuals who shared research materials with me, although here, as in the first edition, I alone am responsible for the use to which the materials have been put. I wish particularly to thank A. Forrester Barker, Martin Durham, Michael Reynolds of the Southern Poverty Law Center, and Christine Xaver.

Preface

The strange story of the Christian Identity movement unfolds in a subculture few know and in which fewer still participate, where deviant religion, spurious scholarship, and radical politics intersect. I first became aware of it in the mid-1980s when, like many other Americans, I was struck by dramatic media accounts of new right-wing extremist movements. They had unfamiliar names, such as Aryan Nations, the Order, and Posse Comitatus, and they were often linked with episodes of violence—the killing of federal marshals, the assassination of a Denver radio personality, a daring armored-car robbery. Journalists tended to linger over the details of these episodes without paying much attention to the ideology of those involved in them. When they did talk about beliefs, the descriptions were as intriguing as they were mystifying. This new radical right, the media sometimes suggested, was connected in some distant way with a nineteenth-century religious movement called "British-Israelism."[1]

I was vaguely aware of British-Israelism, but some casual research on it only deepened the mystery about the new radical right. British-Israelism was a small but vigorous movement in Victorian English Protestant circles that claimed the British were the descendants of the ten "lost tribes" of Israel. It was a curious notion, typical perhaps of the English love for eccentricity, but unfortunately, knowing what British-Israelism was shed little light on the activities of contemporary American rightists.

In the first place, there was no ready explanation for the presumed connection between a marginal religious movement in nineteenth-century Britain and a fringe political movement in late twentieth-century America. If the two did share ideas, how had the ideas crossed the Atlantic? In addition, as I delved further into British-Israelism, I found that it had beliefs about Jews quite different from those held on the radical right. Where right-wing groups typically attributed the world's evils to a Jewish conspiracy, British-Israelism regarded Jews as brother Israelites, the descendants of different but related tribes. How had a philo-Semitic movement engendered groups that were fiercely anti-Semitic? Finally, British-Israelites were staunch defenders of the political status quo. They gloried in England's triumphs and attributed the wisdom of its political institutions to the Israelite heritage, which they believed they had discovered. However, even a cursory examination of press accounts in the 1980s revealed American groups that challenged the very legitimacy of the federal government. What accounted for the metamorphosis?

In seeking answers, I was not helped by the language of news reports, for the media habitually classified right-wing groups under two conventional rubrics, "neo-Nazi" or "white supremacist." Like other stereotypes, these contained a germ of truth. Many of the groups did in fact express admiration for Hitler and the Nazis, and some went beyond that to employ emblems and uniforms that were either Nazi or designed to summon up Nazi associations. Similarly, the groups did believe whites (or, as they preferred to put it, "Aryans") were superior to other races in intellectual and spiritual endowments. The difficulty was not that such categories were untrue but that they were unhelpful. They revealed little about beliefs other than suggesting some fairly obvious sympathies and provided no clues whatever to links with the British-Israelites.

The links indeed existed, as the chapters that follow make clear. Beyond their sympathies for Nazism or their commitment to white supremacy, many on the extreme right are also deeply committed to a distinctive religious position known most often as "Christian Identity." It is as strange as it is unstudied. Few Americans have heard of it, and few scholars have examined it. Yet its elaborate system of religious ideas often provides the driving force for the political agenda of the radical right. It also holds the answers to the questions raised above, for at a point in the recent past, Christian Identity split off from British-Israelism. This book seeks to demonstrate the continuities connecting the two, as well as the discontinuities dividing them.

Christian Identity as a religious orientation is virtually unknown. Its texts are not studied in universities. Its books and magazines are not available in bookstores. It goes unmentioned in all but the most encyclopedic accounts of American religion. No one is sure how many believe in it. It is not organized as a denomination, so that no central organization can be consulted for membership statistics. Made up of numerous small churches, Bible study groups, and Identity-oriented political organizations, it is too fragmented to permit anything but rough estimates. These cover a wide range—from two thousand to over fifty thousand—but the order of magnitude suggests a movement that claims the allegiance of only the tiniest fraction of the American population. So small a group would have little claim on our attention but for the fact that Christian Identity has created the most virulently anti-Semitic belief system ever to arise in the United States and that some of its believers are committed to the eradication of American political institutions.

Christian Identity is built around three key beliefs. First, Identity believes that white "Aryans" are descendants of the biblical tribes of Israel and thus are on earth to do God's work. Second, Identity believes that Jews are not only wholly unconnected to the Israelites, but are the very children of the Devil, the literal biological offspring of a sexual dalliance between Satan and Eve in the Garden of Eden. Third, Identity believes the world is on the verge of the final, apocalyptic struggle between good and evil, in which the Aryans must do battle with the Jewish conspiracy and its allies so that the world can be redeemed. By any criteria, these are beliefs that place Identity at the farthest margins of American religion, but they also suggest its potential political volatility.

This book attempts to answer the questions of where Christian Identity came from, how it was related to British-Israelism, and how the two separated. While I begin the story of Identity with its nineteenth-century ancestry, this is not a complete history of Anglo-Israelism, a subject that deserves a volume of its own. Rather, I concentrate on those aspects of British-Israelism that led to Christian Identity. Other offshoots of the movement, unrelated to Christian Identity, such as Herbert W. Armstrong's Worldwide Church of God, have been omitted or treated in summary fashion.

This inquiry proceeds on two levels, looking first at the visible manifestations of Identity—the organizations, writings, and leading figures—and then at the ideas themselves. We begin with the earliest hints of British-Israelism in the seventeenth century, move through the origin and consolidation of British-Israelism as a social movement in the second half of the nineteenth century, and trace its diffusion from Britain to America. As we move through the story of the American branch of the movement, three figures dominate: C. A. L. Totten, the military-science instructor at Yale who became the movement's first major figure in America; Howard Rand, the dour New England lawyer whose Anglo-Saxon Federation of America gave British-Israelism a firm foothold during the Depression; and Rand's colleague, William J. Cameron, editor and publicist for Henry Ford who linked the American branch with anti-Semitism. The generation that followed took the American brand of British-Israelism that Rand and Cameron had built and transformed it into Christian Identity. Central to this transformation was a cadre of West Coast preachers, most in southern California and all in the orbit of the leading ultra-right-wing figure of the 1940s and 1950s, Gerald L. K. Smith.

But to tell the story solely in terms of organizations and personalities is to leave much unanswered, for the beliefs that separate Christian Identity from British-Israelism lie so far outside even traditional right-wing discourse that they cannot be explained merely in terms of organizational connections. In particular, the belief that Jews are the offspring of Satan is sui generis on the American right. Where did it come from? As we shall see when we move to the beliefs Identity holds, it did not arise suddenly or in a vacuum. Rather, it was gradually pieced together out of strange fragments from religion, fringe scholarship, and the occult, until a final synthesis was achieved after World War II.

Identity doctrine drives a significant amount of extreme right-wing political activity, ranging from the lawful to the violent. It was a subsidiary factor in David Duke's rise, and it was a major force in a string of violent incidents connected with the Order, the Posse Comitatus, and the Covenant, Sword and Arm of the Lord—all groups that combined paramilitary organization with a sense of living in a climactic, apocalyptic time.

Curiously, the subject has never found much favor among scholars. Although Hollywood has recycled elements of it (e.g., *Betrayed*, Costa-Gavras's film based very loosely on the story of the Order), and journalists have been quick to recognize a good story, academics have had little to say. To date, only one work—James Aho's fine study of rightists in Idaho—has provided a sustained discussion of Identity. The journalistic accounts of the extreme right, often colorful and detailed, usually manage to garble its religious aspects. Thus an otherwise useful book on the Order projects Identity anti-Semitism back into the writings of the nineteenth-century British-Israelite Edward Hine, who, as it happens, was a *philo*-Semite.[2]

As Paul Boyer points out, scholarly disdain may also be seen in the failure of academics to explore the prophecy beliefs that pervade evangelical Protestantism, a far more extensive religious phenomenon. The much smaller number of Identity believers might seem to explain the absence of research, but since Christian Identity has become the dominant religious orientation on the extreme right, the failure to examine it is in fact difficult to justify. There are, however, two explanations. First, despite the rise in political militancy of many religious groups in the last twenty years, some scholars continue to regard religion as politically irrelevant. The long-standing belief among social scientists that secularization is an irresistible force dies hard, even in the face of a worldwide resurgence of Fundamentalist groups. Many still find it difficult to accord religious beliefs a significant place among determinants of political behavior. Second, that tendency is exacerbated in the case of Identity by the nature of its beliefs. They are bizarre and seemingly unconnected to recognizable forms of American religious expression. They are also often distasteful, particularly when they address the status of Jews and nonwhites. A movement whose beliefs are both strange and repugnant is difficult for many observers to take seriously, and because they cannot take it seriously, they conclude that it is unimportant.[3]

Unfortunately, odd and repellent belief systems can be important, regardless of what academics may think, if their believers take them seriously and act upon them. The "respectability" of a system of ideas is not a particularly useful test for determining whether it is worthy of study. To close the door on a subject because it is distasteful is to pretend a part of the world does not exist and hence to leave open the possibility of facing unpleasant surprises in the future. The present work seeks to take Identity beliefs seriously, not because I agree with them (quite the contrary) but because of my conviction that they are an important and understudied phenomenon that we ignore at our peril. Hence, I have for the most part sought to suspend my personal views in order to reconstruct as accurately as possible the movement's story.

Because Christian Identity has always been organizationally fragmented, the task of capturing its belief system is unusually difficult. Rivalries among leaders, organizational splits, and the extinction of old and the creation of new groups all make the "mapping" of Identity a frustrating undertaking. My view of this elusive terrain, therefore, may differ from that of others by virtue of the groups upon which I have focused and the time period I have emphasized. Thus, particularly in chapters 6, 9, 10, and 11, I have tried to provide a picture of where Identity theology and politics stood in the mid- and late 1980s, a period defined by the emergence and suppression of the armed group known as the Order.

Two points of style require clarification. The first concerns the use of the word *identity*. It in fact appears early in the literature of British-Israelism as shorthand for the belief in the Israelite descent of the British peoples, who could now become aware of their true identity. Notwithstanding this early usage, I have chosen to limit my employment of the term (always capitalized) to references concerning the contemporary Christian Identity movement, and have avoided employing it in its original, nineteenth-century sense in order to avoid confusion. This practice becomes problematic only for a brief transitional period, in which British-Israelism in America was metamorphosing into Christian Identity, roughly from the early 1930s until shortly after World War II. It is difficult to know what to call the movement at this point, since it still retained significant elements of traditional British-Israelism while becoming hospitable to new and characteristically Identity motifs. I have sometimes tried to finesse this problem with the term "proto-Identity."

The other matter of style concerns citation of sources. In order to avoid the proliferation of notes, I have limited them to the ends of paragraphs. The order in which sources are listed in each note parallels, therefore, the order in which they were employed in the paragraph.

Given the esoteric and ephemeral character of much of the material examined here, I owe special debts of gratitude to the libraries and archival collections that welcomed me. The Library of the British-Israel-World Federation in London extended warm hospitality to me at both their present location in Putney and their former offices at Buckingham Gate. I am grateful to the federation's staff and especially to its secretary, A. E. Gibb. I was also privileged to be able to draw on the extraordinary American Religions Collection at the University of California, Santa Barbara, which covers not only the religious mainstream but also the kinds of exotic tributaries dealt with here. J. Gordon Melton, who assembled the collection, was a gracious and informed guide to its contents. The Wilcox Collection of Contemporary Political Movements at the University of Kansas, the premier collection of right-wing literature in the United States, was of enormous value, and the working conditions provided at the Spencer Research Library could scarcely have been more conducive. I am grateful to Becky Schulte and Sheryl Williams of the Spencer Library and to the collection's donor, Laird Wilcox.

A number of other repositories offered generous aid and access. I wish to express my appreciation to the Anti-Defamation League of B'nai B'rith, and to Gail Gans of the league staff; to the Ford Motor Company Archives in Dearborn, and to Jeanine W. Head, archivist; to the Bentley Historical Library at the University of Michigan; to the Library of Congress; and to the interlibrary loan staff of Bird Library at Syracuse University, my own institution.

John Werly generously shared with me his substantial holdings on and wide knowledge of William Dudley Pelley and the Silver Shirts. Many individuals also provided me with a variety of published and unpublished materials, suggestions, and information not part of the public record. While there are too many to list fully, I wish particularly to acknowledge the assistance of the following: Bruce Barron, Mario DePillis, Floyd Cochran, David R. Elliott, William C. Hiss, Glen Jeansonne, Jeffrey Kaplan, Russell Osmond, Richard V. Pierard, Mrs. Wesley Swift, Eckard Toy, and Laird Wilcox. James Aho and Paul Boyer read the entire manuscript, and I benefited greatly from their comments. I also want to express my special appreciation to Krisan Evenson for her labors in preparing the manuscript for publication.

I also wish to gratefully acknowledge the support I received from Syracuse

University through the Appleby-Mosher Fund of the Maxwell School, the Senate Research Fund, and the Program on the Analysis and Resolution of Conflict.

As in all I have written, my wife, Janet, has been a marvelously acute and perceptive critic.

Part One

The Emergence of Christian Identity

In one sense, Christian Identity is barely half a century old. Its doctrinal basis was established after World War II by a network of independent preachers and writers. It passed rapidly from their hands into a variety of extreme right-wing political movements preoccupied with fears of racial mixing and Jewish conspiracy. Through such organizations as the Aryan Nations and Ku Klux Klan groups, Christian Identity had by the 1970s become, if not white supremacist orthodoxy, at least its most important religious tendency.

In order to understand how Christian Identity developed, the story must be pushed farther back, for Identity's antecedents lay in England, not in America, and in the nineteenth century, not the twentieth. Identity is an outgrowth of what was itself a strange development in religious history, known variously as British-Israelism or Anglo-Israelism (the terms will be employed synonymously here). Although Christian Identity eventually made major changes in British-Israel doctrine, it remains sufficiently related to Anglo-Israelism so that the one cannot be understood without first knowing about the other. Hence, this chapter traces the beginnings of Anglo-Israelism, its key doctrinal concerns, and its growth into a social movement during the late nineteenth century. Succeeding chapters of part I will trace the passage of British-Israel ideas to America; the creation of an American movement by Howard Rand during the 1920s and 1930s; the gradual association of Anglo-Israelism in America with anti-Semitism during the Depression years; and the eventual separation of the American movement from its British roots, when, during the post–World War II years, an autonomous and increasingly strident Christian Identity began to develop in California. This narrative focuses upon three key figures: Howard

1

The Origins of British-Israelism

Rand, whose indefatigable organizing created British-Israel outposts throughout the country during the Depression; his colleague, William J. Cameron, the Ford Motor Company executive who coordinated and largely wrote the notorious anti-Semitic tracts published under Henry Ford's auspices; and Wesley Swift, the California preacher, evangelist, and associate of Gerald L. K. Smith, who, more than anyone else, was responsible for promulgating Identity in the form we know it today.

Part II examines the central ideas in Identity's religious system—its millenarian thrust, its sense of living in the "Last Days," and, particularly, its bizarre theology of anti-Semitism. For more than anything else, Identity has been distinguished from other forms of conservative Protestantism and right-wing politics by its view of the Jews. In the view of Identity, the Jews are the literal biological offspring of Satan, the descendants of Satan's sexual seduction of Eve in the Garden of Eden. This demonization of the Jews—almost without precedent in even the most overheated forms of anti-Semitism—did not emerge from a vacuum. It was instead the result of a synthesis of religious and occult ideas, some centuries old and all marginal. Part II is largely given over to identifying the elements of this synthesis and reconstructing the process by which they were combined.

Part III examines the political consequences and implications of Identity. Identity believers have had two different orientations toward the political system. Some have sought to remain within it, either through the electoral system (for example, the Identity circles around David Duke) or by minimizing their contacts with nonbelievers (the so-called survivalists). A smaller but more widely noted segment of Identity has rejected the possibility of working within the system, seeking instead to overthrow American political institutions (the agenda of such guerrilla groups as the Order) or advancing proposals for the territorial separation of a "white nation," a goal associated with the leader of Aryan Nations, Richard Girnt Butler.

Before we can understand either Identity's theology or its politics, we must first seek its origins, and these lie in the convoluted history of British-Israelism itself.

The Distant Origins of British-Israelism

Just as there is dispute about the origins of Christian Identity, so controversy surrounds the beginnings of its Anglo-Israel parent. British-Israelism, in the most general terms, refers to the belief that the British are lineal descendants of the "ten lost tribes" of Israel. This revisionist view of history did not become the basis for an organized movement until the second half of the nineteenth century. But long before that, there had been suggestions that the British and the biblical Israelites possessed some special affinity for one another. This linkage exerted particular force during the Puritan ascendancy in the mid-1600s, when anticipation of an imminent millennium was strong. Such Puritan sectarians as John Robins and Thomas Tany argued that Britain would play a central role in returning the Jews to Palestine, so that the rest of the millenarian scenario could be fulfilled. In like manner, Puritans in the American colonies saw themselves as a "New Israel" in the wilderness, confronting it for a providential purpose just as the original Israelites confronted the wilderness of Sinai after the Exodus. Two related but distinguishable tendencies were thus at work: either Britain as a nation was specially chosen by God to help realize the divine design in human history, or some spiritually purified portion of it was destined to take on this role.[1]

Nonetheless, this conviction of chosenness was based upon analogy, not upon the presumption of a direct *biological* link between England and the biblical tribes. Indeed, as far as seventeenth-century millenarians were concerned, the descendants of the Israelites were either their Jewish contemporaries or the fabled lost tribes, believed to be hidden somewhere in the fastness of Asia. As the seventeenth century progressed, the belief grew that the tribes would soon reemerge into the light of history, a development appropriate to the "Last Days." Indeed, by 1665 Europe was swept by reports that this reappearance by the lost tribes had already begun, although its locale was variously reported to be Persia, the Arabian Desert, and the Sahara. These reports described a vast Jewish army moving westward, prepared to smite the Turk and, if need be, to enter Europe itself in order to wreak vengeance on anti-Semitic nations. Thus in November 1665, Robert Boulter of Aberdeen published a letter describing the army and one of its vessels: "There is Sixteen hundred thousand of them together in *Arabia*, and . . . there came into *Europe* Sixty Thousand more; as likewise . . . they have had Encounters with the *Turks*, and slain great numbers of them. . . . As for their Ship, . . . in the sails was this Inscription in fair Red Characters THESE ARE OF THE TEN TRIBES OF ISRAEL." A similar letter, originating on the Continent, was published in London in February 1666. Millenarians were attracted to the reports because they believed that the Second Coming and the subsequent millennium could not occur until the Turks were defeated and the Jews regathered in Palestine, where they would accept Christ at the appropriate eschatological moment. As Gershom Scholem has demonstrated, this flurry of rumors in 1665–66 represented much-distorted reactions to the appearance in the Levant of the Jewish false messiah, Sabbatai Zevi. Neither Zevi nor his prophet, Nathan of Gaza, commanded an army, of course, let alone could bring the lost tribes from Tartary, but news of Zevi's messianic pretensions and their electrifying effect on Jewish communities quickly fused with existing legends of the hidden tribes.[2]

The English, absorbed in considerations of the Last Days, consequently found the fate of the Jews an absorbing topic. They also saw in it momentous implications for Christian hopes, and they often regarded England as the ideal instrument for realizing those hopes by assisting Jews in their longing for Palestine. They did not, however, regard themselves as part of Israel, except in the common Christian theological sense that the church was the "New Israel," formed on the basis of a new covenant.

The first indisputably British-Israel figure about whom anything substantial is known appeared much later. He was Richard Brothers (1757–1824), a retired naval officer who began having millenarian visions in 1791. About 1793, he concluded that he had a divine mission to lead the Jews back to Palestine, an idea not unlike those that had circulated among the Puritans in the preceding century. Brothers, however, differed by adding two other ideas. First, he decided that he himself was a descendant of the House of David; and, second, that most Jews were hidden among existing European, and particularly British, peoples, unaware of their exalted biblical lineage. This idea of a "hidden Israel" that believed itself Gentile, ignorant of its true biological origins, marks the initial appearance of what was to become British-Israelism's central motif. Brothers, however, was in no position to translate his beliefs into a social movement, in part because of his disinterest in organizational work, but more significantly because of his escalating personal eccentricity. His behavior become more and more bizarre with his increasing royal pretensions. In the end, Davidic scion or not, he was declared insane and institutionalized from 1795 until 1806. His followers maintained their faith for a time, but after Brothers's release, they drifted away, in part disillusioned, in part stricken with acute social embarrassment. Consequently, although Brothers has some claim to being the first British-Israelite, and is so identified in some accounts, the movement certainly did not begin with him, for by the time of his death, he was a lonely figure.[3]

John Wilson, the First British-Israelite

The British-Israel *movement*, as opposed to the British-Israel *idea*, begins more than a generation after Brothers with the writings of John Wilson (?–1871).

The self-educated son of a radical Irish weaver, Wilson lectured tirelessly in Ireland and England, advancing his claim to have discovered the hidden origins of the nations of northern Europe. His central work, *Lectures on Our Israelitish Origin*, appeared in 1840 and ran through five editions, the last published posthumously in 1876. This work, together with Wilson's lectures and the periodicals he edited, brought the British-Israel message to a large middle-class audience. The *Lectures* depended less on the interpretation of biblical prophecy than on Wilson's attempt to demonstrate empirically that the lost tribes had in fact migrated from the Near East to Europe. Like many writers after him, one of his favorite techniques was to look for words in different languages that sounded the same, assuming, usually erroneously, that if the sounds were similar, then the languages and their speakers had to be connected. Since similar sounds often crop up in otherwise unrelated languages, they allowed Wilson to claim, and to believe, that he had proved that "many of our most common [English] words and names of familiar objects are almost pure Hebrew." He was equally confident that similarities in social institutions were the result of an Israelite legacy directly imported by the migrating tribes themselves, whom he deemed responsible for everything good and British, from limited monarchy to trial by jury. Every strand of evidence seemed to lead Wilson to his conclusion that the search "for the Lost Sheep of the House of Israel" must necessarily end "in the NORTH-WEST—in our own part of the world."[4]

If the British were Israelites, then what of the Jews? Wilson never went so far as to deny the Jews a place in "All-Israel," but he saw nothing to suggest that they held a religious status equal to their newly discovered northern European brethren. In the first place, Wilson and all his successors drew a sharp distinction between the southern kingdom of Judah, from which Jews were deemed to have sprung, and the northern kingdom of Israel, the ancestors of the British and other European peoples. Hence, Jews bore only those divine promises God had given to the few tribes that dwelt in Judah, while the bulk of the prophecies were inherited by descendants of the tribes that dwelt in Israel—preeminently the tribe of Ephraim, which populated the British Isles. In addition, Wilson was skeptical of Jewish claims to undiluted descent from biblical ancestors. Patterns of intermarriage, he maintained, had intermixed Judah's descendants with other, spiritually inferior peoples: "ISRAEL, who were taken out of the land, cannot be more lost among the heathen than were the people called 'Jews' who remained in it," for the Jews, having mingled with "the worst of the Gentiles," had inherited the Gentiles' curse, which could be lifted only with the acceptance of Jesus. Thus Wilson's attitude toward the

Jews was at once fraternal and patronizing. They were erring brothers who needed to be shown the true path to salvation by the spiritually more advanced Israel/Britain, now made aware of its true Identity.[5]

Wilson was not, however, concerned only with the British. He found manifestations of Israel in a range of mostly northern European peoples, "not only among the Germans and their Anglo-Saxon offspring, but also in Italy, and especially in France and Switzerland," as well as in Scandinavia. Britain retained a place of spiritual preeminence, since the British were descendants of the tribe of Ephraim, one of Joseph's sons. Jacob's birthright blessing, which originally had gone to Reuben, was taken from him and transferred to Ephraim and his brother, Manasseh, but Jacob "set Ephraim before Manasseh" (1 Chron. 5:1; Gen. 48:19, 20). Although other peoples might descend from sons of Jacob, it was the descendants of these "adoptive sons," his grandsons, who would lead the way; and since Britain was deemed to flow from the loins of Ephraim, its position was assured. Nonetheless, in Wilson's view, the British needed to recognize their kinship with Germanic peoples across the Channel, a contentious point, for later Anglo-Israel writers were far less willing to share Britain's divine vocation. Wilson's flirtation with "Teutonism" in fact reflected a broader British fascination with Germanic prehistory.[6]

The linkage Wilson made between the British and other Teutonic peoples was reinforced by a number of tendencies in English political thought and intellectual life. There was, in the first place, the prevalent belief that a natural democracy had been practiced by the unspoiled Anglo-Saxon peoples, which presumably developed organically out of their tribal life in Germany and England. This, in turn, was contrasted with the "Norman yoke," the authoritarian and inegalitarian practices that the Norman invaders imposed upon these natural democrats they conquered in 1066. To link England with Germanic peoples was to return to pre-Norman roots and, by implication, to reinvigorate the indigenous democratic inheritance. At a scholarly level, English intellectuals were drawn to the efforts of German philologists who sought to trace the English and German languages to a common Indo-European origin, part of the search for the Aryans from whom both languages were presumed to have sprung. Germanic peoples were therefore deemed to be linked by shared democratic propensities, language, and, ultimately, common descent. By the period 1815–40, which is to say during the time when John Wilson was formulating his version of British-Israelism, these ideas began to take on a more explicitly racial tone. In the hands of Thomas Carlyle and others, links among Anglo-Saxon peoples were increasingly associated with claims to racial superiority. The imperial expansion of England and the settlement of the American West suggested that the Anglo-Saxons had a special destiny to prevail over lesser breeds. Wilson's assertion that the Anglo-Saxons and other Germanic peoples were the very offspring of Israel whom God addressed in Scripture fit in a seemingly natural way with these ambient notions about political institutions, linguistics, and race.[7]

Edward Hine and the Beginnings of a Social Movement

Wilson's book was widely noted, and he worked assiduously to promulgate his ideas from the lecture platform, yet at the time of his death—1871—the task of turning his ideas into a social movement was just beginning. The beginning of British-Israel organizing, however, demonstrated the vulnerability of Wilson's emphasis upon the common destiny of the Germanic peoples, for by the 1870s, Germany was politically unified, economically thriving, and aggressively seeking its "place in the sun." It had, in a word, emerged as Great Britain's chief rival in Europe. At the same time that German and British interests were coming into more frequent conflict, the British Empire continued to grow. And the Empire was taken to be a sign of God's special favor, for had not God promised that Ephraim would become "a company of nations"? Thus, the British-Israelites were not disposed to sacrifice England's imperial mission to Germany at a time when they were experiencing a growing sense of British uniqueness. By the latter decades of the nineteenth century, the Teutonist position fell into increasing disfavor, although, as we shall see, contemporary Christian Identity believers enamored of Hitler's Germany eventually revived it. But insofar as the early British-Israel movement itself was concerned, by the 1870s and 1880s, it felt a pressing need to revise Wilson in order to make the Israelite heritage a more exclusively British concern.[8]

In the 1870s, British-Israel associations began to form in London and elsewhere in England. The Anglo-Ephraim Association continued to advance the Teutonist position, while the Anglo-Israel Association was set up to combat Teutonism. Given political trends, it was inevitable that the anti-Teutonists would prevail, and in 1878 the Anglo-Israel Association absorbed its Anglo-Ephraim rival. By 1886, the association, based in London, boasted twenty-seven affiliated groups throughout the country.

The principal exponent of the anti-Teutonist view was a self-proclaimed disciple of Wilson's, Edward Hine (1825–91), whose indefatigable propagandizing consolidated the movement in England and North America. Hine claimed to have been converted to British-Israelism in 1840 when, as a youth of fifteen, he heard John Wilson lecture. "He [Wilson] lodged a thought in my mind which has lived there ever since," Hine recalled. Despite the powerful impression Wilson made, Hine in fact neither published nor spoke publicly about British-Israelism for nearly thirty years, during which he passed from one modest job to another, all the while privately cultivating the religious interest Wilson had stimulated.[9]

Hine was an avid and effective publicist for the cause, but he proved to be a weak and ineffectual organizer. He gave his first public lecture in 1869, wrote his first pamphlet in 1870, and founded his first magazine in 1873. Tireless though he was in reaching out to new audiences, he had little stomach for the drudgery of organizational work. As Hine reflected, wrote, and spoke, he began to deviate from Wilson's views and promulgated an increasingly Anglocentric doctrine. His message eventually found its organizational instrument in a retired civil servant, Edward Wheeler Bird. Although in the byzantine politics of Anglo-Israelism Hine and Bird became adversaries, Bird in fact supplied the organizational vehicles for Hine's message. Bird's Metropolitan Anglo-Israel Association and his magazine, *Banner of Israel*, were the instruments to rout the Teutonists and define a new mainstream Anglo-Israelism. Hine, despite his distaste for organizational work, could not bear to have institutions outside his control, and he thus saw in Bird a rival rather than an ally. When Hine's attempts to create his own organization, the British-Israel Identity Corporation, and his own magazine failed, he returned to his true métier as missionary and pamphleteer. The movement in England was now centered upon the institutions Bird created, and Hine set off seeking new audiences to woo in North America, where we shall pick up his career in the next chapter.[10]

Whatever Hine lacked as an organizer, he more than made up for it in his ability to reshape and articulate doctrine. To an English public increasingly suspicious of Germany, Wilson's notion that both England and Germany partook of the Israelite inheritance was distasteful. A public accustomed to the seemingly limitless growth of British wealth, power, and prestige were attracted to the notion that their nation's successes were the result of God's will, not luck or brute force. Hine satisfied their appetites.

Hine took strong exception to Wilson's inclusion of all the Teutonic peoples within the newly discovered Israel, but his disagreements were theological rather than political. "The main point of my differing with the late Mr. John Wilson," he wrote in 1885, " . . . is that he sought to identify all the Modern Teutonic Nations as parts of Israel, whereas I stoutly maintain that to accept this view would lead us to terrible inconveniences and calamities." The "inconveniences and calamities" Hine had in mind concerned how biblical prophecies could be fulfilled if "Israel" were parceled out among a large number of nations. As far as Hine was concerned, fulfillment required that "the whole Ten Tribes . . . become consolidated in an Island Nation." For Wilson it was enough that England descended from the tribe of Ephraim, but in Hine's reading of Scripture, "the term Ephraim is synonymous with Israel, and embodies the Ten Tribes as a consolidated people." Only the "thirteenth tribe," Manasseh, lay outside, and British-Israelites in time came to identify it with the United States, so that between them, Britain and the United States constituted all of Israel that was not Jewish.[11]

Hine did more than merely deprive the Teutons of their Israelite status; he placed them in the enemy camp. That is to say he argued that just as the ten tribes of Israel had been "lost," so too had Assyria, and the modern-day Assyrians were none other than the Germans. By implication, therefore, just as Israel and Assyria had fought in the biblical past, so Britain and Germany, their latter-day descendants, were destined to continue the struggle, this time on terms more favorable to Israel.[12]

Hine also parted company with Wilson's view of the Jewish people. While Wilson acknowledged their part in "All-Israel," he emphasized their contaminating intermarriages with the idolatrous peoples around them. Hine, on the other hand, insisted on elevating the Jews' position. While they were subordinated to the ten tribes, they nonetheless remained a valued and important part of "All-Israel," which was made up of the House of Israel and the House of Judah. The House of Judah was comprised of the tribes of Judah and Levi, and "these are the Jews of the present day." Unlike the ten tribes, they were never "lost," so that they might be a reminder of the Jews' rejection of Jesus' messiahship. The House of Judah had once included the tribe of Benjamin as well, Hine went on, but Benjamin had separated from Judah and had become part of the House of Israel, "so that Benjamin is not now with the Jews." Consequently, in a comment often repeated in British-Israel literature, "the Jews are of Israel, but Israel is not of Judah"; "the people of the Ten Tribes were never Jews." The reuniting of All-Israel, inevitable in the Last Days, would require that the present-day ten tribes, that is, the British, come together with the descendants of the remaining tribes, that is, the Jews. A significant part of British-Israel eschatology was to be the common enterprise of Anglo-Jewish resettlement of Palestine as essential to the fulfillment of biblical prophecy.[13]

While John Wilson continued to enjoy respect as Anglo-Israelism's founder, Hine's version, not Wilson's, prevailed. Nonetheless, despite its influence, even Hine's reformulation never amounted to an orthodoxy; British-Israelism never organized as a sect, never required that its adherents break their existing denominational affiliations, and never developed machinery to authoritatively define doctrine and punish deviation. Consequently, from time to time other ideas became engrafted onto Hine's. The most important and improbable of these additions was "pyramidism," the belief that great religious truths were incorporated into the structure and dimensions of the Great Pyramid of Cheops.

At first glance, the only connection between pyramidism and British-Israelism is the fact that both represent "rejected knowledge," ideas outside the academy's definition of respectable knowledge. In fact, their affinity goes far beyond their common pariah status. In the first place, English pyramid literature began to appear at the same time as the publications of Wilson and his followers and therefore was known and available to early generations of Anglo-Israelites. Second, mathematical analysis of the Great Pyramid's dimensions seemed to reveal extraordinary and unexpected numerical relationships. This in turn led pyramidologists to conclude, as a colonialist mentality might dictate, that the ancient Egyptians were too primitive to have created so sophisticated a structure. And, indeed, the more pyramid students experimented with dimensions, the more relationships they were able to find—with pi, with astronomical constants, and with dimensions of the earth. This led to an additional conclusion: not only were the Egyptians incapable of such a feat, but a building incorporating such subtle mathematical relationships must have a purpose beyond merely serving as a pharaoh's resting place. Third, both the pyramidologists and the British-Israelites were engaged in constructing revisionist accounts of the history of the ancient world and consequently were drawn together by a common disposition to question conventional scholarly views. Once the pyramid writers disposed of the Egyptians as the architects, they were prepared to entertain other possibilities, notably that the pyramid had been designed by some biblical figure endowed with divine wisdom. The most common candidates were hazy, prepatriarchal figures, such as Enoch, Noah, and Job. If the structure was not primarily a tomb, what was its function? If a biblical figure had designed it, then, the argument went, its purpose must be related to scriptural truths. Although pyramidologists often argued bitterly with one another about interpretations of the measurements, they agreed that in some way the structure "encoded" biblical truths and had been placed in the world by God to await a generation (their own, of course) sufficiently advanced to understand it and sufficiently close to the Final Days to give the message special significance.

Pyramidism began with the writings of John Taylor (1781–1864), who published *The Great Pyramid* in 1859, when Wilson's British-Israel book was enjoying great attention. In addition to the usual mathematical manipulations, Taylor also believed he had proven that the pyramid was constructed on the English inch-based measurement system. This was a boon to English critics of the metric system, affronted that the hated French would challenge British tradition. It also led to the more fanciful notion that whoever had constructed the pyramid (Taylor's candidate was Noah) later traveled to England, bringing his measurement system with him.[14]

Taylor's work was continued and integrated into British-Israelism by a more substantial figure, C. Piazzi Smyth (1819–1900), the royal astronomer of Scotland. Piazzi Smyth, notwithstanding his scientific background, advanced a theological rather than simply a mathematical theory of the pyramid. If the Great Pyramid had been built by Adam's descendants, he reasoned, it must have been for some divine purpose: "It is the crowning glory of the Great Pyramid to have been prepared by Divine inspiration in the beginning of the world, so as to be now capable of standing up a more than mortal witness to these latter days, both of there being a finite-appointed time for the First, and now, at last a close approaching of the exceeding glories of the Second Coming—though seen through times of trouble." Those who fathered the Israelites had thus built this structure using their own superior measurement system, which later appeared in England after the dispersion of the tribes, and the building that they had built was intended to be read by the present generation as a confirmation and expression of prophecy.[15]

The pyramid functioned for many British-Israelites as a gigantic prophetic clock, in which sacred history was displayed by the length and configuration of its internal passageways. In this system, one "pyramid inch" (which deviated one one-thousandth from the British inch) equaled one year. This equipped British-Israelism with a mechanism familiar to other millenarians, a system of date setting, by which the proximity of apocalyptic events could be precisely ascertained. In the early twentieth century, when this literature reached its greatest influence, some in the movement's umbrella organization, the British-Israel World Federation, attempted to suppress date setting, on the ground that "the exact date of our Lord's appearing . . . is known to God . . . yet the precise time is hidden, and probably will be till the end." Nonetheless, a vast date-setting literature proliferated. Its central figure was a structural engineer, David Davidson, who, in his magnum opus, *The Great Pyramid: Its Divine Message*, and a stream of other books and articles, sought nothing less than a revision of the entire history of the ancient Near East—an enterprise that was to touch a surprising range of figures in both England and North America.[16]

A Movement without a Center

The inability of British-Israelism to suppress date setting was symptomatic of a doctrinal permissiveness present when the movement began and continuous throughout its history. Although sects developed that were influenced by it (notably, Herbert Armstrong's Worldwide Church of God), British-Israelism itself remained a movement without a head, steadfastly latitudinarian where matters of belief were concerned. While various umbrella organizations sought to define views on theological issues, they were neither able nor willing to read those with divergent views out of the movement. (Thus, Mrs. Sydney Bristowe, whose eccentric views about Cain, discussed in chapter 8, significantly influenced Christian Identity, was published by the Covenant Publishing Company, an arm of the British-Israel World Federation, even though the federation dissociated itself from her position.)

In keeping with this permissiveness, the movement avoided elaborate creedal statements, even in its widely used theological compendium, *British-Israel Truth*. In it, the influential Canadian Anglo-Israelite William Pascoe Goard rejected the notion that the volume defined orthodoxy: "The book does not profess to be a complete statement, neither is any part of it to be looked upon as an authoritative statement, but simply as a contribution of each writer from his own view point." Far from constituting a "handbook," the volume was based upon the belief "that the only handbook of British-Israel Truth is the Bible, by which all other contributions must be tested." That extended to such controversial but critical questions as the timing and sequence of millennial events such as the tribulation, rapture, and Second Coming. In light of such attitudes, it was scarcely surprising that when a British-Israel group was organized in Vancouver in 1909, its members resolved at their second meeting to be "strictly unsectarian."[17]

A contemporary academic student of British-Israelism calls it "an interdenominational fellowship," open to any Protestant believer, "a party which could operate within any of the Protestant denominations." Since "it does not claim to have a monopoly of the saving truth," believers can, and indeed are encouraged, to retain active church memberships. Since Anglo-Israelism does not claim to have a message necessary for salvation, it can do little more than exhort followers, assuming that those doing the exhorting can themselves agree on the limits to be placed on beliefs or actions.[18]

The movement in England appears to have peaked in the 1920s, when it had approximately five thousand members. While the number even then was exceedingly small, the movement was staunchly middle class, leavened by conspicuous numbers of aristocrats and high military officers, which assured it resources and visibility out of all proportion to its size. Its decline has been precipitous, and by the early 1990s there were barely seven hundred members, with virtually none of the titled individuals who once served as its patrons.[19]

Anglo-Israelism thus advanced a novel view of both the Bible and of ancient history. Its identification of the ancient Israelites with contemporary Britons gave its antiquarianism a peculiarly modern twist, for no one outdid British-Israelites in their support of the British Empire. They espoused their ideas while remaining in existing mainstream religious denominations, predominantly the Church of England. Since British-Israelism never presented itself as a road to salvation, it did not object to adherents retaining their traditional religious loyalties. Finally, by refusing to organize as a sect, British-Israelism never developed machinery to impose doctrinal discipline, so that it remained open not only to the disparate religious views of its members, but to a variety of eccentric ideas about the relationship between sacred and secular history that it was powerless to exclude. This openness later allowed Christian Identity to draw in equal measure from the traditional and the bizarre.

It was inevitable that British-Israelism would reach America. If Britain was Ephraim, the more blessed of Joseph's two sons, America sprung from his brother, Manasseh, with a critical though subordinate role to play in the economy of salvation. Although Anglo-Israelites sometimes had their organizational problems, they spread their teachings with vigor, and British-Israel literature soon began to find its way across the Atlantic. No one can say with assurance where such material made its first American impact, but there was a demonstrable American presence by the late 1870s. In this chapter, I shall trace the American branch of the movement through its diffusion in the late nineteenth and early twentieth centuries, until it began to falter in the 1920s. That interruption turned out to be the prelude to British-Israelism's American surge in the Depression years, the subject of chapter 3.

The First American Anglo-Israelites?

Whether or not he was the first American Anglo-Israelite, Joseph Wild, pastor of the Union Congregational Church in Brooklyn, was surely among its earliest authors. Although Wild's pamphlets date from 1879, he tells us that his acquaintance with British-Israelism went back to the late 1850s, when he came upon a copy of John Wilson's book. At about the same time, he also became acquainted with pyramidology. By 1876, he felt confident enough in his British-Israelite views to begin preaching about them and claimed to have delivered 130 Anglo-Israel sermons in the next three years. Some time between 1876 and 1879, Wild met a fellow Brooklynite better read on the subject than he, who introduced him to the writings of Edward Hine. Like so many other Anglo-Israel authors, Wild

2

British-Israelism in America

The Early Years,
1870–1928

too concluded that "the United States fulfills the role of the tribe of Manasseh," heir to all that had been prophesied concerning it; "The inference is clearly this, that if England stands for Ephraim, and the United States for Manasseh, why then, politically they must be superior to all other nations."[1]

Wild was not operating in a vacuum. His New York publisher issued and sold British-Israel books, periodicals, and sheet music in amounts ample enough to justify a catalog. Wild, in addition to his regular sermonizing, had another venue for his Anglo-Israel message, an organization called the Lost Israel Identification Society of Brooklyn. This quaintly named group met twice a month "to develope and disseminate the truth of the proposition that the Anglo-Saxon race is descended from the lost Ten Tribes of Israel; and To promote research into the general history of Israel and Judah." It was open to anyone willing to pay dues of fifty cents a year.[2]

Other British-Israelites soon followed. By the 1880s, W. H. Poole, a Toronto clergyman, was active in both Ontario and the United States. In 1887, M. M. Eshelman, a Kansas-based writer steeped in Edward Hine's ideas, published *Two Sticks; or, The Lost Tribes of Israel Discovered*. Eshelman claimed to have learned about British-Israelism in 1886 from an elderly English expatriate.[3]

Lieutenant Totten and His Followers

Wild and Eshelman were essentially local figures. Neither devoted himself to the British-Israel cause with the single-mindedness of Hine, and neither sought to shape an American movement. The first person with such grandiose aims was a later and altogether stranger figure, C. A. L. Totten. His name still surfaces from time to time in Christian Identity literature, usually, as in the sermons of Wesley Swift, as "Prof. Totten of Yale." While Identity writers disdain intellectuals and academics, they seem pathetically grateful for any instance in which the halo of academic prestige shines on their ideas. In Totten's case, however, the tie to Yale was tenuous indeed.[4]

In 1868, the Sheffield Scientific School at Yale was designated Connecticut's land-grant college. While that carried financial benefits for the institution, it also obligated Sheffield to provide military instruction for its students. Yale was able to secure a waiver of the drill requirements and was obliged only to provide senior students with a mandatory course of lectures in "military science." These proved unproductive, and in 1877, Sheffield adopted a slightly different plan in cooperation with the United States Engineering School, whose officers were to provide six lectures each year on strategy, ordnance, fortification, and similar topics. One of the early officers detailed to this position as professor of military science and tactics was a lieutenant in the artillery named Charles Totten, who held the post from 1889 until 1892. Totten's course appears to have been more successful than earlier military training programs at Yale, but his affiliation with the university was not substantially different from that of Reserve Officers' Training Corps instructors later on.[5]

Lieutenant Totten's interest in British-Israelism was of uncertain origin, but it unquestionably predated his days at Yale. He first published on the subject in 1883, and when his work was reprinted in England, it attracted the favorable attention of C. Piazzi Smyth, the astronomer-cum-pyramidologist whom we met in the previous chapter. Piazzi Smyth contacted Totten and subsequently provided the introduction for Totten's book, *The Order of History*. Totten turned out to be a prolific writer. He penned a series of articles for the *New Haven Register* and, beginning in 1890, published a British-Israel periodical, *Our Race: Its Origin and Destiny*. Totten continued to write and publish from New Haven until his death in 1909, and disciples continued to issue *Our Race* for another six years.[6]

By the mid-1880s, Totten's reputation was formidable enough to attract Edward Hine's attention. Anxious to escape the Anglo-Israel turf wars in England, Hine sailed for America in 1884 on a visit that was to stretch over four years. He first found accommodations in a New York hotel, but Totten soon invited him to New Haven. Hine stayed with Totten several weeks and wrote glowingly at the beginning of December that "Lieut. Totten is a great help to me, and has a good score of marvelous identifications of the Americans with Manasseh. . . . Professor Totten intends to publish his researches for the Good of America." After he left New Haven, Hine crisscrossed the northeast quarter of America and adjacent areas of Canada, lecturing from 1884 until 1888. He appeared in New York City, Long Island, Hartford, Boston, Cleveland, Detroit, Buffalo, Chicago, Grand Rapids, and Ann Arbor; Windsor, London, Stratford, Guelph, Hamilton, and Toronto, in Ontario; and a host of smaller communities. In the first eleven months alone, he traveled over two thousand miles, speaking to apparently large and enthusiastic audiences. While in Brooklyn during the early part of his American stay, Hine built on the following Joseph Wild had cultivated (although gloating over the fact that the *Brooklyn Eagle* wrote lengthy reports on him, even though it "never gave five lines to Dr. Wild"). Hine conducted regular services in Brooklyn and lectured to its "Anglo-Israel Association," which may have been the old Lost Israel Identification Society, before which Wild had appeared. By the time Hine returned to England in February 1888, he had become a highly visible figure in North America, reinforcing his voluminous output of pamphlets and tracts with a forceful platform presence.[7]

While British-Israel doctrine appeared eccentric to many, it was not surprising that some Americans found it attractive and even plausible. There was no shortage of Americans convinced that the country would fulfill a millennial role, and many saw in the history of Israel a template that carried the pattern of American destiny. As Herman Melville put it, "Escaped from the house of bondage, Israel of old did not follow after the ways of the Egyptians. To her was given an express dispensation; to her were given new things under the sun. And we Americans are the peculiar, chosen people—the Israel of our time; we bear the ark of the liberties of the world." What Melville said metaphorically, others were prepared to regard literally. The Mormons foretold an American Zion to which, in the end of days, the lost tribes would return, and, in like manner, Anglo-Israelites linked biblical prophecy with American fulfillment.[8]

Because Anglo-Israelism had no central structure, the pattern of its diffusion depended largely on the chance acquaintance individuals made with its teachings. Totten's works, for example, fell into unpredictable hands with equally unpredictable effects. In about 1895, a Maine evangelist named Frank Sandford became acquainted with Totten's writings. Sandford had founded a millenarian movement known as the Kingdom in 1893, which in turn established Shiloh, a large communal settlement near Durham, Maine. Sandford pronounced Totten to be "to Bible study what Galileo was to astronomy." Not surprisingly, after that endorsement, Totten's works became part of the course of study at the Shiloh Bible school.[9]

In 1900, two of Sandford's Bible students came to Topeka, Kansas, where they met a young local evangelist, Charles Fox Parham. What the Shilohites told Parham excited him sufficiently so that he spent a month studying under Sandford at the Maine commune. He also accompanied Sandford on a month-long evangelistic campaign to Winnipeg. When Parham returned to Topeka, he organized his own Bible college on the Shiloh model. There, on January 1, 1901, speaking in tongues began. This experience led Parham to found the Pentecostalist movement. Pentecostalism diffused through the lower Midwest and the Southwest, and many Pentecostalists, Parham included, eventually made their way to southern California, where the British-Israel themes they incorporated helped prepare the ground for Identity a generation later. It is also possible that Parham had independently become aware of Anglo-Israelism earlier, in 1899, from another source, the midwestern evangelist J. H. Allen, who was to become a significant Anglo-Israel figure.

Whether Parham first heard a British-Israel message from Sandford or Allen, his close association with Sandford in 1900 provided a crucial conduit for the transfer of Totten's ideas from New England to the Midwest and Far West.[10]

Whether or not his path crossed Parham's, J. H. Allen (1847–1930) became an influential figure in the American branch of the movement. He was a vice-patron of the British-Israel World Federation and the author of one of the movement's central texts, *Judah's Sceptre and Joseph's Birthright*. Originally an Illinois Methodist, Allen moved in 1879 to Missouri and became one of the founders of the Church of God (Holiness), organized in 1883. Doctrinally distinct from Parham's Pentecostalism, this was one among many Holiness churches established in the late nineteenth century. Their members, often seceding Methodists, were committed to Wesley's demand for complete sanctification, although without the Pentecostalists' speaking in tongues.[11]

Together, Parham and Allen infused British-Israelism into the premillennial evangelical sects that were emerging out of midwestern Methodism. As migratory currents took believers westward, they brought their brands of Anglo-Israelism to the Pacific Coast. The most famous of the Pentecostal outpourings, the Azusa Street revivals, took place in Los Angeles in 1906. Parham preached extensively in Los Angeles in 1924, and by 1936, 11.2 percent of all Pentecostals lived on the West Coast. Beginning at the turn of the century, J. H. Allen evangelized throughout the West and eventually moved to Pasadena—hence the rise of Identity in California during the 1930s and 1940s (described in chapter 4) built upon the foundation established by Parham, Allen, and their followers earlier in the century.[12]

Thus Totten's and Hine's labors had created three centers for future British-Israel growth in America: the Northeast, where the two had lectured and published; the Midwest, where their teachings struck a responsive chord among some evangelical Protestants; and ultimately, in the Far West, where many evangelicals had moved. In the Northeast itself, Anglo-Israelism continued to grow after Totten's death in 1909. A major force in nurturing the movement was a Boston publisher, A. A. Beauchamp.

Beauchamp took over Totten's role as the principal Anglo-Israel publisher in America. *Our Race*, Totten's periodical, had ceased publication in 1915. In 1918, Beauchamp introduced his own monthly, the *Watchman of Israel*, devoted to demonstrating that "the English-speaking peoples of today are the lineal descendants of the Lost Ten Tribes of Israel and must fulfill in these latter days the responsibilities decreed for them through the patriarchs and prophets." Beauchamp's magazine was a collection of brief and nontechnical religious essays, together with bits of news about British-Israel activities in the

United States, Canada, and Great Britain. Beauchamp also became the publisher of choice for Anglo-Israel writers in North America, including such older figures as J. H. Allen, for whom Beauchamp published a string of books, and rising younger writers such as the Canadian W. G. MacKendrick, who became a significant figure in the 1920s and 1930s under his nom de plume, "The Roadbuilder" (writing was a sideline of MacKendrick's paving business). Beauchamp's activities made him a central point of contact for the dispersed and fragmented American British-Israelites.[13]

Foreshadowings: Reuben H. Sawyer and the Ku Klux Klan

One of the far-flung contributors to Beauchamp's journal was an Oregon clergyman, Reuben H. Sawyer. In 1921 alone, he published articles in five of the twelve issues. His story is instructive not only because it demonstrates the decentralized character of the movement but because Sawyer's career anticipates those of Identity figures almost half a century later. Sawyer was one of the first British-Israelites in America to combine his religious commitments with active work on behalf of right-wing political causes, prefiguring the fusion of religious and political radicalism so conspicuous in Christian Identity.[14]

In spite of ample documentation about Sawyer's political and religious activities, recent attempts to identify him have been astonishingly incomplete or fanciful. Ralph Lord Roy, in the only previous history of the Identity movement, simply calls him a "West Coast writer." Stranger still is the theory advanced by Albert Lee in his 1980 work, *Henry Ford and the Jews*. Lee suggests that there was no such person, and that despite publications by him, "no individual by that name ever made an appearance." Indeed, he suggests that "R. H. Sawyer" was none other than the pen name of William J. Cameron, the Ford Motor Company public-relations executive whose career as a British-Israel organizer and anti-Semitic editor will be detailed in the next chapter.[15]

Whatever else might be said of Sawyer, he could never be accused of not having "made an appearance," for he was an accomplished speaker in demand for both the pulpit and lecture platform. Born in 1866, Reuben Sawyer was pastor of the East Side Christian Church in Portland, Oregon. By the 1920s, Portland had a vigorous British-Israel group, due in no small way apparently to Sawyer's efforts. The Anglo-Israel Research Society met twice monthly and supported a bookshop and lecture bureau. Sawyer himself was much in demand as a lecturer. Indeed, by early 1921, his British-Israel activities had become so time consuming that he was compelled to resign his pastorate, much to the distress of his congregation. He lectured throughout the Pacific Northwest and western Canada, especially in Vancouver, a city that was to become critical to the development of Identity ideas in the 1940s. Sawyer was still lecturing in the region as late as 1937, when he was seventy-one and living in Washington State.[16]

To the extent that a movement as diffuse as British-Israelism had an inner circle, Reuben Sawyer was in it. In 1919–20 he was instrumental in the establishment of the movement's umbrella organization, the British-Israel World Federation. He helped draft the federation's constitution and attended the first federation congress in London in 1920 (as did J. H. Allen). At the congress, Sawyer gave three addresses and presided over a session. He also spoke to large British-Israel audiences elsewhere in England. When the head of the federation, Herbert Garrison, journeyed to Canada in 1929, Reuben Sawyer was on hand in Toronto to greet him, and he appears on the list of the federation's vice-patrons with the likes of the Marchioness Dowager of Headfort and Admiral Sir Richard H. Peirse.[17]

Busy as British-Israelism kept Sawyer, his religious activities evidently did not exhaust his time, for he was able simultaneously to maintain a second career. This parallel career also involved lecturing and organizing, but on behalf of a very different organization, the Ku Klux Klan. The early 1920s were of course the heyday of the so-called "second Klan," founded shortly after the end of World War I. Unlike its post–Civil War predecessor, the Klan of the 1920s spread beyond the South to become a powerful national organization, whose support of "Americanism" and traditional morality, together with its contempt for "alien elements," made it politically formidable in many regions, including Oregon. The leader of the Oregon Klan, Fred L. Gifford, was the most prominent KKK official on the Pacific Coast.[18]

The Oregon Klan occupied Sawyer from 1921 until 1924. His first task was to make the Klan acceptable to the general community by packaging its nativist politics in soothing rhetoric. He introduced the Klan to Portland with an address before six thousand people at the Municipal Auditorium on December 22, 1921. Sawyer reassured his fellow citizens that the organization stood only for "a cleansed and purified Americanism where law abiding citizens will be respected and their rights defended, irrespective of race, religion or color so long as they make an honest effort to be Americans, and Americans only." He spoke in a similar vein the following year in Eugene, where he appeared on a stage decorated with a sword, Bible, flag, and image of a burning cross. When he lectured again in Portland, fifteen hundred people had to be turned away from a packed hall guarded by robed Klansmen.[19]

As he had in Anglo-Israelism, Sawyer combined the lecture platform with organizing activities. The Oregon Klan leader, Fred Gifford, was anxious to make a place for women in the all-male organization, and in the summer of 1922 founded a women's auxiliary, the Ladies of the Invisible Empire (LOTIES). He placed Reuben Sawyer at its head. Sawyer ran LOTIES and wrote its rituals until some time in 1923 or 1924, when he had a falling out with Gifford, possibly over division of the organization's substantial revenues. In any case, in 1924 LOTIES was dissolved, replaced by a new women's organization headed by Gifford's wife, and Sawyer disappeared from Klan affairs.[20]

Sawyer's period in the Klan posed a doctrinal problem for him. The Oregon Klan was less hostile to Jews than it was to Catholics, Asians, and the foreign born in general, but it shared with other Klan branches a pervasive anti-Semitism. This obviously presented difficulties for a British-Israelite in the Edward Hine mold, for Anglo-Israelism continued to take a protective, if patronizing, attitude toward Jews. Until such time as the segments of All-Israel were reunited in Palestine, Jews were to be protected and their longing for a homeland supported. Sawyer's British-Israel writing was very much in this vein. He wrote in April 1919 of "the great Jewish people [and] their brethren Israel." He was in demand as a speaker before Jewish organizations. After a talk to the Portland B'nai B'rith, the group's president wrote him that "your reception and the enthusiastic greeting which the members accorded you upon the completion of your address was a physical evidence of how much your auditors enjoyed your remarks." As late as July 1921, Sawyer presented himself as a protector of Jews against anti-Semitism:

> The world fears a Jewish peril, and the Jews fear a renewal of their worldwide persecution. A satisfactory solution of the problem . . . may be found in God's plan, "declared from the beginning," "In his days Judah shall be saved, and Israel shall dwell safely." Fear of a Jewish peril is but the result of the dim impression being made on the minds of men as Jehovah reveals something of His great purpose of making Israel known as that people of influence and power through whom He will restore Judah and bless all the nations of men.

Scarcely the rhetoric of a Klan spokesperson.[21]

And in fact by the time Sawyer emerged as a public Klan figure at the end of 1921, he had begun to leave his philo-Semitic views behind. In his first Klan address in Portland, he spoke about "the Jewish question." He began by distinguishing those Jews "who are of the true lineage and faith of their father Judah" from "objectionable Jews," persons who have "usurped [an] ancient and honorable title." These "objectionable Jews . . . are not of the same mental and spiritual calibre" as their erstwhile coreligionists. Sawyer even speculated that "true Jews" would be qualified to join the Klan if only Christian rituals were not there to inadvertently offend them. Sawyer also addressed the issue of a Jewish conspiracy, or, as he put it, "a 'government within our government.'" With the *Dearborn Independent*'s anti-Semitic articles no doubt in the minds of many of Sawyer's listeners, he went on to warn that the Knights of the Ku Klux Klan opposed any who "attempt to dictate to the American people concerning many important customs, usages and laws which do not meet their approval." But he hastened to add that such persons were opposed "not because they are Jews, but because of their lack of loyalty to American ideals."[22]

By 1922, however, this innuendo had been replaced by full-blown anti-Semitism that was as crude as it was open:

Jews are either bolshevists, undermining our government, or are shylocks in finance or commerce who gain control and command of Christians as borrowers or employers. It is repugnant to a true American to be bossed by a sheenie. And in some parts of America the Kikes are so thick that a white man can hardly find room to walk on the sidewalk. And where they are so thick, it is bolshevism they are talking, bolshevism, and revolution.

The transformation is so startling that one wonders at first if it is the same person speaking. The key lies in the distinction Sawyer had begun to make in late 1921 between authentic and inauthentic Jews, the former ill-treated and in need of protection, the latter masquerading as genuine members of All-Israel even as they plotted the destruction of Christendom. As we shall see in chapter 3, this distinction was becoming increasingly prominent in American anti-Semitism during the early 1920s, greatly assisted by the anti-Semitic articles in the *Dearborn Independent*, overseen and often written by its British-Israel editor, William J. Cameron. In time, as the concept of authentic and inauthentic Jews developed, it became common to assign larger and larger proportions of Jews to the counterfeit category, so that only a minority (the "good" Jews) remained worthy of protection. In the most extreme version of this position, all Ashkenazic, Eastern European Jews were counterfeit, and only Sephardic Jews could legitimately claim Israelite lineage. Since American Jewry was overwhelmingly Ashkenazic, one could maintain a theological position of Jewish defense while excoriating virtually all American Jews as traitorous. This position in fact became increasingly prominent in American and Canadian British-Israelism. As to Sawyer, he obviously saw no incongruity between his British-Israelism and the sentiments he expressed as a Klan leader, for he continued to be active in British-Israel circles throughout and subsequent to the Klan period. Although Sawyer's contributions to A. A. Beauchamp's magazine disappeared during his Klan period, doubtless because of the pressure on his time, they resumed briefly in 1924.[23]

Beauchamp Defects

The cessation of Sawyer's articles in the *New Watchman* (the periodical's name changed in late 1922) was due less to changes in Sawyer than to a dramatic shift in the affiliations of the magazine's publisher, A. A. Beauchamp; in 1924, Beauchamp converted to Christian Science. Beauchamp's shift to Christian Science occurred in the context of a complex interaction between Christian Science and British-Israelism that had begun during Mary Baker Eddy's lifetime. An English convert, Julia Field-King, had read and been impressed by the work of Totten. Totten had, among other things, engaged in a common British-Israel genealogical exercise, attempting to prove the Davidic ancestry of the British royal family. Field-King sought to extend this dubious project with the even more bizarre hypothesis that Eddy too was a descendant of King David. Eddy herself was briefly attracted by this notion, in part because it might bolster the movement in England. However, Field-King's genealogical consultations finally convinced her that the idea was without merit, and it was put to rest.[24]

This, however, was not the end of the matter. Eddy continued to maintain an interest in British-Israelism, although she kept it out of her doctrinal writings. Its attractions remained as Christian Science began to establish itself in England after 1897. After Eddy's death in 1910, British-Israelism reappeared in a schismatic offshoot from the mother church, the Christian Science Parent Church, organized in 1924 by an English Christian Scientist, Annie Cecilia Bill. A disillusioned Christian Scientist, John V. Dittemore, became interested in British-Israelism and ultimately was a contributor to Beauchamp's magazine. After Dittemore became a follower of Bill's, he persuaded Beauchamp that her doctrines were correct. Beauchamp followed Dittemore into the Parent Church and presented the *Watchman* to his newfound ecclesiastical colleagues. In Bill's messianic view of history, she was destined to become the head of a universal church and saw this process beginning with the unification of the English-speaking peoples under her spiritual headship. Dittemore's and Beauchamp's British-Israelism therefore played to her messianic pretensions and, on the practical side, opened up a new body of potential converts, namely, Anglo-Israelites. This promise was apparently at least in part fulfilled: "Our hope was realized in a large measure: many of the subscribers to the original *Watchman of Israel* became members of our Church."[25]

Beauchamp, of course, did not see this as a defection from British-Israelism. The latter had always been permissive about church affiliations, and, in any case, Bill was at great pains to demonstrate harmony between British-Israelism and her own religious views. Nonetheless, the movement of Beauchamp and his publication into a schismatic Christian Science group effectively ended its role as a central point of communication and coordination among British-Israelites in North America, for it was now, after all, the organ of a specific sectarian group. The result was to leave British-Israelism in America—diffuse at best—in an acutely disorganized condition. Coteries of believers remained, defined by such widely available writings as Totten's, or maintained by the force of such personalities as Parham and Allen, or consolidated in a few localities, such as Portland. But the movement, which had always been segmented, lacked any structure to bind its parts together or even keep them aware of one another. This condition persisted from 1924 until 1928. In that year matters were taken in hand by a remarkable organizer who would dominate British-Israelism in America through the 1930s and early 1940s, the crucial period that directly preceded the emergence of Christian Identity itself. That person was an obscure Massachusetts lawyer, Howard Rand.

Howard Rand

British-Israelism in America, fragmented at best, was left without any center after A. A. Beauchamp cast his lot with Christian Science in 1924. Although neither he nor the Christian Scientists of the Parent Church regarded Science and British-Israelism as incompatible, Beauchamp's involvement in the Parent Church effectively removed him as a linchpin of Anglo-Israelism. His periodical, which had linked the disparate British-Israel groups in the United States, now turned to other matters.

The gap, however, was soon filled, indeed, in a manner beyond anything Beauchamp had contemplated. His de facto successor was a bland New Englander, Howard B. Rand, who would dominate British-Israelism in America from the late 1920s until the end of World War II. Rand brought a distinctive background and agenda to Anglo-Israelism, for he was a second-generation British-Israelite, reared in a home already committed to the doctrines. His father had been a reader of Totten's work, and as a young man, Howard was promised five dollars by his father if he would read J. H. Allen's *Judah's Sceptre and Joseph's Birthright* and write a book report on it.[1]

Rand's British-Israel agenda set him apart from his predecessors, including Totten, Allen, and Beauchamp, for from the beginning, he was committed to creating a truly national movement, something more than merely a collection of local coteries. In the course of doing so, he also embraced political causes with a pronounced right-wing cast. This linkage had been anticipated in the career of Reuben H. Sawyer, described in the previous chapter. Sawyer, however, was less concerned with establishing links between British-Israelism and the Klan than he

3

British-Israelism and Anti-Semitism

The Anglo-Saxon Federation of America, 1928–1945

was with simultaneously advancing the separate interests of each, and in any case, his Klan career lasted only from late 1921 until sometime in 1924. Rand, an extraordinary organizer, single-mindedly pursued a coordinated set of objectives: to spread British-Israelism, to build a national organization, and to provide it with a political agenda. Rand thus emerges as a critical bridging figure between mainstream British-Israelism and its subsequent American variant, Christian Identity, for he completed the consolidation of British-Israelism in the United States while opening it to right-wing and anti-Semitic influences that were to be amplified in the postwar years.

Rand was born in 1889 in Haverhill, Massachusetts. In 1913 he received his bachelor of laws degree from the University of Maine, and over the next fifteen years combined legal practice with forays into insurance and construction. In 1927 the distinguished Canadian British-Israelite William Pascoe Goard lectured in Haverhill, very likely under Rand's auspices, for by the spring of the following year, Rand began organizing in the United States as the American representative of the London-based British-Israel World Federation. Beginning in New England, his work spread to Detroit by early 1930, when he met with a group of businessmen to establish a branch of his new British-Israel organization, the Anglo-Saxon Federation of America. The federation held its first convention in Detroit in May 1930 and made the city its headquarters. Beginning in the following summer and fall, Rand set off on marathon organizing trips. If his own account is to be believed, he traveled eighteen thousand miles through the South; twelve thousand miles through the Middle West; and fifty thousand miles during eight months in the West.[2]

Anglo-Saxon Federation branches began to appear rapidly. By September 1930 there were enough members in California to warrant a state convention. An Oregon branch was organized early in 1931, almost certainly based on the earlier organization in Portland. The second convention, which Goard attended, was held in Chicago in 1931. At the Chicago meeting, Rand announced that the Totten Memorial Trust had turned over to the federation C. A. L. Totten's unsold books, together with their cuts and printing plates, for a total of between five and six tons of material. In addition, Victor Morris Tyler, a trustee of the Totten Trust, was made a member of the federation executive committee. Thus in both tangible and symbolic terms, Rand made the Anglo-Saxon Federation of America the instrument for the continuation of Totten's enterprises. Immediately afterward, branches were organized in Chicago, St. Petersburg, Florida, and Miami. A Pacific Coast District now covered not only California, Oregon, and Washington, but also Idaho, Nevada, and Utah. There were bookrooms in Los Angeles and Oakland and a weekly radio program in Los Angeles. In the late summer of 1932, a third convention was held in Philadelphia.[3]

Meanwhile, tracts and pamphlets were being issued at a prodigious rate. In the federation's first two years, fifteen thousand pieces of literature were distributed; but between May 1930 and September 1931, fully forty-two thousand more appeared. Rand worked full-time for the federation without salary. But other factors were at least as important as Rand's devotion and energy. The Great Depression, now at its height, made millenarian ideas of every stripe appear both more plausible and more attractive, for surely such suffering and disorder must presage a cosmic overturning. The federation said of the Depression that "prophecy has foretold such a time will come upon the world." At the same time it asserted that if only the country would legislate "the [biblical] law pertaining to debts, interest and release . . . the co-operative system of Jehovah [would] completely remove the present depression."[4]

William J. Cameron and Anti-Semitism

Another factor was also responsible for the Anglo-Saxon Federation's growth, the involvement in its affairs of William J. Cameron. Cameron and Rand apparently met at federation meetings in Detroit in 1930. He was certainly present at the Detroit convention in May of that year, when he was named to the federation's executive committee. He served as the organization's president in the mid-1930s and remained in leadership positions until the end of the decade.[5]

While Rand was a faceless functionary, Cameron was a public figure, indissolubly linked to the career of the man he served from late 1918 until 1946— Henry Ford. Cameron had begun as a writer for Ford's weekly, the *Dearborn Independent*. He became its editor in early 1921 and remained in that post until the paper ceased publication in 1927. However, by about 1920, Cameron had also begun to serve in a broader capacity as Henry Ford's link with the media. He remained in complete charge of Henry Ford's personal press relations from the mid-1920s until the early 1940s. Since Ford spoke little and was often incomprehensible when he did speak, Cameron became the indispensable interpreter and intermediary, bringing the great man's thoughts to a public hungry for the wisdom of its premier industrial statesman.[6]

In addition to his involvement with Henry Ford, however, William J. Cameron was a committed British-Israelite. While it is not entirely clear how he acquired his religious bent, it was independent of his association with Howard Rand. Cameron was born in Hamilton, Ontario, in 1878. His family moved to

Michigan when he was nine but returned to Canada for his secondary and postsecondary education. This area was systematically covered by Edward Hine, who between 1885 and 1887 made countless appearances in Michigan and Ontario, including two weeks in Hamilton. Thus, it is entirely possible that Cameron, like Rand, received British-Israel teaching from his parents. In any case, by the time Rand met him, he was an accomplished lay preacher.[7]

Cameron brought substantial assets with him into the federation, including the prestige of his close and continuing association with Henry Ford, his public-relations savvy, and his network of contacts in the Detroit business community. He also had access to financial resources in a time of stringency, and even though the federation was plagued by rising deficits in the early Depression years, Cameron, as we shall see, became a source of financial support at a key juncture.[8]

The Anglo-Saxon Federation and the Right

From the perspective of the development of Christian Identity, however, Cameron's chief contributions were of a different sort. In collaboration with Rand he facilitated the first systematic attempt to link British-Israel religious ideas with the political right. Unlike Reuben Sawyer, who pursued the two activities separately, the two men made a concerted effort to reach the political right with Anglo-Israel teachings. Cameron entered the federation already publicly identified with the most notorious program of anti-Semitic publications in American history. His presence at the federation's helm, therefore, implied the compatibility of British-Israelism and anti-Semitism, and at one stroke undercut the philo-Semitism of Edward Hine.

The linkage with ultraconservative politics arose in September 1931. Rand was on his way back to Massachusetts from the federation convention in Chicago, and stopped in Detroit, where he met with Cameron. Since the formation of the Anglo-Saxon Federation, it had published a monthly newsletter, then titled merely the *Bulletin*, which would eventually grow into a slick-paper magazine, *Destiny*. Cameron suggested to Rand that the federation produce "a special issue of our paper sent out to the leading men in this country" and wondered how such a mailing list could be secured. Rand knew just the person to furnish such a list, a small-time conservative political operator named Fred R. Marvin. Marvin had "formed a Coalition of patriotic organizations . . . to fight subversive activities in America." Rand and no doubt

Cameron already knew Marvin, who had just delivered an address at the Chicago convention.[9]

Marvin was one of those who play out their lives on the margins of great events. He began as a newspaperman at the turn of the century, and later served as an aide to legislators and as a publicist. In 1924, he had played a bit part in Teapot Dome and was accused of attempting to smear Senator Thomas Walsh of Montana as an associate of "the radical element." By 1928 he was publishing "daily data sheets" on persons and organizations "designed to destroy" the American system of government, a precursor to the blacklists of the 1950s. Along the way he was accused of using his blacklisting power to favor the more conservative elements within the Daughters of the American Revolution—a relative distinction, to be sure, but enough to lead some to suggest that Marvin was able to gain control of the DAR's internal politics. In addition to these activities, Marvin founded or ran a number of conservative political organizations, particularly the Key Men of America and the American Coalition of Patriotic Societies. It was presumably the latter's mailing list that Rand was able to secure for Cameron's project. In 1930, Marvin had told a group of army reserve officers that he had "documentary evidence that as far back as 1890 the movement to break down government and abolish national defense had started." It must have given him some satisfaction to learn that the Anglo-Saxons, as instruments of God's will, were now in a position to save the nation and eventually the world from such evil and subversion. Cameron agreed to finance the production of the special issue, to be distributed by the patriotic organizations to their members. The special issue came out in a printing of thirty thousand the following February, so that Rand's British-Israel message could blanket the American right in the darkest days of the Depression.[10]

Cameron as an Anti-Semitic Journalist

By this time, Cameron was a figure of some note on the right by virtue of his association during the 1920s with the *Dearborn Independent*. More especially, it stemmed from the *Independent's* publication of a series of anti-Semitic articles that ran on a virtually weekly basis from May 22, 1920, until January 14, 1922. A selection of them later appeared in four volumes that together bore the title of the first (and most famous) of the articles, "The International Jew." Cameron's special association with the series was well known as the result of a highly publicized libel suit filed in 1925 by Aaron Sapiro. Sapiro's suit did not in fact grow out of "The International Jew" series itself, which had already been concluded, but rather was a response to a second set of articles, "Jewish Exploitation of Farmer Organizations." The Sapiro lawsuit went to trial in March 1927 and offered the first opportunity for an extended public examination of the *Independent's* anti-Semitism. The trial was widely reported. Henry Ford engaged as his attorney Senator James A. Reed, Democrat of Missouri. Cameron himself was on the stand for fully six-and-a-half days. In his testimony, Cameron completely absolved Henry Ford of any responsibility for the *Independent's* contents and insisted that he as editor was the sole determiner of what appeared. Although the suit ended in a mistrial, in July Ford apologized to the Jewish community and promised to cease publication of any anti-Semitic material. On December 30, 1927, he closed the *Independent*.[11]

Ford's and the *Independent's* foray into anti-Semitism took place against the background of growing anti-Jewish activities. These were of two separate but mutually reinforcing varieties. First, there was what David Gerber has referred to as "ordinary" anti-Semitism, which consisted of negative representations of Jews in popular culture; social, residential, and occupational discrimination; and random instances of physical and verbal harassment. These relatively unorganized forms of anti-Semitism grew through the first half of the twentieth century and did not begin to decrease significantly until after the Second World War. The second variety of anti-Semitism—the "extraordinary" form— consisted of explicitly anti-Semitic ideologies proposed as explanations for the problems of society, and the expression of these ideologies in political movements. Among them were the so-called "pseudo-agrarian" movements, which, beginning in the 1890s, sought to blame rural and small-town social dislocations on an urban, plutocratic conspiracy. More often than not, this cabal was identified as explicitly Jewish, and it became a convenient scapegoat for those troubled by departures from traditional social values. It was ironical that Henry Ford, himself an agent of some of these changes, became, along with the Ku Klux Klan of the 1920s, one of the principal voices for an anti-Semitic politics of resentment. Until the Sapiro case caused Ford to close the *Independent*, the weekly was the major media outlet for anti-Semitic ideology in America.[12]

The Sapiro case had two significant implications. First, its high public visibility, together with Cameron's extensive testimony, meant that the articles and Cameron were closely linked in the public mind. The articles themselves constituted the first and widest American popularization of *The Protocols of the Elders of Zion*, the czarist forgery that became the most famous anti-Semitic book of the twentieth century. Cameron was therefore known not merely as an anti-Semitic journalist but as one whose anti-Semitism was of a particularly virulent sort. Hence, by the time he became active in the Anglo-Saxon Federation, just three years after the trial, he was arguably one of the best known anti-Semitic writers in the country. An organization in which he played a leading role could reasonably be assumed to be either supportive of or at least compatible with the vision of a world Jewish conspiracy portrayed in the *Independent*.

Beyond that, however, there was a second implication to Cameron's testimony, for it raised the question of whether his admission of responsibility was accurate. What did it say about Cameron's personal views, Ford's beliefs, and the editorial process at the *Independent*? It was argued by some that Cameron had, as it were, merely "fallen on his sword" in order to protect his employer, implying a commitment to "The International Jew" and similar articles that he did not feel. This was, in fact, the view that Cameron himself sought to cultivate in later years. When he participated in Ford's Oral History project in 1952, he claimed not simply to have been marginal to the series but to have opposed it from the outset. However, his version, recounted after the other major figures had died, may charitably by characterized as disingenuous. He sought to place principal responsibility on the *Independent*'s first editor, E. G. Pipp, who had previously been Cameron's boss at the *Detroit News* and had brought Cameron to the *Independent*. Cameron recalled that "the first I ever heard of the Jew intention was from Pipp. He was telling me that was what they were going to do and he seemed to be in agreement with it. I was in total disagreement with it. I said you can't get away with anything like that in this country, just racial prejudice. It was after I was out there [at the *Independent*]. . . . I was the only voice in disagreement." This scenario seems unlikely, however, since Pipp himself resigned in disgust in April 1920, and the series went forward under Cameron's editorship with no discernible moderation in tone.[13]

Cameron always maintained that Henry Ford himself was largely ignorant of the project, the position he had taken at the trial and continued to take after Ford's death: "I can't recall Mr. Ford discussing a single point about them [the articles]. He did have a strong feeling about international financiers. . . . But about the details that were brought up by various investigators, I don't think he even knew. I don't know whether he ever read the stuff." That Cameron would have continued to publish such controversial material without Ford's explicit instructions seemed unthinkable to those who knew both men. Mrs. Stanley Ruddiman, a Ford family intimate, remarked that "I don't think Mr. Cameron ever wrote anything for publication without Mr. Ford's approval."

Despite his eagerness to present himself as the lone opponent of "The International Jew," Cameron conceded under an interviewer's gentle prodding that he himself had written the initial article, but claimed not to be able to remember any of the other authors in the series of anonymous articles: "Well, there were various persons. I don't know their names."[14]

An interested observer of Cameron during the 1920s was the Nazi propagandist Kurt G. W. Ludecke. Ludecke was an early and devoted supporter of Hitler, who came to America after the 1923 Munich Beer Hall Putsch debacle. He initially set himself up as a one-person, unofficial Nazi propaganda and fund-raising bureau. By 1932, with the Nazis on the verge of taking power, Ludecke was rewarded for his prior service by being made the party's official representative in the United States, where the Nazis hoped to cultivate support. His recollections of those years were not written until the late 1930s, by which time his life had taken some unexpected turns. He had returned to Germany, been imprisoned in a concentration camp, escaped to the United States, left the party, and testified before Congress on his earlier activities.[15]

Ludecke met Cameron on at least three occasions: briefly on a visit in 1921, and for more extensive conversations in 1924 and 1927. When he read the *Independent*'s anti-Semitic articles, he leaped to the conclusion that the Nazi party could gain financial support from Henry Ford. He was never in doubt that Cameron had written the articles and that they accurately represented Ford's views, although Ford consistently rebuffed Ludecke's appeals for money. Immediately after Ford issued his retraction of the series and apologized to the Jewish community, Ludecke rushed to Cameron's side, eager to find him "before he could make himself invisible." He found the editor stunned and depressed. Ludecke tried in vain to get Cameron to publicly disavow Ford's statement, "for the sake of historical truth," but after a few moments, "his courage visibly [ebbed] again." Nonetheless, he quotes Cameron as having said with some emotion that "it is certain that I for my part will never make any retraction. What I have written will stand. Not one thing will I take back. You can be sure of that. . . . I know Ford too well not to be absolutely sure that the views set forth . . . are still his views, and that he thinks today as he always did. I simply cannot understand his alleged statement." Since Ludecke's memoirs contain long stretches of conversation by a variety of figures in many settings, there is an excellent chance that in this case he placed his own paraphrasing in Cameron's mouth. Nonetheless, the substance is sufficiently consistent with other evidence to make it credible, particularly in light of Ludecke's vivid account of Ford's refusal to contribute funds to the party.[16]

Both in his 1952 "Reminiscences" and elsewhere, Cameron himself left powerful clues that the views expressed in "The International Jew" articles were not merely Henry Ford's but were Cameron's own, as well. These clues fall into three categories, of significance not merely for an understanding of Cameron's journalistic career but for an understanding of the role he played in the development of British-Israelism in the United States. There is, first of all, the equivocal manner in which he continued to regard the central source for the series, *The Protocols of the Elders of Zion*. Even thirty years later, he professed astonishment and a measure of respect for the auspices under which *The Protocols* were published: "They were printed by Eyre and Spottiswoode, the King's printers. . . . The auspices were quite astonishing to me, [that] the King's printers would publish them. . . . What astonished me was the quality of the publishers." He balked at referring to *The Protocols* as a forgery: "I don't know what they mean by forgery yet." He conceded they might be called a "fiction," but then remarked that "laid alongside actual happenings in the world, why . . . there was a similarity between what was written in the book and what had occurred here and there." That Cameron would volunteer such observations in the 1950s suggests that his involvement with anti-Semitism in the early 1920s was neither nominal nor reluctant.[17]

In reflecting on the *Independent*'s articles, Cameron never seemed sure whether they were wrong because they were untrue or wrong because they had embarrassed him and his esteemed employer. As a public-relations man, he recognized that in retrospect the whole affair had been imprudent: "A manufacturing corporation has no right to enter into the publication of controversial matter." On the matter of the articles' truthfulness, he was equivocal, suggesting that while they were "untrue," the series "was true in spots as far as actuality was concerned." Ten years before the "Reminiscences," in May 1942, his friend, the Canadian British-Israel writer Colonel W. G. MacKendrick had asked Cameron's opinion about a manuscript on the religious meaning of the Second World War. Cameron's major criticism concerned MacKendrick's harsh treatment of the Jews. Cameron, doubtless reflecting his own experiences with the *Independent*, observed that "no author is going to be read who promotes Anti-Semitism," the words of someone governed more by prudence than by principle.[18]

If some clues can be derived from Cameron's comments on *The Protocols*, and others from his reluctance to condemn unequivocally the *Independent*'s anti-Jewish campaign, a final and even more pertinent set of indicators comes from Cameron's British-Israelism. His religious views were widely known at Ford, as well as in the greater Detroit area, where he was in demand as a preacher. An in-house Ford publication in the mid-1930s said of him: "His discourse on the Economic Law of Moses is a classic, and famous. He is an earnest student of what has been called the British-Israel movement; at its last national convention was elected National President." In fact, the "discourse on the Economic Law of Moses" was an address, "The Economic Law of God," that Cameron had given at Christ Episcopal Church in Dearborn, April 30, 1933, and that was published in periodicals of both the British-Israel World Federation and the Anglo-Saxon Federation of America.[19]

When Cameron preached, we may presume that he spoke only for himself, not for Henry Ford or the Ford Motor Company. His lectures and sermons were more muted in their racism and anti-Semitism than were his newspaper articles, and after the humiliation of the Sapiro trial in 1927, Cameron sought to protect himself from public scorn. His views, however, are unmistakable. In a set of lectures at the Dearborn Inn in late 1933, he elaborated on his view that the Bible is "a racial book," and that "the racial question will never be properly stated, and its meaning will never be found, except on Biblical principles." The Bible, according to Cameron, was the story of the "Anglo-Saxon race," and he was careful to make clear that he was not using *race* as a synonym for *nationality*. Germans, Bohemians, Dutch, Scandinavians, and Britons "all belong to one race stream," descended from the ancient Israelites. In a much-published presentation given in Detroit the following year, "What I Believe about the Anglo-Saxon," Cameron described the Bible as *"the only reliable racial guide I know."* It tells the story, he went on, of the struggle of the race of Israel with its adversary, the "Esau race," "an anti-Israel power that endures to this day." The "Esau race," once separate, had "amalgamated with the Jews, and began their terrible work of corrupting the Jewish religion from within." This clearly drew not on the philo-Semitic tradition of Edward Hine but on the older notion of John Wilson's that the Jews had been irrevocably contaminated by intermarriage with the Edomites, Esau's putative descendants.[20]

Much the same material had already appeared in the *Independent*, where, alongside discussion of the Jewish conspiracy, there was a good deal of British-Israel doctrine. Examinations of the *Independent* have, understandably, focused on its anti-Semitic content rather than on its excursions into Anglo-Israelism. There is no reason to believe that any on the newspaper's staff other than Cameron were British-Israelites. Hence, its theological slant may be wholly attributed to him, and we may reasonably presume that he wrote all British-Israel articles that did not carry a byline, and commissioned those that did.

Between May 1921 and April 1927, the *Independent* published ten articles with significant British-Israel content, the last three by named authors: Mark John Levy, a British Jew who had converted to Christianity; Paul Tyner, who also wrote for the *Independent* on Major Douglas's Social Credit movement; and the Canadian British-Israelite, Colonel MacKendrick. The anonymous articles fell within the series of virtually weekly articles on the Jews' capacity to create mischief in their host societies. For this purpose, British-Israel ideas had obvious advantages, since by seeming to prove that Jews were distinct from Israel, they could show that Jews were not "God's chosen people," were not of the same stock as Jesus, and had been subject subsequently to unique racial mixing that allegedly had obliterated their original links to the tribe of Judah.[21]

The article that appeared on Christmas Day 1920 was typical of the manner in which British-Israelism was integrated into the idea of a world Jewish conspiracy. The author (presumably Cameron) begins by distinguishing Judah from Israel, from which he infers that the Jews' claim to chosenness "is not warranted by the Scriptures themselves." The essay then moves swiftly to *The Protocols*, "the most perfect plan for the destruction of Christian society ever brought to light." If, as Jews contend, *The Protocols* are a forgery, "let them prove" the book's falsity. British-Israelism and *The Protocols* can now be brought together: members of the tribe of Judah were the mischief makers of ancient Israel, "its least progressive tribe," characterized by "darkness and perversity," a people with whom "the rest of their nation could not live." Thus the enmity between Jews and Gentiles is rooted in conflict between Judah and Israel. The evil design of Judah/Jews must be unmasked through publication of documents such as *The Protocols* before further damage is done.[22]

The link between Cameron the anti-Semitic journalist and Cameron the British-Israel preacher is even clearer in a bizarre piece of parallelism. An anonymous 1923 *Independent* article observed that the prophet Jeremiah, although technically a Judean, must have been an Israelite, because "seldom is a Jew named 'Jerry.'" A decade later, in an Anglo-Israel lecture at the Dearborn Inn, Cameron remarked that "though I have searched through many lists of Jewish names, I have never found a Jew named after this great prophet of Judah, Jeremiah."[23]

Despite the openness with which Cameron expressed his views, at least one later author, Albert Lee, suggests that Cameron's involvement in the Anglo-Saxon Federation of America generated so much negative publicity that the company forced him to step down from the organization's presidency. This, Lee believes, accounted for the federation's headquarters' move from Detroit to Haverhill, Massachusetts. It is impossible to determine with absolute certainty why Cameron left the presidency and why the headquarters were changed. Most of Cameron's correspondence at Ford has been lost or destroyed, including all that might have spoken directly to this issue. As already indicated, his oral history recollections were often inadvertently or willfully distorted, and in any case do not address his federation activities.[24]

Howard Rand himself was never president of the Anglo-Saxon Federation. While others held that office, Rand was content to bear more modest titles, such as national commissioner or general secretary. However, as the organization's founder and full-time functionary, he, rather than the federation's president, ran the organization. Further, Cameron had not been its only titular head; in 1923 Reverend Frank Hancock "was appointed Chairman to consider all matters pertaining to the Movement," suggesting that at that point in its existence the federation did not have a president. In addition, in the early period dues continued to be paid to Rand's office in Haverhill, although the decision to make Detroit the official center had been taken in 1930.[25]

Cameron in Decline

Cameron was succeeded as president by A. F. Knoblock. Knoblock had been recruited as a result of the February 1932 mailing to members of Fred Marvin's patriotic coalition. He was at the time an executive of the Bundy Tubing Company. By 1933 he was a member of the federation's national executive committee and the head of an arrangements committee that organized an intensive series of meetings of the Detroit Anglo-Saxon Group in the spring of that year. That he rose to the presidency in 1937 was, therefore, not particularly surprising, and may simply have been the result of normal rotation. Certainly, there is no evidence that pressure on or from the Ford Motor Company was the reason, nor that the decision was Cameron's rather than the organization's. Although Rand insisted that the shift of headquarters to Haverhill was merely a matter of convenience, the way in which the change was announced in the January 1938 issue of *Destiny* suggests that the reasons for it were linked to the internal politics of the organization. In addition to making that announcement, the issue is the first to omit a list of staff members and officers. Only Rand is named as editor, suggesting some breach between him and the Detroit group.[26]

Cameron remained intimately involved with British-Israelism until the mid-1940s, long after he had ceased to occupy any position in the leadership of the Anglo-Saxon Federation. Through most of World War II, he was part of a three-way Anglo-Israel correspondence on the mystic eschatological meaning of the war and the manner in which pyramid calculations might predict the time and nature of the war's end. Although Cameron's side of the correspondence no longer exists, those of the other parties—Colonel MacKendrick and William McCrea—show that McCrea produced the interpretive materials and sent them to MacKendrick, who in turn passed them on to Cameron with his glosses. But despite Cameron's continued British-Israel commitment, his ability to act effectively on its behalf diminished.[27]

Cameron's star was declining at Ford, due in part to the rise in the company of the unscrupulous Harry Bennett, whose influence over Henry Ford brought him dominance not only over Ford's labor policy but over large segments of its bureaucracy. Bennett loathed Cameron and was eager to see him go, but Ford remained loyal to Cameron, who stayed with the company longer than did Bennett. Nonetheless, Bennett began to assume increasing responsibility as an intermediary between Ford and the press, as did Ford's public-relations and advertising firms and the company's own news bureau. Cameron's monopolization of media contacts with Henry Ford was broken by 1940. While he retained his office down the hall from Ford's and continued to lunch daily with Henry and Edsel in the private dining room at the engineering laboratories, he ceased to be a power in the corporation by the early 1940s.[28]

Cameron's problems went beyond company politics, for he was a heavy drinker whose attachment to the bottle grew worse with time. Mrs. Stanley Ruddiman suggests that Cameron may have had a drinking problem as early as his days on the *Detroit News*, when he needed to be "one of the boys" in a hard-drinking profession. By the time of his service at Ford, and particularly by the late 1920s, he was an alcoholic. There is some suggestion that he was able to curb his drinking just before and during the Sapiro trial, but he was drinking more heavily than ever after the trial ended. His responsibilities at the time remained substantial, even though the *Independent* had been closed. In addition to his role as press intermediary for Henry Ford, he was the company's spokesperson on its radio program, the "Ford Sunday Evening Hour," from October 1934 until March 1942. At its peak, in 1936–37, the "Sunday Evening Hour" attracted a national audience of 16–20 million for its programs of concert music. Midway in the broadcast, Cameron gave a six-minute homily on behalf of the company, a concoction of bromides on life and events. He delivered many of these platitudinous sermonettes in an inebriated state, but, like many alcoholics, he could give a reasonable imitation of sobriety when the need arose, and only those familiar with the natural timbre of Cameron's voice knew by the telltale huskiness that he was in his cups. The company and N. W. Ayer, its advertising agency, routinely detailed men to make sure Cameron got to and from the broadcast, and a Ford functionary, Fred L. Black, was always on call to read Cameron's script if needed. Ironically, that became necessary only when Cameron contracted the flu.[29]

None of this sat well with Henry Ford, a teetotaler, but he insisted that Cameron's indulgence was a "sickness" from which he might in time be cured. He provided Cameron with an attendant when necessary, as well as medical care at Henry Ford Hospital. During Prohibition, Cameron was necessarily dependent upon bootleggers and speakeasies. Whenever Ford discovered a Cameron source, he had it closed down. This seems to have engendered a certain suspiciousness in Cameron, so that when he once met another Ford employee at a bootlegging source, he became enraged, certain the man had been sent by Henry Ford to spy on him.[30]

Cameron's drinking problem had several implications for his role in British-Israelism. In the first place, insofar as it weakened his ability to fight corporate battles, it may have contributed to the decline of his influence at Ford, which in turn indirectly reduced his prestige outside the company. Second, it may well have caused friction between him and Howard Rand. Cameron's alcoholism was particularly serious in the years of his contacts with Rand, which followed shortly upon the conclusion of the Sapiro trial. Rand, however, was a Prohibitionist. Indeed, in 1914, at the age of twenty-five, fresh out of law school, Rand had run for attorney general of Massachusetts on the Prohibition party ticket, and he retained this early temperance commitment. He ran again on the Prohibition party ticket in 1944, 1950, and 1952. As late as 1946, he wrote: "Jesus informs us that by their fruits we shall know them, and the fruits of the liquor traffic, saloon and tavern are far removed from righteousness. . . . [The] statement that no drunkard will inherit the Kingdom of God . . . [is] sufficient reason to question the accepted views of the school of thought that would use the Bible to justify their desire for intoxicating liquors." Since Rand lived in Massachusetts, he met Cameron only intermittently, as the affairs of the Anglo-Saxon Federation required, and it is possible that Cameron concealed his alcoholism in their early contacts. But it is not plausible that he could have done so for a decade, nor that the rigid Rand would have taken as charitable a view as the paternalistic Ford. Recently, Rand authorized a staff member to state that the federation's headquarters were moved from Detroit to Haverhill solely because it was Rand's home. However, Rand's cryptic announcement of the change in January 1938, explaining the shift as the result of "certain differences in policy [that] have arisen," suggests some incompatibility, and it is possible that Cameron's alcoholism may have played a role.[31]

Whether or not Cameron's drinking was the cause of a breach between him and Rand, two points are clear. First, Cameron ceased to play a significant role in the federation after the late 1930s, although he remained committed to British-Israelism for some time thereafter. Second, Cameron eventually left British-Israelism altogether as a direct consequence of his drinking. As perhaps the most prominent American to have publicly championed British-Israelism, his defection was significant. The alcohol issue caused Cameron eventually to join the Missouri-based religious sect Unity. The introduction to Unity came through Cameron's wife, who, despairing of his ability to become sober on his own, was attracted to the Unity movement's program of prayer on behalf of those who solicited their help, the so-called practice of "Silent Unity." Mrs. Cameron was sufficiently impressed with the Unity literature she read to attend two educational sessions at the Unity school, located outside Kansas City in Unity Village, Missouri. Cameron himself appears initially to have been uninvolved. However, in the mid-1940s he was shaken by his own heart and ulcer problems, no doubt exacerbated by heavy drinking, and by Henry Ford's final illness. Cameron was "morose and unapproachable." Henry Ford ceased active participation in the company in 1945. In April 1946 Cameron retired, and in 1947 Ford died. Ford's death was the apparent catalyst in Cameron's conversion. When his wife made her third trip to Unity in 1947, Cameron accompanied her.[32]

Thereafter, Cameron ceased drinking completely. As Mrs. Ruddiman put it: "He has had a rebirth. . . . He's been born again. He knows now that his body is God's temple." The faith to which Cameron now clung was an offshoot of the turn-of-the-century New Thought movement, out of which Christian Science had also sprung. Founded in 1889 by Myrtle and Charles Fillmore, Unity emphasized healing through prayer. Unlike Christian Science, it was devoid of associations with British-Israelism. So complete was Cameron's conversion that in his retirement he entered the Unity ministry. In 1949, he moved to Oakland, California, as assistant minister of a Unity church, the position he occupied when he died in 1955. In light of the conversion, his 1952 oral history interview, in which he sought to minimize the anti-Semitism of the 1920s and 1930s, may reflect both his desire to present himself in a more flattering light and perhaps his feeling that earlier religious positions were now of no consequence.[33]

Rand's Withdrawal

Howard Rand's situation was quite different, for Rand lived on to an extraordinary age. He died October 17, 1991, four months after his 102d birthday.

Nonetheless, his British-Israel activities peaked in the 1930s, the period of his association with Cameron. While the subsequent decline in his level of activity may be ascribed to age, the principal reason was undoubtedly the fact that British-Israelism in America found its most favorable environment in the uncertainties of the Depression. At a time when political, social, and religious orthodoxies were crumbling or under attack, even the most exotic alternatives were likely to get a sympathetic hearing. The message that Americans were indeed God's chosen people, in a literal rather than merely a metaphorical sense, must have been solace to many who had begun to doubt the validity of the American experience.[34]

However, the institutional framework of the Anglo-Saxon Federation of America decayed rapidly after the Second World War. Rand devoted his attention primarily to writing and editing rather than to organizing. Only in Portland, Oregon, where British-Israel activity predated Rand, did a branch survive, under the name of the Anglo-Saxon Christian Association of the United States of America. But it too eventually succumbed to an aging membership, and its periodical ceased publication in mid-1964, ending with the hope "that our thirty years of earnest effort has not been in vain." The Anglo-Saxon Federation of America continued to maintain a paper existence. Its substantial and well-produced periodical *Destiny* appeared monthly until early 1969, when it briefly changed to a quarterly before ceasing publication altogether in the following year. Rand continued to issue pamphlets, however, as well as an Editorial Letter Service, which as late as 1983 claimed twenty-five thousand readers.[35]

It is often the curse of the long-lived either to sink into obscurity or to see his or her life's work changed at the hands of others. Rand suffered a measure of both. While his longevity was a major factor, it was not the only explanation. He was, after all, only in his late fifties when the Second World War ended. But he clearly had developed a stronger preference for writing than for the tedious business of keeping the federation's branches alive. His output was enormous. He wrote much of *Destiny*, together with a torrent of books and pamphlets. Not surprisingly, when the Depression and Cameron left the scene, the Anglo-Saxon Federation, without Rand's scrupulous tending, withered. While Rand continued to be treated as a revered elder by those in the British-Israel fold, he became increasingly an object of respect rather than a vital force, the kind of person of whom it is said in awe and surprise, "Is he still alive?"

By the time Rand died, Christian Identity had cast off even the most nominal link with the British-Israel World Federation, whose American representative Rand had once been. He himself clearly regarded Identity as a deviation that he chose not to acknowledge by name, and he maintained significant theological disagreements with it in his old age (these will be·discussed in part II). Nonetheless, in complex and significant ways Rand and the Anglo-Saxon Federation made Identity possible. First, they distributed large amounts of British-Israel materials on a national basis and brought its ideas to hitherto untouched audiences. Second (and here the linkage with Cameron was paramount), they created a movement in which racists, anti-Semites, and those generally on the political right felt welcome. Third, they built an Anglo-Israel infrastructure, a network of publications and local organizations that, although they did not survive their founder, did last long enough to become the foundation for Identity activities later. In particular, the federation facilitated critical contacts between American British-Israelites on the West Coast and their opposite numbers in western Canada. As the next chapter will show, these U.S.-Canadian contacts, begun in the late 1930s, were an important mechanism for introducing an even more intensely anti-Semitic theology than anything Cameron or Rand had contributed. Given the chronic inability of British-Israelism to enforce an orthodoxy, the motifs that filtered down from Vancouver through Rand's network made possible the creation of that American variant we know as Identity.

Beginning in the late 1930s, Anglo-Israelism underwent the final set of organizational transformations that produced Christian Identity. The ties to the original movement in England—nurtured by Totten, Beauchamp, and Rand—became attenuated to the point of rupture. By the beginning of World War II, and certainly by the war's end, what remained was a distinctively American movement. It might contain doctrines of English provenance, but organizational ties to the British-Israel World Federation had ended and such terms as "British-Israel" and "Anglo-Israel" had themselves fallen into disrepute. These changes were tied to two other transformations, one geographical, the other doctrinal.

American British-Israelism experienced a change in geographical focus beginning in the late 1930s. The movement had originally been centered in the Northeast, with Joseph Wild in New York, Charles Totten in New Haven, A. A. Beauchamp in Boston, and Howard Rand in Haverhill, Massachusetts. There were secondary centers in the Middle West (e.g., Eshelman in Illinois, J. H. Allen in Kansas), greatly strengthened in the Depression era with William Cameron's ascendancy in Detroit. However, the movement had not achieved much prominence in the West. There had been, it is true, an active group in Portland associated with Reuben H. Sawyer, and Rand had organized assiduously in California beginning in the late 1920s. But notwithstanding these outposts, the movement's center of gravity remained northeastern and midwestern.

By the late 1930s, however, that had begun to change. In part it was a matter of old areas weakening. As the Depression ended, recruitment became more difficult. Cameron, as we saw in chapter 3, began to withdraw from leadership,

4

Creating Christian Identity, 1937–1975

possibly as the result of disagreements with Rand. Rand himself ceased to put as much time into organizing and became more involved with writing and editing. But whatever changes might be attributed to the decline of strength in the East and Midwest, the major sources of change came in the West itself. Along the Pacific Coast, British-Israelism began to grow and change as a result of two factors.

First, a vigorous British-Israel group in British Columbia began to push down the coast. At a point when American energies were flagging, this Canadian influence produced a burst of activity, first in the Pacific Northwest and later in California. Second, demographic changes and religious developments in Los Angeles created an increasingly receptive climate for Anglo-Israel activities. Indeed, these changes are partly reflected in the American folklore of the period that identified southern California with bizarre forms of religious expression. By the late 1940s, a critical mass of British-Israel-related groups were active in Los Angeles and adjacent areas, most now so distant from British origins that Christian Identity can conveniently be dated from this time and place.

In addition to the change in geographical focus, British-Israelism in the West exhibited subtle but significant doctrinal alterations, concerned primarily with the view of Jews and the movement's political orientation. As chapter 7 describes in greater detail, even "mainstream" British-Israelism harbored latent anti-Semitic tendencies, which developed from British-Israelism's core belief that Judah and Israel were different. These tendencies became especially prominent in the 1940s among Vancouver British-Israelites. This may partly be ascribed to rising anti-Zionism in Anglo-Israel circles, since the desire of Jews for an independent homeland in Palestine was seen as repudiation of the British peoples' claim to be the true Israel. It was well and good for Britain, as the mandatory power in Palestine, to aid Jewish settlement paternalistically, quite another matter for the Zionist movement to demand British withdrawal. In addition, the Vancouver group appears to have contained some figures whose anti-Semitism was unusually open and intense.

The openness of anti-Semitism in these circles represented a new phase, beyond that which had characterized the Anglo-Saxon Federation of America. The presence of William Cameron in the leadership of the federation, and his identification with the *Dearborn Independent* and the *Protocols*, had signaled the compatibility of British-Israelism with radical anti-Semitism. However, these themes still remained subordinate in the federation. On the West Coast, they were to become increasingly central and, moreover, began to take forms beyond anything with which Cameron or Rand had been associated. One begins to find, for the first time, the suggestion that the Jews might be more than simply an unassimilable or evil force, but rather the very quintessence of evil, the literal offspring of Satan.

This new and more virulent strain of anti-Semitism came also to be more frequently linked with right-wing political causes. Rand and Cameron had explored this as well in their association with Fred Marvin during the Depression, but as with their anti-Semitism, the right-wing linkages had been occasional and unsystematic. During the 1940s in Los Angeles, Christian Identity established systematic and pervasive ties with right-wing political circles. At the center of these networks stood the doyen of American anti-Semitism, Gerald L. K. Smith. The story of Christian Identity in southern California can be told largely through the activities of Smith's associates. One of these—a former Methodist named Wesley Swift—became by the 1950s and 1960s Christian Identity's central figure. Identity's development in the 1970s and 1980s was largely a function of those influenced in one way or another by Wesley Swift's writing and preaching. By the time Swift died in 1970, therefore, Christian Identity had separated from its English roots; was developing most vigorously in southern California; and promulgated a theology of battle against demonic Jews and a political program of racial supremacy.

The Canadian Connection

A major force in disseminating British-Israelism on the West Coast was a group centered in Vancouver. Anglo-Israelism had taken root in eastern Canada in the nineteenth century, particularly in Ontario, but took longer to penetrate the western region. An organization was established in Vancouver, however, in July 1909 called the British Israel Association. By 1922 there were four branches in the Vancouver area, amalgamated under the name of the British Israel Association of Greater Vancouver. By the early 1930s, the Greater Vancouver organization began to think in Canada-wide terms and began organizing a Dominion Federation, unaware that a similar effort was underway in Toronto. The Vancouver effort was eventually dissolved in favor of the Toronto-centered federation, but the tension between eastern and western Canada was to surface again.[1]

Through much of this period—at least from 1919 on—there had been contacts between the Greater Vancouver group and smaller British-Israel coteries in the Pacific Northwest. As we saw in chapter 2, Reuben H. Sawyer had, in addition to his Klan activities, propagandized vigorously for British-Israelism not only in Oregon and Washington, but also in British Columbia.

Sawyer's role as a founder of the British-Israel World Federation in London positioned him in an international network that included Canadians as well as Britishers and Americans. Nonetheless, the links between the United States and the Vancouver group were informal rather than systematic, the result of personal ties and proximity rather than policy. This was about to change.

Although the Vancouver association had relinquished its claim to organize the movement for all of Canada, it was not in the end pleased with the direction the Toronto group had taken. In 1935 the Dominion organization in Toronto, now called the British Israel World Federation (Canada), decreed that "no group in the Dominion of Canada is, or can be recognized as belonging to the British Israel World Federation excepting as they are registered through the Canadian organization." This shift from a loose federation to a centrally governed organization appeared to threaten the independent programming that had characterized activities in Vancouver, with its radio programs, publications, and branches. In addition, between 1934 and 1937 key figures in Vancouver who had direct access to federation leaders in London died. The Vancouver association, fearful that its independence was threatened and unable to rescind the centralization policy, effectively withdrew from the federation in Toronto by 1937 and ceased to be recognized by the umbrella group in London. Isolated from the rest of Canadian British-Israelism and cut off from the London organization, the Vancouver group turned its attention to the United States.[2]

The Vancouver association began to systematically cultivate contacts on the West Coast. The principal vehicle was a series of conferences between 1937 and 1947 that was an important catalyst for the eventual emergence of Christian Identity. The first conference, in May 1937, was called the Convention of the Anglo-Saxon Association of North America, made up of the western segment of Howard Rand's Anglo-Saxon Federation of America and the British-Israel Association of Greater Vancouver. The meeting, held in Seattle, drew from Washington, Oregon, Idaho, California, and British Columbia. Rand himself attended, and so did Reuben Sawyer. Thirty representatives came from British Columbia, including the Vancouver leadership and Clem Davies, a Victoria clergyman who later operated out of Los Angeles. For its part, Rand's group resolved that "the Regional Convention of the Northwest District of the Anglo-Saxon Federation of America, desires and hereby enters into a friendly and reciprocal affiliation with the [Greater Vancouver] Association for the purpose of co-operating together in the free exchange of guest speakers and in order to mutually further the interests of the Kingdom of God in our respective territories." Subsequent meetings were held in Vancouver in

1939–40, in Portland in 1941–43, and in Los Angeles in 1945–47. The result was a Canadian-American network that stretched from Vancouver to southern California, independent of activities in Toronto, London, and the eastern United States.[3]

When the Vancouver group shifted its attention from east to south, from Canada to the United States, the consequences were more than merely organizational; the Vancouver group nurtured ideas that were more clearly conspiratorial and anti-Semitic than what might be found in the run of British-Israel literature. In the early and mid-1940s, Vancouver-based writers produced a stream of apocalyptic and anti-Semitic materials that could now be diffused along the lines of communication that had been established with the United States.

This literature had two main components. The first was a series of books and pamphlets that reached its climax in a pseudonymously authored novel, *When?: A Prophetical Novel of the Very Near Future*, by "H. Ben Judah," published in 1944 by the British-Israel Association of Greater Vancouver. This work stands as one of the first statements of what was to define Christian Identity doctrine, the belief that the Jews are the offspring of Satan. Because of its significance, it will be examined at length in chapter 9. *When?* was preceded by two pamphlets, which, although published with no indication of authorship, almost certainly came from the same hand. They share motifs and subject matter, as well as an elaborate "Chart of Racial Origins." The first version, *The Morning Cometh*, issued in Vancouver in 1941 by the otherwise obscure Anglo-Saxon Christian World Movement, is a relatively unexceptional apocalyptic tract with little overtly anti-Semitic material. But an augmented edition, published in 1944 by the association, was quite different. This version, *When Gog Attacks*, is closely related in subject matter to *When?*, published the same year, save that *When Gog Attacks* employs the traditional format of a religious tract rather than the novelistic devices of *When? When Gog Attacks* presents a number of themes crucial in subsequent Identity thinking: Cain as the founder of the "synagogue of Satan"; the "Turko-Mongol" origins of Ashkenazic Jews; the blood of fallen angels among Jews; and the historicity of *The Protocols of the Elders of Zion*. As the pamphlet's author concludes, "The Ashkenazim are neither Jews nor Semitic by blood or race."[4]

If one part of the Vancouver group's literary production was the work of the *When?* author, the other principal contribution came from a clearly identifiable source, C. F. Parker. Parker had impeccable British-Israel credentials. His father, J. W. Parker, was an early member of the Vancouver group, part of its executive committee by 1924, and a delegate to the 1937 Seattle conference. His son had studied at the British-Israel teacher's training college in England. C. F. Parker exemplified a hidden but increasingly significant strand of anti-Semitism within British-Israelism itself. Where British-Israelites had previously emphasized a fraternal, although patronizing, relationship with the Jewish people, this philo-Semitism was increasingly challenged from two quarters: by those who argued that sinful out-marriage had corrupted Jewry's All-Israel blood, and by those resentful of Zionism's opposition to British rule in Palestine. Parker gave full vent to both views.[5]

The blood of Esau and his descendants, the Edomites, had infiltrated and corrupted the Jews. They were now a tainted people: "Esau-Hittites comprise no small portion of modern Jewry; and . . . we must be prepared to look for the continuation of Esau-Edom within the Jews." Worse, these racial tendencies had spawned all manner of subversive and revolutionary forces, notably communism and Zionism, with the result that by 1948, "Palestine Jewry . . . a Communist and Atheist-ridden monstrosity," had "seized the Holy Land from the rightful owners—Israel-Britain."[6]

Consequently, the Vancouver Anglo-Israelites, now connected far more directly with Americans in the West than with fellow Canadians, became a catalyst and a conduit, at once stimulating the growth of British-Israelism on the Pacific Coast and infusing the anti-Semitic doctrines of Parker and the *When?* author.

British-Israelism in Los Angeles

The Vancouver group's influence made itself felt initially in Washington and Oregon, but in time British-Israel activity accelerated in California as well, and in the Los Angeles area in particular. This was due in part to the gradual diffusion of Canadian influence southward but also because of changes in the composition of the population in Los Angeles itself. Between 1890 and 1930 Los Angeles was one of the fastest-growing cities in the country, and with its extraordinary population increase came greater social and religious diversity. The religious diversity is difficult to measure, but Gregory Singleton concludes that "the activity of cults in Los Angeles may have been more intense than in other cities." Certainly, the area acquired a national reputation as a hotbed of religious novelty and experimentation. Between 1920 and 1930—the decade immediately preceding the upsurge in West Coast British-Israelism—small sects and cults in Los Angeles grew by 381 percent. These deviant religious organizations recruited not only from recent migrants to the city but from members of Protestant denominations seeking greater religious fulfillment.[7]

These shifts in population and religious affiliation provide the background for the growth of Anglo-Israel and, eventually, Christian Identity activities in southern California. British-Israelism came in part through its own organizations and in part as the doctrinal baggage associated with other groups. The most significant of the latter were the Pentecostalists. As we have already seen, Pentecostalism's founder, Charles F. Parham, had been profoundly influenced by British-Israel ideas early in his career. With the Azusa Street Revivals of 1906, Los Angeles became a major locus of Pentecostalism, and by 1924, if not earlier, Parham was preaching there on British-Israel themes.[8]

By 1930, Howard Rand's Anglo-Saxon Federation had a state organization in California, headquartered in Los Angeles. A key figure in the federation's California operation was Philip E. J. Monson, state secretary in the fall of 1930 but by the end of the year district superintendent for the Pacific Coast, with authority over California, Nevada, Utah, Oregon, Washington, and Idaho. Monson appears to have been a British-Israelite since at least 1928, before Rand recruited him for the federation, and was associated with, and may have founded, the Kingdom Bible College, established in Los Angeles the same year Monson became active in the Anglo-Saxon Federation. Monson's Covenant Evangelistic Association proclaimed itself "an international undenominational movement composed of Spirit-filled Christians" who anticipated "the near return of the Lord Jesus Christ to take up His Kingdom Administration."[9]

By 1935, a colorful southern evangelist with British-Israel views, Joe Jeffers, set up shop in Los Angeles and may simultaneously have been active in William Dudley Pelley's Silver Legion. By the early 1940s Los Angeles had also attracted Clem Davies, a prominent British-Israel preacher from Victoria, British Columbia. By the time he arrived in Los Angeles, Davies had a long right-wing and anti-Semitic past, including involvement with the Ku Klux Klan in the 1920s and sympathetic statements about the Silver Shirts and the British fascists. William Dudley Pelley disdained British-Israelism and took no role in its organized manifestations. He was, however, profoundly influenced by one of its major figures, pyramidologist David Davidson. He turned Davidson's ideas in directions neither their author nor other British-Israelites would have approved, but Pelley did perform two functions in the emergence of Christian Identity: he popularized Davidson's writings among his followers, and he integrated Davidson's work into an unabashedly anti-Semitic political movement.[10]

The Silver Shirts' founder claimed to disdain British-Israelism. However, in the early and mid-1930s, he had appropriated parts of it for his own eclectic ideology, a mixture of fascism and mysticism. His fondness for the occult led him to the pyramid literature, which served him, as it had others, as a device for predicting critical events. Since he remained aloof from organized Anglo-Israelism and incorporated only a small and arguably minor part of its beliefs, the use he made of pyramidism will not be considered here. It will, however, be examined in chapter 5, along with other British-Israel scenarios of the Last Days.

Los Angeles's position in the movement was ratified when it served as the site for the final conferences of Canadian and American British-Israelites in 1945, 1946, and 1947. They were organized by John A. Lovell (1907–74), a Texas Baptist who became acquainted with British-Israelism in the 1930s. He established a magazine, *Kingdom Digest*, in 1941, pastored a church in Long Beach, and extended his ministry through radio broadcasts. He returned to Texas in 1946 and established the United Israel World Fellowship in Fort Worth. During his brief time in Los Angeles, however, he helped make it the center of organized Anglo-Israel activities in the West.[11]

Gerald L. K. Smith in California

Although Lovell departed quickly, the vacuum was soon filled. As British-Israelism was slowly metamorphosing into Christian Identity, its center was a figure at once logical and improbable: Gerald L. K. Smith. Smith had begun his political career as Huey Long's chief lieutenant. Unable to hang on successfully to the Kingfish's political legacy after Long's assassination in 1935, Smith began to adopt positions that were increasingly radical and, after 1942, increasingly anti-Semitic. He made his first visit to Los Angeles in 1943 and came every year thereafter. In the early 1950s, he purchased a home in Los Angeles and moved his headquarters to the city in 1953. None of this would be of more than peripheral significance but for the fact that Smith's activities intersected with those of most of the significant Identity figures on the West Coast—among them, Conrad Gaard, Jonathan Ellsworth Perkins, Bertrand Comparet, William Potter Gale, and, above all, Wesley Swift.[12]

Gerald L. K. Smith's network was not British-Israel, it was unambiguously Christian Identity. Ties with the original group in England were now virtually nonexistent. Much of the organizational work in California had been done by Howard Rand, with London's blessing, fifteen years before the activities of Smith and his colleagues. But Rand himself was a continent away in Massachusetts, and far more interested in writing than in organizing. The early figures on the West Coast, such as Sawyer and Monson, had either moved away, died, or were too old to continue in leadership roles. Many of the pivotal figures in California between the 1940s and the 1970s therefore had no prior involvement with the British-Israel World Federation or groups directly tied to it. In a movement that had always had difficulty in defining orthodoxy and suppressing deviation, those on the West Coast felt themselves at liberty to borrow, modify, and discard doctrines as their own idiosyncrasies dictated. The early phases, marked by the activities first of Rand and then of the Vancouver group, had propagandized and brought believers together, but now the West Coast coteries took on lives of their own, building upon but not beholden to the work of earlier organizers.

The significance of Gerald L. K. Smith was threefold. First, Smith was by the 1940s, and remained until his death in 1976, the most prominent anti-Semite in America. His involvement with Identity therefore recapitulated the role that had been played earlier by William J. Cameron. The association of Cameron with British-Israelism in America, and then Smith with Identity, signaled the linking of religion with anti-Semitism. But whereas Cameron muted his anti-Semitism after the dissolution of the *Independent*, and in any event saw his primary loyalty to Henry Ford, Smith was under no such constraints. He was a full-time propagandist, speaker, and organizer whose influence was a function of the stridency of his rhetoric.

Second, although Smith frequently dealt with religious issues (a point explored further below), he saw his major role as that of political agitator pursuing a right-wing agenda. This agenda was compounded of opposition to the United Nations and other internationalist initiatives, opposition to "communism," loosely defined, and opposition to expanded rights for blacks. Encompassing it all was an obsessive fear of Jewish subversion. The single-mindedness with which Smith pursued his political efforts had a special significance for Christian Identity. Howard Rand had made contacts on the right through Fred Marvin, but they were not systematically built up and sustained. Reuben Sawyer had had an active career with the Klan but kept his Klan activities separate from his religious role. Smith was intent on mobilizing Christian Identity figures in the West on behalf of his own political goals. The consistency with which Smith drew on Christian Identity support linked Identity strongly with the program of the anti-Semitic right.

Third, Smith gave coherence to a fragmented movement. Permissive at best, British-Israelism and derivative groups were always in danger of falling into anarchic and fratricidal strife. By assiduously cultivating prominent Identity figures and using them as vehicles for his political causes, Smith helped shape an Identity network on the Pacific Coast, something far too loose to be called an organization but nonetheless a coherent set of interacting and collaborating churches and individuals.

Was Smith an Identity Believer?

In view of all Smith contributed to Identity, a significant question remains: was he an Identity believer himself? Although the answer may seem obvious in view of his richly textured Identity connections, it is in fact not at all clear. His biographer, Glen Jeansonne, believes he was, based upon the strong Identity views Smith expressed in a 1964 letter. Smith and his Christian Nationalist Crusade also sponsored events that were at least as concerned with Identity doctrine as with politics. A 1956 lecture by Wesley Swift, "The Middle Eastern Crisis in the Light of the Scriptures," Smith promised, would be "one of the richest and rarest experiences of your life." The following year he asked Swift to "speak on the subject 'The Divine Destiny of Our Race,' drawing heavily on the Scriptures." Smith was fulsome in his praise of Swift and his Identity approach to the Bible: "I covet for you and the Israel cause the establishment of a permanent work in Los Angeles that forever will keep alive in the hearts of the people the Scriptural truth concerning the destiny of the white race, the identity of Israel, and other great messages embraced by your fellowship." Near the end of his life, Smith claimed that, over and above all of Swift's political contributions, the "greatest contribution" he made to Smith was that "he opened up the Bible. . . . He identified the 'true Israel' which gave us the Messiah, and demonstrated to me with the proper texts that Christ's worst enemies were not God's chosen people. He identified the 'true Israel' which gave us the Messiah, and demonstrated to me . . . we were indeed Israelites. . . . He demonstrated that the crucifiers of Christ were apostates, sons of Satan, and the seed of Cain." Although Smith's periodical, *The Cross and the Flag,* was mostly concerned with political issues, Smith regularly wrote religious articles. These included the views, by now increasingly common in Identity circles, that the Jews "are not necessarily offspring of the seed of Abraham," that they had intermingled with the Canaanites, and that they are "sons of Satan."[13]

While all of this would argue strongly for Smith's commitment to Identity, there is also evidence that points in the other direction. Much of it comes from religious articles in *The Cross and the Flag,* although by implication rather than direct assertion. Smith rarely opened the magazine's pages to his many Identity associates, at least not for religious articles, although a bland essay by Bertrand Comparet did appear in April 1955. In the same articles that link Jews with Canaanites and Satan, Smith also defined chosenness in decid-edly non-Identity terms. The chosen "are those who have manifested their love of [Christ] by their faith, their repentance, their confession and their baptism. I humbly boast that I am of the House of Israel because I have accepted the Divine seed of Abraham fulfilled in its divinity through the Blessed Virgin and the Holy Spirit." And elsewhere, "The real land of Israel belongs to those who have accepted Christ." Considering how much Smith wrote, and how close his ties with Identity figures were, it is remarkable how few Identity references occur in his publications, and how much of his re-ligious writing maintains the orthodox view that "Israel" consists of all those who have accepted Jesus as Savior. The ambivalence remained even in *Be-sieged Patriot*, the collection of "autobiographical episodes" he wrote a few years before his death. Here, along with encomiums to Wesley Swift, were a host of theologically orthodox, non-Identity observations: that "the true Israel is made up of the people who accepted and praise Jesus Christ as the Son of God," that God's chosen people are those "who have chosen to approach God by way of the name of Jesus Christ." His seven-point list of the "fundamentals of the Christian faith" says nothing that sounds remotely like Identity.[14]

There are a number of possible explanations for this mixed record. The most cynical is that Smith was anxious to flatter potential supporters so that he could exploit them, and recognizing the anti-Semitic strand in Identity, did what was necessary to curry favor with its leading exponents. A less cynical but still nonreligious explanation is that Smith recognized in Identity a group whose interests at least partially coincided with his, particularly insofar as both advanced anti-Semitic ideas, and that he therefore behaved at least some of the time in ways necessary to remain in the good graces of a valued constituency. Alternatively, and more plausibly, Smith may simply have been so theologically unsophisticated (he certainly believed he knew more about theology than he did) that he was unaware of his own inconsistencies and was untroubled by the incoherence of his religious views. Smith had started out as an evangelical preacher, and thrived on platform virtuosity. Jeansonne remarks that his religious views were "highly opinionated and unconven-tional," and it is possible that he was happy to borrow from Identity to buttress his anti-Semitism without feeling the need to recast his broader religious views in Identity terms. Whatever the case, even those who accept Smith as an Identity believer find it difficult to point to a single sustained instance of Identity writing from his pen. His importance lay rather in the role he per-formed as a link between the disparate elements of the West Coast Identity community.[15]

At one time or another, Gerald L. K. Smith had contact with virtually every significant Identity figure in the country, and particularly with those in the West. While it is not possible to exhaustively track all of his Identity affiliations, an examination of some of the principal relationships will provide some sense of how complex the interconnections were. In the absence of central organization, the links through Smith provided some measure of coherence for the movement during the growth period of the 1940s.

Among those in Gerald Smith's circle, Conrad Gaard was a relatively marginal figure, if only because, based as he was in Washington State, he was less able to participate in Smith's California activities. Gaard, however, deserves consideration because, as we shall see at a later point, he was among the first Identity figures to make a sustained written presentation of Identity views, and he was also among the first to present at length the view that Jews were the literal offspring of Satan. Although Gaard taught at a short-lived British-Israel seminary in Dayton, Ohio, during the late 1940s, his base was in Tacoma, Washington, where he led the Christian Chapel Church and the Destiny of America Foundation. He was an active religious broadcaster and issued a regular publication, the *Interpreter*. Gaard spoke widely in the United States and western Canada, where he maintained ties with the Vancouver group. He died in 1969.[16]

Gaard was in contact with Smith at least as early as 1946, and remained in touch with him both directly and through Wesley Swift for at least a decade. Smith was anxious that Gaard address the 1950 convention of his Christian Nationalist party in Los Angeles, something Gaard was unsure he could do given his extensive publishing, broadcasting, and travel commitments, although in the end he participated, advertised as a "Lecturer of influence."[17]

Smith had a far closer but also far more tormented relationship with Jonathan Ellsworth Perkins. Perkins was raised as a Methodist in rural Ohio, although he eventually had ties to the Assemblies of God and Aimee Semple McPherson's International Church of the Foursquare Gospel. He moved to Los Angeles in the early 1930s, where he seems to have been based until sometime in the late 1940s or early 1950s, when he transferred his activities to Tulsa. He met Smith in 1945, when both were in San Francisco attacking the founding of the United Nations. Perkins was firmly in the Anglo-Israel/Identity fold: "I shall not deny that I believe that the White nations of Western Europe are the lost ten tribes of Israel, and an integral part of Israel."[18]

In addition to his association with Smith, Perkins was closely allied to members of the Dixiecrat wing of the Democratic party that had bolted the 1948 convention and formed the States' Rights Democratic party, which nominated Strom Thurmond. Perkins helped organize the States' Rights party convention and attempted to secure a role in the group for Smith, but Smith's endorsement was too dangerous even for southern segregationists, and his assistance was rejected.[19]

A few months later, in September 1948, Perkins broke with Gerald Smith. That was not in itself unusual, since Smith had a way of inviting defections of formerly devoted associates, but in Perkins's case, the break was dramatized by a rambling, vituperative book he published in 1949, *The Biggest Hypocrite in America: Gerald L. K. Smith Unmasked*. Perkins's polemic against Smith makes curious reading. He made three specific attacks upon Smith. First, he argued that Smith's goal was to become the dictator of America: "He eagerly awaits Revolution in America, thinking he is the strong man of the hour." Since Smith could not even get a hearing from Perkins's Dixiecrats, it is difficult to see how he could take over the country. Second, in Perkins's view, Smith was, quite simply, insane, and lived in fear that his emotional problems would be revealed. Perkins's final point is the strangest of all, for he asserted that the break with Smith was ultimately caused by the latter's anti-Semitism. He rested his objections on British-Israel grounds, arguing that "Judah, from whence Jews Sprang, was one of the twelve tribes of Israel." The Second Coming could not take place until all twelve tribes, including the Jewish descendants of Judah, had returned to Palestine. As Perkins saw it, Smith (and Wesley Swift, for that matter) "would put every Jew in America out of business if given authority," and "Smith would kill or have every Jew killed that would not accept his leadership if he were in power."[20]

Perkins's indignation was ironic, because Smith's anti-Semitism was well known before the break between them in 1948, indeed, was clear by the time Perkins first became a Smith associate. In addition, Perkins's own views on Jews were far from unblemished. He had picked up and developed the same themes of racial contamination that had appeared in the Vancouver group and that cast increasing doubt on the role of the Jews in God's plan. As Perkins wrote in *The Modern Canaanites; or, The Enemies of Jesus Christ*: "We have at least 13 Canaanite groups incorporated into the tribe of Judah, giving us a foreign race we know as the Jews. They have some Israel blood in their veins, and in that sense have a definite relation to the covenant that God made with Abraham but because of being largely of foreign to Israel blood are not worthy of being considered the true children of Judah." One can only speculate on the fulsome philo-Semitism suddenly manifested in his book on Gerald L. K. Smith; perhaps his vindictiveness overrode his convictions.[21]

In any case, Smith responded in kind. Writing to Wesley Swift in the spring of 1949, Smith concluded that Perkins had done no political damage, but characterized him as "the vilest, most consciousless human being I have ever known." Smith concluded that Perkins was "either . . . insane or possessed of a devil."[22]

Smith's relationship with Bertrand Comparet was altogether more harmonious. Indeed, Comparet appears to have stood relatively aloof from the factional strife that periodically erupted among Identity sectarians. Comparet was born in San Diego at the turn of the century. Educated at Stanford, he became a lawyer, first serving as a deputy district attorney in San Diego County, then as San Diego deputy city attorney. After 1947, he was in private practice, although he must have been hard-pressed to fit his professional activities into a career already filled with Identity preaching and the publication of his Identity pamphlet series, *Your Heritage*. Comparet died in 1983 at the age of eighty-two.[23]

Comparet's extraprofessional activities were intimately interwoven with the affairs of Smith and Wesley Swift. He served as legal adviser to the California Anti-Communist League, which Swift headed and whose assistant director was Charles F. Robertson, a key Smith aide. He served in all manner of capacities for Smith—as an emissary on missions to Washington in the hope of interesting public officials in Smith's views, as both a planner and a speaker at Christian Nationalist conventions, and as a contributor to *The Cross and the Flag*. In 1955, he successfully defended Smith in a libel suit.[24]

Gerald L. K. Smith and Wesley Swift

However much Comparet may have served Smith as a jack-of-all-trades, he was never as significant for either Smith or Christian Identity as his comrade Wesley Swift. For both religious and political reasons, Swift emerges as the single most significant figure in the early history of Identity. While he conducted his political activities for the most part through Smith's organizations, his influence as a preacher gave him an independent base, so that Smith magnified Swift's position without overwhelming it. This needs to be made clear, because so many published references to Swift repeat Ralph Lord Roy's erroneous description of him as Gerald L. K. Smith's "chauffeur, bodyguard, and research assistant." More than anyone else, Wesley Swift was responsible for popularizing Christian Identity in right-wing circles by combining British-

Israelism, a demonic anti-Semitism, and political extremism. Later Identity figures, such as Richard Girnt Butler and James K. Warner, sought to present themselves as his heir. Swift's influence certainly did not flow from any gifts as a systematic thinker, and he left no extended statement of his religious views. But he was a compelling preacher, whose riveting style is evident from even the technically flawed recordings of his sermons. His widely reprinted articles are essentially sermon texts.[25]

Like many others on the Identity right, Swift moved through successively more conservative forms of evangelical Protestantism to his final theological stance. He was born in New Jersey in 1913, the son of a Methodist minister, Richard Swift. What social views he might have been imbued with as a child are unclear, but much later, in 1958, the older Swift wrote Gerald L. K. Smith thanking Smith for a picture of Joseph McCarthy and a copy of *The International Jew*. Of McCarthy, Richard Swift asserted "that the enemy achieved a great victory when they succeeded in silencing his attacks on the strongholds of Communism." Concerning *The International Jew*, he wrote that "you [Smith] deserve the highest commendation for all you have done to put this very informative book in the hands of our American people, especially where it will do the most good." Whether or not Wesley Swift heard comparable views in his youth, he quickly demonstrated an attraction to religion. He had a born-again experience at seventeen and received his license to preach in the Methodist church the following year. At about that time, he moved to Los Angeles, where he attended Bible college, and the Los Angeles area remained his base thereafter.[26]

Notwithstanding his strong Methodist connections, he left the church in his youth, a move his widow attributes to his distaste for the reformism of the Social Gospel. In California he maintained some ties with Aimee Semple McPherson's International Church of the Foursquare Gospel. In the mid-1930s, by which time Swift was in California, more than half the national membership of the Foursquare Gospel church was on the Pacific Coast. For the most part, however, Swift went his own way religiously, functioning first as an itinerant evangelist and later establishing his own independent church. His early preaching was in the Randsburg area, in the Mojave Desert, but he eventually moved to the Antelope Valley, at the edge of the desert, north of Los Angeles.[27]

Wesley Swift and Identity

Just as Swift's break with Methodism is unclear, so controversy surrounds the question of how he first became acquainted with British-Israel/Identity doctrines. Swift's widow thinks Swift may have first heard about British-Israelism listening to Gerald Burton Winrod, the Kansas evangelist whose political activities made him a defendant in the widely publicized 1942 sedition trial of right-wing figures (William Dudley Pelley was a codefendant). Winrod was certainly in a position to transmit some version of Anglo-Israel doctrine through his fellow Kansan, Charles Fox Parham. Parham had drifted to the right politically, perhaps because of rejection by his black protégé, W. J. Seymour. Parham praised the Klan in the 1920s and, more significantly, wrote for one of Winrod's periodicals.[28]

On the other hand, James K. Warner of the Christian Defense League and the New Christian Crusade church, who considers himself Swift's spiritual heir, offered another theory, that in his late teens, Swift heard a lecture by "a Kingdom Identity minister," not otherwise identified. Yet a third theory came from William Potter Gale, who was once close to Swift but became bitterly hostile after Swift's death, so that Gale's views must be weighed with care. Gale first presented his account in a 1975 printed attack on Swift, five years after the latter's death, and then elaborated upon it in extended interviews with a California reporter, Cheri Seymour, a few months before Gale's own death. In both accounts, he places Swift as a "preacher" in the Foursquare Gospel church, whose way into Identity was facilitated by San Jacinto Capt, who apparently had organized a pyramid study group in Temple City, California. (Capt's son, E. Raymond, became a pyramid author whose works are sold widely by Identity organizations.) When Gale wrote about the relationship between Capt and Swift, he implied that Capt was the source of Swift's Identity beliefs. In the conversations with Seymour, he suggested that Capt's major function was to provide Swift with an audience receptive to the Identity message. In any case, Gale clearly places these contacts in the World War II years, a full decade after Warner's dating. Far more plausible than any of these theories is that Swift acquired his British-Israelism when he attended the Kingdom Bible College in Los Angeles. Kingdom, where he later set up a comparative theology program, had been established in 1930 and was associated with a local British-Israel group, the Covenant Evangelistic Association. Both the college and the association were, in turn, closely linked to Philip E. J. Monson. Monson, who published through the association, had been Howard Rand's man in the West. By 1930, he was in charge of all of the activities of the Anglo-Saxon Federation on the Pacific Coast. Swift came to California shortly after the college was founded, and his association with it very likely was the principal source of his early Anglo-Israel views. While these conflicts cannot be definitively resolved, they point to some salient characteristics of the religious milieu in which Swift moved—that in the southern California of the 1930s and 1940s, Anglo-Israelism impinged from many different sources, including Pentecostal revivalism and the activities of Rand's Anglo-Saxon Federation. British-Israelism was "in the air," accessible to anyone engaged in quests for religious fulfillment through evangelical Protestantism or political activity on the extreme right. As we shall see, Wesley Swift was seeking both.[29]

Swift founded his own church in Lancaster, California, in the mid-1940s. A report by the California state attorney general placed the founding of the church in 1946, but the 1958 celebration of the tenth anniversary of Swift's Los Angeles ministry suggests that the church was not organized until two years later. In any case, its original name was the Anglo-Saxon Christian Congregation, in keeping with the currency given "Anglo-Saxon" in American proto-Identity circles by Howard Rand and his followers. The subsequent name—the Church of Jesus Christ Christian—might have appeared innocuous to the outsider but expressed the Identity belief that Jesus was not a Jew. During the same period in which Swift was founding his church, immediately after the end of World War II, he also attended the Anglo-Israel/Identity meetings organized by John Lovell. These were the final round of U.S.-Canadian conferences begun in the Pacific Northwest in 1937.[30]

Swift was eager to spread his message beyond the Antelope Valley. As we have already seen, he gave well-publicized Bible lectures in Los Angeles under Gerald L. K. Smith's sponsorship on such topics as "Khrushchev's Invasion of America in the Light of Bible Prophecy" (this was at the time of Khrushchev's tour of the United States). When his work for Smith required him to travel to Oklahoma, he combined political activism with Identity meetings in Oklahoma City and Tulsa. While Smith received contributions given at the Christian Nationalist Crusade gatherings, the two agreed that Swift would keep any offerings collected at Identity meetings. In the 1950s, Swift formed a religious coalition with Bertrand Comparet under the umbrella title Anglo Saxon Christian Congregations Incorporated, for which Swift served as president and Comparet vice-president, which listed branches in Los Angeles, Lancaster, San Diego, and San Francisco.[31]

When the tenth anniversary of Swift's ministry was celebrated in 1958, Gerald L. K. Smith organized the celebration. Smith sent out announcements to friends of the Christian Nationalist Crusade "because of my great personal affection for this brilliant Christian statesman [Swift]." Smith sent out personal invitations to such close Swift associates as Bertrand Comparet and John Lovell. Lovell, by then in Dallas, sent an effusive message to be read at the festivities, in which he described Swift as "one of the best informed persons, on public affairs to be found anywhere in America." While he could not himself attend, he asked that "our Heavenly Father continue to guide, protect, bless, and use Dr. Swift and his great ministry." Reverend George Rigler in Oklahoma wrote that Swift was "a Bulward [*sic*] against the Hordes of Antichrist," while Reverend Bob Howard in Little Rock claimed that "no man in America has done more to shape my personal ministry than Dr. Wesley Swift."[32]

Wesley Swift and Political Activism

While Swift was cutting a wide swath through Identity circles, extending his influence through California and beyond, he was simultaneously pursuing an active right-wing political career. His first brush with political notoriety occurred in 1946, when he was involved in an attempt to revive the Ku Klux Klan in Los Angeles. Los Angeles, like many other areas of the country, experienced explosive Klan growth in the 1920s, but the movement declined sharply in the 1930s, and by the end of the war was virtually nonexistent. In February and March 1946, crosses were burned in the mountain town of Big Bear Lake, northeast of Los Angeles. Although the perpetrators were never identified, Swift spoke about "the new Klan" to a Big Bear Lake American Legion post in late March. Swift and a former Kleagle, Ray J. Schneider, refused to cooperate in an investigation by the state attorney general, although Schneider did eventually testify. Gun-permit records revealed that Swift had purchased twelve handguns between 1932 and 1946, including four between the fall of 1945 and April 1946, as well as an undisclosed number of rifles. The attorney general began court proceedings to dissolve the Knights of the Ku Klux Klan, whose state incorporation dated from the 1920s. In the course of these investigations, it was revealed that a deputy sheriff stationed in Lancaster, where Swift's church was located, had a close relationship with Swift and might have been involved in his Klan activities. He was initially transferred, then discharged. Swift himself gained significant press coverage but suffered no penalties as a result of the episode.[33]

At about the same time, Swift met Gerald L. K. Smith. As Smith told it, his speaking engagement at a high school auditorium was picketed by a large and hostile crowd. While police were able to control the picketers and get Smith and his wife to the platform, Smith feared attack by members of the audience: "I turned to the right and there sat a young man about 30 years old [Swift was in fact about thirty-three at the time]. He turned to me and said: 'Don't be afraid, Mr. Smith. Anyone who comes toward you will be sorry.' He lifted up his coat and there he held a black automatic pistol." It was the beginning of an association that lasted more than two decades. Smith's voluminous correspondence with Swift began in early 1946 and extended into the mid-1960s, by which time Smith had left California. Swift toured the West Coast with Smith and participated in a wide range of activities of Smith's Christian Nationalist Crusade. On Smith's behalf, Swift attended a conference of conservative Republicans in Chicago and took on a nebulous mission to Washington "for the purpose of initiating activity in relationship to certain fundamental projects being undertaken by the Christian Nationalist Crusade." In much the same manner as Smith's own writing, Swift's report of the mission insinuates but does not document associations with highly visible conservative politicians, including Senators William Jenner, John Bricker, Joseph McCarthy, and William Knowland. Swift outlined a series of essential projects that required completion as "the exclusive property of most patriotic citizens." They generally involved securing information—"the lowdown"—on various nefarious activities, all somehow linked to evil conspiracies. Thus Swift darkly hinted that "some place, somehow men of great power are covering up awful things. Why has the President [Eisenhower] forbidden employees of certain Government bureaus to report treason to members of Senate committees? . . . Why has this terrible Jew, Matusow, been used as a witness to belittle Senatorial committees? . . . We must know the answers to these questions." Swift's report was sent to Christian Nationalist supporters and duly published in *The Cross and the Flag*. At the same time, Swift was also speaking to Christian Nationalist Crusade conventions and helping to plan the Crusade's "Emergency Congress."[34]

The Christian Nationalist Crusade was not the only vehicle for Swift's political activities or his involvements with Gerald Smith. The California Anti-Communist League, which Swift headed, shared a secretary with his church and had as its assistant director Smith's close associate, Charles Robertson, who became Smith's assistant in 1953 and took over direction of what remained of Smith's activities after the latter died.[35]

Swift's relationship with Gerald Smith weakened, however, by 1962. Smith wrote a strange letter to Swift in which he accused the preacher of slighting him by failing to invite Smith to address Identity meetings, to invite Smith to Swift's home, or to dine out with Smith. Smith speculated "that you [Swift] have obligations which I do not know about to people who are not cordial in their attitude toward me. . . . This may seem like a childish viewpoint, but regardless of any other theories which you may have concerning my restrained attitude, this letter contains the complete and exact truth." While Swift's response does not survive, the two remained in brief but only occasional communication for the remaining few years. In 1964, Smith established a summer home in Eureka Springs, Arkansas, to which he eventually moved. The final letter to Smith in 1965 came, significantly, from Swift's secretary, because "[Mrs. Swift] and Dr. Swift are busy almost 24 hours a day."[36]

Swift, William Potter Gale, and the Christian Defense League

Wesley Swift's political activities survived the weakening of his ties to Gerald L. K. Smith. Indeed, he came to the attention of the California state attorney general again in 1965, this time as part of a report on right-wing paramilitary groups. The report linked Swift to two such organizations, the California Rangers and the Christian Defense League (CDL). A raid on the home of a league member had turned up eight machine guns and an assortment of other weapons. A Ranger was "arrested for selling a machine gun and Sten gun to undercover agents." Swift's association with both groups, and particularly the CDL, was intimately related to the activities of his protégé, William Potter Gale, who in time himself became a major Identity figure, part of the Comparet-Swift-Gale triumvirate that defined Christian Identity in California.[37]

William Potter Gale came to his religious and political vocation after a military career. By his own account, he was the youngest lieutenant colonel in the army when he was promoted at the age of twenty-seven. He served on General Douglas MacArthur's staff during World War II and helped organize guerrilla forces in the Philippines. War injuries required his retirement in 1950, when he was thirty-three. Gale was characteristically inconsistent in describing how he first became acquainted with Identity doctrine. He wrote that he had received his initial training in Identity from S. J. Capt, who, along with Steven Goodyear (an Identity believer with links to Gerald L. K. Smith), took Gale to meet Wesley Swift in 1956. In the same year, Swift ordained Gale as an Identity minister. In Gale's 1987 conversations with Cheri Seymour, ten months before he died, Gale not only elaborated on this story but inserted a slightly different one as well. In this version, he met S. J. Capt at a meeting of conservative Republicans at Gale's home in 1953, when he was just entering right-wing politics. Capt introduced him to Identity and then arranged a "study program" for Gale involving himself and an otherwise unidentified Catholic priest, "Father Eustace." At the same time, according to Gale, he decided to study for the Episcopal ministry, and claimed to have been ordained in 1956 (perhaps not coincidentally the same year Swift ordained him).[38]

However, in the Seymour conversations, he raised yet another possibility. He recalled that he had first heard about Identity in 1946, when the army sent him for a period of study at Yale. In New Haven, he claimed to have discovered the writings of "Professor Charles Totten from Yale University." Given Totten's extremely tenuous association with Yale (described in chapter 2), it is most unlikely that simply being at Yale brought Totten to Gale's attention, although he may fortuitously have run across the *Our Race* volumes. Gale also recalled that a Yale Russian history professor, whose name he does not provide, told him that the Russian czars were descended from the tribes of Israel, and that that first planted the Identity seed. But whatever ideas Gale may have come upon in New Haven, he almost certainly had no sustained contact with Anglo-Israelism or Identity before he retired to California in 1950.[39]

As with so much else in the history of Christian Identity, accounts of the founding of the Christian Defense League are also ambiguous and contradictory. In Gale's account, the CDL was founded by him and S. J. Capt at some point between 1957 and 1962 (Gale tended to be vague about dates). He claimed to have then brought in Swift and Comparet. Comparet, as a lawyer, incorporated the organization. In an alternative account, an anonymous follower of Swift's claimed that the CDL had been "actuated" in 1963 with little or no help from Gale. A CDL brochure gives the date as 1964. During this period Gale and Swift were apparently still on good terms, for in 1959, Gerald L. K. Smith had written Swift mentioning how pleased he was that Swift had reported on Gale's staunch loyalty to the Christian Nationalist Crusade.[40]

Regardless of whether the CDL was founded in either the late 1950s or (as is more likely) in the early 1960s, and regardless of the roles Gale and Swift may have taken, the organization does not initially appear to have been very active. Indeed, both Gale and Swift supporters agree that the organization had to be "reactivated" a short time later. Its alleged paramilitary activities appear to date from this second phase. A journalist, William W. Turner, links the CDL and its members with a variety of illegal schemes ranging from the theft of dynamite to a plot to assassinate Reverend Martin Luther King, Jr. Turner also claims that in June 1964 Swift and associates met with American Nazi party leader George Lincoln Rockwell to attempt an organizational merger. None of these stories can be independently confirmed.[41]

The public face of the Christian Defense League was plain enough.

(a) Its specific and primary purpose is to encourage Christians to join together and cooperate for the promotion of their mutual interests as Christians and the propagation of their religion; to oppose all persecution which may be directed against Christians by reason of their religion and all attacks directed against Christianity; and by all lawful means to defend Christian individuals and institutions against persecution or any attacks made against them by reason of their religion.

(b) To promote the knowledge of and belief in the doctrines and tenets of Christianity and the high standards of morality and ethics advocated therein.

Notwithstanding the broad language, the CDL was an Identity vehicle. Its first president and national director was Richard Girnt Butler, an engineer at Lockheed who had come within Swift's orbit.[42]

Richard Butler reached Swift by a circuitous route. He was first introduced to William Potter Gale by one of Gale's parishioners. Whether or not Gale gave Butler the Identity message, as Gale later claimed, there seems little dispute that Gale brought Butler to Wesley Swift's church. The effect on Butler was electrifying: "He [Swift] was the total turning point in my life. The light turned on. He had the answers I was trying to find." Butler became a member of Swift's church and then ascended to the leadership of the CDL. As we shall soon see, Butler's Identity career was just beginning.[43]

Butler left California in 1973. The leadership of the Christian Defense League then passed to another Swift disciple, James K. Warner. Warner, a Pennsylvanian, had moved first to Alexandria, Virginia, and then, in 1966, to Los Angeles. He carried with him a variety of political and religious baggage, including affiliations with the National Socialist White People's party and Odinism, the putative religion of pre-Christian Nordics. Although he initially moved in neo-Nazi circles in Los Angeles, he too converted to Identity. His New Christian Crusade Church in Los Angeles offered Identity as Swift had preached it. As Warner later proclaimed on the CDL's behalf: "*As a White person YOU ARE A DESCENDANT OF THE TRIBES OF ISRAEL or Judah and as such are THE CHOSEN PEOPLE OF GOD.*"[44]

Successors

Ill with kidney disease and diabetes, Swift died in the waiting room of a Mexican clinic of an apparent heart attack on October 8, 1970. He was fifty-seven. The funeral was held on October 12, and a memorial service on

October 18. The void left by Swift's death was not readily filled, not only because others lacked his zeal as a preacher but because there were so many potential successors in a movement that had no mechanism for establishing leadership, let alone succession.[45]

There was, of course, William Potter Gale, whose own ministry had been established before Swift's death. Gale tried his hand at theology and in fact produced a codification of Identity belief far more systematic than anything Swift had written. After Swift's death, however, he turned on his former patron. Gale had been provoked by an anonymous 1975 article in the Swift-oriented *National Chronicle*, an Identity paper published in northern California and edited by Hal W. Hunt. The article—"Who Is 'Col.' Gale?"—portrayed him as a shifty intriguer who used Swift but secretly betrayed him. Gale's angry response in his own publication in turn portrayed Swift as a Johnny-come-lately to Identity and political activism, and painted his supporters as small-minded people unable to cope with Gale's success. As his version of Identity "spread . . . across the land, they see its success and their ego simply cannot stand up to it."[46]

Not content to direct his attack on Swift's admirers, Gale made a series of allegations against Swift himself, albeit five years after the latter's death. He claimed that Swift had smeared him by spreading the report that Gale was a CIA agent. Swift also attempted, according to Gale, to discredit Gale's Ministry of Christ Church by portraying it as a financial rival, depriving Swift of offerings he might otherwise have received. By the time Gale was finished with his lengthy counterattack, he had burned any remaining bridges to Wesley Swift's followers.[47]

Isolated from those he called "Swiftites," Gale nonetheless continued to be politically active. Along with Henry "Mike" Beach, he was one of the founders of Posse Comitatus in the 1970s. The loosely organized Posse movement was based upon the belief that no entity above the county sheriff's posse possesses constitutional validity. Gale, who fancied himself an expert on constitutional law, wrote that "a County (or Parish) government is the highest authority of government in our Republic." This radical rejection of the state and federal governments Gale carried to its logical conclusion in his battles with the Internal Revenue Service described in chapter 10. Gale was convicted of tax-related criminal charges on October 2, 1987, and sentenced to prison the following January. However, he had been seriously ill with emphysema during the trial and died on April 28, 1988, at the age of seventy-one, while an appeal was pending.[48]

James K. Warner, the second national director of the Christian Defense

League, eventually moved the league and the New Christian Crusade Church to Louisiana, where he continued to publish Wesley Swift's sermons and writings. In time he drew close to another right-wing figure in Louisiana, David Duke, during Duke's days as a Ku Klux Klan entrepreneur. That is a story best left for a later chapter.[49]

The best known of those who tried to follow in Swift's footsteps was, of course, Richard Girnt Butler, who had led the reactivated CDL before Warner. According to Swift's daughter, Joan Nielson, Butler conducted services at the Lancaster, California, church with no encouragement from the church board. Nielson claimed the result was a shrinking congregation made up of Butler's friends. In 1973, Butler moved to Coeur d'Alene, Idaho. Shortly afterward, with the help of Nielson and her husband, Butler established his Church of Jesus Christ Christian. Although it bore the same name as Swift's church, the remaining members and the board of the church in Lancaster refused to grant Butler a charter. Indeed, the Lancaster church continues to maintain an existence under Swift's widow, primarily as an outlet for her husband's tape-recorded sermons and publications. In any case the Nielsons eventually became disillusioned and left Butler's church.[50]

Nonetheless, Butler's enterprises were destined to become the most publicly visible Identity manifestations in America. In addition to the Church of Jesus Christ Christian, he organized a political arm, the well-known Aryan Nations, both housed in a heavily guarded compound. Annual Aryan Nations World Congresses on the grounds came as close to an umbrella organization as the racial movement has had, drawing both Identity and non-Identity racialists from North America and Europe and consolidating Butler's position. Yet in so fractious a movement, leadership is a relative term. By the early 1990s, in his seventies and in uncertain health, Butler attempted to turn leadership over to his "chief of staff," Carl Franklin, a generation younger. In little more than a year, however, Franklin left to form his own church in Montana. With Butler's withdrawal, the possibility of leadership by a major Identity figure drawn from Swift's own circle ended, for Gale was dead and Warner had never been able to attract a significant following.[51]

The highly politicized and often violent Identity groups of the 1970s and 1980s emerged directly out of the movement that solidified in the decade 1936–46. During that period, British-Israelism was transformed from an extension of an English movement to a distinctly American movement, dimly aware of English antecedents but with no ties, organizational or personal, to the British-Israel World Federation. Stimulated by rising levels of anti-Semitism in the writings of the Vancouver group, Identity placed at least as much emphasis upon the diabolical nature of a Jewish adversary as on its sense of chosenness. Concentrated on the West Coast, under the impact of evangelical and Pentecostal groups in southern California, Identity became increasingly a religion of millenarian anti-Semitism. From the fog of names, associations, and rivalries, two points clearly emerge. First, a series of influences converged on southern California in the 1930s and 1940s, bringing British-Israelism in forms that were increasingly linked to anti-Semitism and the political right and ever farther removed from English roots. Second, these influences can be traced back through sequences of American, Canadian, and eventually English Anglo-Israelites to establish, as it were, Identity's lines of descent.

The paths of influence were thus complex but also clear: one line ran from Hine in England to Totten in America, then to Frank Sandford, the Maine evangelist, and from him, through Charles Fox Parham, to the Pentecostal movement. A second line ran from Hine to Totten, then to Howard Rand, and through Rand's Anglo-Saxon Federation of America, to widely scattered groups of American Anglo-Israelites, including Philip E. J. Monson, at whose Bible college Wesley Swift studied. A third line ran from Hine and the others in England across Canada to the group in Vancouver, which established linkages with the Anglo-Saxon Federation on the West Coast. All three streams converged in southern California, to which Pentecostalists had migrated, where the Anglo-Saxon Federation had vibrant branches, and to which the ideas of the Vancouver group had filtered down the coast.

It is important to reconstruct this in order to establish the channels that led from nineteenth-century British-Israelism to twentieth-century Christian Identity. But important as this reconstruction is, it is not enough, for Identity is doctrinally as well as organizationally distinct. It is not merely a matter of the diffusion of ideas but of their metamorphosis as well. At what points and in what ways did old doctrines change and new teachings develop? For this we must turn to the tangled tale of the religious ideas themselves since Identity's millenarian anti-Semitism is not only a function of groups and individuals, writers and publications, but also a product of ideas. Thus far we have examined the conduits of communications, the means by which the ideas were transmitted. It is time now to examine the ideas.

Part Two

Christian

Identity

Doctrine

Christian Identity believers think of themselves as living in the "Last Days," when history will reach its consummation, a millennialist outlook they inherited from British-Israelism. The latter was concerned not merely with identifying the "Anglo-Saxon-Celtic peoples" as true Israelites but in drawing from this knowledge inferences about the fulfillment of biblical prophecies. Hence British-Israelism acquired an early concern for millenarian matters, as followers sought to demonstrate that the English-speaking peoples would be the beneficiaries of God's redemptive power. Despite its idiosyncratic character, British-Israelism was significantly influenced by broader late nineteenth-century Protestant millennialist currents, and since British-Israelites had no sectarian ambitions of their own, the movement sought to demonstrate its compatibility with millenarian ideas circulating in evangelical circles.

Christian Identity received this millenarian legacy but then proceeded to alter it significantly. It was moved to do so for two reasons. First, the main carrier of millenarian ideas in contemporary America has been Protestant Fundamentalism. While British-Israelites maintained a generally open attitude toward much Fundamentalist theology, Identity was not inclined to be so receptive, in part because of the extent to which contemporary Fundamentalist millennialism depends upon the existence and security of the state of Israel. Clearly, no such flirtation with philo-Semitism could coexist with Identity's demonization of Jews. Second, by linking Jews with the Devil, and the "Jewish conspiracy" with Satan's struggle to subvert humanity, Identity has come perilously close to dualism, the view that history is a clash between good and evil forces. Indeed, partly for that reason the major dualist

5

British-Israel
Millennialism

on the extreme right, the late Robert Miles, regarded Identity as compatible with his own views. Christian Identity, having raised the power of Evil to a status scarcely different from God's, has made the attainment of the millennium a more problematic enterprise. The greater the power of the Jewish conspiracy, the more difficult, and therefore the less likely, its defeat. And while no Identity writer has abandoned the idea of inevitable redemption, the focus has shifted from the goal itself to the process of reaching it, a process fraught with considerably greater risks for Identity than for Anglo-Israelism.

This chapter and the next explore the development of millenarian ideas in the religious continuum that runs from nineteenth-century British-Israelism to modern Christian Identity. But before sketching British-Israel views of the End-time, it is first necessary to briefly examine where ideas of the millennium stood at the point when British-Israelism appeared on the Anglo-American religious scene.

Protestant Millenarian Thought

Under the stimulus of the French Revolution and the Napoleonic Wars, British millennialism flourished in the early nineteenth century. While British chiliasm never again manifested the zeal it had shown during the Puritan Revolution of the seventeenth century, it did awake from its eighteenth-century slumber. It was "premillennialist," in the sense that the Second Coming was to precede the millennium itself. The premillennialism of the 1800s is best viewed as a dialogue between two approaches ("schools" would imply greater doctrinal organization than was the case). The two positions are most commonly labeled "historicist" and "futurist." As the terms themselves suggest, the former looked to past events for evidence of prophetic fulfillment, while the latter placed such fulfillment in the future. Historicism, meditating upon the key texts of the biblical books of Daniel and Revelation, concluded that most of the prophecies they contained had already been realized by the events of European history, and that by carefully analyzing political and ecclesiastical chronologies, millenarians could determine with considerable certitude the few remaining unfulfilled prophecies. Beyond this general attitude, historicists had also developed techniques for teasing precise meanings out of biblical texts, as in their practice of converting biblical "days" into historical years. The historicists' combination of prophecies fulfilled by past history and devices for calculating the rest of the chiliastic scenario reached a climax in America during 1843–44, when William Miller became the center of a mass movement in anticipation of an imminent Second Coming. The traumatic failure of the Millerites' predictions deeply undercut the credibility of historicism.[1]

As the Millerites' "Great Disappointment" suggested, the historicist position carried the seeds of potential public embarrassment. The more specific the predictions, the more massive the disconfirmation. But even before the Millerite debacle in America, some British millennialists had begun to advance an alternative position. Futurism was in some respects historicism's opposite, for it rejected the latter's reliance on history in order to validate prophetic utterances. To the contrary, futurism argued that nothing in the church's past could be taken as fulfillment of prophecy. The crucial events described in the Book of Revelation were yet to occur. Further, futurists rejected the year-day equation, with all the date-setting temptations associated with it. The futurist position was articulated in the most influential manner by John Nelson Darby (1800–1882), a member of the Plymouth Brethren. Darby's views were well formed by the 1830s but were not widely circulated in the United States until the early twentieth century, when they were incorporated into a Bible commentary prepared by C. I. Scofield (1843–1921).[2]

Darby's version of futurism, known as "dispensationalism," offered a profound challenge to the historicist position. Darby divided sacred history into a series of ages, or dispensations, each characterized by a change in the manner in which God dealt with humanity. Darby, however, had not invented the concept of dispensations, nor was use of the idea limited to futurists. Nonetheless, the process of periodization became in time so closely associated with Darby's other, and more contentious, views, that *dispensationalism* came to mean only that version of millennialism that Darby had devised. Darby's contribution lay in two unrelated ideas. First, he argued that at a point in the distant past, prophecies had ceased to be fulfilled, introducing a "parenthesis" into history, an era when the "prophetic clock," as it were, had ceased to tick. The resumption of prophetic fulfillment, therefore, lay in the future. Second, at a future time impossible to calculate, as the key prophecies came to fulfillment, the saved would be secretly lifted off the earth by Christ in a supernatural event most commonly referred to as the "rapture."[3]

Darby's concept of the parenthesis, during which the fulfillment of prophecy ceased, was an outgrowth of his concept of the church, an entity unrelated in his mind to the organized church on earth. It was instead a nonworldly, spiritual entity. In the futurist rendering, when Jesus came and was rejected by the Jews, the original eschatological scenario was violated. Jesus was unable to make his originally intended rapid return, and God of necessity had to create a new people from among the Gentiles to take the place of the original Israel, the church as it is commonly regarded. Scriptural passages, therefore, existed in two sets, one concerning the newly created church and the other concerning the Jews. This division of Scripture came to be referred to by dispensationalists as "rightly dividing the word of truth." Most prophecies, in Darby's view, referred to the Jews, and inasmuch as their continued dispersion and failure to recognize Jesus as the Messiah continued, there seemed to be no immediate prospect of the "clock" resuming its tracking of prophetic time.[4]

Darby's approach left dispensationalists with a profoundly ambivalent attitude toward the Jews. On the one hand, God's promises to the Jews—for example, restoration to their own land—would be fulfilled. On the other, they had rejected the Savior. Dispensationalists consequently adopted a paternalistic attitude toward Jewish national aspirations, a theme that was to be echoed in British-Israelism. At the same time, however, they often interpreted persecution as divine chastisement. As far as the Last Days were concerned, the Jews would indeed be restored to their homeland in Palestine, but during the Tribulation, they would suffer bloody persecution at the hands of Antichrist, until only a remnant was left to convert at the time of the Second Coming. Hence, dispensationalism advanced a philo-Semitic agenda, while at the same time not wholly abandoning the view that Jews were targets of wrath from both God and Satan. British-Israelism expressed a similar ambivalence. It emphasized philo-Semitic themes in the nineteenth century, but by the 1940s, as we shall see, increasingly emphasized that Jewish suffering was merited.[5]

The insertion of this Darbyite parenthesis into history placed the church in the awkward position of being unable to affect or accelerate the attainment of the Second Coming and millennium. The parenthesis, however, might be removed by external intervention. This in turn was linked to Darby's teaching concerning the rapture. Darby believed that at some unknowable future time, the true, spiritual church—unrelated to its often corrupt organizational manifestations—would be removed by Christ from the earth and dwell with him in heaven, to return with him to earth once again to inaugurate the millennium. In this sense, the Second Coming would occur twice, once in secret when Christ would come to snatch up the church, the truly saved, and again in a public Second Coming that would include Jesus' physical return to rule over the thousand-year kingdom of the saints. Once the secret rapture occurred, the interrupted sequence of prophetic fulfillment would resume, including the seven-year period of violence and persecution known as the Tribulation, during which Antichrist would appear and great armies would marshal at Armageddon.[6]

Through the nineteenth century, Darby's ideas continued to acquire influence in Great Britain, especially among evangelicals within the Church of England and the Scots Presbyterian church. With the exception of the Plymouth Brethren themselves, Darbyite dispensationalism made little headway in the dissenting churches. These futurist inroads were particularly striking in view of Darby's pronounced antiinstitutional views, associating ecclesiastical organizations with worldliness and corruption. The rise of British-Israelism occurred simultaneously with the rise of dispensational premillennialism, and within many of the same denominations. Hence, in its formative decades, British-Israelism could not help but be touched by powerful millenarian currents. Darby was anxious to avoid the mathematical calculations and date setting associated with historicism. The Millerite episode only served to reinforce this aversion. Nonetheless, the prospect that the rapture and ensuing millenarian events might occur at any time produced an understandable desire to know when the present dispensation was approaching its end. Hence, although futurists have by and large retained their dislike for date setting, a countervailing desire for closure on so momentous a subject has continued to tempt them to seek "signs of the times" that might presage the imminence of the "latter days."[7]

Millennialism in Edward Hine

In light of the simultaneous growth of British-Israelism and a new millenarian consciousness in English evangelical circles, it is not surprising that early Anglo-Israelism manifested a strong belief that the world was entering the final days of history. The same apocalyptic mood appears in writings by American British-Israelites as well, for by the time the movement had put down roots in the United States, American Protestants had begun to be influenced by English millenarian developments. Yet British-Israelism professed no orthodox position on eschatological matters, reflective of the fact that it never developed along fully sectarian lines and that Protestants themselves were not entirely certain how the road to the end ran. This can be seen clearly in the speculations of Edward Hine, the leading late-Victorian British-Israelite, who was fascinated by the prospect that the final dispensation was coming to a close but was not certain when it would occur.

Hine, like many millenarians before him, believed that the literal millennium—the thousand-year reign of Christ and his saints prior to the Last Judgment—would be a sabbath of sorts for the world, and would therefore be the seventh one-thousand-year period of history. Hence Hine was curious as to when the sixth such age would come to a close. His speculations suggest both vacillation and millennial yearning. Since he believed that the six thousand years of history had begun with the creation, he looked to biblical chronologies in order to see where humanity presently was. Responding in 1871 to an inquiry concerning the Battle of Armageddon, Hine suggested that it would be the final event of the six thousand years and that it would occur in another 125 years, that is, in 1996. By 1880, however, he had expanded this interval to 360 years (to the year 2240) in order to provide enough time to spread the British-Israel message. For inasmuch as the tribes now resident in England were to be at the forefront of the millennial age, they could scarcely occupy that exalted role until they accepted their true "identity." In 1889, two years before his death, Hine was apparently satisfied that the movement had grown with sufficient rapidity (in no small measure as a result of his own efforts) so that the end was not nearly so far off:

> Twenty years ago Israel was not known, now they are. Twenty years ago Manasseh [i.e., the United States] was lost, now he is not. . . . *The fulness of the Gentiles* had not come in, now it has. The wars and rumours of wars were not about, now they are, and 20,000,000 armed men on the battle-fields, prepared for the deadliest war yet told of. Twenty years ago the Bible was neither corroborated nor confirmed, nor God Himself established as a God of truth. Then there were 700 promises of prophecy not known to be fulfilled, and God could not possibly be established as true unless they were fulfilled. We have waited for their fulfillment, 777 in number, and they have all come to pass. These have all belonged to the past. Now we wait for future events.

We can see numerous millenarian crosscurrents in Hine's thinking—the futurist aversion to date setting together with the historicist search for prophetic fulfillment in the past. British-Israelism always harbored a historicist strain, since its assertion that the Anglo-Saxon-Celtic peoples were Israel compelled it to find in aspects of their history demonstrations that one or another biblical prophecy concerning the Israelites had been fulfilled by British descendants. In place of Darby's great parenthesis, British-Israelism saw less reason to stop the prophetic clock. If the Jews were not Israel, their rejection of Jesus posed less of a problem in millenarian terms, although to be sure they would eventually have to be regathered in Palestine and convert. If Israel was another group, and a Christian one at that, it was entirely possible that prophecies had continued to be fulfilled throughout the Christian era. The obstacle in this case was the fact that these putative Israelites were unaware of their true identity, a problem the movement felt obliged to solve with any persuasive techniques available.[8]

Millennialism among American British-Israelites

The same conviction of accelerating apocalypse may be found in American British-Israelites. Thus Joseph Wild, one of the earliest Anglo-Israelite writers in America and a contemporary of Hine's, saw numerous signs of prophetic fulfillment, "these being the latter days." M. M. Eshelman detected in greater civil and political rights for Jews the threshold of that critical time when Jews would regather in Palestine so that events linked to the final consummation of history could begin. But among American believers, none bore down more heavily on millenarian themes than C. A. L. Totten. In part, the strength of Totten's chiliasm was a function of the time in which he wrote, a decade after Eshelman and almost twenty years after Wild. Totten's work reflected rising social tensions in an America beset by economic dislocations and inequality and the adjustments required by mass immigration. Internationally, tensions continued to build toward the coming flashpoint of the First World War. There was, finally, the more diffuse sense of expectation generated by the approaching end of the century itself. Thus in 1897, Totten observed that

> the fall of Turkey is in sight, the nations are literally gathering toward Armageddon, the heathen rage, the waves roar, the signs increase in heaven and upon earth, and all things portend the ending of an age that has at least established the science of prophecy. . . . The establishment of the Fifth and final universal monarchy is now due, for the "times of the Gentiles" certainly run out with "this generation," and the century now wanes!

While none of this reflects a particularly acute theological mind, it clearly suggests that the millenarian speculation rising in Protestant circles generally made a comparably deep impact upon British-Israelites.[9]

Systematizing British-Israel Millennialism

As British-Israelism matured, it eventually sought to present its millenarian views in a more logically connected fashion, although its theological efforts were limited by the fact that the movement never took fully sectarian form.

It had, therefore, to contend with a membership that retained a range of denominational affiliations and the impossibility of enforcing orthodoxy on questions where believers were already divided. The most ambitious attempt to codify British-Israel beliefs took the form of a collection of extended essays, *British-Israel Truth*, first issued in 1891 and revised numerous times through the 1930s. Its authors laid out as clear a statement of Anglo-Israel millennialism as the permissive character of the movement allowed.

In this presentation, the prevalent concept of periodized, or dispensational, sacred history was retained. Those blessings the Bible promises to Israel that refer to temporal power and wealth must be fulfilled before the end of the present dispensation and, therefore, before the Second Coming. These include any prophecies that deal with the regathering of the tribes. Consequently, they cannot be fulfilled until the true Israel becomes fully aware of its real "identity." This position is fully and unambiguously premillennialist—that is, it is deemed necessary that Christ return prior to the millennium rather than at its conclusion: "Our Lord's second, personal, and premillennial advent is one of the foundation-stones on which we build our argument." Nonetheless, H. Aldersmith, one of the volume's editors, felt constrained to separate fundamental beliefs from those about which British-Israelites might legitimately differ:

> Those holding British-Israel views may differ—like other students of prophecy—about the exact position of the translation of the then living true Christians [i.e., the rapture]; with regard to the ending of "the Times of the Gentiles"; the last "Great Tribulation"; and other events during the closing years of this Dispensation; they are practically unanimous in looking forward to THE PERSONAL AND PRE-MILLENNIAL ADVENT OF CHRIST.

In short, the movement strove to avoid taking a firm position in the still-ongoing debate between the historicists and the futurists, both of whom were premillenarians but were separated, as we have seen, on details of scriptural interpretation and apocalyptic chronology.[10]

In seeking to maintain a balance between premillennial orthodoxy and latitude concerning details, British-Israel writers nonetheless were often tempted to provide details of the Last Days. Hine himself had described how, prior to the Battle of Armageddon, the emperor of France would rise to greater power, Paris would be burned (by whom Hine does not say), and the Latin nations would form a confederation under the French emperor, ruling from Rome. With Napoleon III thus identified as the Antichrist, he goes on to identify

Russia with the apocalyptic Gog, a common millenarian practice. Russia would then defeat the Antichrist's confederacy and move toward Palestine, which in the meantime had been resettled by Israel. Hine had also inscribed a millenarian scenario into the flyleaf of his Bible, probably around 1870:

1. Restoration of the Jews.
2. Pouring out of the Spirit.
3. The Universal acceptance of the Gospel.
4. The Great Tribulation.
5. The Resurrection of the Faithful.
6. The Second Coming of the Lord.
7. The Millennial Age.

The American Eshelman had worked out two such scenarios. In one, England conquers Palestine and opens it to settlement by Jews and "Israelites," who elect an enlightened and learned ruler. Those Jews who have not returned to Palestine come under the rule of the Antichrist, who, unlike Hine's Antichrist, becomes an ally of the czar. Their combined armies advance on Palestine, only to be decisively defeated by the Israelites aided by the returned Jesus. Alternatively, Eshelman has Palestine secured by an unknown power, the country now ruled by a Davidic descendant who rebuilds Jerusalem and the Temple, where services are reinstituted. "Russia and her allies" arrive for the Battle of Armageddon, where Christ destroys them.[11]

By the post–World War I period, such speculations required additional attention in light of the defeat of the Ottomans and League of Nations' assignment of a British mandate over Palestine. The defeat of Turkey had long had special significance for millenarians. Indeed, the Millerites and their Seventh-Day Adventist successors expended considerable ingenuity linking the fall of Turkish power with the sixth trumpet of the Book of Revelation. Throughout the nineteenth century, however, despite numerous international crises connected with "the Eastern question," the Ottoman Empire survived, albeit in an increasingly enfeebled condition. British-Israelites looked back upon General Allenby's conquest of Jerusalem in 1917, the subsequent defeat of Turkey, and the assignment of Palestine to Britain as a mandate territory in 1923 as the fulfillment of prophecy and, more specifically, as the vindication of decades of Anglo-Israelite teaching: "It will be seen that we fully expected this great European war-woe, the drying up of the Turkish power, the occupation of the promised land by Great Britain, and the return of the Jews to Palestine."[12]

In the wake of these events, British-Israel millennialism took on both greater urgency and greater specificity. "The Anglo-Saxon race," represented by England and the United States, was destined to have "the ultimate dominion of the world" during Christ's millennial reign. Before that time comes, however, this latter-day Israel was to undergo disasters and trials to purge her of accumulated sins. In the time before the final Tribulation, the Jews would return to Palestine under British sponsorship and protection, effecting the ingathering, with the Anglo-Saxons, of "All-Israel." In the days that will follow this ingathering, Gog in the form of Russia will invade the Holy Land at the end of the Tribulation period. As the Battle of Armageddon is joined, the Jews will acknowledge Jesus as the Messiah, the Anglo-Saxons will call upon God for deliverance, and Christ will descend to save his people. In setting out this consensus position, however, British-Israelites were careful to note that theological divergences remained.[13]

This was nowhere more evident than in the gingerly manner in which they approached the issue of the rapture, perhaps the major source of division between historicists and futurists. While acknowledging that representatives of the twelve tribes would be reunited in Palestine at the time of the Second Coming, Aldersmith assured his readers that "the *exact* relation of 'the rapture of the Church' to the other closing events in this dispensation, has but little to do with the main question discussed in this book." The church would be raptured and the saints would return with Christ, "but the time that will intervene between the two events is a matter that is much disputed by students of the prophetic Word." Aldersmith's personal view was that all the believers in Christ would be raptured near the end of the Tribulation, but "we distinctly assert, in the name of our Association, that we teach no dogmatic views on the relative position of future events connected with our Lord's return, and everyone is free to hold his own opinion as to when these things will come to pass." The significance of this theological toleration is not merely restricted to the British-Israelites' desire to include both historicists and futurists. Rather, this acceptance of diverse viewpoints was to develop subsequently in unforeseen ways. American Fundamentalism came to be dominated by Darby's futurist position, and, as we shall see, Christian Identity developed theological positions far more restrictive than those of its Anglo-Israel forebears. Where British-Israelites were content to let the two camps continue their debate as long as they accepted the Anglo-Saxons as Israel, Christian Identity has rejected futurism and the Darbyite dispensational model in unequivocal terms, in the process accusing Fundamentalists of ignorance, corruption, and distortion of God's word. They reject the rapture and all the apparatus of interpretation that accompanies it, a matter to be taken up in greater detail in the next chapter. Hence, British-Israel latitudinarianism, welcoming millennialists of every stripe, was to give way to a cleavage between Christian Identity and the Fundamentalist community.[14]

Millennialism and Pyramidism

If one of futurism's pillars was the doctrine of the rapture, another was the aversion to setting dates for the final events of history. There were, of course, practical as well as doctrinal reasons for this reluctance, since a movement could be destroyed by false predictions, as Millerism had been. British-Israelism, however, began increasingly to edge toward precisely this date-setting abyss, coming toward it, however, from an idiosyncratic direction. British-Israelism had since the late nineteenth century been fascinated by the mathematical properties of the Great Pyramid at Gizeh, and it had become commonplace to ascribe its design to one or another of the Israelites' ancestors, such as Enoch or Noah. By the 1920s, however, this occult fascination with the pyramid's dimensions crystallized into a system for dating the events of millenarian history. This enterprise was principally connected with the work of a Scots engineer, David Davidson.

Davidson created a system that involved the correlation of pyramid measurements with dates from both scriptural and secular history, employing the formula of one "pyramid-inch" (which deviated slightly from the English measure) equaling one year. This formula was then applied to the structure's internal passageways, which led to the so-called King's Chamber. Davidson's system was in fact not unlike the historicists' equation of one biblical day with one historical year, except that while biblical references to days were scattered throughout the Scriptures, the pyramidal system of passages was a well-bounded entity with demarcations in the form of changes in the height, dimensions, and direction of the tunnels. The advantage of the pyramid studies was that they gave the appearance of precision, indeed even of archaeological science, to British-Israel interpretations of prophecy. If God had indeed had the pyramid created to encode a message for humanity, and if in fact its internal dimensions could be precisely measured (which indeed was the case), then the divine design for both past and future history was displayed for "objective" study. The disadvantage of the approach, beyond the association of pyramid studies with occultism, was the same as that of more conventional historicist calculations, namely, that it raised the temptation of predicting the future and, inevitably, of being embarrassed by the results. Nonetheless, the sheer bulk and detail of Davidson's work led to wide acceptance in British-Israel circles and, with it, entry onto the dangerous terrain of date setting.

The futurist message had been sufficiently strong to lead Aldersmith to write that

> the Second Advent is *near*, though we are not foolish enough to try to fix the date of it (as is too common in these last days), knowing full well that nothing does more harm to the study of prophecy than the unwise attempt of trying to determine the exact date of our Lord's appearing. That time is known to God; and though many signs of its near approach may be apparent, . . . yet the precise time is hidden, and probably will be till the end.

These sentiments notwithstanding, Aldersmith was also the coauthor of Davidson's most influential work, *The Great Pyramid: Its Divine Message*, although his listing as coauthor was largely a courtesy extended by his senior collaborator. Aldersmith in fact died before the book was written, having been involved with the research that led to it, and there is no way of knowing what he would have made of the result. In the book itself, Davidson made no secret of his belief that the Last Days had begun and that he had predicted their onset.[15]

Davidson claimed, for example, to have predicted the Great Depression, when in the original edition of the book he claimed that the pyramid foretold "that a period of Tribulation on the British world order should extend from May 29, 1928, to September 16, 1936." He regarded it, therefore, as no accident that London commodity prices began to fall on May 29, 1928, and that the pound reached its highest 1928 value on May 30, only to begin falling the following day. In fact, he claimed for pyramid prophecy the same precision that a century earlier William Miller and his followers had claimed for their calculations based on Daniel and Revelation. In Davidson's case, the purpose of the pyramid was not only to make a divine proclamation of Jesus as the Savior, but "*to announce the dated circumstances relating to His Coming.*" Davidson had, in effect, fused pyramidal numerology, the manipulation of the building's measurements, with prophetic interpretation. The result was to give British-Israelism a means of relieving the anguish millenarians always feel that comes from not knowing when the inevitable will occur. It also gave British-Israelism a further claim to uniqueness, beyond that which already attached to its revisionist identification of Israel.[16]

Pyramid Millennialism in North America

Davidson's work had particular influence upon the millenarian expectations in North America. Three individuals in particular used it to help construct detailed and politically charged millenarian scenarios: the Canadian writer W. G. MacKendrick, a close friend of William J. Cameron; Howard Rand, the founder of the Anglo-Saxon Federation of America; and, significantly, William Dudley Pelley, the organizer of such Depression-era political organizations as the Silver Legion and the Christian party.

Beginning with his first book in 1921, W. G. MacKendrick's writings were saturated with millennial expectation and a thirst for precision about apocalyptic dates. Thus he concluded that the war that would climax in Armageddon was only a few years off, although his dating was sometimes difficult to follow. "This war is to take place in the Holy Land and will be finished by 1936 according to the best authorities," he writes, only to observe a few pages later that "Armageddon will be upon us about eleven years from the time we took Jerusalem." If that refers to Allenby's conquest in 1917, it would put Armageddon at 1928. If MacKendrick means the assumption by Britain of the mandate over Palestine in 1923, that would push Armageddon to 1934, still two years shy of his 1936 prediction. It is unclear whether at the time MacKendrick wrote he had had any contact with Davidson. The latter began to publish only in 1925. However, both 1928 and 1936 were key dates in Davidson's system. Nineteen twenty-eight marked the beginning of the Final Tribulation, while 1936 marked its conclusion.[17]

MacKendrick's prophetic chronology became much more complicated during the years of World War II. This complexity was no doubt attributable to separate factors: the apocalyptic expectations generated by the war itself; the publications by Davidson, with whom MacKendrick was acquainted by this time; and a three-way correspondence he maintained with William McCrea, a Canadian British-Israelite, and William J. Cameron. The letters make clear MacKendrick's acceptance of Davidson's conclusions, which he melded with related but independent speculations based upon the pyramid and other ancient artifacts undertaken by McCrea.[18]

The tensions of the war clearly drove both McCrea and MacKendrick to increasingly desperate efforts to calculate its end. Thus McCrea wrote MacKendrick, apparently in the bleak summer of 1940, "You know that I have never, never liked this 'date' business. It was that reluctance of mine, then, to investigate the future which kept me from giving you the whole plan of the war sooner. . . . 1940 is THE YEAR of retribution, though the end does not come until March 2nd, 1941, five days after Feb. 25th, which is indicated as something terrific." MacKendrick passed this letter on to William J. Cameron, as he did McCrea's numerous other pieces of correspondence. Since 1940 obviously passed without an Allied victory, McCrea was forced to push the apocalypse further along, and by early 1942 he had settled upon March 6, 1942, with the cautionary note that it would mark not the end of the war but "a definite step in what Davidson calls 'the Round-Up.'" "The Round-up" was Davidson's term for the rounding-up of the powers of evil that would precede the final consummation. By the fall of 1942, it was clear that McCrea's hopes would not be realized, and MacKendrick had to confess to Cameron, as so many other millennialists had in the past, "'His ways are not our ways' we are subject to error [sic]." McCrea had shifted by this time first to August 31 and then to September 10, and even as late as September 4 confessed to Mac-Kendrick, "August 31st would be the start of the ten days that would see the end of hostilities. . . . August 31st . . . IS THE GREAT DAY. *There is no possibility of error. . . .* If I am wrong . . . then I shall be completely baffled." As for MacKendrick himself, he was assuring Cameron on September 22, that a major earthquake would take place December 8–10 and hoped the Ford Motor Company plants would survive. After so many apparently missed predictions, McCrea dug in his heels concerning September 10: "I DID NOT MAKE A MISTAKE." Something *had* occurred on September 10, he concluded, but it was a mystic end of hostilities, the beginning of "that very short period during which Christ fights the battle alone." Although none could see it, this was the war's "real climax."[19]

During the year of the McCrea-MacKendrick correspondence—1942—MacKendrick gave public voice to his own growing feelings of millennial imminence in a brief book, *This IS Armageddon*. He concluded that the conflict in progress had a finality none of its predecessors could claim: "This is the war of God's Great Day—the final war of this age of wars." He concluded that since Hitler "cannot possibly last until the fall of 1943," the climactic events of this climactic struggle would begin momentarily, in the venue prophecy had set aside for it—not in the areas of central combat in Europe or the Pacific, but in Palestine. So certain was MacKendrick that the war would conclude in Palestine, and sooner rather than later, that two years previously, in the fall of 1940, he had set out a detailed military-religious scenario for the war's conclusion and sent it off to General A. G. McNaughton, the commander of Canadian troops in Britain.[20]

The description MacKendrick sent to General McNaughton was extraordinary both in its specificity and in its author's conviction that God required events to play out in this way and in no other, and that those who had the ear of policymakers must make certain that strategic plans were drawn up accordingly. As MacKendrick had it, Germany would seek to capture the pipeline that led to the Haifa oil refinery, as well as to the Iraqi and Iranian oil fields, bombing Britain's Mediterranean fleet in the process. Egypt would not hold: "Egypt is going to let us down and we will lose out there—that's Biblical and certain." As a sequel to these grim events, Mussolini would conquer both Egypt and Palestine, but a coalition of Russia, Turkey, and Iran would defeat and kill him there. The combined armies of Germany, Russia, Italy (presuming any forces remained), Turkey, and Iran would gather against Jerusalem, and in this atmosphere of direst need, King George VI would declare a national day of prayer. As England (i.e., Israel) placed itself in God's hands, "by the Omnipotent power of our Lord . . . we will be saved to carry on into the NEW ERA as decreed in Holy Writ." It is not known what response, if any, General McNaughton made to this remarkable letter.[21]

MacKendrick, however, did not limit such highly detailed predictions about the Last Days to his correspondence. In 1921 he had not only sought to date the Battle of Armageddon, as described above, but had written a totally different scenario for it, as reflective of the post–World War I political ambience as his letter to General McNaughton was of the World War II environment. His initial stab at Armageddon politics placed Britain in a common cause with India and with the Arabs, playing upon the romanticization of desert tribesmen by T. E. Lawrence. He dropped this imperial coalition under the pressure of events in the 1940s and in *This IS Armageddon* continued to elaborate the ideas outlined in the McNaughton letter. In the published version of his apocalyptic script, he foresees a successful attack by Hitler (not Mussolini) on Palestine, Egypt, and the Suez Canal in June or July 1942. Hitler literally sets up his tent between Mt. Carmel and the sea. But before he can take control of Iraqi oil, Russian forces ("Gog's hordes") march down the east bank of the Jordan and cut the Germans off. After the chastened Anglo-Saxons call upon God's help, a series of natural calamities ("the Day of the Lord") saves the day, including clouds of carbon monoxide generated when great earthquakes release and ignite subterranean pools of oil and "fire and brimstone" raining down from sudden volcanic eruptions. It is a picture as lurid as anything that came from the Millerite imagination in the nineteenth century.[22]

While MacKendrick may have been unusual in the specificity of his predictions, he was by no means the only British-Israelite who combined Davidson's predictive apparatus with a belief that the Second World War was part of the final clash between good and evil. A contemporary, Frederick Haberman, who was also heavily dependent upon Davidson's work, exclaimed shortly after war broke out that *"Great Pyramid Prophecy has been fulfilled."* Indeed, Haberman was vulnerable to the same predictive mania as McCrea and Mac-

Kendrick. He felt sure that if the German forces reached Palestine by the end of June 1941, *"we may expect startling developments over there by the 25th of that month."* Davidson himself, interestingly, was far more circumspect in his approach to the war. He was anxious to demonstrate that he had predicted it and equally anxious to indicate what lay on the other side, but he did not succumb to the temptation to give a day-to-day forecast of military events.[23]

Davidson presented two public lectures on the war in London on July 8 and October 8, 1942, while the McCrea-MacKendrick-Cameron correspondence was at its height. He reminded his audiences that he had unveiled God's pyramid messages in the 1920s, predicting both the Depression and the Second World War. With his customary facility, he was able to note that on pyramidally significant dates, *something* had always happened that might be linked to later, larger developments. Insofar as the war itself was concerned, Davidson had no doubts about its ultimate significance: "It is a war which is to end in the utter demolition of the tools and works of civilisation, to prepare the world for the foundations of the Kingdom of Heaven on earth. . . . If this war goes on as it is now going and as it must continue to a settlement, there will be *nothing left for any nation to covet of another.* It is the purpose of God Almighty that this should be so." The purpose of the war, as he saw it, was to force submission to God's will, to lead "modern Israel [to] the Kingdom of Heaven on earth." Rather than anticipating an imminent Armageddon, as followers such as MacKendrick and Haberman had, Davidson focused on a somewhat more distant set of dates: the political union of Britain and America by January 31, 1947; the extension of unification "to every element of the race by 10th November 1948"; and "attaining cooperation with God" by August 20, 1953. As to the millennium itself, that was still further off, but datable nonetheless. "The millennial reign of righteousness" would begin, Davidson predicted, on September 17, 2001. The gap between Davidson's views and those of what one might call the prophetic strategists in Canada at the same time suggests that Davidson's system of pyramid calculations had, like other forms of millenarian date setting, taken on a life of its own, independent of the views of its creator. It had the twin virtues that it had sufficient precision to suggest to believers that they had access to a "science of prophecy" and was sufficiently ambiguous so that it could be molded to fit changing circumstances and differing tastes. No matter who employed it, however, the aim remained the same, to predict the millennium and to identify events on the road to it.[24]

Davidson's system excited millenarians not only in Canada but in the United States. As far back as the mid-1930s, it had captivated a figure not

usually associated with British-Israelism, right-wing mystic and political organizer William Dudley Pelley.

William Dudley Pelley

William Dudley Pelley, the founder of the Silver Shirts, did not consider
himself a British-Israelite, and, indeed, it is difficult to imagine a person of
such idiosyncratic views subordinating himself to any belief system he had not
invented. He mocked British-Israelism as an ideology based upon a flawed
conception of the covenant between God and Israel. Nonetheless, Pelley's entire vision of history was structured around the pyramid chronology of David
Davidson. While it is not clear how early Pelley first became acquainted with
Davidson's ideas, Pelley reports that his lieutenant, Robert Summerville, was
in correspondence with Davidson by March 1933. Summerville interrupted
Pelley with a letter and a pamphlet "from Professor [sic] David Davidson, the
eminent Great Pyramid authority." Summerville asked him whether he was
familiar with the pamphlet Davidson had sent, the title of which Pelley does
not report. Pelley had not previously seen the pamphlet but is vague about
whether he knew Davidson's other writings. The general tenor of the passage
in which the incident is described, however, suggests that this was not his first
exposure to Davidson. Davidson had been publishing since the mid-1920s
and had issued two works in the early 1930s that spoke directly to current
political and economic issues, *The Great Pyramid's Prophecy on the Current
Economic Oppression* (March 1931) and *The Great Pyramid's Prophecy Concerning the British Empire and America* (September 1932). It may well have
been one of these that Summerville received.[25]

In any case, Davidson's work evidently made a profound impression on
Pelley. In 1935 Pelley announced the organization of the Christian party, on
whose ticket he intended to run for president in 1936. For the inner circle of
the party—its Councils of Safety—he created a set of *Master Councillor's
Addresses*, in which he laid out his application of Davidson to both world and
American history. The *Master Councillor's Addresses* cite Davidson copiously.
Indeed, Pelley appropriated most of Davidson's system of pyramid chronology
unaltered. Even when Davidson is not explicitly cited, his system permeates
Pelley's view of events.[26]

Despite Pelley's disdainful comment on British-Israelites, he retained a
good deal of British-Israelism. Although he occasionally implied that Jews
were descended from Israelites—as when he referred to the latter's Exodus as
"their petty and spleenish experiences"—he was inclined to accept British-

Israelism's distinction between the two. Intellectual rigor, never Pelley's strong suit, collapses in a heap of contradictions. On the one hand, the people led out of Egypt by Moses were "Hebrews and Israelites. By no means were they Jews." On the other hand, "it's from the tribe of Judah that we get modern Jews." The tribe of Judah, according to Pelley, were the bane of Moses' existence, as "disruptive [and] cantankerous" in the desert as their descendants were subsequently. Pelley's confusion apparently arises from his emphasis upon the period of the Exodus rather than upon the subsequent division of the Israelite polity into the kingdoms of Israel and Judah. Pelley also adopted the notion, occasionally found among Anglo-Israelites, that descendants of Abraham also migrated east and south to become ancestors of the Hindus. A similar idea—this time that some members of the ten lost tribes fathered modern Hindus—appeared at the turn of the century in the writings of the founder of Pentecostalism, Charles F. Parham, also a believer in British-Israelism.[27]

Pelley held back, however, in tracing other modern descendants of the Israelites. He clearly had little patience with the claim that the British were descendants of the lost tribes and was apparently unaware of the British-Israel belief in the central role to be played by the descendants of Ephraim (the British) and Manasseh (the Americans). As for the place of the United States in Pelley's cosmic drama, he was characteristically muddled, uncertain how much to embrace the biological determinism of British-Israelism. Thus he seemed to interpret American chosenness figuratively when he asserted that "my Chosen People aren't composed of a *race*. They're those who've given their allegiance to a *king*." But in nearly the same breath he announces that "the *real* Chosen people . . . are here in America. It's the Twelve Tribes here in the United States." Whether his tribes are symbolic or literal, however, is never explained.[28]

The key to understanding God's design for Pelley, as for Davidson, lies in the configuration and measurements of the passageways of the Great Pyramid, what British-Israelites were fond of referring to as "the Bible in stone." He saw in pyramid prophecy an infallible guide to history: "Great Pyramid prophecy has never been wrong," although there can be difficult problems in correlating the prophecies with the right kind of evidence. The pyramid is always right about issues of timing; if the date comes up, something *must* have happened. As Pelley put it, "The quandary which we, as reasonably enlightened students of universal affairs, are faced with, isn't WHEN great events are due to occur, but WHAT the nature of those great events is to be in each case when chronology arrives at Great Pyramid markings." In other words, the assumption that pyramid prophecy is infallible implies that something must have occurred on the assigned date.[29]

This approach to prophetic fulfillment effectively eliminates a major vulnerability of date-setting schemes, the danger that specific, empirically testable predictions will produce massive public embarrassments for a religious movement, of the sort experienced by the Millerites in 1844. Such predictions customarily involve statements that some particular event, most frequently the Second Coming, will occur on a particular date; hence its nonoccurrence is traumatic. Pyramidologists emphasized the significance of the date and then looked to see what had happened on it. Given the intrinsic ambiguity of events, they were almost always able to find an event that could be appropriately classified.

Pelley, however, was reluctant to place all of his confidence in a single view of history, especially one concocted by someone else, if only because it appeared to make him dependent upon the insights of others. Accordingly, he was at pains to make clear that whatever Davidson had discovered had already been vouchsafed to him (Pelley) independently. Pelley always claimed special access to divine or supernatural forces, beginning with a revelatory, out-of-body experience he claimed to have gone through in 1928. He assured his followers that before he had ever read or heard of the pyramid literature, his "Oracle" had already revealed to him the significance of a key pyramid date: "'Your True labors in this nation begin on the morning of September 17, 1936,'" the date the Silver Shirts were founded. The work of Davidson could then function as a confirmation of the prophet's revelation.[30]

The principal alteration Pelley made in Davidson's system lay in the radically changed significance of the Exodus of Israel from Egypt. For Davidson, as for other mainstream British-Israelites, the Exodus was a central episode in the history of the "Adamic race," Davidson's term for the white race, the spiritual elite that was subsequently to populate Britain. Indeed, for Davidson it was one of the "three chief occasions of Divine Interference in the normal course of human history," the other two being the Resurrection and the final, apocalyptic "Exodus of civilisation from Economic Bondage under the rule of Money-Power." Pelley took a very different view of things, suggesting that the travails of the escaping Israelites were less a significant set of events in themselves than they were a prefiguration of later history. He was inclined to see in the events of the Exodus merely a microcosmic anticipation of the future. The Israelites of the Exodus were "little" Israel, "petty and spleenish," people temperamentally unworthy of performing great events. What they experienced was important only because it provided "a literal model for the Program of the Greater Israel coming out of *real* Egyptian bondage 3,000 years afterward." And who was this latter-day "Greater Israel"? It was none other than the white Christians of Pelley's own day. And *"real* Egypt"? In language the Populists might have appreciated, Pelley described it as "the economic structure founded on gold, where the true followers of Christ must make bricks without straw."[31]

Pelley was prepared to go a good deal further in identifying "Egypt." In an inversion whose irony Pelley himself seems to have realized, the Jews became "Egypt": "Now we've got the ironical situations of the tables being turned. . . . The 'Egyptians' are the racial plunderers who imagine they're Israelites because they've descended from the one tribe of Judah. . . . The Jews are the Egyptians, and the Gentiles are the Israelites." In a way, Pelley simply completed the theme of reversal begun in British-Israelism. The latter, by rejecting Jewish chosenness and asserting Anglo-Saxon chosenness, had reversed the positions of Jews and Gentiles. Now Pelley's version of the Exodus reversed the roles of Israelites and Egyptians. Not only were the Jews merely a tiny fragment of the Israelites ("from the one tribe of Judah"); they now played Egyptians to the "Christian Israelites," as Pelley called them. In this replay of the Exodus as modern economic allegory, the story of escape from Egyptian slavery became something "not to glorify the Jews, but to give us a Code Book for all that is to happen in the 65 years ahead." The crossing of the Red Sea even became the passage "unscathed through the great sea of Red Bolshevism."[32]

All of this was keyed, of course, to Davidson's pyramid chronology, which marked off dates on a sacred calendar. Using his formula of one "pyramid inch" for one solar year, Davidson calculated that there would be a two-phase Tribulation as part of the Last Days, the outcome of "the Great Pyramid's Scientific prophecy." The first phase would run from August 4, 1914, to November 11, 1918, the second and greater phase from May 29–30, 1928, to September 15–16, 1936. Then, "between September 16, 1936, and August 20, 1953, the English-speaking peoples should be guided, as the nucleus of the Theocratic (or Theocentric) World-State, to receive Divine Protection ensuring racial isolation and true safe-guarding under the Law of the Kingdom of Heaven on earth." Pelley proceeded to incorporate into Davidson's eschatology his own conceptions of a war against the Jews and his own metahistoric role in human redemption.[33]

Not surprisingly, Pelley focused on the year in which he was writing, 1936, the year of the foundation of the Christian party, when he would attempt to vindicate himself at the polls. Davidson had predicted great events for September 16, when the Tribulation would give way to the final march toward "the Theocratic [i.e., millennial] . . . World-State." According to Pelley, September 16 would mark a "crisis," *the lowest ebbs of this depression.* In his idiosyncratic reading of the Exodus story, September 16, 1936, was going to mark the beginning of freedom from "Jewish-Egyptian economic bondage." Davidson's pyramid date was anticipated by Pelley's Oracle, who had independently revealed to him that " 'your true labors in this nation begin on the morning of September 17, 1936.' " After September 16, 1936, nations would have the next seventeen years to decide whether to adopt theocratic government, after which those who rejected it would be destroyed.[34]

The Jews played rather a different role in Pelley's scheme than they did in Davidson's. As we shall see in a later chapter, Davidson, together with other twentieth-century British-Israel writers, incorporated covertly anti-Semitic themes. However, he regarded Britain as divinely charged with rescuing Jews from persecution and facilitating their ingathering to Palestine. Pelley, of course, considered the Jews responsible for the Depression as well as much else in the way of the world's evil, although he was willing to forego genocidal massacre, largely on the grounds that "so long as one Jew remained, in the furthest corner of Patagonia, the deed down distant years would have to be repeated." He was perfectly willing to tolerate "incidental" violence but was confident that the establishment of "Christian economics" would drastically alter Jewish behavior. Consequently, he was impatient with Davidson's seeming disinterest in "the Jewish question." Indeed, as a result, he said, Davidson had entirely missed the significance of January 31, 1933, when Hitler came to power "and began smashing the predatory clutch of Judah on civilized institutions." It was the struggle against the Jews that was central for Pelley, for that was "THE GREAT ARMAGEDDON OF ANCIENT PROPHECY," the battle of Gog and Magog.[35]

This struggle would inexorably lead, in Pelley's view, to both the end of the Depression and the millennium. He held out little hope that the Depression would end any time soon, however; surcease would come only on the night of September 16, 1969, *and not one moment sooner!* As to the millennium, he was of two minds. In one sense, he expected the millennium to begin in a matter of months, on September 16 of the year in which he was writing, for everything from then on would be improvement. On the other hand, that position reflected a kind of postmillennialism, the point when beneficent forces would begin to operate in America, thanks presumably to the Silver Legion and the Christian party. The true, world millennium was farther off, on September 17, 2001, at which point the entire world would be incorporated into "the Christ form of government." Although the date was distant, the finality of the outcome allowed Pelley to indulge his premillennialism as well.[36]

The Christian party's performance in the 1936 election was pathetic even by minor party standards. Indeed, Pelley's efforts were paltry compared with the far more conspicuous campaign by the Union party, the coalition formed by Dr. Francis Townsend, Gerald L. K. Smith, and Charles Coughlin. Although Pelley claimed significant efforts in sixteen states, the party appeared on the ballot only in the state of Washington. Of the nearly 70,000 votes cast in Washington in 1936, the Union party received 17,463. Only 1,598 went to Pelley, 300 fewer than the Communist party received and only 550 more than the Prohibition party garnered.[37]

Notwithstanding Pelley's failure to draw any significant electoral support, such grass-roots activity as the Silver Legion and Christian party had generated was heavily concentrated in a few areas of the country. Pelley's followers clustered in the Great Lakes region and the Pacific Coast, probably never amounting to more than fifteen thousand at any one time. Modest though the size of the movement was, its concentration, particularly on the West Coast, may have nurtured coteries of proto-Identity believers, persons who had been exposed to Pelley's personal fusion of British-Israelism and anti-Semitism and hence were more receptive to other such combinations later. Among them was Henry L. "Mike" Beach, who in 1969 was one of the founders of Posse Comitatus. In the mid-1970s Beach's organization, CLERC (Citizens Law Enforcement and Research Committee), reprinted a turn-of-the-century extract from C. A. L. Totten's *Our Race*, and in so doing brought Identity from its roots in late nineteenth-century British-Israel missionizing, through Pelley's mystic anti-Semitism in the mid-1930s, to the militantly antiauthority stance Identity took in the 1970s.[38]

Howard Rand

Howard Rand, as the American representative of the British-Israel World Federation, assiduously promulgated the millenarian views of the parent organization. In keeping with the position of other Anglo-Israelites, Rand also shaped his millennialism to the date-setting apparatus developed by Davidson. On the occasion of Davidson's death in 1956, Rand wrote of him: "He was a man called of God to proclaim the meaning of the Structural measurements of the Great Pyramid of Gizeh. . . . The material he so carefully compiled . . . will yet be used mightily of God to glorify His own Name and demonstrate the accuracy of the revelation measures built so many centuries ago into this Great Witness in the midst of the land of Egypt." Rand's extraordinary longevity—he remained active as a writer and publisher from the late 1920s into the early 1990s—compelled him to maintain his millenarian views through a variety of economic, religious, and political circumstances, including the Depression, World War II, the Cold War, and the development of Christian Identity.[39]

Rand rejected the futurist view associated with John Nelson Darby in a manner consistent with British-Israelism's rejection of Darby's belief that the prophetic clock had stopped. Indeed, to believe that prophetic fulfillment temporarily ceased after the Jewish rejection of Jesus would fly in the face of the Anglo-Israelite belief in the redemptive history of the Anglo-Saxons:

> The Bible gives no warrant to the common view of a "Gentile Parenthesis" [wrote Hanan and Aldersmith]. . . . From Genesis to Revelation we can easily trace . . . the grand chain of God's providential scheme of rescue from the ruin of the fall, in the *redemption* of Israel; and, by the revelation made to them, and their carrying the Gospel to the uttermost parts of the earth, the deliverance of the whole human family from the bondage of Satan.

Rand's objection to the parenthesis theory was in part founded on divergent readings of key scriptural passages, particularly from the Book of Daniel. But by the late 1940s, Rand's view of futurism was also colored by his hostility to Zionism. As we shall see in chapter 7, anti-Zionism had become relatively common among British-Israelites in England as a result of the Zionist challenge to the British mandate in Palestine. In Rand's case, this hostility was compounded by the anti-Semitism that had been endemic in the Anglo-Saxon Federation of America virtually since its founding in 1928 and that had been personified in the 1930s by William J. Cameron.[40]

Rand rejected the futurist view that the establishment of a Jewish state in Palestine constituted the fulfillment of prophecy. Instead, he asserted that the return of Jews to Palestine was part of a different divine plan, which would see "the gathering of the enemies of our Lord for the final execution of judgement upon them for their rejection of Him." Hence, in Rand's view, Jews were returning to the Holy Land "under an urge which they themselves cannot wholly define . . . so that they may arrive in time at the place of execution when the sentence will be carried out." In short, the setting up of a Jewish state, far from being a sign that a dormant "prophetic clock" had begun to run, was rather a sign of the imminence of "the Great and Terrible Day of the

Lord." In words that did not require much elaboration, Rand broadly hinted that the state of Israel would be destroyed by God and its Jewish inhabitants would be killed to punish them for their and their ancestors' refusal to convert to Christianity.[41]

As was the case with many British-Israelites, Rand looked more kindly at the Zionist movement when it did not appear to threaten British hegemony in Palestine. In 1943 he saw "the program to again make the Jewish people an independent nation" as evidence that "the fig tree is truly budding again." If that were the case, then his would be the generation of the latter days: "We are witnessing an age coming to an end; and we will see the resurrection and return of Our Lord." A year later, Rand saw in Britain's refusal to recognize Zionist claims the catalyst for a political situation that would ultimately draw Russia ("the hosts of Gog") into Palestine, and when that occurred, the final events of history were bound to follow, that complex of battles and disasters Rand habitually referred to as "the Great and Terrible Day of the Lord."[42]

Although nuances changed in Rand's voluminous millenarian writings, his views remained staunchly premillennial, although more closely wedded to the historicists than to the futurists. Like generations of premillennialists before him, Rand adopted the view of "the worse, the better," in the sense that the millennium would be preceded by rising "evil and corruption" rather than by the waxing of virtue and spirituality. Every sign of multiplying vice was evidence that divine judgment was imminent. When that judgment came, it would destroy "all evil, after which the righteous will shine forth as the sun." Jesus would return to physically rule over the earth and to "establish the millennial rule of righteousness." Rand never wavered in his belief in the imminence of the apocalypse. Nonetheless, like other Anglo-Israelite millenarians such as W. G. MacKendrick and the pseudonymous "Ben Judah," author of the chiliastic novel *When?*, Rand's millenarian passions reached their peak during the Second World War.[43]

Like MacKendrick, with whom he was almost certainly in contact, Rand was tempted to spin elaborate religiomilitary scenarios of the manner in which the forces of good and evil would engage one another in Palestine. In a 1944 essay, "Final Theater of War," Rand elaborated his narrative in terms strikingly similar to those employed by MacKendrick, although unlike MacKendrick in 1942, Rand had given up on an apocalyptic role for the Axis powers. The British fleet would anchor the "Israel" line in the north opposite Armageddon and in the south off of Aqaba. The land fortifications would then run from the Gulf of Aqaba to Haifa. Russian forces (Gog), deterred by the

British fleet from moving on Palestine by sea, would be forced to march overland from the area between the Black and Caspian seas through Iran and Iraq, turning west to cross the Jordan River north of the Dead Sea. At the same time, Palestine would be threatened by two other armies, one coming east through Turkey from "a Sovietized Europe," and the other "composed of Asiatic hordes," crossing the Jordan south of the Dead Sea. A threat from the southwest would materialize when "an enemy coup" in Egypt closed the Suez Canal to British shipping (Rand, like MacKendrick, distrusted the Egyptians).

The European confederacy, led by the Soviet Union, would threaten both the British forces at Haifa and those at Armageddon. Jerusalem would fall. The Asiatic army would occupy the valley of Jehoshaphat, and if it could link up with the Soviets coming in from the north, the forces of Israel-Britain could be decisively defeated. Like MacKendrick, at this desperate juncture, "the governments of Israel call for a solemn assembly of their people to petition God for deliverance." In the ensuing destruction of enemy forces, a great earthquake would destroy the southern army and cause the northern army to flee in terror. World War II was only the prologue, setting up the circumstances for Gog's confederation of Europe and invasion of the Middle East.[44]

Once the Second World War was in fact over, Rand turned his attention to more systematically integrating these predictions into a larger framework of sacred history. He placed the "Times of the Gentiles" in the period between the reign of Nebuchadnezzar and the First World War. When Allenby captured Jerusalem in 1917, "it came into possession of its rightful heirs again" (i.e., Britain-Israel), but symbolic though this may have been, it did not "finally bring Gentile rule in all of its ramifications to an end." That process required, among other things, the defeat of Babylon, which Rand identified with the Germany of both Kaiser and Hitler. Once the "Babylonian Succession of Empires" had ended in 1945, the way was clear for the advance of Gog (the Soviet Union). As to the Great Pyramid, he saw in its measurements evidence "that in these years of ours the time is fulfilled."

> Here [i.e., in the pyramid predictions] the consummation of the ages is indicated as beginning in 1909 A.D. to be completed by 1953 A.D. This forty-four years is highly marked by many prophetic and chronological times converging upon this Pyramidal time-period. It is also the period during which the *Dispensation of the Fullness of Times* would begin and be completed, for 1914 A.D. saw the beginning of intensified judgment. The Great Pyramid indicates an increase in the intensification of judg-

ment between 1941 A.D. and 1948 A.D., while by 1953 A.D. the new social order will have become manifest to all.

Insofar as pyramid numerology is concerned, the key date was August 20, 1953, the point at which measurement reaches the far wall of the so-called King's Chamber. Once the date had passed, Rand had no difficulty demonstrating that it "marked a distinct change in God's dealings with His people." And what was the evidence of this epochal change? The announcement that the Soviet Union possessed the hydrogen bomb—for "it was immediately recognized, and so stated by thoughtful men and women, that, to curb the mad rush toward self-destruction, a new order must be born."[45]

The most evident characteristics of British-Israel millennialism have been not only its pervasiveness but its extraordinary elasticity. No matter the shifts in political alignments and military power, confidence in the validity of predictions never decisively flagged. This enduring quality is not merely a confirmation of cognitive dissonance theory, the desire to achieve harmony between cherished beliefs and external evidence. If that were true, Millerism would have retained its following after the Great Disappointment of 1844. (In fact, while some Millerites retained their commitments and set about constructing rationalizations for the failed prediction, the movement as a whole foundered.) The difference between Millerite collapse and British-Israel resilience lies in the fact that Millerite date setting concentrated upon a single visible event, the return of Jesus to earth. In British-Israel millennialism, particularly in the complex numerological form developed by David Davidson, the Endtimes could be almost indefinitely stretched out through innumerable transitions, anticipations, stages of fulfillment, and periods of probation and judgment. On the one hand, something could be discovered to give significance to almost any date. On the other hand, no single date was so pivotal as to place the entire system in jeopardy.[46]

The implications of this malleability for Christian Identity were considerable. Had British-Israelism possessed the rigidity of Millerism, it—or at least its millenarian propensities—would have been extinguished long before Christian Identity emerged in the United States. However, its capacity to be bent and reinterpreted, its potential for adaptation to changed conditions, and its balance between specificity and vagueness—all of these characteristics permitted this idiosyncratic millenarian system to persist from the late nineteenth century to the mid-twentieth. Operating outside the dispensationalist framework of most Fundamentalists, it provided an alternative understanding of history that purported to give believers leverage over otherwise incomprehensible events. As we shall see in the next chapter, Christian Identity, anxious to maintain independence from Fundamentalist conceptions of the millennium, which depended on the creation and security of the state of Israel, had at hand a parallel eschatology, at once complex, adaptable, and resistant to falsification. It became in their hands not merely a predicter of Anglo-Saxon triumph, but a vision of a racist apocalypse.

When Christian Identity defined its vision of the
end of history, it was at once dependent upon the
apocalyptic views already developed in British-
Israelism and anxious to develop its own distinctive outlook on the future. From Anglo-Israelism
it took belief in the imminence of the Last Days
and in a premillennialism with a distinctive historicist tinge, for sacred history was a record of
Israel's continuation in the form of the Anglo-
Saxon-Celtic peoples. At the same time, Identity
began to distance itself from the pyramid studies
that so enthralled British-Israelites and greatly
accentuated racist and anti-Semitic motifs.
These changes could be ascribed to a number of
factors—the organizational developments, already described in chapters 3 and 4, that broke
Identity free of remaining English connections;
the tendency of Identity figures, less cerebral and
less widely read than their English counterparts,
to prefer simpler ideas; and the obsessive anti-
Semitism that defined the American movement.
There was, however, an additional element, specific to the religious environment in which Identity grew.

Beginning in the 1970s, one of the most dramatic developments in American religious life
was the resurgence of Protestant Fundamentalism. It was reflected in the rapid growth rates
of evangelical denominations, the rise of such
celebrity preachers as Jerry Falwell and other
televangelists, and the political mobilization
of Fundamentalists for conservative political
causes. Casual observers often incorrectly
lumped Identity with this "New Christian Right."
The confusion is understandable, since the Fundamentalist New Christian Right has been theologically as well as politically conservative. But,
as we shall see, the two have always been adversaries. Fundamentalism has rejected Identity's

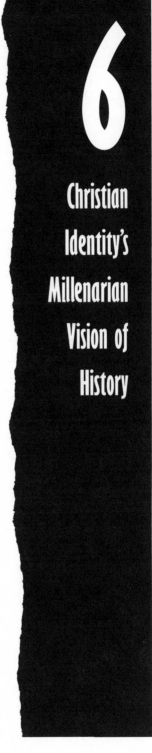

6

Christian
Identity's
Millenarian
Vision of
History

racism and anti-Semitism, and Identity has rejected Fundamentalism's mille-narian theology. More specifically, most Fundamentalists accept in one form or another John Nelson Darby's dispensationalist view of history, with its unfolding sequence of the rapture of the saved, the violence of the Tribulation, the conversion of the Jews, Armageddon, and the Second Coming—a view unacceptable to Identity.

Identity and Fundamentalism

Even more than British-Israelism, Christian Identity rejects the dispensational premillennialism associated with the futurist perspective. Far from constitut-ing an offshoot of Fundamentalism, as is often supposed, Christian Identity rejects the futurist orientation of most Fundamentalists. Its hostility is par-ticularly directed at the rapture, a doctrine it regards as without scriptural foundation. Beyond questions about the meaning of biblical texts, however, Identity's rejection of the rapture is linked to the disdain for anything that promises to rescue the saved from the rigors of the Tribulation. The rapture, as most Fundamentalists understand it, will remove the saved from the earth at the beginning of the Tribulation, sparing them the dangers associated with the Tribulation's seven years of persecution, war, and violence that are to precede the Second Coming. Identity, however, far from wishing to avoid this period of tumult, yearns for an opportunity to engage the forces of evil in apocalyptic battle. Hence the rapture to them smacks of cowardice and retreat.

There is, of course, little doubt as to the nature of the evil Identity seeks to confront. Identity singles out Jews as the personification of cosmic evil, at once the offspring and instrument of the Devil. Hence any struggle during the Tribulation will, in their view, be between Aryans and Jews and is to be welcomed rather than avoided. The centrality of anti-Semitism in Identity belief provides a second basis for its rejection of dispensationalism, beyond its opposition to the rapture. In the view of John Nelson Darby and his British and American followers, biblical prophecies addressed to "Israel" had to be read literally. The church traditionally interpreted such prophecies meta-phorically, applying them to itself as the "New Israel." British-Israelism, of course, also insisted on a literal reading, but saw the Anglo-Saxons as Israel. Mainstream dispensationalists in the Darby mold, however, assumed that in postbiblical history, "Israel" meant "Jews." In their view, the Jewish rejection of Jesus had halted any further fulfillment of God's promises to Israel (the Jewish people) as part of the Great Parenthesis. But within the last half-century, Fundamentalists have become convinced that the fulfillment of these prophecies has once more begun, validated by such events as the founding of the state of Israel, the regathering of Jews on its territory, the reunification of Jerusalem, and the expansion of Israel toward its biblical boundaries. Fundamentalist concern for Jewish national aspirations and Israeli security coexists with predictions of enormous Jewish casualties when the warfare of the Tribulation focuses on the Middle East. Only a remnant of Jewish survivors will remain to convert at the time of the Second Coming. Despite this dispensational ambivalence, Fundamentalist End-time scenarios remain sufficiently philo-Semitic to arouse deep Identity mistrust. As a result, Christian Identity seeks to define a millennialism that is simultaneously distinct from that of Fundamentalism and consistent with Identity's theological anti-Semitism.

Christian Identity regards traditional churches as impure. Each denomination may begin in a state of purity but eventually succumbs to corruption at the hands of Jews. The churches have been deluded into believing that Jews are God's chosen people when in fact they descend from Canaanites, pagan Khazars, and other impure peoples. Fundamentalism is believed to be in a state of "spiritual bankruptcy," its members "very spiritually depressed" and hence easily gulled by "false prophets" promising an imminent rapture. As Dan Gayman puts it, "Their theology is on the rocks," but this very corruption may provide Identity with an unparalleled opportunity for proselytizing among "sincere fundamentalist Christian people . . . yearning for a fresh breath of Bible truth." This allegedly disillusioned and spiritually malnourished multitude may provide "the greatest opportunity for evangelical work in the history of the Kingdom-Israel message," although to date, there has been no significant shift of religious allegiances.[1]

Identity and the Rapture

Identity's hostility to the rapture is unwavering and cuts across organizational lines. Although Identity writers differ on why the rapture will not occur and what will happen to Christians during the Tribulation, they are of one mind in condemning it. Indeed, few would quarrel with Sheldon Emry's assertion that "the rapture 'doctrine' has done more to disarm and make American Christians impotent than any other teaching since the time of Christ." To Emry, the rapture is a subversive notion, invented by Jesuits and insinuated into Protestantism. Borrowing from an anti-Catholic tract by Duncan McDougall, Emry concluded that John Darby allowed himself to be used as a tool for the promulgation of a pernicious, Jesuit-devised doctrine.[2]

Rejection of the rapture deprives believers of the assurance that they will be spared the dangers of the Tribulation. Jack Mohr of the Christian-Patriots Defense League viewed a raptureless future in light of his belief in an imminent Soviet attack and an American military defeat: "Then Christians will learn what is meant by the GREAT TRIBULATION, and you, my Christian friend, will be right in the middle of it. Don't count on a RAPTURE to rescue you." The Tribulation will be the final battle, and many Identity writers seem to welcome the closing of an escape hatch. The risk is, as Emry puts it, that "rapture-deceived Christians have deserted their posts on the frontiers of Christendom."[3]

But some influential Identity figures, while rejecting the rapture as "false doctrine," nonetheless manage to salvage a view of the latter days that places believers at minimal risk, even though they must stay on earth through the Tribulation. For some, God's protection will be direct and absolute: "We shall endure the tribulation period, but we shall escape the wrath of God when His judgments are meted out. . . . God's people will be divinely protected . . . not raptured OUT OF IT, but kept and protected THROUGH IT." Wesley Swift directed his attention at a key point of rapture doctrine, whether there would be one Second Coming or two. He concluded that there would be only one, and it would be anything but secret and spiritualized. Instead, "He shall come with a triumphant shout. He shall come with the fleets and hosts of Michael; and He comes to defeat the enemy." That being the case, neither Satan nor the Antichrist will be permitted to defeat the Anglo-Saxon lands, although they will come close to doing so. But at the moment when doom seems inevitable, rescue will occur, not through the rapture but by the kind of physical descent of Christ in majesty familiar to the Millerites: "YAHWEH—Christ—Yashua will come to earth at the climactic part of this last battle." Swift's Second Coming will even be televised; satellite transmission of the event will not be needed, for a divine ray will overcome any attempts at satanic jamming, and "television sets will lock into this . . . signal."[4]

The issue of the rapture is of more immediate importance than might be suggested merely by doctrinal considerations. Identity rejection of it is believed to carry real and imminent consequences because of Identity's conviction that the Last Days are about to begin, if they have not done so already. Bertrand Comparet spoke of the "death-agonies" that mark the demise of the present and the "birthpangs" necessary to usher in the new era. Swift, too, emphasized the nearness of apocalyptic events. He referred simultaneously to the violence that would attend the end of the age and the protection believers would enjoy. On the one hand, "with violence shall Babylon be destroyed! . . .

The world is being plunged into its agony and its travail by an attempt to collectivize it, to socialize it, and this is being done by the same children of darkness [read: 'Jews'] who designed the earliest catastrophes against your race, in order to carry out their objectives." On the other hand, he assured his audiences, "you are not little people; you are the children of the Most High." As the literal "sons and daughters of the Most High God," Identity believers would be protected in the period of chaos and emerge from it to help rule the millennial kingdom: "We . . . have an assurance . . . that the God Who is not only with you, but is on your side . . . has ordained that His Kingdom shall triumph." Hence, believers could face a raptureless Tribulation, perhaps already underway, from whose sound and fury they themselves would be spared.[5]

A Militarized Apocalypse

While Comparet and Swift spoke of millennial imminence in the somewhat abstract language of scriptural exegesis, others on the Identity right, notably those associated with paramilitary and survivalist groups, view the onrush of eschatological events in more concrete terms, as challenges to be overcome by organization, training, and discipline. By the same token, the orientation of such groups toward combat introduces an element of uncertainty into assurances of salvation, for what if preparations are inadequate or believers insufficiently resolute? John Harrell's Christian-Patriots Defense League (for which Jack Mohr serves as "minister of defense") is part of a constellation of affiliated organizations, including the Citizens Emergency Defense System, the Save America Gun Club, and the Christian Conservative Churches of America. In the early 1980s, the latter informed its members that "our nation is now rapidly rushing into the Valley of Decision." If a "spiritual, political, and moral housecleaning" is delayed, evil will triumph in an outcome that will be *"terrible, irreversible, and eternal."* In Harrell's survivalist pamphlet, "The Golden Triangle," he urged retreat to an area in the center of the continent as a redoubt where the faithful can wait out the "ruthless Communistic dictatorship" or the total anarchy that will overwhelm North America during the Tribulation: "Prepare now, begin this day—whether you be saint or sinner; the storm's almost upon us. Believe it or not, 'We are in training for the Tribulation.' Time is exceedingly short. Remember, it wasn't raining when Noah started building the Ark." The Covenant, Sword and Arm of the Lord, perhaps the most thoroughly militarized Identity commune, introduced its *Survival Manual* by announcing that "those who endure to the end shall be saved," and that the compendium of guerrilla warfare tips, first-aid information, and camping advice is intended "for now, in the period before the collapse of the world as we know it. . . . Christians are headed for the tribulation. The days ahead are a chance to truly show our love and faith in God. Do not let the judgments that are about to fall turn you against God. Understand that this is the cleansing process needed before the kingdom of our Lord Jesus Christ can be established." In the meantime, "the planet earth is about to become the battleground between the forces of God, led by Jesus Christ . . . and the serpent, father of deceit, Satan and his seed, the satanic blood-line Jews."[6]

The Millenarian Scenario

Aryan Nations in the late 1980s published a potpourri of apocalyptic predictions, whose sources ranged from David Davidson, to an interpretation of the Aztec calendar, to religious gossip. Disparate though their origins, they all identified events in the 1980s as central to the Last Days and, more particularly, as miraculously correlated with events in the life of Aryan Nations. Thus the author is able to wring from biblical numerology the conclusion that the date of the Aryan Nations Congress—July 7, 1983—is 2,520 years plus 252 days after the supposed fall of Babylon (assumed to be October 29, 539 B.C.). The presumed significance lies in the belief that since Israel was to be punished, according to the Bible, seven times; and that since by exegetical tradition, conservative interpreters considered a "time" to be 360 years; therefore, seven times 360 yields 2520. Since the exercise begins with the observation that "most are aware today that these are the End times," the assorted predictions, prophecies, and deductions appear to the author, and doubtless to readers, to be self-evident. Consequently, it appears equally plausible to report that a friend of the group's pianist is alleged to have been told by *her* friend in Boise in 1979 that "a little Identity church in North Idaho with a cross on the steeple 'would become the light of the world' (or words to that effect)." Millenarian date setting thus takes on a reassuring circularity: these are the latter days because predictions say so, and predictions say so because these are in fact the latter days.[7]

In a description reminiscent of those written forty years earlier by W. G. MacKendrick and Howard Rand, Bertrand Comparet described the details of the final days. The Russian Gog will form a vast coalition of its own satellites—Iran, Ethiopia, Afghanistan, Egypt, Libya, and other Arabs. In addition, the Soviets will be aided by "the mixed breeds of Asia and Africa and India, who . . . will ally themselves with anything which promises them that they can pillage and rape in the lands of the White Man." Finally, the alliance will include "those who hate Jesus Christ," Jewish "Edomites" and their bought political agents. "The Russian hordes" and their associates will attack along two fronts, seizing the eastern Mediterranean and the Suez Canal to shut off the flow of oil and then directly attacking the United States across the Bering Straits and by missile, submarine, and aircraft. After "nomadic warriors disperse . . . through the vast forests of the western Canadian mountains . . . the Asiatic hordes [will] roll in like a flood in our northwestern States." This double assault will, of course, fail. The various Soviet armies will mutiny and the satellites revolt. God will send all manner of natural calamities against the invaders: epidemic diseases, storms, showers of meteors, and volcanic eruptions spewing toxic gases, until the enemy forces are utterly destroyed. The level of detail approaches that of earlier British-Israel millenarians (and, incidentally, that of such contemporary futurist millenarians as Hal Lindsey). But a number of distinctive differences emerge. One is the dramatic shift in the locus of action, away from traditional sites in Palestine and toward the United States. While the attack on the Suez Canal is reminiscent of more traditional accounts, Comparet makes clear that events in the eastern Mediterranean are a sideshow, a means of strangling Europe while the main battle centers on the United States. Where British-Israelites continued to reflect the historic link between British interests and the Near East, and especially to reflect British hegemony over Egypt and Palestine, Christian Identity had separated itself from the political loyalties of its parent. Howard Rand's Anglo-Saxon Federation persisted in speaking of an Anglo-American partnership, of Ephraim and Manasseh doing God's work together. Christian Identity insists on the centrality of America in God's plan, an element made all the easier by the bipolar character of the Cold War. If indeed the United States and the Soviet Union were the only powers of significance, as was the case until the late 1980s, then surely the millenarian script concerned only the Soviet Union (Gog) and the United States (Israel). Hal Lindsey, in his best-selling book, *The Late Great Planet Earth*, insisted on a salvationist role for the United States even though he was hard-pressed to find much biblical warrant for it. Comparet and other Identity writers, operating on the assumption that the United States is Israel, have no such constraints to limit their speculations.[8]

Identity flourished during the Cold War and constructed its millenarian scenario against the backdrop of U.S.-Soviet conflict. In this they were no different than their adversaries, the Fundamentalists. Both groups face the necessity of recalibrating their visions of the Last Days, adapting them to a world in which neither the Cold War nor the Soviet Union exists. The adaptability of millenarians, however, can scarcely be underestimated, and their capacity to revise their understanding of the future in the light of changed political circumstances will doubtless allow them to meet the challenge of a post–Cold War world. Thus Paul Boyer's perceptive comments on Fundamentalist views of Armageddon apply to Identity as well. Because of

> the resourcefulness of prophecy writers in adapting their scenarios to shifting events . . . this theme seems likely to continue to figure prominently among those invoked by prophecy writers in documenting humankind's bleak prospects. Like frugal homemakers, they learned over the centuries to recycle their basic themes. The genre grows by accretion—rarely abandoning a theme, simply adding new ones as world conditions change.[9]

Surviving the Tribulation

In the meantime, during the run-up to the final conflagration, the conditions of organized social life can only worsen. It is the nature of the Tribulation that this should be so and, in the absence of a rapture, natural also that Identity believers note with particular care the character of the decay that will attack social institutions during the period. They, after all, expect to have to live through it. Hence the Tribulation is cast not in general terms but in terms of specific developments, against which believers need to take immediate protective action. George Stout, the leader of Aryan Nations in Texas, asserts that "as we enter into the Kingdom Age, we will see the greatest tribulation period ever known to our race." Dan Gayman of the Church of Israel is more concrete:

> The fall of the American government is imminent. We are living already in the preparatory throes of a national and world wide revolution . . . as the agents of Satan who head their world wide conspiracy of anti-Christ, plot and plan the total demise of Christian civilization and of the white race. . . . A blood-bath will take place upon the soil of this great nation, that will end only in victory for Christ or Satan. We of the Nordic race who believe in Jesus Christ are determined that this nation will remain ours.

The question that remains is that of the appropriate response to this onrushing chaos. Gayman's church believes that "like Noah we seek to build an *Ark of*

Safety in this time of national and world travail," which entails the "people of God . . . [making] an exodus to the land" in the form of settlements of groups of families "in isolated places across the country, principally west of the Mississippi River." Both the groups and the families that comprise them should strive for maximum self-sufficiency. The same survivalist imperative lay behind the Covenant, Sword and Arm of the Lord's purpose, "to prepare a physical refuge for God's people during the time of upheaval in America." Lest the undercurrent of violence be forgotten, William V. Fowler, a follower of Wesley Swift's, advises his readers to arm themselves, for even if the dire predictions prove incorrect, the guns and ammunition can always be sold at a profit: "I firmly believe, right or wrong, that if you GET YOUR GUNS AND AMMUNITION NOW and prepare for war, you have nothing to lose. If you sell your guns later, after you proved me wrong, you are going to make a profit. . . . But the best possible investment you can make is to get enough guns, foods, and ammunition for a half a dozen families. . . . TIME IS SO SHORT." As we shall see in chapter 10, such responses to Tribulationist predictions carry a dangerous potential for becoming self-fulfilling prophecies, in which millenarians create the very climate of violence they seek to flee.[10]

The coming disasters will be both familiar and novel. Some resemble not only those cataloged by British-Israelites but those favored by millenarians since the seventeenth century—plague, flood, earthquake, and eruption. An Aryan Nations author predicts cataclysmic seismic events throughout the West Coast and Pacific Northwest, which would not only destroy major population centers but cause the waters of Lake Tahoe to pour down on the Carson Valley in Nevada. But other disaster fears are of a distinctly novel character, growing out of Identity's pervasive racialism. For Identity, the ultimate disaster is not natural but demographic, and they harbor an obsessive concern with racial obliteration. This fear that the Tribulation may result in the destruction of the white race, that believers will not survive intact, pushes Tribulationist fantasies away from millenarian expectation and toward apocalyptic despair, an issue to which we shall return at the end of the chapter. The alleged plots of ZOG (the movement's habitual acronym for Zionist Occupation Government, i.e., the federal government) are all directed toward "destroy[ing] from the earth our Aryan Race and Heritage," principally through the sale of drugs and the right of abortion. "Those who are spared this genocide and grow into adults have the threat of jew wars ever present to dampen the promise of any kind of plausible future." David Lane, a member of the Order who is now in prison, puts the matter in even grimmer terms: "The political entity known as the United States of America has attempted with near single-minded determination, almost from its inception, to destroy any White territorial imperative, of any size and on any continent where such a state could be found. Genocide of the White Race has been the aim and result of the American political entity." Such circumstances were never dreamed of in the British-Israel tracts of an earlier era, written under the impress first of British imperial expansion and then of the American rise to superpower status. Christian Identity therefore harbors an altogether less stable set of millenarian ideas, in which the determinism of the divine plan is in constant tension with the apparently limitless power of Satan.[11]

Nonetheless, Identity remains committed to a literal Second Coming and millennial reign of the saints. Thom Robb, Klan leader and pastor of the Christian Identity Church in Harrison, Arkansas, affirms belief "in the literal return to this earth of Yashua the Messiah (Jesus Christ) . . . to take the Throne of David and establish His everlasting Kingdom." When that occurs, "righteous government" will be restored to the earth and "a day of reckoning will come" for evildoers. Dan Gayman foresees a comparably final consummation of history, to which his Church of Israel adds the regathering of the tribes of Israel to Palestine, presumably only in representative form, since most "will be apportioned throughout much of the globe." This suggests that Israel (the Anglo-Saxon-Celtic peoples) will then exercise dominion over their spiritual inferiors. Jerusalem, or rather "the New Jerusalem," will serve as the headquarters of the millennial theocracy. In like manner, Aryan Nations believes "that there is a day of reckoning. The usurper will be thrown out by the terrible might of Yahweh's people as they return to their roots and their special destiny. We know there is soon to be a day of judgment and a day when Christ's kingdom (Government) will be established on earth as it is in heaven." The last sentence of the Aryan Nations' position is taken up word for word in the creedal statement of James K. Warner's New Christian Crusade church.[12]

Identity and British-Israelism

While Identity retains the sense of millenarian imminence inherited from British-Israelism, the manner in which the vision of the Last Days is conceived has undergone subtle but significant changes. The emphasis on the centrality of America has already been mentioned. In addition, British-Israel pyramidology—central to Anglo-Israelite millennialism at least since the time of Davidson—has been deemphasized in Christian Identity. North American British-Israelites, such as Howard Rand, retained a central place for date calculations based upon pyramid measurements. Some, like W. G. Mac-

Kendrick and William McCrea, often seemed to lose themselves in a maze of mathematical manipulations, certain that if they could only perform the correct operations, the millennial dates would flow with absolute accuracy. Without repudiating pyramidism, Christian Identity has deemphasized it, especially as a date-setting device. At one level, this appears symptomatic of the movement's desire to separate itself definitively from English antecedents. The English movement never seemed sufficiently racist or anti-Semitic to suit Identity tastes. In addition, the reliance upon Davidson's methods and conclusions left a trail of incorrect predictions. While these failures were more easily rationalized away than those of the nineteenth-century Millerites, one senses that by the 1950s, devotees of pyramidism were wearied by two decades of disappointments and by ever-more-intricate rationalizations. Some, like Rand, appeared to have had boundless faith that Davidson had been correct, but fewer and fewer American believers seemed interested in pursuing such an elusive quarry. Finally, just as Identity was anxious to distinguish itself from British-Israelism, so it was committed to sharpening the boundary between itself and the dispensational Fundamentalists.

One of dispensationalism's early virtues appeared to be precisely its hostility toward date setting. Indeed, in the wake of the Millerite fiasco, this aspect of dispensationalism particularly commended it to wary millenarians. The fact that the rapture and Second Coming could occur at "any moment" rendered the embarrassing matter of date-setting moot, according to the futurists. Nonetheless, when Fundamentalism experienced its most recent surge as a result of the changed politics of the Middle East, latent date-setting propensities began to surface once again. As Timothy Weber observes, "Since the founding of Israel in 1948 and the Six-Day War in 1967, many of premillennialism's most popular writers have become rather reckless in their predictions." Weber points especially to the very widely read Hal Lindsey, who, although careful not to specify precise dates for apocalyptic events, nonetheless comes perilously close to making falsifiable predictions. As a result, he and other "modern premillennialists may find themselves in the same position as the Millerites." For reasons already discussed, Identity finds dispensationalism scripturally invalid and theologically repugnant, particularly in the role assigned to the Jewish people. This view has engendered a visceral Identity rejection of anything associated with the Fundamentalist perspective on the End. Hence, as Fundamentalism moved closer to date setting, Identity sought reflexively to move even further from date-setting tendencies. The movement from pyramid chronology may thus reflect a desire to distance Identity from its rival. Indeed, the connection between the pyramid literature and date setting has led some Identity figures to repudiate pyramidology completely. Among them is Thom Robb, who lumps pyramid writers with other *"crystallball prophets"* who believe "they can pinpoint the time of the return of Christ." Instead, they practice a corrupt "scriptural gymnastics."[13]

For the most part, the Great Pyramid appears in Identity literature merely as an occasional reminder of the distant glories of the "Adamic race." There are exceptions, as in William V. Fowler's fears that a communist invasion of the United States was about to take place in early 1979 in order to set the final eschatological events in motion, because "the Pyramid points to September of 1979, as being a very important date in Israel, which I believe to be the sealing date for the Bride." And *Calling Our Nation* reprinted an article on biblical chronology by Bertrand Comparet that relies heavily on Davidson's calculations. On the whole, however, the pyramid receded to a distinctly subordinate position. It is taken as evidence of a mysterious ancient priesthood in Egypt, whose modern descendants are "the White Christians." The "nonwhite priests" hid the fact that Noah and his sons were "the builders and designers of the great marvels of constructions," and that Shem himself had built the Great Pyramid. Shem was "the greatest Adamite after Jesus Christ," and God chose him for the task so that the pyramid could stand "as an eternal testimony to the advanced civilization of His chosen people, the Adamic race." It would stand as one of "God's Silent Witnesses . . . beyond the reach of destructive tampering of the modernists and the higher critics." But of elaborate deductions concerning the meaning of present and future events, there is scarcely a word. The pyramid becomes simply one other testimonial to the greatness of long-dead Aryan patriarchs. Even where the mathematics of pyramid measurements enter, as they do in the publications of the Lord's Covenant church, they do so in the manner of the nineteenth-century pyramid writers, who saw it as conclusive evidence that the structure could never have been built by the Egyptians themselves, who, the British "knew" from their colonial experience, were lazy, superstitious heathens. Hence, the more remarkable the pyramid seemed to be in the mathematical complexity of its dimensions, the greater the likelihood that someone like themselves had built it, and who better than the dim figures of Genesis, from whom the British-Israelites liked to trace their own descent? Davidson's elaboration of this early literature to produce a millenarian time-clock, however, seems to Identity a different and potentially more embarrassing matter, threatening to enmesh them in a web of failed predictions. Better to leave the pyramid as an "Adamic" testimonial and go no further.[14]

Identity millennialism differs from that of British-Israelism in another respect as well: its inner conflicts about the certainty of the outcome. While Identity writings give ample evidence of faith in the inevitability of the Second Coming and millennium, they provide equally vivid testimony concerning the obstacles to their achievement. These difficulties fall into two related categories: the extraordinary power imputed to the Jewish conspiracy, and the soft and corrupt character of the American people, which prevents them from resisting evil. The New Christian Crusade church of James K. Warner concludes that "our White race enters the twilight of its very existence. . . . Without your help, this truly is—The End." Karl Schott observes that "we seem powerless to break this bondage," something only God can do. As *The Turner Diaries* (not an Identity work but widely read on the Identity right and consequently discussed in chapter 11) puts it, "Americans have lost their right to be free." Thus Identity seems precariously balanced between a belief that no matter how great the obstacles, the deterministic millenarian script will be played out, and the fear that the power of evil will thwart divine intentions. As with other practitioners of "the paranoid political style," Christian Identity seems caught between optimism and pessimism, much in the manner of the nineteenth-century Populist writer, Mrs. S. E. V. Emery, who dedicated *Seven Financial Conspiracies* to "the enslaved people of a dying republic." If the people were really enslaved and the republic in fact dying, there would have seemed little point to her book, but she was obviously unsure that even her propagandistic efforts would be sufficient to rouse the citizenry for the final battle against the conspirators. Christian Identity exhibits the same ambivalence.[15]

Identity, Satan, and the Jews

This ambivalence is ultimately traceable to the one tenet that most clearly distinguishes Christian Identity from British-Israelism: the belief in the satanic origin of the Jews, a belief traced in the next three chapters. While British-Israelism manifested considerable anti-Semitism, particularly by the 1940s, its Jews were always salvageable. Their alleged corruptions could be cast off and their crimes purged by the act of conversion to Christianity, which they were expected to perform eventually, if not now, then surely at the time of the Second Coming. It is no accident that the North American writers whose millennialism is most detailed, consistent, and free from ambivalence are those most closely tied to the British-Israel mainstream, figures such as Howard Rand, William J. Cameron, and W. G. MacKendrick. All were prepared to engage in vicious libels against the Jewish people (none more than Cameron), but each left the door of salvation open, as had Christian anti-Semites throughout history. Christian Identity definitively closed that door by declaring that the taint was one of blood, and that the diabolical nature of the Jew could never be altered, either by him or by anyone else. Identity's "final solution," scarcely original but here placed in a novel theological context, is the obliteration of the Jewish people. Identity writers differ only in the instrumentality of a future Holocaust, whether at the hands of revolutionary millenarian Christians or at those of an enraged racial deity.

By its elaboration of a line of descent from the Devil/Serpent in the Garden, through Cain, the Edomites, and the Khazars, to contemporary Jews, Identity has fused belief in a world Jewish conspiracy with that of a cosmic satanic conspiracy. The latter belief flourished in the late Middle Ages and early modern period, and ensnared thousands of hapless old women and social deviants in accusations of witchcraft. The former, its secularized counterpart, achieved "canonical" form with the late nineteenth-century publication of *The Protocols*. The plot outlined in *The Protocols* was bent on economic dominance and political supremacy, and one could believe in it, as William J. Cameron did, and still urge Jews to repent and renounce it. The satanic cabal, on the other hand, could potentially be regarded as providing the central theme for the history of the cosmos, describing a struggle between light and darkness that began with the revolt of Lucifer and the fallen angels and would end only with the Devil's destruction in a lake of fire at the end of time. Identity fused the two conspiracy theories, theologizing that of *The Protocols* to bring its machinations within the larger context of the transhistorical battle between light and darkness.

Having done this, Identity has created a form of millennialism that is not only unstable, hovering uncertainly between optimism and pessimism, but that has a distinctly dualistic character. Its Devil is no mere pesky upstart or insubordinate underling; he is an adversary with the resources potentially to unseat his master. This potential for dualism is nowhere better exemplified than in the writings of the late Robert Miles. Despite the idiosyncrasies of his theology, the avuncular Miles functioned as a kind of elder statesman of the racial movement and was largely divorced from its feudings. He is important both for the explicitly dualistic theology he developed and for the manner in which others systematically misperceived his beliefs. He was frequently classified as a major Identity figure by organizations that monitor extreme right-wing activity, such as the Anti-Defamation League and the Center for Democratic Renewal. The confusion is understandable, since Miles was involved in numerous collaborative activities with Identity groups and leaders, and because his theology, while not an explicit Identity creed, does in fact accentuate precisely that dualistic element that is latent in so much Identity thought itself.[16]

Miles's dualism was based on a struggle between the true God and a false God, Satanael. Satanael had been Lucifer, the "chief angel, first or eldest son of God," before his rebellion. Jesus, by contrast, was "the Younger, Loyal Son." Some of the "astral seed" (i.e., angels) followed Satanael-Lucifer into rebellion against his father, while others remained loyal. "The ongoing stellar civil war," spreading through the universe, continued to be fought on earth. The whites to whom Miles preached he presumed to be the loyal astral seed who took "the flesh form," and thus had an angelic existence prior to their lives on earth and would return to that spirit state once their battle with evil had been completed. Yet Miles's neo-Catharist myth was not simply a description of a struggle between rival angelic forces, for it was complicated by his account of the process by which the contending angelic armies assumed human form on earth.[17]

Miles believed that in addition to the warring groups of angels, human beings were created on earth not once but twice. In an account of dual creations reminiscent of Charles Fox Parham's, God the Father created human beings on the sixth day. They, however, were not Adam and Eve; Adam and Eve were created on the eighth day by God's rival, Satanael, in the hope that they would be sufficiently attractive to tempt the loyal angels. Adam and Eve, however, turned out to be less than perfect or manageable and, hence, inadequate to the task. Thus in this primal age there were four different creatures: two groups of angels, representing the contending deities; and two groups of creatures of flesh, created respectively by God and the Devil. Since the angels possessed sexual urges, angelic warriors of both camps "fraternized" with "the daughters of men," thus embedding their respective "astral seeds" in flesh form. The offspring of the mating between the two types of human beings and the loyal angels "produced a towering ethnic strain . . . your strain . . . the true seed of the North!" (i.e., the white race).[18]

After this complex series of interminglings, the "stellar civil war" continued on earth between the angels-made-flesh. Notwithstanding descent from Adam and Eve, "God had interceded with His grace" and made Noah a "blessed man . . . beyond reproach." Thereafter, the battle became a competition for the loyalty of Noah's descendants. "If God wins Noah and his descendants, despite their flesh mixes, despite the impurities which such contain, God wins the eternal war. Satanael will repent. Satanael may be forgiven for the mercy of God the Father is boundless and endless. Harmony will then reign on earth as it once was in heaven. The balance of the forces of life will be restored." On the other hand, a victory by Satanael will give him dominion over the earth, converting it into "part of the darkness, the anti-matter void which we call in other areas, the black holes." That will deliver the world to the Jews, for "a jew . . . is anyone who believes only in the flesh and this world, and follows the Prince of Darkness."[19]

While dramatically different in its symbolism from Christian Identity, it is, as far as Miles was concerned, compatible with Identity. The respective groups of believers are "true cousins in the present, but from the same household in the past." The difference lies in point of view. Dualists and Identity begin sacred history at different points, according to Miles. The dualists move it back to "the arrival of the Sons of God to the earth," while Identity begins with Abram/Abraham. Miles's dualism linked the arrival of the angels to a mythic era of the "ice ages," whereas "Identity sees a need to concentrate on that period subsequent to the ice ages." Identity is "totally correct," Miles says, but is preoccupied with the descendants of Shem, while the dualists know that their own history long predates the period of the patriarchs. As a courtesy, however, "we do not stress [these differences] in their company."[20]

The idiom Miles employed, with its mélange of references to Norsemen, Cathars, and astral beings, is distinctive, as well as remote from much of the language employed by Identity. That Miles was so frequently considered an Identity figure despite these differences is not simply the result of the fact that outsiders tended to lump him together with Identity associates (he had, for example, been a conspicuous participant in the Aryan Nations congresses). Rather, it reflects the fact that he unabashedly advanced a Manichaeanism that exists in much less open form within Identity itself. For Identity, having conjured up an adversary of seemingly overwhelming power, finds its millennialism transmuted as a consequence. Eschatological events cannot be presumed to occur in an automatic way under conditions of warfare with an equal or possibly superior enemy. The millennium, together with the racial triumph it is taken to represent, continues to be the goal, for if it were not, what else would keep believers at their tasks? But millennial expectation has become shadowed by the fear that the consummation of history will be undone at the last moment.

Identity as a Spiritual Elite

The tension between confidence and despair that casts a shadow over millenarian certainty is reinforced by the fact that Identity is, even by the standards of American sectarianism, a tiny movement. Accurate estimates of its size are impossible to obtain because of its decentralized character. It has no denominational structure, merely shifting and overlapping groups with family resemblances to one another. However, even the guesses have placed its maximum size at no more than one hundred thousand, and it may be less than half that. Further, there is no evidence Identity can attract large numbers of new members, although it has proselytized among small populations of the alienated (e.g., skinheads and white prison inmates). Consequently, it cannot look forward to a foreseeable future as a mass movement.

That being the case, Identity believers must resolve the dissonance between, on the one hand, their belief that they are God's instruments on earth and, on the other hand, their manifest failure to convince others. Resolution of the dissonance is key not only to the survival of the Identity coteries but to their continued confidence in the predicted millennial outcome. This they have done through two interrelated means. First, they lay claim to possessing special knowledge—knowledge of the workings of social institutions, American society, world politics, and, ultimately, the universe itself. Second, they assert on the basis of this claim to special knowledge that they have been the victims of a gigantic, cosmic swindle engineered so successfully that nonbelievers cannot see that the crime has occurred. The deception that obsesses them is that, in their view, the Aryans' claim to being God's real chosen people was stolen from them by the Jews, who now masquerade as chosen while the true spiritual elite languishes in obscurity.

Hence, Identity's millenarian scenario is interwoven with the need to expose this "crime," convince others of its occurrence, and reverse its consequences, at which point history will achieve its consummation. The motifs of election and theft—of a granted and stolen birthright—produces a theology of resentment. Unable to convince others that the theft has occurred, Identity simultaneously fastens upon the retelling of the myth, together with the elaboration of political scenarios that would restore them to what they see as their rightful place as the world's spiritual elite. But before the political strategies can be understood, we must first unravel the myth that the arrival of the millennium is frustrated by the theft of the true Israel's birthright. The myth describes Satan's plot, carried out by those Identity asserts to be his progeny, the Jewish people. The diabolization of the Jews lies at the heart of Identity millennialism, for the Jews are deemed to be those who stole and will not relinquish the prize.

The anti-Semitic theology of Christian Identity has been woven of many strands. The most commonplace consist of various racial explanations of Jewish origins, all designed to cast doubt on Jewish connections to the biblical Israel and to give to Jews a variety of unsavory characteristics. Some of these ideas were nurtured within British-Israelism itself, but most were the common property of anti-Semites of a variety of persuasions, both religious and secular.

While British-Israelism never manifested the systematic, sustained, and intense anti-Semitism currently found on the Identity right, it did nurture a number of covertly, and occasionally overtly, anti-Semitic themes. These were to provide the basis for future elaboration by Identity writers. By its nature, British-Israelism radically reduced the religious claims that they believed could legitimately be made by Jews, since Anglo-Saxons were the true Israel. At best, Jews would have to content themselves with the secondary affiliation of Judah, part of All-Israel to be sure, but with only a minor role to play in God's plan. Some British-Israel writers used this concept of "religious disenfranchisement" to further diminish the already attenuated tie between Jews and All-Israel. They did so by questioning the one form of religious identification that British-Israel permitted to Jews, the link with the tribe of Judah. By introducing concepts of "interracial" marriage, these writers called into question even the diminished connection that Hine and others had acknowledged.

These aspersions cast upon Jewish origins took two major forms. One linked Jews with non-Israelite peoples of the ancient world, whose vices they had allegedly absorbed through intermarriage. The most common version of this theory was the charge that Jews had been absorbed

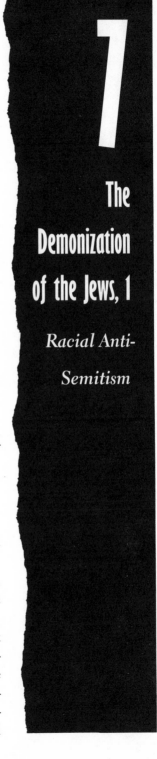

7

The Demonization of the Jews, 1

Racial Anti-Semitism

into the Edomites, the putative descendants of Esau. This found much subsequent favor with Identity writers, although they, along with some earlier authors, interchangeably employed such labels as Edomite, Canaanite, Hittite, and Amorite—regarded as equally defiling. The charge of an Edomite connection became notably stronger in British-Israelism during the mid- and late 1940s as a result of rising Zionist demands for an independent Jewish state in Palestine. Since the creation of such a state necessarily required Great Britain to give up its mandate to govern Palestine, Zionism was taken by British-Israelites to be an affront to God's plan, which required Israel (i.e., Britain) to control the Holy Land.

The second type of attack upon Jewish antecedents took a more radical form, arguing that in fact those who called themselves Jews were members of two different "races," one authentically linked by Judean ancestry to All-Israel, but the other stemming from a wholly unrelated biological source. This had the effect of dividing the Jewish people into "good Jews," who could rightfully claim a Judean pedigree, and "bad Jews," who were impostors masquerading as Judeans. The most common form this theory took was the belief that the Ashkenazic Jews of Eastern Europe were in fact descendants of the Khazar people who had lived in the area of the Black Sea and had converted (to what extent is in fact unknown) to Judaism. While the Khazar hypothesis was not originated by British-Israelites, some found it attractive, and it subsequently became a virtual article of faith not only in Identity but upon the extreme right generally. As chapter 8 will demonstrate, the process of religious disenfranchisement in general, and the claim that at least some Jews have a distinct racial origin, was to contribute to Identity's most novel and sinister doctrine, the belief that Jews are the offspring of Satan.

Philo-Semitism and Anti-Semitism in Early British-Israelism

In fact, much early British-Israelism was philo-Semitic. While insisting upon the need for Jews to eventually convert to Christianity, early British-Israel writers emphasized their ties to Jews and sought to exercise a protective and paternalistic role toward them. Thus, M. M. Eshelman, in one of the first British-Israel books published in America, wrote:

> The Jews and the Israelites are upon amicable terms. For ages the Jews have been hated, hunted, persecuted, and cast out in many countries. In Russia they are abhorred, shut out, and debarred from nearly every profit-

able employment. Among the English they find sympathy, friends, kindness and benevolence. Why are they hated in one country and loved in another? God said they would be persecuted and scattered among the heathen; He also said they should be joined to Ephraim [England] in the latter days. The latter days are at hand, and the way is preparing in the East [Palestine] for a glorious union.

Eshelman's point of view was not atypical and followed the line laid down by Edward Hine. Since the final millennial consummation required the unification of All-Israel in Palestine, Jews had to be protected and aided in their aspiration for return so that they could join representatives of the other tribes.[1]

Despite this philo-Semitic strain, British-Israelism operated in an environment rife with anti-Semitism. The movement's heyday at the turn of the century was a time when racial theorizing was rampant in Western intellectual circles, and racial inequality was accepted as both socially necessary and scientifically established. Racialism extended to perceptions of Jews, since for most late nineteenth-century writers, lines between "race," "ethnicity," and "nationality" ranged from vague to nonexistent. Beyond the intellectual acceptability racial theories had achieved, social and political circumstances in America guaranteed a sympathetic hearing for them, since they appeared to strengthen and make respectable the hostility to mass immigration articulated by American nativists. If the masses arriving from Europe were not merely different but racially inferior, efforts to block their entry would be strengthened.[2]

Among the best known of the American racists, Madison Grant described Eastern European Jews in terms that rendered them subhuman: "dwarf stature, peculiar mentality and ruthless concentration on self-interest." Worse yet, in his view, the admission of such racial inferiors would irrevocably weaken "the stock of the nation," for there was no possibility that the weaknesses and vices they brought would be diluted through intermarriage. Instead, a leveling down would occur, with the resulting racial mixture "reverting to the more ancient, generalized and lower type." Thus, intermarriage between whites and blacks would always produce black offspring. As far as Jews were concerned, the result would be the same: "The cross between any of the three European races and a Jew is a Jew."[3]

The confluence of intellectually respectable racial theories with the drive for immigration restrictions ultimately made itself felt in British-Israel circles. The leading American Anglo-Israelite of the period, C. A. L. Totten, began in the early 1890s by following the position laid out by his friend and mentor, Edward Hine. Thus the 1891 edition of his treatise *Our Race* is free of anti-

Semitic references and, indeed, generally avoids any extensive comments on Jews. By 1897, however, Totten felt it necessary to write expansively on the subject. He did so, however, with an ambiguity that suggests something of the conflicting forces that played upon the British-Israel movement. On the one hand, he took for granted the necessity of Jewish restoration to Palestine, in fulfillment of the divine mandate for the unification of Israel. He took comfort in the travails of Ottoman Turkey as evidence that the time of restoration was near: "All things portend the ending of an age." Thus far, he reflected both the philo-Semitism of Hine and the millennial expectations widespread in Protestant circles as the century approached its end. However, Totten appended to this conventional view a series of seemingly gratuitous remarks on Jews less reflective of British-Israelism per se than of anti-Semitic currents in the larger society.

Totten, like many others at the time, imputed to Jews enormous power and wealth—indeed, so much so that he suggested God's plan, as revealed in British-Israelism, would be best advanced by a tripartite "racial alliance" of England, America, and "the Kingdom of Judah." The advantage of such an arrangement for the Jews was obvious, for it would give them essential political backing for a return to Palestine. But, in Totten's view, there was great future benefit for England and America as well, for once the return was effected, the Palestinian Jews "will necessarily develop into a strong, if not the strongest Nation upon earth; and they are by blood, by letter, and by inheritance the natural allies of the Anglo-Saxon Race. A word to the wise is sufficient." The Jews, in other words, would shortly become a world power to be reckoned with, and those who had earned their gratitude would be rewarded. This conception was echoed a quarter-century later in William J. Cameron's *Dearborn Independent*, in an article which predates "The International Jew" series. The *Independent* suggested that when the Jews did return to Palestine, they might establish a monarchy there, with a Rothschild as king; the Rothschilds might perhaps even "make Palestine the center of their banking operations." Totten, and the *Independent* after him, tapped into the widespread popular notion of hidden Jewish power, particularly commercial and financial, which might be used for good but, then again, might not. The conspiratorialism of *The Protocols* lay only a short step beyond.[4]

In addition to his speculations on Jewish power in Palestine, Totten had also absorbed the contemporary penchant for racial analysis. Disclaiming personal prejudice ("Personally, I like Jews"), he went on to cast a balance sheet of racial virtues and vices. On the one hand, they are thrifty, industrious, and philanthropic. But on the other hand, they are so "clever in the trade of money-making" that "collectively they are a serious danger." His fear was that while the Christian rich were nationals of their respective countries first and foremost, and thus incapable of uniting in a common enterprise, Jews, in Totten's opinion, "are Jews first, and Englishmen, Frenchmen, Russian, afterwards." They have used their wealth, he said, to buy newspapers in order to mold public opinion and thus "render all policies subservient to the Jewish supremacy." The outcome he foresaw was "Jewish conquest of the world." Thus, even as Totten denied all prejudice, he prefigured the conspiracy theory of *The Protocols* and the *Dearborn Independent*. While there is no evidence to suggest that Cameron was aware of his writing, Cameron's own British-Israelism makes this likely, and in any case, this side of Totten surely anticipates the linkage of conspiratorialism and British-Israelism that Cameron worked so assiduously to effect.[5]

Having cast up his balance sheet, Totten was uncertain as to the consequences. He certainly advocated no systematic persecution or legal disabilities. As long as Jews obeyed the law, he wrote, they should ply their trades and put forward their opinions in the same way as their Gentile compatriots. "No one would dream of persecuting them." But he clearly regarded them as "a real and serious danger" and had no short-term answer to his imagined concentration of Jewish power. In the longer term, however, he saw in British-Israelism a solution to what was stereotypically called "the Jewish problem," for once the Jews were restored to Palestine, "under the protectorate of England and America," all problems about the place of Jews in Western societies would be solved. It was a position with curious similarities to that of classical Zionism, which argued that only in a Jewish state could the status of Jews be "normalized." Totten's emphasis upon the supervisory power of England and America established them not only as guarantors of a Jewish homeland but as bulwarks against the concentration of Jewish power. In sum, Totten maintained Hine's emphasis upon the responsibility of the Anglo-Saxon peoples for the return of the Jews to Palestine, and he reiterated Hine's belief that contemporary Jews were the lineal descendants of the tribe of Judah. However, Totten was clearly touched by the rising anti-Semitism of the Gilded Age, and its preoccupation with the "otherness" of the Jew and his alleged plutocratic power.[6]

British-Israelism had already significantly reduced the religious claims Jews might make, by transferring the chosenness of Israel to the Anglo-Saxons and reducing Jews to a Judean remnant. Even the popular anti-Semitism that filtered into Totten's writings was counterbalanced by this residual claim that Jews were a part of All-Israel. Anti-Semitism would not become a major element in British-Israelism until this residual claim was somehow neutralized, so that Jews were not only not-Israel but also not-Judah. In fact, the seeds for such a second stage of religious delegitimization had been present from the very beginning of British-Israelism in the writing of its "founding father," John Wilson.

Wilson and His Heirs

John Wilson wished to make the point that the descendants of the lost tribes had retained their identity even though they had been "lost among the heathen." He did so in part by the kind of spurious linguistic analysis that was to become commonplace among British-Israelites, arguing, for example, that on the basis of similarities of sound, "Many of our most common words and names of familiar objects are almost pure Hebrew." However, he also sought to reinforce the "racial integrity" of Israel-in-Europe by showing that the Jews were just as "lost" even though they seemed to have a greater degree of intactness. He did so by suggesting that while Jews had stayed for a longer period in Palestine (presuming as he did that Jews were descendants of the kingdom of Judah), they had spent much of that time in intermarriage with proscribed heathen populations: "If one people were cursed above another, it was Edom, of the children of Abraham, and Canaan among the more immediate descendants of Noah; and with both of these 'the Jews' have become signally mingled, so as to become one people with them, and inherit the curse of both." This motif initially was a minor one, since Hine in later years vigorously advanced the view that Jews were Judah, pure and simple. However, particularly in the twentieth century, other British-Israel writers were to incorporate and elaborate upon the hypothesis Wilson had advanced in 1840.[7]

This process may have begun first in America. It certainly was conspicuously present among key American British-Israelites by the 1930s, and in their British counterparts a decade later. William J. Cameron, in a sermon delivered in a Detroit church in 1934, placed Israel in a continuing struggle with "the Esau race," the descendants of Jacob's rival. Those descendants had "amalgamated with the Jews, and began their terrible work of corrupting the Jewish religious from within." These Esau descendants had become the Edomites and later the Idumeans, from whom the family of Herod had descended. By implication, then, whatever there had been of Judah in the Jews had been corrupted and displaced by the blood of "the Esau race" until the Jews were indissolubly, biologically linked with Jesus' persecutor. Much the same view was put forward in the same year by Frederick Haberman, a British-

Israel writer in St. Petersburg, Florida, in a work that has been republished by both British-Israel and Christian Identity organizations up to the present day. Haberman acknowledged that Jews had originally been descendants of the tribes of Judah and Benjamin. However, they had intermarried so extensively with other peoples that their very appearance had changed: "During their stay in Palestine they intermarried with the masters of Palestine, the Edomites, the Idumeans, and Syrians, and took on the dark complexion and features of these people. Generally, the Israelites were tall and fair, the cream of the Aryan race." Four years later, in 1938, George R. Riffert took a slightly different but related tack. The "pure Jews are very few in number." As to the others, their "originally fine, Israelitish countenance" has been marred by "continuous intermarriage with the Hittites and Canaanites." Riffert asks why Jesus and the disciples in religious paintings do not "look like a Jew." It never seems to have occurred to him that these images reflected local religious and artistic conventions rather than portraits made from life. Jews look different, he believed, because God has punished them for race mixing.[8]

Not surprisingly, Howard Rand, the editor of *Destiny*, in which both the Cameron and Riffert articles appeared, accepted the intermarriage theory, except that he concentrated on the Hittites rather than on the Edomites or Canaanites. It was Hittite blood that "gave the Jew his dark hair and eyes and the facial characteristics by which he is known and recognized today." Rand's emphasis upon Hittite intermarriage was by no means original. It was already present in the racial anthropology that passed as social science well into the interwar period. The influential racial theorist Lothrop Stoddard (1883–1950), who wrote widely in the popular press during the 1920s, had advanced the same position on allegedly scientific grounds completely divorced from British-Israelism. In a widely cited 1926 article, "The Pedigree of Judah," he noted a "striking . . . parallel between the ancient Hittites and a large proportion of the modern Ashkenazim." "One cannot look at a Hittite sculpture," he wrote, "without being struck by the 'Jewishness' of the faces there depicted." While Stoddard had no interest in British-Israelism, his racial analysis of Jewish facial features fitted perfectly with that strain of British-Israelism anxious to further diminish the ties between Jews and All-Israel.[9]

Jews and Edomites

The link with the Edomites, which had originated with John Wilson in 1840, eventually found its way back into mainstream British-Israel writing, and from no less a figure than David Davidson, whose pyramidology dominated the movement in the 1920s and 1930s. By 1944, Davidson concluded, as Americans had earlier, that Jews had "completely absorbed" the Edomites. As a result, "the Jews become racially the medium of expression for the Edomite ideals to which Herod the Great had first given political formulation." The Jews were thus an irredeemably corrupt hybrid in which heathen vices had overwhelmed any All-Israel virtues. The most systematic exposition of this position was given four years later by the Vancouver Anglo-Israelite, C. F. Parker, in A Short History of Esau-Edom in Jewry, issued by the British-Israel publishing house in London.[10]

Parker developed themes already latently present in Cameron, Rand, and Davidson. He spoke, for example, of Esau-Hittites, thus collapsing the distinction between Edomites and Hittites. He also advanced an elaborate argument concerning the consequences of the racial corruption produced by intermarriage. He did so by asserting that there was a division within the Jewish people between a small portion who were "true Judah," undefiled by racial admixtures, and the larger group of "Idumean-Hittites, masquerading as the true seed of Abraham and seeking to expel the direct descendants of Jacob." As Parker saw it, there was no great difficulty in distinguishing the two. Authentic Jews were pious and placed their fate in God's hands. Esau's descendants had rejected traditional Judaism in favor of atheism, embraced violence and revolution, and favored Zionism. More concretely, the authentic Jews are the Sephardim, while the Esau-Hittites are the Ashkenazim, concentrated historically in Eastern and Central Europe and now in America. The influence of Parker's formulation lay in its explicit fusion of religious categories (Jacob-Esau, Israel-Edom) with "racial" categories (Ashkenazim-Sephardim), building upon the older hostility to Eastern European Jews as a racially unassimilable group. This aversion, particularly strong in countries to which large numbers of Russian and Polish Jews had emigrated, Parker now traced to the primordial struggle between the children of Jacob and the children of Esau. In so doing, he reinforced the view that Jews, rather than constituting a homogeneous group, were divided into those who were authentic and worthy and those who were counterfeit and corrupt. Parker's views were to resonate subsequently in Christian Identity. Thus Conrad Gaard, writing about 1960, cited Parker approvingly in his discussion of "pseudo-Jews."[11]

This line of development, emphasizing intermarriage with heathen peoples, contained a curious irony, for traditionally British-Israel had understood "Edom" in quite different terms, having nothing to do with Jews. The Jews were not Edom. Esau's descendants were the Turks. M. M. Eshelman, for example, took it for granted in his discussion of the politics of the Ottoman

Empire in 1887: "Edom now owns and controls the holy mountain—Jerusalem—and rejoices over the house of Judah, not the house of Israel; but the time will come when 'the house of Jacob shall be a fire, and the house of Joseph (Israel) a flame, and the house of Esau (the Turks) for stubble.' All this because Israel and Judah must possess the land, hence the Turks must be removed, not by Russia but by Israel." This remained the position, and, if anything, it was strengthened, after Britain's defeat of Turkey in World War I. The identification of Edom with the Turks was so strong, in fact, that when Parker came to write his book in the late 1940s he found it necessary to begin with a special justification, noting that attempts to identify "the seed of Esau with modern Jewry have caused a certain amount of perplexity to those who have been accustomed to regard the Turk as the progeny of Jacob's twin brother." In defense of his revisionist view, he insisted that the traditional position was without historical evidence, while he was prepared to offer "an abundance of evidence" that the Jews, not the Turks, were the real latter-day Edomites.[12]

The significance of the new identification lay not only in the damage it did to Jewish authenticity, by suggesting that most Jews descended from racially inferior interlopers, but also in the ease with which the old religious language lent itself to new political implications. "Edom" meant "red." In addition, some medieval biblical interpreters had argued that the Jews were the offspring of Esau, whereas the Christians stemmed from Jacob. This tradition may account for (or, alternatively, be the by-product of) legends that the lost tribes were "red Jews" who would one day pour into Europe through a pass in the Caucasus Mountains. The color designation of Edom, and its occasional legendary association with Jews, took on new and sinister political overtones in the twentieth century, for it became the basis for assertions that there was a natural affinity between Jews and Red politics. Parker had hinted as much when he claimed that most Russian communist revolutionaries were descendants of Esau-Edom. Howard Rand claimed it was "renegade Jews" who had allowed the Bolsheviks to achieve victory. Christian Identity writers later made the connection in much more explicit terms, as in this comment by a follower of Wesley Swift: "We are all aware that Red and Edom are interrelated, and that the Amalek seed line, the Canaanite seed line, merging with the Edomite seed line, is the house of Red Jewry, Communism today." In similar fashion, the Identity minister Karl Schott anticipates the day when God "moves . . . against the armies of Communism and the Edomites." Thus the symbolism of medieval legend, refracted through British-Israel exegesis, identifies the Edomites not only with the Jews rather than with Turks, but makes them a fount of political radicalism whose source lies in the interracial couplings of the ancient Near East.[13]

Christian Identity and Jewish Origins

As this use of the Edom-equals-Jews-equals-communists equation suggests, the British-Israel argument on the racial origins of Jews has been fully incorporated into the Christian Identity belief system. Bertrand Comparet fastened upon Judah's marriage to a Canaanite woman, whose son, Shelah, fathered a "half-breed, mongrel line," to which were added descendants of Hittites, Amorites, and Edomites. As a result, according to Comparet, no Jews "were any part of any tribe of Israel." Even the remnant of undefiled Judah descendants has been eliminated. In Comparet's version, the Jews had never been Israelites. Instead, they were the indigenous Canaanites who were in the land when the Israelites entered it, and with whom the latter intermarried. When the tribe of Judah went into Babylonian exile, the Edomites, who had themselves intermarried with Canaanites, "moved westward into the vacant lands of Judah." Thus, a mixture of Canaanites and Edomites took the geographical and historic place of the tribe of Judah under the name of "Jews." Not surprisingly, a similar position was adopted by the most prominent of American anti-Semites, Gerald L. K. Smith, who while not himself an Identity figure, was affiliated (as we have seen) with many important Identity preachers.[14]

William Potter Gale was among the few Christian Identity figures to attempt a systematic statement of doctrine, in his 1963 pamphlet, "The Faith of Our Fathers." His position closely resembled Comparet's. Those Gale called "Yehudi" also spring from Shelah, "a mongrelized son of Judah." Shelah's descendants are then twice "mongrelized" by becoming "joined with the mongrelized descendents of Esau who had taken Canaanite wives in the days of Jacob and all were called 'Yehudi.'" Once this amalgamation is effected, the Shelahites become Edomites and bear the curses associated successively with Cain, putative ancestor of the Canaanites, as well as with Esau and Judah. As we shall see in the next chapter, the link with Cain and the Canaanites eventually becomes even more theologically significant than the stigma associated with Esau and Edom.[15]

By the 1970s, Identity writers vie in the number and depravity of heathen peoples with which they link the Jews. For one the Jews are "Canaanites/Essauites" and Edom a fusion of "Canaanites" and Amalekites. The result is "a perpetual hatred of us as we of them . . . [that] goes all the way back through Esau/Amalekites-Esau/Canaanites back to Cain." For another, Sheldon

Emry, Esau intermarried with Canaanites, and his descendants "infiltrated true Israel to become its rulers and religious leaders (scribes and Pharisees) in Jerusalem." Jarah Crawford, one of Identity's more systematic biblical exegetes, incorporates nineteenth-century attitudes toward race mixing. Believing Jews to be a "half-breed, race-mixed polluted people . . . the products of fornication," he concludes that as a result they are necessarily inferior, for "race-mixing always and forever produces an inferior being." Dan Gayman, of the Church of Israel, writes of an amalgamation of the "apostate branches of the Abrahamic family"—a conglomeration of cursed peoples, "all claiming descent from Abraham, and yet none of them being legitimate seed," since all were involved in forbidden marriages. Mark Thomas, the Pennsylvania state chaplain of the Invisible Empire, Knights of the Ku Klux Klan, sees racial intermarriage as an apparently uncontrollable predilection of Esau's descendants, who allegedly "followed his evil example." When Esau's son's concubine gives birth to Amalek, she begins yet another line of Israel's enemies. From "Amalek," Thomas derives the epithet "kike," which he tells his readers is merely a contraction of Amalek and "refers to the true family tree of the 'Jew.'"[16]

One of the more systematic efforts to untangle these biblically derived genealogies appeared in a chart of descent published in *Calling Our Nation*, the publication of the Aryan Nations and Church of Jesus Christ Christian in Hayden Lake, Idaho. In its derivation, the descendants of Cain and Ham produce the Hittites, with whom Esau intermarries, producing the Edomites. They in turn intermarry with "part of Judah" (presumably the descendants of Shelah) to become the Idumeans, who include "mixed blood (so-called Jews)." Interestingly, this Aryan Nations rendering retains the British-Israel concept of a "pure bloodline" of Judahites, who in time produce not only Jesus but a category labeled "Sephardic Orthodox true Judahite," with no indication any longer that "Sephardic" has anything whatever to do with Jews. Jews have been so completely redefined as to exist within this genealogical system merely as a synonym for the defiled and corrupted.[17]

In short, the link with Edom, originating in John Wilson's original formulation of the British-Israel position and developed with special force in the 1940s, became the foundation on which was erected an increasingly complex and convoluted line of Jewish descent, ever more heavily freighted with sinister connotations. As the Anglo-Saxon-Celtic peoples represented all that was pure, so Jews became little more than a receptacle for every source of evil and impurity in the biblical narrative. What had turned the once philo-Semitic tendencies of British-Israelism in so pernicious a direction?

In large measure, the association of Jews with biblical impurity is tied to British-Israel's rising hostility to Zionism. British-Israelism, particularly under the impress of Edward Hine, took a traditionally paternalistic view of Jewish national aspirations. For M. M. Eshelman, as for others in the movement, the return to Zion was testimony to the nearness of the final days. Support for Jewish settlement in Palestine was predicated on Britain's continued role, first as its facilitator and then as its guarantor. Events appeared to confirm this view, particularly with General Allenby's capture of Jerusalem from the Turks (the traditional Edom) in 1917. Britain was required not simply as a guarantor, however, but as a coparticipant, for since it, along with America, constituted the key elements of Israel, Ephraim and Manasseh, Britain must be in Palestine, too. Jews were at best only Judah, not Israel, and had not prophecy promised a comprehensive regathering? Thus did the argument go, the result of which was a highly qualified support for Zionism. Settlement was permissible and even necessary for the fulfillment of the divine plan, but sovereignty was not. Indeed, the very concept of a sovereign Jewish state in Palestine was anathema, for it could exist only if Britain retreated or was expelled, and if that occurred, Palestine would be left with Judah but without Israel. Hence, any movement toward a Jewish state at Britain's expense had to be resisted at all costs.[18]

This anti-Zionist strain was suppressed through most of the Second World War, due in part to the inability of the Zionist movement to muster significant international support up to this point. It was also due to the view, widespread in British-Israel circles, that the war was about to produce the climactic time of which millenarian prophecies spoke, the events foretold in Revelation of a great battle at Armageddon, of the descent of Christ in glory, and the inauguration of the millennial age. Since these events were considered imminent, and necessarily had to occur in Palestine, Jewish political goals appeared of little moment.

The apocalyptic scenario for World War II was advanced in astonishing concreteness, due perhaps to the large number of retired military officers in the movement. As has already been mentioned, Colonel MacKendrick went so far as to write a letter on October 25, 1940, to Lieutenant General A. G. McNaughton, the commander of Canadian troops in Britain, alerting him to the shape the war was about to take. Germany would attempt the capture of the Iranian and Iraqi oil fields, along with the pipeline to Haifa, and attack the British fleet in the Mediterranean. Mussolini, in the meantime, would initially conquer Egypt and Palestine, but would be defeated and slain in Palestine, as the combined armies of Russia, Turkey, Persia, and Germany gathered against Jerusalem. But the king of England would meet the challenge by calling a National Day of Prayer, and supernatural forces would defeat the unholy coalition "in the Great Day of Almighty God by the Omnipotent power of our Lord and we will be saved to carry on into the NEW ERA as decreed in the Holy Writ." There is no indication of General McNaughton's response to this curious religiomilitary analysis, but MacKendrick's approach was by no means unique.[19]

MacKendrick prepared a modified and much elaborated version for public consumption the same year, an enterprise for which he consulted his friend William J. Cameron (see chapter 4). Although he and Cameron apparently disagreed about the reference to Jews in MacKendrick's original manuscript, the discussion of Jews was scant in the published version. He clearly regarded Jewish claims to Palestine as scarcely worth discussing on the eve of Armageddon, and limited himself to observing that Jewish claims "will not stand in the overturning that we shall witness in Palestine." Since the "consummation of prophecy" was to occur within the coming year, the politics of Zionism were deemed distinctly peripheral.[20]

Although neither 1943 nor 1944 brought the prophetic fulfillment MacKendrick expected, his analysis remained influential, for it reappeared in at least two other versions from different hands in 1944. A strikingly similar analysis, with comparable emphasis upon the military strategies the belligerents would employ, came from Howard Rand in the fall of 1944. Rand, however, was now aware of the fact that World War II was likely to end without the climactic events in the Middle East that MacKendrick had anticipated, and he therefore extended the millenarian script to encompass a postwar struggle with the Soviet Union: "The first phase of World War II will end with the capitulation of Germany and the second phase will follow immediately with the Sovietization of Europe and the formation of a world confederacy of the nations who are to join in the great combination that will move against the Anglo-Saxon-Celtic peoples in the bid for world domination and power." Here, too, the imminence of world-shaking events left little room for a consideration of Jewish claims to Palestine.[21]

But another work, also published in 1944, suggested that as British-Israelites looked past the war, or toward its extension following the defeat of Germany, Zionism would loom larger in their awareness. Canadian British-Israelites in Vancouver issued the pseudonymously authored apocalyptic novel *When?: A Prophetical Novel of the Very Near Future*, by "Ben Judah," which set the coming military conflict in Palestine in a fictional framework. The protagonist, one Brian Benjamin, a Sephardic Jew who has converted to Christianity, visits Palestine on an obscure, presumably British, intelligence mission, arriving in time to witness the British retreat from Jerusalem, the city's capture by the forces of Gog, and the storms, earthquakes, and sundry other interventions that prevent Gog's final triumph. After the heaving earth, sulphurous fire, and hailstones save the British army, Christ returns and establishes the millennial kingdom. Unlike MacKendrick's and Rand's earlier narratives, however, the *When?* author is careful to note that Gog's capture of Jerusalem was significantly aided by collusion with Zionists. Indeed, the Zionist fifth column is none other than the inauthentic Jews who are the descendants of the interracial marriages in ancient times. One of Brian Benjamin's informants is happy to enlighten him about these racial differences. There are, he says, "two races of so-called Jews, the Sephardim, or true Semitic Jews of Israel blood, and the Ashkenazim . . . who are not Semitics, nor are they Jews except by religion. . . . There was great animosity between the real Semitic Jews and the greater part of the Zionists [who] were usurpers of Gentile blood."[22]

With the growth of the Zionist movement and the realization that World War II was not to bring the fulfillment of prophecies, the belief grew that not only were there distinct "races" of Jews, one authentic and the other inauthentic, but that the latter provided the wellsprings of Zionism. For if God had intended that Palestine go to Israel (the Anglo-Saxon-Celtic peoples) as well as to Judah, how could "authentic" Jews pursue a contrary course?

One of the earliest suggestions of Zionism's illegitimacy had appeared in the *Dearborn Independent*, in 1921, with the suggestion that Zionists were pawns of Bolshevism. The *Independent* foresaw a rebellion of Palestinian Jews against the British, aided by their Russian kinsman, but to no avail, for Great Britain "and perhaps the United States will defend the old pure vision of a Jerusalem redeemed." Although Howard Rand had omitted Zionism from his military analysis of the coming Battle of Armageddon, he left no doubt as to his views on the illegitimacy of Zionism: "God has overruled the endeavor to give to Jewry what does not belong to them through an increasingly Arab opposition to Jewish demands. Jewry cannot nor will they ever be able to administer the affairs of Palestine. Their nationhood ended in 70 A.D. and will not again be restored." And, like "Ben Judah," Rand suggested that the Zionists might work hand-in-glove with the forces of Gog. This army of evil would shortly "march toward Palestine." England's refusal to accept Zionist claims would trigger the advance of Gog's forces on Palestine, thus setting the stage for the final act of history.[23]

C. F. Parker, writing in 1948, the year of the creation of the state of Israel, synthesized the growing antipathy to Zionism with his belief in "two races of Jews." The Zionists were in his view almost all Ashkenazim, and therefore "Esau-Edomites." While the Sephardim were presumed to be pious, apolitical, and reliant only upon God's mercies, the Ashkenazic Zionists used the financial and political influence of European and American Jewish communities to foster their political program for statehood. Parker regarded the result as both odious and blasphemous:

> The newly declared Jewish State of "Israel" is as ersatz and barren as its predecessor, the Herodian-Jewish nation, for it still rejects Jesus Christ. It is a pretender. Palestinian Jewry is a Communist and Atheist-ridden monstrosity whose only ambition is not to serve the world but to rule it. . . . The Jews have seized the Holy Land from the rightful owners—Israel-Britain, who has blindly and stupidly, and yet for a divine purposes—permitted her heritage to pass to them.

The Herodians, we will remember, were themselves regarded as the tainted offspring of forbidden liaisons, and so the new state is linked with the "racial" violations of an earlier generation.[24]

The events of 1948 solidified Howard Rand's resolve as well. Two months after the proclamation of the Jewish state, he branded it the work of "renegade Jews," not "true Israelitish Jews." These "renegades" were the same impostors who thirty years earlier "were instrumental in taking over Russia." A year later, Rand was even more explicit in his identification of Zionism with cosmic evil. The Zionists were part of "a Great Conspiracy," a "program of evil," whose fundamental tactic was the deception practiced by its members. These false Jews had successfully deceived Christians so that Jews rather than Christians would appear to constitute Israel, the better to further their acquisition of world power. Rand went on to characterize Zionists in language reminiscent of *The Protocols*: "Thoughtful men and women have long recognized the existence of a secret group of would-be world rulers whose activities have been manifested principally through the power of money and financial control. For example, a study of the history of the Nihilists, the *Illuminati*, the Fabians and the House of Rothschild supplies ample evidence of the existence of such a cabal." The Zionists were merely the Great Conspiracy's most recent manifestation.[25]

The intensity of anti-Zionist sentiment among British-Israel writers contrasted sharply with the very different response to Jewish statehood among other Protestant millenarians. The principal expression of Protestant millennialism—dispensationalism—did what British-Israelites found so unacceptable: it identified prophecies concerning Israel with the history of the Jewish people. Consequently, for those evangelical Protestants within the dispensationalist fold, the creation of the state of Israel was cause for rejoicing, as was the reunification of Jerusalem nineteen years later. Indeed, the resentments of British-Israelites, and of Christian Identity believers later, have been directed not only against Zionists but toward the influential and vocal body of pro-Zionist Christians whose scenario for the millennium is premised upon the reestablishment of a Jewish state in Palestine.

Jews as Asiatics: The Khazar Hypothesis

The anti-Zionist tenor of British-Israel writing, particularly in the late 1940s, centered upon the assertion that plans for the state had been made and advanced by counterfeit Jews, with no claim to biblical authenticity. They were the offspring of idolators, whose very genes carried the predilection for evil that had existed in their remote ancestors. As we have seen, these "false Jews" were invariably identified as Eastern European and were frequently contrasted with their allegedly authentic and pious Sephardic coreligionists. We have also seen that hostility toward Russian and Polish Jews was by no means unique to British-Israelism. It pervaded the native-born elites of countries that experienced large-scale Jewish immigration from Eastern Europe. Hence, hostility to Ashkenazic Jews was shared by a wide range of individuals for a variety of motives, some theological (in the case of British-Israelites), but some on the grounds that this Jewish in-migration was unassimilable, disease-ridden, harbored political radicalism, and fostered unethical business practices. Because so many outside British-Israelism exhibited bias against the Eastern Europeans, elements of this larger hostility found their way into British-Israelism.

Foremost among these external anti-Semitic motifs brought into British-Israelism was the charge that Eastern European Jews were in fact not Europeans at all but were "Asiatics." The specific form this took was the accusation that Jews from the czar's empire were descendants of the Khazars, a people that had once lived near the shores of the Black Sea, and whose leadership stratum and an unknown portion of its populace had converted to Judaism in the seventh century. The Khazar theory never figured as a major component of anti-Semitism. Indeed, it receives only scant attention in Léon Poliakov's monumental history of the subject. However, it came to exercise a particular attraction for advocates of immigration restriction in America. Since they already had a well-developed position on the exclusion of "Orientals," particularly the Chinese, the suggestion that Jews were Asiatics rather than Europeans made it possible to include them within an existing category of inadmissible foreigners. Hence in the 1920s when immigration restrictionism reached a peak, the Khazar theory enjoyed a vogue in America, although it had in fact existed for several decades before that.[26]

The earliest suggestion that Khazar ancestry played a significant role in determining the composition of Ashkenazic Jewry appears to have been in a lecture given by Ernest Renan, "Judaism as Race and as Religion," on January 27, 1883. Although the conversion of the Khazar ruling group was well known, Renan seems to have been the first to suggest that Khazar converts may have been numerous enough to constitute a major proportion of Eastern European Jewry. Renan's suggestion was consistent with his long-standing belief that a racial distinction separated Jews from Aryans. There was, however, no immediate reason for such a view to exercise an attraction for British-Israelites, except insofar as they might for their own reasons have harbored an antipathy toward Ashkenazic Jews. There was nothing in the Khazar theory per se that commended it to British-Israelites, for—ironically—legend had for generations associated the Black Sea Khazars with the ten lost tribes of Israel.[27]

This association seems to have had its origin in the complex of medieval legends concerning Alexander's Gate, a barrier Alexander the Great was alleged to have had constructed in one of the mountain passes of the Caucasus, for the purpose of shutting out from the civilized world barbarian masses until such time as the wars of Gog and Magog in the Last Days should require their presence. Those behind the gate were sometimes Scythians, sometimes Turks, sometimes the lost tribes, and sometimes Khazars. Although tales of the gate faded out by the Renaissance, it is possible that since both the Khazars and the lost Israelites were candidates for enclosure behind it, their names were first linked and then fused. What is not speculative is that John Wilson, the founder of British-Israelism, in his effort to track down stray descendants of the lost tribes, did in fact link them quite explicitly with the Khazars, who sprang from Israel and "who are of the same race with the Anglo-Saxons." Having been brought so explicitly within both the Israel and Anglo-Saxon folds by Wilson, how did the Khazars become linked a century later to Esau-Edom, Bolshevism, and the Zionist conspiracy?[28]

To get some sense of the manner in which the Khazars came to function as an anti-Semitic symbol, it is instructive to look at the use made of them by perhaps the most widely read American racialist of the interwar period, Lothrop Stoddard. Even more than Madison Grant, Stoddard spread a racialist gospel to a mass audience, not only through nearly two dozen books but through numerous articles in the popular press. Stoddard brought impeccable credentials to the enterprise. Born of an old New England family, he received a law degree and a doctorate from Harvard. While Stoddard was a prolific author, the work that reverberated longest was his 1926 magazine article, "The Pedigree of Judah." The editors of the *Forum*, where it appeared, disclaimed any wish to sow prejudice or hatred: "We believe that a vast majority of our readers realize that only good has come from the fearless airing of honest differences of opinion." In "seeking out the underlying cause of the symptoms [of] the Jewish question," they commended Stoddard's approach as "broad and scientific." Stoddard too claimed only the desires of a scientist for sure and objective knowledge: "Surely no factor is more vital than that of Jewry's racial make-up. Modern science teaches us the basic importance of race." Yet Stoddard's analysis appeared strangely similar to those made by persons of no particular scientific pretensions.[29]

Stoddard too spoke in terms of two races of Jews, and in nearly the same way as theologically inclined British-Israelites, with whom he had no discernible links. There were the "aloof" and "aristocratic" Sephardic Jews, who were Semites. But there were also the Ashkenazic Jews, whose "coarse features . . . reveal[ed] a mixture of diverse bloods." Their "Jewish nose" had been acquired through intermarriage with the ancient Hittites. The Sephardic Jews had entered the Mediterranean world, "absorbing much Mediterranean blood." But their eastern brethren had wandered into southern Russia, where they met up with and blended into the Khazars. The latter Stoddard regarded as a combination of Turkish and Mongoloid strains from the fastnesses of Asia. "The result was a population prevailingly round-headed and thick-set, but with two outstanding facial types: the full-faced, hook-nosed Armenoid; and the flat-faced, squat- or pug-nosed Mongoloid." The physical differences between Sephardic and Ashkenazic Jews were merely the external sign of "profound differences . . . in mentality and temperament." As far as the presence of "genuine Hebrew blood" was concerned, it was "very small" among the Sephardim, "while among the Ashkenazim it must be infinitesimal." To his analysis, Stoddard appended a series of Jewish portraits with predictably clinical explanatory notes.[30]

Stoddard was, of course, operating from a set of underlying ideas that did not derive from British-Israelism at all. Rather, they reflected nineteenth- and early twentieth-century concepts of race, in which small variations in facial features as well as presumed accompanying character traits were deemed to pass from generation to generation, subject only to the corrupting effects of marriage with members of other groups, the result of which would lower the superior stock without raising the inferior partners. Racial inequality had become accepted scientific opinion by the mid-1800s, and on this foundation were erected increasingly elaborate racial typologies, which attempted to make increasingly fine distinctions among racial groups, a tendency both reflected and extended by Stoddard.[31]

Although Stoddard was in fact an atheist, his approach to Jewish origins was profoundly congenial to British-Israel thought. British-Israelites were prone toward sympathy with racial anthropology because it shared an important characteristic with their religious views, namely, the belief that important human traits were heritable. To be sure, British-Israelites were not completely deterministic. They still believed, for example, that the acceptance of Christ was essential for salvation. But the dividing line between themselves and other Christians lay in their insistence that a special role in facilitating salvation in the form of both rewards and obligations had been given to a group defined in terms of biological ancestry. Unlike other Christians, who spoke in terms of a "New Israel" defined by belief rather than by blood, British-Israelites insisted that blood mattered in the divine scheme. Therefore "pedigree" (to use Stoddard's own term) was religiously significant. Had not John Wilson himself cast doubt upon the "pedigree of Judah" when he raised the specter of intermarriage with the heathen? Stoddard's supposedly scientific analysis of bloodlines, with its intimations of moral as well as physical variation, could not help but strike a responsive chord. As has already been shown, British-Israelites had begun by the 1920s to return to and elaborate Wilson's ideas of Edomite and Canaanite connections with the Jews. The suggestions by Stoddard and others that Jews' share of Semitic ancestry might have been further debased by a Khazar connection did not seem implausible to those already predisposed to pay attention to biological antecedents.

The Khazar theory therefore was in no sense peculiar to British-Israelism but was in fact imported from a larger universe of fashionable racial discourse. It did, however, find a particularly accepting audience in British-Israel circles. The *Dearborn Independent* under William J. Cameron was one such venue. As early as 1923—well before Stoddard's article—he had observed that Khazar ancestry meant that at least as far as Ashkenazim were concerned, "this indiscriminate mass known as Jews are not the Jews of old, nor even their remote descendants." Paul Tyner, who contributed an article on the British-Israel movement to Cameron in 1925, included lengthy extracts of an interview he had had in London with one of British-Israelism's most prominent figures, Reverend William Pascoe Goard. Goard assured him that the Zionists lacked a valid claim to Palestine, since the Jews, far from being exiles from the land, were in large measure offspring of Khazar proselytes. In the *National Message*, organ of the British-Israel World Federation, Reverend Frank Hancock, an early leader of the Anglo-Saxon Federation of America, left little room for misunderstanding when he assured readers that "we hasten to endorse the writings of Lothrop Stoddard, Geno Speranza, Madison Grant and others, because the racial question touches all others." By the mid-1930s, the Khazar connection, along with the racial anthropology that distinguished between "long-headed" Sephardim and "round-headed" Ashkenazim, was accepted seemingly as a matter of course.[32]

By the 1940s, with the fuller development of the Esau-Edom thesis and more intensely anti-Zionist sentiments, the Khazar theory acquired a decidedly sharper edge. The Canadian *When?* author disposed of Eastern European Jews as "a minor Asiatic mongrel breed, with a strong admixture of Turko-Mongol blood." In like manner, C. F. Parker regarded Khazar ancestry as strengthening sinister tendencies already present through the Esau-Edomites. Howard Rand noted that not only did mixture with a "non-Semitic, Turko-Finn, Mongolian tribal people" deprive Jews of any claim to Palestine; it also guaranteed, to Rand's evident relief, "the non-Jewish lineage of our Lord."[33]

The Khazar theory had arisen outside of British-Israelism to begin with. While British-Israelism proved to be a particularly hospitable home for it, it was not the only place where the theory came to rest. It continued to lead a more or less separate life in right-wing circles, at least to the extent that these were sympathetic to anti-Semitic arguments. This connection with political extremism served as a reinforcing factor later on, with the full development of Christian Identity, for many Identity believers were well placed to take "Khazarism" from two sources: the religious literature that issued from British-Israelism and the political literature that came from more secular right-wing sources.

Khazar ancestry of the Jews assumed particular prominence in two books widely read on the extreme right, John Beaty's *Iron Curtain over America* (1951) and Wilmot Robertson's *Dispossessed Majority* (1972). Beaty exhibited a particularly obsessional concern with the roots of Russian Jewry. Like Lothrop Stoddard before him, Beaty brought academic credentials to his work, which gave it the appearance of objective research. After earning a doctorate in English at Columbia, he joined the faculty of Southern Methodist University, where he eventually became chair of the English Department. During World War II he was chief of the Historical Section of the War Department General Staff. The ideas in *Iron Curtain over America* circulated widely not only in the circles around Gerald L. K. Smith but in those linked to Willis Carto's Liberty Lobby. The book was therefore exceptionally well placed to reach the emerging Christian Identity right.[34]

Beaty devoted an entire chapter of the book to Russia and Khazars, although in fact, like earlier writers, he relied upon such outdated sources as Heinrich Graetz's late nineteenth-century history of the Jews. In Beaty's version of the story, the conversion of the Khazars had allowed "the imported rabbis and their successors . . . complete control of the political, social, and religious thought of [the] people." The reforms of Czar Alexander II, misguided in Beaty's view, gave the "Judaized Khazars" the ability to infiltrate and corrupt Russia as a whole. They did so with four aims in mind: the development of communism, the fomenting of revolution, the growth of Zionism, and the transfer of their numbers to America. Hence, he argued, they were able not only to seize control of Russia but to provide their conspiracy with an American base as a minority "obsessed with its own objectives which are not those of Western Christian civilization." Beaty did not employ the religious language familiar in British-Israel tracts; there was no suggestion, for example, of a tie between Khazars and Edomites. But Beaty, by giving currency to the Khazar theory on the extreme right, provided a familiar reference point for Christian Identity in the future. The more prevalent the Khazar theory, the less exotic were religious positions based upon the contaminated racial stock of Jews. Indeed, Christian Identity could be seen as merely pushing the point of racial intermarriage further back in history. Instead of occurring only with the Khazar episode of the seventh century, the conversion of the Khazars could be placed in a framework of Jewish intermarriage extending into the biblical period.[35]

By the time Wilmot Robertson's *Dispossessed Majority* appeared in 1972, Christian Identity was well established. Without adopting an Identity position, and purporting merely to correct distortions in traditional history, Robertson repeated virtually unchanged the view of the Khazars presented almost half a century earlier by Stoddard. He too distinguished between a race of "olive-skinned, long-headed Sephardim" and round-headed Eastern European "Armenoid Khazars." Like Stoddard, Robertson also concluded that Jews were mistaken in believing they were descended from the biblical Hebrews. Robertson's book had a particularly strong influence on David Duke.

Indeed, Duke's Knights of the Ku Klux Klan also subsequently reprinted Stoddard's 1926 article in its entirety. Although Duke offered the disclaimer that neither he nor the Klan agreed completely with Stoddard, the article was being republished as "a landmark in bringing an understanding of Jews to non-Jews." Duke has been careful never to identify himself with Identity or any other religious position. On the other hand, he was lionized in Identity circles and cultivated Identity support, a matter I shall return to in chapter 10.[36]

In short, by the time Christian Identity took hold as a force on the right in the 1960s and 1970s, the Khazar ancestry of the Jews was a virtual article of faith that emerged simultaneously from two sources: it came by way of British-Israelites anxious to further impugn Jewish racial origins in the wake of the establishment of Israel, for only some innately evil group would oppose God's will by driving Britain from Palestine. However, as we have seen, Renan's original suggestion about the Khazars had also found its way into the writings of immigration restrictionists. This association with nativism brought the Khazar theory into prominence among secularists on the right who knew nothing of Anglo-Israelism but were also anxious to find whatever "evidence" was available that might characterize Jews as evildoers. In this connection, the Khazar theory was particularly attractive, since rightists already argued that Jews had been responsible for the Bolshevik Revolution. If they could now also argue that the revolution's perpetrators were "Turko-Mongol Asiatics" (i.e., barbarians), the revolutionist label would seem all the more plausible. Hence, Christian Identity was able to incorporate the Khazar theory on both religious and political grounds.

Jewish Origins in Christian Identity

Thus, Wesley Swift, the most influential of the first generation of Christian Identity preachers, effortlessly incorporated virtually every element of the racial intermarriage literature, although with some significant modifications. Swift began with the assumption that God's primal command to Adam's descendants was the prohibition on racial intermarriage. The Jews, however, were those who systematically violated the commandment and "mongrelized with every people on the face of the earth." They intermarried with the Hittites and Canaanites "to produce a very cutting type of Jew," and then with the Khazars to produce "the Mongolian Ashkenazi of our time." Unlike most earlier writers, however, Swift saw little to distinguish the Sephardim from the Ashkenazim. There was, to be sure, a different skull shape, a matter Stoddard was particularly keen on. But Swift was clearly influenced by the suggestion, made by Stoddard and others, that even the Sephardim carried the blood of Hittites and other infidels. While most early writers who stressed Sephardic-Ashkenazic differences were willing to grant the Sephardim a measure of racial distinction, Swift dismissed them as "thin faced Hittite Jew[s]," in no way preferable to "the round headed Mongolian [Ashkenazic] Jew." All were equally sullied by crimes of miscegenation, although for some the offenses took place in the remote past, while for others, the descendants of Khazars, they occurred in comparatively recent times. However, like many racialists before him, Swift regarded the taint of distant race mixing as undiluted by time; the recency of the union was insignificant.[37]

The views of Conrad Gaard were not as widely disseminated as those of his contemporary, Swift, but Gaard too had ties to Gerald L. K. Smith, and Gaard was among the few Identity figures who attempted to present his position in a systematic fashion. Gaard had read and approved of Stoddard's 1926 article, which he proceeded to place in a theological framework the patrician Stoddard would have found incomprehensible. Those who converted and intermarried among the Khazars were "Babylonian pseudo-Jews" who had never been part of "All-Israel." They were "Shelahite-Canaanites," who found the absorption with the Khazars attractive because, in Gaard's curious version of history, the Khazars could become "one of the largest and strongest nations in Europe." The Khazar base only whetted their appetite for greater conquests, a plan that Gaard, like Howard Rand, referred to as the "Great Conspiracy," a cabal "so far-reaching in scope and so audacious in purpose, that it staggers the imagination of men of good will." Racial mixture not only removes the Jewish people from God's design, according to Gaard, it creates a mass of unassimilable evildoers for whom each racially forbidden liaison is a step in the direction of world conquest, a theory that fused the obsessive concern for racial purity with *The Protocols*'s fixation upon a Jewish conspiracy.[38]

In 1962, Bertrand Comparet added another twist, further integrating the Khazar theory into Identity theology. Comparet claimed that according to the Khazars' tradition, their ancestors had originally come from the vicinity of Mt. Seir, "which is Edom, the home of the Edomite Jews." The implication is clear. When the Jews intermarried with the Khazars, they were not becoming further defiled racially; they were merely marrying their own distant kin, since they had themselves lost any Israel connection by virtue of prior fusion with the Edomites. Where Edom had originally been construed as the Turks by British-Israel, and had slowly metamorphosed into the Jews, Edom now became a source of evil from which many streams departed and joined, some

Jewish, some Khazar—but, Comparet implies, these are in the end meaningless distinctions. Subsequent Identity writers occasionally accepted Comparet's reversal of the Khazar theory, suggesting that Esau-Edomite Jews were the ancestors of the Khazars, rather than the Khazars being forebears of Ashkenazic Jews.[39]

The more common version—that Khazars were the ancestors of Eastern European Jews—spread throughout the Identity movement, from Richard Girnt Butler's Aryan Nations to Dan Gayman's Church of Israel. It appeared on the margin of Identity, in John Harrell's paramilitary Christian-Patriots Defense League, and in pamphlets by the league's "minister of defense," Colonel Gordon "Jack" Mohr, a late convert to Identity. The doctrine's malleability was evident in the use made of it by Bob Hallstrom, a successor to Sheldon Emry at the America's Promise Ministry. Hallstrom, in an article originally published by America's Promise and then republished by Aryan Nations, links the Khazar theory to the medieval ritual-murder libel, according to which Jewish ritual required the blood of Christians. He assures us that such murders continued to be "well documented up until the early 1900s," and that "to this day young children and adults mysteriously disappear, never to be heard from again." He implies not only that ritual murder has been verified and continuous, but that its authenticity is rejected because "mainline 'Christian-dumb'" fails to recognize that Jews are actually "a mixed race of Turko-Finn, Mongolian tribal people from Khazaria." By implication, such people from beyond the frontiers of civilization would engage in any act, no matter how barbaric.[40]

The Khazar theory received reinforcement from an unexpected quarter with the publication in 1976 of Arthur Koestler's *Thirteenth Tribe*. Coming near the close of a life of rare intellectual force, Koestler's eccentric work, on behalf of the Khazar theory, was bound to attract considerable attention. By unhappy accident, its publication coincided with the rise of Christian Identity. Although unequipped with the specialist background the subject might be thought to require, Koestler nevertheless made an amateur's serious attempt to investigate and support the theory. In so doing, he reinforced, however inadvertently, many of the positions British-Israelites and others supportive of the Khazar connection had advanced. He concluded that "the Khazar contribution to the genetic make-up of the Jews must be substantial, and in all likelihood dominant," and therefore that it was scientifically impossible for Jews to have biologically "descended from the biblical tribe." He implied, as had racial theorists before him, that the "Jewish nose" might well have been acquired from the "'nostrility' . . . frequent among Caucasian peoples [i.e., the

Khazars]." He seems only to have partially understood the implications of his thesis. He does indeed disclaim any desire to impugn the legitimacy of the state of Israel, a status he saw as flowing from United Nations action, not from either an Abrahamic covenant or the genetic profile of contemporary Jews: "The problem of the Khazar infusion a thousand years ago . . . is irrelevant to modern Israel." However, Koestler seems to have been either unaware of or oblivious to the use anti-Semites had made of the Khazar theory since its introduction at the turn of the century. Indeed, even in his own lifetime, Christian Identity writers fastened upon his book as the ultimate validation of their own position, for if such a view was advanced by a leading Jewish intellectual and, moreover, advanced as scientifically valid, then it must be more than merely the creation of anti-Semites.[41]

Identity writers quickly seized the opportunity Koestler had unwittingly provided, selling his book through their mail-order services and putting it to uses its author could scarcely have imagined. Notwithstanding what Koestler himself had written, the New Christian Crusade Church, led by James K. Warner, asserted that "if Koestler (a Jew) is correct, 95% of world Jewry today has Turkish rather than Semitic ancestry. This invalidates their claim to Palestine as a historical home." This conclusion, although clearly at variance with Koestler's intentions, was altogether consistent with Identity theology. Koestler accepted the legitimacy of Israel because he saw its claim to sovereignty as assured by the legality of the United Nations partition plan of 1947. Identity, however, had absorbed British-Israelism's radically different position, premised upon the significance of putatively "pure" bloodlines and the identification of Israel with the Anglo-Saxon-Celtic peoples. Hence, no showing of legality could override the racial conception of salvation.[42]

The America's Promise Ministry regarded *The Thirteenth Tribe* as sufficiently important to warrant issuing a special newsletter in 1977, reissued a year later, completely devoted to the book. It bore the headline:

FINALLY AVAILABLE TO ALL AMERICANS
ABSOLUTE HISTORICAL PROOF
JEWS ARE NOT ISRAELITES!

"We cannot stress enough," they wrote, "how absolutely imperative it is for all Christian Americans to consider the startling proof in Arthur Koestler's book that today's Jews are not Israelites." Here, as elsewhere on the Identity right, the implication was that a veil had been pulled away, and what was hidden now stood revealed, although in fact the Khazar episode had long been noted, going back to the medieval Jewish poet-philosopher Judah ha-Levi. America's

Promise took note of the fact that the non-Israelite origin of the Jewish people had much earlier been "Henry Ford's conclusion," and that "Ford further proved" that these inauthentic Jews used their Jewish identification as a "cloak" to "take economic and political control of America." As we have already seen in chapter 3, while this may well have been Ford's view, the words were those of the British-Israelite William J. Cameron, advanced in the *Dearborn Independent,* in the volumes that made up *The International Jew,* and in the Anglo-Saxon Federation of America. Finally, America's Promise was quick to include what Koestler had omitted, that those who intermarried with the Khazars were "Edomite descendants of Esau," who would go on after the Khazar period to become communist revolutionaries. In the process, they would "call . . . [communism's] followers 'Reds' after their Abrahamic ancestor Esau-Edom."[43]

Thus by stages the religious authenticity and racial homogeneity of the Jews had been called into question, by British-Israelites, by secular anti-Semites, and by Christian Identity. At first, they came only from the tribe of Judah. Then they were said to have mingled with the offspring of Esau to become Edomites. Along the way, Canaanite and Hittite blood had further compromised them, until whatever was left of Semitic association vanished in the Asiatic gene pool of the Khazars. As this process of delegitimation went forward, the Jews were successively seen as younger brothers who would be protected by the more significant Israel; as weak and sinful harkers after strange peoples; as the carriers of tainted and cursed blood; and finally as impostors masquerading as a biblical people. In this final incarnation, they took on the characteristics compatible with the conspiracy theory of *The Protocols of the Elders of Zion*. Skilled in the art of concealing their true mixed origins, dissemblers who presented themselves as a people they were not, they now possessed the attributes of guile and clandestinity perfectly suited to participants in a secret organization bent on world conquest. Consequently, religious and political agendas converged. According to the religious beliefs of British-Israelism, Jews were in a subordinate role. Not they but the Anglo-Saxon-Celtic peoples were to have primacy in Palestine. The failure of Jews to acknowledge the "true Israel" was bad enough; to repudiate the British role in Palestine was beyond forgiveness or understanding. Only some peculiarly benighted people could so thoroughly seek to subvert God's plan. It was precisely this concept of the Jews' commitment to evil and deception that would likewise be required in order to breathe life into the belief that a Jewish conspiracy sought to rule the world.

But this process of dehumanization had one more road to traverse. The acceptance of Jewish "mongrelization" permitted the rejection of Zionism and the adoption of a conspiracy theory of history. But these beliefs, while rendering the Jew less human, did not render him less *than* human. Jews came increasingly to be viewed as loathsome and dangerous as such labels as "Edomite" and "Khazar" were applied, but they were in the final analysis lowered in the human racial hierarchy rather than removed from it altogether. That final step in the dehumanization process would come.

Loaded as Jews now were with imputations of evil and corruption, it is difficult to believe that they could be further besmirched. Yet Christian Identity took the final step, a step British-Israelism never allowed itself. British-Israelism regarded Jews with increasing disdain and annoyance, as unworthy and duplicitous, but it considered them human beings of some order. Christian Identity ultimately removed them totally from the domain of "humanity," not, as with blacks, by identifying them with lower animals, but by linking Jews with transcendent, cosmic evil. Christian Identity began to assert with increasing vigor and consistency that Jews were the literal children of the Devil.

The most distinctive doctrine associated with Christian Identity is the belief that Jews are the direct biological offspring of the Devil. This belief is the final extension of a process of delegitimation described in the preceding chapter, according to which Jews became progressively more racially contaminated through marriages with forbidden heathen peoples. This view, saturated though it was with anti-Semitism, accepted that Jews were human beings who had sprung from the stock of Abraham. Hence, the obsessive concern with out-marriages was premised on the notion that no matter how impressive the religious pedigree of Jews, it had been forfeited by their own misconduct. Although British-Israelism manifested increasingly anti-Semitic reactions to Zionism, it never adopted the view that Jews were nonhuman, demonic creatures. Christian Identity, while it accepts the theory of Jewish out-marriage, seeks to demonstrate that the Jews were never human beings, a position fundamentally different from that of their Anglo-Israel parent.

The theory of satanic origins differs not only from the position of British-Israelism but from that of the most ferocious period of Christian anti-Semitism, the Middle Ages. Late medieval popular religious culture, as well as the writings of theologians, associated Jews closely with the Devil. They were represented as having horns and tails, and were believed capable of summoning the Devil, as well as being an intermediary for those anxious to sell their souls to him. Jews were alleged to be allies of the Devil in continuing warfare against Christ, and they were even thought to teach in the Talmud that the Devil was their parent. Yet ultimately these charges could all be reduced to affiliations with the Devil and metaphors of demonic paternity but not to

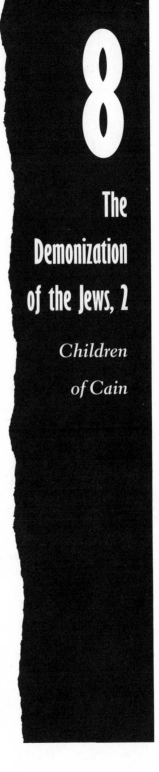

8

The Demonization of the Jews, 2

Children

of Cain

assertions of actual biological descent. They constituted variations upon volatile New Testament phraseology: "they [Jews] are of their father the Devil," and "the synagogue of Satan." But obsessed though late medieval Christians were with the Devil as a real force, they in the end shrank from advancing the demonic descent of Jews with the literalness Christian Identity was to adopt. In other words, Christian Identity might associate itself with ancient strands of anti-Semitic belief—the Jew as the Devil's ally—but more was clearly required in order to carry that belief to the point of asserting a biological link.[1]

The theory of the Jews as the Devil's seed may be summarized as follows, although, as the succeeding chapter demonstrates, there are small variations among Identity writers. According to the theory, either the Devil himself or one of his underlings had intercourse with Eve in the Garden of Eden. Cain was the product of this illicit union. Hence Cain and all his progeny, by virtue of satanic paternity, carry the Devil's unchanging capacity to work evil. These descendants of Cain became known in time as "Jews." This theory, with no real precedents in either medieval anti-Semitism or British-Israelism, did not in fact emerge out of a vacuum, nor was it purely the product of some anti-Semitic writer's inventiveness. The ideas themselves—Eve's seduction, Cain's satanic paternity, and the demonic origin of the Jews, for example—may be found in Gnostic writings from the early centuries of the Christian era. This Gnostic literature was almost certainly unknown to the Identity writers who put this anti-Semitic theology together, since they tended to be either autodidacts or the graduates of small Bible colleges. There is no evidence that they knew of or used these ancient sources. To the extent that Gnostic precursors had any influence at all, it was in highly mediated form, through untraceable layers of intervening texts.[2]

What can be traced with some accuracy are the more immediate sources, although even some of these go back several centuries. Identity's anti-Semitism was synthesized from a number of separate elements. Most were in existence by the end of the nineteenth century, and all were in place by the end of the 1920s. There were five such elements. Sometimes two or three might be found together, but the five were not fully fused until the mid-1940s, and it was not until about 1960 that the full-blown Devil's seed theory began to circulate widely in Christian Identity circles.

The five elements of the theory were these:

1. God made a primal distinction between two types of human beings according to their paternity. Some, called Adamites, were descended

from Adam. Others, called Pre-Adamites, were created separately, long before Adam.

2. The serpent in Genesis's story of the Fall was not a reptile. He was an intelligent, "humanoid" creature associated with the Devil, if not the Devil himself.

3. Original sin consisted of Eve's sexual relationship with this quasi-human "serpent."

4. Because of this liaison, the world contains two "seedlines." One (Adam's seedline) consists of the descendants of Adam and Eve. The other (the serpent's seedline) consists of the descendants of Eve and the "serpent."

5. Cain was a historical figure associated with evil in general and with the Devil in particular, and passed his propensity for evil to a line of descendants.

A significant and interesting attribute of these beliefs is that none refers to the Jews. The utilization of these elements in Christian Identity's theology of anti-Semitism was a comparatively late development. Only with the synthesis of the five into a single theory were they clearly associated with anti-Semitism. This chapter is concerned with explicating the five original elements, whose presence was necessary before such a synthesis could take place, while the synthesis itself will be described in the following chapter.

The Pre-Adamites

The oldest of the five elements is the belief that Adam was not the ancestor of all human beings. While bibliocentric religions regularly asserted a common ancestry for all people, in a line that led back to Adam, doubts were frequently expressed concerning its validity. This skepticism in fact predated the much-better-known debate that occurred over scientific accounts of human origins. Pre-Adamism can occasionally be found in ancient Jewish scriptural exegesis. It was developed in tenth-century Islam by al-Maqdisi, and began to appear in Christianity by the fourteenth century. During the Renaissance it was advanced tentatively by Paracelsus and directly by Giordano Bruno, whose views were adopted by Christopher Marlowe. But its most systematic exposition was by Isaac de la Peyrère in 1655. La Peyrère (1594–1676) was a Calvinist who may have been of Jewish descent. Indeed, Léon Poliakov and Richard Popkin suggest that he may have been a Marrano, a crypto-Jew who professed Christianity while secretly retaining his Jewish identity. Be that as it may, his advocacy of Pre-Adamism brought immediate retaliation from civil and ecclesiastical authorities. In Paris, his book was burned by the public hangman. Its author was imprisoned and subsequently recanted both his opinions and Protestantism. He appears to have remained at least nominally a Catholic convert from the late 1650s until his death.[3]

According to La Peyrère, there had been two creations, the first to create the Gentiles, and the second, beginning with Adam, to father the Jews. La Peyrère also found Pre-Adamites convenient in order to explain the life of Cain after Abel's murder. Since the account in Genesis mentions Cain taking a wife and building a city, La Peyrère, like many after him, wondered from what stock Cain's wife came and who the inhabitants of Cain's city were. Postulating Pre-Adamites appeared to solve the problem. Despite attempts to suppress La Peyrère's writings, his work was widely and often favorably noted by contemporaries in France and England. His arguments, if not direct knowledge of his books, survived into the Enlightenment among deists, all the way down to Voltaire. By the eighteenth century, the body of writing that challenged the traditional account of human origins was sufficiently large that one can discern separate "monogenetic" and "polygenetic" accounts, the former continuing to trace human origins back to Adam, the latter arguing for two or more separate creations. While polygenesis remained a minority opinion, its ranks were growing. In the first place, voyages of exploration demonstrated the multiplicity of different human societies and made it increasingly difficult to believe that all peoples had diffused from one couple in Eden and subsequently differentiated themselves by race and culture. In the second place, unlike La Peyrère, eighteenth-century polygenists could speculate without incurring the same risks of prosecution.[4]

By the nineteenth century, polygenesis and Pre-Adamism were even more attractive; acquaintance with non-Western peoples had developed in Europeans not only an intellectual curiosity about where they had come from, but an increasingly acute desire to demonstrate their racial inferiority. While differences were often explained environmentally, those more attuned to racial theories found it unpleasant to contemplate a common ancestry with nonwhites. This was especially the case in America, where Charles Caldwell, Josiah C. Nott, and Samuel G. Morton rejected the view that nonwhites were descendants of Adam and Noah. Morton, the most influential, combined Pre-Adamism with cranial measurements to construct a theory of racial differences, which especially appealed to defenders of Southern slavery. Indeed, as Reginald Horsman observes, "by the early 1850s the inherent inequality of races was simply accepted as a scientific fact in America, and most of the discussion now concerned the religious problem of accepting polygenesis as an explanation of racial differences or the problem of exactly defining the different races."[5]

In such an intellectual atmosphere, Pre-Adamism appeared in two different but not wholly incompatible forms. Religious writers continued to be attracted to the theory both because it appeared to solve certain exegetical problems (where did Cain's wife come from?) and exalted the spiritual status of Adam's descendants. Those of a more scientific bent found it equally attractive but for different reasons, connected with a desire to formulate theories of racial difference that retained a place for Adam while accepting evidence that many cultures were far older than the few thousand years humanity had existed, according to biblical chronology. The two varieties differed primarily in the evidence they used, the one relying principally upon scriptural texts and the latter on what passed at the time for physical anthropology.

Among the religious treatises, Dominick M'Causland's *Adam and the Adamite*, first published in London in 1864, was among the most influential. He took as the fundamental problem a reconciliation of the biblical Creation account with the fact that among known human societies of his time, "there are many gradations of civilization." He attempted to resolve the problem by positing ancient races that had long been in existence at the time of Adam's creation, and "that must have ever remained in that low state [of civilization] without some . . . special interposition of the Almighty." Hence by the time of Adam's creation, all the races save one were already in existence. That one, with Adam as its progenitor, M'Causland called the "Adamic race," a term that was to assume particular importance in Christian Identity.[6]

If M'Causland was representative of those anxious to preserve the traditional biblical account, the scientific position had its own advocates, some, such as Louis Agassiz, of considerable eminence. However, one of the most sustained scientific arguments came from the American geologist Alexander Winchell, a Methodist minister as well as a scientist. Winchell dismissed M'Causland's work as unsupported speculation. He also found M'Causland's polygenism too extreme, for Winchell believed it was possible to simultaneously accept the existence of Pre-Adamites and to believe that at some point of infinite remoteness, all human beings did in fact have a common ancestor. Winchell divided all human beings into three groups, the "White Race," the "Brown Races," and the "Black Races." He regarded Adam and the other figures in the early chapters of Genesis as historical latecomers, who branched off of nonwhite stock long after the latter had been created. Hence, instead of

asserting "the descent of Negroes and Australians from Noah and Adam"—
something he viewed with repugnance—Winchell reversed the traditional
ordering, so that the White Race came into existence last. As far as Adam was
concerned, he "was the progenitor of the Mediterranean race in its *Blonde*
and *Brunette* and *Sun-burnt* subdivisions, and of other peoples descended
from Seth or Cain, or other sons, who have constituted other races,—*swarthy*
tribes of the Mongoloids and Dravidians; or still other types of ruddy complexion, who have been displaced from existence before our times." These biblical
figures, then, collectively brought the White Race into existence in a previously nonwhite world. The Pre-Adamites among whom they emerged were
closely related physiologically, yet in comparison to them, Adam "may have
represented a decided and even a sudden step in organic improvement . . . a
noble and superior specimen."[7]

Pre-Adamites and Racial Inferiority

Despite their differences, both M'Causland and Winchell agreed that the Pre-
Adamites were nonwhites and the Adamites were whites. Their concern was
less in demonstrating the harmony of the biblical text or in resolving contradictions between religion and science as it was in lending scriptural authority
to doctrines of racial superiority. M'Causland considered the view that Adam
was the common ancestor of all humanity repugnant, for it compelled him to
see himself and blacks as related through a common ancestor. The Adamic
origin of humanity was equally pernicious in Winchell's view, for it placed a
specimen of the most "advanced" race temporally earlier than the less advanced and thereby threatened a Victorian article of faith, inevitable progress.

Like La Peyrère, M'Causland was perplexed by Cain's ability to marry and
found a city after his expulsion from the home of Adam and Eve. But La
Peyrère had conjured up Pre-Adamites to give Cain a wife and subjects without
suggesting what these people might have been like. M'Causland believed that
he knew. They were members of "inferior tribes," over whom Cain "gained
that ascendancy . . . that a strong-minded resolute man, endowed with capacity
and attainments superior to those of his new associates, might naturally obtain
under such circumstances." These tribesmen were not whites but were rather
nonwhite "Mongols" and thus the more easily dominated by the Adamite,
Cain. As far as M'Causland was concerned, the evidence was "conclusive" that
"the paternity of the Mongol or Negro races [is] wholly different from Adam."[8]

Winchell was equally concerned to emphasize racial separation. This was
particularly so for the division between "Black Races" and others. The "Black

Races" comprised the "Negro Race," "Hottentot Race," "Papuan Race," and "Australian Race." As far as the "Negro Race" was concerned, Winchell wrote, it is "an inferior race" based upon "anatomical, physiological, psychical and historical facts." To make them Adam's descendants would be to assert that "the world has witnessed a general scene of degradation and retrogression." Only by making Adam a recent creation could Winchell's conception of progress remain undisturbed. "Preadamitism means simply that Adam was descended from a Black race, not the Black races from Adam."[9]

The views of M'Causland and Winchell were thus deeply rooted in a nineteenth-century racialism that demanded that the inferiority of nonwhites be blessed by Scripture and ratified by science. It is important to recognize, however, that no matter how archaic such a view may seem now, it continued to be transmitted well into the twentieth century. When, as we shall see in a subsequent chapter, Pre-Adamism appears in contemporary Christian Identity, its presence does not require a century-long leap. Rather, the worldview out of which M'Causland and Winchell came continued to be espoused, albeit in more and more marginal ways.

As far as Christian Identity is concerned, the channel of greatest influence was a curious book, *Sargon the Magnificent*, published in 1927 by Mrs. Sydney Bristowe. Bristowe's Pre-Adamism might have been lifted unaltered from a work of M'Causland's time, although she subsequently claimed to have been unacquainted with his work. In her version, too, Cain arrives among Pre-Adamites to "become the leader, teacher and absolute lord and master of an inferior race." The Pre-Adamites were blacks.

> The Bible, by showing that only eight of Adam's race were saved in the ark, demands a belief in a previous black race to account for the existence of blacks in later history, for how could the Ethiopian who, the prophet remarks, could no more change his skin than the leopard his spots, have descended from Noah? Science, by discovering the fundamental physical differences between the black and white races, has shown the fallacy of the old idea that they had a common origin.

Thus a racialism that may seem incomparably remote from us continued to appear virtually unaltered in the twentieth century.[10]

The "Adamic Race" and the Aryan Myth

If M'Causland, Winchell, and other believers in the Pre-Adamite theory were certain Pre-Adamites were nonwhites, the corollary was that Adam and his descendants—the "Adamic race"—were whites, and that the sacred history recorded in the Bible was therefore best understood as neither universal nor tribal, but as racial. Adam was "the first of the Caucasian race," and the Bible is his history, M'Causland writes. For Winchell, "Adam was a ruddy white man, possessed of the higher range of faculties of the Mediterranean race." The American antiblack author Charles Carroll, writing at the turn of the century, assures his readers not only of Adam's and their whiteness but of the closeness to God that racial ancestry implies: "Adam was as literally and truly the son of God as was Isaac the son of Abraham. And the descendants of Adam, of pure Adamic stock, are sons and daughters of God, throughout all time." This strong link between Adam and the Caucasian race was not merely a general feature of racialist writing; it also rapidly passed into the work of individuals within the British-Israel fold.[11]

The myth of an Adamite people racially distinct from Pre-Adamites found its way into the work of perhaps the twentieth century's most influential British-Israelite, David Davidson. This may seem an odd point of contact between Pre-Adamism and British-Israelism, for Davidson's primary interest was to prove the divine character of the Great Pyramid at Gizeh. This enterprise, however, quickly ramified into a far stranger and more ambitious effort to reconfigure the entire history of the ancient Near East, including all of the accounts in Genesis. The effect was to project British-Israel into the patriarchal age and beyond, to the time of Adam himself. Concerned as British-Israelites always were with lines of descent, Davidson took the lineage back to the primal man.

Davidson accepted both the racial distinctiveness of Adam and the racial character of the biblical account. Genesis described not the creation of the human species but rather only a part of it, "the special creative selection or election of the First Adam and his seed—the Adamic race." This "elect race" was, in Davidson's view, indisputably white, and by virtue of its whiteness possessed physical and spiritual faculties absent in the nonwhite races around it. Even after the Deluge, the surviving descendants of Adam continued to manifest these characteristics:

The restless energy and the "spiritual" stamina—as distinct from purely *bestial* stamina—characteristic of the white race, their dominating influence over other races, and their so-called "conquest" of nature and of nature's science and elements, all indicate their retention, to a certain extent, of the power—not yet entirely latent—and the faculties—not yet completely atrophied—attributed in the First Book of Genesis to the founder of the Adamic race, and, in a lesser degree, to the Adamic race.

Although Davidson's work was to embed in British-Israelism the Pre-Adamite thesis and the identification of the Adamites with the white race, the introduction of these ideas apparently encountered some initial resistance in British-Israelite quarters. This is evident less from Davidson's work than from Bristowe's, published about the same time. Although her book on Cain contained no distinctively British-Israel material, it was issued by the English movement's publishing house, the Covenant Publishing Company. She found it necessary to state in the introduction that the British-Israel World Federation "does not associate itself with my views about the preadamites and the deluge." Nonetheless, largely because of the enormous prestige that attached to Davidson's pyramid studies, these and related doctrines came to be intimately interwoven in the doctrinal fabric of the movement.[12]

Davidson's fascination with Adam and his descendants was part of a more general interest in human origins that had developed in the nineteenth century. Those more religiously inclined sought to infuse Adam and the other figures of biblical antiquity with historical reality, the better to defend scriptural accounts in an age when the prestige of both the natural sciences and of critical historical scholarship were rising. Thus, like a Renaissance geographer, Dominick M'Causland wrote with assurance that the river of Paradise "must be the Shat-el-Arab," and that Paradise itself had been located just west of the waterway, "yet not quite extending down to the Persian Gulf." But Adam had of course been expelled from Paradise, sent "to the East of Eden," and it fell to Victorian scholars to try to locate the new home of the antediluvian Adamites.[13]

This search for some locale east of present-day Iraq was strongly reinforced by the simultaneous efforts of European linguistic scholars to trace the origin of European languages. As early as the eighteenth century, it had become common to trace the human race to a birthplace between the Indus and the Ganges. By the mid-nineteenth century, the tracking of linguistic relationships had given rise to the belief that Europeans had indeed had an Asian origin, not in the Indian river valleys but rather in "the high plateau of Asia." The inhabitants of this elevated hinterland were the "Aryans," the putative invaders of India and the ancestors of Europeans. M'Causland himself was clearly touched by this influential myth, for he places the Adamites before the Flood as "elements of expanding civilization . . . active in Central

Asia," the nodal point from which in post-Deluge years Noah's descendants dispersed.[14]

The principal channel for bringing the Aryan myth into British-Israelism was, again, the writings of David Davidson. In Davidson's reconstruction of Genesis as a historical narrative, Adam and his family left the Euphrates Valley to migrate east into Asia. Davidson then searched for a region that he believed would fulfill the geographical requirements of the biblical account of the post-Edenic world: a mountain-ringed basin sufficiently unstable geologically to make possible later flooding (the Deluge) from subterranean water sources. He discovered it to his own satisfaction in the Tarim Basin in eastern Turkestan, the region of the Takla Makan Desert in westernmost China. In view of the tendency of nineteenth-century racial theorists to make central Asia the original home of the white Adamic race, Davidson's choice hardly seems accidental. Rather, it emerges as simply another indication of the overlap between British-Israelism's racial interpretation of Adam's ancestry and the tendency of Victorian science to ground racial beliefs in specious scholarship.[15]

Race Mixing and the Flood

This racialist interpretation of the Bible extended from Adam to his descendants. As we have already seen, Cain was deemed to have established dominion over a Pre-Adamite race of nonwhites. At a later point in the biblical narrative, the story of the Deluge underwent a similar racial reinterpretation. The Pre-Adamite literature sought to make two major points about the Flood: first, that it was geographically localized rather than universal and was directed against the wickedness of the Adamites; and, second, that this wickedness, far from merely being some generalized will to do evil, was a much more specific transgression: the sin of race mixing. To M'Causland, "it is plain that the moving cause of the destruction of the Adamites, with the exception of Noah's family, was that their race had become corrupted by the admixture of non-Adamite blood." Like many later writers in this tradition, M'Causland fastened upon the obscure reference in the sixth chapter of Genesis to marriages between the "sons of God" and the "daughters of men," a legend that now became the prototypical example of miscegenation. The "sons of God" were no longer supernatural beings but were nonwhite Pre-Adamites with whom Adamite women illicitly cohabited. In America, Charles Carroll advanced a somewhat similar thesis in even more overtly racialist terms: " 'The sons of God' were the white males who traced their pedigree through a line of pure-blooded ancestors to Adam; and . . . 'the daughters of men' were mixed-blood females who traced their pedigree to men, on the paternal side, and to negresses on the maternal side. Their fathers were men, but their mothers were negresses—apes—beasts." The Deluge was their punishment.[16]

Charles Fox Parham, the founder of Pentecostalism, provided yet another variation that linked Pre-Adamism, race mixing, and the Deluge. In Parham's version, God had created two races. On the sixth day of Creation he had made a race "having everlasting human life, and [bearing] the stamp and attributes of divinity." Two days later, he created Adam. The sixth-day race "had dominion and authority," while "the Adamic race of the eighth day" had been formed from the earth and was meant to tend the Garden of Eden. The sixth-day race, however, was "sensual" and expressed its lust by marrying Adamic daughters. The Flood obliterated the earlier race as punishment for their sins, but God, "having made a promise to Adam of a Savior, was compelled to preserve the Adamic race." Parham's version was clearly of a far less virulent sort than Carroll's, but both they and M'Causland before them agreed on three points: that no matter how the biblical narrative had been traditionally read, it sanctioned the view that at least one race had been created before Adam's; that this primeval multiracialism created temptations for sexual relationships across racial lines; and that God would punish such liaisons in the severest fashion. These views too passed into British-Israelism through Davidson. The "sons of God" now became fallen angels, malevolent spirits that took possession of the souls of Adamic men, who "were compelled by the lust of the spirits possessing them to seek wives of the daughters of the gentile races." Although the Adamic world was ringed with mountains, its isolation was not total, and the Adamites could find women from the Pre-Adamite peoples outside the Tarim Basin. Initially, only "outcasts and renegades" did so, but in time more and more wives were chosen from inferior, external races, "resulting in a raising of the physical standard [presumably because the Pre-Adamites possessed bestial strength] and the lowering of the spiritual standard." When spirituality fell to an intolerably low level, God destroyed the sinning Adamites, with the sole exception of Noah's family.[17]

The Two Seedlines

The existence of Pre-Adamites bearing the taint of race mixing would later become part of Christian Identity's myth of satanic Jews, when these animalistic Pre-Adamites became connected to the progeny of Cain. Cain functions in the myth as the link between the Devil, the representative of primal evil and chaos, and the Pre-Adamites, who will carry the Devil's work and message into the world. In order for Cain to fulfill this mythic function, he had to be linked to Satan in a way not evident in the biblical text itself. Here, too, a racialist gloss was required, in this case through a radical reinterpretation of the story of the Fall.

Satan enters Eden, as one might expect, by a circuitous path. This consisted of a redefinition of the nature of the "serpent." If the serpent were not a snake, he might have capabilities that even the biblical snake did not have and could go beyond merely conversing with Eve about the fruit of the tree in the center of the Garden. Indeed, if he could be changed into something resembling a man, he could not merely converse but have sexual intercourse, which would push miscegenation back in time from the days before the Flood to the period just before the Fall. A significant step was taken in this direction by the early nineteenth-century Scottish exegete, Adam Clarke. Clarke, by a combination of ingenious speculations on the text itself and searches for words in Arabic that might be related to the Hebrew, reached a number of conclusions. In Clarke's view, the "serpent" (Hebrew, *nachash*) walked erect, had the capacity to reason and speak, and was most probably "a creature of the *ape* or *ouran outang* kind," which Satan then employed as "the *most proper* instrument for the accomplishment of his murderous purpose against the life and soul of man."[18]

In the full flood of racial anthropology that followed the publication of Clarke's commentary, it became commonplace to seek links between human races and primates. Comparative anatomists suggested that different primates were affiliated with different races. The orang-outang was variously linked to Malays, Europeans, Mongols, and the "yellow races" in general. What matters here is not the precise racial linkage, but the suggestion of sufficient affinities so that those with a desire to do so could argue that an apelike *nachash* could function not only as a tempter of Eve but as a sexual seducer.[19]

The concept of a humanoid "serpent" who cohabited with Eve makes an appearance in Charles Carroll's antiblack diatribe in 1900. Carroll's views enjoyed some popularity among less educated southerners. He asserted that "the tempter of Eve was a beast—a negro." Explicitly utilizing Clarke's commentary, Carroll, who regarded all blacks as biblical "beasts of the field," saw the black seducer of Eve as the first in a continuing line of nonwhite adversaries of the Adamic race. Stripped of the racist associations Carroll gave it, the serpent-as-seducer maintained an existence in fringe evangelical circles into the present.[20]

Its most significant modern exponent, outside the Identity fold, was Indiana

Pentecostalist William Branham (1909–65). Branham saw the serpent as a creature occupying a niche somewhere between animals and humans, "a beast," to be sure, but with unspecified human characteristics. As he put it in a 1959 sermon, "The serpent was a—like a prehistoric man, something next to God—or next to man. . . . This animal that will mix the seed is complete—it's extinct. God turned him to a snake." According to Branham, the creature had sexual relations with Eve and fathered Cain, a connection particularly significant to the development of Identity's view of the Jews as the seed of the Devil through Cain. Branham, however, was careful to distinguish between serpent paternity and the Devil. When a follower asked him about "your theory that Eve conceived Cain of the devil," Branham responded, "I never said that; I said Eve conceived Cain of the serpent." Yet the fact that his listeners could regard the Devil and the serpent as interchangeable suggests that the conception of the serpent as a quasi-human sexual predator could easily lend itself to associations with Satan. This was particularly so in the context of the story of the Fall, since the serpent's act of seduction now became the basis for Original Sin and the introduction of death, transgression, and divine curse into the world.[21]

The human characteristics that were imputed to the serpent became plausible not simply because Adam Clarke had suggested that the serpent was more likely to have been a primate than a reptile; the idea had the further attraction of interlocking with a deviant doctrine of human sinfulness which had been in existence in conservative Protestant circles in America since the early 1800s: the "two seeds" doctrine of Daniel Parker. Parker (1781–1844), born in the South but active most of his career in Illinois, was a Baptist preacher of a distinctively predestinarian cast. In his 1826 pamphlet, *Views of the Two Seeds*, he argued that Eve contained two kinds of "seed," later to be transmitted to her descendants. One was good and had been implanted by God, the other by Satan in the form of the serpent. Hence, from Eve two "seedlines" descended, one good and elect, the other evil and nonelect, the former the offspring of the Woman, the latter the offspring of the Devil/ Serpent. No action by man could alter this primal division. Those who were of the serpent seedline could not be brought into the domain of the saved, so missionary activity among them was fruitless. Parker's views were reflected in the sect of Old Two-Seed-in-the-Spirit Predestinarian Baptists, who numbered almost thirteen thousand in 1890 but fell to scarcely two hundred by the end of the Second World War.[22]

Although it is not clear whether William Branham was directly influenced by Parker's views, he grew up in Baptist circles where the two-seed theory was well known. While Branham attempted to maintain the position that the

Serpent rather than the Devil copulated with Eve, he clearly regarded the humanoid, prereptilian "serpent" as the medium through which Satan's seed passed: "What did Satan pregnate Eve with? To disbelieve the Word." Branham either embellished Parkerite views or developed them himself, but in either case, he implied the existence of two genetic strains in humanity, such that one could trace the descendants of the two seedlines through history. The seed of the Woman had produced Seth, Noah, Abraham, Isaac, Jacob, David, and Jesus. That of Satan had produced Cain, Ham, Ahab, and Judas Iscariot. But Branham became a good deal more vague when it came to contemporary manifestations of the Devil's seed. To the extent that he tried to identify them, he regarded them as those persons with a dangerous proclivity to learning and reasoned thought: "Through Cain came all the smart, educated people down to the antediluvian flood." After that, they were the "intellectuals," a category in which he grouped Bible colleges and other institutions of higher education: "They know all their creeds . . . but know nothing about God."[23]

Parker and Branham thus added to speculations about the sexual prowess of the serpent by concluding that out of his dalliance with Eve had come vast numbers of people who carried in their very nature the bestial, God-defying tendencies of their ancestral sire. But both Parker and Branham stopped short at identifying the children of Satan and the serpent with any distinctive group; certainly, they never suggested that they were Jews. But the idea of a sexually potent agent of the Devil, through whom the latter's seed could have continuing human expression, opened up new channels of speculation. It is also tempting to speculate that the prevalence of British-Israel ideas among some Pentecostalists, a tendency that goes back to Pentecostalism's founder, Charles Fox Parham, may have favored the introduction of Branham's ideas into Christian Identity. Branham first spoke about the serpent seed in about 1958–59, the point at which the full statement of the demonic origin of the Jews began to appear in Christian Identity.

Cain and History

However, the attachment of two-seed theology to anti-Semitism was not possible without connecting links, most specifically in the form of a vastly increased role for the figure of Cain. Cain becomes the means by which the concept of the serpent seedline can be linked first to the Pre-Adamites and then to the Jews, and in the process, the evolving British-Israel belief that Jewish blood had been corrupted by sexual contacts with forbidden peoples was incorporated.

Cain comes to loom over Identity interpretations of Genesis in a manner that is seemingly disproportionate to the role he plays in the biblical text. The apparently excessive attention paid to a figure who quite literally is expelled from the narrative stems from a peculiar bias of the pseudo-scholarship engaged in by British-Israel writers. Just as British-Israelites sought to document empirically the meanderings of the Israelite tribes from Middle Eastern exile to European sanctuary, so their concern for establishing lineage and pedigree caused them to push the genre backward in time. The identification of the Israelites with European nations in the recent period had its counterpart in the identification of them with the "Adamic race" in the more distant past. Thus, "Israel" was deemed to be in some sense hidden both after and before the collapse of the kingdom of the ten northern tribes. For the postcollapse period it was necessary to separate the Israelites' true "identity" from what British-Israelites insisted was only the apparent and much less important identity of nationality. This had, of course, been the main thrust of the movement from its beginnings. But it also became concerned with the period before the kingdom collapsed—indeed, with the period before Israel entered Palestine—and pushed bloodlines ever farther back. If purity of blood was all, then purity had to be established all the way back to the source, Adam and his children. To this problem, British-Israel writers applied the same style they had applied to establishing the Israel identity of the British peoples, namely, by mimicking techniques of historical scholarship so that conclusions might be advanced not merely as statements of faith but as intersubjectively testable knowledge. Hence, there arose a literature that treats the pre-Abrahamic figures in Genesis neither as religious icons nor as revelation, but as historic figures. Adam and Noah were deemed to be as objectively real as any Egyptian pharaoh. This, of course, continued a practice already well established among the Victorian writers on Pre-Adamites, for whom Adam's and Noah's families possessed a palpable reality that in principle was amenable to scientific analysis as well as scriptural exegesis. Cain, consequently, became merely a particularly conspicuous object of this approach.

The genre found its master practitioner in Davidson, who set his pyramid studies within the context of a reconfiguration of ancient history. In more specific terms, Davidson sought to establish a connection between the chronology that could be teased out of Genesis and "the chronological system of the ancient Egyptian king lists." Figures such as Seth and Enoch, who had been customarily treated as inhabiting a domain of legend, took their places with the pharaohs, for whom both written and monumental evidence were often abundant, in a single, synoptic account. Indeed, he came to believe that a similar synthesis could be effected between Genesis, on the one hand, and Babylonian and Chinese records on the other, yielding a single, bibliocentric chronological system covering all of Asia from remote antiquity: "The Book of Genesis," he wrote, "is a true statement of the history of the Adamic race and of the origin of the people of Israel."[24]

The role Cain was to play had been foreshadowed by the Pre-Adamite writers. They had found Cain a figure of special interest for two reasons. First, because he had been expelled from Eden for the murder of his brother, Abel, he was the first of the Adamites compelled to mingle on a continuing basis with the Pre-Adamites. Second, because advocates of Pre-Adamism clearly saw Pre-Adamites as nonwhite and Adamites as white, they regarded Cain as the earliest representative of a particularly sinister figure, the race mixer, who did not simply move among nonwhites but became involved with them sexually as well, tainting the offspring.

M'Causland has Cain moving to a Pre-Adamite area of Asia, where his natural superiority permitted him to easily assume dominance. According to M'Causland, since the Deluge affected only the area of Adamite settlement, which Cain had been compelled to leave, the "Cainites" survived the Flood and in time moved ever farther eastward from "the land of Nod" to eventually settle China. There, their superior knowledge and skill, albeit by now diluted through racial intermarriage, served as the foundation of Chinese civilization. While Alexander Winchell's self-proclaimed allegiance to science rendered his account somewhat less deferential to the Bible, Cain played a significant role in it. The Pre-Adamites among whom Cain dwelled were, Winchell speculated, possibly one of "the Black races," but were more likely "primitive Dravidians, or primitive Mongoloids," both segments of "the Brown Races." While Winchell speculated that Cain may have taken a black wife (a theory we shall return to shortly), he eventually dismissed it as "not sustained by anthropological evidence." His wife instead came from one of the brown peoples, "a daughter of the preadamite race." This was, however, a forbidden marriage, the first of many associated in the Cain literature with his line. Here Winchell picks up a strand other nineteenth-century writers had associated with the period immediately before the Deluge, namely the passage in Genesis 6:1–2 concerning the marriages of "sons of God" and "daughters of men." Cain was the archetypical case, "violating the law of caste . . . a mark of primeval wickedness." Having settled among such people, Cain not only married but "built up a city and developed a *secular* civilization."[25]

While Winchell was reluctant to give Cain a black wife, the southern racialist Charles Carroll had no such qualms. Indeed, the union of Cain with a black woman was central to Carroll's contention that "the Bible is simply a history of the long conflict which has raged between God and man, as the result of man's criminal relations with the negro." Carroll implies that Cain's first sexual experience with a black woman occurred before the murder of Abel, indeed, that it provided the motive for the murder, since an outraged God reacted by compelling Cain to marry "his paramour of strange flesh," while providing Abel with a "beautiful Adamic woman [of] virginal loveliness." Furious at his brother's good fortune, Cain slew him. In this version, therefore, Cain does not secure a wife from among Pre-Adamites in the land of Nod but from among Pre-Adamites in Eden itself. As a result of the forced marriage, Cain's offspring were "mixed-bloods," and therefore, his descendants "were thrust out of the line of descent from Adam to the Saviour." Carroll's most audacious suggestion is that Cain's new father-in-law was none other than the "serpent" that had seduced his mother, Eve, the black man who had made possible the primal sin before Cain's birth and had been cursed for it. The serpent's curse was now "fulfilled in Cain's ultimate banishment from the Adamic family." Cain was now linked both to the Pre-Adamites and to the serpent, the representative or embodiment of Satan. While Carroll's identification of the serpent with Cain's father-in-law was not reflected in other speculations about the Pre-Adamites, Carroll was not alone in regarding Cain's wife as nonwhite. Charles Parham regarded Cain's marriage to a woman from the land of Nod as the first step in "the woeful intermarriage of races for which cause the flood was sent in punishment."[26]

In keeping with his desire to fuse sacred and secular history, Davidson treats Cain's journey to the land of Nod as a literal movement that can be mapped in terms of conventional geographical coordinates. Since Davidson believed that Eden had been located in present-day Iraq, and that the post-Fall "Adamic earth" was in eastern Turkestan, he concluded that Cain traveled to some point between the two. The "land of Nod," therefore, occupied an "isolated land-locked area somewhere East of the Tigris." This supposition was to serve as the basis for a fancifully detailed "history" of Cain by Mrs. Sydney Bristowe which, along with Davidson's own work, was to have enormous influence upon the development of Christian Identity theology.[27]

Ellen Bristowe's 1927 life of Cain, *Sargon the Magnificent*, was not, strictly speaking, a British-Israel work. Since, however, it was issued by the movement publishing house, it was guaranteed an audience among Anglo-Israel believers. Bristowe attempted, through an examination of Near Eastern inscriptions and artifacts, to reconstruct Cain's life after he arrived in the land of Nod. She concluded that in this post-Edenic phase of his life, he was identical to "the great Babylonian monarch Sargon of Akkad." Sargon was a Mesopotamian king who reigned about 2300 B.C. Bristowe proceeded to superimpose upon this historical figure the characteristics she regarded as quintessentially Cain's.[28]

According to Bristowe, the history and features of Babylonian life could now be explained as a result of the arrival of the fugitive murderer. Babylonian civilization advanced rapidly, she said, because Cain was, after all, an Adamite and possessed the "super-human knowledge" that such ancestry conferred. Since the early Babylonians were nonwhite Pre-Adamites, in her view, they could scarcely have become civilized without the promptings and innovations brought by a white visitor. In keeping with others, such as Davidson, Bristowe had no qualms about simultaneously accepting archaeological dating for secular societies while continuing to regard Bishop Ussher's chronology of the Bible as valid. She thus satisfied herself that Cain could have lived during Sargon's time. So extraordinary were Sargon-Cain's "powers of body and mind," the inheritance from his divine parents, that he not only transformed Babylonia but was responsible for prehistoric monuments in Crete, Cyprus, Greece, and "possibly" Britain, "since the monuments seem to show that Sargon travelled to all these places." Like other writers on Pre-Adamism and British-Israelism, Bristowe was intrigued by the possibility of links between biblical characters and the peoples of the Orient. In part perhaps because of her racial views, she was less disposed than others to make East Asians descendants of either Israel or Abraham. Instead, she traced "the Yellow race" to a mixture of "Cain's race with a black race," suggesting further that Cain himself might have journeyed to China.[29]

This bizarre view of history might be dismissed as no more than eccentricity were it not for the fact that it was widely cited by British-Israelites and by their Christian Identity offspring, who invariably have regarded it as an authoritative source on the early Near East. The American British-Israelite Frederick Haberman so regarded it in the early 1930s, and a decade later the *When?* author in Canada included a lengthy synopsis of *Sargon* in his book, treating its conclusions as established facts. Christian Identity writers from 1960 on have similarly deferred to Bristowe. No less a figure than Wesley Swift incorporated her views wholesale, although, as was his custom when dealing with the ideas of others, he neglects to mention her name. Conrad Gaard, more generous in his treatment of the writing of others, acknowledged *Sargon* as the source of "a great deal of evidence from secular sources that Cain not only founded . . . a hybrid serpent race, but also that he established the first Super World government." As late as 1980, the *Christian Vanguard*, published by the

New Christian Crusade Church in Louisiana, was offering one of Bristowe's other books, *The Man Who Built the Great Pyramid*, as a premium to new subscribers.[30]

The attraction of *Sargon* lay not merely in its author's belief that Cain was a historic personage but in her insistence that his role in history had made him one of the greatest, if not the greatest, sources of human evil, an instrument of the Devil himself. At the Devil's instigation, Cain had originated idolatry, presumably as revenge against the God that had expelled him from his home. This led Bristowe to suggest, in language Christian Identity was quick to appropriate later, that Cain's innovation led to "a great conspiracy cunningly devised to catch the souls of men." The introduction of death having destroyed physical immortality, the "great conspiracy" built on idolatry would now cause human beings to sacrifice their spiritual immortality as well. In support of idolatry, Cain was believed to have established a peculiarly evil Babylonian cultic apparatus built upon cannibalism. Although Bristowe's book is notably free of anti-Semitism, her preoccupation with the alleged cannibalistic rites practiced in ancient Babylon fitted with disturbing neatness the medieval ritual-murder libels. Hence, Cain was the origin of a continuing plot to undermine human spiritual integrity, and for that purpose had had his Babylonian minions construct an evil priesthood based upon the worship of false gods and the eating of human flesh.[31]

All of this Bristowe traced back to the Devil. The "Prince of Darkness" was only too happy to utilize Cain as a way of revenging himself upon God. Indeed, Bristowe went so far as to suggest that in the furtherance of the demonic plot, Cain himself created Babylonian deities based upon Adam, Eve, the Devil, his deceased brother, Abel, and himself, the latter in the form of Marduk. The Devil consequently served Cain "as his advisor," so that Cain might more effectively dominate the Pre-Adamites who served his, and the Devil's, will. Thus, between Cain and the Devil there was a kind of contract, in which the former received power while the latter gained instruments for the conquest of the earth. The Devil's ultimate contribution to Cain's evil regime lay in having gotten Cain to institute cannibalism, for "who but Cain, who was 'of that evil one,' could have invented it?" As Frederick Haberman later paraphrased Bristowe's thesis, Cain brought to the Euphrates Valley "the Devil worship, as he was of that Evil One, the Devil." Nothing in *Sargon* suggests that its author knew anything of the two-seed theology discussed earlier; indeed, she considered herself a historian of sorts, not a theologian. Nonetheless, while not declaring Cain to have been the offspring of anyone but Adam and Eve, she so closely associated him with the Devil that a biological connection was a relatively easy step to take for those already familiar with the concept of a "serpent seedline."[32]

Ellen Bristowe was in fact plowing a field others had worked before her. While substantively different in its emphasis upon Cain, *Sargon the Magnificent* strongly resembled an anti-Catholic tract, *The Two Babylons*, published in Edinburgh in the 1850s. Its author, Alexander Hislop (1807–65), believed, as did Bristowe, that he had unlocked the origins of human evil by fusing biblical narrative with an assortment of archaeology, myth, and folklore. In Hislop's case, his point of biblical reference was not Cain but the equally obscure Nimrod and Nimrod's father, Cush. Cush, according to Hislop, had founded Babylon, and Nimrod had built up the city. With his consort, the licentious Semiramis, Nimrod organized a cult based upon idolatry, prostitution, and human sacrifice. When the evil Nimrod was finally slain by Noah's son, Shem, Hislop went on, he became a deity in the Babylonian pantheon, and the cult he had founded was forced underground. Its obscene rituals continued out of public view until in time the entire Babylonian system reemerged to public view in the form of the Catholic church. The church was to Hislop none other than the "Mystery Babylon" of the Book of Revelation. The church was the "Beast," and while the pope was its "visible head," its invisible head was none other than Satan, using the church as "one vast system of Devil-worship." Hislop's book continued to be reprinted well into the twentieth century and is still occasionally cited in right-wing conspiratorial literature, although not on the Identity right; for there it seemed far more appealing to accept Bristowe's idea that Cain had founded the Babylonian cult, the better to link it with Jews.[33]

Although Bristowe clearly believed that she had stumbled upon some great truth missed by others, her eccentric work stands in a long line of speculation about Cainite evil. Popular religion had long associated Cain with the invention of sorcery. The notion that Cain was the mastermind of "a secret demonic religion" had been advanced in 1869 by Gougenot des Mousseaux, who suggested, as Christian Identity would a century later, that Cain's malevolent and esoteric cult was eventually passed down to the Jews, "as 'the representatives on earth of the spirit of darkness.'" Similarly, there had been earlier suggestions of an intimate association between Cain and blacks. A 1733 essay by Father August Malfert, derived from La Peyrère's original discussion of the Pre-Adamites, suggested that the "mark of Cain" was black skin, and that from him all nonwhites with the exception of the American Indians had descended. This, of course, prefigures elements of one of the most sustained discussions of Cainite evil, which developed in nineteenth-century Mormonism.[34]

Early Mormon doctrine associated Cain with conspiracy, diabolical evil, and nonwhite races. He obeyed Satan's order to make an offering to God, an offering whose rejection eventually led to Abel's murder. This relationship with Satan led in time to a Cainite conspiratorial tradition. In Joseph Smith's *Pearl of Great Price*, Cain entered a covenant with Satan, "a secret combination, and their works were in the dark." Cain's lineage survived the Flood, because Ham married one of Cain's descendants. Cain became the first person to whom Satan revealed diabolical skills for doing evil, in the form of "oaths, vows, and *secret combinations*." He was also the first person to take an oath to Satan and to form a secret society in his service. In subsequent generations, others whose nature was malevolent (but who were not necessarily Cain's descendants) imitated his behavior. The result was a series of secret societies tied to the Devil and directed against the righteous. While this teaching did not assert a blood link among the conspirators, it did claim the existence of "an organization founded anciently by Satan (with Cain), periodically renewed in ancient times by Satanic revelation, internally protected by covenants of the blackest sorcery, and established for the express purpose of murdering and plunder." D. Michael Quinn suggests that Smith may have tapped into currents of popular religion referred to earlier, in which Cain had been identified as the first sorcerer, thus recasting a much older folk tradition.[35]

In addition to Cain's link with conspiracy, he was also tied to the possession of a black skin. Joseph Smith appears to have first characterized blacks as "sons of Cain" in 1842. After Smith's murder, Orson Hyde linked blackness with events in the preexistence, humanity's "first estate," when individuals possessed a spiritual existence prior to their physical embodiment on earth. Lucifer's rebellion in heaven occurred in this premortal condition, and Hyde suggested that those later born with dark skin had been premortal spirits who were insufficiently vigilant in defending God's cause during the revolt. Brigham Young rejected Hyde's theory, and instead linked blackness to the fact that blacks' ancestor, Cain, had been the first murderer.[36]

There is no evidence that Bristowe knew anything about the place of Cain in early Mormon doctrine, nor is there any direct evidence of Mormon influence on Christian Identity, despite the presence within it of a significant number of former orthodox and schismatic Mormons. What is more likely is that both Mormon and non-Mormon writers about Cain reflected legendary associations of him with evil, sorcery, and conspiracy, and that the "mark" he wore (interpreted by Bristowe as a talisman) was easily converted into darkness of skin. The particular manifestation of the Cain legends in Christian

Identity was shaped more decisively by Bristowe than by anyone else, but given the similarities of theme, Christian Identity's version, in which Cain is the offspring rather than merely the partner of the Devil, must resonate with the views of some Mormons. Hence, Mormon doctrine is less a shaper of Christian Identity than it is a factor predisposing some believers to regard Christian Identity's myth of evil as plausible.

Jews and Cain

The only element remaining to give completeness to the synthesis was a more explicit link between Jews and Cain. This was ready at hand through the mechanism described in the previous chapter. Jews had already come to be regarded in late British-Israelism as a mélange of different racial stocks, most of them considered impure. While much of this speculation had centered on connections with the Edomites, the putative descendants of Esau, there were also alleged connections with other ancient peoples, including the Canaanites, putative descendants of Cain. Sometimes the connection took the form of random patterns of intermarriage. More frequently, the linkage was in the form of Judah's liaison with a Canaanite woman, from which came a son, Shelah (Gen. 38). As the elements of the myth coalesced, the Canaanite connection began to become dominant, overshadowing links to the Edomites or Hittites. If the Satan/Serpent had had intercourse with Eve; and if Cain had been the offspring of the relationship; and if Cain's birth inaugurated a human "seedline" linking descendants with satanic paternity; and if Cain's sojourn in Nod had equipped his followers with knowledge of the Devil's plan for earthly dominion—then an intersection of Cain's line of descent with the tribe of Judah was sufficient to link the Jews irrevocably with the Devil.

As it turns out, this became in fact the weak version of the myth, since it locates the point of contact between Jews and Cain at a relatively late point, after the separation of the northern and southern kingdoms. As the myth became further developed and embroidered upon in Christian Identity, the point of contact was pressed ever farther back, until in some versions Cain himself became "the first Jew." In the weak version, Jews were dangerous because they were related to Cain. In the strong version, Cain was a Jew because he was dangerous, for to be associated with evil and the Devil was, ipso facto, to be a Jew.

An ancient body of folklore connected Cain with satanic conspiracies. Bristowe gave these motifs a gloss of pseudo-scholarship by claiming to demonstrate through archaeological evidence that Cain had founded a satanic religion in Babylon. Hence, Cain could function not merely as a symbol of evil, the first malefactor on earth, but as the organizer of an ongoing plot against God, the Devil's emissary. When this reinterpretation of Cain was combined with the other elements described earlier in this chapter, a full-blown anti-Semitic theology became possible.

This worldview began with the radical separation of a white, Aryan "Adamic race" from evil and inferior Pre-Adamites. The Adamic race itself, however, was endangered from two sources. In the first place, the Devil, having taken human form through the creature referred to as the "serpent," sexually seduced Eve. This primal sin was responsible not only for Adam and Eve's expulsion from Eden but for the creation of a hybrid creature, Cain, part devil and part human; or rather, like his father, a devil in human form. His descendants, superficially indistinguishable from those whose father was Adam, continued to manifest Cain's own quintessentially diabolical character. In addition, Cain had institutionalized his plot against God and the Adamic race in a secret organization, to which his descendants belonged and gave loyalty. These descendants Christian Identity understands to be Jews, although Identity writers sometimes differ in making the connection with Cain from the very beginning or adding Cain's blood to the Jewish line through Judah and Shelah. The result, in any case, ties Jews to the Devil through links of paternity and biological descent, and casts Jews in the role of God's adversaries on earth.

The attraction of this fabric of legend, deviant exegesis, and racialism is that it was compatible with existing secular conspiracy theories about Jews. One could accept the notion of the Jews as "the Devil's spawn" without rejecting beliefs about cabals of international Jewish bankers, Jewish Bolsheviks, or the Elders of Zion meeting to plot world conquest. All could be assimilated to the belief in satanic paternity, which created a kind of superconspiracy—what Conrad Gaard called "the great conspiracy"—of which all the smaller plots were elements. The grand conspiracy had existed from the creation of the world, and all the other clandestine arrangements could take their places as components or manifestations of this demonic master plan. To people who tend to think of history in terms of conspiratorial machinations, this was doubly comforting, for it meant that all conspiracy theories retained their validity, since they were all derived from a single source; and it imposed a common scheme upon both sacred and secular history, which allowed both to be read as expressing the same struggle between forces of light and darkness, since the primary conspiracy ran from the outset of the biblical narrative to contemporary politics and economics. Since the essence of conspiracy theories is their claim to parsimony—explaining all evil through single causes—the incorporation of satanic paternity into already existing theories of a world Jewish conspiracy gave to the theory ultimate parsimony: everything that was or is undesirable in the world has come from a single source. If that source is destroyed, the world will be perfected and the millennium will begin. Further, as with all conspiracy theories, this one defies falsification. A plot of such cunning is presumed to be able to mislead those who would try to detect it, so that any evidence that appears to contradict the theory must necessarily have been fabricated by the conspirators themselves. Paradoxically, as far as conspiracy theorists are concerned, the more innocent the putative conspirators appear to be, the more clearly they are implicated, for their apparent innocence is taken to be proof of their complicity. Thus the theory becomes a closed system of self-referential ideas, from which all contradictory information has been excluded.

The individual elements that were to make up the theory of the satanic origins of the Jews were already in place by the 1920s. Indeed, as we have seen, some of them, such as the belief in Pre-Adamite races, extended back to the seventeenth century. Many of the components—not only Pre-Adamism, but the linking of the Flood with race mixing and the elaboration of a secular history for Cain—had appeared in British-Israel literature, either in works devoted to British-Israel themes, such as Davidson's pyramid studies, or in books that, while not explicitly Anglo-Israelite, were issued by British-Israel publishers, such as Ellen Bristowe's influential essay on Cain. Those elements of the satanic origins thesis that had not appeared in British-Israel venues circulated widely in the conservative Protestant religious culture to which many in Christian Identity were already atuned. This was particularly true of the so-called two-seed theory that gave to the Serpent/Devil an earthly seedline.

What remained to turn these disparate elements into the satanic thesis was a synthesis that would place them within a logical structure. Such a synthesis was approximated as early as the mid-1940s, but the first full versions began to appear about 1960. They came from the first generation of Christian Identity preachers associated with Gerald L. K. Smith: Conrad Gaard, Bertrand Comparet, William Potter Gale, and Wesley Swift. Gale and Swift produced particularly elaborate versions, engrafting onto earlier elements ideas not previously found in the British-Israelite milieu. Thus they gave to the Adamic race a spiritual existence that preceded its life on earth (reminiscent of the Mormon concept of the "preexistence,") and, especially in the case of Swift, superimposed upon the warfare between God and the Devil the imagery of space-

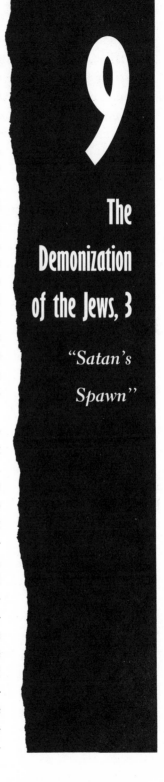

9

The Demonization of the Jews, 3

"Satan's Spawn"

ships and flying saucers that circulated widely in the 1950s. The ideas of Gaard, Comparet, Gale, and Swift were taken over largely intact by such succeeding individuals and groups as the Identity Bible commentator Jarah Crawford, the Church of Jesus Christ Christian/Aryan Nations, Pastor Dan Gayman and his Church of Israel, and the communal group the Covenant, Sword and Arm of the Lord (CSA). These more recent statements of the diabolical origin of the Jews were shorn of some earlier aspects, such as Wesley Swift's fascination with flying saucers, and other elements were given new prominence, such as the CSA's fixation upon the Illuminati. Nonetheless, the positions developed by the older generation of Identity figures in the 1960s became Identity orthodoxy by the 1980s.

Curiously missing from this roster was Howard Rand. Rand, at the center of American British-Israelism in the 1930s, continued to publish throughout the period of Christian Identity's maturation. Nonetheless, while Rand's anti-Semitism had been in evidence throughout his public career, he shrank from acceptance of the satanic theory. While accepting certain of its elements concerning Cain and the Pre-Adamites, Rand made clear during the 1960s that he found unacceptable the notion that Satan had fathered a race of earthlings to fulfill his designs. Rand's explicit rejection of what had become mainstream Identity doctrine not only confirmed the marginal role he had come to occupy in a religious tradition he once dominated, but also confirmed the increasingly explicit separation between British-Israelism and Christian Identity. Rand, as Anglo-Israelism's chief spokesperson in America, saw himself as the representative of an international movement, whereas Swift and the other Identity figures had no formal ties with the British movement and spoke from within an American religious subculture.

The Satanic Theory in the 1930s

In 1934, when Frederick Haberman published his influential and much reprinted tract, *Tracing Our Ancestors*, he did little more than combine ideas of David Davidson and Ellen Bristowe to produce an account of the lives of Adam and his descendants. According to this synthetic narrative, Cain and "the later sons of Adam" married "wom[e]n of the Turanian or Mongolian race," that is, Pre-Adamites, and, as Davidson had earlier asserted, the result was offspring of prodigious physical size and strength but diminished spiritual capacities. The Adamites had been living in the "Forty Cities of Takla Makan," in the Turkestan desert, where their sins were overtaken by a localized Deluge, again following Davidson. Cain, however, was condemned to wander and had "migrated into the valley of the Euphrates as early as 3800 B.C." Here, Haberman adopts Bristowe's account, according to which Cain created the first civilization and introduced worship of his patron, the Devil. However, Haberman, like other British-Israel writers of the time, does not expand the Devil's role further, and certainly does not imply that Cain's father was anyone other than Adam. As to the Jews, they were corrupted physically and morally by marriages to idolaters, but as we saw in chapter 7, that had become a steady Anglo-Israel motif that prepared the way for the theory of satanic origins but certainly did not imply it. However, at about the same time that Haberman was writing, another author incorporated other features of the satanic theory.[1]

The satanic theory was more closely approximated in a tract by Philip E. J. Monson. Monson, it will be remembered, was Howard Rand's top man in the West, in charge of the Anglo-Saxon Federation's Pacific Coast operations. He also was closely associated with the Kingdom Bible College in Los Angeles, from which Wesley Swift graduated. Monson's thesis appeared first in 1928, was republished in 1936, and issued in a third, expanded version, undated but almost certainly from the late 1930s. Monson had some but not all of the theory's elements. He argued the two-seedline position, one ("the Satan line") stemming from Cain, and the other ("the God line") from Abel. The two had to be kept separate and "the blood stream pure." Many of the "Satan line" had been killed in the Flood, Monson reports, but enough survived to be a continuing threat. But here he invokes not Bristowe, whose work he was apparently unfamiliar with, but her precursor, Alexander Hislop. The "Satan line" was Nimrod's religion, preserved in the Catholic church. The pope was "Prime Minister of the Devil," and it was against him that British-Israelites had to be vigilant.[2]

The When? Author

About a decade after Haberman and Monson, another series of publications appeared—this time in Vancouver—that even more closely approximated the full Identity position. Their authorship is unknown. The author is referred to here as the When? author, after the title of his/her major work. The works are tied together by style, subject matter, place of publication, and the presence in each of an unusual "Chart of Racial Origins from Biblical Sources." The first two pamphlets appeared anonymously. The first, The Morning Cometh, was issued in Vancouver in June 1941, and successively revised in October 1941 and February 1942. It was filled with apocalyptic expectations but had little to say about Jews. Its "Chart of Racial Origins" placed Jews in a line of corrupted descendants of the House of Judah without conspicuously linking them with Cain.[3]

A greatly enlarged version of *The Morning Cometh* appeared in January 1944, reprinted in June, under a new title, *When Gog Attacks*. Its author was clearly familiar not only with Hislop but with Bristowe and found Bristowe the more persuasive. Reviewing the position Bristowe took in *Sargon the Magnificent*, the author concluded that "it was Cain (Sargon) who founded the 'synagogue of Satan,' and not his descendant Nimrod." *When Gog Attacks* cited Lothrop Stoddard's article on Jewish racial types approvingly, noting especially the Asiatic origins of Ashkenazim. As to the biblical account of Jewish origins, Satan's fallen angels had had children by Canaanite women, and this "Canaanite blood" had survived the Deluge and was passed on by Canaan himself to "the Jewish remnant." As to more modern events, *When Gog Attacks* regarded *The Protocols* as a factual account of Jewish plans and viewed Zionists as Ashkenazim "of Turko-Mongol blood." "The cry of 'anti-Semitism' raised by the Zionists . . . is purely propaganda, and has no basis of fact, as the Ashkenazim are neither Jews nor Semitic by blood or race."[4]

The final step was a book-length work, *When?: A Prophetical Novel of the Very Near Future*, also published in Vancouver in 1944. It is ascribed, clearly pseudonymously, to one "H. Ben Judah." *When?* incorporated much of the material in *When Gog Attacks*, set in the context of a novel. Although *When?* begins in a clearly imperfect society, its author adopts the conventions of the utopian novel. A naïve but curious visitor finds himself in a strange land, where he is taken in hand by knowledgeable natives who serve as his guides. These guides enlighten the visitor about the true meaning of human life through a series of didactic monologues and responses to his questions. In this case, however, the locale is Palestine, not some mythic "no-place." The visitor, Brian Benjamin, is a Sephardic Jew converted to Christianity. A retired army officer, he has been sent to Palestine on a mission for British Intelligence. His cousin, Samuel Josephus, equips Benjamin with a letter of introduction to Amos Ben Jacob, a "Semitic" (as opposed to an "Asiatic") Jew. Together, Josephus and Ben Jacob educate the neophyte in British-Israelism and the sins of the Zionists. Benjamin's education takes place against the backdrop of End-time events, for *When?*, published during World War II, incorporated the apocalyptic scenario current in Anglo-Israel circles: Gog has attacked Palestine, but a sulphur-producing earthquake destroys much of Gog's forces. A tank battle follows at Megiddo, where a second earthquake, together with storm, sulphurous fire, and hailstones, destroys Gog's remaining troops, so that Christ can return and usher in the millennial kingdom.

Before this climax occurs, however, Benjamin learns the real nature of Ashkenazic Jews and their relationship to Cain. Cain, it seems, founded a secret society to do the Devil's work on earth and had in fact been so successful in this endeavor that everyone on earth with the exception of Noah and his family, "appears to have come under the control of Satan." Unfortunately, Noah's line was poisoned when Ham married a descendant of Cain's, "and thus the contaminated blood was brought through the Flood." Cain's conspiracy continued on through history, controlled "by certain of the Ashkenazim Jews." On the matter of Cain's paternity, however, the *When?* author was ambivalent. Adam "may have been" Cain's physical father, "but he certainly was not his spiritual father." Indeed, Ben Judah accepts the existence of the serpent's seed on earth without specifying how such people might be identified. Ben Judah, too, followed Bristowe's account of Cain's life as Sargon the Devil-worshipper, who had made a Faustian bargain. Through the Fall, the earth had been delivered into the hands of Cain and the serpent's seed. *When?* carefully notes that Cain's descendants, the Canaanites, intermarried with Judah, and the children of that union were "those Jewish leaders who continually opposed Messiah." Ben Judah shrank from the final steps, which would have involved acknowledging Satan as Cain's physical father, and the Jews as the Devil's descendants. Nonetheless, his reference to Cain's "contaminated blood" and his willingness to consider the Devil as Cain's "spiritual father" places *When?* in the direct line of Identity development, with its conspiracy of Ashkenazic Jews doing the Devil's bidding.[5]

Conrad Gaard

It is unclear who cobbled together the first complete account of the alleged diabolical origin of the Jewish people, in part because the writings of Comparet are often undated and those of Swift are often transcripts of undated sermons. Conrad Gaard had published a full version of the theory by 1960, and William Potter Gale by 1963. Since Gaard's appears to be the earliest complete version to which a specific date can be assigned, it is best to begin with it.

Gaard considers the "serpent" a Pre-Adamite "beast of the field," who, acting as "Satan's agent," fathered Cain. He accepts the idea of a liaison between the serpent and Eve on "considerable evidence of a circumstantial nature . . . [but] it makes little difference whether or not he [Cain] was actually the son of the serpent," since in any case Cain married a Pre-Adamite. Hence, Cain's descendants constituted a "mongrel, hybrid race," whether because of copulation with the serpent or with Pre-Adamites. This line of "mongrel" offspring makes up the "serpent race," set in eternal opposition to "the pure seed . . . of the Woman." With the addition of Ham to the serpent line, Cain's race survived the Flood. Cain himself had (and here Gaard too cites Bristowe) previously set the conspiracy moving by establishing "the first Super World government" to accomplish Satan's purposes, an enterprise continued by his descendants to the present day: "Satan has controlled his Kingdoms of this world through earthly Masters, who received their orders occultly from Secret Hidden Masters, and . . . he controls his Kingdom today, including even Communist Russia and Red China, in the same way." Central to this Cainite conspiracy are the Jews. While there are some genuine Jews from the tribes of Judah and Benjamin, most are "Babylonian pseudo-Jews," who became part of "the Serpent Seed Race" when Judah had offspring by a Canaanite woman. When Judah's corrupted offspring were carried into Babylonian exile, according to Gaard, they joined with "the various Edomite-Amalekite Shelanite-Canaanite elements of the serpent race . . . and under Satanic inspiration they were united in one Conspiratorial group, which became known as the 'Diaspora,' or Dispersion, of the 'Jews.'" By fraudulently posing as God's chosen people, these "pseudo-Jews" have disguised their true origin and design. Gaard gives Satan not one but two conspiracies, the second of which, "Great Babylon," brought with it "a counterfeit King-Priest Order" and a diabolical "Babylonian Financial System" built on gold and usury. The two conspiracies cooperate, so that Jews can use the financial system for their own benefit. Gaard implied that at the top of the conspiratorial pyramid, the otherwise unidentified "Secret Hidden Masters" keep the cabals in tune with Satan's master plan.[6]

Gaard's convoluted theory allowed him to incorporate not only the elements of the Devil theory but more familiar right-wing motifs as well. Thus, he utilized variant meanings of *nachash* to convert the serpent into a humanoid "beast of the field" capable of having intercourse with Eve. He accepted Bristowe's life of Cain, as well as C. F. Parker's attempt to demonstrate that the Jews, rather than the Turks, are Edom. He found room for an approving citation of Lothrop Stoddard's discussion of the Jews' alleged Khazar ancestry as well. But in addition to these authorities, familiar in both British-Israel and Identity literature, he accommodated themes neither specifically Anglo-Israelite nor Identity. The Illuminati, an alleged force for evil ever since early nineteenth-century nativism, reappear as an instrument "directed occultly by hidden masters." "Great Babylon" becomes the origin of the hatred of gold and the fixation upon monetary conspiracies that fed Populist fears of Jews and cities. Thus, Identity theology is readily linked to the fears of economic conspiracy that Richard Hofstadter identified with the "paranoid political style."[7]

Bertrand Comparet

Bertrand Comparet wielded great influence in the Identity movement, in part because he appeared better able than such contemporaries as Gale and Swift to avoid factional conflict. He rarely wrote at length, however, and his positions must be stitched together from published sermons and brief articles. He outlined a by-now-familiar position: there were races before Adam and Eve, and hence, all people on earth are not their descendants. However, in discussing the Pre-Adamites, Comparet gave older views a somewhat novel twist in suggesting that a satanic race was among them. The "serpent race" did not begin with Cain; rather, the serpent himself was one of its members. This position resembles that of Charles Carroll and some other earlier racists, who believed the serpent was a black Pre-Adamite. Like other writers, Comparet tries to tease new meanings from the Hebrew word translated as *serpent*, although, like them, his ignorance of Hebrew betrays his reliance on the commentaries of others: "The word mistranslated 'serpent' is the Hebrew word 'naw-khash,' which literally means 'enchanter' or 'magician'—and, no doubt Satan, still possessing angelic powers, was able to be an enchanter or magician." As the passage indicates, Comparet suggested at some points that the serpent was merely a member of the satanic race but at other times that it was Satan himself who seduced Eve.[8]

Although casual in citing the work of others, Comparet so precisely paraphrased Davidson's revisionist history of the Near East that his debt is clear. He had the post-Fall Adam migrating east "into what was formerly called Chinese Turkestan," where Adam, Eve, and their descendants take up residence in "the Tarim Basin . . . identified as the site of Noah's flood." His reliance upon Bristowe seems equally clear when he asserted that "Yes, Cain is a well-known historical character, not found only in the Bible (but he is known in history under another name). He established an empire which extended from the Persian Gulf to the Mediterranean Sea, and even took in some of the larger islands in the Mediterranean Sea." As to the Jews, they are "the children of Satan," Canaanites and the offspring of Canaanite-Israelite intermarriage, augmented by Edomites, who took over the territory of Judah when the latter were deported to Babylon.[9]

William Potter Gale

While Comparet was prone to sketch out the Devil theory in brief sermonic statements, William Potter Gale sought to make a more systematic exposition in his 1963 booklet, *The Faith of Our Fathers*, as well as in essays and articles. Gale predictably traced sacred history from the Pre-Adamites through the Fall, the rise of Cain and his descendants, and the Jewish conspiracy. Adam and Eve were preceded by other races, "Asiatics and Negroes," who had been created "hundreds of thousands of years and possibly millions of years before the two children of the Creator were placed in Eden." By contrast, Adam and Eve, and therefore the white race, were created in 5500 B.C. But in fact, for Gale the "Adamic race" had a far older ancestry. The placement of Adam and Eve in Eden merely marked the point when they were "born into the flesh body on earth." Here Gale overlaid the biblical narrative with a quasi-Gnostic myth of preearthly origins. In this preearthly era, Lucifer and his fallen angels fought a "great and mighty space battle" through the reaches of the universe with the forces of God, led by the archangel Michael. The battle between opposing spaceships led, of course, to Lucifer's defeat, and when he and the other rebels had been defeated, they were "cast down," falling from space to the planet Earth. These fallen angels deposited on a planet not their own were the nonwhite Pre-Adamites. Hence, Pre-Adamites are distinguished not merely by a general racial inferiority but by a primal association with Lucifer and complicity in rebellion against God, a heritage of criminality that pre-dates the existence of humanity of earth.[10]

As to the Adamites themselves, Gale—like Davidson and such "Aryanists" as Renan—placed them in central Asia. Davidson, however, had distinguished between Eden, located in present-day Iraq, and the land "east of Eden," to which Adam and Eve were forced to migrate. Thus Davidson had them travel eastward from the Euphrates Valley to the Tarim Basin, which would be the Adamite/Aryan home until the Flood. Gale passed over any distinction between the locus of Adamic activity before and after the Flood. "All circumstances," he wrote, "point to the Tarim Basin, lying just east of the Great Pamirs, as the home land of the Adamites," simultaneously identifying it as Eden and as the land the Adamites occupied subsequent to the Fall.[11]

But the Adamites were destined to a life of sin and retribution, for their Asiatic home was placed in the midst of Pre-Adamite peoples. Satan, seeking to thwart God's purposes, caused the Adamites to "mongrelize . . . with the fallen angel line of people [i.e., the Pre-Adamites] who had lost their first estate." The Flood, submerging only the land in which the Adamites lived, was the punishment for racial sin. Only those few—Enoch, Methusaleh, Lamech, and Noah—who refused the invitation to racial mixing would survive the Flood.[12]

But evil was present not merely in the person of the Pre-Adamites but more intimately in the form of Cain. As might be expected at this point in the evolution of Identity doctrine, Gale unambiguously attributed Cain's paternity to the Devil: "Satan seduced Eve and she had a son by him who was named Cain." Because "Cain was evil and not acceptable to the Creator," he left his mother and foster father after the murder of Abel "and joined Satan's hosts," that is, became a member of the Pre-Adamite society formed by the fallen angels. Gale's conception of a universe divided between the warring powers of God and Satan pushed him toward an anti-Semitism even more radical than that of his predecessors. Cain is the first "white Jew," but even before Cain's birth, "Satan had . . . mixed his seed with the pre-Adamic races, thus producing Asiatic Jews and black Jews." "Jews" for Gale, in other words, are any people who contain the Devil's seed, regardless of racial characteristics or religious beliefs. Nonwhites are therefore "Jews" by definition, the descendants of Lucifer's minions with whom Satan intermingled his seed prior to the creation of Adam and Eve. Notwithstanding this expansive conception of the satanic "Jew," Gale also understood "Jew" in a more restricted, quasi-biblical sense to mean a people who lived in Palestine during scriptural times.[13]

In his restricted, biblical meaning, Gale considered "Jews" Cain's descendants who intermarried with Judah. Cain and his offspring were prolific "because they married often and had no morals." Judah's son by a Canaanite woman produced Shelah, who "was of the Mongrelized seed, some white from Judah and the balance of Negro and Asiatic mixture." These so-called Shelahites were subsequently known as Edomites when "they were joined with the mongrelized descendants of Esau." This group, clustered in southern Judea, was, in Gale's view, the Jews as they first entered history. Gale distinguished them from the generic "Jews" (who included nonwhites) through the term "Yehudi." In time, these Yehudi, following the bidding of Satan, "gained control of the money and wealth of most of the nations they had invaded." From bases in Holland and Switzerland, they utilized financial leverage to infiltrate other European countries for the purpose of dominating "Adam's family."

The evening is slowly approaching as many children of Ad-am [sic] leave their original nations and come across to the new Jerusalem [America]. The new nation of God's Kingdom and His people is to be founded during the evening hours with darkness slowly approaching. It will flounder in darkness for the period of time ordained by the Creator of the Universe. Then there will be a new dawn and a new day.

In Gale's hands, the theory of satanic ancestry became the basis for a conception of the world and history that teeters uneasily between hope and despair but ultimately anticipates a millenarian salvation in which the war between God and the Devil, now transposed into a conflict between the children of Adam and the children of Cain, finally produces divine victory.[14]

Gale was not one to cite his sources, but he occasionally made respectful gestures toward "Professor Davidson." But Davidson saw himself as a student of history, however bizarre his account might seem to academic historians. While Gale was perfectly willing to incorporate the work of Davidson, Parker, and others in the British-Israel tradition, he operated at the level of myth, where eternal forces battle with spaceships in a cosmic void and defeated angels take on earthly bodies. Then, when this evil multitude grows to fill the earth, the "Creator" sends his own children, "celestial beings," to recapture the earth, initiating a new round in the war between good and evil. The figure of the Jew in this mythic portrayal is now totally dehumanized, a literal devil in human form, taking on a variety of racial complexions, infiltrating nations and institutions in a nearly successful attempt to undo Lucifer's original defeat. So described, it is an adversary to whom no quarter can be given.[15]

Wesley Swift

William Potter Gale saw Wesley Swift both as a mentor and rival, toward whom he directed a stream of vilification and accusations (much of it after the latter's death), most having to do with alleged financial improprieties and unfair competitive tactics. Nonetheless, Swift's views were closely parallel to Gale's own. Indeed, before their falling-out in the mid-1960s, they were close associates. Swift, however, was destined to have the greater influence. After his death in 1970, his widow and followers disseminated his sermons widely in pamphlets, cassettes, and as articles in the Identity press, which gave Swift's message a distribution Gale's never had. Swift also had the advantage of having been a member of Gerald L. K. Smith's inner circle, which brought Swift to the attention of many rightists who were otherwise not inclined to patronize religious services. Since Swift eschewed systematic exposition, his doctrinal positions must be reconstructed from the fragments contained in his innumerable sermons and short articles. However, since so much of what Swift asserted closely resembled Gale's ideas, we may move through Swift's system more rapidly.

Wesley Swift's view of Genesis differed only marginally from that of Gale and other Identity writers. Far from beginning with the creation of humanity, it is a racial text, as indeed is the Bible as a whole, "the Book of the Adamic race," "written to the white people who constitute Christian civilization." This white Adamic race was not, however, created on earth, but consists of the direct, spiritual offspring of God, who were created "before the creation of the solar system" and subsequently sent to earth, where they were physically embodied as the Adamic race, "the vessels for our arrival." As to nonwhites, the blacks were "brought . . . in from other planets in the Milky Way" by Lucifer in the great angelic rebellion, so that the battle with God could be continued on Earth.[16]

The Pre-Adamites consequently had a nonearthly origin. They were allies of Lucifer, who originally lived elsewhere in the galaxy. Swift, like Gale, placed the Pre-Adamites within the context of Lucifer's rebellion. The forces of Lucifer deployed "vast space crafts" against the space fleets of the archangel Michael. Lucifer's crews were made up of the newly recruited blacks. Lucifer's defeated fleet was driven into the solar system, where the surviving ships eventually crashed into Earth. This had the twofold consequence of introducing the Pre-Adamites and of transferring the cosmic conflict between Lucifer and God from the cosmos to the earth.[17]

The Adamites whom God embodied on earth to battle the Luciferians began as the Aryans of central Asia. Swift, somewhat more careful with geography than Gale, distinguished Eden, which he located on the Pamir Plateau in southeast Turkestan, from the area to which Adam and Eve were driven after the Fall, the Tarim Basin. There, before the Flood, the Adamites performed scientific wonders based on celestial knowledge. But much of "their knowledge, their wisdom, and their science" was to vanish in the Deluge, the price paid for race mixing with the Pre-Adamites. Far from the Flood ending the battle between good and evil, it simply shifted the struggle to a postdiluvian world in which the Adamites would be confronted not simply with the Pre-Adamites but with Pre-Adamites in combination with Jews.[18]

In furtherance of his designs, Lucifer seduced Eve, who begat Cain: "The moment that Lucifer brought about the seduction of Eve, the AURA or light emanation that surrounded this physical body departed from Eve, and later from Adam, and the very day the Aura departed, the processes which would maintain permanently, the structure of the physical body, and maintain Immortality, at that very moment when the Aura that connects the power of Spirit to sustain the physical body, passes off it." Cain's own children, "the sons and daughters of Lucifer," "are the people you know today as Jews." In general Swift asserted that Lucifer seduced Eve, destroying the primal couple's immortality at the same time as he insured himself an earthly confederate. But he occasionally entertained another idea, namely, that when Satan's minions fell to earth, they "intermingled" with its inhabitants to produce "unassimilable" demonic offspring, a notion similar to Gale's concept of white, black, and yellow "Jews." Swift then designated Cain "the white one [i.e., devil]," who, however, would have been produced by Eve having had intercourse with one of the shipwrecked fallen angels rather than with Lucifer himself. At still other points, Swift combined the two ideas to declare that the Jews "are the offspring of Lucifer and the fallen angels which came with Lucifer." Swift's Jews, too, like Gale's, are shape-changers, a generic form of evil with multiple manifestations: "The jews are Hittites and Amalekites and Canaanites. They are red, black, yellow, and brown, as well as off-colored white."[19]

Notwithstanding the bewildering varieties of evil in Swift's universe, he was still able to maintain a special place for Cain and his descendants. When Cain fled his homeland, he settled among the Akkadians, "a pre-Adamic race of people," and "mongrelized himself" with them. Without explicitly referring to Bristowe, Swift nonetheless appropriates her notion that Cain "may well have become Sargon the Magnificent." Cain's followers and descendants—the Canaanites—become a major vehicle for "Jewish" infiltration of Israel. All Swift's strands now come together in his version of the "Great Conspiracy." Swift's conspiracy is "Mystery Babylon," the "great harlot" revealed by the angel in the seventeenth chapter of Revelation, with seven heads and ten horns: "And the woman was arrayed in purple and scarlet, and decked with gold and precious stone and pearls, having in her hand a golden cup full of abominations, even the unclean things of her fornication, and upon her forehead a name written, MYSTERY, BABYLON THE GREAT, THE MOTHER OF THE HARLOTS AND OF THE ABOMINATIONS OF THE EARTH." Earlier generations of chiliasts, including Alexander Hislop, had identified the image with the pope, but Swift, like Conrad Gaard, linked it to Jews and their alleged financial manipulations. "Jewry has been the head and the manipulating force behind the system of Mystery Babylon . . . controlled and run by these descendants of Lucifer." This cabal, wrote Swift, has used its financial cunning and power to control and enslave by economic means, but he foresaw an apocalyptic time when "the uprising of the peoples of the world" will destroy the conspiracy and "organized world Jewry" with it. "*When Mighty Babylon falls, it will be the falling of the symbolic mystery system that controls all pagan religions and false theology, and philosophies, and economic manipulation—all parts of the Luciferian kingdom, Great will be the fall of that kingdom.*" Immersed in the apocalyptic imagery of gold, abominations, and Lucifer, Swift, like the writer of Revelation itself, lapsed into an incantatory style in which words lose connections with their referents, and the very act of employing language appears to be an act of violence against a phantom enemy, an enemy the more feared for its very invisibility.[20]

In fact, little of substance separated Swift from his protégé, Gale. Their style suggests, however, something of why Swift emerged as the more influential figure. Gale, reflecting perhaps his military background, plods through tedious exposition, so that every nook and cranny of doctrine is illuminated. Swift, by contrast, races breathlessly although not always logically through a tangle of images. As has already been mentioned, neither was scrupulous about citing sources. But there is ample contextual evidence for their joint reliance upon Bristowe's idiosyncratic account of Cain's life as a Near Eastern potentate, and more concrete evidence that both were familiar with Davidson, even if neither cited him nearly as often as the occasions warranted. To Gale, he is "Professor Davidson," whose pyramid studies establish biblical chronology as "authentic history." Swift's evocation of the Adamic cities of Takla Makan might have been lifted directly from Davidson but for a few changes of wording.[21]

Gale, Swift, and the Question of Mormon Influence

There is circumstantial evidence of other influences upon Gale and Swift from outside the circumscribed domain of British-Israelism. Both Gale and Swift placed considerable emphasis on the nonearthly origins of the Adamic race, which was originally made up of purely spiritual "celestial beings" who were the direct offspring of God. Thus the physical form that "Aryans" presently take is deemed to reflect a relatively recent embodiment rather than their "true" nature, spiritual rather than material. Pre-Adamic, nonwhite peoples, by contrast, are "created beings," brought into existence by God as a creative act, but not his offspring. In any case, their association with Lucifer's rebellion has rendered them morally unfit. By utilizing these myths of origins,

Gale and Swift added a strongly Manichaean aspect to the conception of Jewish diabolism, for the warfare between Jews and Aryans must now be set within a far larger struggle between God and Lucifer that began before the creation of the earth and will end only with Lucifer's final defeat in the Last Days. While this concern with preearthly history is not in conflict with the British-Israel sources on which their theology mainly rests, it is a motif not found among Anglo-Israel writers. What might be its source?

One possible source lies in Mormon doctrine. The relationship between Mormonism and Identity is complex. On the one hand, Mormons also see themselves as Israel. Joseph Smith believed that many who converted to Mormonism were, unknown to themselves, blood Israelites, for some of the lost tribes had so intermingled with other populations that their descendants were scattered over the earth. As James E. Talmage, an apostle of the church, put it, "many of those belonging to the Ten Tribes were diffused among the nations." Nonetheless, Smith and those who followed believed that the bulk of the ten tribes remained intact, somewhere in "the north," and that in the latter days they would reemerge: "And then shall the work of the Father commence at that day, even when this gospel shall be preached among the remnant of this people. Verily I say unto you, at that day shall the work of the Father commence among all the dispersed of my people, yea, even the tribes which have been lost, which the Father hath led away out of Jerusalem." "The leading of the ten tribes from the land of the north" would be a hallmark of the end of history. Smith's teaching was consolidated before the development of British-Israelism, although he, like the Anglo-Israelites, followed the clues to the ten tribes laid out in the Apocrypha.[22]

Like Anglo-Israelites, Mormons place great emphasis upon the dispersion and eventual reemergence of the ten tribes. Where British-Israelites concentrated upon tracing migrations to Europe, the Book of Mormon described the journey of members of the tribes to the Western Hemisphere. Others of the tribes, however, had been dispersed, their Israelite origins obscured. Like British-Israelism, Mormonism too gives centrality to Ephraim and Manasseh, and many Mormons believe themselves to be lineal descendants of Ephraim, either by blood relationship or subsequent adoption.[23]

Mormonism, however, is free of virulent anti-Semitism. Jews suffered the penalty of exile as punishment for rejection of Jesus, but Mormons regard Jesus as a Jew and consider Jews to be part of Israel. Their preservation is considered essential and miraculous, so that the creation of the state of Israel became a demonstration of God's action in history, "a harbinger of the great gathering which will involve the ultimate conversion and sanctification of the chosen of Judah." This doctrinal framework has led James Aho to suggest that Mormons are resistant to Identity, despite the latter's similarity to Mormon beliefs about the lost tribes. Thus in Aho's sample of 384 Idaho "Christian patriots" for whom religious data was available, 159 were "Christian constitutionalists," whose right-wing philosophy omitted mention of a Jewish conspiracy, while 185 were considered adherents of Christian Identity. Sixty-five percent of the Christian constitutionalist group had been raised, and in most cases continued, as Mormons. By contrast, those of Mormon background comprised only 9 percent of the Christian Identity group. This finding was reinforced by the fact that Christian Identity respondents resided overwhelmingly in Idaho's northern and western counties, rather than in the southeastern counties with large Mormon concentrations. Nonetheless, while Mormons figured less prominently than those of Fundamentalist background among Aho's Identity respondents, individuals raised as Mormons seem far more likely to affiliate with Identity than is true of the American population in general.[24]

The possibility of Mormon doctrinal influence cannot be rejected out of hand. No direct evidence links either Wesley Swift or William Potter Gale to Mormonism. However, both lived in southern California, which had a significant Mormon population, including pockets of Mormon doctrinal schismatics. They may well have picked up and selectively appropriated some Mormon teachings or interpretations and, as non-Mormons, would have been unconstrained by the discipline of the church. Intriguing doctrinal parallels suggest that this may have been the case, particularly for the concept of the preexistence.

In Mormon teaching, every form of earthly life had a prior, nonphysical existence. In a revelation Joseph Smith received in 1830, God said, "And I, the Lord God, formed man from the dust of the ground, and breathed into his nostrils the breath of life; . . . nevertheless, all things were before created; but spiritually were they created and made according to my word." In one of Joseph Smith's papyrus translations, God showed Abraham "the intelligences that were organized before the world was." This nonphysical "first estate" of human existence came to be called the "preexistence of spirits," in which "the souls of mankind passed through a stage of existence prior to their earthly probation." The concept of the preexistence is echoed in later Identity sources.[25]

Wesley Swift's very language strongly suggests some exposure, however partial and distorted: "Being born of incorruptible seed, is a process of the

Father, by which you were begotten in the beginning, before even these worlds were framed." Dan Gayman, pastor of the Church of Israel, asserted that major biblical figures in the Adamic line had had earlier spiritual lives, including Enoch, Noah, Abraham, and Sarah: "*Our Christian Fathers were strangers to this terrestrial plane, having existed in spirit essence before time*, to take on a *flesh body in time.*" Significantly, the Church of Israel is an offshoot of a schismatic Mormon group, the Church of Christ (Temple Lot), with which Gayman's father was involved. As Gayman moved closer to British-Israel and Identity teachings, direct Mormon associations were dropped, including the Book of Mormon, but it is reasonable to suppose that Gayman's belief in the preexistence reflects his and the church's origins. A slightly different conception of the preexistence appeared in the Aryan Nations' journal, *Calling Our Nation*. Here, God decides to "manifest" a family of his made up of "Elohim" by giving them physical form. While these materialized divine beings may reproduce with one another, they cannot be born of unions with human beings of nondivine origin (i.e., interracial unions).[26]

By placing white origins in a purely spiritual preexistence, Identity establishes yet another contrast between Aryans and Jews. As the latter are considered lineal offspring of the Devil, so the former are the literal children of God. As the latter are trapped in the corruption of material existence, so the former are presumed to have a spiritual essence that remains even though they have taken on physical form. Indeed, once Identity had committed itself to the doctrine that Jews were not simply "of the Devil" in some metaphorical sense but were "of the Devil" *biologically*, it was essential to provide a doctrinally symmetrical account of Aryan origins. Consequently, the Adamites are conceived to be not simply "in the image of God" but to be his literal children. Not only did the belief in Aryan preexistence give whites a status as exalted as that of Jews was degraded; it also provided a theological basis for the link between two episodes of conflict between God and the Devil. In the first episode, which took place in the preexistence, Lucifer and his minions rebelled against God and the loyal angels, led by Michael. In the second episode, on earth during historic time, Satan continued the war against God and his people through the instrumentality of a Jewish conspiracy. Hence, Identity Christians can see themselves as participants in a struggle that began before the creation of the world and will end only at the end of time. This allows them to integrate their own racist and anti-Semitic activities into a conception of the cosmic struggle between the forces of light and darkness, elevating what might otherwise seem petty to a level of ultimate significance.

The Satanic Theory:
The Second Identity Generation

The satanic theory had been hammered together by the first generation of Identity leaders, principally Conrad Gaard, Bertrand Comparet, William Potter Gale, and Wesley Swift. By the 1970s, a second generation appeared, and while they generally acknowledged the contributions of their elders, they were prepared to offer their own elaborations and modifications. In light of Identity's fragmented structure—made up of independent congregations, organizations, and publications—second-generation figures were free to chart their own courses. In this segmented religious milieu, what is surprising is not the degree of dispute but the extent of consensus. The number of Identity groups and writers is so large that it is impossible to fully describe the doctrinal positions of them all. Instead, the remainder of the chapter will be devoted to an explication of the positions of five representative organizations and individuals: Richard Girnt Butler's Aryan Nations and the Church of Jesus Christ Christian; Jarah Crawford, an influential Identity Bible exegete; Dan Gayman's Church of Israel; the Covenant, Sword and Arm of the Lord, the religious communal settlement led by James Ellison; and, finally, by way of contrast, Howard Rand. The first four offer statements of the theory of Jewish origins that closely resemble the position first systematically articulated by Comparet, Gale, and Swift. Rand's strong dissent reflects the now unbridgeable gap between organized British-Israelism (or what was left of it), and Identity.

In its creedal statement, Aryan Nations and the Church of Jesus Christ Christian state the Satanic theory in clear and unmistakable terms:

> WE BELIEVE that there are literal children of Satan in the world today. These children are the descendants of Cain, who was a result of Eve's original sin, her physical seduction by Satan. We know that because of this sin, there is a battle and a natural enmity between the children of Satan and the Children of The Most High God. . . .
>
> WE BELIEVE that there is a battle being fought this day between the children of darkness (today known as Jews) and the children of light (God), the Aryan race, the true Israel of the Bible.

From this acceptance of "serpent seedline" anti-Semitism, Aryan Nations writers have elaborated descriptions of the satanic conspiracy and its operations. George Stout, the Aryan Nations leader in Texas, attributed to the conspiracy control over "the world's political movements through the Babylon system of banking, finances, and economics." The Aryan Nations periodical, *Calling Our Nation*, has also offered frequent descriptions of alleged Jewish human sacrifice. These articles, often written by members of other extreme right-wing organizations, derive not only from the medieval literature of ritual murder but from Ellen Bristowe's contention that when Cain organized his kingdom in Babylon as Sargon, he introduced a human sacrificial cult at Satan's urging. Although Bristowe never suggested any association between Cain and Jews, the fact that so many British-Israel and Identity writers did has made it possible to assimilate her speculations to the older ritual-murder theme in anti-Semitic literature. Michael Hudson, director of the Christian Nationalist White People's party, wrote in *Calling Our Nation* that ritual murder had been "originated in Babylon," adopted by the Cainite priesthood, and "carried out continuously by the Jews for more than 2500 years . . . in the name of . . . Satan." *Calling Our Nation* also reprinted an article that originally appeared in the periodical of the Lord's Covenant church suggesting that Jewish ritual murder had begun in biblical times and was continuing into the present.[27]

Jarah B. Crawford, a former Assembly of God minister, is the foremost contemporary Identity Bible interpreter. His work, *Last Battle Cry*, is cast in the form of a "racial interpretation" of the books of the Old and New Testaments. Crawford found that all but five of the books—Letter of Paul to Philemon, Job, Nahum, Habakkuk, and Zephaniah—have a hitherto unexplicated racial character, and in seeking to derive a "racial understanding" of the texts, Crawford found biblical warrant for the satanic theory. While his conclusions purportedly derive from scriptural passages, they in fact simply restate positions contained in the literature reviewed in this and the preceding chapters. However, since Crawford desired to link Identity beliefs with specific biblical passages, he regarded the idea of Satan's seduction of Eve as based on circumstantial evidence. Nevertheless, "we are led to believe [by the text] that Satan seduced Eve. Eve then introduced sexual intercourse to Adam." However circumstantial the evidence might be, Crawford has no doubts about Cain's paternity: "*Cain was the Son of Satan*! Satan had seduced Eve and impregnated her with his evil seed." In reaching this conclusion, he respectfully cited the writings of Conrad Gaard, not only on the matter of Cain's father but to support his belief in the existence of the Pre-Adamites. Similarly, he explicitly relied on Bristowe's account to settle the matter of the Pre-Adamites' race (black) and the fact that Cain married one of their number. The Jews are "half-breed, race-mixed, polluted people not of God. . . . *They are not God's creation.*" Instead, they are "the children of Satan," "the serpent seed line" that derived from Cain.[28]

Although Dan Gayman adopted positions close to those of many other Identity figures, his writings present perhaps the most elaborate theological discussions to be found in the movement. The Church of Israel's *Articles of Faith and Doctrine* assert that a multiplicity of races was created at different times, with Adam as "the father of only one race on this earth, that is the caucasion race." The law of God requires that races "remain segregated in the habitat given each of them by the Eternal God." Satan placed his offspring on earth through the instrumentality of the serpent. Gayman has elaborated the notion of a serpent seedline in greater detail than has any other Identity writer. In a series of essays on the third and fourth chapters of Genesis, Gayman argued that Cain and Abel were fraternal twins sharing a mother but having different fathers. Because Eve had been "beguiled and deceived by Satan," she did not realize that Satan had seduced her. She had released two ova, one of which had been fertilized by Satan and one by Adam. This, then, was the origin of the two seedlines. In support of the two-seedlines theory, Gayman went so far as to find medical evidence for its physical possibility, arguing that the different paternities claimed for Cain and Abel rest on a scientific basis. Specifically, he grounded the two-seedlines idea in cases where two eggs have been released or "a true ovum divides into identical halves," each of which is then fertilized by sperm from a different father and develops separately but simultaneously in the womb.[29]

The consequence of the two seedlines is a relationship of continuing conflict between the satanic offspring of Cain and the Adamic descendants of Abel. More than most Identity writers, Gayman used indirection to identify the Jews with the serpent seedline. This may reflect difficulty in rejecting the Mormon position on Jews. In any case, Gayman's conclusions are unmistakable. Thus, among the scriptural passages he cited as devices for tracing the seedline of Satan is the passage in Revelation 2:9 identifying Jews with "the synagogue of Satan." He asks rhetorically, "If Cain were not the offspring of Satan, there is no basis for the age old conflict between Jews and Christians. Moreover, there are no reasonable grounds for the Jews themselves claiming to be from Cain. Why is the snake chosen as the symbol of the serpent's seed in *The Protocols of the Learned Elders of Zion?*" In a like vein, he concluded that the Crucifixion proves that Jews are not Adamites, a position he regarded as having been conclusively demonstrated by the fact that a Jewish film company produced *The Last Temptation of Christ.*[30]

If Gayman occasionally utilized indirection in his argument, there is nothing approaching subtlety in the writings published by the Covenant, Sword and Arm of the Lord. The CSA was best known for its communal settlement, Zarephath-Horeb, in southern Missouri, the most heavily militarized of all Identity communes. Its utilization of the theory of satanic origins is noteworthy primarily for the intricacy with which it was interwoven with a conspiratorial view of politics and history. As we have seen, most Identity writers who accept the belief in the Devil as progenitor of the Jews link this myth with a concept of the "great conspiracy," a largely Jewish cabal dedicated to realizing the Devil's designs. Nowhere has this linkage been more elaborately explicated than in CSA's book, *Witchcraft and the Illuminati*, published without indication of authorship in 1981, but most likely attributable to the CSA's leader, James Ellison.

CSA identified the serpent of Genesis not only with the Devil but with a Pre-Adamite black. The emphasis on an etymology for the Hebrew word *nachash*, linking it to "the Arabic words AKHNAS, KHANASA, and KHANOOS, all of which mean 'Ape,'" connects the exegesis firmly with Adam Clarke's nineteenth-century Bible commentary. By making the serpent simultaneously diabolical and nonwhite, CSA made Cain both "serpent's seed" and a black man. Cain also takes a black wife once he reaches the land of Nod. Since the "mixing of races always produces evil and chaos," Cain is defined here as "the first JEW," and the remainder of Cain's line Jewish.[31]

To this point, there is little in the CSA view of the Bible to differentiate it from other Identity writings. However, a new note entered when the author linked the diabolical origin of the Jews to a theme favored in American nativist and right-wing circles since the beginning of the Republic, an Illuminatist conspiracy. Despite the fact that the liberal, Masonic order of the Illuminati had had an existence in Europe only between 1776 and 1787, it lived on in the minds of some Americans as a continuing conspiratorial threat to American institutions. This view of an atheistic, foreign fifth column enjoyed initial success among some New England Federalists in 1798–99, only to reemerge periodically among those in search of secret enemies. In the CSA's version of the Illuminatist conspiracy, the plot is hatched not only by Adam Weishaupt, the Bavarian law professor who founded the actual Illuminati, but by the Rothschilds, who were seeking an instrument for Jewish conquest of the world. As the nineteenth century rolled on, according to the CSA, the Illuminati founded communism, worked out advance plans for the world wars, assassinated Lincoln and John Kennedy, and defeated the Mafia. This complex Illuminatist plot is heavily dependent upon the writings of a contemporary non-Identity conspiracy theorist, Des Griffin, who in *Fourth Reich of the Rich* outlined what he called (always in capital letters) "the MASTER PLAN": "THE MEN WHO CONCEIVED THE DIABOLICAL CONSPIRACY AS LAID OUT IN THE PROTOCOLS, WERE NOT ATHEISTS. THEY WERE MEMBERS OF THE ILLUMINATI, FOLLOWERS OF THE ORIGINAL 'LIGHT BEARER,' SATAN THE DEVIL. THEY WERE WORSHIPPERS OF SATAN. THIS IS THE PLAN OF SATAN." Although most recent authors have favored Bristowe over Alexander Hislop, Griffin relied upon the nineteenth-century account of Nimrod's satanic cult that Hislop included in *The Two Babylons*. As a result, the Covenant, Sword and the Arm of the Lord adopts an interpretation of the Bible that has room for both Cain's and Nimrod's plots. Cain is the first Jew, but in some obscure way that is never clearly described, Cain's machinations are reinforced by the Babylonian perversions of Nimrod and Samiramis as Satan's plot continues to unfold.[32]

Witchcraft and the Illuminati can scarcely contain its excitement about all of this secret knowledge: "Only about 5000 people in the entire world know the true purpose of the Illuminati and its conspiracy to rule the earth." They know because they possess the key that allows them to unveil the true meaning of the encoded text of Illuminati plans, which turns out to be Ayn Rand's novel *Atlas Shrugged*. Much of the rest of the CSA volume purports to be a decoding of the sinister plans allegedly contained in Rand's best-seller. Among them is to be a plan code-named "Helter Skelter," in which the government will stop all nonmilitary transportation while "an army of some 200,00 [*sic*] white prisoners and motorcycle gang members will create mass insanity in the streets by bombing church buildings, raping, murdering, and other fear tactics." CSA reported that "90% of the conspiracy plan has been fulfilled on schedule." The components of the conspiracy include the "House of Rothschild," a thirteen-member "Grand Druid Council," "the 33 highest Masons in the world," and the world's five hundred richest families, all coordinated by a gigantic computer in Brussels. It is scarcely surprising that, having this view of the world, the members of the Covenant, Sword and Arm of the Lord retreated behind their fortifications in the Ozarks.[33]

Rand's Dissent

The Covenant, Sword and Arm of the Lord represents the furthest extension of the Devil theory of the Jews, with the most highly elaborated version of the "great conspiracy." While all Identity writers do not, as we have seen, reach so paranoid a set of conclusions, they share a perspective in which evil is ultimately attributable to Satan's seduction of Eve in the Garden, not in the sense of having introduced sin into the world, but by the act of fathering a demonic race. Only one figure, Howard Rand, dissented strongly from this view. Rand's rejection did not stem from any philo-Semitism—indeed, his writings had been anti-Semitic for decades. Rather, it results from the fact that Rand was always more closely linked to British-Israelism than to Identity.

Rand rejected the idea that Cain had been fathered by the Devil. His periodical, *Destiny*, began to publish such views in the early 1960s, when Gaard, Comparet, Gale, and Swift were all active, and it is doubtless they whom Rand had in mind when he wrote that "there are those who undertake to suggest that when Eve succumbed to the serpent's temptation, Satan became the father of Cain." In addition to an essay by Rand himself in 1961, *Destiny* gave prominence to an anonymous two-part article in 1966 that purported to present "the undeniable truth" of the inferiority of "the colored races." This material together constitutes a systematic statement of Rand's position.[34]

The 1966 articles both cite and follow Charles Carroll's antiblack tract of 1900, *"The Negro a Beast,"* already discussed in previous chapters. While Adam and Eve lived a sinless life in Eden, "progenitors of the purebred Negroes . . . followed the chase in the Land of Nod." Adam employed these "beasts of the field" to perform manual labor. As Carroll had speculated, the "serpent" might have been a black overseer Adam employed to supervise his nonwhite laborers. Like other authors who deal with this material, the unnamed writer of the 1966 articles struggles with the Hebrew *nachash*. He knows and cites Adam Clarke's *Commentary* but concludes (as Clarke did not) that *nachash* was not a word for serpent but merely the name of "a highly intelligent beast of the field . . . a pure bred Negro." *Nachash* became "a willing tool" of Satan's in the latter's "diabolical scheme to corrupt mankind." As others had already suggested, Cain is made to take a Pre-Adamite black "paramour," and the author strongly intimates that this "shameless crime," rather than the slaying of Abel, was the reason for Cain's expulsion and wanderings. The narrative follows Carroll in asserting that Cain was also punished by being made to remain with and marry his black mistress, and thus to father "humanoids," "a mixed breed among the races of mankind." Yet despite its ferociously antiblack tone, there is no suggestion that Satan's role was anything but that of a corrupter, and no suggestion that Cain's father had been anyone but Adam.[35]

This was in line with Rand's own statement of a few years before that "the entire speculation about Eve's seduction by Satan is preposterous and contrary to all known facts." Rand too speculates on the meaning of the serpent's

Hebrew name, which he renders as *nasha*, and concludes that it means merely to seduce or deceive, implying mental rather than physical defilement. He accepts that Cain and Abel had the same father. Just as Satan was not the father of Cain, so his relationship with the Jews, wrote Rand, was "not . . . physical fatherhood but . . . spiritual fatherhood [by] the Evil One." A virtually identical view was published two years after Rand's article, in 1963, in the periodical of the Anglo-Saxon Christian Association of the United States of America, based in Portland, Oregon, which was probably an offshoot of the organization Rand had founded in the late 1920s, the Anglo-Saxon Federation of America. But by the 1960s, Rand's formerly central role in the formation of an American Anglo-Israelism had given way to marginality, as he was displaced by the post–World War II generation of Identity preachers described in chapter 4. Rand continued to hew to the line that Jews had been corrupted by intermarriage with heathen peoples, had been cursed for rejecting Christ, and had taken on all manner of unsavory personal and communal traits, but nonetheless had origins that originally went back to the tribe of Judah. Unrelenting in his anti-Semitism, Rand nonetheless saw the Devil theory of the Jews as an outgrowth of invalid scriptural interpretation.[36]

While Rand attempted to maintain British-Israel orthodoxy, Identity had meantime passed into the hands of younger men who saw the British movement as an effete exercise in half-measures. For them, the Jews were necessarily evil incarnate, and the struggle against them, a cosmic battle begun "before the world was made" and destined to end only in the coming final struggle between good and evil.

Identity Confronts British-Israelism

To those like Rand who rejected the Satan theory, Identity—now with a firm sense of its own distinctiveness—was prepared to respond in kind. While few were willing, as one correspondent to an Identity publication put it, to condemn British-Israelism as "tied in with Anti-Christ forces," many were convinced that it was shot through with theological errors. Gordon "Jack" Mohr called it "misleading," while William Potter Gale charged it with "serious theological errors." Most important of these was Anglo-Israelism's identification of Jews with the tribe of Judah, when in fact, Gale argued, "ALL of the white-Christian nations make up the 'House of Israel.'" He cautions, however, against blanket condemnation of British-Israelites, since "they are all anti-communist, opposed to the United Nations and are classified by the Jews as being anti-Jewish."[37]

Others in Identity were not so charitable. Notwithstanding Gale's suggestion that British-Israelism was considered "anti-Jewish," an Aryan Nations leader warned that "those who follow after British-Israelism are generally pro-Jewish." Tom Metzger, an Identity minister associated with James K. Warner before he joined forces with David Duke, labeled British-Israelism as "Kosher-Identity," and warned that "our people must shun British Israel as the plague," since it promotes a sense of common heritage among Jews and Gentiles.[38]

While some in Identity regarded British-Israelism as a partial truth, now outgrown, others viewed it as a rival. The latter were not fearful of the small coteries associated with the British-Israel World Federation; rather, the rivalry was with the one British-Israel-derived group that took sectarian form in America, Herbert W. Armstrong's Worldwide Church of God, a proselytizing sect free of anti-Semitism. Indeed, the *End Time Revelation Newsletter* warned that "Armstrong is reported to have Jewish blood and look at the lies he spread about the Anti-Christ Jews being Judah." With the full demonization of the Jews within Identity theology, British-Israelism had come to be regarded as at best a quaint relic, at worst a source of error and competition designed to lead the faithful astray.[39]

Part Three

Christian

Identity

and the

Political

System

As is the case with other groups of religious believers, Christian Identity adherents vary greatly in the degree to which they have integrated their political behavior and their spiritual lives. There is no evidence that more than a minority have taken Identity beliefs to their logical political conclusions. Those who have, however, have often reached political judgments that skirt and at times cross the boundary separating legal from illegal conduct.

Forms of Political Action

Christian Identity doctrines have political corollaries, implied consequences for the structure and operations of political institutions. While not all Christian Identity authors and organizations have identified the same political implications, many have addressed issues of law, the distribution of power, and the rights of "non-Aryans." These political orientations lie along a continuum of legally permissible behavior. At one end lie those behaviors that are unambiguously sanctioned by prevailing legal and political norms. At the other end are actions that are just as unambiguously prohibited. In the middle are activities whose acceptability is uncertain, which are in the penumbral area where behavior may be marginally acceptable but easily leads to unacceptable consequences. Thus, for example, participation in election campaigns is a clearly accepted form of political behavior, while seeking to overthrow the government by force just as clearly is not. But retreating to paramilitary communes has a more ambiguous status, for even if the members of such communities obey firearms regulations, their armed posture toward the larger society may well provoke violent confrontations with authority.

10

Racial

Politics

Christian Identity has given rise to at least six distinct forms of political action. Two lie clearly within the system's norms, two outside them, and two in the penumbral area. The two clearly legitimate positions are campaigns to bring the American legal system into conformity with laws spelled out in the Bible and to garner support for political candidates whose positions are deemed compatible with Identity views. Two other activities lie in the gray area between the permissible and the prohibited. One is the organization of self-sufficient, "survivalist" communities whose members have minimal contacts with the larger society. To the extent that the members of such communities are armed and reject the legitimacy of the society they have fled, the potential for violent confrontation exists, for the likelihood that any group of people could wholly separate itself from the society around it is slight. At some point, that society will make claims on citizens, even if the latter wish only to be left alone. A second such problematic tactic is the development of local political groups as an expression of the radical right's frequently expressed view that only local political institutions are legitimate. This, of course, implies that the state and national governments are illegitimate. While involvement in local government is surely no crime, it may lead to criminal activity if it carries with it an implied opposition to the requirements of state and federal law, such as the obligation to pay income tax, which many rightists oppose.

Finally, two Identity positions lie unambiguously outside the boundaries of acceptable political behavior. One consists of planning, organizing, and attempting to overthrow the federal government through campaigns of terrorism and guerrilla warfare. While rightists do not believe that insurgency alone will accomplish this end, some believe that it can serve as a catalyst for a popular uprising. A second proscribed form of behavior is territorial secession, widely advocated on the Identity right during the 1980s. Although there have been various schemes for dismembering the United States, all require that a large section of the country be broken off as an independent "Aryan nation." Advocates of this quasi-nationalist option suggest that this will happen when "white supremacists" constitute a working majority in the putative homeland, but they fail to address the issue of why the federal government would permit territorial fragmentation, and what could be done, short of civil war, were the government to actively seek to prevent it. Let us now examine each in greater detail.

"Biblicizing" American Law

Identity's goal of "biblicizing" American law—making it conform to the law presented in the Bible—must be distinguished from two related ideas. First, it is not the same as some concepts of natural law, according to which God's revealed law provides a standard for measuring the adequacy of man-made statutes. This idea presumes the existence of two rule systems, one of divine and one of human origin, the latter subordinate to the former. When Christian Identity speaks of the Bible as an ultimate source of law, it looks to a future in which man-made law will not exist, having been displaced by the superior divine version. Second, Identity's view is not the same as that of Protestant Fundamentalism, which accords to the Bible attributes of completeness, perfection, and inerrancy. While in principle Fundamentalists accord equal status to all segments of the biblical text as the inerrant word of God, they rarely urge the incorporation of detailed biblical rules of law into existing positive law. An important exception, however, is the "reconstructionist" or "theonomist" position among some contemporary postmillennialists, which will be considered below. Their position, although strikingly similar to that of Christian Identity, was independently derived and represents the views of only a very small segment of Fundamentalism. Influential Identity writers regard the Bible as a sourcebook for rewriting positive law, which, particularly in the economic realm, must reflect biblical legislation in order to produce a righteous society.

This position received early attention from Howard Rand and William J. Cameron through the Anglo-Saxon Federation of America, and in Rand's subsequent writings. Their demand for a wholesale restructuring of the American legal system gained momentum from the general dissatisfaction with American economic institutions during the Depression years, when the federation was most active. Indeed, Rand and Cameron advanced biblical ideas about law as a means for pulling the country out of its economic slump. In a more general way, however, ideas about biblical law have resonated in a distinctive manner within both British-Israelism and Christian Identity, for dependence upon biblical law may be shown to be a logical outcome of British-Israelism's and Christian Identity's central doctrine.

That doctrine is, of course, the belief that the biological descendants of Israel are peoples who live or whose forebears lived in the British Isles and/or parts of Western Europe. Traditionally, the church had portrayed itself as the "new Israel," the nonbiological successor to the biological Israel as the carrier of God's design in history. British-Israel, by insisting upon a biological criterion for identifying Israel, asserts a radical continuity between the biblical people and their putative contemporary descendants. Hence, it sees itself not as superseding biblical Israel but as continuing its mission, and therefore, biblical imperatives directed toward Israel are deemed to be directed toward the Anglo-Saxon-Celtic peoples as well, for they *are* Israel. The temptation to interpret biblical laws metaphorically, or to view them as outmoded, is substantially neutralized, although for the most part British-Israel and Christian Identity regard the ritual ordinances as having been made unnecessary by Jesus' mission. Nonritual rules, however, are regarded as in principle binding on "Israel" today as in the past. Hence, biblical law is taken to be rules specifically addressed by God to the Anglo-Saxon-Celtic peoples.

Howard Rand, a lawyer by training, first published his *Digest of the Divine Law* in 1943; it has been reprinted many times since. Reflecting the events of the Depression and the Second World War, Rand asserted that

> our nation faces a political and economic crisis today. . . . We shall not be able to continue in accord with the old order. Certain groups are already planning an economy of regimentation for our nation; but it will only intensify the suffering and want of the past and bring to our peoples all the evils that will result from such planning by a group of men who are failing to take into consideration the fundamental principles underlying the law of the Lord.

Rand went no further in intimating who these individuals might be. However, his long-standing antipathy toward economic planning, Jews, and racial desegregation suggests that he had some liberal cabal in mind. By way of neutralizing the conspiracy, he offers divine legislation as "the only possible solution which will prevent ultimate economic chaos and political oblivion."[1]

The "divine law" Rand had in mind was not that handed to Moses at Mount Sinai. Regarding Moses as a mere codifier, Rand argued that divine law had existed "from the very beginning of human history." Indeed, he traces its observance back to Job, "a few hundred years after the Deluge," at the same time intimating that it was revealed even earlier as a way of preventing a repetition of the corruption that had provoked the Flood. Despite the alleged antiquity of these rules, heathen empires, beginning with Babylon, insisted on ignoring them, with predictably catastrophic consequences. Yet Rand regarded the punishments visited on law-breaking societies as edifying to the extent that they pushed humanity back toward a Bible-based legal system: "Our economic troubles and the difficulties and trials of the present are for the purpose of compelling a national awakening to this: our responsibility as His Kingdom People." This view was shared by Rand's associate in the Anglo-Saxon Federation, William J. Cameron, who insisted that biblical laws were intended "to be administered as the law of the land."[2]

Rand's and Cameron's Christian Identity successors have continued to advance the same ideas. The Lord's Covenant church, founded by the late Sheldon Emry, distributed a "concordance" of "the laws, statutes, and judgments of God." It consists of an index of scriptural references from the New Testament as well as the Old under an elaborate series of headings and subheadings, ranging from "health laws" to "property laws." Although the compilers do not seek the immediate implementation of the code, its study is enjoined, because "in the New Order Divine Law will become the law of the land." An even stronger position was advanced by Pete Peters of the Church of LaPorte (Colorado), one of the largest and most active Identity churches. A project of Peters's has been the "Remnant Resolves," a statement of principles of governance for Identity believers. The Remnant Resolves Committee sought to register the statement with units of local government, a process that will be examined in a subsequent section of this chapter. For present purposes, however, what is more important is the concept of law articulated in the statement. God is "the Great Lawgiver." His law is "binding . . . on all men, regardless of their political persuasion or personal beliefs." As far as the function of government is concerned, "the role of Civil Authority is to administer God's Law." Since Identity Christians possess "unique access to the knowledge of God and His Truth, they have a responsibility to influence civil law to conform to God's standards."[3]

However, this professed fidelity to divine law carries the potential for violent confrontation with "civil authority." Government, for example, may choose to ignore admonitions that it follow God's law and may act contrary to it. At that point, it loses its legitimacy and, presumably, the claim of Christians to obey it: "Any man or group of men who seek to plunder under the cloak of law, or who seek to negate the Law of God, forfeit their authority, and becomes a despot and a tyrant. They are a *'terror to good works,'* and must be exposed and resisted by whatever means Heaven has provided us." "Resisted by whatever means Heaven has provided us" is both ambiguous and open-ended, suggesting anything from civil disobedience to armed uprising. The position in "Remnant Resolves" carries Rand's and Cameron's views forward to their logical conclusion, by stating that no secular authority can be wholly legitimate, that no legal system is valid unless it incorporates "God's law," and that believers have both the right and obligation to resist. Indeed, at a later point in the "Resolves," the courts and prisons are condemned because they "are being used to hold many men and women without due process of law"—presumably, those who resisted authority. Belief in the Bible as the ultimate legislative authority may be variously regarded as a blueprint for the millennial age, a model to be gradually realized in mundane legal systems, or a source of claims overriding those of worldly government, with whatever political implications that implies.[4]

Although advocates of biblical law proclaim its encompassing character, they invariably concentrate upon its economic implications. This appears to stem from two main causes. First, much of the British-Israel literature that cast the longest shadow over Christian Identity was either published during the Great Depression or shortly thereafter. This was true not only of the work of Rand and Cameron but of David Davidson as well. By the Second World War, Davidson was inveighing against "the Money Power" with the fervor and seemingly the very language of late nineteenth-century American Populism. Second, as Richard Hofstadter has pointed out, economic panaceas have exerted a traditional fascination for the American right. The literature on gold, silver, paper currency, the Federal Reserve System, and related issues is vast, and much of it presumes the existence of a financial conspiracy to subvert American institutions. While the tradition of monetary cranks and economic plots long predates Christian Identity, its very prominence on the American right made it inevitable that its categories would fuse with Identity. Clearly, not all who believe in economic plots believe in Identity doctrines, but a very large proportion of Identity followers believe in economic plots, either because they believed in them before they found Identity or because Identity has facilitated their inclusion in broader right-wing networks.[5]

At the end of April 1933, William J. Cameron, in his address "The Economic Law of God," argued that "Biblical economics" mandated individualism and at the same time produced social justice. It did so primarily through what Cameron saw as God-given principles of taxation and credit. Land, and by extension other forms of property, must not be taxed, nor must that part of the land's produce that its owners consume. "Only the surplus over and above a livelihood was taxed, and that in slight degree." As to credit, "Divine economics" requires that it be given without the payment of interest. *"The creation of credit without the multiplication of debt* is a masterpiece of economic legislation." It is scarcely surprising that ideas such as these should have commended themselves to the desperate victims of a failing economy, nor is it surprising that Cameron, with his obsessive concern for Jewish financial plots, would have made an attack on usury central to his exposition of biblical economic law.[6]

These concepts reappeared in elaborated form in the subsequent writings of Howard Rand, who contrasted, as Wesley Swift was to do later, "the Israel standard" with "this Babylonian system." Relying upon biblical laws concerning weights and measures, Rand concluded that God required a different monetary system, one in which there was "a fixed standard of value in relation to gold and silver." The effect, he believed, would be price stability achieved by expansion in the money supply, the same prescription that had been offered in the late nineteenth century by the Populists. Like them, Rand condemned the demonetization of silver and what he regarded as excessive dependence upon gold. Nebuchadnezzar, he related, had convened "the first great economic conference of which we have any record," and there instituted the gold standard as "the Babylonian system." The answer must be new legislation that would allow silver along with gold to constitute money (for Rand, paper money was mere "currency"), assuring level prices.[7]

The same themes reappeared in exaggeratedly conspiratorial form among later rightists. The Federal Reserve "is the modern version of the 18th century 'Illuminati,'" still seeking "to get control of the monetary power of the major countries of Europe and thus enable the conspirators to create a One-World government." Sheldon Emry, in his pamphlet *Billions for the Bankers*, advanced the same argument as Rand, urging expansion of the money supply in order to stabilize prices and tracing economic iniquities back to Babylon and its gold. Lest the reader miss the numerous cartoons of hook-nosed, bearded Jewish bankers, Emry took note of "the 'almost hidden' conspirators in politics, religion, education, entertainment, and the news media [who] are working for a Banker-owned United States in a Banker-owned world under a Banker-owned World Government!" Pete Peters's "Remnant Resolves" similarly included a resolution for "return to a Biblical economic system" based on "'just weights and measures.'" Instead, at present, America has been "enslaved" by an economic system that contradicts God's law.[8]

Thus both British-Israelism and Christian Identity read the Bible as a mandate for a soft-money policy, excusing or prohibiting debt, and cheap money to place more purchasing power in the hands of individuals. As already noted, both approaches were part of a long-standing current of economic radicalism as likely to be couched in secular as in religious terms. A more volatile, but far less common, variety of economic protest lay in resistance to taxation. Here, too, Cameron and Rand laid the groundwork. Cameron's "Divine system of taxation" rejected property taxes as "a form of piecemeal confiscation." Instead, he read the Bible's references to tithes and offerings as implying a tax only on the produce of the land beyond what was required for the owners' subsistence. He also rejected any taxes imposed on goods during their passage from manufacturer to consumer, since that implied that some would be required to bear the tax burdens of others. Finally, and most curiously, a portion of biblically ordained taxes reverted back to the taxpayer as a fund to cover "vacation trips and attendance upon national and seasonal festivals by himself and family, and for the aid of those temporarily distressed." Written at a point when the Depression was scarcely over, this concept of a divinely sanctioned tax rebate must have appeared particularly attractive.[9]

Howard Rand's "Israel system of taxation" also claimed to be grounded on the biblical system of tithes. Rand's views were similar to those of Cameron, although he drew some distinctive inferences from them. Thus, since property taxes were invalid, and taxes could legitimately be levied only upon "profitable increase," no tax burden could properly fall upon the jobless or destitute, nor could a farm be seized for nonpayment. He noted that "tithe" as "one-tenth" needed qualification, so that it was clear the obligation was to pay one-tenth of earnings, although once that was uniformly done, Rand saw the tenth eventually increasing to a maximum of one-fifth, since the Bible referred to more than one tithe. The result would be a prosperity in which "all men will become capitalists."[10]

Cameron and Rand advocated changes in tax policy but did not advocate resistance to existing tax policy, although they clearly regarded that policy as in violation of God's law. Nonetheless, they were implicitly willing to acquiesce in the "Babylonian system" until increasing piety brought about the desired changes. In this sense, they continued to operate within the existing political and economic system, while advocating alterations to it. Indeed, Cameron, as a ranking Ford executive with many ties to the larger business community, had a vested interest in economic tranquility. However, others in Christian Identity who came after Cameron and Rand were often not content to leave the matter at a critique of existing tax laws. Thus, what some construed as working within the system could for others be a mandate for law violation.

This was certainly the case for Gordon Kahl, the North Dakota Identity farmer who killed two federal marshals and was subsequently himself killed in Arkansas by the FBI in 1983. Kahl ceased paying taxes in 1967, when he wrote the Internal Revenue Service that "he would no longer 'pay tithes to the Synagogue of Satan.'" In a statement Kahl wrote after fleeing the North Dakota murders, he concluded "that our nation has fallen into the hands of alien people. . . . These enemies of Christ have taken their Jewish Communist Manifesto and incorporated it into the Statutory Laws of our country and thrown our Constitution and our Christian Common Law (which is nothing other than the Laws of God as set forth in the Scriptures) into the garbage can." If Kahl was essentially a practitioner of Christian Identity tax resistance, its principal theoretician was William Potter Gale.[11]

In addition to his activities as a Christian Identity preacher and writer, Gale was instrumental in organizing two related political organizations, the United States Christian Posse Association, one of several Posse Comitatus groups; and the Committee of the States, which sought to revive the governmental structure of the Articles of Confederation. Gale began with the proposition that the Articles of Confederation, which shaped the national government from 1781 until 1789, remained in effect even after the adoption of the Constitution. "These articles, being perpetual, remain in effect to this day. They've never been altered, amended nor repealed. They cannot be." Further, in Gale's mind, they were divine: "The source of the Articles of Confederation for a Perpetual Union is the Holy Bible. . . . It contains God's laws for his people, for their nations and their governments. . . . The source is the Bible, otherwise known as the common law." Gale's ideas had a number of elements. First, they incorporated a political fundamentalism not unlike his religious fundamentalism, in the sense that he believed a complete, inerrant account of American government could be derived from the literal texts of charter documents. Second, since "Israel"/America was God's chosen people, God had revealed to it the political truths necessary for its governance. Third, this truth had been concealed or misrepresented by malevolent forces, so that a vast body of constitutional interpretation had obscured the eternal verities of the Articles of Confederation. These principles turned out to have considerable implications for the tax laws.[12]

Gale rejected the entire Internal Revenue Code as "a string of unconstitutional abuses which attempt to require a citizen's consent to the repudiation and violation of his God-given and Constitutional rights." Gale drew from this the ominous inference that all government officials who attempted to enforce the tax code should be "removed from office," by the Posse Comitatus if necessary. Since the loose governmental system of the Articles of Confederation was deemed to still be in effect, Congress had overstepped its bounds in taxing: "The states are sovereign in this Republic. . . . By what authority do they bring any citizen in for willful failure to file a communist graduated income tax, when they, in fact, have no jurisdiction over that sovereign citizen, who is a citizen of a state and a county in a state." Gale then turned his attention to reconstructing what he saw as the only valid governmental structure for the United States.[13]

Gale's ideal polity revolved around two types of organizations, the Committee of the States and an enforcement body termed variously the Posse Comitatus and the Unorganized Militia. The committee was mentioned in the Articles of Confederation as a group appointed by Congress to manage the nation's affairs when Congress was not in session. Gale, however, regarded it as a kind of superlegislature capable of overruling an errant Congress. Consequently, on July 4, 1984, largely at his instigation, a group of right-wing activists met at his California ranch to sign a "Compact," subsequently filed with the county recorder, reestablishing "the Committee of States in Congress," that is, themselves. They quickly concluded that the Congress in Washington, D.C., had overstepped its authority, particularly by taxation, and was in consequence "indicted." For this purpose the Compact contained a provision called the Caveat: "Any interference or attempt to interfere with the functions and activities of this Committee of the States or its delegates by any person or agency of government shall result in the death penalty being imposed upon conviction by said Committee sitting as the Congress of the United States." The enforcement of the penalties in theory devolved upon what Gale sometimes referred to as the Posse and sometimes as the Unorganized Militia (of which he was the chief of staff), consisting of the males in a community between fifteen and forty-five.[14]

Associates of Gale, many of whom had failed to file tax returns, began sending "indictments" and copies of the Caveat to those they regarded as having trespassed on local sovereignty. In October 1986, Gale and five associates were arrested and charged with interfering with the administration of the tax laws by mailing death threats to IRS employees and with threatening the life of a Nevada justice of the peace. On October 2, 1987, all were convicted on all counts. Gale was sentenced to a year and a day in jail with five years' probation, fined five thousand dollars, and assessed four hundred dollars in charges and penalties. He died before the sentence could be carried out.[15]

Clearly, then, the desire to model the American legal system after the legal system supposed to have been authorized by God in the Bible in practice led to behaviors that ranged from advocacy and civil disobedience to attempts to disable the existing system through threats and violence. Examples of intimidation and threats of violence are exclusively found in Christian Identity, and appear never to have been present in British-Israelism itself. In this as in other cases, Christian Identity exhibits a far greater propensity for violence.

The theme of Bible-centered law cannot be left before examining one final element: the striking resemblance between the concept of Bible-centered law in British-Israelism and Christian Identity, on the one hand, and its counterpart among some contemporary evangelicals, on the other. These so-called "Reconstructionists" are part of the dominion theology movement that urges the reconstruction of society on Christian lines prior to the Second Coming. The Reconstructionists, including such figures as Rousas John Rushdoony,

David Chilton, and Gary DeMar, consider biblical law binding and wish to see American law recast in biblical terms. There is, however, no evidence of any connection between the small but influential Reconstructionist movement and the British-Israel or Identity groups considered here. Indeed, there is no evidence that either is even aware of the other. Where British-Israelism drew legal inferences from its claim of Israelite ancestry, Reconstructionism reflects a quite different Calvinist tradition transmitted through Dutch Reformed scholars and institutions. Nonetheless, should Reconstructionism expand beyond its currently small coterie, it may create a climate of opinion from which similar Christian Identity doctrines will inadvertently benefit. Since Reconstructionist leaders are trained intellectuals (something Identity figures are certainly not), the rigor of their approach may confer a halo of respectability on all ideas of Bible-centered law, including Identity's, despite the latter's completely separate origins.[16]

Electoral Politics

Christian Identity has not directly entered the electoral arena. Nonetheless, three individuals with strong Identity connections—James Wickstrom, Tom Metzger, and David Duke—have done so. While Duke's political career has been far more successful and widely reported, all three careers are worth examining because they partake of a process of opportunistic searching, seeking openings and interstices in the political system that may be exploited for larger ideological ends. They found, for example, that loose party organizations and the vagaries of the nominating process allowed individuals with no history of party participation to achieve surprisingly rapid advancement.

Of the three, James Wickstrom was the least successful. He ran for the U.S. Senate in Wisconsin in 1980 and lost but still gathered 16,000 votes; a run for the governorship two years later brought 7,700 votes. In 1974 or 1975 Tom Metzger was ordained as a minister of the New Christian Crusade church, an Identity church founded in 1971 by James K. Warner. As Reverend Tom Metzger, he directed the church's "active arm," the Crusaders, and by July 1976 was listed as a contributing editor of *Christian Vanguard*, the church periodical, where he contributed such articles as "Forming an Identity Sunday School." By November 1977, however, about the time he left the church, he had been dropped from the masthead, and the following month, the church revoked all ordinations and required its clergy to seek new ordination certificates. That mandate appears to coincide with the period in which Metzger was seeking other organizational vehicles.[17]

At about the time Metzger joined the New Christian Crusade church, he had become acquainted with David Duke. He joined Duke's Knights of the Ku Klux Klan about 1975, after he had met Duke at James Warner's home. Metzger maintained simultaneous affiliations with Duke's Klan and Warner's New Christian Crusade church, but as his commitment to the Klan grew, his involvement in the church waned. In late 1979, he and Duke parted company, and Metzger founded a group of his own, the California Knights of the Ku Klux Klan. His falling out with Warner and the church thus occurred sometime between 1977 and 1979. Once he turned his attention exclusively to the Klan, he was no longer "Reverend" Metzger, and Identity themes disappeared from his rhetoric. Metzger's Klan eventually metamorphosed into White American Resistance and then into his present organization, WAR, White Aryan Resistance.[18]

Shortly before Metzger broke with David Duke, he made his first foray into electoral politics. Metzger ran for San Diego County supervisor in 1978. He lost but still accumulated 11,000 votes. In June 1980, he sought the Democratic nomination for a congressional seat, which he won by polling 43,000 votes in the primary. Repudiated by the Democratic party, he lost in the general election. In 1982, Metzger entered the California state Democratic primary in search of a U.S. Senate nomination. While he secured only 2.8 percent of the vote, that nonetheless amounted to 75,593 votes at a time when Metzger's racial views were scarcely a secret.[19]

David Duke's political exploits, of course, received far greater attention, a result both of his greater success and his flair for media coverage. Unlike Metzger, Duke was never as clearly linked to Christian Identity. There is no evidence that he was ever a believer, but he maintained close ties with major Identity figures—ties he found it expedient to deny or minimize as his political ambitions grew. His relationship with James Warner was sufficiently close so that in 1975, Warner became director of information for Duke's Klan. Warner provided new opportunities for Duke to build his reputation as a rising racist leader. When the New Christian Crusade church sponsored a "patriotic conference" in Los Angeles in 1975, the church's (and Warner's) newspaper hailed the appearance of the twenty-four-year-old Duke: "He *already* towers over everyone in the patriotic movement in his ability to speak, convince, debate, and inspire." In 1980, when the post of national chaplain of the Knights of the Ku Klux Klan fell vacant, Duke appointed an Identity preacher, Thom Robb, later pastor of the Church of Jesus Christ and the Christian Identity Church, both in Harrison, Arkansas.[20]

Duke's political career fell into three segments: his activities in Louisiana in the late 1970s; his presidential candidacy in 1988; and his electoral races in Louisiana from 1988 to 1991. Duke ran for the Louisiana State Senate as a Democrat in 1975 and 1979. In the first race, he attracted 11,000 votes, one-third of the total. Four years later, he received almost as many votes, finishing second among four candidates, one of whom was the incumbent, Joseph Tiemann. While Tiemann could claim a two-to-one victory over Duke, Duke ran better against him than challengers had in the past.[21]

Duke ran as a minor party presidential candidate in 1988 on the Populist party ticket. The party had been organized in 1984 by Willis Carto, publisher of the *Spotlight* and head of the Liberty Lobby. As the best-funded anti-Semitic organizer in recent American history, Carto had the resources to try to create an umbrella organization for political efforts by both the Identity and non-Identity right. The 1984 Populist candidate, former Olympic athlete Bob Richards, rejected anti-Semitism, despite the prominence of anti-Semites in the party organization. When these associations became widely known, Richards "virtually quit campaigning." Duke maintained his associations with Willis Carto. Indeed, later, when Duke ran as a successful candidate for the Louisiana legislature, the Populist party was a major source of campaign funds, and when he took office, Carto's personal assistant became his legislative aide.[22]

Four years later, Duke was himself the Populist party's presidential candidate. His original running mate was the flamboyant former Green Beret officer Lieutenant Colonel James "Bo" Gritz, said to have been the model for Rambo. Although Gritz is a Mormon convert, he has had extensive Identity connections. In 1990, he spoke three times at an Identity "camp meeting" sponsored by Peter G. Peters's Scriptures for America and attended by such well-known Identity figures as "Jack" Mohr and James K. Warner. In 1992, Gritz became the Populists' presidential candidate. In an otherwise obscure campaign, Gritz secured national press coverage when he served as a go-between, mediating an armed standoff between law-enforcement officials and an Identity family on an Idaho mountaintop. In 1988, however, Gritz's involvement with Duke turned out to be brief, for Gritz decided to withdraw in order to run (unsuccessfully) for a congressional seat. His place on the ticket was taken by an obscure New Mexican, Dr. Floyd Parker. The Duke-Parker ticket had difficulty securing a place on most state ballots and in fact appeared on only a dozen: Arkansas, Iowa, Kentucky, Louisiana, Minnesota, Mississippi, New Jersey, Pennsylvania, Rhode Island, Tennessee, Vermont, and Wisconsin. They attracted write-in votes in seven others: Arizona, California, Colorado, Florida, Michigan, Missouri, and Oregon. Duke's total national vote was 47,047, roughly .04 percent of the total. The state from which the largest number of votes came was, not surprisingly, Louisiana, where he drew 18,612. The next four, in descending order, were Arkansas (5,146), Kentucky (4,494), Mississippi (4,232), and Pennsylvania (3,444). By any standards, Duke's vote was pathetically small.[23]

Drawing what was perhaps the natural conclusion, that his political base, if any, lay in Louisiana, Duke devoted the rest of his energies to state office, and with some conspicuous success. In January 1989, he won the Republican nomination in a special primary election for a seat in the state House of Representatives from a district in economically depressed Jefferson Parish. He received 3,995 votes, one-third of the total, among seven candidates. His nearest rival managed only 19 percent of the vote. The general election a month later was far closer. Indeed, Duke won by only 234 votes out of 16,688. Narrow though it was, his victory as a major party candidate and his seating in the legislature was a major embarrassment to the Republican party and conferred the appearance of legitimacy on Duke.[24]

While individuals associated with Christian Identity have generally fared poorly at the polls, the electoral process continues to be intermittently attractive to them. Duke's ability not only to mobilize voters but to secure media attention suggests that persons with Identity connections can enter the political mainstream, as long as they avoid overtly religious appeals and soften the most controversial white-supremacist issue positions. Duke's career also suggests that the major factor in electoral success is a candidate's general attractiveness and articulateness rather than past political or religious affiliations.

On the other hand, an inevitable tension arises between the attractions of political success and Identity's fundamentally millenarian character. If the world is believed to be entering the final phase of history, then normal politics becomes trivial and irrelevant. Like other millenarians, including the Fundamentalist-oriented New Christian Right, Identity adherents face a basic dilemma: to the extent that they continue to be committed to a belief in an imminent millennium, politics, with its compromises and its acceptance of the status quo, must be repudiated. On the other hand, if millennial change is delayed, the prospect of partial victories through the political process becomes more attractive, albeit at the price of watering down religious positions. Hence, should Christian Identity members move more decisively into the political arena, perhaps on Duke's coattails, they can only do so by diluting the importance of their millenarian beliefs.

Survivalism

The political positions discussed thus far—reshaping law on a biblical basis and entering electoral politics—imply an active engagement with the political system through lobbying, campaigns, and other conventional modes of participation. As was pointed out at the beginning of the chapter, however, Identity figures have also sometimes opted for political orientations that lie in a gray area between permissible and impermissible behavior. Two will be discussed here—survivalism and an emphasis upon local sovereignty.

"Survivalism" has become an omnibus term for a life-style of physical withdrawal and self-sufficiency that has as its aim surviving some imagined future calamity. The survivalist writer Kurt Saxon, who claims to have coined the term in 1976, defines a survivalist as "one who anticipates the collapse of civilization and wants to save himself and his loved ones and bring something to the movement, if you would, which will contribute to the advancement of the next generation." Survivalists include individuals with a broad array of beliefs. Some are secularists who believe themselves threatened by nuclear war, environmental pollution, or racial conflict. Some are religionists who adopt the so-called post-Tribulationist position, asserting that saved Christians will have to live through the Tribulation instead of being raptured off the earth for this period. Those in this camp, such as Jim McKeever, argue that Christians must be prepared to survive in a hostile and violent world until the Second Coming takes place. But there are also Christian Identity survivalists who anticipate imminent catastrophe and believe that as the self-identified remnant of Israel, they must withdraw from an increasingly dangerous world until such time as their enemies have been defeated. In its most strident form, this dread may be seen in William V. Fowler's advice: "If you GET YOUR GUNS AND AMMUNITION NOW and prepare for war, you have nothing to lose."[25]

In theory, and often in practice, survivalists desire no quarrel with the existing political order. They wish only to be left alone in their rural enclaves, with their stockpiles of food, ammunition, medicine, and other essentials. They may despise their fellow citizens as Pollyannas, but they accept the existing governmental authorities as a fact of life. However, the act of radical withdrawal can engender a siege mentality, a sense that one is surrounded by enemies and that the battle is even now beginning. Thus survivalists are prey to the self-fulfilling prophecy, in the sense that their very preparations may lead them into actions that set them at odds with political authorities.

We can see the variations among Identity survivalists by examining three groups: those associated with Dan Gayman's Church of Israel; John Harrell's

Christian-Patriots Defense League; and James Ellison's Covenant, Sword and Arm of the Lord.

Although rejecting the violence of such groups as the Order (to be considered in the next chapter), Dan Gayman believes that disaster awaits America and that, as a result, "that small remnant of Germanic nordic peoples, the Israel of God," must organize themselves "in self-sufficient groups upon the land and away from the cities. These people will maintain a defensive posture throughout the terror of the revolution." Since the impending "red revolution financed by the anti-Christ money changers" will produce those traditional apocalyptic terrors, famine and pestilence, "families should settle in groups in isolated places across the country, principally west of the Mississippi River. . . . A *return to the land is imperative!* We must learn to become self sufficient. . . . Each group should provide for their own individual needs *in addition* to the group program." This community-formation process will require acts of radical withdrawal but, in theory, can be accomplished without violence.[26]

However, the boundary between detachment from government policies and potential conflict with the authorities is often a difficult line to mark out. Thus, the Church of Israel abjures the advocacy or use of violence and terror, but strongly supports the "Biblical right to keep and bear arms in defense of . . . lives and property." They advocate strict racial segregation, separating the races "as much as is humanly possible to do . . . in a multiracial society." They also oppose being "marked in any way by a government agency at any level of operation." While not rejecting Social Security numbers as such, they reserve the right to reject them should they "become the universal number of identification." Finally, they reject immunization on biblical grounds. Although it is not clear how willing church members would be to press these points against local authorities, the prohibitions are part of the church's official *Articles of Faith* and therefore hold the potential for placing the church in confrontation with civil powers.[27]

The church, however, has concentrated on increasing its self-sufficiency, likening itself to Noah, "build[ing] an *Ark of Safety* in this time of national and world travails." The church seeks to free itself from dependence upon external institutions and upon the larger economy, advocating home birthing rather than hospital birthing, home schooling rather than public schooling, and self-employment. In addition, the church developed a two-hundred-acre organic farm. These enterprises are viewed as doubly beneficial, contributing not only to self-sufficiency but also reducing contact with institutions regarded as contaminating. Thus home birthing is considered safer, part of a larger Identity suspiciousness concerning conventional medicine. Home schooling will protect children "from sex education courses, inoculations, profanity, peer pressure, and one world anti-Christian information presented in the textbooks used in the public schools." Organic farming will protect members from dangerous chemical fertilizers and pesticides.[28]

Because the Church of Israel is a small, locally based organization, it has been able to implement projects that advance its survivalist program. However, survivalism has also been framed in broader terms, aimed at protecting a relatively large area in some future emergency. This approach was most conspicuously advanced by the Christian-Patriots Defense League and its founder, John Harrell. While Harrell himself is not known primarily as a Christian Identity spokesperson, his "minister of defense," "Jack" Mohr, is a visible and prolific Identity writer. The CPDL and the affiliated Christian Conservative church see an America prey to "subversion, nuclear blackmail, nuclear attack, invasion, negotiated treaty, surrender, run-away inflation, famine, or a combination of any two or more." John Harrell therefore proposed the creation of a secure area in the center of the country, "the Golden Triangle," "that may be defended and remain free when the present governmental systems of Mexico, Canada, and the United States collapse or precipitate into an absolutely ruthless Communistic dictatorship." While Harrell conceded that the size of the Triangle might have to be reduced if people are not available to fully defend it, he envisioned an area whose baseline would extend from Texas to northern Florida and whose sides would meet at the Canadian border. Thus the area to be defended would include virtually all of the South, most of the lower Midwest, and a significant part of the upper Midwest.[29]

Unlike Dan Gayman's modest efforts to detach his flock from the surrounding society, Harrell's proposal implies a shadow system of authority over a large portion of the country, clearly beyond either the financial or legal capacities of a private organization. Notwithstanding problems of feasibility, Harrell made a number of proposals to begin implementation of the Golden Triangle plan. Those within its borders should stock up on food and other emergency supplies. They should condition themselves physically, mentally, and spiritually for the coming onslaught, and they should meet with like-minded individuals. To establish an infrastructure for the Triangle, Harrell claimed to have purchased, through an organization known as Outposts of America, rural sites to which the faithful could repair in time of emergency and which could be used for paramilitary and survival training until that time. He left no doubt concerning what he believed to be at stake: "Prepare now, begin this day—whether you be saint or sinner; the storm's almost upon us. Believe it or not,

'We are in training for the Tribulation.' Time is exceedingly short. Remember, it wasn't raining when Noah started building the Ark." The retreatism he advocated goes beyond the creation of small, self-sufficient communities (although it is not incompatible with such efforts) to plan, however fragmentarily, the outlines of a rurally based, militarily potent, parallel structure of authority.[30]

Harrell's plans clearly had a far more substantial existence at the level of rhetoric than at the level of action, if only because of the number of people required to carry them out. A more modest but in the end more politically volatile approach was taken by James Ellison's Covenant, Sword and Arm of the Lord (CSA), which combined the community-organization thrust represented by Gayman with Harrell's paramilitary emphasis. CSA set up perhaps the most militarized of all Identity communal settlements, a place to which other rightists went for training in guerrilla warfare and related skills. Located in northern Arkansas, the community, called Zarephath-Horeb, was established by Ellison in 1976 on a 224-acre tract. Its life effectively ended in 1985, when it was raided by the Bureau of Alcohol, Tobacco, and Firearms. In a series of prosecutions, Ellison was convicted of the manufacture of automatic weapons and acts of bombing and arson. He received a twenty-year prison sentence, and the compound was eventually sold.[31]

The original CSA emphasis was upon developing the capacity to survive the Tribulation, because "those who endure to the end shall be saved!" They anticipated an imminent period in which "the planet earth is about to become the battleground between the forces of God, led by Jesus Christ, King of Kings, Lord of Lords, and the serpent, father of deceit, Satan and his seed, the satanic blood-line Jews and those who have been deceived or bought off." However, the increasing involvement of CSA members and others living at Zarephath-Horeb in felonies, and the ensuing pressure by state and federal law enforcement agencies, led the group to move toward increasingly militant positions. By the late summer of 1984, it appeared to them that "it is inevitable that war is coming to the United States of America. . . . It is predestined!" The recommended response was to meet force with force: "Terror will succeed only until it is met with equal terror!" By late fall, the mood was even more aggressive, and members were told "to attack the enemy at every opportunity." The rhetoric increasingly suggested not merely actions to keep the community and its property intact, but the beginning of the apocalyptic battle itself. This was no longer a time for retreat from the larger society:

> CSA is not content with being "a nation within a nation." We want the outer nation to fall. . . . We strive as much as possible to live peaceably

with all MEN—but not with aliens and traitors! . . . We will lay out the ATTACK [an acronym for Aryan Tactical Treaty for the Advancement of Christ's Kingdom] plan at various Aryan gatherings. The time has come for the Spirit of Slumber to be lifted off our people! Arise, O Israel, and Shine, for thy light is come, and the glory of our Father is risen upon thee! We shall Attack and Advance into enemy territory within the next two years. Be prepared!

Before the two years were up, of course, the community had disbanded and its leader was in custody. In retrospect, the survivalist orientation and the expectation of an imminent Tribulation created a self-fulfilling prophecy. The Zarephath-Horeb population believed itself to be at war, behaved accordingly, and created in the authorities precisely the patterns of behavior the community had predicted, which were now used to justify additional acts of violence. While the story of Zarephath-Horeb was unusual because of its heavily militarized character, the path the community took suggests how unstable the retreatist/survivalist position can be.[32]

Survivalists take steps to cut themselves off from the larger environment because they feel threatened by it. Often that sense of threat engenders nothing more than a desire for solitude and noninvolvement. However, the environment is sometimes characterized as dominated by active and expanding forces of evil, implying that each time separatists attempt to disengage, they will be assailed by these expanding forces of pollution and contamination, whether identified with Jews, blacks, or some other allegedly malevolent force. Those sensitized to see the world as the product of conspiracies easily interpret neutral or ambiguous data as validation of their fears, so that what others construe as innocent may strike them as proof of imminent danger. A world read according to conspiratorial and apocalyptic scenarios may thus lead to courses of action that are anything but retreatist, when a sense of survival and a millenarian view of history seem to demand active engagement with the putative forces of evil. When that occurs, the retreatist leaves his encampment and may violently assault whatever symbols of authority can be found.

Radical Localism

The movement's emphasis upon self-sufficient communities prepared to survive a general calamity reflects a broader emphasis upon the primacy of local political units. This pervasive localism is the product of many elements: hostility toward the policies of the federal government, the inability to mobilize a mass following, and a highly romanticized vision of the past. Thus, many rightists, both Identity and non-Identity, picture a preindustrial past of free Aryan yeoman farmers, governing themselves under a common law that allegedly allowed no outside political intervention in these self-governing rural communities. This medieval dream was then followed, according to the usual scenario, by a long process of corruption in which political and economic centralization reduced the independence of local communities to the vanishing point; it is the aim of contemporary rightists to return to this earlier mythic time.[33]

Identity leaders and groups have sought to assert local primacy in both symbolic and concrete ways. The former includes rhetorical statements of political, moral, and religious principles given the appearance of legality by being registered with county clerks. The latter has consisted of setting up local law-enforcement organizations deemed to be more legitimate than those of state and national governments. Both rest upon a naïve contractarianism that assumes politically and legally valid decisions may be taken by the mere fact of agreement, even if the agreement takes place outside constitutionally mandated channels.

On July 11, 1982, fifty-nine members of right-wing organizations met in northern Idaho to sign a document entitled the Nehemiah Township Charter and Common Law Contract. In certain respects it prefigured William Potter Gale's 1984 Compact, but where the Compact attempted to resuscitate the Articles of Confederation, the Nehemiah Township Charter concentrated on the legal arrangements to be instituted in a local community of "Aryan Freemen." Where Gale's political fundamentalism was directed toward the text of the Articles, the charter adopted a legal fundamentalism in its attempt to reconstruct ancient Anglo-Saxon law. The document was replete with references to "socage," "scutage," and "wergild." The signatories included figures well known in Identity circles, including Richard Girnt Butler, Thom Arthur Robb, and Robert Miles. Randolph Duey, later a prominent member of the Order, and Carl Franklin, Jr., who eventually succeeded Butler as head of Aryan Nations, also signed. The charter drafters set a pattern repeated with the Compact and with the "Remnant Resolves" (considered below) by filing the document with the recorder of Kootenai County. This gave it the appearance of official recognition, while also connecting the charter with the one jurisdiction the Identity right has always acknowledged to be valid, the county.[34]

The charter signers professed the desire to "covenant and combine ourselves together into a Civil Body Politic for our better ordering and preservation under and by GOD's Law." They did so in clear Identity fashion by invoking "our Father and God, YAHWEH, YAHSHUA, JESUS THE CHRIST, the only rightful originator of Law." The polity envisioned was for "the preservation, protection and sustenance of our Aryan Race." Only "white freem[e]n" could be members. Much of the document was devoted to describing the community's legal system, which was to have sole jurisdiction over the conflicts among its members. While these provisions sometimes appeared to be no more than a private, alternative dispute-resolution mechanism, other articles made clear that the township's courts would brook no opposition from existing units of government.[35]

Any conflicts between the claims of Nehemiah Township and the county, state, and federal governments would have to be resolved in the township's favor. Thus, the township would determine for itself whether and when it was "subject to 'equity' enforced by municipal governments or federal governments." If these demands violated "GOD's Law," they would be rejected. The township would decide for itself whether the laws of any governmental unit would be enforced within its boundaries. "No member of this Association or Guilds shall be bound by State, Municipal, local, or Federal statute, ordinance, usage, or taxation except as he himself may will." Lest this implied claim of sovereignty appear ambiguous, the charter gave the township the right to "conduct diplomacy for peace, [and] declare and wage war against the enemies of our Race and our God."[36]

Nehemiah Township consequently claimed for itself the prerogatives of a miniature state. Its instrumentalities for doing so were to be—as they would be later for William Potter Gale—the Posse Comitatus and the Militia. If the local sheriff agreed to command the Posse Comitatus for the purpose of enforcing God's laws, he could function as its leader; if not, the Posse would choose its own officers. To the extent that the Posse and the Militia could be differentiated, the former "shall confine its activities to the Shire wherein it is chartered" (except in times of war or rebellion), while the Militia would be free to operate anywhere its services were required. Officials of other governments, particularly state and federal officials, were to be subject to trial in the township's courts if their behavior warranted.[37]

It is difficult to know how the charter was meant to be taken, whether merely as a solemn statement of ideal future political and legal arrangements or as the blueprint for an imminent challenge to authority. If the drafters intended to try to implement it in the immediate future, their timing was poor. Robert Mathews organized the Order in late September 1983, fourteen months after the charter was signed, and in the same area. As actual violence supplanted rhetorical violence, federal pressure on the Identity right in the Pacific Northwest increased dramatically, and greatly increased the risks of trying to implement a plan as confrontational as the Nehemiah Township Charter.

A similar but far less confrontational project was undertaken in the late 1980s by Pete Peters through the "Remnant Resolves," an effort "to awaken and stimulate slumbering Christians to action as Christian soldiers." The "Resolves" consisted of a series of positions on political, economic, legal, and moral issues which together constituted a "covenant . . . to establish the Lordship of the God of Israel." Among the thirty-eight separate resolutions were statements asserting the submission of wives to husbands, the Christian character of America, the need for "scriptural" methods of taxation, opposition to abortion, "sodomy," and interracial marriage, and opposition to Jews holding public office ("It is blasphemous to regard antichrists as 'God's chosen people' and allow them to rule over or hold public office in a Christian Nation"). In addition to the general aim of rousing Christians to action, the "Remnant Resolves" project sought to file the statement of principles "in every one of the 3,049 county courthouses in the nation. . . . This is an important action because it makes the Resolves a matter of public record—an official document, as it were. Furthermore, it does so at a level of government which is closest to the people." The effort reflected Identity's ambivalent attitude toward government, which is generally regarded as corrupt and controlled by a Jewish conspiracy but whose local manifestations continue to be idealized as a survival of a mythic Anglo-Saxon past. Nonetheless, even local governments might find themselves targeted if they fail to fulfill their duty. As one "Remnant Resolves" supporter put it, "When government officials ignore your Resolves, we must be ready with 'Plan B' which will serve notice that we intend to obtain our objectives UNLESS the Lord Himself stops us."[38]

"Plan B" was in fact already in existence in many areas in the form of the Posse Comitatus movement. Posse Comitatus groups were always fragmented, not only because they appear to have emerged at the same time at different sites but also because their ideology demanded fragmentation. "Posse Comitatus"—literally, the "power of the county"—technically refers to citizens summoned by a law-enforcement official in order to deal with lawbreaking. As interpreted by the founders of the Posse Comitatus movement, the Posse represents the only legitimate legal authority, since Posse Comitatus members reject any authority above the county level. Further, the ideology of Posse Comitatus holds that the adult males in a county may constitute themselves as a posse and enforce the law according to their lights.

Posse Comitatus organizations began to appear about 1969 and can claim two separate but almost simultaneous beginnings, one in Portland, Oregon, under Henry L. "Mike" Beach, and the other in southern California under William Potter Gale. While Posse Comitatus is not an Identity movement per se, Identity figures have been extremely prominent in it. The extent of Mike Beach's Identity commitment is unclear. In the interwar period he had been a member of William Dudley Pelley's Silver Shirts, and, as we have seen, Pelley was drawn to some elements of British-Israelism. During the 1970s, after Beach had established his Posse organization, the Citizen's Law Enforcement and Research Committee, he reprinted material originally published in C. A. L. Totten's *Our Race* series. William Potter Gale, of course, was one of the triumvirate of early Identity ministers in California, along with Bertrand Comparet and Wesley Swift. An Identity minister, James Wickstrom, was a highly visible Posse figure in Wisconsin, and Richard Girnt Butler led the Kootenai County, Idaho, Posse Comitatus from 1974 to 1976, when its members rebelled against what they considered his high-handed leadership.[39]

Gale formed the United States Christian Posse Association as an offshoot of his Ministry of Christ church. Like other Posse supporters, Gale insisted that "the County Sheriff is the only legal law enforcement officer in the United States of America." Like them, as well, Gale argued that the acts of higher governmental officials were often unconstitutional, null and void, particularly where taxation was involved, and that it was the duty of the sheriff and his Posse to oppose such state and federal actions. But Gale placed his distinctive stamp on the Posse by tying it directly to Identity theology. The United States "emerges as a direct result of the militant advance of the Kingdom of God, holding aloft a triumphant banner—the Name of Yhvh [*sic*] our Yashua, He whom we call Jesus the Christ." Since the United States was, according to Gale, a Christian nation, its law-enforcement apparatus had to reflect its essentially religious character. Gale's associate, Colonel Ben Cameron, expanded upon Gale's ideas. According to Cameron, when the Bible required Israel to observe the Lord's statutes and possess the land God had given to his people, Scripture was in fact referring to the legal obligations of Christians in "the NEW JERUSALEM, the United States of America." "The People known today as Christians," wrote Cameron, "are the People of the Bible and are literal descendants of the God of this nation, Jesus Christ." In Cameron's view "the PEOPLE are the Church," and consequently, the people mobilized in the form of the Posse Comitatus is the church manifested as a governing body. In conjunction with the Compact and the Committee of States, which Gale oversaw in 1984, the Posse was part of a governmental scheme that was at once theocratic and radically decentralized. Constitutional arrangements, laws, and enforcement mechanisms were all traced directly to God. Thus, the Posse was doing the Lord's work when it acted against evildoers. At the same time, by tying the Posse to his belief in the eternal, divine, and irrevocable character of the old Articles of Confederation, Gale conceived of a national government far different from the one that actually evolved. It would be more a shell than a government, with so many powers reserved to localities as to make them in fact and in name sovereignties accountable to no national institutions.[40]

It was central to the Posse Comitatus movement, therefore, that every county organization was independent, a veritable law unto itself, subject only to its own understanding of what God required in a particular time and place. The danger lay in a group of heavily armed men acting as a vigilante band, for vigilantes too claimed to represent the true law as against its allegedly corrupt official representatives. Thus Gordon Kahl, the North Dakota farmer who killed two federal marshals in 1983, was an Identity believer who had organized a Posse chapter. Kahl also embraced radical localism in his efforts to set up Continental Township, a shadow government in the Medina, North Dakota, area that would preserve order when the expected political, economic, and social collapse occurred. The shootings occurred immediately after a meeting of the township's supporters.[41]

Radical localism thus might take the essentially rhetorical form of such documents as the Nehemiah Township Charter and the "Remnant Resolves." But it might also manifest itself as an armed force in potential opposition to the power of the state, as the Posse Comitatus chapters often did. Hence, Identity political strategies have had a way of slipping from permissible to impermissible spheres of conduct, and back again. Biblicizing American law might be advanced as no more than intellectual exercises or conventional lobbying, but by questioning the legitimacy of, for example, the state's power to tax, might also create the rationale for illegal acts by others. Conversely, electoral politics might serve as an avenue of legitimation for those previously tainted by extremist associations, as was the case with David Duke. Retreatists in their survivalist enclaves might carry on their distinctive life-styles merely by restricting their contacts with nonbelievers, but they might also become so wedded to the belief that they constitute an encircled, besieged remnant that the use of armed force appears inevitable. In somewhat the same manner, the radical localists, insistent that only local government is legitimate, could by stages be drawn into violent confrontations with state and federal authorities.

Consequently, while all the political approaches discussed in this chapter can be utilized in legal, constitutionally protected ways (one could be a radical localist without being a member of Posse Comitatus), even those activities engaged in within the system have had a way of slipping into law violation. They have also sometimes fed more grandiose and manifestly illegal political designs—particularly plots to overthrow the federal government and proposals for outright territorial secession, ideas to which we turn in the following chapter.

As we saw in the preceding chapter, many political activities that are legally permissible may be transformed into illegal activities by individuals certain they are targets of a diabolical conspiracy. Believing that they face imminent disaster, they feel the need to strike out at the imagined adversary before it is too late. Many of the violent confrontations between Identity believers and law-enforcement personnel have arisen when Identity members perceived themselves to be encircled by enemies.

However, in addition to political activities that retain a potential for such violent transformation, Identity rightists have also advocated and occasionally engaged in conduct that is manifestly outside the realm of sanctioned politics. Two such types of activity will be examined here. The first is the organization and practice of guerrilla insurgency for the purpose of either igniting a popular struggle against federal authority or wearing that authority down in a war of attrition. The second is the widely publicized plan to organize an "Aryan" state in the Pacific Northwest that would achieve independence by seceding from the United States. Advocating such a scheme is, of course, protected by the First Amendment. However, it is virtually impossible to imagine its implementation without open rebellion.

The Turner Diaries

Both ideas have roots in a work of fiction, the underground right-wing novel, *The Turner Diaries*. While not an Identity work per se, it has circulated so widely and been cited so frequently and approvingly in Identity circles that its importance to the movement is unquestioned. While *The Turner Diaries* purports to be the work of one

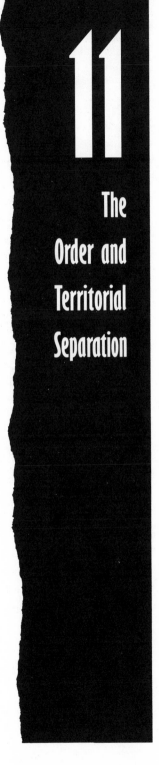

11

The Order and Territorial Separation

"Andrew MacDonald," it was written by William L. Pierce. Pierce received a doctorate in physics at the University of Colorado and taught briefly at Oregon State University. He worked for Pratt and Whitney before becoming an aide to George Lincoln Rockwell, the leader of the American Nazi party. After Rockwell's assassination in 1967, Pierce became associated with the National Youth Alliance (NYA). The alliance grew out of the activities of Willis Carto, one of the best funded and most indefatigable right-wing organizers. In 1968 Carto had been instrumental in founding the alliance as an anti-Semitic outgrowth of a campaign organization originally associated with Governor George Wallace, Youth for Wallace. Once Carto had created the new NYA, it became increasingly strident in its racism and anti-Semitism. However, the NYA was itself unstable, for it quickly divided into one wing dominated by Carto and another dominated by Pierce. By 1971 the NYA had split. Carto's faction was renamed Youth Action, and Pierce's eventually, in 1974, shortened its name to National Alliance.[1]

The Turner Diaries first appeared in serial form in the National Alliance publication *Attack!* between 1975 and 1978. The first paperbound version of the novel was published by the Alliance in 1978. The book purports to be a diary kept by its eponymous hero, Earl Turner, from the fall of 1991 until the period immediately before his death a little more than two years later. Turner finds himself repelled by new gun-control legislation (the novel's fictional Cohen Act), by ever-more-drastic forms of racial integration, and by a variety of urban ills attributed to blacks and Jews. A reluctant revolutionary, Turner nonetheless eventually finds and joins a clandestine group, the Organization, dedicated to unseating the existing government. In time, he is also admitted to the Organization's quasi-monastic inner circle, the Order. While *The Turner Diaries* concentrates upon the mechanics of insurgency rather than upon religious beliefs, just prior to his initiation into the Order, Turner states, "I understand the deepest meaning of what we are doing. I understand now why we *cannot* fail, no matter what we must do to win and no matter how many of us must perish in doing it. Everything that has been and everything that is yet to be depend on us. We are truly the instruments of God in the fulfillment of His Grand Design." The initiation ceremony itself is an affair of robes, candles, and oaths, which leaves Turner feeling that "today I was, in a sense, born again." After combat begins, he participates in the successful seizure of most of southern California, from which nonwhites are quickly expelled.[2]

The Organization has also seized Vandenberg Air Force Base, with its nuclear missiles. Turner's assignment is to help carry a set of nuclear warheads to the outskirts of Washington. The racial enclave in California will be secured by emplacing nuclear weapons around the country, in areas still controlled by "the System," and detonating a few to demonstrate their deterrent effect. In a final suicide mission, Turner flies a small plane armed with one of the warheads into the Pentagon. Thereafter, as an epilogue explains, the System begins to disintegrate, and in time, the Organization comes to control first North America and then Europe. In a genocidal assault on nonwhite areas of the world, "the Organization resorted to a combination of chemical, biological, and radiological means, on an enormous scale, to deal with the problem. Over a period of four years some 16 million square miles of the earth's surface, from the Ural Mountains to the Pacific and from the Arctic Ocean to the Indian Ocean were effectively sterilized." *The Turner Diaries* is not a Christian Identity tract. Indeed, Pierce made clear in a later novel, *Hunter*, that he held Identity in the same contempt as other supernatural religions. As one of *Hunter*'s characters puts it, "The reason they can't recruit anyone but uneducated hicks is that their doctrine is crazy." Notwithstanding Pierce's low opinion of Identity, however, *The Turner Diaries* had great appeal to Identity readers, who saw it as another demonstration that the Jews are the enemy, victory is assured, and those dedicated to the racial struggle are doing God's work.[3]

Pierce's novel was in certain respects curiously similar to another work of political fiction, virtually contemporaneous with it but of a vastly different ideological character—Ernest Callenbach's *Ecotopia*, which has been to the radical environmental movement what *The Turner Diaries* has been to the racist right. Like *Turner*, *Ecotopia* purports to present a first-person account, in this case the notebooks of William Weston, the first outsider allowed to visit the new environmentalist country of Ecotopia. As in *Turner*, the secessionist nation was carved out of sections of the West Coast, in this case the northern as opposed to the southern section. Although the Ecotopians have no desire to kill their enemies, they too use nuclear means to assure independence: "It was . . . believed that at the time of secession they had mined major Eastern cities with atomic weapons which they had constructed in secret or seized from weapons research laboratories. Washington, therefore, although it . . . mined their harbors, finally decided against an invasion." The parallels are all the more curious in light of the fact that *Ecotopia* was first published in condensed form in Oregon, Pierce's former home, in 1975, the year in which the serialization of *The Turner Diaries* began. However, there is no way of knowing whether Callenbach's utopian novel influenced Pierce, or whether the two authors independently hit upon nuclear terrorism as the means by which small and militarily weak groups of dissidents could overwhelm or hold at bay vastly more powerful adversaries.[4]

Since *The Turner Diaries* is cast as a narrative, with only a few brief ideological digressions, it appeals to an audience that may agree about little else beyond the inferiority of nonwhites and the irremediable evil of Jews. Most attractive to its readers is the book's scenario for attaining power, since it argues that a very small but highly committed group can compensate for its initial lack of numbers and resources by strength of will, stealth, and other attributes associated with unconventional warfare.

The Order

In September 1983, *The Turner Diaries*' premises took actual form with the founding, in Metaline Falls, Idaho, of an organization most often referred to as the Order but more commonly known to its members as the Bruders Schweigen, or Silent Brotherhood (it will be referred to here as the Order). It was founded by Robert Mathews, a clean-cut young man originally from Arizona with a history of right-wing associations that began in high school. Mathews sought to create a small, tightly knit group with the will and resources to overthrow "ZOG," the "Zionist Occupation Government." This group would first require money and then arms to begin the campaign of guerrilla actions that would, in his view, eventually stimulate a mass uprising of the white population. To this end, the Order engaged in large-scale counterfeiting and armed robbery. In July 1984, members of the Order stole $3.8 million from a Brinks armored car in Ukiah, California. Mathews contributed significant sums to a number of right-wing causes and individuals, some associated with Christian Identity, including, it is thought, $10,000 for Dan Gayman. The bulk of the money, however, was never traced or recovered. In addition to filling its coffers, the Order also engaged in other acts of violence, most conspicuously the murder in 1984 of Alan Berg, a Jewish radio talk-show host in Denver well known for baiting rightists on the air. Berg was a last-minute substitute for the original assassination target, Morris Dees, founder of the Southern Poverty Law Center. The FBI ultimately traced Mathews to Whidbey Island, Washington, where on December 8, 1984, he was killed in a dramatic shoot-out. The other members of the Order were apprehended during 1985 and 1986 and reached plea agreements with the government or were tried and convicted.[5]

This very brief description of the Order's history raises three questions relevant in the present context. What was the relationship between the organization and the secret society described in *The Turner Diaries*? What was Robert Mathews's own religious orientation? What was the relationship of the Order to Christian Identity?

There is strong circumstantial evidence to suggest that the Order was consciously modeled after the organization described in William Pierce's book. Mathews had joined Pierce's own organization, the National Alliance, in 1980 and is known to have spoken about the *Diaries* well before founding the Order. In the novel, the insurrectionist group referred to as "the Organization" contains within it "a select, inner structure" known as "the Order," to which Earl Turner is admitted. Mathews told potential members that his organization was patterned after the fictional group, and handed out copies of the book to his members. James Aho traces numerous parallels between the fictional and actual groups, including the use of code names, the creation of "hit lists," the execution of unreliable members, and the initiation of members through ritual oath taking. He concludes that the modeling was conscious, despite statements of some Order members to the contrary. Earl Turner's oath taking is described in detail, but the text of the oath is not given. The Order oath, reproduced at one of the subsequent trials, leaves little doubt concerning the group's goals:

I, as a free Aryan man, hereby swear an unrelenting oath upon the green graves of our sires, upon the children in the wombs of our wives, upon the throne of God Almighty, sacred be His Name . . . to join together in holy union with those brothers in this circle and to declare forthright that, from this moment on, I have no fear of death, no fear of foe, that I have a sacred duty to do whatever is necessary to deliver our people from the Jew and bring total victory to the Aryan race. I, as an Aryan warrior, swear myself to complete secrecy to the Order and total loyalty to my comrades. Let me bear witness to you, my brothers, that should one of you fall in battle, that I will see to the welfare and well-being of your family. Let me bear witness to you, my brothers, that should one of you be taken prisoner, I will do whatever is necessary to regain your freedom. Let me bear witness to you, my brothers, that should an enemy agent hurt you, I will chase him to the ends of the earth and remove his head from his body. And furthermore, let me witness to you, my brothers, that if I break this oath, let me forever be cursed upon the lips of our people as a coward and an oath breaker. My brothers, let us be His battle axe and weapons of war. Let us go forth by ones and twos, by scores and by legions, and as true Aryan men with pure hearts and strong minds face the enemies of our faith and our race with courage and determination. We hereby invoke the blood covenant, and declare that we are in a full state of war and will not lay down our weapons until we have driven the enemy into the sea and reclaimed the land which was promised to our fathers of old, and through his will and our blood, becomes the land of our children to be.

The oath bears all the hallmarks of Mathews's other brief writings, reaching as it does for an elevated style and an invocation of primeval themes. There is certainly nothing in it that contradicts Identity teaching, but neither is it a plainly Identity text, which raises the issue of Mathews's own religious beliefs.[6]

A lapsed Mormon convert, Mathews managed to leave behind a blurred picture of his own religious convictions and loyalties. A Fundamentalist preacher, Bob LeRoy, records an interview with Mathews's wife, Debbi, in 1989, in which she said that "her husband was not any special religion." Kevin Flynn and Gary Gerhardt, the most ambitious journalistic chroniclers of the Order, indirectly confirm this statement by describing Mathews's religion as a private pastiche of elements drawn from numerous sources, including Odinism, the putative religion of pre-Christian Norse peoples, which they consider the dominant element. Others—notably his mistress, Zillah Craig, by whom he had a child—have been at pains to link him more explicitly to Identity. Craig was herself an Identity believer. Mathews told her he was as well, but Flynn and Gerhardt imply that he did so primarily to ingratiate himself with her. However that may be, Craig has maintained the position. In a 1991 television interview, when asked whether Mathews was a member of her church, she replied: "He did say that he'd been to Aryan Nations in Idaho. And their beliefs were similar to what mine are." Mathews had briefly attended Richard Girnt Butler's services, but seems to have let this connection lapse. However, after the Brinks robbery in Ukiah, when discussing the disposition of the loot, he told his members, in good Identity style, that "we must share what Yahweh has given us." All that one can conclude is that Mathews had some familiarity with Identity, and sometimes represented himself as a believer, without evincing any continuing interest in either its doctrines or its churches.[7]

If there is uncertainty concerning Robert Mathews's commitment to Identity, there is substantially less doubt concerning the Identity links of the Order's members and sympathizers. When the organization was first detected by law-enforcement officials, they assumed that it was completely made up of

Identity believers, although subsequent investigation revealed that this was not the case. Thus a memorandum from the Butte, Montana, field office of the FBI to "All Agents" on October 2, 1984, correctly attributed a string of western crimes to a single group, but misidentified the group. The memorandum traced both the crimes that had been committed and the goal of insurrection to the Aryan Nations and its religious affiliate, the Church of Jesus Christ Christian. Although a quarter of the Order's recruits was ultimately made up of persons with Aryan Nations or Church of Jesus Christ Christian associations, the organization as such was never an arm of either. The Order eventually grew to almost forty members, although some individuals had relatively tenuous connections. In time, tensions arose between committed Identity believers and others in the organization. Mathews attempted to smooth these over (his invocation of "Yahweh" is best seen in this light), but in the end, he had to recognize the reality of the cleavage. Although the Order never split, it did divide into Identity and non-Identity wings. The Identity branch, consisting of sixteen men, women, and children, was led by Bruce Carroll Pierce, an Aryan Nations member.[8]

However, Aryan Nations was not the only Identity organization with which the Order maintained ties. Two key members of the Order, David Lane and Robert Merki, attended Pete Peters's Church of LaPorte, an important Identity congregation. Through Lane, Robert Mathews met Zillah Craig, who had also attended services in LaPorte. Lane, who subsequently drove the getaway car in the Alan Berg assassination, brought Mathews to Peters's church several times. He also wrote prolifically for the Identity press, both before and after his arrest. In a "statement to the world" on behalf of "the twelve loyal soldiers of the Holy Order of the Bruder Schweigen," Lane restated the Order's mission in Identity terms, incorporating the key concepts of a divine racial "seedline" that identifies God's chosen and the battle between the divine seedline and the Devil's Jewish progeny: "We declare our God-given right as descendents and members of the seedline who founded these United States to continue our racial existence . . . so that our people may fulfill the mission allotted them by the Creator of the universe." Lane sees the Jews ("the devil's children") as very nearly omnipotent, controlling "the media, finance, politicians, government, and judiciary of almost all nations." Yet notwithstanding his Manichaean vision of the world, he assumes that in the end God rather than the Devil will triumph. However, one detects in Lane, as in many other Identity writers, a deeper pessimism, a fear that their millenarian hopes will ultimately be submerged by a more powerful demonic principle.[9]

Once law-enforcement agencies and the courts had broken the Order,

Identity writers outside the organization began to reflect on the experience. Some glorified it, treating Robert Mathews as a holy martyr to the racialist cause. In a eulogy published by Aryan Nations, Robert Mansker saluted Mathews as one of the first casualties in the "Final Battle," a phrase frequently used by Identity to refer to the ultimate struggle between Aryans and Jews: "One hundred keys to heaven and they were all yours! Yahweh has surely Blessed thee above thy brothers and sisters! Now thou art in his Arms, thy battle fought and thy race run! Hallelujah!" Mansker assured Mathews that "we shall continue on. . . . We shall bring forth the Kingdom you so longed for, and we shall sit with thee in it!" Not all in Identity, however, were willing to heap such fulsome praise on Mathews and his followers. A strong dissent came from Dan Gayman of the Church of Israel, despite the fact that he had been a likely recipient of Mathews's largesse after the Ukiah robbery.[10]

In the Church of Israel's *Articles of Faith*, published in 1982, just before the Order was organized, Gayman had rejected the violence as an instrument of Identity ends: "We *do not* advocate, nor do we believe in the use of violence for any cause. We *deplore all acts of terror* and believe that they that live by the sword will die by the sword. . . . Christians do have a moral and Biblical right to keep and bear arms in defense of their lives and property." After the unraveling of the Order, Gayman directly addressed it, speaking on behalf of the church: "This body of Christian believers [does] not believe in and would not condone crimes including counterfeiting, armed robbery, murder of law officers, and a variety of other crimes spawned by the ORDER and openly condoned and sometimes encouraged by a variety of militant organizations and groups throughout the United States." Indeed, Gayman directly blamed the Order not only for its criminal activities but for weakening Identity organizations. While asking his readers to pray for the incarcerated Order members, he asserted that "no singular group in post World War II history has done so much to discredit, malign, and retard the growth of the Gospel of the Kingdom in North America." Gayman's criticism of the Order was also a thinly veiled attack on such movement rivals as Richard Girnt Butler, with whom so many Order members had been associated. Gayman, who testified as a prosecution witness at the Fort Smith sedition trial of right-wing figures in 1987, asked believers to "pray . . . for the ministers whose rebellious counsel caused them to take the path of unlawful resistance."[11]

A less direct repudiation of the Order came from the Association of the Covenant People, a British Columbia–based Identity organization with a significant following across the border in the Pacific Northwest. The association was a direct outgrowth of the British-Israel group in Vancouver that had played such a critical role in reshaping British-Israel doctrine in the 1940s and spreading it along the West Coast (a process described in chapter 4). In the fall of 1985, after the apprehension of Order members, the association found it necessary to respond to "recent media reporting on Para-Military and Neo-Nazi groups who call themselves 'Identity.'" Its statement identified it as "an autonomous body" with "no affiliation with any other organization." As "a Christian scholarly society," it declared itself "not aligned with any political persuasion" and protected under Canadian law to worship and express itself freely.[12]

Reactions to the Order episode clearly reflected a schism in the movement between groups oriented toward withdrawal, such as the Church of Israel, and those that took an activist stance, such as Aryan Nations/Church of Jesus Christ Christian. On the other hand, the breakdown between sympathizers and opponents of the Order was never so neat. Thus, there were numerous links between the Order and the survivalist Covenant, Sword and Arm of the Lord, some of whose members were affiliated with the Order and which provided sanctuary for some Order fugitives.[13]

The failure of the Order to accomplish more than a minimal fundraising goal and the comprehensive character of the subsequent prosecutions clearly had a chastening effect. Those who were not repelled because of moral scruples about violence concluded that, at least for the foreseeable future, recourse to guerrilla activity posed problems beyond anything suggested by *The Turner Diaries*. Perhaps not coincidentally, therefore, the years immediately following the collapse of Robert Mathews's organization saw a burst of enthusiasm for another approach, equally ambitious but seemingly not directed at the violent overthrow of the government: territorial separation.

Territorial Separation

While the views of separatists diverge on certain points, all agree that short of overthrowing ZOG, the best path for the racialist right lies in somehow carving out a separate state. This new entity, referred to variously as the "Aryan Nation," "white American bastion," and "homeland," is almost always located in the Pacific Northwest, although the proposed boundaries have fluctuated. In one sense, no doubt, the choice of the Northwest reflected accidental and expediential factors: the migration of some major Identity figures, such as Richard Girnt Butler, from California to the Northwest; the availability of cheap land in areas of low population density; and the absence of large Jewish and black communities. However, a sense of the area's separateness appears to have developed independently of rightists' political aspirations. Eckard Toy points out that in the nineteenth century for many in the East, "the exploration and acquisition of the Pacific Northwest renewed the national promise in a place far distant from the corrupting influences of slavery, immigration, Catholicism, and the factory." In keeping with this tradition, white supremacists seemed to believe that within this region, they could definitively cut themselves off from everything they loathed in the larger American society.[14]

This sense of separateness was reflected in contemporary perceptions of the region by observers entirely removed from the white-supremacist ambience. In 1981, the reporter Joel Garreau sought to remap North America as nine distinct "nations," each with special attitudinal, cultural, and economic characteristics that cut across state and provincial boundaries. Garreau's mapping did not precisely match the territorial claims later made by Robert Miles, Richard Girnt Butler, and others, but it captured much of the sense of regional difference. Garreau saw the Pacific Northwest as part of two "nations." One, "Ecotopia" (the name borrowed from the Ernest Callenbach novel discussed above), was a coastal strip of ecological activism stretching from Santa Barbara north to Alaska. The other, much closer to right-wing preferences, was a vast interior territory of great mineral resources but few people. Garreau, reminded of the Arabian Desert, christened it "the Empty Quarter." Garreau's Empty Quarter stretched from northern Arizona to arctic Canada and from just east of Seattle to the North Dakota border, and skirted the grain-growing areas of the Canadian prairie provinces to encompass northern Canada up to northern Quebec. Garreau recognized in this sparsely populated region something of the same blank slate that later attracted rightists: "It represents to a lot of people," he found, "a freedom that is meaningful only when compared to the confines of the city." The Ecotopia of Callenbach's 1975 novel was in fact a good deal closer to Identity preferences: Washington, Oregon, and northern California, missing only the crucial Idaho panhandle where many Identity believers have clustered.[15]

Although Richard Girnt Butler advocated a territorial "homeland" as early as 1980, selection of the Northwest came later. Butler originally thought in terms of a midwestern location similar to John Harrell's Golden Triangle. While Butler switched to a preference for the Northwest by 1986, the original suggestion for the Northwest appears to have come from the dualist pastor Robert Miles as early as 1982.[16]

Miles called his idea the "Mountain Free State." Unlike Callenbach's Ecotopia but like Garreau's Empty Quarter, it avoided the coastal strip; Miles thought it too vulnerable to nuclear attack and too racially diverse. The Free

State would contain "all of Washington, all of Oregon, all of Idaho except for the corner southeast of Pocatello perhaps because of the large Mormon population, most of Nevada and California north of Santa Barbara." He also implied that "most of Montana" would be included as well. By 1985, however, Miles had changed his territorial demands to Washington, Oregon, Idaho, Montana, and (newly included) Wyoming. California and Nevada no longer figured in the plan, nor did Miles pay any attention to excluding the coastal fringe.[17]

However the territory was configured, it invited comparison with the Golden Triangle. In 1982, when Miles was more preoccupied with nuclear war, he sought to justify the Mountain Free State's boundaries in terms of relative freedom from attack. Since he then assumed that U.S.-Soviet nuclear war was inevitable, he sought to anticipate "impact areas" and plot bands of potential radioactive contamination. He assumed the five principal impact areas would be Seattle, Los Angeles, New Orleans, Chicago, and the Boston–New York–Washington megalopolis. After drawing impact circles and contamination bands, he concluded that the remaining areas would be "sanctuaries," including both his Free State and Harrell's midwestern Golden Triangle. His only reservations about the latter had to do with the possibility that in the postattack period, the Triangle would be a mixture of "strong state governments, many areas with chaos, and some Free State Republics." Hence, the Golden Triangle was compatible with a Mountain Free State in the Pacific Northwest, since Aryan communities would develop in the Triangle, and possibly even in the South, and thus would open the possibility of collaboration among many independent white units.[18]

By 1985, however, Miles began to have serious doubts about the Triangle as a locus for homelands. The Golden Triangle "is intriguing but illusionary." His change of heart appears to have been the result of a greatly diminished expectation of nuclear attack. If territories did not have to be evaluated in the context of a postattack environment, then they might appear very different. As far as the Triangle was concerned, it was too important for ZOG to give up "without a bitter and a protracted struggle." Its lack of a geographically defined boundary made it militarily indefensible, and "it has no outlet to the sea," a point Miles clearly regarded as a defect, suggesting that the newly configured Mountain Free State would include the Washington and Oregon coastlines instead of beginning thirty miles east of Seattle.[19]

In 1986, Tom Metzger's White Aryan Resistance (WAR) offered still another map, based on discussions at the Aryan Nations Congress that year, where Miles had spoken about his territorial plans. The WAR map gave the

"White American Bastion" a vast domain: Washington, Oregon, Idaho, Montana, Wyoming, Nevada, California, large chunks of Utah and Arizona, British Columbia, Alberta, a corner of Saskatchewan, much of the Northwest Territories, and a bit of the Alaskan panhandle. On the opposite side of the country, ZOG was to be squeezed into Massachusetts, Rhode Island, Connecticut, New Jersey, and small parts of New York, Pennsylvania, and Maryland. Most of the space between went to the "Nation of Islam," this at a time when Metzger harbored ambitions of white separatists negotiating with black separatists over national dismemberment. The three domains were to be separated by ample buffer zones. Thus Metzger included all Miles had in both his plans, together with new territory in the Southwest and far north.[20]

The territorial proposal has been strongly advanced by Identity rightists. This is true even in Miles's case, since he regards his dualism as theologically distinctive but compatible with Identity. Yet the territorial imperative does not appear to flow from a distinctively religious position. Rather, a number of arguments have been made as justifications for this form of radical separatism.

Only Miles seems to have made any special point of seeking religious justifications, on the grounds that Aryan spirituality will be contaminated by contact with "earth worshippers," that is, non-Aryans: "Our Faith, our very religious concepts, require that we be free to live in as natural an environment as is possible. If we are to be free, all peoples must be free. We can not be free of their influence unless they are free of ours. They must separate for their own sake. . . . Only the earth worshippers who came from the mud, direct and dust creations, and wish to bring everyone else down to that level, try to say otherwise." "Racial freedom," however, was deemed to be endangered not simply by contact with the impure and inferior but by the nature of modern political institutions. The state, by centralizing power and authority, intruded itself into personal life choices and thus made racial segregation impossible. Thus, whether Miles meant to say it or not, he argued that every significant political development since the Renaissance militated against his racial utopia, which he believed had once existed in a distant, premodern, European past when there were "only City-States and vast clan holdings in between."[21]

The irony in Miles's belief that state authority subverted racial purity is that other writers in the movement held out the prospect of statehood as a panacea. David Lane, obsessed by the belief that "Genocide of the White Race has been the aim and result of the American political entity," insisted that unless there was a racial state in which Aryans "are the exclusive residents and governors," the race would vanish. This implied not only the defensibility of borders but an elaborate apparatus for determining racial composition and rooting out the impure. The linkage of a racial state with racial survival pervaded Identity literature on the homeland.[22]

There was also a sense of diminishing options, brought on by the Order's collapse and the movement's inability to significantly increase the size of its following. In his influential essay, "Common Sense," Louis Beam, who moved from the Klan into Identity, observed that rebellion was futile. No conceivable armed action could prevail over the federal government. In like manner, he acknowledged that there was also no reason to believe the system would collapse from within. He had given up on prospects of depression, hyperinflation, or catastrophic default by debtor nations. In part, Beam's unwillingness to entertain scenarios of economic disaster flowed from his belief that the Jewish conspiracy was too powerful and effective to permit it. Hence, the United States government would not be overthrown and would not collapse from within, a belief that led Beam to conclude, as though there were no other alternatives, that only statehood remained an option.[23]

How such a radical restructuring of the American polity might be accomplished was an altogether different matter. Those on the racist right who entertained secessionist agendas remained extraordinarily vague about means. Whether for reasons of tactics or in reaction to the Order episode, they insisted that it would be accomplished peacefully. Robert Miles talked in nebulous terms about mass migration:

> How to gain separation from the others? That is a question. We have ever proposed a peaceful out trek. It is why we asked you to know who lives around you where you are now. Not to hurt anyone but to be sure that you will be able to commence the trek, at your time and in your own manner, when you desire. It is why we asked you to prepare yourself for the ways and means of moving out from where you are. For it has to come. It will come. It must come.

He elsewhere suggested that the territory would be voluntarily surrendered by the government as a way of getting rid of a minority so indigestible that five states would be a small price to pay for their departure. He spoke of "bringing in some 30 million more or less," although no basis for the figure was presented, and it was most unlikely that the racial right, by even the most generous estimate, included more than 100,000 sympathizers.[24]

A more common argument for the feasibility of separation was that it would somehow develop spontaneously from a pattern of migration. Louis Beam believed that the mere announcement of the separatist goal would produce a self-fulfilling prophecy: "Let the banner of a flowering renaissance of White

Culture be raised, of Anglo-Saxon Law enforced, and Constitutional rebirth in the making, and the best of what is left in America will flock to it." Coupled with a policy of maximum family size, "in one generation of child rearing—*we will be in the majority.*" In any case, Beam said, "America already is being . . . partitioned." That meant, in his view, that different ethnic groups already dominated different areas of the country and that the Aryan homeland would merely constitute one additional element.[25]

Such scenarios paid scant attention to those already living in the putative homeland. Robert Miles acknowledged that most would choose to leave and should be allowed to "go in peace." Should any wish to remain, non-Aryans among them would face a grim existence. The grim nature of this existence was suggested by the Aryan National State Platform, a proposed constitution. Citizenship would be limited to "Aryans (White Race)"; all others could live there "only under the custodianship of a citizen," a status not otherwise defined. Even this servile condition would be closed to "hybrids called Jews," who would be expelled after forfeiting their property. The killing of a white by a nonwhite would be a capital offense, and as a general policy, "a ruthless war must be waged against any whose activities are injurious to the common interest." Media would be heavily censored and the educational system restructured to support the "White Aryan Heritage."[26]

The arguments in favor of such a racial state were fraught with internal contradictions. On the one hand, none who espoused it suggested that it be brought about by force, doubtless a response to the Order's failure and to the federal prosecutions that followed. On the other hand, none of separatism's advocates suggested even a minimally persuasive argument for its political feasibility, short of violence. Given the fact that the only remotely similar experiment in American history ended in a bloody military defeat, there is little reason to suppose that any subsequent central government would acquiesce in the detachment of a large and rich area. Nor was there any indication of why even an area with a majority of racialists (assuming migration could produce so unlikely a result) would be able to translate its preferences into law, much less political autonomy, given the gulf that separated their views from those of the country as a whole.

White supremacists presented the separatist option as a choice that lay within the system; that is, an alternative that could be pursued nonviolently through normal political channels. Yet the improbability of such a development suggested more complex factors at work. One possibility was that those who advocated separatism did so in the full knowledge that any serious attempt to pursue such a policy could lead only to open conflict, but chose for prudential reasons not to acknowledge the link between separation and violence. If this was the case, then the territorialists were simply continuing at a rhetorical level the policies of the Order, cloaking the invitation to violence out of fear of government reprisals. The other possibility was that the territorialists genuinely believed their goal could be achieved peacefully. If that were so, they were clearly out of touch with political realities, and so invited catastrophic disillusionment at some future time. At the moment, the internal evidence does not indicate clearly the relative weight of disguised aggression and self-delusion. Whatever balance might be struck between them, the potential for violence persists, either by those who would try to emulate the Order or by those frustrated by seeking an unattainable goal.

The territorial option was clearly beyond any foreseeable twist in the political process. With neither a mass base nor the prospect of securing one, and with the necessity of confronting central authorities fully capable of preserving public order, there was no conceivable prospect for a successful secessionist political program. Lacking the cultural cohesion of nationalist irredentist movements elsewhere, the racist right continued to nurture dreams of sovereignty that were beyond its capacity to realize and remained caught up in a cycle of extravagant dreams, frustration-releasing violence, and governmental suppression, which then engendered a new phase of speculation.

Identity and Politics

Millenarian movements carry inevitable political baggage, for the anticipation of total societal transformation implies that political arrangements too will be reordered. Millennialists vary, however, in the degree to which they regard the transformation as the result of outside forces, the efforts of believers themselves, or some combination of the two. Where there is a strong commitment to an imminent millennium (change now rather than in the distant future), and where a significant role is assigned to believers as participants rather than as spectators, the potential for a violent clash with authorities is considerable. Such groups usually maintain their commitments until they suffer catastrophic defeat, at which time they deflect their aspirations in safer directions: the millennium may be made more distant, the changes sought may be redefined as spiritual rather than physical, the role of human action may be deemphasized, or an institutional and ritual structure may be substituted for a program of social change. This is a pattern that can be found in many times and places where millennialists have faced defeat and disappointment—among the revolutionary millenarians of the Radical Reformation no less than among the Cargo Cults of Melanesia. Where, then, does Identity fit in this dialectic of confrontation and sublimation?

Christian Identity clearly believes that the Last Days are imminent, a characteristic shared with most millennialists in contemporary America. Unlike many of their fellow chiliasts, however, a high proportion of Identity believers adopt an active rather than a passive stance. While some, such as Dan Gayman, advocate watchful waiting, many others assign a "frontline" role to believers, largely for two reasons. First, rejection of the rapture means they must try to survive the rigors of the Tribulation, a period uniformly described in imagery of battle and conflict. Second, history up to and including the present is conceptualized in terms of race war. Where other millenarians may contrast the evil and corruption of the present with the perfection of the coming millennium, Identity attributes the evil and corruption to a conspiracy actively at work in the world and willing and able to defend itself. As the Tribulation approaches, the forces of evil are expected to push toward victory, with only a thin line of Aryan warriors left to defend the good.

As Identity theology developed, the forces of Satan were concretely identified with a Jewish cabal, so that the conspiratorialism of *The Protocols of the Elders of Zion* was subsumed under a more comprehensive concept of Satan's struggle against God. As Identity writers have elaborated upon the conspiracy's malevolence and cunning, its tentacles have been portrayed as reaching into virtually every sector of American life: the churches, the universities, the mass media, and, not least, the government. The federal government especially has come to be viewed as little more than an appendage of the Jewish-satanic conspiracy. Hence every action of the government is seen as sinister, duplicitous, and illegitimate. A worldview premised upon such ideas sees politics in confrontational terms, with choices that range from disengagement to struggle.

The political choices such a theology offers are necessarily limited. One is psychological disengagement, a kind of "inner emigration" in which the individual ceases to feel connected to political life and directs his or her energies to other pursuits. The intangible character of such behavior makes its incidence difficult to measure, but one suspects that a large number of Identity believers have taken this path. A more concrete manifestation of disengagement is survivalist withdrawal, described in the preceding chapter. While this permits a high degree of detachment from the political system, it is not without risks, as the history of the Covenant, Sword and Arm of the Lord demonstrates, for the line between feelings of detachment and encirclement can easily become blurred. Finally, there are the transformational options discussed in this chapter, such as armed conflict and territorial secession. These alternatives are not and will not be politically viable. Indeed, they are suicidal. Yet because they flow directly out of Identity's millenarian sensibility and because they promise immediate (though temporary) psychological satisfactions, violence-producing outbursts will occasionally occur.

Among the least likely paths are those connected to pragmatic politics, such as participation in the electoral system. It is significant that those who have run for office have been individuals with Identity pasts (Metzger) or Identity associations (Duke and Gritz) but not current Identity believers themselves. Identity believers would have extraordinary difficulty in reconciling the norms of American politics, which emphasized incremental adjustment and coalition building, with Identity's sense of apocalyptic expectation. Duke has, however, demonstrated that Identity associations themselves (not to mention a neo-Nazi past) are not a bar to electoral success at the local level, and that Identity believers will support a candidate deemed compatible with their social philosophy.

Finally, there is the question of whether the trauma of defeat can produce a fundamental political reorientation of Identity, as it has of earlier millenarian movements. Identity did in fact suffer significant defeats in the second half of the 1980s. The breakup of the Order has already been described. With it went most dreams of imminent revolt and insurgency. A few years later, in 1988, the federal government prosecuted thirteen major right-wing figures for seditious conspiracy, alleging they had plotted to overthrow the government and set up an Aryan nation in the Pacific Northwest, thus activating the territorial option by systematically violent means. Although there were non-Identity defendants, significant Identity figures were in the dock, including Richard Girnt Butler, Louis Beam, and Richard Wayne Snell, as well as some with close Identity associations, such as David Lane and Robert Miles. The Fort Smith trial, named after the Arkansas community where it was held, resulted in acquittals for all defendants, but the length, cost, and risks of the case clearly made an impact on both the defendants and the movement; and some have argued that Fort Smith, along with the Order proceedings, forced Identity in nonviolent directions.[27]

There seems little doubt that the aggressiveness of law-enforcement agencies and prosecutors has significantly reduced the potential for future violence. However, the reduction seems the result not of a fundamental theological reorientation but of prudence and calculation. Identity appears not yet to have faced defeats so definitive as to force a basic rethinking of its orientation toward the political system. Some, like Dan Gayman, who testified for the prosecution at Fort Smith, have always rejected violence. For those who have not, however, the issue remains one of assessing risks, not of altering principles.

In any case, the potential for violence depends not only on Identity theology but upon the stance taken by authorities responsible for public order. The extent to which government decisions may control the outbreak and intensity of violence was driven home in 1993 at the sectarian compound of the Branch Davidians outside Waco, Texas. Although the Branch Davidians were unrelated to Identity theologically, their interactions with the authorities reproduced dynamics that can occur in Identity settings as well. The Branch Davidians were communal and separatist in their life-style, heterodox in their beliefs, and millenarian in their expectations about the future. They believed themselves to be living in an evil but doomed world, and, partly as a result, were heavily armed. The violence at the compound developed, however, because of miscalculations by federal authorities. A mistimed assault by agents of the Bureau of Alcohol, Tobacco, and Firearms on February 28, 1993, cost the lives of four agents. After a fifty-one-day armed standoff with the FBI, a final assault on the compound resulted in the fire that claimed the lives of nearly eighty Branch Davidians. However responsibilities are apportioned, it remains true that the violence was the result of a complex interaction in which both apocalyptic sectarians and governmental authorities possessed some measure of control.[28]

A similar but less violent episode with Identity participants had already occurred in 1992. The Randy Weaver family, Identity believers, were besieged for eleven days in August 1992 by federal authorities seeking to serve a firearms-violation warrant. In the first two days of the standoff, a deputy U.S. marshal and Weaver's wife and son were killed. Ironically, Weaver's trial took place during the Waco episode the following year; he and a family friend who was present were acquitted of all but the original firearms charges. The Waco and Weaver episodes suggest that the potential for violence in Christian Identity depends upon both the beliefs and strategies adopted by Identity groups and the responses made by local and national authorities. In some cases (the Order is the clearest instance), Identity believers have been first users of violence as part of a revolutionary strategy. In other cases, such as the Randy Weaver episode, violence has been a by-product of government tactics, a consequence of misperceptions and miscalculations. Therefore, the potential for Identity-related violence in the future depends as much upon the responses made by law-enforcement agencies as it does upon changes internal to the movement.[29]

This book has been a study in the transformation of ideas. What began as an eccentric but benign religious movement—British-Israelism—became a movement that, while still at the intellectual margins, took on a hate-filled political agenda. This metamorphosis might be regarded as little more than the internal concerns of obscure coteries but for the fact that here, as elsewhere, ideas have consequences. Beliefs can both drive and justify actions. As the belief system of Christian Identity incorporated more and more explicitly political components, it became capable of producing more serious societal consequences.

This chapter examines the process of *ideological mutation*, through which a benign and politically conformist movement turned into a movement obsessed with enemies and conspiracies. As the process of transformation went forward, Christian Identity was opened up to additional influences, emanating from the *cultic milieu*, the society's domain of rejected and stigmatized ideas. This openness to rejected knowledge was a product of the pervasive fear of conspiracy. When that conspiratorialism was joined with a belief in the imminence of the apocalypse, Identity could become a breeding ground for *revolutionary millenarianism*, the final assault of the pure on the citadel of corrupt authority.

Ideological Mutation

If the British are indeed a people both productive and tolerant of eccentricity, then Anglo-Israelism must surely be a quintessentially English phenomenon. Its devotees ordered their organizational and publishing lives around the curious belief that they alone had discovered the true Israelite origins of the British peoples, and they saw in it the fulfillment of biblical prophecy. De-

12

Conclusion

The Politics

of Ultimacy

spite their failure to convince most of their countrymen, British-Israelites persevered, unswervingly committed to the "identity message." They were curious but essentially harmless. As we have seen, British-Israelites tended to be middle-class Anglicans, leavened by other Protestants and by a surprising number of titled aristocrats and military officers. None surpassed them in loyalty to the sovereign, the putative descendant of King David, and the Empire, which Britain was deemed to have acquired in fulfillment of divine promises. The achievements of British law and parliamentary institutions they attributed to the Israelite legacy brought by the tribes from their ancient Near Eastern homeland. In short, British-Israelism idealized and defended the political status quo.

While Christian Identity maintained and even extended the core belief in Israelite origins, it departed in significant ways from British-Israelism. Having abandoned the Anglophilic sentiments of American British-Israelism, Identity also left behind the traditional defense of the political status quo. While Identity believers idealized the Constitution and proclaimed their devotion to the common law, they regarded American political institutions as corrupt beyond any hope of reform. The political system had been captured by the Jewish conspiracy. The Jews, as "Satan's spawn," were here to do the Devil's work on earth, and in furtherance of the demonic plan had taken over the governmental apparatus. Hence, in Identity's view, government was illegitimate, and Christians owed no loyalty to it. They were obliged to yield to its demands only as tactical prudence dictated. In short, where British-Israelism rhapsodized about the goodness and virtue of the British political system, American Identity believers saw around them only hostile and malevolent forces.

What made this transformation possible? How did an English movement once unswerving in its support of the status quo give rise to an American successor at potential war with government? The transformation was facilitated by two factors: organizational form and intellectual style. As we have seen, almost from its inception British-Israelism was plagued by tension between centrifugal and centripetal forces. On the one hand, there were continual attempts to create overarching organizational structures that would draw British-Israelites together. These, however, always took the form of *federations*, groupings of at least semiautonomous units over which the center exercised only nominal control. While at least one tightly governed religious sect did eventually emerge from British-Israelism (the Worldwide Church of God), Anglo-Israelites in Britain and North America generally rejected the sectarian model. Members were encouraged to retain their denominational affiliations, for which British-Israelism was supposed to supply reinforcement rather than competition.

Thus the center—the offices of the various federative structures—lacked the machinery and the sanctions to enforce doctrinal conformity. Often as a matter of principle they rejected the desirability of such conformity. British-Israelites could believe as they pleased, provided they accepted some notion of Israelite ancestry. As a result, the movement lacked an orthodoxy but possessed an organizational structure so segmented that multiple centers of doctrinal variation could be sustained within it. Whether in Detroit, Vancouver, or Los Angeles, British-Israelites felt free to elaborate their own interpretations. In this multicentric organizational environment, a wide range of interpretations proliferated, some close to the views of such influential Anglo-Israel publicists as Edward Hine, others idiosyncratic and deviant. For example, many British-Israelites were content to follow Hine's lead in regarding Jews as part of All-Israel, but as we saw in chapter 7, ideological permissiveness allowed some, like C. F. Parker, to argue that Jews had forfeited their place by intermarrying with heathens. Hence, British-Israelism was structured in a manner likely to produce a high degree of ideological variation—a reservoir of ideas, continually replenished with new and different contributions. Those at the center had limited capacities for controlling both what went into the reservoir (e.g., Ellen Bristowe's notions about Cain) and what was drawn out (e.g., that the Jews, rather than the Turks, were modern-day Edomites). As the American movement began to draw increasing numbers of anti-Semites in the 1930s and 1940s, they found a congenial milieu. There were ample materials on which they could draw to reinforce and express their own predilections, and they could embellish those themes without being stigmatized as heretics.

The organizational structure existed in a reciprocal relationship with intellectual style. British-Israelism was from the outset a *revisionist* movement, that is, it offered a new version of orthodox beliefs. Further, it was doubly revisionist, for it claimed to offer both a new interpretation of the Bible (making it religiously revisionist) and a new account of historical events connected with migration patterns that populated Europe and the British Isles (making it a form of revisionist history). British-Israel writings were genteel and mannerly, avoiding the accusations, name calling, and stridency common in the later Christian Identity literature. But it was abundantly clear that British-Israelites regarded the common Protestant understanding of biblical prophecy to be incomplete at best and likewise considered accounts of both biblical and British history to be deeply flawed. They thus set themselves in decorous but clear opposition to both religious and academic authorities. If both sets of authorities were in error, who then was correct? British-Israelism's problem was always its inability to find a clear source of authority once it had rejected those of both the church and the academy.

The problem of authority was intertwined with that of organization. Having chosen not to found a sect, British-Israelites lacked the means to set up their own fount of authority. Like the Millerites before them, they seemed ever confident that the sheer force of their arguments would eventually win over denominational Protestantism. But having no authority structure of their own, and having rejected key views of both religious and secular authorities, they found it even more difficult to control doctrinal mutation. Not only did new ideas and interpretations grow because local centers were autonomous and little could be done to discipline deviation; in addition, the commitment to revisionism proved in practice to be unstoppable. If churches and universities were teaching errors, then institutionally sanctioned truth was suspect. If received biblical interpretation and history were false, then nothing was as it seemed. The real truth was hidden and had to be uncovered. In practice, British-Israelism gave the benefit of the doubt to certain institutions, such as the British monarchy. But their substitution of a daringly different picture of both sacred and secular history from that accepted by others had far-reaching implications.

Revisionism, once launched, proved difficult to control. It stimulated increasingly ambitious searches for hidden meaning, the truth concealed behind conventional ideas. The work of David Davidson codified British-Israel revisionism, extending it into new domains of revisionist history and supplying it with a new tool for separating false appearances from the concealed truth beneath. While Davidson's date-setting exercises bothered some British-Israelites, they could scarcely fault him for logically extending the revisionist enterprise.

While British-Israelism did not apply its revisionism to political institutions, Identity had no comparable inhibitions. British-Israelism had already demonstrated to its adherents' satisfaction that received knowledge is at best an illusion or, at worst, a deception. Identity merely extended the revisionist enterprise to new domains, notably politics. Unencumbered by the British-Israelites' devotion to the Crown, Identity saw in political institutions the operation of sinister plots. Their belief that a Jewish cabal had seized control of government and the media thus merely took revisionism a step further. Similarly, it explains the readiness of Identity believers to accept Holocaust revisionism not only because they hate and fear Jews but also because every historical account has become suspect, whether of Egyptian pharaohs, the origins of European peoples, or Nazi genocide.

In two respects, therefore, British-Israelism provided necessary, though not sufficient, conditions for the emergence of Identity: by an organizational structure that encouraged the proliferation of doctrines without being able to control the directions doctrinal development took; and by an intellectual style that encouraged a skepticism so radical that ordinary canons for distinguishing truth from falsehood seemed useless. When the fragmented organization and revisionist skepticism of British-Israelism impinged on the American right in the 1930s and 1940s, Identity was the result, and Anglo-Israelism's harmless eccentricities took on a decidedly more sinister appearance.

The Cultic Milieu

The skepticism that British-Israelism encouraged and that Identity intensified made an already diffuse body of beliefs more nebulous still. Received ideas—those that bore the imprimatur of prestigious institutions—were stigmatized. The converse was also the case—that is, those ideas not associated with prestigious institutions ipso facto appeared more credible. The more doubt that was cast on accepted notions, the more persuasive unaccepted ideas seemed, for to be linked with churches and universities was to be tainted. British-Israelism could keep its tendency toward skepticism partially in check because of its loyalty to Crown and Empire and because of its members' social backgrounds—middle class, leavened by the aristocracy and armed forces. Consequently, despite their suspicion of traditional Bible interpretation and history, they retained powerful links with the established order. Christian Identity, with a more plebeian social profile, had distinctly weaker institutional loyalties.[1]

Identity's more thoroughgoing skepticism had opened the movement to a bewildering variety of influences beyond those that may be directly traced to British-Israelism and anti-Semitic politics. Many influences emanated from the "cultic milieu," a concept described by the British sociologist Colin Campbell that has two significant aspects. First, it refers to a society's "rejected knowledge," beliefs considered unacceptable by such authoritative institutions as conventional religion, universities, the state, and the mass media. Second, the cultic milieu refers not simply to this body of rejected knowledge but to its expression in the form of a "cultural underground," a "network of individuals, groups, practices, institutions, [and] means of communication."

The cultic milieu's conception of the world is therefore a virtual mirror image of that shared by the majority. What institutions of orthodoxy consider error, the cultic milieu regards as truth—the occult, the crank, and the pseudo-scientific. The cultic milieu therefore implies a distinctive, even forbidden, vision of the world.[2]

The cultic milieu was in evidence from the early days of British-Israelism. The Israelites' presence in Europe and the British Isles was inferred from deviant interpretations of archaeological evidence. According to it, Jeremiah had brought the daughter of the last king of Israel to Ireland, the Ark of the Covenant had been buried in the mound at Tara, and the Stone of Scone below the Coronation Throne at Westminster Abbey was the stone on which Jacob had lain his head at Beth El. The intersection of Anglo-Israelism with pyramidology introduced an additional body of cultic material, which achieved increasing prominence. By extension, other ancient monuments throughout the world, including Stonehenge, were also given Israelite provenance.[3]

Initially, the cultic milieu exercised influence in areas that reinforced the central religious message. Speculations about migrating peoples and mysterious structures were ransacked for confirmation of the Israelites' wanderings in strange lands. But given the dynamic of historical revisionism, there were temptations to draw in cultic materials less immediately germane. As Wesley Swift and William Potter Gale pushed the battle between good and evil back before biblical times, they drew on the imagery provided by science fiction and the flying saucer/UFO literature. The rebellion of the fallen angels had been fought by armadas of spaceships, one commanded by Lucifer and the other by the archangel Michael. In anticipation of such later occult writers as Eric van Däniken, some of the ships crashed and brought celestial creatures to earth.

The reach of the cultic milieu extended to nonreligious areas as well. Christian Identity literature combined its discussions of religion and race with encomiums to the medicinal value of garlic, attacks on processed food, and analyses of UFOs. Indeed, but for the agenda of religion and race, Christian Identity exhibited striking parallels with New Age literature. While the two may seem radically opposed, both drew on the cultic milieu, a common reservoir of excluded ideas, whose very exclusion from common discourse is taken as evidence of their validity.[4]

The cultic milieu was attractive for several reasons. In the first place, as has already been indicated, British-Israelism drew from and contributed to the cultic milieu by the very nature of its central beliefs. Second, the uncontrollable dynamic of historical revisionism tended to take speculation into new fields, so that it was virtually impossible to limit the cultic milieu's influence to a single facet of the belief system. Third, the power of the cultic milieu was enhanced as the theme of conspiracy became increasingly prominent.

Conspiratorialism, of course, was itself an idea nurtured in the cultic literature, in such concepts as that of the Illuminati, the shape-changing secret society alleged to have been at the bottom of every untoward event in Western history since the French Revolution. At the same time, the more Identity fastened upon a conspiratorial view of history, the more attractive the cultic milieu became as a source of themes and "verification"—and not simply because conspiracy theories tend to be relegated to the cultic milieu. Rather, there was an additional reason. The more seriously conspiracies are taken, the less trust can be placed in centers of authority. If the conspiracy is everywhere—embedded in the churches, universities, governments, banks, the mass media—then no knowledge promulgated by such institutions can be trusted. Hence, seekers after knowledge must by default go to the cultic milieu, precisely that body of ideas condemned by the centers of authority. According to the line of reasoning employed, if the conspiracy has co-opted authority, and if authority has rejected certain ideas, then those rejected ideas must be the really true ones, for if they were not true, then why would the conspiracy have condemned them?

Thus the fixation upon conspiracy drove Identity deeper into the cultic milieu by rendering all noncultic ideas suspect. Since the plot of satanic Jews was regarded as all-encompassing, social institutions and the ideas they produced were deemed untrustworthy. Just as conspiratorialism accentuates tendencies toward the reception of occult and other heterodox ideas, so conspiratorialism leads to a conflict-laden political agenda.

Revolutionary Millenarianism

Identity constructed a Manichaean universe, divided into realms of light and darkness. The central figures of each, God and Satan, are in combat. Each is aided by coalitions made up not only of allies but of literal descendants, white Aryans who are the children of God and Jews who are the children of Satan. A universe structured along dichotomous lines leads to a characteristic form of politics, a politics of ultimacy.

The politics of ultimacy rejects conventional political norms of coalition building, compromise, and incrementalism. There can be no coalition building, except in the most limited sense, for other groups are almost certainly either willing participants in the conspiracy or its hapless dupes. The range of potential coalition partners is limited to coteries regarded as racially self-conscious and untainted. In like manner, compromise is unacceptable, for that means complicity in the program of Satan. Further, if Identity's political program fulfills God's requirements for racial redemption, then it becomes nonnegotiable. Flowing from a divine source, it constitutes the ultimately valid scheme of social organization and governance. Modification of it can result only in replacing virtue with sin. Conventional politics as a practical necessity accepts not only the need for coalition building and compromise but also the inevitability of piecemeal achievements, acquired bit by bit over a long period of time. Here too prevailing norms conflict with Identity theology, for Identity's millenarian consciousness argues the imminence of the Last Days. Gradualism is a luxury that requires endless future time, precisely the commodity deemed to be in shortest supply. Victory must come soon and totally, or not at all.

Such unconventional politics, intolerant of others' interests and impatient of slow-moving political processes, resembles what Norman Cohn has called "revolutionary millenarianism": "It is characteristic of this kind of movement that its aims and premises are boundless. A social struggle is seen not as a struggle for specific, limited objectives, but as an event of unique importance, different in kind from all other struggles known to history, a cataclysm from which the world is to emerge totally transformed and redeemed." The motifs of Christian Identity place it within the revolutionary millenarian fold: "Israel" as a self-identified spiritual elite, which as God's progeny must fight his battles in the world; the belief that they face the ultimate adversary, Satan and his minions; the siege mentality that flows from the perception that God's forces are encircled; and the conviction of an approaching, apocalyptic battle that will determine for all time whether good or evil prevails. This is at once an invitation to violent confrontation and a prescription for political defeat. The collision of revolutionary millenarians preaching a politics of ultimacy with a refractory reality sets in motion Identity's unstable political dialectic.[5]

On the one hand, much in the religiopolitical message imparts a drive toward continual confrontation, even at the price of defeat and suppression at the hands of law-enforcement agencies and courts. The defeated are God's martyrs, simultaneously role models and the objects of cultlike devotion. Figures such as Robert Mathews and Gordon Kahl became objects of movement hagiography. The closed character of Identity's belief system tends to filter out contradictory messages and information. Whatever does not fit or is inconsistent comes by definition from the enemy, a worldview that encourages the overestimation of one's own strength and the underestimation of the adversary's. Finally, like all millenarians, Identity counts on God to provide. What they lack in numbers and resources will be amply compensated for by divine assistance. Since victory is assured, what appear to be defeats need not be taken seriously.

Counterpoised against these factors, however, are others that work against revolutionary millenarianism. When defeats are dramatic and governmental pressure strong, even the most committed can doubt the direction of history. Failure feeds forces of quietism and withdrawal, nurtured by Identity's post-Tribulationism. Since the rapture will not rescue the saved, they must be prepared to separate themselves from the world and hunker down until God is ready to act. At the same time, traditional politics exerts occasional temptations, as the career of David Duke demonstrates. While Identity rejects the legitimacy of conventional politics, the success of Duke and those with similar views sometimes suggests that the political arena has its uses—to lessen pressure by hostile prosecutors, to spread aspects of the Identity message, and to draw in recruits who might otherwise not be reached. Finally, as has already been indicated, Identity's very Manichaeanism can sap millenarian vitality. The more formidable the conspiracy appears, the more difficult victory may be to attain, and the harder it is to maintain confidence and optimism.

The balance between these factors is in part a function of the *dynamic of withdrawal and engagement.* Identity believers are rejecting of, and rejected by, the larger society. They regard that society as dominated by Satan, and they in turn are regarded as supporters of bigotry. Their contempt for the world as it is causes them to withdraw from it, and the opposition they stimulate confirms them in their view that they face a diabolical adversary. If, as they often believe, the rule of Antichrist is imminent, and if Christians cannot count on the rapture and thus must survive Antichrist's rule, then believers feel the necessity to disconnect themselves from the larger environment. They do so by adopting a survivalist life-style, moving to sparsely populated areas, and minimizing contacts with public institutions. Regarding the outside world as evil, and predicting the imminent breakdown of order in apocalyptic racial conflict, they arm themselves and train for what they call "the final battle."

But as their fears engender withdrawal into armed enclaves, the result can only be yet greater suspiciousness from those outside, which confirms Identity's original apocalyptic fears. Since "the great conspiracy" is deemed to be the source of all evil, the actual source of opposition is immaterial. Few distinctions are made between pressure from the news media, the FBI, and the Anti-Defamation League; all are part of ZOG, different manifestations of the same adversary.

However, the very factors that stimulate withdrawal—belief in the imminence of the Last Days and fear that the world is about to fall into the hands of primal evil—make it impossible for that withdrawal to be complete. Paradoxically, the very efforts to cut themselves off bind communally based millenarians to the environment they detest. The more radical the withdrawal, the greater the likelihood that those who withdraw will be tempted to ignore, circumvent, or violate the complex network of laws and regulations that governs a modern society, whether in the regulation of firearms, tax payments, or the treatment of children. Conflicts between withdrawing millenarians and the administrative state are inevitable.

In this respect, contemporary sectarians fare differently than most of the communal groups of the pre–Civil War period, such as the Shakers. Antebellum communitarians were generally dealt with more gently by the state (the Mormons were of course the great exception) for a number of reasons: the governments they faced were weaker and less intrusive; the groups were eager to present themselves in a favorable light in order to increase their followers; and while they viewed the outer world as corrupt, they often regarded it as salvageable.

The conflict between revolutionary millenarianism and quietistic withdrawal makes the course of Christian Identity difficult to predict. The former is undaunted by battles against hopeless odds, while the latter desires only to wait on God's timetable. The uncertainty is amplified by organizational forces that govern the content of beliefs. Decentralization and reliance upon the cultic milieu create their own form of instability—not an instability that results from clashes with political authority, but an instability that results from multiple centers of authority and the indiscriminate embrace of diverse bodies of ideas. Identity constantly mutates in a process dictated by the whims and interests of autonomous leaders and the ingestion of new themes from the cultic milieu. In complex ways, these intrinsic forces interact with extrinsic forces from the larger political environment. As a result, the movement may change rapidly in the future, toward either greater militancy or greater disengagement. It may also fission if the family resemblance among the groups within it weakens.

An imponderable concerns changes in Identity leadership. By the late 1980s and early 1990s, an entire generation of leadership had left the scene. The first generation of leaders—figures such as Swift, Gale, and Comparet—had given way to a second generation in the 1970s. Usually younger, this second generation had come to Identity through the preaching and message of the first. Now members of the second generation have themselves succumbed to death or the infirmities of age, such as Robert Miles (important to Identity although not strictly speaking an Identity figure) and Richard Butler; or, like James Ellison and James Wickstrom, they were removed from active religious and political activity by incarceration. There is some evidence that their places are now being taken by a third generation of leaders, not simply younger than their predecessors but better educated, more polished, and more adroit in shaping their message to a skeptical audience, having learned from David Duke's example how effectively appearance and manner can deflect hostility.[6]

Even if disengagement wins out against militancy, and the revolutionary millenarian drive weakens, however, Christian Identity will not have lost a capacity for future disruption, for it has already introduced into American life—albeit thus far only at the margins—motifs not present before, which for sheer virulence are virtually unprecedented. Should Christian Identity disappear through internal transformation, membership erosion, or fissioning, it will still have created dangerous new potentialities. Whatever may happen to Identity as a religious movement, or to its organizational parts, its doctrines of demonic conspiracy and apocalyptic battle exist where they did not before, for others to exploit in the future.

Earlier chapters have described a subculture steeped in exotic religious beliefs, deviant politics, and racial and ethnic stereotypes—a world whose beliefs and agenda seemed totally divorced from that inhabited by most Americans. Despite occasional news coverage of groups such as the Order, until recently few Americans were more than dimly aware of the radical right, the larger subculture in which Christian Identity is embedded. That changed with dramatic suddenness in the spring of 1995 with the bombing of the federal building in Oklahoma City. Not since the assassinations of the Kennedy brothers and Martin Luther King, Jr., in the 1960s had a domestic crisis evoked such a sense of national shock or elicited such saturation coverage by the media.

As the investigation of the bombing expanded through right-wing circles during April and May, a once-invisible milieu became the subject of countless news reports and daily conversations, revealing a world of apocalyptic fears, baroque plots, and paramilitary organizations. This chapter explores the bombing's implications for, and possible connections with, Christian Identity, focusing on the radical right's obsession with the destruction of the Branch Davidian compound outside Waco, Texas, the spread of ideas about a New World Order conspiracy, the execution of Identity believer Richard Wayne Snell on the day the Oklahoma City bombing occurred, and the explosive growth of the militias.

Christian Identity, as we have seen, has had two basic organizational characteristics. The first is a capacity for rapid ideological and tactical mutation, which flows from its fragmented and decentralized structure. The second is Identity's ability to blend with other elements of the radical right, from secular racists to neo-Nazis and

13

Epilogue

Oklahoma City and the Rise of the Militias

Klan members. Developments in the 1990s have confirmed these predispositions, as Identity has become a leading force in building broad antigovernment coalitions. These alliances, which might once have operated in a clandestine netherworld, now increasingly seek to shed their stigma and function as open political forces.

The Bombing

On Wednesday, April 19, 1995, a bomb detonated in a truck parked near the Alfred P. Murrah Federal Building in Oklahoma City, destroying most of the building and killing 168 people, including 15 children. It was the most destructive terrorist attack ever committed on American soil. In keeping with prevailing stereotypes, initial suspicion fell on persons or groups from the Middle East, and a Jordanian-American was briefly held for questioning. By Friday, however, foreign connections had been rejected, as agents arrested Timothy McVeigh and, a short time later, McVeigh's friend, Terry L. Nichols. Both were indicted on August 10. Suspicion also fell on several of their relatives and acquaintances and on an as-yet-unidentified individual (referred to by law-enforcement agencies as "John Doe #2"), but by the end of the year, only McVeigh and Nichols faced trial.[1]

McVeigh and Nichols are alleged to have acted without the knowledge or sponsorship of any organization. However, the possibility of connections with other individuals on the radical right has been a recurring motif in the case. Early in 1996, for example, Stephen Jones, a lawyer for Timothy McVeigh, was reported to be investigating right-wing activists in Great Britain, on the theory that extremists in England, and possibly in Germany as well, had conspired with Americans to build the Oklahoma City bomb. At this writing, Jones's theory remains unconfirmed. What is clear is that through the spring of 1995, investigators and journalists established a pattern of associations linking the suspects to radical right-wing organizations, activities, and literature. Michigan Militia literature was reportedly found on the farm of Terry Nichols and his brother James, both of whom were apparently ejected from a Michigan Militia meeting for "hyperbolic language." McVeigh was seen at a militia meeting early in 1995. In 1993, McVeigh had tried to sell military equipment by placing ads in the Liberty Lobby newspaper, *The Spotlight*. Those who had known McVeigh in the army remembered his fondness for *The Turner Diaries*. While on one level McVeigh and Nichols emerge as loners operating outside any conventional organizational framework, on another level they appear to have moved continuously through a pervasive right-wing subculture, a world of paramilitary groups and gun shows, underground literature and videotapes, post office boxes and mail drops.[2]

Most Americans never knew that such a world existed. After McVeigh's arrest on April 21, saturation media coverage of the radical right described a kind of alternative reality. Suddenly exposed to national notoriety were the previously invisible militias, a conspiratorial worldview built around fears of a sinister New World Order, and a literature in which more often than not the enemy was the U.S. government. At the same time, developments in the wake of the Oklahoma City bombing cast new light on two earlier events, the siege at the Ruby Ridge, Idaho, cabin of Randy Weaver and his family in 1992 and the standoff at the Branch Davidian compound near Waco, Texas, the following year (both discussed at the end of chapter 11). One thread connecting the events was the violence that can erupt between self-identified outsiders and the government. Another was the fact that outsiders on the right themselves saw a pattern in events. It was apparently no coincidence that both the fire at Waco and the Oklahoma City bombing took place on April 19.

Thus the hermetic right-wing subculture suddenly entered mainstream consciousness. It did so in the context of a collective national trauma, an event that unsettled conventional ideas about social and political order as much as did the 1992 Los Angeles riots and the assassinations of the 1960s. Inevitably, Christian Identity organizations and personalities were involved, for by 1995, Identity so pervaded the radical right that even though McVeigh and Nichols do not appear to have been believers, they moved through much the same world as did believers.

The "New World Order" Conspiracy

Central to the worldview of the militias and those in their orbit is belief in a "New World Order" (NWO) conspiracy. Although the phrase "New World Order" swept right-wing circles in the early 1990s, it predates that period by at least a decade. The same term, as a catch-phrase for "One World Government" under "the All Seeing Eye of Lucifer," appeared in a 1981 publication of the Christian Identity commune, the Covenant, Sword and Arm of the Lord (discussed in chapters 9 and 10). When George Bush talked about a "New World Order" at the time of the Gulf War, he meant only to suggest a newly revived system of collective security. Those on the right, however, saw such talk as confirmation of their worst fears: this child of "the establishment" was "going public" about the conspiracy's secret plans for world domination. To many fundamentalists—preeminently Pat Robertson—the New World Order resonated with apocalyptic expectations of the Antichrist's world dictatorship that will mark the Tribulation.[3]

The most common version of NWO theory contains the following elements. At the heart of the new order lies an unscrupulous secret organization of immensely wealthy men. They are often identified with the mysterious order of Illuminati, a demonic presence previously drawn from the cultic milieu by Christian Identity and some of its British-Israel precursors. The New World Order itself refers to the conspiracy's plan for world domination, which it intends to implement through its control of the United Nations. According to NWO theorists, the conspiracy's plans are already well advanced. Hundreds of thousands of foreign troops are allegedly stationed in the United States. New and sinister law-enforcement organizations, often believed to incorporate urban youth gangs, have been established. Gun owners and other "patriots" will soon face massive repression, including incarceration in a vast network of concentration camps being built by FEMA, the Federal Emergency Management Agency. The symbol of these malevolent designs is the ubiquitous black helicopter, which is believed to be the conspiracy's favored means of transport and surveillance.[4]

NWO conspiratorialists claim extraordinary certainty. Their literature is filled with names, dates, and places—the location of every concentration camp and the size and armament of every foreign military detachment. This is, as Richard Hofstadter noted in his famous essay on the "paranoid political style," a genre of pseudo-scholarship in which "the very fantastic character of conclusions leads to heroic strivings for 'evidence' to prove that the unbelievable is the only thing that can be believed."

In its secular versions, NWO theory focuses on a cabal of the super-rich whose uncontrollable greed feeds a drive for world domination. In religious versions, the New World Order is the reign of Antichrist, fulfilling End-time prophecy. In both versions, the American constitutional system will be an early casualty, for the conspiracy must quickly dismantle republican government in order to exercise the control it seeks. Hence, as we shall see, NWO theory becomes a principal justification for paramilitary organization, necessary for repelling the invader in order to safeguard American institutions. This is in many respects a variation on Identity's idea of the "Great Conspiracy," save that in this version anti-Semitic themes have been suppressed—a mutation we will examine presently. Those who favor religious interpretations of the New World Order concentrate most of their attention on the enigmatic passage in Revelation 13 concerning "the mark of the beast": "And he causeth all, both small and great, rich and poor, free and bond, to receive a mark in their right hand, or in their foreheads: and that no man might buy or sell, save he that had the mark, or the name of the beast, or the number of his name." NWO speculation about the mark has extended in two directions: it is viewed both as a total means of surveillance and control, not merely as a means of regulating economic activity, and as a prophecy about the role microelectronics will play in the End-times. The latter has led to elaborate discussions of how microchips could be implanted under the skin, simultaneously fulfilling prophecy and giving the Antichrist conspiracy the means of exercising dictatorial control. One Michigan-based right-wing periodical claims that in the 1970s computer scientists began working on a microchip small enough to be implanted with a hypodermic needle in order to fulfill the requirements of Revelation 13.[5]

These concerns may well have had an impact on Timothy McVeigh. A few days after McVeigh's arrest, Philip Morawski, an acquaintance of McVeigh and the Nichols brothers, told a reporter: "He [McVeigh] had this real sharp pain in his rear. He thought they had planted one of those chips that they have for identifying cattle, sheep or goats so the all-seeing eye of the government could keep an eye on him and know where he was." This story soon took on a life of its own. By the time it reappeared in the *Chicago Tribune* three weeks later, the chip had been "injected." Those on the radical right were quick to seize on the story. Linda Thompson, whose antigovernment videotapes about Waco will be discussed below, thought that the aim was to turn McVeigh into a "Manchurian Candidate," a "brainwashed" or programmed assassin. Jack Oliphant, who had been associated with the paramilitary Arizona Patriots, told a reporter that "the government did plant that microchip in McVeigh's butt. They can control behavior through that, you know."[6]

All of these motifs—concentration camps, black helicopters, implanted microchips—are connected by the idea of forces that are at once immensely powerful and skilled in the arts of concealment and dissimulation—a hidden "they," one step away from conquest of the United States, whether the purpose of their conquest is to enrich an evil plutocracy or to bring Satan's triumph closer. It is scarcely surprising that some of those surrounded by these messages of menace and danger would try to strike first.

One of the most puzzling aspects of the April 19 bombing was its location. Why Oklahoma City? As many pointed out at the time, its very location magnified the horror, for if a relatively small and typical "heartland" city could experience such violence, where could one be safe? The bombing of the World Trade Center in Manhattan was less traumatic, not only because of the far lower loss of life, but because for many people New York was already perceived as a place of danger and sudden violence.

Many theories have developed to explain the choice of Oklahoma City: that it was chosen randomly, that it was close to Timothy McVeigh's old army post(Fort Riley, Kansas), that it was near Waco. But in some of the conspiracy literature itself, Oklahoma City was not just another small metropolitan area. It was, rather, one of the nodal points in the New World Order plot.

In the 1970s, William Pabst, one of the early writers on alleged government concentration camps, singled out Oklahoma City. Pabst claimed there were only four such campsites (later writers would suggest over a hundred), but one of the four was said to be thirty miles from Oklahoma City. At the time, Pabst thought the camps would be run by the Law Enforcement Assistance Administration, but by 1990, FEMA was the consensus candidate among NWO conspiratorialists. In the early 1990s, Oklahoma City was given even greater prominence by Mark Koernke, the University of Michigan custodial employee whose shortwave radio broadcasts and videotapes had large followings in militia circles. Koernke announced that all "patriots" detained west of the Mississippi would be processed in Oklahoma City. A similar idea appeared in Jim Keith's 1994 book, *Black Helicopters over America*, one of the most widely read statements of NWO theory: "There are confirmed reports that . . . a huge FEMA prisoner transfer terminal is being constructed in Oklahoma City." In 1995, the year of the bombing, the Michigan-based American Freedom Network added that Oklahoma City was the site of one of four enormous crematoria, able to incinerate three thousand corpses a day in a ten-story facility over whose entrance gates there is "the New World Order symbol, the all-seeing Satanic eye above a pyramid."[7]

A plan to blow up the Oklahoma City federal building had apparently been discussed more than a decade before. The plot was allegedly revealed by James Ellison, the leader of the Covenant, Sword and Arm of the Lord, in conversations with Steven N. Snyder, a prosecutor at the Fort Smith sedition trial (discussed in chapter 11). Snyder recalled that Ellison described a 1983 plot centered on the federal building. According to Snyder, Ellison described discussions that were said to have taken place in 1983 in Hayden Lake, Idaho, site of the Aryan Nations compound. Angered by news of Gordon Kahl's death (see chapter 10), Ellison and a group of rightists met to plan a strike against the government. In Snyder's recollections, Ellison attributed the choice of an Oklahoma City target to Richard Wayne Snell. Snell, whose life and Identity associations will be discussed in detail below, was executed for murder the day the Oklahoma City bombing occurred, April 19, 1995.

The 1983 plot apparently went no further than an examination of the building and the sketching out of placements for rocket launchers that could be used against it. As Snyder recalled twelve years later:

> I remember this because I thought it was strange that they would go all the way to Oklahoma City [from Arkansas]. Ellison said that Snell was bitter toward the government because of the I.R.S., and I think these were agents from the Oklahoma City office, and they had taken him to court, and his property had been seized by the F.B.I. and other agents in a raid. But you can't be sure about any of this, because a Federal raid, to a lot of these people, is any time the postman brings the mail.

There is no evidence that Timothy McVeigh and Terry Nichols had any direct contact with persons involved in the alleged 1983 plot or any knowledge of it. Nor is there clear evidence concerning Snell's reasons for choosing Oklahoma City. Although his difficulties with the IRS may have been the principal reason, the independent appearance of Oklahoma City in later conspiracy theories suggests that it was emerging in right-wing thought as an important locus of the New World Order.[8]

The Bombing and Waco

The Oklahoma City bombing occurred on the second anniversary of the fire that destroyed the Branch Davidian compound, Mount Carmel, outside Waco, Texas. That the relationship between the two events was not coincidental is strongly suggested by two facts: first, Timothy McVeigh visited the ruins of Mount Carmel a few months after the fire and made no secret of his anger at the government; second, he allegedly rented the truck linked to the bombing with a forged driver's license whose date of issue was "4-19-93." McVeigh's fixation with Waco was, however, more than a personal idiosyncrasy. It was the reflection of a belief widespread in antigovernment circles that actions against the Branch Davidians were part of a larger plan directed at unpopular religious and political causes.[9]

On the face of it, the right's appropriation of the Branch Davidians' suffering as part of their own struggle appears implausible. The multiracial Davidians shared neither the religious beliefs of Christian Identity nor the political agenda of the radical right. Nonetheless, almost immediately after the end of the episode in April 1993, the radical right began to claim the Mount Carmel community as its own. In their eyes, the victims of the fire were martyrs to the same cause, their deaths indisputable evidence of the federal government's ruthlessness.

While this was in part an opportunistic exploitation of the misery of others, it was also fed by the issue of gun control. The proximate cause of the original raid on the Branch Davidians by agents of the Bureau of Alcohol, Tobacco, and Firearms was the community's alleged violation of federal firearms laws. NWO conspiracy theory asserts that to seize power, the conspiracy must disarm the American population; hence, to believers, any vigorous enforcement of firearms regulations is prima facie evidence that the New World Order is on the march.

Months after the raid, *The Spotlight*, the most widely circulated right-wing periodical, continued to devote double-page spreads to Waco. And even after attacks on the government died out in right-wing print media, some on the right continued to champion the Branch Davidians' cause through video-cassettes. The most influential of the Waco cassettes were two issued by the Indianapolis-based American Justice Federation, *Waco: The Big Lie* and *Waco II: The Big Lie Continues*. Among other charges, the tapes asserted that some ATF agents at Waco had actually been executed by the government, that tanks penetrating the compound were equipped with flamethrowers, and that survivors of the fire were shot as they tried to escape.[10]

The American Justice Federation is headed by attorney Linda Thompson, who had been at Mount Carmel during the standoff. On March 18, 1993, she sought unsuccessfully to enter the compound. On April 4, she asked "the 'Unorganized Militia of the United States' to come to Waco with their (legal) weapons to demonstrate and show support for Koresh." Thompson claims to be "Acting Adjutant General" of the "Unorganized Militia." She called for a militia march on Washington to take place on September 19, 1994, to seek repeal of the Fourteenth, Sixteenth, and Seventeenth Amendments, the Brady Law, and the North American Free Trade Agreement. When support for the march failed to materialize, she canceled it. Thompson's attack on the government's Waco policy blends into a broader New World Order conspiratorialism. Her *Waco II* tape acknowledges the assistance of Mark Koernke, a major conspiracy theorist, and she claims that the Waco raid was related to "reported citings [sic] of UN tanks going into Portland, Oregon."[11]

It was scarcely surprising, therefore, that Thompson saw the Oklahoma City bombing in conspiratorial terms. The truck blast was a decoy "probably" arranged by the FBI to hide the real explosions. "We have a seismographic report from the University of Oklahoma that shows there were two distinct blasts." She noted on April 19 that FBI Special Agent Bob Ricks, who handled press briefings during Waco, was based in Oklahoma City. "My guess on this is it could be: (1) CIA, tired of waiting on the concerned citizens; (2) ADL/FBI in order to blame it on 'Militia.'" For Thompson and others, what happened in Waco and Oklahoma City were not isolated events; they were parts of a pattern in which nothing was as it seemed.[12]

So thoroughly did the radical right co-opt the Branch Davidians' cause that one publication, *Criminal Politics*, insinuated that the Davidians were actually part of Christian Identity, contending that "they . . . believe that the Anglo-Saxons are the true Israelites." One Davidian, the article claimed, "believes that the 10 'lost' tribes of Israel in ancient times migrated over the Caucasus Mountains and into Europe, and the present day Jews are not true Israelites." This clearly shows elements of the Khazar hypothesis, discussed in chapter 7. In fact, of course, it has nothing whatever to do with the actual Branch Davidians, who were free of anti-Semitism and considered the founding of the state of Israel to be the fulfillment of prophecy. It may, however, dimly reflect the fact that in the mid-1970s, the then-leader of the community, Ben Roden, ruled that the observance of biblical festivals, such as Passover, was required of the Branch Davidians—a practice that is also common in Christian Identity.[13]

Ironically, the most dramatic manifestation of right-wing concerns with the Waco episode was scheduled to occur on April 19, 1995—the day of the Oklahoma City bombing. Morning and afternoon ceremonies were scheduled to take place that day on the now-desolate site of the compound. The speakers announced for the morning remembrance ceremony and the afternoon memorial service were a mixed group. They included a former attorney general, Ramsey Clark, as well as lawyers, journalists, and academics, all critics of the government's actions two years before. But mixed in among them were two other figures of a quite different sort: Ralph Turner, spokesperson for the North Texas Constitutional Militia, and James "Bo" Gritz, whose Christian Identity associations and leadership role on the radical right are noted in chapter 10. The militia placed a stone marker on the site, dedicated to "a church and its members . . . [who] came under attack by ATF and FBI agents."[14]

The Death of Richard Wayne Snell

The radical right has appropriated the Branch Davidian victims as its own. They are among its martyrs, the honored dead who must be avenged, if only because they had the same putative enemies, the federal government, the faceless NWO conspiracy, the Anti-Defamation League (ADL), and other assorted fronts for plots and cabals. But if the Branch Davidians are the most frequently honored of the martyrs, commemorated even on Timothy Mc-Veigh's forged driver's license, they are by no means the only ones. Another also linked to April 19 is Richard Wayne Snell, whose execution for murder occurred on the day of the bombing. A London press report, attributed to McVeigh's defense team, suggested that the bombing was in fact timed to coincide with Snell's execution, although no confirmation of this has yet been offered. Snell's attorneys sought a stay of execution as late as the day of the bombing, but Snell's appearance at an April 10 clemency board hearing had made execution virtually inevitable, since he quoted Rudolph Hess and said he "probably" would shoot an Arkansas state trooper again if the circumstances of his original crime were repeated. Snell had been sentenced to life imprisonment without parole for the killing of Trooper Lewis Bryant, who was black, and sentenced to death for the murder of a pawnbroker, Bill Stump, whom he erroneously believed to be Jewish. According to his wife, Mary Snell, the conflict with Bryant began when Snell "reprimanded" Bryant for "harassment of white women."[15]

Snell's impending execution was well known in right-wing circles. Mary Snell secured the support of the Militia of Montana in a letter-writing campaign directed at Governor Jim Guy Tucker of Arkansas in advance of the clemency hearing. The militia's newsletter, *Taking Aim*—which was reproduced on Snell's own copying machine, donated to the militia by his wife—gave prominent coverage to the case as early as December 1994 under the headline, "AN AMERICAN PATRIOT TO BE EXECUTED BY THE BEAST." In March 1995, *Taking Aim* reprinted a lengthy letter from Snell that tied his coming execution to a long series of Arkansas scandals allegedly connected with Bill Clinton, in which twenty-five victims were said to have met strange deaths. Indeed, he claimed to have evidence of twelve more such deaths. Snell was to die, according to the Militia of Montana, because he "was and still is heavily involved in exposing Clinton for his trail of blood to the White House."[16]

Whether the accused Oklahoma City bombers timed the blast to coincide with Snell's execution is not known at this time, but it is highly unlikely that anyone familiar with radical right-wing literature would have been unaware that the execution would take place sometime shortly after April 10, 1995. Even if revenge for Snell's death was not a motive for the bombing, his execution is important for three reasons. First, the juxtaposition of his death with the bombing and the Waco anniversary strongly reinforces the significance of the date in right-wing circles. Second, Snell maintained a complex series of links among Christian Identity figures. Third, one of those Christian Identity connections may have drawn the attention of Timothy McVeigh in the weeks before the bombing.

Richard Wayne Snell was associated with three Christian Identity organizations, the first two of which figured prominently in preceding chapters: the Christian-Patriots Defense League, founded by John Harrell; the Covenant, Sword and Arm of the Lord, led by James Ellison; and the Oklahoma-based Christian Identity communal settlement, Elohim City, led by Robert Millar. At various times, Snell also maintained ties with Gordon Kahl and Gordon "Jack" Mohr. Between November 1983 and June 1984—just as the Order was becoming active in the West—Snell, besides committing two murders, was involved in unsuccessful attempts to bomb a natural gas pipeline and an electricity transmission tower. In these activities, he was acting out the imagery of the war between "Aryan Israel" and its enemies that suffused Identity teaching.[17]

Snell was born in 1930, the son of a Church of the Nazarene preacher. He followed his father's calling, but eventually he left organized religion, "disillusioned with what he saw in the church and became an avowed atheist." After a period of increasing opposition to the IRS, he discovered Identity at a 1981 meeting of the Christian-Patriots Defense League. His Identity views remained unmellowed by his time on death row. "The Jew," he wrote, "then and is endeavoring now to steal the birthright of true Israel. And it appears they have succeeded to the extent of stealing our wealth and our nation, and we have swallowed the lie of the Jew being 'the chosen.'"[18] Snell was still a member of the CPDL at the time of one of his trials, in October 1984. The "Minister of Defense" of the CPDL, Jack Mohr, a late convert to Identity, testified on Snell's behalf: "I met him at a meeting of the Christian and Patriot Defense League . . . and we became quite well acquainted. We saw each other, I guess, on about a yearly basis, but corresponded back and forth and he also supported me off and on with contributions towards my work which is called 'Crusade for Christ and Country' which is a patriotic/Christian endeavor." At some point in the early 1980s, Snell also became a member of James Ellison's Covenant, Sword and Arm of the Lord. Mary Snell testified that she herself was not an active member of CSA, but acknowledged that she had visited the group's compound, Zarephath-Horeb, and received an award there.[19]

The fate of Gordon Kahl was closely intertwined with that of Snell. Kahl, it will be remembered, was the Posse Comitatus member who, after killing two federal marshals in North Dakota, was finally found and killed by law-enforcement authorities in Arkansas. Kahl's death was a catalytic event for Snell, as it was for many on the radical right. Snell was apparently a courier aiding Kahl while the latter was in hiding in Arkansas, or so his wife's testimony suggests:

> Q: Is your husband a member of the Posse Comitatus?
> A: No, sir.
> Q: But he was a courier for Gordon Kahl, wasn't he?
> A: For the people who were involved with Gordon Kahl, I believe, rather than—
> Q: For him personally? Okay.
> A: As I understood.

Kahl's death led Snell "to fear for his life because he felt he was in the same category as Gordon Kahl." The feeling that Kahl's fate awaited him too also appeared in conversations Snell had with Mohr and with another Christian Identity minister, Robert Millar. Yet Kahl's death in June 1983 did not lead Snell to renounce violence; rather, it was the prelude to his own war. As he told Mohr, he believed he himself "would be dead in a few weeks."[20]

Movement Martyrology

Two alternative movement martyrologies have developed on the radical right. The first is linked to a date, April 19, and includes as signs of martyr status not only sacrificial deaths or suffering but also acts of resistance. The second is only partially linked to a date and remains fixed on acts of alleged martyrdom, regardless of when they occurred.

The date of April 19 became talismanic for the movement in large part because of the fire at the Branch Davidian compound, but there is evidence that a movement numerology, associating many events with the same date, did not begin until Snell's execution date was set. As the Militia of Montana's newsletter put it:

If this date does not ring a bell for you then maybe this will jog your memory. 1. April 19, 1775: Lexington burned; 2. April 19, 1943: Warsaw burned; 3. April 19, 1992: The fed's [*sic*] attempted to raid Randy Weaver, but had their plans thwarted when concerned citizens arrived on the scene with supplies for the Weaver family totally unaware of what was to take place; 4. April 19, 1993: The Branch Davidians burned; 5. April 19, 1995: Richard Snell will be executed—UNLESS WE ACT NOW!!!

In other words, the linking of Snell's execution with the Branch Davidian fire, treating April 19 as a sacred date, began before, not after, the Oklahoma City bombing. Subsequently, still other April 19 events were added. The Texas Militia seeks to associate the date with the battle of San Jacinto, April 21, 1836. Militia members and sympathizers are seeking formal recognition of April 19 as "Militia Day," celebrating the Second Amendment. "Martyrs," the Texas Militia believes, "will serve the Movement better than victors."[21]

The alternative martyrology devotes less attention to a single date and more to personalities. This fixation on a line of heroic dead began in the mid-1980s with the deaths of Kahl and Robert Mathews. As a member of Aryan Nations rhapsodized about Mathews, "What greater Honor than to have been among the first to have died in the Final Battle!" Randy Weaver's family entered the same line as a result of the death of his wife and son at Ruby Ridge in 1992. In response to Ruby Ridge, the Identity pastor Pete Peters convened a meeting of Identity and non-Identity movement figures in October 1992 at Estes Park, Colorado. In an "Open Letter to the Weaver Family," the group sounded the notes of martyrdom: "Impelled by the spirit of our HEAVENLY FATHER, and hearing the cry of innocent blood shed in the land, WE, 160 Christian men assembled for three days of prayer and counsel. . . . We are determined to employ HIS strength and to work continually to insure that Vickie and Samuel's mortal sacrifices were not in vain." The Branch Davidians, according to this martyrology, fall into a line defined not by date but by person and cause: from Kahl, to Mathews, to the Weavers, to Waco.[22]

Those who died in the Oklahoma City bombing cannot be readily incorporated in either martyrology, whether by concentrating on the date or the cause. Yet that has not prevented rightists from seeking to appropriate them for their cause, principally by insinuating that the government, not the defendants, bears responsibility for the blast. In conspiratorialism's world of mirrors, where appearances mean nothing, such inversions are commonplace. In the case of Oklahoma City, a bewildering variety of alternative explanations has emerged to either exculpate McVeigh and Nichols, reduce their bomb to a decoy, or make them tools of a government-sponsored conspiracy. Some versions of events claim that there were multiple blasts; others that McVeigh was a dupe (conspiratorialists frequently invoke the example of the Reichstag fire); and still others that McVeigh and Nichols were one of a much larger band of plotters who operated with government connivance. The consequences of these theories are threefold. First, by holding McVeigh and Nichols guiltless or making them little more than tools, conspiratorialists remove their right-wing associations as a factor in their alleged guilt. Indeed, so the right-wing argument goes, they were specially selected so that their associations would provide the pretext for suppression of "patriots." Second, if a government conspiracy is responsible, then the Oklahoma City victims can be assimilated in the larger category of movement martyrs, co-opted in death like the Branch Davidians. Finally, the bombing-as-government-conspiracy explanation reinforces April 19 as a sacred date, when the forces of darkness again attacked the forces of light.[23]

Timothy McVeigh and Christian Identity: A Connection?

In the dogged media pursuit of Timothy McVeigh's past, only a single link has been found connecting him with Christian Identity, but it is an odd and tantalizing link, for it also connects him indirectly to Richard Wayne Snell. On April 5, 1995 — exactly two weeks before the bombing — Timothy McVeigh is reported to have made two telephone calls to Elohim City, a Christian Identity communal settlement in eastern Oklahoma, near the Arkansas border. The leader of Elohim City, Robert G. Millar, claimed neither to have known McVeigh nor to have spoken to him: "I don't think I've ever seen him. I don't think he's ever been in any of my audiences to the best of my knowledge. He may have gotten our telephone number from someone if he used our telephone number, and if he phoned, nobody here has any knowledge of ever talking to him." The calls were apparently brief and made to a telephone in a common room. It is impossible to determine whom McVeigh called or why, although, according to one report, he was attempting to reach a German national he knew who was then living at the commune. Nonetheless, one may speculate that his call might have been prompted by the pending execution of Richard Wayne Snell, to whom Robert Millar was closely linked.[24]

Millar's ministry developed from a visionary experience he is reported to have had in 1948, in his native Canada. He founded the Bethel Christian Church and School in Maryland in the late 1950s, moved to Oklahoma in 1972, and claims congregations in Florida, Virginia, North Carolina, and Maryland. By 1985, sixty people were living in the Elohim City community. A reporter who visited ten years later found slightly less than a hundred there. Millar has continued to teach Identity doctrine: "I believe that the inheritors of the promises of the 12 tribes of Israel are primarily the Celtic tribes, the Germanic people and the Scandinavian people, not inclusively, and not exclusively, but primarily."[25]

At some point in the late 1970s or early 1980s, Millar began an association with James Ellison of the Covenant, Sword and Arm of the Lord. In time, he became Ellison's "spiritual advisor." In 1982, after Ellison had declared himself a descendant of King David, Millar performed an anointing ceremony at Zarephath-Horeb. During the standoff with federal law-enforcement agents at Zarephath-Horeb in 1985, Ellison asked to see Millar, who was flown to the compound by the FBI. Millar served as an intermediary in the negotiations that led to an end to the standoff, including Ellison's surrender, much as Bo Gritz was to do in the Ruby Ridge affair seven years later. Ellison later served a sentence on weapons and racketeering charges. On May 19, 1995, after his release from prison, he married Millar's granddaughter.[26]

It is scarcely surprising that, given his close association with Ellison, Millar would also come to know Richard Wayne Snell. As he testified at Snell's trial, Millar met Snell in 1981 at "a gathering in southern Missouri of Christians and concerned citizens" where Millar spoke. The conversation begun there was sufficiently intense to continue "for a number of days." Subsequently, Snell visited "one of our communities," although which community is not clear. Snell also accompanied Millar on some of his speaking engagements and stayed with one of Millar's sons in Oklahoma. "We had extensive sharing on a general basis and on a theological basis," Millar reported, "and although it wasn't formalized it seemed that I sort of in a sense became his pastor." Millar, in other words, came to perform the same function of spiritual adviser for Snell that he had for Ellison. Millar was a frequent visitor to Snell's death row cell, was present for his execution, and escorted Snell's body to Elohim City for burial on April 20.[27]

The residents of Elohim City live reclusive lives at the end of a six-mile dirt road. Unlike the congregation of Pete Peters, for example, this is not an Identity group known for its aggressive outreach activities. Nor is Timothy McVeigh known to have had prior contacts with Millar or any of the community's residents. As a local Methodist minister put it, "I guess they pretty much keep to themselves." The community is also a substantial drive from Oklahoma City. It seems unlikely, therefore, that McVeigh phoned Elohim City for some casual reason. It is far more likely that he either wished to reach a specific individual (in which case the brevity of the calls suggests that he failed) or to acquire a specific piece of information, perhaps concerning the fate of Richard Wayne Snell.[28]

The Turner Diaries

Much has been made of the role *The Turner Diaries* may have played in the planning of the Oklahoma City bombing. In the first place, those who knew McVeigh in the army have emphasized his attachment to the book, arguably the single most widely read work on the radical right. In addition to McVeigh's fondness for the book, observers were struck after April 19 by the similarity between the Oklahoma City bombing and an episode that occurs early in Turner's narrative. As the first major act of violence in the racist revolution, Turner's organization is assigned the task of blowing up the FBI building in Washington. Unable to secure the desired supply of TNT or a comparable explosive, the plotters build a device that is "a little under 5,000 pounds, and nearly all of that is ammonium nitrate fertilizer," which was, of course, one of the main components of the Oklahoma City bomb. The fertilizer, mixed with heating oil, is then packed into a stolen delivery truck that the plotters drive into the building's freight entrance.[29]

William Pierce, the book's author, was immediately placed on the defensive when the parallel became widely publicized. When reporters reached Pierce at the National Alliance compound near Hillsboro, West Virginia, he scoffed at the idea that his novel might have been the model: "It's just ridiculous. This is a fictional account I wrote 18 years ago. Why should there be any similarities between a fictional account in a novel with this bombing in Oklahoma City? It's really, really grasping. . . . You can go to any newsstand or drug store, find a dozen adventure novels, spy novels in which there are bombings of some sort or other." A week later, however, Pierce decided to make a more extended statement, aired on a shortwave radio program used by the radical right. Pierce's statement is notable for both what it includes and what it omits.[30]

The statement, "OKC Bombing and America's Future," is remarkable for its failure to make any mention of *The Turner Diaries*, even by way of exculpating its author in the manner of Pierce's earlier interview. Pierce's statement is nevertheless worth examining, because his opinions are influential in both Identity and non-Identity circles. Pierce linked Oklahoma City with Waco in two ways, arguing, first, that those who died at Waco were no less victims than those who died in Oklahoma City and, second, that what happened at Waco too was an act of terrorism: "They [the government] did it simply because the Davidians were different. Their religion was odd." In Pierce's view, the bombing was a "desperate and foolish" act. Attempting to walk a narrow line between commentary and incitement, Pierce continually distinguished "disorganized terrorism," such as the bombing in Oklahoma City, from "planned, organized terrorism," presumably of the kind described in *The Turner Diaries*. He predicted an increasing amount of the disorganized variety by "exasperated, fed-up Americans" angered by nonwhite immigration, corrupt politicians, Jewish media, multiculturalism, and other assorted ills. But, he concluded, "Such disorganized terrorism, motivated by anger rather than by a plan, will never bring down the government." To accomplish this aim, Pierce prescribes, rather than the risky advocacy of planned terrorism, an informational campaign to "help . . . people understand who America's real enemies are, by helping them understand the underlying causes of terrorism, and by encouraging them to stand together in a united front against government terrorism."[31]

For obvious legal reasons, Pierce has chosen not to develop the logic of *The Turner Diaries* in a public forum, preferring instead to characterize it as a mere work of fiction on a par with airport paperbacks. Yet his reiterated contrast between disorganized and futile terrorism, on the one hand, and planned, potentially effective terrorism, on the other, is of a piece with the *Diaries*. If only, Pierce appears to be saying, there were a cadre of disciplined and totally committed individuals, people like Earl Turner and his colleagues, anything would be possible, even the overthrow of the government, with a racist "utopia" to follow. But curiously absent both from Pierce's statement and from his novel is the organization most closely associated in the public mind with the Oklahoma City bombing—the militias.

The Rise of Militias

Timothy McVeigh and Terry Nichols were, at most, hangers-on of the militia, drifting occasionally into meetings. Yet despite their lack of formal militia ties, public awareness of the militias was perhaps the most dramatic by-product of the bombing. Militias are locally based private armed groups that possess a command structure, engage in military training or exercises, and claim to fulfill essential public functions: protection of the community against "tyranny," assertion of the right to bear arms, and defense of the Constitution. In seeking to fit the militias into the larger picture of radical right-wing activity, two preliminary observations are essential. First, the groups now called militias did not emerge from a vacuum. They are, rather, the latest manifestation of a long-standing right-wing paramilitary tendency. Second, as potential instruments of violence, the militias and militialike organizations are in a relationship of constant tension with a competing organizational model. The military model, with its mobilized cohorts and chain of command, competes with what might be described as an atomistic or cellular model, in which the means of violence are held by single individuals or very small coteries, independent of one another rather than nested within a larger, more complex structure.

The militias are the offspring of a tendency described in chapter 10—"radical localism," the belief that local governmental units, usually the county or township, are the most fundamental and legitimate units of government. Hence, they must take responsibility for their own defense. As David Bennett points out in his history of the American right, the militias, although creatures of the 1990s, have paramilitary antecedents that go back to armed anticommunist groups of the Cold War era, such as the Minutemen. The militias, however, focus not on invasion or foreign subversion, but on an enemy within, the government itself. In the post–Cold War era, with America's most obvious external enemy defeated and in disintegration, a once-coherent world, with its clear and dramatic distinctions between good and evil, suddenly became much more complicated. Now, the world seems to be a muddled, confusing place, where—whether in Somalia, Haiti, or Bosnia—American national interests are often difficult to discern.[32]

The theory of a New World Order reimposed a simple conflict between good and evil; but now evil lay within, in the form of a federal government bent on imposing tyranny upon its citizens. Where earlier examples of radical localism rested primarily upon constitutional theories that asserted the invalidity of larger governmental units, the militias add the belief, drawn from NWO theory, that localities are in imminent danger of attack from the national government. John Trochmann, head of the Militia of Montana, paints an apocalyptic picture:

> When the troops come in, they'll come in such force it will be incredible! In forty-eight hours, they can have one hundred million troops here. They'll come out of the ground! They'll come from submarines!

They'll come from air drops! They'll come from everywhere! . . . We're here to defend our community, not just ourselves, but the whole community. These hills out here, my county has about five thousand hunters, and every hunter is a sniper. And the enemy that would come in here to destroy our way of life knows that.[33]

The paramilitary groups that served as models for militias often had important Identity components. Among these was the Christian-Patriots Defense League, whose "Minister of Defense," the Identity writer and evangelist Jack Mohr, was a comrade of Richard Wayne Snell, and the Posse Comitatus, the quintessential expression of radical localism, loose associations of armed county "posses." Indeed, as we saw in chapter 10, a key figure in the posse movement was the Identity preacher William Potter Gale. In Gale's thought, the Posse Comitatus often merged with the "Unorganized Militia." At his trial on charges of tax resistance, Gale's attorney described the Unorganized Militia as

a law of the United States of America codified in the United States Code, which says that every person, every male, who is between the ages of seventeen and forty-five who is not an active member of the armed forces, is a member of the Unorganized Militia. The evidence will show that the Unorganized Militia is not a figment of this man's imagination, it is a law, albeit one that few know about. So the Unorganized Militia, or being a member of that, is not a crime.

The militias of the 1990s, therefore, constitute not so much a departure from as an extension of ideas that circulated widely in the Identity–radical right milieu in the two preceding decades.[34]

The size of the militia movement is difficult to calculate with accuracy. The militia groups themselves have often made extravagant claims of their size. The Chemung Division of the Citizens Militia of Chemung County, New York, claims one thousand members; the Michigan Militia claims twelve thousand. Such figures cannot be tested, and no corroboration is provided. The best guess of those who monitor such groups is that there may be about fifteen thousand members nationally, divided into more than four hundred groups operating in all fifty states. Whatever their exact size, collectively the militias dwarf paramilitary organizations of earlier decades.[35]

The militias claim to be organizations called into existence and legitimated by the Second Amendment, and whose function is to protect the American constitutional system from the predations of the New World Order. The Michigan Militia, with which McVeigh and Nichols had at least passing contact, lists as its goals, besides providing military training, to "inform its members of local, national, and global events impelling [*sic*] the Constitution and impacting the direction of the country" and to "encourage its members to stand against tyranny, globalism, moral relativism, humanism, and the New World Order threatening to undermine our form of government and these United States of America."[36]

Like other conspiracy theories, NWO theory is a closed system. It resists falsification, because any fact or argument that might be advanced against it can be incorporated into the theory. Thus, allegedly contradictory evidence has been fabricated by the conspiracy, some opponents of the conspiracy may be dupes or confederates of the plotters, or the contradictory evidence is erroneous. Whichever option is chosen, the conspiracy theory itself is left intact. NWO theory is comparably nonfalsifiable. NWO forces, with their alleged wealth and political influence, are deemed to be in control of the media, academia, and many of the world's governments. It is scarcely surprising, therefore, that so many people in militia circles were prepared to believe that McVeigh and Nichols either were not the bombers or had been set up to deflect attention from the "real" bombers, the NWO forces in the federal government who sought a pretext for suppressing "patriot" activity. *The Spotlight* claimed in August 1995 that the Pentagon, in collaboration with the FBI and the Bureau of Alcohol, Tobacco, and Firearms, had developed a plan to "decapitate" militias by seizing their leaders and instructors. In the process, a national emergency might be declared (a frequent component of NWO theory), along with the "virtual elimination" of the Second and Fourth Amendments.[37]

Militias, consequently, exist in an atmosphere of continual fear of conspiracies and their agents. They are exemplars of what Richard Hofstadter three decades ago called "the paranoid political style." While such individuals "tend to be overheated, oversuspicious, overaggressive, grandiose, and apocalyptic in expression," they see plots not as directed toward them personally, but as "directed against a nation, a culture, a way of life whose fate affects . . . millions of others."[38]

While militia ideology is often presented in secular terms, as a response to an Illuminatist-UN plot, there is also a significant religious dimension to its belief system. A 1994 militia field manual contains the usual constitutional arguments about gun ownership and popular sovereignty, but these are preceded by a theological chapter grounded in the Bible as "word-for-word the word of God." On that basis, the field manual's author asserts, "Jesus Christ was not a pacifist." Furthermore, "since Jesus was not a pacifist, we cannot say that Christians renounced all armed conflict. And while force should be a last resort, it is sometimes necessary for self-defense and to resist tyranny. . . . [Jesus] gives authority to governments to maintain law and order, not to abuse citizens or to perpetrate evil." When government officials engage in abuse or evil, they forfeit their authority, and they, not citizens who employ force against them, are the ones engaged in rebellion. The Michigan Militia calls the Bible "the greatest single guiding influence for all nations desiring to be free" and claims as one of its goals to "seek the protection, wisdom, and leadership of Almighty God as we submit to Him and to do His will in protecting the liberty and freedom He has given to all Americans." As the Michigan Militia's former leader, Norman Olson, put it: "Our God is not a wimp. . . . He's the God of righteousness and wrath. Our way of looking at God and country is not passive Christianity."[39]

Given the militias' conspiratorialism and religious undertone, it is not surprising that Christian Identity has been connected with them. E. Tom Stetson of Concerned Citizens of Idaho and Martin J. "Red" Beckman of Montana attended the 1992 Estes Park conference convened by Pete Peters. John Trochmann, co-founder of the Militia of Montana, spoke at the 1990 Aryan Nations Congress. Indeed, as we shall see, one consequence of the militia movement has been to provide Identity figures with new opportunities for recruitment and coalition-building. They can now present themselves not as religious sectarians but as pioneers in the struggle against the federal government.[40]

The Roots of the Militias

As we have seen, the militias were in part modeled on older paramilitary organizations. But their sudden growth beginning around 1990 had different origins. Two factors seem particularly significant: the growth of antigovernment sentiment in the population at large and evidence of government misconduct at Ruby Ridge and Waco.

Surveys taken shortly after the Oklahoma City bombing reveal that although direct support for militias was low, a surprisingly large number of respondents held negative views of the government. A *Washington Post*–ABC News poll, taken between May 10 and 14—roughly three weeks after the bombing—found that only 2 percent of respondents said they strongly support militia groups, together with 11 percent who "support them somewhat." While the tiny proportion of strong supporters is not surprising, the aggregate 13 percent expressing some degree of support signaled the existence of a larger pool of antigovernment sentiment, and indeed the existence of such a pool is clear in the findings of both the *Washington Post*–ABC survey and a USA Today/CNN/Gallup poll, taken less than a week after the bombing.[41]

The latter survey asked respondents whether "the federal government has become so large and powerful it poses an immediate threat to the rights and freedoms of ordinary citizens." Thirty-nine percent agreed with the statement, a finding that remained largely consistent across lines of gender, age, income, region, and political affiliation—although agreement was particularly strong among individuals who had not completed college, made less than $20,000 a year, and lived in rural areas. An almost identical question in the *Washington Post*–ABC News survey produced nearly the same results. Thirty-six percent of those surveyed claimed they feared the government as a threat to their "personal rights and freedoms." Even though only 6 percent were willing to call the government an enemy, more than a third of respondents regarded it as a personal threat. Regardless of how this fear may have originated, it defines a sufficiently large mass of disaffected citizens to provide a significant reservoir for militia organizing.[42]

If such free-floating antigovernment feeling has been one force driving the militias, a more specific goad to action can be found in government conduct at Ruby Ridge and Waco. Most Americans knew little about the incident at Ruby Ridge, which was not widely covered when it occurred in 1992, and the vast majority of Americans supported government actions taken against the Branch Davidians. However, there is persuasive circumstantial evidence that for the substantial minority who expressed fear of the government, the two incidents were taken as proof that their fears were well founded.

Rising hostility to the federal government was partially reflected in the extreme conservatism of newly elected members of the House of Representatives in 1994. In the period that followed the Oklahoma City bombing, this was manifested in renewed interest in government actions at Ruby Ridge and Waco, and both incidents were the subjects of well-publicized congressional hearings.

At the Ruby Ridge hearings in the fall of 1995, an FBI sharpshooter invoked the Fifth Amendment, while the bureau's director, Louis J. Freeh, conceded that "at Ruby Ridge, the F.B.I. did not perform at the level which the American people expect or deserve from the F.B.I." While public controversy centered on whether the Ruby Ridge deaths were the result of flawed rules of engagement, internal FBI investigations produced their own, less visible conflicts. The reports apparently dealt with both the events on the ground in Idaho in 1992 and the manner in which the subsequent internal investigation was conducted. Although neither report has been released, subsequent events suggest highly critical conclusions. Shortly before the beginning of Senate hearings, five FBI administrators were suspended, including a former deputy director. Their suspensions were based on the possibility that they had obstructed earlier investigations of the Weaver incident by destroying documents or providing false accounts. These cases have yet to be resolved. Four days after the suspensions were announced, the government agreed to pay $3.1 million to the Weaver family in settlement of a civil suit—tacit acknowledgment, perhaps, that an even larger judgment would have resulted if the case had gone to trial.[43]

The impact of the Oklahoma City bombing on attitudes toward the Waco affair was more ambiguous, although here too a civil suit has been brought but remains pending. The high level of public support for government actions during the siege made it less likely that the Branch Davidians would be the recipients of belated sympathy. Nonetheless, government officials were compelled to restate their positions in widely covered congressional testimony. Little new information emerged, however, because the principals had already gone on record in earlier hearings, in internal Treasury and Justice Department inquiries (the reports of which had been made public), and in the criminal trials of surviving Davidians. Although the hearings were scheduled before the bombing, it is difficult to imagine that they would have been as widely noted in the absence of the bombing and the publicity it generated about the militia subculture. Clearly, those who convened and conducted the hearings did so knowing the symbolic importance Waco had assumed for the right generally and, by all accounts, for Timothy McVeigh personally; they knew as well that for a vocal right-wing constituency, whose perceptions had been shaped by Linda Thompson's Waco videotapes and other antigovernment materials, the government's conduct at Waco was a live and potent issue.[44]

For the radical right, the renewed life breathed into these cases after April 19 had a double significance. On one level, it suggested a latent but tappable political force. If senators and representatives perceived these issues to be so significant that open hearings had to be held, then presumably the antigovernment constituency was strong and important. As we shall see, this was one of a number of signs that the radical right's sense of isolation from the political "mainstream" was breaking down and that a once-insular subculture was becoming linked to broader political tendencies. On another level, the seriousness with which charges of governmental misconduct at Ruby Ridge and Waco were taken at the highest legislative levels—indeed, the virtual admission of misconduct in the Weaver case—was taken by the right as validation of its own worldview. But, of course, this was not quite the case, for the radical right did not see the causes of misconduct as stupidity, ineptitude, or misjudgment. Instead, everything that was done was deemed to have been done intentionally, in fulfillment of a grand conspiratorial plan, the New World Order. Hence the lessons taken from Ruby Ridge and Waco might be quite different depending upon one's perspective. Many not on the radical right who criticized government action in the harshest terms saw the outcomes at Waco and Ruby Ridge as institutional failures that could be addressed and solved. But NWO conspiratorialists criticized them as signs that a demonic plot was in progress to destroy American liberties.[45]

"Leaderless Resistance"

Militias tread a fine line between radical localism and a hierarchical military model. They must maintain at least the semblance of a command structure, while simultaneously granting a significant measure of autonomy to local units. Placing too much emphasis on central control would destroy their claim that sovereignty resides in local communities. Completely sacrificing a command structure risks vitiating their claim to speak for the majority of Americans and makes a mockery of their claim to possess credible military force.

However, there is a significant number of people on the radical right who are profoundly suspicious of the military model—not for ideological reasons, but because they believe large, open organizations are too vulnerable to government penetration and suppression. Instead, they argue, violent opposition to the government and to racial traitors and inferiors must be undertaken by individuals or, at most, by very small groups without visible links to one another. The circumstances of the Oklahoma City bombing suggest that this view may have had more influence on McVeigh and Nichols, the alleged bombers, than the more widely publicized militia movement. The concept of individual and small unit violence has been most notably advanced in three works: William Pierce's novel *Hunter*, Richard Kelly Hoskins's *Vigilantes of Christendom*, and Louis Beam's influential essay, "Leaderless Resistance."

Although far less well known than *The Turner Diaries, Hunter*, published in 1989, presents an even more frightening scenario of America's future. There, writing again under the pseudonym of Andrew MacDonald, Pierce presents the story of a single individual, Oscar Yeager, who undertakes a one-man war against Jews and nonwhites. Whereas "the Organization" in *Turner* resorted to open warfare, including the use of nuclear weapons, Yeager limits himself to bombings and assassinations. *Hunter* features yet another ammonium nitrate–fuel oil bomb packed in a delivery van. Yeager's acts of violence achieve political impact through their coordination with the activities of a charismatic televangelist and a closet racist in the FBI. The message is clear: small-scale acts of violence can destabilize the government if the public's racial consciousness is raised. Unlike *The Turner Diaries*, however, *Hunter* is openly contemptuous of Christian Identity. As one of Yeager's associates puts it: "The reason they can't recruit anyone but uneducated hicks is that their doctrine is crazy. . . . They have this completely nutty version of history, which no one who's paid attention in his high school history class can believe." (Curiously, Pierce's anti-Identity diatribe has done nothing to diminish his influence in the movement.) *Hunter* placed Pierce in the forefront of those who reject organized, open armed struggle with the federal government in favor of difficult-to-trace acts of individual violence that might have a catalytic effect if the public mood is right. In retrospect, *Hunter* may be seen as one of the first systematic responses to the defeat of the Order (1985–86) and the Fort Smith sedition trial (1988). The federal government was too powerful; violence would work only outside a vulnerable organizational framework.[46]

In 1990, a year after the publication of *Hunter*, Richard Kelly Hoskins published *Vigilantes of Christendom*. Hoskins, a Virginia-born racist in the mold of Lothrop Stoddard, believes that the "Nordic race" must struggle against the "Yellow Peril," "the Khazar," and "the hybrid Mexicans." *Vigilantes of Christendom* purports to retell world history in terms of the exploits of "the Phineas Priesthood." The name derives from an enigmatic reference in the 106th Psalm. The psalm, alluding to a plague that God sent against the rebellious Israelites in the wilderness, credits Phineas with "executing judgment" so that "the plague was stayed." By extension, according to Hoskins, disease appears whenever "strangers seek . . . to force their way into Christian society," bringing corruption and decay. Hoskins identifies a string of "Phineas Priests" through history who engage in acts of violent purification against "strangers" and "aliens." They ranged from King Arthur and Robin Hood to the Klan and the SS.[47]

When Hoskins reaches the contemporary period, his Christian Identity leanings become clear. He distinguishes between two types of Christians, "the Lawful and the Lawless. Those who believe and obey the Laws, Statutes, and Judgments, and those who don't. Those who believe look to God as their governor. Those who don't look for pronouncements from the ruling establishment for their cue as to what to believe. . . . The two are bitter opponents." Lawful Christians "simply call themselves 'Christian' or 'Christian Identity' instead of Catholic, Baptist, Presbyterian, etc." Hoskins points approvingly to Identity claims that biblical prophecies concerning Israel have been fulfilled by the history of Europeans. Hoskins never suggested that the "Phineas Priests" constituted a real organization, merely that God had commissioned individuals in different ages to use violence to preserve racial purity. Nonetheless, this metaphorical use of Phineas—a figure so obscure that many meanings could be read into him—might be understood by right-wing zealots to be a grant of divine authority for violent acts. Similarly, some law-enforcement personnel believed Hoskins might have been describing a previously unknown organization of right-wing assassins.[48]

Pierce and Hoskins conjured up the same image almost simultaneously. In each image, single individuals or very small groups would engage in acts of violence engendered by a racist worldview. Pierce relied on an essentially secular conception of race as the moving force of history, while Hoskins sought to ground his tactical imperative in scriptural texts and the history of Christianity. What remained was to associate their atomistic style of violence with a strategic vision, a task that was to be accomplished by the Identity figure Louis Beam. Louis Beam, once a leader in the Texas Klan, became an Identity believer and was a defendant at the Fort Smith trial. His increasing involvement with Identity was reflected in his relocation from Texas to northern Idaho in 1993. His influential essay, "Leaderless Resistance," was included in the report of Pete Peters's 1992 Estes Park conference, following the shooting at Ruby Ridge.[49]

Beam argued that antigovernment "resistance" organized along conventional hierarchical lines, with a command structure, was suicidal. Such an organization could too easily be penetrated and destroyed through infiltration and electronic surveillance. An alternative was the cellular model associated with Soviet communism, in which the destruction of a single cell left the rest of the organization intact. While Beam found this model attractive, he ultimately rejected it on the grounds that coordinated action by such cells required a degree of central direction and external resources that the movement could not afford. This led him, finally, to "leaderless resistance," or "phantom cells." These units, some as small as a single person, would have no central direction and no outside resources. "It becomes the responsibility of the individual to acquire the necessary skills and information." Beam believed that central direction was unnecessary in any event, since "in any movement, all persons involved have the same general outlook, are acquainted with the same philosophy, and generally react to given situations in similar ways." These uniform attitudes could be reinforced by alternative communications media, "allowing for a planned response that will take many variations." From the government's standpoint, Beam wrote, leaderless resistance would be an "intelligence nightmare." While Beam's essay carefully avoids any direct mention of violent acts, his use of the language of resistance, his emphasis on secrecy, and his invocation of the example of the Committees of Correspondence during the American Revolution make it clear that phantom cells are groups expected to engage in extralegal activity.[50]

"Leaderless Resistance," consequently, sought to provide a reasoned argument in favor of precisely the kind of individualized violence that had been described by William Pierce and Richard Kelly Hoskins. The attractions of such an approach were many: it promised security from government penetration; it evaded the embarrassing question of why the movement could not attract a mass following; and it implied that stealth and daring could accomplish what Robert Mathews and David Duke could not. By implication, however, leaderless resistance also stood in an ambiguous relationship to the militia movement. The militias sought to be large; they addressed the public directly; they claimed to be completely legal; and, despite the ideology of radical localism, they set great store by some kind of command structure. They had, in other words, all of the vulnerabilities Beam had associated with pyramidal organizations. If militias are the radical right's public face, leaderless resistance by phantom cells is its hidden face. The uneasy coexistence of the two masks a certain dependence, for militias can become "feeder organizations" for leaderless resistance. Those who find militias too timid or constrained have somewhere else to go, an outlet for revolutionary millenarianism. One can speculate that the accused Oklahoma City bombers represented leaderless resistance as opposed to militia action, that Timothy McVeigh's flirtation with the Michigan Militia drew him further into the movement, even as the militia's relative restraint frustrated his urge for dramatic action—an urge that leaderless resistance encourages each individual to act upon.

As the radical right entered the 1990s, two new motifs became evident among some of its adherents: first, the claim that it was neither racist nor anti-Semitic and, second, the assertion that the extreme right, far from being radical, was in fact the carrier and guardian of mainstream American values.

Militia groups have been particularly keen on presenting themselves as free of racist or anti-Semitic taints. This is especially true of two of the most highly publicized groups, the Michigan Militia and the Militia of Montana. The Michigan Militia, for example, advances as one of its goals "to insure that all citizens regardless of race, color, religion, sex, physical characteristics or national origin shall have the right and opportunity to due process of law." In its literature, the militia claims to be

Non-Denominational (Not following any one particular tenet or religious group)
Non-Political (Not recognizing any one particular political candidate,
  group, or party)
Non-Racial (Not discriminating against any racial or ethnic group)

Despite such sentiments, militia members seem overwhelmingly to be white Christians.[51]

The Militia of Montana presents a more complex and ambiguous case, in part because one of its founders, John Trochmann, was associated in press reports with Aryan Nations. In 1994, Trochmann denied that he was a white supremacist: "I'm not a supremacist . . . No being is supreme except our creator. All I'm trying to do [with militia meetings] is to make people aware of the military takeover of our country and the erosion of our constitutional freedoms, especially the Second Amendment, the one amendment that guarantees all the rest." He conceded that he had once spoken at the Aryan Nations compound, but claimed he "never had ties with them" and stated disapprovingly that he had noticed on his visit that they were "teaching their young men to disrespect women."[52]

Trochmann has not explicitly condemned anti-Semitism. Instead, in "answering allegations of . . . Anti-Semitism," the Militia of Montana emphasizes the various activities of the Anti-Defamation League, which it claims does not represent American Jews. Trochmann and two associates appeared at Senate hearings on militias in June 1995. The militia's attorney, John De Camp thought "they wanted John Trochmann because he is 'dripping blood' since he's supposedly 'anti-Semitic.'" In an interview after the hearings, neither De Camp, Trochmann, nor militia spokesman Bob Fletcher explicitly denied the charge. As De Camp put it, "they [the Senators] couldn't document anything as far as their claims of anti-Semitism." Again, the ADL surfaced as the Militia's anathema. "We walked into an Anti-Defamation League–orchestrated set-up," Trochmann claimed, "but it totally backfired on them. . . . When they started chopping us up as the lackeys for the ADL, we pulled the plug and let them have it." Explicit anti-Semitism vanishes and in its place is a fixation on an ADL conspiracy.[53]

The Militia of Montana claims the ADL had an office in the Oklahoma City federal building, implying that in some unspecified way this was related to the bombing. More sinister still, the ADL, along with Morris Dees, they assert, is an instrument "used in furthering the plan for *world governance*," that is, the New World Order. Since the Militia of Montana is part of "the patriot community" seeking to expose the plan for a "one-world-socialist-society," those who attack it must be among the conspiracy's allies. Hence organizations can forswear anti-Semitism while freely venting their hostilities on an organization intimately tied to the American Jewish community. There is no way of knowing whether this is a conscious employment of code words to evade public censure, but the militia's audience clearly contains many people who are amply prepared to read "ADL" as "Jews."[54]

Militia organizations are not the only venues on the right in which such circumspection may be found. The 1992 Estes Park conference, led by Pastor Pete Peters, demonstrated similar care in avoiding any explicitly racist or anti-Semitic themes. Indeed, in discussing the Ruby Ridge incident, Peters implied that accusations of racism were part of a media-government conspiracy: "Not only has the media used the labeling terms of White Supremacist and White Separatist but it has used them with the term criminal." But in summarizing the conferees' "Other Thoughts and Dessenting [*sic*] Opinions," the report included troubling language: "Some felt more emphasis needed to be placed on the command in Deut. 17:14–15 [that Israelites should not be ruled by foreigners] and that the destruction of white Christian people will continue until the stranger is removed from the position of being over His people." This Identity language equates America with Israel, emphasizes the religious importance of racial purity, and denigrates "the stranger." But who is "the stranger"? While the statement may refer to immigrants, a common theme in nativist writing, "stranger" is almost certainly a code word for "Jew." It is employed in precisely that sense by Richard Kelly Hoskins in *Vigilantes of Christendom*, where strangers are "disease factories," carriers of plague and bearers of "God's curse." To prevent contamination, "God's chosen people always attempt to stamp out the lesser evil to avoid the greater one."[55]

As the radical right has expanded with the growth of the militias, it has become chary of utilizing the openly racist and anti-Semitic rhetoric customarily employed, as it were, "within the family." Speaking now to broader audiences, including many attracted by nonracist, antigovernment appeals, discretion seems advisable, with euphemisms and code words substituting for the hard-edged rhetoric of an earlier period. At the same time, the right increasingly positions itself as an exemplar of core American values, arguing that even as these values are imperiled by the New World Order, they have found a stalwart and incorruptible guardian on the "patriot right." This is in part a replay of earlier right-wing motifs, in which those on the political fringe sought legitimization by linkage with venerated American symbols. This was notably the case with the Ku Klux Klan of the 1920s. As we saw in chapter 2, the proto-Identity clergyman and Klan functionary Reuben Sawyer preached "a cleansed and purified Americanism" on the Klan's behalf.

At the ideological level, the radical right seeks to make the same connection by portraying itself as the stronghold of "constitutionalists," that is, those whose primary fidelity is to the values incorporated in the American foundational document. At the social level, the link is made through "bridging mechanisms," that is, organizations that connect the core of the radical right to segments of American society considered more "mainstream" and non-stigmatizing.

Constitutionalism

Just as the radical right has embraced religious fundamentalism, so it has been associated with what might be called "legal fundamentalism." Like its better-known religious counterpart, legal fundamentalism insists on the literal reading of authoritative legal texts and holds that the true meaning of those texts has been lost through distortions allegedly introduced by corrupt interpreters in the past. It is necessary, therefore, to recapture a submerged authentic tradition. Just as Christian Identity believes that Protestant clergy have corrupted the true meaning of Scripture, so on the legal level constitutionalists believe judges and lawyers have collectively perverted constitutional principles.

Some legal fundamentalists advance the idea of the "organic constitution," the original constitutional text plus the Bill of Rights, on the theory that this alone was the product of the Founding Fathers. By implication, then, the remaining amendments, particularly the Civil War amendments (the Thirteenth, Fourteenth, and Fifteenth) are not constitutionally valid. The remaining authoritative text is further subject to minute linguistic analysis. As Red Beckman, a participant in the Estes Park conference, explained: "We have a little stricter discipline in the use of words than you will see in most dictionaries." A widely circulated militia handbook argues that the Sixteenth Amendment, which permitted the taxation of income, "WAS NOT ratified in the same language by three fourths of the United States as required . . . and is therefore invalid."[56]

The Constitution is intentionally severed from traditions of interpretation, with the goal of restoring its literal meaning. This has two consequences. The first is to effectively delegitimize the actions of courts and legislatures for those who seek the document's "plain meaning" or the framers' "original intent." The second consequence is to raise the Constitution to a status of near-scriptural infallibility: "Apart from Original Intent, we break faith with those who founded this great nation. How do you like it when people interpret the Bible to suit their fancy instead of as God meant it? . . . *Documents mean what their authors meant!*" According to Reyond E. McFarland, an Iowa constitutionalist, the organic constitution "is not quite the Bible, but it is awfully close." The connection between the Constitution and the Bible had been made earlier by William Potter Gale (see chapter 10), although Gale pushed divine inspiration back further to include the Articles of Confederation. The line of divine inspiration continued to the Constitution itself: "The Constitution was lifted from the Articles of Confederation, therefore the source of the Constitution is the Holy Bible."[57]

When constitutionalists have been prosecuted, as Gale was, they regard the government's action as tyrannical and unconstitutional. In their eyes, it is they rather than the government that abides by the intent of the framers, and actions taken against them are construed as the misuse of power, cloaked in specious legal justifications. These tendencies, present at least since the 1970s, have intensified in the 1990s, with the rise of the militias, who trace their legitimacy to the Second Amendment and who claim, "Our purpose is solely to defend these [Bill of Rights] rights for ourselves and our neighbors." In June 1995, John Trochmann and Bob Fletcher of the Militia of Montana appeared before a Senate subcommittee. In their prepared statement, they asserted that "the [militia] movement is made up of a cross section of americans from all walks of life, with one singular mandate which is public and overt: THE RETURN TO THE CONSTITUTION OF THE UNITED STATES, *AND TO YOUR OATH TO DEFEND THAT CONSTITUTION.*" By implication, then, those who oppose such activities either value the Constitution less or seek to subvert it.[58]

A dramatic demonstration of these principles occurred in the spring of 1996 with the conflict between federal law-enforcement personnel and the group calling itself Freemen in Garfield County, Montana. The Freemen were an Identity group whose legal doctrines led them to claim virtually total freedom from the state's authority. The ranch that served as their base— "Justus [*sic*] Township"—was declared to be a sovereign, self-governing unit beyond the government's reach, empowered to convene its own grand juries and courts. The Freemen were an extreme example of what I referred to in chapter 10 as "radical localism," and it is not surprising that their members faced legal charges—in this case, the use of fraudulent financial instruments.[59]

The Freemen's Identity views were explicated in a "Common Law Memorandum" filed with a local court by Rodney Skurdal in 1994. Skurdal, who was in charge of Freemen security, joined the group in the fall of 1995. The memorandum begins with a lengthy presentation of Identity beliefs, including two-seed theology, and then goes on to draw legal implications. Not only are members of "the white race" Israelites, but "'America,' i.e., 'United States of America,' is the New Land of 'milk and honey', the new 'Zion,' as contained in the Bible, . . . in which Israel will never move from, [*sic*] and the Land which Almighty God promised Israel." If whites are Israel, living on land promised by God, then the only law applicable to them is that of the Bible, along with whatever nonbiblical norms are judged to derive from Scripture. The Freemen discovered this fundamental, divinely enjoined law in the "organic constitution" and in a vision of common law drawn from an idiosyncratic reading of English legal history in the Middle Ages, conjuring up an imagined utopia of free Anglo-Saxon yeoman.[60]

An important corollary of this argument is that regulations that fall outside the biblical–common law corpus do not bind members of the white race, and obedience to such norms is a form of idolatry. The Skurdal memorandum considers as acts of "worshipping Baal" even seemingly innocent legal requirements, such as applying for a driver's license, marriage license, or building permit; securing a Social Security card; or paying income, property, or inheritance tax. "Once you have applied for these benefits, via your 'application forms' . . . from your '*new gods*,' you have voluntary [*sic*] become their new 'slaves,' to 'tax' at their will, for you are no longer 'Free,' i.e., a 'freeman.'" By this reasoning, conforming to the law is no longer merely a violation of a fundamentalist reading of the Constitution; it is the most profound kind of sin.[61]

The Freemen manifest a number of ideas described in earlier chapters. They resemble the armed radical localism of the Posse Comitatus. Their "sovereign township" harks back to an earlier separatist declaration, the Nehemiah Township Charter. Their fusion of law and the Bible has roots in the writings of Howard Rand and his followers. Together, these elements form a volatile mix that made conflict with authority virtually inevitable.

Having learned some of the bitter lessons of Waco, the FBI approached the Freemen in a radically different manner. Agents remained as inconspicuous as possible, the operation was directed by specialists in crisis management, and the authorities carefully avoided the appearance of a military operation. The FBI avoided self-imposed deadlines and relied instead upon patience and the passage of time in the hope of slowly eroding the Freemen's resistance. The wisdom of this strategy was borne out when, on June 13, 1996—the eighty-first day of the standoff—the sixteen Freemen still in the compound surrendered to federal authorities.

Bridging Mechanisms

The increasing association of the radical right with core American values suggests its fundamental repositioning within American politics and society. As recently as the late 1980s, the radical right was an isolated, insular subculture, detached from and shunned by the larger society, if indeed the latter was even aware of its existence. It was blocked from access to major communications media, where notice of it was taken only intermittently when it was associated with actual or threatened violence. Its boundaries were maintained by a combination of distaste for a world it regarded as corrupt and by the world's rejection. The subculture's cohesion was maintained by an intricate alternative communications system made up of books, periodicals, mail-order services, electronic bulletin boards, shortwave broadcasts, video and audio tapes, gun shows, and the like.

But the chasm that once separated the radical right from less stigmatized forms of association and expression has narrowed appreciably in the last five years. It has become linked to the mainstream of American politics and culture by a series of bridging mechanisms. First, some on the radical right have deliberately sought to repackage themselves in order to deflect opposition and attract larger audiences. Second, ideas incubated on the radical right have found partial acceptance in some mainstream venues, particularly some of those associated with evangelical Protestantism and the New Age. Third, the militia movement provides a way station for the disaffected between the outermost fringe of acceptable political discourse and the core of the radical right.

Emblematic of this mainstreaming is the case of Larry Pratt, the executive director of Gun Owners of America. Pratt was a featured speaker at the 1992 Estes Park conference attended by important Christian Identity and militia figures, as well a contributor to the Identity periodical *Jubilee*. In 1996, Pratt served as one of four co-chairs of Pat Buchanan's campaign for the Republican presidential nomination. In February 1996, Pratt's earlier associations became public knowledge, and, although he denied any racist sentiment, he was compelled to step down from his campaign post. Two conclusions seem clear. First, Pratt would have continued to serve had his sharing of a platform with Louis Beam and Identity's Richard Butler not become public knowledge. It is perhaps not coincidental that the information about him was released shortly after Buchanan's strong showing early in the campaign, as he was increasingly employing anti–New World Order rhetoric. Second, since Pratt's supportive view of militias was scarcely a secret, it seems reasonable to suppose that his appointment to the top echelon of a national campaign was made after a calculation that the stigma attaching to his views and activities was less important than his ability to mobilize a valued constituency.[62]

The "repackaging" of the radical right is tied to the rhetoric discussed earlier in this chapter: the New World Order theories that seek to explain America's problems by attributing them to a conspiratorial threat. In a society where conspiracy theories have always flourished, NWO conspiracy theories appear different largely in degree. These tales of plots and cabals coexist with the constitutionalism described earlier. Indeed, the two are often combined: the threat posed by the New World Order requires extraordinary efforts if the Constitution is to survive. Whether for opportunistic reasons or out of conviction, this rhetorical style is largely free of the strident anti-Semitism and racism that previously was so conspicuous a part of ultra-right discourse. Such themes, however, often remain just below the surface in variants that link the conspiracy to Jewish bankers or see world government designs in affirmative action proposals.

In part because these conspiracy theories are often devoid of the most objectionable racist language, they have found places outside the radical right subculture itself. They have been transplanted to some evangelical Protestant and New Age circles. Among evangelical Protestants, for example, New

World Order ideas, with elaborate discussions of the Illuminati's role, appear in the ministry and publications of Texe Marrs, whose works may be found in religious bookstores to which conspiratorial literature would ordinarily not gain access. A weaker but still fully recognizable version of NWO theory also appears in Pat Robertson's 1991 volume, *The New World Order*. Although Robertson has disclaimed any anti-Semitic intentions, his tale of Illuminatist plots is drawn in large part from the anti-Semitic writings of Nesta Webster and Eustace Mullins. The appearance of such material in religious writings is not entirely surprising, however, since fears of world government have been linked by millenarians to the rise of Antichrist in the End-times.[63]

More surprising, though, is the fact that some of the same ideas appear in New Age publications, which themselves are reviled by fundamentalists as manifestations of paganism and Satanism. Yet some New Age publications have found conspiracy theories attractive for their own reasons, as examples of what might be called stigmatized knowledge—ideas rejected or ignored by such institutions as universities, the scientific community, and the mass media. Just as these institutions have generally rejected UFOs, herbal medicine, and the story of Atlantis, so they have turned their backs on conspiratorial theories of history. Indeed, to some in the New Age movement such theories are doubly attractive, for they are not only themselves examples of stigmatized knowledge; they can also be used to explain why other ideas have been shunned. As with conspiratorial religious literature, New Age conspiratorialism is rarely subject to informal censorship and gains access to mainstream distribution outlets.[64]

Finally, the militias themselves are a bridging mechanism, with their public face and patriotic rhetoric. Yet even when they themselves eschew racial appeals, they are part of the subculture's communications system and facilitate contacts by their members with groups and ideas that are far more extreme. They are less fronts than they are transition points on individual journeys from conventional politics to political extremism. Rather than shift abruptly from "normal" to "abnormal" politics, one can move by stages.

What are the consequences of these bridging mechanisms? Will they transform formerly isolated coteries into socially acceptable mass movements? Or will they dilute extremist doctrines in order to build greater pubic acceptance? When a formerly small and insular group aspires to be a major social movement, it often faces a trade-off between doctrinal purity and a mass membership. It can rarely have both. This poses a special dilemma for Christian Identity, whose idiosyncratic belief system seems particularly ill suited to mass organization. Identity can cloak its beliefs, seeking instead to establish a leadership position in a broader coalition of antigovernment forces, somewhat as Pete Peters did at the Estes Park conference. Alternatively, it can retain and nurture a unique message, in the hope that an enlarged recruiting pool will find it attractive. Which of these courses it will take, and what impact bridging mechanisms will have, are questions that, unfortunately, can be answered only after the fact.

The experiences of the last five years, culminating in the bombing in Oklahoma City, have confirmed and strengthened the conclusions drawn in the original edition of this book. The analysis of Christian Identity suggested that it had, throughout its brief history, been a movement peculiarly susceptible to rapid doctrinal mutations. That may be said as well for the larger right-wing milieu in which it is enfolded. Precisely because it is a fragmented world, with leaders who often compete, organizations that rapidly form and split, and a disinclination to accept a comprehensive structure of coordination, its development is subject to sudden swings. In this respect, the growth of militias is merely the latest in a long series of examples. In the absence of a charismatic figure capable of welding its disparate elements together, the radical right, including Identity, may be expected to undergo future changes, only some of which can be anticipated.

What is most striking about the Oklahoma City bombing's implications for Identity and the radical right, therefore, is its irony: the circumstantial ties between the bombing and the radical right should have definitively delegitimized the radical right. But instead of reinforcing its pariah status, the bombing helped move it toward the mainstream, supplying it with the kind of media access it never previously enjoyed and attributing to it a power about which it had only fantasized. Such media access, in a time of rising antigovernment sentiment, has opened new recruiting possibilities, while the attribution of power has made the fringe right an increasingly attractive prize for some mainstream politicians to covet.

Notes

Preface

1. A list of acts that resulted in fatalities appears in James A. Aho, *The Politics of Righteousness: Idaho Christian Patriotism* (Seattle: University of Washington Press, 1990), pp. 8–9. Aho lists twenty such incidents between 1979 and 1985 that collectively resulted in fifty-one deaths. Roughly half of the incidents involved individuals with Identity associations.

2. In contrast to Aho, Stanley Barrett gives Identity only scant attention in his study of Canadian rightists, *Is God a Racist?: The Right Wing in Canada* (Toronto: University of Toronto Press, 1987), pp. 334–36. The incorrect characterization of Edward Hine appears in Kevin Flynn and Gary Gerhardt, *The Silent Brotherhood: Inside America's Racist Underground* (New York: Free Press, 1989), p. 51.

3. Paul Boyer, *When Time Shall Be No More: Prophecy Belief in Modern American Culture* (Cambridge: Harvard University Press, 1991), pp. 15–17.

Chapter 1

1. Clarke Garrett, *Respectable Folly: Millenarians and the French Revolution in France and England* (Baltimore: Johns Hopkins University Press, 1975), p. 184.

2. Quoted in Gershom Scholem, *Sabbatai Sevi: The Mystical Messiah, 1626–1676* (Princeton: Princeton University Press, 1973), p. 348 and pp. 332–54 passim, emphasis in original.

3. Garrett, *Respectable Folly*, pp. 179–222; *The Dictionary of National Biography*, 22 vols. (London: Oxford University Press, 1967–68), 2:1350–53.

4. John Wilson, "British Israelism: The Ideological Restraints on Sect Organization," in Bryan R. Wilson, ed., *Patterns of Sectarianism: Organization and Ideology in Social and Religious Movements* (London: Heinemann, 1967), pp. 353–54; John Wilson, *Lectures on Our Israelitish Origin*, 5th ed. (London: James Nisbet, 1876), pp. 189, 315, emphasis in original, first published in 1840. The two John Wilsons are, of course, separated by a century of time and a universe of discourse.

5. Wilson, *Lectures on Our Israelitish Origin*, pp. 108, 111, 368, emphasis in original.

6. Ibid., p. 191, 270, 368.

7. Reginald Horsman, *Race and Manifest Destiny: The Origins of American Racial Anglo-Saxonism* (Cambridge: Harvard University Press, 1981), pp. 32, 37–38, 63.

8. Wilson, "British-Israelism," p. 357.

9. Alexander Beaufort Grimaldi, *Memoirs, and a Selection of Letters from the Correspondence of Edward Hine* (London: Robert Banks and Son, 1909), pp. 9–13.

10. Ibid., pp. 12–13, 17; Wilson, "British Israelism," pp. 363–75.

11. Edward Hine, *Forty-seven Identifications of the Anglo-Saxons with the Lost Ten Tribes of Israel, Founded upon Five Hundred Scripture Proofs*, new ed. (New York: James Huggins, 1885), pp. v, 2.

12. Grimaldi, *Memoirs*, pp. 14–15.

13. Edward Hine, *England's Coming Glories: Being the Fourth Part of the "Identifications of the Anglo Saxons with Lost Israel"* (New York: James Huggins, 1880).

14. James Webb, *The Occult Underground* (La Salle, Ill.: Open Court, 1974), p. 233; Kurt Mendelsohn, *The Riddle of the Pyramids* (New York: Praeger, 1974), pp. 206–7.

15. C. Piazzi Smyth, "The Glory of the Great Pyramid," in Hine, *England's Coming Glories*, p. 230.

16. H. Aldersmith, "The Second Advent of Christ," in Denis Hanan and H. Aldersmith, eds., *British-Israel Truth*, 14th ed. (London: Covenant Publishing Company, 1932), p. 210, first published in 1891; M. Alma Hetherington, *70 Years Old!: An Outline History of Our Work since 1909* (Burnaby, British Columbia: Association of the Covenant People, [1979]), p. 14. A list of David Davidson's publications appears in D. Davidson and H. Aldersmith, *The Great Pyramid: Its Divine Message—An Original Co-ordination of Historical Documents and Archaeological Evidences*, 11th ed. (London: Williams and Norgate, 1948), pp. xii–xiii, first published in 1924. Although the work is designated volume 1, volume 2 was never issued. Notwithstanding the joint authorship, the work is generally regarded as predominantly Davidson's.

17. Pascoe Goard, "Introduction," in Hanan and Aldersmith, *British-Israel Truth*, p. ix; Aldersmith, "The Second Advent of Christ," p. 209; Hetherington, *70 Years Old!*, p. 2.

18. Wilson, "British Israelism," pp. 345, 376; John Wilson, "The Relation between Ideology and Organization in a Small Religious Group: The British Israelites," *Review of Religious Research* 10 (1968): 51–60.

19. Wilson, "The Relation between Ideology and Organization," pp. 52–55. The figure on contemporary British-Israelism membership is from an interview with A. E. Gibb, secretary of the British-Israel-World Federation (a second hyphen was recently added to the name), London, June 1992.

Chapter 2

1. Joseph Wild, *The Lost Ten Tribes And 1882* (New York: James Huggins, 1879), preface (unpaginated); idem, *Manasseh and United States: An Essay* (New York: James Huggins, 1879), pp. 9–10.

2. Wild, *The Lost Ten Tribes*, catalog of publications follows p. 280; idem, *Manasseh and United States*, announcement of the Lost Israel Identification Society of Brooklyn follows p. 16.

3. W. H. Poole, *Anglo-Israel or the Saxon Race Proved to Be the Lost Tribes of Israel* (Toronto: William Briggs, n.d. but probably early 1880s); M. M. Eshelman, *Two Sticks; or, The Lost Tribes of Israel Discovered: The Jew and the Israelite Not the Same* (Mount Morris, Ill.: Brethren's Publishing Company, 1887), p. 11.

4. Wesley A. Swift, *Standards of the Kingdom* (Hollywood, Calif.: New Christian Crusade Church, n.d.), p. 30.

5. Russell H. Chittenden, *History of the Sheffield Scientific School of Yale University, 1846–1922*, 2 vols. (New Haven: Yale University Press, 1928), 2:503–4. Chittenden misidentifies Totten as Charles E., rather than Charles A. L.

6. Charles A. Totten, *Our Race: Its Origin and Destiny—A Series of Studies on the Saxon Riddle* (New Haven: Our Race Publishing Company, 1891), p. 250; idem, *The Order of History: The Coming Crusade. Palestine Regained, or The Relation of Our Race to the Restoration of Israel: The Means Towards the End* (New Haven: Our Race Publishing Company, 1897); Thomas F. Gossett, *Race: The History of an Idea in America*, rev. ed. (New York: Schocken, 1987), pp. 191–92.

7. Alexander Beaufort Grimaldi, *Memoirs, and a Selection of Letters from the Correspondence of Edward Hine* (London: Robert Banks and Son, 1909), pp. 20–50.

8. Quoted in Ernest Tuveson, *Redeemer Nation: The Idea of America's Millennial Role* (Chicago: University of Chicago Press, 1968), pp. 156–57; on the Mormons, see pp. 175–86 passim.

9. William C. Hiss, "Shiloh: Frank W. Sandford and the Kingdom, 1893–1948" (Ph.D. dissertation, Tufts University, 1978), pp. 166–71; Shirley Nelson, *Fair Clear and Terrible: The Story of Shiloh, Maine* (Latham, N.Y.: British American Publishing, 1989), pp. 102–5.

10. James R. Goff, Jr., *Fields White unto Harvest: Charles F. Parham and the Missionary Origins of Pentecostalism* (Fayetteville: University of Arkansas Press, 1988), pp. 57–58, 208; Robert Mapes Anderson, *Vision of the Disinherited: The Making of American Pentecostalism* (New York: Oxford University Press, 1979), p. 50.

11. Charles Edwin Jones, *A Guide to the Study of the Pentecostal Movement*, 2 vols. (Metuchen, N.J.: Scarecrow Press, 1983), 2:721; Clarence Eugene Cowan, *A History of the Church of God (Holiness)* (Overland Park, Kans.: Herald and Banner Press, 1949), pp. 17, 26–27, 34, 75; Martin E. Marty, *Modern American Religion: The Irony of It All, 1893–1919*, 2 vols. (Chicago: University of Chicago Press, 1986), 1:241–42; Charles F. Parham, *A Voice Crying in the Wilderness*, 2d ed. (Baxter Springs, Kans.: Apostolic Faith Bible College, 1910), first published in 1902; Sarah E. Parham, *The Life of Charles F. Parham, Founder of the Apostolic Faith Movement* (1930; reprint, Joplin, Mo.: Hunter Printing Company, 1969), p. 305.

12. J. Gordon Melton, *The Encyclopedia of American Religions*, 2d ed. (Detroit: Gale Research Corporation, 1987), p. 41; S. Parham, *The Life of Charles Parham*, p. 305; Anderson, *Vision of the Disinherited*, pp. 116–17; Cowan, *A History of the Church of God (Holiness)*, p. 75.

13. *Watchman of Israel* (Boston), later called *New Watchman*; "The Roadbuilder" [W. G. MacKendrick], *The Destiny of America* (Toronto: T. H. Best Printing Company; Boston: A. A. Beauchamp, 1921), a catalog of Beauchamp's publications appears after p. 267.

14. Sawyer's 1921 *Watchman* articles included the following: "The American Idea," 3 (March 1921), pp. 81–85; "Who Are the Americans?," 3 (April 1921), pp. 114–15; "Who Are the Americans?," 3 (August 1921), pp. 182–85; and "Israel's Great Prophet," 4 (November 1921), pp. 7–9.

15. Ralph Lord Roy, *Apostles of Discord: A Study of Organized Bigotry and Disruption on the Fringes of Protestantism* (Boston: Beacon Press, 1953), p. 97. Roy's was the only history of Identity (see pp. 92–117 passim) until the last few years. Albert Lee presents his bizarre

theory about Sawyer and Cameron in *Henry Ford and the Jews* (New York: Stein and Day, 1980), p. 89.

16. Sawyer's birthdate is given in the *National Union Catalog Pre-1956 Imprints* (London: Mansell, 1977), 522:527; "Anglo-Israel Claims Entire Time: Portland Pastor Retires," *Watchman of Israel* 3 (March 1921), p. 99; "Communication," *Watchman of Israel* 4 (November 1921), pp. 18–19; a letter from a representative of the Victoria, British Columbia, British-Israel group appears in *Watchman of Israel* 3 (January 1921), p. 57; "The British Israel World Federation," *Watchman of Israel* 3 (May 1921), pp. 136–37; additional news of Sawyer's lecturing activities appears in *Watchman of Israel* 3 (June 1921), p. 158; M. Alma Hetherington, *70 Years Old!: An Outline History of Our Work since 1909* (Burnaby, British Columbia: Association of the Covenant People, [1979]), p. 26.

17. "Anglo-Israel Claims Entire Time," p. 99; "British-Israel World Federation Congress: A Report of the London Meetings, July 5–10, 1920," *Watchman of Israel* 2 (August 1920), pp. 181–89; a list of the federation's vice-patrons appears after p. 267 in [MacKendrick], *The Destiny of America*.

18. Malcolm Clark, Jr., "The Bigot Disclosed: Ninety Years of Nativism," *Oregon Historical Quarterly* 75 (1974): 108–90.

19. R. H. Sawyer, *The Truth about the Invisible Empire Knights of the Ku Klux Klan: A Lecture Delivered at the Municipal Auditorium in Portland, Oregon, on December Twenty-second, Nineteen Twenty-one, to Six Thousand People* (n.p., n.d.), pamphlet, p. 5; Eckard V. Toy, "Robe and Gown: The Ku Klux Klan in Eugene, Oregon, during the 1920s," in Shawn Lay, ed., *The Invisible Empire in the West: Toward a New Appraisal of the Ku Klux Klan of the 1920s* (Urbana: University of Illinois Press, 1992), pp. 153–84; Kenneth Jackson, "The Ku Klux Klan in the City, 1915–1930" (Ph.D. dissertation, University of Chicago, 1966), pp. 282–83.

20. Clark, "The Bigot Disclosed," pp. 176, 180–81, 190; Kathleen M. Blee, *Women of the Klan: Racism and Gender in the 1920s* (Berkeley: University of California Press, 1991), p. 63.

21. R. H. Sawyer, "The Stone of Destiny," *Watchman of Israel* 1 (April 1919), pp. 127–30; "Anglo-Israel Claims Entire Time," p. 99; R. H. Sawyer, "Who Are the Americans?," *Watchman of Israel* 3 (July 1921), p. 168.

22. Sawyer, *The Truth about the Invisible Empire*, pp. 11–12.

23. Eckard V. Toy, Jr., "The Ku Klux Klan in Oregon: Its Program and Character" (M.A. thesis, University of Oregon, 1959), p. 137; R. H. Sawyer, "Israel the Man," *New Watchman* 6 (March–April 1924), pp. 21–23; idem, "The Evolution of Israel," *New Watchman* 6 (May–June 1924), pp. 41–45.

24. Robert Peal, *Mary Baker Eddy: The Years of Authority* (New York: Holt, Rinehart, and Winston, 1977), pp. 16–18.

25. Altman K. Swihart, *Since Mrs. Eddy* (New York: Henry Holt, 1931), pp. 186, 222, 231, 265–66.

Chapter 3

1. Rand's recollections are contained in a letter to the author from S. B. Campbell of Destiny Publishers, January 28, 1991.

2. "Congratulations to Howard B. Rand," *Prophetic Expositor* (Toronto) 26 (August 1989), p. 24; Thomas F. Gossett, *Race: The History of an Idea in America*, rev. ed. (New York: Schocken, 1987), pp. 191–92; "Business Report of the Federation," *Bulletin* (Anglo-Saxon Federation of America) 2 (October 1931), pp. 75, 78; M. Alma Hetherington, *70 Years Old!: An Outline History of Our Work since 1909* (Burnaby, British Columbia: Association of the Covenant People, [1979]), p. 14; "Annual Report of the British-Israel World Federation for 1929," *National Message and Banner* (London) 9 (April 26, 1930), p. 278; "British-Israel World Federation Annual Report and Review for 1930," *National Message* (London) 10 (May 23, 1931), p. 330; "Congress Addresses at Central Hall, Westminster," *National Message* 14 (October 19, 1935), pp. 664–67. Notwithstanding changes of name, the *National Message and Banner* and the *National Message* are the same periodical, the official organ of the British-Israel-World Federation.

3. *Bulletin*, no. 10 (October 1930), pp 83–84; *Bulletin*, no. 12 (December 1930), pp. 99–100; "Remedy for Depression," *Bulletin* 2 (July 1931), p. 49; *Bulletin* 2 (November 1931), p. 87; *Bulletin* 2 (January 1931), p. 8; "The Third Annual All-American Convention: A Turning Point in the American Movement," *National Message* 11 (October 8, 1932), p. 652.

4. "Business Report of the Federation," p. 79; "Is It Destruction Instead of Depression?," *Bulletin* 2 (October 1931), p. 73.

5. S. B. Campbell to author; "British-Israel World Federation Annual Report and Review for 1930," p. 330; "Congress Addresses at Central Hall, Westminster," p. 665; W. J. Cameron, " 'The Economic Law of the Lord,' " *National Message* 13 (January 13, 1934), p. 21; *Bulletin*, no. 10 (October 1930), p. 84; "Detroit, Michigan: Special Meetings," *Bulletin* 4 (May 1933), p. 40.

6. William J. Cameron, "Reminiscences," interview by Owen Bombard, reel 1, June 5, 1952, Ford Oral History Project, Ford Archives (hereafter, FA; all subsequent references to the "Reminiscences" are on reel 1); David L. Lewis, *The Public Image of Henry Ford: An American Folk Hero and His Company* (Detroit: Wayne State University Press, 1976), pp. 193, 222, 376.

7. Cameron, "Reminiscences"; Alexander Beaufort Grimaldi, *Memoirs, and a Selection of Letters from the Correspondence of Edward Hine* (London: Robert Banks and Son, 1909), pp. 27–43.

8. "Business Report of the Federation," p. 79.

9. "Congress Addresses at Central Hall, Westminster," p. 665. Rand describes this meeting as having taken place "after the third Convention, returning to the East." Federation materials make clear that the official third convention took place in Philadelphia, so that Rand could hardly have passed through Detroit on his way back to Massachusetts. In addition, the Philadelphia convention occurred after the publication of the proposed special issue. Rand evidently thought of the organizational meeting in Detroit as a convention, although subsequent federation material did not formally treat it as such. Dr. John W. Stephens, "Our Chicago Convention," *Bulletin* 2 (October 1931), p. 76.

10. *New York Times*, March 4, 5, 1924; April 9, 10, 1928; July 21, 1930; July 15, 1939 (Marvin's obituary); "Congress Addresses at Central Hall, Westminster," p. 665; "Convention Report Continued," *Bulletin* 3 (November 1932), p. 93.

11. Lewis, *The Public Image of Henry Ford*, pp. 143–46. The most detailed discussion of

the anti-Semitic articles that appeared in the *Independent* is Leo P. Ribuffo, "Henry Ford and *The International Jew*," *American Jewish History* 69 (1980): 437–77.

12. David A. Gerber, "Anti-Semitism and Jewish-Gentile Relations in American Historiography and the American Past," in idem, ed., *Anti-Semitism in American History* (Urbana: University of Illinois Press, 1986), pp. 20–22, 29–30. Gerber borrows the term "pseudo-agrarian" from John Higham.

13. Cameron, "Reminiscences."

14. Ibid.; "Reminiscences of Mrs. Stanley Ruddiman," March 1952, p. 32, Ford Oral History Project, FA. The Ford and Ruddiman families had been friends since Henry's childhood, and he had named his son after his boyhood friend Edsel Ruddiman. Norman Cohn, in his otherwise authoritative history, *The Protocols of the Elders of Zion*, mistakenly attributes authorship of the *Independent* articles to three European émigrés, Dr. Edward A. Rumley, Dr. August Muller, and Boris Brasol, a conclusion shared by virtually no one else and convincingly refuted in Ribuffo, "Henry Ford and *The International Jew*." Norman Cohn, *Warrant for Genocide: The Myth of the Jewish World-Conspiracy and "The Protocols of the Elders of Zion"* (Chico, Calif.: Scholars Press, 1981), pp. 160–61.

15. Alton Frye, *Nazi Germany and the American Hemisphere, 1933–1941* (New Haven: Yale University Press, 1967), pp. 32–33, 59; Kurt G. W. Ludecke, *I Knew Hitler: The Story of a Nazi Who Escaped the Blood Purge* (New York: Charles Scribner's Sons, 1938).

16. Ludecke, *I Knew Hitler*, pp. 192–93, 197, 200–201, 204, 313–14, 315.

17. Cameron, "Reminiscences."

18. Ibid.; undated penciled note in what appears to be Cameron's handwriting, subsequently marked "May 1942," FA; W. G. MacKendrick to William J. Cameron, May 31, 1942, emphasis in original; MacKendrick to Cameron, accession 44, box 1, FA.

19. Cameron's religious views receive superficial treatment in Alan Nevins and Frank Ernest Hill, *Ford: Expansion and Challenge, 1915–1933* (New York: Charles Scribner's Sons, 1957), pp. 125–26; "W. J. Cameron—Voice of the Sunday Evening 'Mike,' " *Ford Digest* (November 7, 1936), p. 15, FA; W. J. Cameron, "The Economic Law of God," *National Message* 12 (July 1, 1933), pp. 403–6; idem, "Economics of the Bible: As They Were Practiced for a Thousand Years by Our Anglo-Saxon-Israel Forefathers," *Destiny* 8 (September 1937), pp. 7–11. *Destiny* succeeded the *Bulletin*, the *Messenger*, and the *Messenger of the Covenant* as the periodical of the Anglo-Saxon Federation of America.

20. W. J. Cameron, *The Covenant People* (Merrimac, Mass.: Destiny Publishers, 1966), pp. 3–5. The text was originally delivered as lectures at the Dearborn Inn in Dearborn, Michigan, in 1933, and published in a special issue of *Destiny* (April 1938). W. J. Cameron, "What I Believe about the Anglo-Saxon," *Destiny* 29 (August 1958), pp. 183, 184, 185, emphasis in original; John Wilson, *Lectures on Our Israelitish Origin*, 5th ed. (London: James Nisbet, 1876), p. 368.

21. The following articles in the *Dearborn Independent* contained significant British-Israel materials: "Gentile Fall Involved in Hope of Jewish Rule," December 25, 1920; "Angles of Jewish Influence in American Life," May 21, 1921; "Will Jewish Zionism Bring Armageddon?," May 28, 1921; "Candid Address to Jews on the Jewish Problem," January 7, 1922; "An Address to 'Gentiles' on the Jewish Problem," January 14, 1922; "Are the Jews 'God's Chosen People'?," September 22, 1923; " 'Was Jesus Christ a Jew?'—An Inquiry," October 6, 1923; Paul Tyner, "Where Are Israel's Lost Tribes?," May 23, 1925; Mark John

Levy, "Why the Anglo-Saxons Are the Descendants of the Lost Ten Tribes of Israel," February 19, 1927; Lieutenant Colonel W. G. MacKendrick, "Does the Bible Predict Peace?," April 16, 1927.

22. "Gentile Fall Involved in Hope of Jewish Rule," pp. 8, 9.

23. "Are the Jews 'God's Chosen People'?," p. 2. Strikingly similar language appears in Cameron's 1934 lecture, "What I Believe about the Anglo-Saxon," first published in *Destiny* in 1934 and reprinted in *Destiny* 29 (August 1958), pp. 183–87. W. J. Cameron, "Israel as Two Nations: Part II," *National Message* 13 (April 21, 1934), p. 247; idem, *The Covenant People*, pp. 27–28.

24. Lee, *Henry Ford and the Jews*, pp. 89–90.

25. "The Third Annual All-American Convention," p. 652.

26. "Congress Addresses at Central Hall, Westminster," p. 665; "Detroit, Michigan: Special Meetings," p. 40; *Destiny* 8 (May 1937), masthead; S. B. Campbell of Destiny Publishers on Howard Rand's behalf to the author, January 28, 1991; *Destiny* 9 (January 1938), p. 3.

27. See W. G. MacKendrick to W. J. Cameron correspondence, FA.

28. Lewis, *The Public Image of Henry Ford*, p. 376.

29. John A. Spalding, "'A Nice Man Saying Sensible Things': An Analysis of the Radio Speaking of William John Cameron," n.d., small accession, accession 665, box 15, FA; "Reminiscences of Mrs. Stanley Ruddiman," p. 31; Lewis, *The Public Image of Henry Ford*, p. 377; Spalding, "'A Nice Man Saying Sensible Things'"; Lewis, *The Public Image of Henry Ford*, p. 326.

30. "Reminiscences of Mrs. Stanley Ruddiman," p. 33; "Reminiscences of F. W. Loskowske," November 1951, p. 102, Ford Oral History Project, FA.

31. Ralph Lord Roy, *Apostles of Discord: A Study of Organized Bigotry and Disruption on the Fringes of Protestantism* (Boston: Beacon Press, 1953), p. 93; "A Tribute to Howard Benjamin Rand," obituary leaflet, 1991; Howard B. Rand, *Documentary Studies*, 3 vols. (Merrimac, Mass.: Destiny Publishers, 1950), 2:110 (reprinted from *Destiny*, December 1946); *Destiny* 9 (January 1938), p. 3; S. B. Campbell to the author.

32. "Reminiscences of Mrs. Stanley Ruddiman," pp. 30, 31, 33, 35.

33. Ibid., p. 31; J. Gordon Melton, *The Encyclopedia of American Religions*, 2d ed. (Detroit: Gale Research Corporation, 1987), p. 797; Charles S. Braden, *Spirits in Rebellion: The Rise and Development of New Thought* (Dallas: Southern Methodist University Press, 1963), pp. 254–56; *Oakland (Calif.) Tribune*, August 2, 1955.

34. "A Tribute to Howard Benjamin Rand."

35. "To Our Subscribers," *Reminder of Our National Heritage* (Portland, Oreg.) 27 (July–August 1964), p. 1; letter from *Destiny* editors to readers, January 30, 1969, letter to subscribers, January 19, 1970, and questionnaire response from the Anglo-Saxon Federation of America to the Wilcox Collection, 1983, all in Wilcox Collection, Spencer Research Library, University of Kansas.

Chapter 4

1. M. Alma Hetherington, *70 Years Old!: An Outline History of Our Work since 1909* (Burnaby, British Columbia: Association of the Covenant People, [1979]), pp. 1–2, 7, 9, 20.

2. Ibid., pp. 26–27, 30. In 1968, the Vancouver group—now with offices in both British Columbia and Washington State—changed its name to the Association of the Covenant People.

3. *National Message* 17, no. 800 (May 1, 1937), p. 285; Hetherington, *70 Years Old!*, pp. 26–27.

4. H. Ben Judah [pseud.], *When?: A Prophetical Novel of the Very Near Future* (Vancouver: British Israel Association of Greater Vancouver, 1944); *The Morning Cometh* (Vancouver: Anglo-Saxon Christian World Movement, June 1941), 2d ed., rev. (October 1941), 3d ed., rev. (February 1942); *When Gog Attacks* (Vancouver: British Israel Association of Greater Vancouver, January 1944), 2d ed. (June 1944), p. 17. The similarities among the three publications are so striking that the conclusion that they are all by the same hand is inescapable. Nonetheless, I have thus far been unable to identify the author.

5. Hetherington, *70 Year Old!*, pp. 10, 17, 26, 27.

6. C. F. Parker, "The Desecration of the Jewish Nation by the Seed of Esau," *National Message* 25 (September 25, 1946), p. 291; idem, *A Short History of Esau-Edom in Jewry* (London: Covenant Publishing Company, 1948), 2d ed. (1949), pp. 39, 40, 70, 77.

7. Gregory H. Singleton, *Religion in the City of Angels: American Protestant Culture and Urbanization, Los Angeles, 1850–1930* (Ann Arbor, Mich.: UMI Research Press, 1979), pp. 119, 148, 159, 168–69.

8. Sarah E. Parham, *The Life of Charles F. Parham, Founder of the Apostolic Faith Movement* (1930; reprint, Joplin, Mo.: Hunter Printing Company, 1969), p. 305.

9. *Bulletin* (Anglo-Saxon Federation of America), no. 10 (October 1930), pp. 83–84; "Anglo-Saxon Federation of America: Pacific Coast District," *Bulletin*, no. 12 (December 1930), pp. 99–100; "Pacific Coast District," *Bulletin*, no. 13 (January 1931), p. 8; Philip E. J. Monson, *Satan's Seat: The Enemy of Our Race* (Los Angeles: Covenant Evangelistic Association Zion Press, n.d.).

10. Ralph Lord Roy, *Apostles of Discord: A Study of Organized Bigotry and Disruption on the Fringes of Protestantism* (Boston: Beacon Press, 1953), pp. 101–3. John M. Werly has found the name "Rev. Joseph C. Jeffries" on a Silver Legion membership list for California, as well as a "Reverend Joe Jeffires" mentioned in House Un-American Activities Committee testimony on the Silver Legion. They are presumably the same person, and identical with "Joe Jeffries." I am grateful to John Werly for bringing this information to my attention. David R. Elliott, "Fundamentalism, Fascism, and Human Rights," *McMaster Journal of Theology* 2 (1991): 68.

11. Hetherington, *70 Years Old!*, p. 27; "Anniversary Issue," *Kingdom Digest* 16 (March 1956), p. 14; "Editor's Monthly Letter," *Kingdom Digest* 24 (April 1964), pp. 4–5; Richard V. Pierard, "The Contribution of British-Israelism to Anti-Semitism within Conservative Protestantism," unpublished ms.; Roy, *Apostles of Discord*, pp. 99–100.

12. Glen Jeansonne, *Gerald L. K. Smith: Minister of Hate* (New Haven: Yale University Press, 1988), pp. 99–100, 105–6, 150.

13. Ibid., p. 103; mass mailing letter from Gerald L. K. Smith, February 1956, box 46, Smith to Wesley Swift, January 15, 1957, box 48, and Smith to Swift, April 5, 1949, box 29, all in Gerald L. K. Smith Collection, Michigan Historical Collection, Bentley Historical Library, University of Michigan (hereafter, GLKS); Gerald L. K. Smith, *Besieged Patriot: Autobiographical Episodes Exposing Communism, Traitorism and Zionism from the Life of*

Gerald L. K. Smith, ed. Elna M. Smith and Charles F. Robertson (Eureka Springs, Ark.: Elna M. Smith Foundation, 1978), pp. 238, 239; idem, "Who Are God's Chosen People?: Certainly Not the Jews! (As We Now Know Jews)," *The Cross and the Flag* 26 (September 1967), pp. 2, 23–24; "Who Owns Palestine?," *The Cross and the Flag* 27 (July 1968), p. 21.

14. Bertrand Comparet, "Destiny Is on Our Side," *The Cross and the Flag* 14 (April 1955), pp. 5, 35–37; Smith, "Who Are God's Chosen People?," p. 24; "Who Owns Palestine?," p. 21; Smith, *Besieged Patriot*, pp. 136–40, 162–63, 177.

15. Jeansonne, *Gerald L. K. Smith*, p. 177.

16. Pierard, "The Contribution of British-Israelism"; Hetherington, *70 Years Old!*, p. 27; Roy, *Apostles of Discord*, p. 107.

17. Wesley Swift to Gerald L. K. Smith, August 6, 1948, box 25, Opal M. Tanner (Smith's secretary) to Smith, May 3, 1955, box 44, Conrad Gaard to Smith, May 21, 1950, box 30, and Gaard to Smith, January 12, 1950, box 30, all in GLKS; "Christian Nationalist Convention," *The Cross and the Flag* 9 (June 1950), p. 20.

18. Roy, *Apostles of Discord*, p. 114; Jonathan Ellsworth Perkins, *The Biggest Hypocrite in America: Gerald L. K. Smith Unmasked* (Los Angeles: American Foundation, 1949), pp. 11–15, 23, 29, 106.

19. Jeansonne, *Gerald L. K. Smith*, p. 157.

20. Perkins, *The Biggest Hypocrite in America*, pp. 21, 105, 106, 108.

21. Jonathan Ellsworth Perkins, *The Modern Canaanites; or, The Enemies of Jesus Christ* (Metairie, La.: Sons of Liberty, n.d.), p. 23.

22. Gerald L. K. Smith to Wesley Swift, April 5, 1949, box 29, GLKS.

23. Bertrand L. Comparet, *Israel's Footprints: Who Are the Jews? Was Jesus Christ a Jew? An Identification of the True Israel by Biblical and Historical Sources* (Flagstaff, Ariz.: Patriot Associates Publishers, 1962); "Two Great Men in Israel Have Fallen," *America's Promise Newsletter* (November 1983), p. 1.

24. Wesley Swift to Gerald L. K. Swift on League letterhead, November 15, 1950, box 33, Smith to Swift, August 16, 1955, box 44, and Smith to Swift, March 6, 1956, box 46, all in GLKS; "Christian Nationalist Convention," *The Cross and the Flag* 9 (June 1950), p. 20; *The Cross and the Flag* 14 (August 1955), p. 12; *The Cross and the Flag* 14 (October 1955), pp. 16–17; "Sixty-seven Subjects—Eyewitness Account—A Diary—A Survey—An Interpretation," *The Cross and the Flag* 15 (June 1956), p. 15.

25. Roy, *Apostles of Discord*, p. 103.

26. "Dr. Wesley Swift Passes," *The Cross and the Flag* 29 (March 1971), pp. 14, 26; Richard Swift to Gerald L. K. Smith, September 5, 1958, box 49, GLKS; *Christian Vanguard*, no. 118 (October 1981), p. 9.

27. Mrs. Wesley Swift to the author, April 13, 1992; William P. Gale, "A Reply to the National Chronicle," *Identity* 8 (November 1975), pp. 5–7. In light of Gale's bitter hostility toward Swift expressed in this article, his assertions must be weighed with care. Robert Mapes Anderson, *Vision of the Disinherited: The Making of American Pentecostalism* (New York: Oxford University Press, 1979), pp. 116–17; "Dr. Wesley Swift Passes," pp. 14, 26.

28. James R. Goff, Jr., *Fields White unto Harvest: Charles F. Parham and the Missionary Origins of Pentecostalism* (Fayetteville: University of Arkansas Press, 1988), p. 157; Anderson, *Vision of the Disinherited*, pp. 116–17, 190.

29. *Christian Vanguard*, no. 118 (October 1981), p. 9; Gale, "Reply to the National

Chronicle"; Cheri Seymour, *Committee of the States: Inside the Radical Right* (Mariposa, Calif.: Camden Place Communications, 1991), pp. 80, 83–84, 217; Mrs. Wesley Swift to the author, August 26, 1992; Monson, *Satan's Seat*; "Anglo-Saxon Federation of America: Pacific Coast District," *Bulletin*, no. 12 (December 1930), pp. 99–100.

30. *Los Angeles Times*, April 13, 1965; leaflet for anniversary celebration, June 22, 1958, box 49, Wesley Swift to Gerald L. K. Smith, September 5, 1949, box 29, and Swift to Smith, October 10, 1949, box 29, all in GLKS.

31. Undated mailing piece from Gerald L. K. Smith, 1959, box 51, Smith to Opal Tanner, May 17, 1954, box 42, Smith to Tanner, May 25, 1954, box 42, Smith to "Miss Harris" (probably Louva Harris, Wesley Swift's secretary), May 31, 1954, box 42, and Louva Harris, addressee unknown, on Anglo Saxon Christian Congregations' letterhead, March 10, 1956, box 46, all in GLKS.

32. Gerald L. K. Smith to Wesley Swift, March 17, 1958, box 49, Smith to Bertrand Comparet, June 13, 1958, box 49, Smith to J. A. Lovell, June 13, 1958, box 49, Lovell to "Christian Brethren," [June 1958], box 49, George D. Rigler to the Church of Jesus Christ Christian, June 19, 1958, box 49, and Bob Howard to Swift, June 18, 1958, box 49, all in GLKS.

33. *Los Angeles Times*, April 6, 10, 12, 17, May 3, 1946.

34. Smith, *Besieged Patriot*, p. 238; "Dr. Wesley Swift Passes," pp. 14, 26; Wesley Swift, "Washington—Chicago—A Memo," n.d., distributed by the Christian Nationalist Crusade, probably summer 1955, and reprinted in *The Cross and the Flag* 14 (April 1955), pp. 31–33; "Christian Nationalist Convention," *The Cross and the Flag* (June 1950), p. 18; *The Cross and the Flag* 14 (October 1955), pp. 16–17.

35. Jeansonne, *Gerald L. K. Smith*, pp. 100, 211–12; Wesley Swift to Gerald L. K. Smith, September 5, 1949, box 29, GLKS.

36. Gerald L. K. Smith to Wesley Swift, February 26, 1962, box 54, GLKS; Jeansonne, *Gerald L. K. Smith*, p. 188; Sharon Schoonmaker (Wesley Swift's secretary at the time) to Mr. and Mrs. Gerald L. K. Smith, February 15, 1965, box 56, GLKS.

37. *Los Angeles Times*, April 13, 1965; William W. Turner, *Power on the Right* (Berkeley: Ramparts Press, 1971), pp. 101–2.

38. Seymour, *Committee of the States*, pp. 80–81, 217.

39. Ibid., pp. 36, 203.

40. Gale, "Reply to the National Chronicle"; The Jutlander, "Who Is 'Col.' Gale?," *National Chronicle* 24 (October 23, 1975); "Why, What, Who, Where, When," Christian Defense League brochure, Baton Rouge, La., undated but probably from the late 1970s, Wilcox Collection, Spencer Research Library, University of Kansas; Gerald L. K. Smith to Wesley Swift, February 26, 1959, box 51, GLKS.

41. Gale, "Reply to the National Chronicle"; The Jutlander, "Who Is 'Col.' Gale?"; Seymour, *Committee of the States*, pp. 68, 87; Turner, *Power on the Right*, pp. 101–2.

42. Mass mailing letters from Christian Defense League, Whittier, Calif., and Baton Rouge, La., both undated, Wilcox Collection.

43. Gale, "Reply to the National Chronicle"; Butler is quoted in James Aho, *The Politics of Righteousness: Idaho Christian Patriotism* (Seattle: University of Washington Press, 1990), p. 55; *Idaho Statesman* (Boise), September 14, 1980. In the Seymour interviews, Gale claimed that Richard Butler first came to him in connection with Butler's efforts to

mobilize support for an anticommunist bill in the state assembly. According to this account, after converting Butler to Identity, Gale became his minister and "he [Butler] became a member of my church." Swift goes unmentioned. Seymour, *Committee of the States*, pp. 81–82.

44. "Why, What, Who, Where, When"; Turner, *Power on the Right*, p. 113; James K. Warner to "Dear Christian Patriot," Christian Defense League, Baton Rouge, La., September/October 1981, emphasis in original, Wilcox Collection.

45. *Idaho Statesman* (Boise), September 14, 1980; *Los Angeles Times*, October 12, 1970; *The Cross and the Flag* 29 (December 1970), p. 23; "In Memory of Dr. Wesley A. Swift," *National Chronicle* 19 (October 22, 1970), p. 1.

46. William P. Gale, "The Faith of Our Fathers," *Identity* 7 (January 1974), pp. 1–4; idem, "The Faith of Our Fathers," *Identity* 7 (April 1974), pp. 1–3; The Jutlander, "Who Is 'Col.' Gale?"; Gale, "A Reply to the National Chronicle."

47. Gale, "A Reply to the National Chronicle." In the Seymour conversations, Gale added the charge that Swift had hoodwinked "two elderly ladies," former clients of Gale's mutual funds business, in an investment scheme that involved Swift's son. Seymour, *Committee of the States*, pp. 92–93.

48. "United States Christian Posse Association," *Identity* 6 ([1972]), pp. 2–3; *Jubilee* 1 (May 1988), pp. 1, 4; Seymour, *Committee of the States*, pp. 343, 345–47, 356.

49. "Why, What, Who, Where, When."

50. *Idaho Statesman* (Boise), September 14, 1980; Mrs. Wesley Swift to the author, April 13, 1992.

51. "Aryan Nations Showing Ominous Signs of Life," *Klanwatch Intelligence Report*, no. 60 (April 1992), pp. 1–6; "Low-Key Atmosphere, Small Attendance Mark Annual Aryan Youth Assembly," *Klanwatch Intelligence Report*, no. 61 (June 1992), p. 16; "Ex–Aryan Nations' Leaders Start New Hate Group in Montana," *Klanwatch Intelligence Report*, no. 69 (October 1993), p. 8.

Chapter 5

1. On historicism, see Ernest R. Sandeen, *The Roots of Fundamentalism: British and American Millenarianism, 1800–1930* (Chicago: University of Chicago Press, 1981), pp. 36–37; and Timothy P. Weber, *Living in the Shadow of the Second Coming: American Premillennialism, 1875–1982*, 2d ed., rev. and enl. (Grand Rapids, Mich.: Academic Press, 1983), pp. 9–10. The most comprehensive and perceptive study of American millennialism in its cultural context is Paul Boyer, *When Time Shall Be No More: Prophecy Belief in Modern American Culture* (Cambridge: Harvard University Press, 1992). On Millerism, see the following: Sandeen, *The Roots of Fundamentalism*, pp. 51–52; Michael Barkun, *Crucible of the Millennium: The Burned-over District of New York in the 1840s* (Syracuse: Syracuse University Press, 1986); and Ruth Alden Doan, *The Miller Heresy, Millennialism, and American Culture* (Philadelphia: Temple University Press, 1987).

2. Sandeen, *The Roots of Fundamentalism*, pp. 37, 222; Weber, *Living in the Shadow of the Second Coming*, pp. 10–11; Boyer, *When Time Shall Be No More*, pp. 97–100.

3. Sandeen, *The Roots of Fundamentalism*, pp. 68, 86.

4. Ibid., p. 67; Weber, *Living in the Shadow of the Second Coming*, pp. 17–20.

5. Boyer, *When Time Shall Be No More*, pp. 183, 209, 211, 213–14.

6. Sandeen, *The Roots of Fundamentalism*, pp. 62–63; Weber, *Living in the Shadow of the Second Coming*, pp. 20–23.

7. Sandeen, *The Roots of Fundamentalism*, pp. 89–90.

8. Alexander Beaufort Grimaldi, *Memoirs, and a Selection of Letters from the Correspondence of Edward Hine* (London: Robert Banks and Son, 1909), pp. 15–16; Edward Hine, *England's Coming Glories: Being the Fourth Part of the "Identifications of the Anglo Saxons with Lost Israel"* (New York: James Huggins, 1880), p. 276; Grimaldi, *Memoirs*, p. 53, emphasis in original.

9. Joseph Wild, *The Lost Ten Tribes And 1882* (New York: James Huggins, 1879), p. 64; M. M. Eshelman, *Two Sticks; or, The Lost Tribes of Israel Discovered: The Jew and the Israelite Not the Same* (Mount Morris, Ill.: Brethren's Publishing Company, 1887), p. 202; Charles A. Totten, *The Order of History: The Coming Crusade. Palestine Regained, or The Relation of Our Race to the Restoration of Israel: The Means Towards the End* (New Haven: Our Race Publishing Company, 1897), pp. ix–xxiii.

10. H. Aldersmith, "The Pre-Millennial Fulfillment of the Promises Made to the 'House of Israel,'" p. 34, Rev. E. J. Wemyss-Whittaker, "An Appeal to the Clergy and Ministers of All Denominations," p. 175, and H. Aldersmith, "The Second Advent of Christ," pp. 208–9, all in Denis Hanan and H. Aldersmith, eds., *British-Israel Truth*, 14th ed. (London: Covenant Publishing Company, 1932), emphasis in original.

11. Grimaldi, *Memoirs*, pp. 15–16, 59; Eshelman, *Two Sticks*, pp. 247–48.

12. Eric Anderson, "The Millerite Use of Prophecy: A Case Study of a 'Striking Fulfillment,'" in Ronald L. Numbers and Jonathan M. Butler, eds., *The Disappointed: Millerism and Millenarianism in the Nineteenth Century* (Bloomington: Indiana University Press, 1987), pp. 78–91; Douglas A. Onslow, "The Distinctive Marks, Characteristics, and Location of the 'House of Israel' in the 'Latter Days,'" p. 101, and H. Aldersmith, "Appendix E, Part II," p. 256, both in Hanan and Aldersmith, *British-Israel Truth*.

13. Onslow, "The Distinctive Marks," p. 87; Rev. J. Idrisyn Jones, "Some Objections Answered," in Hanan and Aldersmith, *British-Israel Truth*, pp. 163–64; Aldersmith, "Appendix E, Part II," p. 256.

14. Aldersmith, "The Second Advent of Christ," pp. 209–10, 211–12, 233, emphasis in original.

15. Ibid., p. 210, emphasis in original; D. Davidson and H. Aldersmith, *The Great Pyramid: Its Divine Message—An Original Co-ordination of Historical Documents and Archaeological Evidences*, 11th ed. (London: Williams and Norgate, 1948), p. ix.

16. Davidson and Aldersmith, *The Great Pyramid*, pp. vii–viii, 458, emphasis in original.

17. "The Roadbuilder" [W. G. MacKendrick], *The Destiny of America* (Toronto: T. H. Best Printing Company; Boston: A. A. Beauchamp, 1921), pp. 194, 233; Davidson and Aldersmith, *The Great Pyramid*, plate following p. 390.

18. W. G. MacKendrick to William J. Cameron, June 11, 1933, and William [?] McCrea to MacKendrick, n.d., filed after letter of July 1, 1942, both in FA.

19. William McCrea to W. G. MacKendrick, n.d., filed after letter of August 26, 1940, emphasis in original, McCrea to MacKendrick, February 6, 1942, McCrea to MacKendrick, September 21, 1942, McCrea to MacKendrick, September 4, 1942, emphasis in original, MacKendrick to William J. Cameron, September 22, 1942, McCrea to MacKen-

drick, September 17, 1942, emphasis in original, McCrea to MacKendrick, September 23, 1942, and McCrea to MacKendrick, December 1, 1942, all in FA.

20. W. G. MacKendrick, *This IS Armageddon* (Toronto: Commonwealth Publishers, 1942), pp. 28, 92.

21. W. G. MacKendrick to William J. Cameron, November 5, 1940, emphasis in original, FA.

22. [MacKendrick], *The Destiny of America*, p. 191; idem, *This IS Armageddon*, pp. 93–94, 101, 103, 105.

23. Frederick Haberman, *The Climax of the Ages Is Near* (St. Petersburg, Fla., 1940), unnumbered page, emphasis in original, 3d ed. (1941), p. 7, emphasis in original.

24. David Davidson, *The Path to Peace in Our Time: Outlined from the Great Pyramid's Prophecy* (London: Covenant Publishing Company, 1942), pp. 14, 18, 22, 32, 56, 48, emphasis in original.

25. "Abraham's Seed," *Master Councillor's Address* (Councils of Safety of the Christian Party, n.d.), p. 11; William Dudley Pelley, *The Door to Revelation: An Intimate Biography* (Asheville, N.C.: Foundation Fellowship, 1936), p. 262; Davidson and Aldersmith, *The Great Pyramid*, p. xii; cf. Leo Paul Ribuffo, "Protestants on the Right: William Dudley Pelley, Gerald B. Winrod, and Gerald L. K. Smith" (Ph.D. dissertation, Yale University, 1976), pp. 250, 306–7.

26. Eckard V. Toy, Jr., "Silver Shirts in the Northwest: Politics, Prophecies, and Personalities in the 1930s," *Pacific Northwest Quarterly* 80 (1989): 139–46; John M. Werly, "Premillennialism and the Paranoid Style," *American Studies* (1977): 39–55. Pelley's most detailed references to Davidson's work occur in the following *Master Councillor's Addresses*: "The Pillar of Cloud," pp. 8, 9, 12; "Those Who Pass the Judgement," p. 16; and "The Pendulum of the Cosmos," pp. 1, 4–5, 13.

27. "The Pillar of Cloud," p. 10; "Abraham's Seed," pp. 10–11; Charles F. Parham, *A Voice Crying in the Wilderness*, 2d ed. (Baxter Springs, Kans.: Apostolic Faith Bible College, 1910), p. 105.

28. "Deserts of Roses," *Master Councillor's Address*, p. 3, emphasis in original.

29. "The Splendors of Tomorrow," *Master Councillor's Address*, p. 14; "The Pendulum of the Cosmos," p. 1, emphasis in original.

30. "The Pillar of Cloud," p. 13.

31. David Davidson, *Through World Chaos to Cosmic Christ*, 2d ed. (Toronto: Periscope Publishing Company, 1944), pp. 184–85; "The Pillar of Cloud," p. 10, emphasis in original.

32. "The Pillar of Cloud," pp. 10, 11, 12, 17.

33. Davidson and Aldersmith, *The Great Pyramid*, p. viii, text accompanying plate 65.

34. "The Splendors of Tomorrow," p. 14; "The Pendulum of the Cosmos," p. 6, emphasis in original; "The Pillar of Cloud," pp. 8, 13, 16.

35. Davidson and Aldersmith, *The Great Pyramid*, p. 416; "Abraham's Seed," p. 6; "The Pendulum of the Cosmos," pp. 1–2, 16, emphasis in original.

36. "The Pillar of Cloud," p. 6, emphasis in original.

37. David H. Bennett, *Demagogues in the Depression: American Radicals and the Union Party, 1932–1936* (New Brunswick, N.J.: Rutgers University Press, 1969); Ribuffo, *Protestants on the Right*, p. 343; Toy, "Silver Shirts in the Northwest," p. 143.

38. Toy, "Silver Shirts in the Northwest," p. 144; "George Washington's Vision" (Mosinee, Wis.: Sheriff's Posse Comitatus, Citizen's Law Enforcement and Research Committee, n.d.), brochure.

39. "David Davidson," *Destiny* 27 (September 1956), p. 200.

40. Denis Hanan and H. Aldersmith, "The Old and the New Covenants: Israel in the New Testament," in Hanan and Aldersmith, *British-Israel Truth*, p. 77, emphasis in original.

41. Howard B. Rand, *A Crisis in Fundamentalism* (Merrimac, Mass.: Destiny Publishers, 1958), p. 10.

42. Howard B. Rand, "When the Boy Falls in Battle," in Howard B. Rand, *Documentary Studies*, 3 vols. (Merrimac, Mass.: Destiny Publishers, 1950), 1:393 (originally published in *Destiny*, July 1943); idem, "The Kingdom of God Is at Hand," in Rand, *Documentary Studies*, 1:74–75 (originally published in *Destiny*, December 1944).

43. "The Question Box," *Destiny* 27 (September 1956), p. 212.

44. Howard B. Rand, "Final Theater of War," in Rand, *Documentary Studies*, 1:202 (originally published in *Destiny*, September 1944).

45. Howard B. Rand, "The Fullness of the Ages," in Rand, *Documentary Studies*, 2:63–67, emphasis in original (originally published in *Destiny*, August 1946); Davidson and Aldersmith, *The Great Pyramid*, chart facing p. xiv; Howard B. Rand, "When Ye Think Not," in Rand, *Documentary Studies*, 3:415–16.

46. Leon Festinger, Henry W. Ricken, and Stanley Schachter, *When Prophecy Fails: A Social and Psychological Study of a Modern Group That Predicted the Destruction of the World* (1956; reprint, New York: Harper and Row, 1964); Lawrence Foster, "Had Prophecy Failed?: Contrasting Perspectives of the Millerites and Shakers," in Numbers and Butler, *The Disappointed*, pp. 173–88.

Chapter 6

1. Jarah B. Crawford, *Last Battle Cry: Christianity's Final Conflict with Evil* (Knoxville, Tenn.: Jann Publishing Company, 1984), p. 386; John Coleman, "Who Are the Jews, and Where Do They Come From?," *Christian Vanguard*, no. 131 (November 1982), pp. 1–2; "The Aborted Rapture," *Watchman* 11 (Fall 1988), p. 9; "Theology on the Rocks," *Watchman* 11 (Fall 1988), p. 10.

2. "A Vain Waiting for the 'Rapture,'" *America's Promise Newsletter*, December 1983, p. 1; Duncan McDougall, *The Rapture of the Saints* (Phoenix, Ariz.: Lord's Covenant Church/America's Promise Broadcast, 1982).

3. Gordon "Jack" Mohr, *The Satanic Counterfeit* (Muskogee, Okla.: Hoffman Printing Company, 1982), p. 83, emphasis in original; "A Vain Waiting for the 'Rapture.'"

4. Ed Robinson, "'The Rapture' When? And Where?" *Identity* (Burnaby, British Columbia) 4 (April–May 1984), p. 15, emphasis in original; Wesley A. Swift, "The 'Rapture,'" *Christian Vanguard* 157 (April 1987), p. 1, emphasis in original. A position similar to Swift's appears in David K. Stacy, "Seed of the Serpent!," *Grace and Race*, undated supplement to the *National Chronicle*, p. 4.

5. Bertrand L. Comparet, *Birthpangs of the New Age* (San Diego: Your Heritage, no. 92, n.d.), p. 1; Wesley A. Swift, "With Violence Shall Babylon Be Cast Down," *Christian*

Vanguard, no. 86 (February 1979), p. 8; idem, *Testimony of Tradition and the Origin of Races* (Hollywood, Calif.: New Christian Crusade Church, n.d.), p. 34; idem, *You: Before the World Was Framed* (Hollywood, Calif.: New Christian Crusade Church, n.d.), p. 29; idem, *Testimony of Tradition*, p. 34.

6. John R. Harrell, Christian Conservative Churches of America, to "Dear Patriot and/or Christian," n.d., Wilcox Collection, Spencer Research Library, University of Kansas; John R. Harrell, *The Golden Triangle* (Flora, Ill.: Christian Conservative Church, n.d.), pp. 6, 13; *C.S.A. Survival Manual* (Pontiac, Mo.: C.S.A. Enterprises, 1982), pp. 1–2.

7. J. R. Taylor, "End Times," *Calling Our Nation*, no. 56 (n.d.), inside back cover.

8. Bertrand L. Comparet, "Russia in Bible Prophecy," *Christian Vanguard*, no. 123 (March 1982); Hal Lindsey, with C. C. Carlson, *The Late Great Planet Earth* (1970; reprint, New York: Bantam, 1973).

9. Paul Boyer, *When Time Shall Be No More: Prophecy Belief in Modern American Culture* (Cambridge: Harvard University Press, 1992), p. 151.

10. George Stout, "Apocalypse Now," p. 7; Dan Gayman, "The Road to Revolution," *Zion's Restorer* 5, no. 8 (n.d.), pp. 1–2; idem, *Articles of Faith and Doctrine for the Churches of Israel, Diocese of Manasseh, United States of America* (Schell City, Mo.: Church of Israel, 1982), p. 17, emphasis in original; idem, " 'Survival of the Elect,' " *Zion's Restorer* 5, no. 12 (n.d.), p. 3; "War Is at Hand," *Newsletter* (Covenant, Sword and Arm of the Lord) (August–September 1984), p. 1; "Who Is the Anti-Christ King Today?," *End Time Revelation Newsletter* (Coeur d'Alene, Idaho) 2, no. 7 (1977), p. 10, emphasis in original.

11. "Last Days of ZOG," *Calling Our Nation*, no. 59 (1989), p. 25; David Lane, "Migration," *Calling Our Nation*, no. 59 (1989), p. 8.

12. Christian Identity Church, Harrison, Ark., undated brochure; Gayman, *Articles of Faith and Doctrine*, p. 13; "This Is Aryan Nations," point 12, undated brochure; "Beliefs of the New Christian Crusade Church," *Christian Guide*, no. 169 (April–May 1988), p. 6.

13. Timothy P. Weber, *Living in the Shadow of the Second Coming: American Premillennialism, 1875–1982*, 2d ed., rev. and enl. (Grand Rapids, Mich.: Academic Press, 1983), p. 242; *Message of Old*, no. 1 (1982), p. 1.

14. "Who Is the Anti-Christ King Today?," p. 10; Bertrand L. Comparet, "The Great Jubilee," *Calling Our Nation*, no. 50 (n.d.), pp. 18–20 (originally published in *Special Alert No. 69*, Destiny Editorial News Service); Michael DeBeck, "Tracing Our Ancestors," *Calling Our Nation*, no. 45 (n.d.), pp. 21–22; John Coleman, "God's Chosen Race," *Christian Vanguard*, no. 135 (March 1983), p. 2; "God's Silent Witnesses," *America's Promise Newsletter* (January 1988), p. 1.

15. "Land of the ZOG," *CDL Report* (Metairie, La.), no. 112 (n.d.), special edition, p. 16; Karl I. Schott, "Come My People Hide Thyself for a Little While" (Spokane, Wash.: Christian Gospel Fellowship Church, n.d.), pamphlet; Andrew MacDonald [William Pierce], *The Turner Diaries*, 2d ed. (Washington, D.C.: National Alliance, 1980), p. 33; Richard Hofstadter, *The Paranoid Style in American Politics* (New York: Knopf, 1965); Mrs. S. E. V. Emery, *Seven Financial Conspiracies* (1894; reprint, Westport, Conn.: Hyperion Press, 1975).

16. "The 'Identity Churches': A Theology of Hate," *ADL Facts* 28 (Spring 1983): 10–11; *Extremism on the Right: A Handbook* (New York: Anti-Defamation League of B'nai B'rith, 1983), pp. 112–13; Leonard Zeskind, *The "Christian Identity" Movement: A Theological*

Justification for Racist and Anti-Semitic Violence (Division of Church and Society of the National Council of the Churches of Christ in the U.S.A., n.d.), p. 9.

17. *From the Mountain* (July–August 1985), p. C; (September–October 1984), p. 1; "Minor Error" (May–June 1989), p. 8.

18. *From the Mountain* (September–October 1984), p. 1; (March–April 1985), p. 3; (July–August 1985), p. D.

19. *From the Mountain* (July–August 1985), pp. D, E; "What Is a Jew?," (September–October 1982), p. 3.

20. "Coming Soon," *From the Mountain* (September–October 1982), p. 3; "Kissing Cousins" (September–October 1982), p. 3; (March–April 1985), pp. 2–3.

Chapter 7

1. M. M. Eshelman, *Two Sticks; or, The Lost Tribes of Israel Discovered: The Jew and the Israelite Not the Same* (Mount Morris, Ill.: Brethren's Publishing Company, 1887), p. 261.

2. Léon Poliakov, *The Aryan Myth: A History of Racist and Nationalist Ideas in Europe* (New York: Basic Books, 1974); David Bennett, *The Party of Fear: From Nativist Movements to the New Right in American History* (Chapel Hill: University of North Carolina Press, 1988).

3. Madison Grant, *The Passing of the Great Race, or the Racial Basis of European History* (1918; reprint, New York: Arno, 1970), pp. 16–18.

4. Charles A. Totten, *Our Race: Its Origin and Destiny—A Series of Studies on the Saxon Riddle* (New Haven: Our Race Publishing Company, 1891); idem, *The Order of History*, pp. i, ix, xi, 73; *Dearborn Independent*, September 13, 1919; Totten, *The Order of History*, p. 297.

5. Totten, *The Order of History*, pp. 297–98.

6. Ibid., pp. 299–300.

7. John Wilson, *Lectures on Our Israelitish Origin*, 5th ed. (London: James Nisbet, 1876), pp. 111, 189.

8. W. J. Cameron, "What I Believe about the Anglo-Saxon," *Destiny* 29 (August 1958), p. 185; Frederick Haberman, *Tracing Our Ancestors* (1934; reprint, Vancouver: British Israel Association, 1962), p. 144; George R. Riffert, "Judah—The Jews and the Bible in a False Light," *Destiny* 9 (October 1938), p. 13.

9. Howard Rand, "Jesus Was Not a Jew," in Howard B. Rand, *Documentary Studies*, 3 vols. (Merrimac, Mass.: Destiny Publishers, 1950), 1:415 (originally published in *Destiny*, March 1943); Thomas F. Gossett, *Race: The History of an Idea in America*, rev. ed. (New York: Schocken, 1987), p. 390; Lothrop Stoddard, "The Pedigree of Judah," *Forum* 75 (March 1926), p. 325.

10. David Davidson, *Through World Chaos to Cosmic Christ*, 2d ed. (Toronto: Periscope Publishing Company, 1944), pp. 90, 154.

11. C. F. Parker, *A Short History of Esau-Edom in Jewry*, 2d ed. (London: Covenant Publishing Company, 1949), pp. 25, 35, 36, 38, 39, 43; Conrad Gaard, *Spotlight on the Great Conspiracy* (Steilacoon, Wash.: Destiny of America Foundation, n.d.; reprints articles from Gaard's journal, the *Interpreter*, originally published in 1960), pp. 46, 49–51.

12. Eshelman, *Two Sticks*, p. 195; L. G. A. Roberts, "Preface to the Thirteenth Edition,"

in Denis Hanan and H. Aldersmith, eds., *British-Israel Truth*, 14th ed. (London: Covenant Publishing Company, 1932), p. v; Parker, *A Short History*, p. 17.

13. Léon Poliakov, *The History of Anti-Semitism* (London: Routledge and Kegan Paul, 1974), p. 159; Andrew Runni Anderson, *Alexander's Gate, Gog and Magog and the Inclosed Nations* (Cambridge, Mass.: Mediaeval Academy of America, 1932), pp. 72–73; Howard Rand, "The Incredible Hoax," in Rand, *Documentary Studies*, 2:134 (originally published in *Destiny*, July 1948); "Two Witnesses," *End Time Revelation Newsletter* (Coeur d'Alene, Idaho) 2, no. 7 (1977), p. 2; Karl I. Schott, "Come My People Hide Thyself for a Little While" (Spokane, Wash.: Christian Gospel Fellowship Church, n.d.), pamphlet.

14. Bertrand L. Comparet, *Israel's Fingerprints: Who Are the Jews? Was Jesus Christ a Jew? An Identification of the True Israel by Biblical and Historic Sources* (Flagstaff, Ariz.: Patriot Associates Publishers, 1962), pp. 23, 24, 29–30, 34; idem, "The Bible Is Not a Jewish Book," *Christian Vanguard*, no. 30 (May 1974), p. 3; Gerald L. K. Smith, "Who Are God's Chosen People?: Certainly Not the Jews! (As We Now Know Jews)," *The Cross and the Flag* 26 (September 1967), pp. 2, 23–24.

15. William P. Gale, "The Faith of Our Fathers," *Identity* 7 (April 1974), p. 1.

16. "Mystery of Ezekiel," *End Time Revelation Newsletter* 2 (January 1977), pp. 3, 8; *America's Promise Broadcaster* (Phoenix, Ariz., 1977; reprint, 1978), special issue; Jarah B. Crawford, *Last Battle Cry: Christianity's Final Conflict with Evil* (Knoxville, Tenn.: Jann Publishing Company, 1984), p. 7; " 'My People Are Destroyed For Lack of Knowledge . . . ,' " *Klansman*, no. 142 (September–October 1989), p. 1.

17. *Calling Our Nation* (Hayden Lake, Idaho), no. 55 (1987), p. 26.

18. Eshelman, *Two Sticks*, pp. 202–3.

19. W. G. MacKendrick to William J. Cameron, November 5, 1940, accession 44, box 1, FA.

20. W. G. MacKendrick, *This IS Armageddon* (Toronto: Commonwealth Publishers, 1942), p. 61.

21. Howard B. Rand, "Final Theater of War," in Rand, *Documentary Studies*, 1:206 (originally published in *Destiny*, September 1944).

22. H. Ben Judah [pseud.], *When?: A Prophetical Novel of the Very Near Future* (Vancouver: British Israel Association of Greater Vancouver, 1944), pp. 77, 88.

23. "Will Jewish Zionism Bring Armageddon?," in *Jewish Influences in American Life*, vol. 3 of *The International Jew: The World's Foremost Problem* (Ford Motor Company, [1921]), p. 124 (originally published in the *Dearborn Independent*, May 28, 1921); Howard B. Rand, "The Kingdom of God Is at Hand," in Rand, *Documentary Studies*, 1:74 (originally published in *Destiny*, December 1944); idem, "Who Shall Possess Palestine?," in Rand, *Documentary Studies*, 1:550 (originally published in *Destiny*, February 1944).

24. Parker, *A Short History*, pp. 38–39, 70, 77.

25. Howard B. Rand, "The Verdict of Time," in Rand, *Documentary Studies*, 2:133–34 (originally published in *Destiny*, October 1947); idem, "The Plot to Seize the Kingdom," in Rand, *Documentary Studies*, 2:169–70 (originally published in *Destiny*, June 1949); idem, "The Iniquitous Empire: A Great Mystery," in Rand, *Documentary Studies*, 3:263 (originally published in *Destiny*, March 1950).

26. Despite the prominence of the Khazar theory in contemporary anti-Semitic writing, it receives little, if any, attention in most histories of anti-Semitism. An exception is Robert

Singerman, "The Jew as Racial Alien: The Genetic Component of American Anti-Semitism," in David A. Gerber, ed., *Anti-Semitism in American History* (Urbana: University of Illinois Press, 1986), pp. 103–28. The best-known recent work on the Khazars, which, although not anti-Semitic is frequently cited by anti-Semites, is Arthur Koestler, *The Thirteenth Tribe: The Khazar Empire and Its Heritage* (New York: Random House, 1976).

27. Ernest Renan, "Le Judaisme comme race et comme religion: Conférence faite au Cercle Saint-Simon le 27 janvier 1883," in Henriette Psichari, ed., *Oeuvres complètes de Ernest Renan*, 10 vols. (Paris: Calmann-Lévy, n.d.), 1:925–44; Léon Poliakov, *The Aryan Myth*, pp. 207–8.

28. Andrew Anderson, *Alexander's Gate*, pp. 103–4; John Wilson, *Lectures on Our Israelitish Origin*, p. 369.

29. Gossett, *Race*, pp. 390–91, 394–95; Stoddard, "The Pedigree of Judah," pp. 321–23.

30. Stoddard, "The Pedigree of Judah," pp. 324–25, 329–30, 331.

31. Reginald Horsman, *Race and Manifest Destiny: The Origins of American Racial Anglo-Saxonism* (Cambridge: Harvard University Press, 1981), pp. 134–35.

32. *Dearborn Independent*, September 22, 1923, pp. 2–3; May 23, 1925, p. 27; Frank Hancock, "Anglo-Israel as a Racial Movement," *National Message* 12 (October 7, 1933), pp. 628–29; W. H. Fasken, *Israel's Racial Origin and Migrations* (London: Covenant Publishing Company, 1934), p. 51.

33. Ben Judah, *When?*, p. 11; Parker, *A Short History*, pp. 36, 41; Howard B. Rand, "The Incredible Hoax," in Rand, *Documentary Studies*, 2:133 (originally published in *Destiny*, July 1948); idem, "Mishandling the Scriptures," in Rand, *Documentary Studies*, 3:158 (originally published in *Destiny*, November 1949).

34. Frank P. Mintz, *The Liberty Lobby and the American Right: Race, Conspiracy, and Culture* (Westport, Conn.: Greenwood Press, 1985), pp. 51–52; Ralph Lord Roy, *Apostles of Discord: A Study of Organized Bigotry and Disruption on the Fringes of Protestantism* (Boston: Beacon Press, 1953), p. 84.

35. John Beaty, *The Iron Curtain over America* (Dallas: Wilkinson Publishing Company, 1951), pp. 19, 25, 42.

36. Wilmot Robertson [pseud.], *The Dispossessed Majority*, rev. ed. (Cape Canaveral, Fla.: Howard Allen, 1973), pp. 27–28, 156; Evelyn Rich, "Ku Klux Klan Ideology, 1954–1988" (Ph.D. dissertation, Boston University, 1988), p. 182; "Gallery of Jewish Types," *The Crusader: The Voice of the White Majority*, no. 26 (October 1977), p. 11.

37. Wesley Swift, "Who Are the Jews?," *New Beginnings* 18 (December 1988), p. 10.

38. Gaard, *Spotlight on the Great Conspiracy*, pp. 40–42, 51–52, 54.

39. Comparet, *Israel's Fingerprints*, pp. 32–33; K. R. McKilliam, "Conspiracy to Destroy the Christian West," *End Time Revelation Newsletter* 1 (October 1976), pp. 2, 3.

40. *Calling Our Nation*, no. 55 (1987), p. 26; Dan Gayman, *In Search of Abraham's Children* (Schell City, Mo.: Church of Israel, 1987), p. 7; *Newsletter*, Christian-Patriots Defense League, September 1983, p. 1; Col. Jack Mohr, "Who Is True Israel?" (Bay St. Louis, Miss., n.d.), brochure; Brig. Gen. Jack Mohr, "Exploding the 'Chosen People' Myth" (Bay St. Louis, Miss., n.d.), pamphlet, p. 11; Bob Hallstrom, "Oprah, the Jews and Ritual Murder," *Calling Our Nation*, no. 50 (1989), pp. 22, 24 (reprinted from *America's Promise Newsletter*).

41. Arthur Koestler, *The Thirteenth Tribe*, pp. 180, 199, 200, 223.

42. "Land of the ZOG," *CDL Report* (Metairie, La.), no. 112 (n.d.), special edition, p. 2.

43. *America's Promise Broadcaster.*

Chapter 8

1. Léon Poliakov, *The History of Anti-Semitism* (London: Routledge and Kegan Paul, 1974), 1:142, 144; Joshua Trachtenberg, *The Devil and the Jews: The Medieval Conception of the Jew and Its Relationship to Modern Anti-Semitism* (New Haven: Yale University Press, 1943), pp. 21, 41–42.

2. Neil Forsyth, *The Old Enemy: Satan and the Combat Myth* (Princeton: Princeton University Press, 1987), pp. 236, 312, 328, 330.

3. Léon Poliakov, *The Aryan Myth: A History of Racist and Nationalist Ideas in Europe* (New York: Basic Books, 1974), pp. 131–32; Richard H. Popkin, *Isaac La Peyrère, 1596–1676: His Life, Work and Influence* (Leidon: E. J. Brill, 1987), pp. 21–23; David Rice McKee, "Isaac de la Peyrère: A Precursor of Eighteenth-Century Critical Deists," *PMLA* 59 (1944): 458–59; Popkin, *Isaac La Peyrère*, pp. 14–15.

4. McKee, "Isaac de la Peyrère," pp. 461, 463, 473, 479, 484; Reginald Horsman, *Race and Manifest Destiny: The Origins of American Racial Anglo-Saxonism* (Cambridge: Harvard University Press, 1981), pp. 45, 48.

5. Horsman, *Race and Manifest Destiny*, p. 52, 119, 120, 134–35; Popkin, *Isaac La Peyrère*, pp. 149–50.

6. Dominick M'Causland, *Adam and the Adamite; or, The Harmony of Scripture and Ethnology* (1864; reprint, London: Richard Bentley and Son, 1872), pp. 70, 164.

7. Alexander Winchell, *Preadamites; or, A Demonstration of the Existence of Men Before Adam; Together with a Study of Their Condition, Antiquity, Racial Affinities and Dispersion Over the Earth* (Chicago: S. C. Griggs and Company, 1880), pp. v, 52–53, 161–62, 191–92, 193, 385.

8. M'Causland, *Adam and the Adamite*, pp. 197–98, 284.

9. Winchell, *Preadamites*, pp. 52–53, 245, 268, 284–85.

10. E. S. G. Bristowe, *Cain—An Argument* (Leicester, England: Edgar Backus, 1950), p. 90; Mrs. Sydney Bristowe, *Sargon the Magnificent* (London: Covenant Publishing Company, 1927), pp. 16, 28. Despite the difference in names, both books have the same author.

11. M'Causland, *Adam and the Adamite*, pp. 295, 307; Winchell, *Preadamites*, p. 294; Charles Carroll, *"The Negro a Beast"; or, "In the Image of God"* (St. Louis: American Book and Bible House, 1900), p. 23.

12. D. Davidson and H. Aldersmith, *The Great Pyramid: Its Divine Message—An Original Co-ordination of Historical Documents and Archaeological Evidences*, 11th ed. (London: Williams and Norgate, 1948), pp. 424, 425, 431, emphasis in original; Bristowe, *Sargon the Magnificent*, p. viii.

13. M'Causland, *Adam and the Adamite*, pp. 178–79.

14. Poliakov, *The Aryan Myth*, pp. 188, 256; M'Causland, *Adam and the Adamite*, pp. 201–2.

15. D[avid] Davidson, *A Connected History of Early Egypt, Babylonia and Central Asia* (Leeds, England: D. Davidson, 1927), chart on p. 23.

16. M'Causland, *Adam and the Adamite*, 208–9; Carroll, *"The Negro a Beast,"* p. 153.

17. Davidson and Aldersmith, *The Great Pyramid*, p. 425; Charles F. Parham, *A Voice Crying in the Wilderness*, 2d ed. (Baxter Springs, Kans.: Apostolic Faith Bible College, 1910), pp. 82, 84.

18. Adam Clarke, *The Holy Bible containing the Old and New Testaments, The Text Carefully Printed from the Most Correct Copies of the Present Authorized Translation, Including the Marginal Readings and Parallel Texts with a Commentary and Critical Notes Designed as a Help to a Better Understanding of the Sacred Writings* (New York: Abingdon Press, n.d.), 1:48–49.

19. Poliakov, *The Aryan Myth*, p. 279.

20. Carroll, *"The Negro a Beast,"* pp. 219, 220, 221, 228.

21. C. Douglas Weaver, *The Healer-Prophet, William Marrion Branham: A Study of the Prophetic in American Pentecostalism* (Macon, Ga.: Mercer University Press, 1987), pp. 98, 113; William Marrion Branham, *Questions and Answers—Book 7, June 28, 1959* (Jeffersonville, Ind.: Branham Tabernacle, n.d.), p. 39.

22. Sydney E. Ahlstrom, *A Religious History of the American People* (New Haven: Yale University Press, 1972), pp. 721–22; William Henry Brackney, *The Baptists* (New York: Greenwood Press, 1988), pp. 241–42; Henry Warner Bowden, *Dictionary of American Religious Biography* (Westport, Conn.: Greenwood Press, 1977), p. 351.

23. Quoted in Weaver, *The Healer-Prophet*, p. 124; Branham, *Questions and Answers*, p. 39, quoted in Weaver, *The Healer-Prophet*, pp. 113–14. A view opposed to Branham's is presented in Rev. A. W. Post, *The "Serpent's Seed" Doctrine Refuted!* (Fredericton, New Brunswick, n.d.), pamphlet.

24. Davidson, *A Connected History*, chart 19; Davidson and Aldersmith, *The Great Pyramid*, p. 438.

25. M'Causland, *Adam and the Adamite*, pp. 197–98, 208–9, 262; Winchell, *Preadamites*, pp. 189, 191, 295, emphasis added.

26. Carroll, *"The Negro a Beast,"* pp. 146, 150, 220, 221; Charles Parham, *A Voice Crying in the Wilderness*, p. 83.

27. Davidson, *A Connected History*, chart 22; Davidson and Aldersmith, *The Great Pyramid*, p. 424.

28. Bristowe, *Sargon the Magnificent*, p. 3.

29. Ibid., pp. 26, 28, 28–29, 32, 135, 144, 147.

30. Frederick Haberman, *Tracing Our Ancestors* (1934; reprint, Vancouver: British Israel Association, 1962), p. 25; H. Ben Judah [pseud.], *When?: A Prophetical Novel of the Very Near Future* (Vancouver: British Israel Association of Greater Vancouver, 1944), p. 70; Wesley Swift, "Who Are the Jews?," *New Beginnings* 18 (December 1988), p. 9; Conrad Gaard, *Spotlight on the Great Conspiracy* (Steilacoon, Wash.: Destiny of America Foundation, n.d.; reprints articles from Gaard's journal, the *Interpreter*, originally published in 1960), p. 5; *Christian Vanguard*, no. 103.

31. Bristowe, *Sargon the Magnificent*, pp. 55, 58, 127.

32. Ibid., pp. 55, 70, 80–81, 95, 127; Haberman, *Tracing Our Ancestors*, p. 25.

33. Alexander Hislop, *The Two Babylons; or, The Papal Worship Proved to Be the Worship of Nimrod and His Wife* (reprint, New York: Loizeaux Brothers, 1943), pp. 25, 28, 34, 211,

224, 232, 274–75. A brief first edition was published in Edinburgh in 1853 and a much expanded second edition in 1858.

34. D. Michael Quinn, *Early Mormonism and the Magic World View* (Salt Lake City, Utah: Signature Books, 1987), p. 167; Norman Cohn, *Europe's Inner Demons* (New York: Basic Books, 1975), pp. 41–42; McKee, "Isaac de la Peyrère," p. 479.

35. Daniel H. Ludlow, ed., *Encyclopedia of Mormonism*, 5 vols. (New York: Macmillan, 1992), 1:245–46; *The Pearl of Great Price: A Selection from the Revelations, Translations, and Narrations of Joseph Smith* (reprint, Salt Lake City, Utah: Church of Jesus Christ of Latter-day Saints, 1973); Moses 5:30, 5:51, 7:22; Bruce McConkie, *Mormon Doctrine*, 2d ed. (Salt Lake City, Utah: Bookcraft, 1966), pp. 108–9, 527, 698, emphasis in original; Quinn, *Early Mormonism*, pp. 165–67.

36. Newell G. Bringhurst, *Saints, Slaves, and Blacks: The Changing Place of Black People within Mormonism* (Westport, Conn.: Greenwood Press, 1981), pp. 86–87, 101–2.

Chapter 9

1. Frederick Haberman, *Tracing Our Ancestors* (1934; reprint, Vancouver: British Israel Association, 1962), pp. 18, 19, 25, 144.

2. Philip E. J. Monson, *Satan's Seat: The Enemy of Our Race* (Los Angeles: Covenant Evangelistic Association Zion Press, n.d.), pp. 4, 22–23, 27. The work's publication history appears on p. 2.

3. *The Morning Cometh* (Vancouver: Anglo-Saxon Christian World Movement, June 1941), 2d ed., rev. (October 1941), 3d ed., rev. (February 1942).

4. *When Gog Attacks* (Vancouver: British Israel Association of Greater Vancouver, January 1944), 2d ed. (June 1944), pp. 9, 12, 13–14, 15, 17.

5. H. Ben Judah [pseud.], *When?: A Prophetical Novel of the Very Near Future* (Vancouver: British Israel Association of Greater Vancouver, 1944), pp. 16–17, 21, 69–71, 73–74.

6. Conrad Gaard, *Spotlight on the Great Conspiracy* (Steilacoon, Wash.: Destiny of America Foundation, n.d.; reprints articles from Gaard's journal, the *Interpreter*, originally published in 1960), pp. 1, 4, 5, 10, 13, 14–16, 38, 42, 43, 45–46, 64–65, 79, 97–98.

7. Gaard, *Spotlight on the Great Conspiracy*, pp. 5, 40–42, 49–51, 65, 79; David Bennett, *The Party of Fear: From Nativist Movements to the New Right in American History* (Chapel Hill: University of North Carolina Press, 1988), pp. 23–26, 245, 317; Richard Hofstadter, *The Paranoid Style in American Politics* (New York: Knopf, 1965), pp. 29–32.

8. Bertrand L. Comparet, "Adam Was Not the First Man," *Your Heritage*, no. 15 (n.d.), p. 2.

9. Bertrand L. Comparet, "Noah's Flood Was Not World-Wide," *Christian Vanguard*, no. 47 (November 1975), pp. 6–8; idem, "Let's Examine the Evidence," *Your Heritage*, no. 105 (n.d.), p. 1; idem, "The Bible Is Not a Jewish Book," *Christian Vanguard*, no. 30 (May 1974), p. 3.

10. William P. Gale, "Racial and National Identity," *Identity* (n.d.), p. 4; idem, "'The Faith of Our Fathers,'" *Identity* 7 (January 1974), pp. 1–2.

11. Gale, "Racial and National Identity," pp. 6–7.

12. Gale, "'The Faith of Our Fathers'" (January 1974), p. 2; idem, "Racial and National Identity," p. 11.

13. Gale, "'The Faith of Our Fathers'" (January 1974), p. 2; idem, "Racial and National Identity," p. 11.

14. Gale, "'The Faith of Our Fathers'" (January 1974), p. 2; idem, "'The Faith of Our Fathers'" (April 1974), pp. 1, 4.

15. Gale, "Racial and National Identity," p. 10; idem, "'The Faith of Our Fathers'" (January 1974), p. 2.

16. Wesley Swift, *Testimony of Tradition and the Origin of Races* (Hollywood, Calif.: New Christian Crusade Church, n.d.), p. 6; idem, "Preserving Our Racial Self-Respect," *National Chronicle* 20 (March 4, 1971), p. 1; idem, *Testimony of Tradition*, pp. 4–5, 29.

17. Swift, *Testimony of Tradition*, pp. 25, 29; idem, "Who Are the Jews?," p. 8.

18. Swift, *Testimony of Tradition*, pp. 9–10, 13.

19. Ibid., p. 15; idem, "Who Are the Jews?," p. 9; idem, "The Redemption, towit [*sic*], of the Body," *National Chronicle* 22 (July 12, 1973), p. 3, emphasis in original; idem, "The Children of the Beast," *Christian Vanguard*, no. 103 (July 1980), p. 6; idem, "With Violence Shall Babylon Be Cast Down," *Christian Vanguard*, no. 86 (February 1979), p. 5; idem, "The Jews! Who Are They?," *Christian Vanguard*, no. 64 (April 1977), pp. 9–10.

20. Swift, "Who Are the Jews?," p. 9; Rev. 17:2–5; Swift, "With Violence Shall Babylon Be Cast Down," pp. 5, 6, emphasis in original.

21. Gale, "Racial and National Identity," p. 10; Swift, *Testimony of Tradition*, p. 10.

22. *The Book of Mormon* (reprint, Salt Lake City, Utah: Church of Jesus Christ of Latter-day Saints, 1951), 3 Nephi 21:26. New editions of Mormon scriptures appeared in 1981. Earlier editions are cited here, however, since any appropriation of Mormon teachings by Gale and Swift would have occurred prior to the new editions. James E. Talmage, *A Study of the Articles of Faith*, 50th ed. (Salt Lake City, Utah: Church of Jesus Christ of Latter-day Saints, 1971), p. 340; *Doctrine and Covenants of the Church of Jesus Christ of Latter-day Saints* (reprint, Salt Lake City, Utah: Church of Jesus Christ of Latter-day Saints, 1973), 110:11.

23. Daniel H. Ludlow, ed., *Encyclopedia of Mormonism*, 5 vols. (New York: Macmillan, 1992), 2:461–62, 706, 708–9.

24. Bruce McConkie, *Mormon Doctrine*, 2d ed. (Salt Lake City, Utah: Bookcraft, 1966), p. 856; James A. Aho, *The Politics of Righteousness: Idaho Christian Patriotism* (Seattle: University of Washington Press, 1990), pp. 177, 254.

25. *The Pearl of Great Price: A Selection from the Revelations, Translations, and Narrations of Joseph Smith* (reprint, Salt Lake City, Utah: Church of Jesus Christ of Latter-day Saints, 1973); Moses 3:7; Abraham 3:22; Talmage, *A Study of the Articles of Faith*, p. 192; R. Clayton Brough, *Our First Estate: The Doctrine of Man's Pre-Mortal Existence* (Bountiful, Utah: Horizon Publishers, 1979).

26. Wesley A. Swift, *You: Before the World Was Framed* (Hollywood, Calif.: New Christian Crusade Church, n.d.), p. 3; Dan Gayman, *The Holy Bible, The Book of Adam's Race* (Schell City, Mo.: Church of Israel, n.d.), p. 11, emphasis in original; J. Gordon Melton, *The Encyclopedia of American Religions*, 2d ed. (Detroit: Gale Research Corporation, 1987), p. 462; Steven L. Shields, *The Latter-day Saints Churches: An Annotated Bibliogra-*

phy (New York: Garland, 1987), pp. 256–57, 267; Philip Jones, "The Kingdom of Yahweh—The White Man's Hope," *Calling Our Nation*, no. 25 (n.d.), p. 14. The fullest discussion of Gayman and his church is Jeffrey Kaplan, "The Context of American Millenarian Revolutionary Theology: The Case of the 'Identity Christian' Church of Israel," *Terrorism and Political Violence* 5 (1993): 30–82. Jones, "The Kingdom of Yahweh," p. 14. In late 1992, the Mormon Church excommunicated a number of members with right-wing connections, some of whom appear to have been suspected of harboring Identity sympathies. In the 1992 presidential election, Utah contributed almost one-third of the votes for the fringe candidacy of James "Bo" Gritz, a Mormon convert with close Identity connections to such figures as Pete Peters. *Salt Lake Tribune*, November 6, 29, 1992.

27. "This Is Aryan Nations," undated brochure; George Stout, "Apocalypse Now," *Calling Our Nation*, no. 48 (n.d.), p. 7; Michael Hudson, "Jewish Ritual Murder," *Calling Our Nation*, no. 36 (n.d.), pp. 6–7; Bob Hallstrom, "Oprah, the Jews and Ritual Murder," *Calling Our Nation*, no. 50 (1989).

28. Jarah B. Crawford, *Last Battle Cry: Christianity's Final Conflict with Evil* (Knoxville, Tenn.: Jann Publishing Company, 1984), pp. 7, 321, 333–34, 337, 339–40, 346, emphasis in original.

29. Dan Gayman, *Articles of Faith and Doctrine for the Churches of Israel, Diocese of Manasseh, United States of America* (Schell City, Mo.: Church of Israel, 1982), p. 5; idem, "Cain and Abel: Fraternal Twins from Different Fathers," *Watchman* 11 (Fall 1988), pp. 21, 23; idem, "Genesis 4:1: An Exegetical Review," *Watchman* 11 (Fall 1988), p. 28.

30. Gayman, "Cain and Abel," p. 21; idem, "Genesis 4:1," pp. 30, 31.

31. *Witchcraft and the Illuminati* (Zarephath-Horeb, Mo.: Covenant, Sword and Arm of the Lord, 1981), pp. 4–7.

32. Bennett, *The Party of Fear*, pp. 23–26; Hofstadter, *The Paranoid Style in American Politics*, pp. 10–14; Des Griffin, *Fourth Reich of the Rich* (South Pasadena, Calif.: Emissary Publications, 1981), p. 195.

33. *Witchcraft and the Illuminati*, pp. 14–18, 30–31.

34. Howard B. Rand, "Knowledge of Good and Evil," *Destiny* 32 (July 1961), p. 157; "In the Image of God: The Origin and Destiny of Races," *Destiny* 37 (1966), p. 216; "In the Image of God: The Origin and Destiny of Races, Part II," *Destiny* 11 (1966), pp. 234–46.

35. "In the Image of God, Part II," pp. 238, 239, 240, 243, 245.

36. Rand, "Knowledge of Good and Evil," pp. 157, 158; "Cain," *Reminder of Our National Heritage* 26 (May–June 1963), pp. 1–3.

37. *National Chronicle* 10 (March 25, 1971), p. 2; Brig. Gen. Jack Mohr, *Proofs of Identity* (Bay St. Louis, Miss., n.d.), unpaginated. The rank is an honorific conferred by the Christian-Patriots Defense League. "The Truth about British Israel," *Identity* 7 (February 1975), p. 8, emphasis in original.

38. Philip Jones, "Aryan 'Identity' Divided," *Calling Our Nation*, no. 37 ([1983]), p. 23; Rev. Tom Metzger, "Let's 'Can' Kosher-Identity Practices," *Christian Vanguard*, no. 52 (April 1976), p. 8.

39. Mohr, *Proofs of Identity*; Jones, "Aryan 'Identity' Divided"; "Who Is the Anti-Christ King Today?," *End Time Revelation Newsletter* 2, no. 7 (1977), p. 4.

Chapter 10

1. Howard B. Rand, *Digest of the Divine Law* (Merrimac, Mass.: Destiny Publishers, 1943), p. xiii.

2. Ibid., pp. 14–15, 22.

3. Warren Fennell and Joyce Fennell, *An Index to the Laws, Statutes, and Judgments of God* (Phoenix, Ariz.: Lord's Covenant Church, 1979).

4. "Remnant Resolves" (LaPorte, Colo.: Scriptures for America, n.d.), brochure.

5. Richard Hofstadter, *The Paranoid Style in American Politics* (New York: Knopf, 1965), p. 249; James A. Aho, *The Politics of Righteousness: Idaho Christian Patriotism* (Seattle: University of Washington Press, 1990), pp. 91–92.

6. W. J. Cameron, "The Economic Law of God," *National Message* 12 (July 1, 1933), pp. 403–6; idem, "Economics of the Bible: As They Were Practiced for a Thousand Years by Our Anglo-Saxon-Israel Forefathers," *Destiny* 8 (September 1937), pp. 8–10, emphasis in original.

7. Rand, *Digest of the Divine Law*, pp. 88, 203, 206–7.

8. "The Fed's Role in the Grand Conspiracy," *Primrose and Cattleman's Gazette* 10 (June 12, 1984), p. 10; Sheldon Emry, *Billions for the Bankers Debts for the People* (Phoenix, Ariz.: Lord's Covenant Church, n.d.), p. 24; "Remnant Resolves."

9. Cameron, "Economics of the Bible," pp. 8–9.

10. Rand, *Digest of the Divine Law*, pp. 93–94.

11. James Corcoran, *Bitter Harvest: Gordon Kahl and the Posse Comitatus—Murder in the Heartland* (New York: Viking, 1990), pp. 51–52, quoted in Aho, *The Politics of Righteousness*, p. 246.

12. Quoted in Cheri Seymour, *Committee of the States: Inside the Radical Right* (Mariposa, Calif.: Camden Place Communications, 1991), p. 200.

13. "United States Christian Posse Association," *Identity* 6 ([1972]), pp. 6–7; Seymour, *Committee of the States*, p. 199.

14. Seymour, *Committee of the States*, pp. 5, 8, 272, 290. On the Committee of the States, see Robert W. Hoffert, *A Politics of Tension: The Articles of Confederation and American Political Ideas* (Niwot: University Press of Colorado, 1992), pp. 31, 34.

15. Seymour, *Committee of the States*, pp. 267–68, 343, 347; *Jubilee* 1 (May 1988), pp. 1, 4.

16. Bruce Barron, " 'Let's Not Change the World, Let's Run It': Movements and Ideologies of Social Takeover within the New Christian Right" (paper presented at the annual meeting of the Society for the Scientific Study of Religion, 1989); idem, "Re-Christianizing America: The Reconstruction and Kingdom Now Movements in American Evangelical Christianity" (Ph.D. dissertation, University of Pittsburgh, 1991), pp. 25–30.

17. Seymour, *Committee of the States*, p. 169; *Extremism on the Right: A Handbook* (New York: Anti-Defamation League of B'nai B'rith, 1983), pp. 110–11, 145–47; Tom Metzger, "Crusader Action," *Christian Vanguard*, no. 52 (April 1976), p. 8; *Christian Vanguard*, no. 55 (July 1976); Tom Metzger, "Forming an Identity Sunday School," *Christian Vanguard*, no. 53 (May 1976), p. 11; *Christian Vanguard*, no. 71 (November 1977); *Christian Vanguard*, no. 72 (December 1977), p. 2.

18. *Extremism on the Right*, p. 110; Evelyn Rich, "Ku Klux Klan Ideology, 1954–1988" (Ph.D. dissertation, Boston University, 1988), pp. 195, 239–40.

19. Rich, "Ku Klux Klan Ideology," pp. 239–40; *Extremism on the Right*, p. 111.

20. Rich, "Ku Klux Klan Ideology," pp. 210–11, 272, 296; William B. McMahon, "David Duke and the Legislature," in Douglas D. Rose, ed., *The Emergence of David Duke and the Politics of Race* (Chapel Hill: University of North Carolina Press, 1992), p. 118; "Victory in Los Angeles," *Christian Vanguard*, no. 40 (March–April 1975), p. 1, emphasis in original.

21. Rich, "Ku Klux Klan Ideology," pp. 237–38.

22. On Carto and the Liberty Lobby generally, see Frank P. Mintz, *The Liberty Lobby and the American Right: Race, Conspiracy, and Culture* (Westport, Conn.: Greenwood Press, 1985). The Populist party's 1984 campaign is described in Leonard Zeskind, *It's Not Populism—America's New Populist Party: A Fraud by Racists and Anti-Semites* (Atlanta: National Anti-Klan Network, 1984); *Ballot-Box Bigotry: David Duke and the Populist Party*, Center for Democratic Renewal Background Report, no. 7 (Atlanta: Center for Democratic Renewal, n.d.), p. 15; Elizabeth A. Rickey, "The Nazi and the Republicans," in Rose, *The Emergence of David Duke*, p. 62.

23. *Ballot-Box Bigotry*, p. 17; "Identity Camp Meeting," *Christian Vanguard Newsletter*, no. 194 (August 1990), p. 8; *New York Times*, August 30, 1992; Richard M. Scammon and Alice V. McGillivray, *America Votes 18: A Handbook of Contemporary American Election Statistics* (Washington, D.C.: Congressional Quarterly, 1989). A different total, as well as percentage figures, appears in the *New York Times*, November 22, 1988.

24. Lawrence N. Powell, "Slouching Toward Baton Rouge," in Rose, *The Emergence of David Duke*, p. 28; *New York Times*, January 23, February 20, 1989, October 9, 1990; Douglas D. Rose with Gary Esolan, "DuKKKe for Governor," in Rose, *The Emergence of David Duke*, pp. 227, 231. Duke unsuccessfully sought the U.S. Senate seat held by J. Bennett Johnston in 1990 but still managed to secure 44 percent of the vote and carry twenty-five of sixty-four parishes. In 1991 he forced Edwin Edwards into a nationally publicized Republican gubernatorial primary runoff. Edwards won decisively (61 percent), but Duke's vote, concentrated in rural areas, included heavy majorities among born-again Christians. He subsequently fared badly in early Republican presidential primaries, and dropped out of electoral politics.

25. *Knocking on Armageddon's Door* (documentary shown on the Public Broadcasting System program "P.O.V.," July 19, 1988); "Two Witnesses," *End Time Revelation Newsletter* 2, no. 7 (1977), p. 10, emphasis in original.

26. Dan Gayman, "The Road to Revolution," *Zion's Restorer* 5, no. 8 (n.d.), p. 3; idem, " 'Survival of the Elect,' " *Zion's Restorer* 5, no. 12 (n.d.), pp. 1, 3, emphasis in original.

27. Dan Gayman, *Articles of Faith and Doctrine for the Churches of Israel, Diocese of Manasseh, United States of America* (Schell City, Mo.: Church of Israel, 1982), pp. 14–16.

28. Ibid., p. 17, emphasis in original; "Organic Farming," *Watchman* 11 (Fall 1988), p. 10; "Home Schooling Going Well," *Watchman* 11 (Fall 1988), p. 10; "Home Birthing Going Well," *Watchman* 11 (Fall 1988), p. 10; "Life in the Country," *Watchman* 11 (Winter 1989), p. 15.

29. John R. Harrell, *The Golden Triangle* (Flora, Ill.: Christian Conservative Church, n.d.), pp. 6–7.

30. Ibid., pp. 8–12, 13.

31. *Extremism on the Right*, p. 7; *The Hate Movement Today: A Chronicle of Violence and Disarray* (New York: Anti-Defamation League of B'nai B'rith, 1988); *New York Times*, May 19, 1988.

32. *C.S.A. Survival Manual* (Pontiac, Mo.: C.S.A. Enterprises, 1982), p. 1; *Newsletter* (Covenant, Sword and the Arm of the Lord) (August–September 1984), p. 2; "ATTACK!," *Newsletter* (Covenant, Sword and the Arm of the Lord) (November–December 1984), p. 2, emphasis in original.

33. On rightist legal doctrine, see Aho, *The Politics of Righteousness*, pp. 47–50.

34. Nehemiah Township Charter and Common Law Contract, County of Kootenai, Idaho, July 12, 1982; Alan D. Sapp, *Ideological Justification for Right Wing Extremism: An Analysis of the Nehemiah Township Charter Document* (Warrensburg: Center for Criminal Justice Research, Central Missouri State University, 1986).

35. Nehemiah Township Charter, preamble, emphasis in original.

36. Ibid., articles 4, 6, 12, 13, emphasis in original.

37. Ibid., articles 9, 14, 22.

38. James Bruggen, "Making The Remnant Resolves 'Official' (A Personal Experience)," *Remnant Resolves Report* (n.d.), unpaginated, emphasis in original. Elsewhere in the publication, the author's name is given as "Bruggenman."

39. Aho, *The Politics of Righteousness*, pp. 45–46; *Extremism on the Right*, pp. 43–45; "George Washington's Vision," *Idaho Statesman* (Boise), September 14, 1980.

40. "United States Christian Posse Association," pp. 3, 10; Ben Cameron, "The Constitutional Republic," *Identity* 6, no. 1 (n.d.), pp. 16–17, emphasis in original.

41. Corcoran, *Bitter Harvest*, pp. 29, 49, 77.

Chapter 11

1. On William Pierce, see James A. Aho, *The Politics of Righteousness: Idaho Christian Patriotism* (Seattle: University of Washington Press, 1990), p. 275. On the National Youth Alliance and the National Alliance, see Frank P. Mintz, *The Liberty Lobby and the American Right: Race, Conspiracy, and Culture* (Westport, Conn.: Greenwood Press, 1985), pp. 129–31.

2. Andrew MacDonald [William Pierce], *The Turner Diaries*, 2d ed. (Washington, D.C.: National Alliance, 1980), pp. 71, 76, emphasis in original.

3. Ibid., p. 210; Andrew Macdonald [pseud.], *Hunter* (Hillsboro, W.Va.: National Vanguard Books, 1989), p. 157.

4. Ernest Callenbach, *Ecotopia: The Notebooks and Reports of William Weston* (reprint, New York: Bantam, 1977), p. 57.

5. This account is based on the narrative in Kevin Flynn and Gary Gerhardt, *The Silent Brotherhood: Inside America's Racist Underground* (New York: Free Press, 1989), especially pp. 95–99, 110, 193, 201–6, 228, 247, 249, 252, 392–99.

6. Flynn and Gerhardt, *The Silent Brotherhood*, pp. 81, 93, 140, 194; [Pierce], *The Turner Diaries*, p. 73; Aho, *The Politics of Righteousness*, pp. 62–63; "An Oath to Read and One to Ponder," *From the Mountain* (September–October 1987), p. 10.

7. Bob LeRoy, "My Interview with Mrs. Bob Mathews," *Alarming Cry* (Spring 1989), p.

8; Flynn and Gerhardt, *The Silent Brotherhood*, pp. 25–26, 84, 120, 249, 252; "Racist Women," "Sally Jessy Raphael" transcript 613, air date, January 9, 1991.

8. FBI Memorandum from Special Agent in Charge, Butte, Montana, to "All Agents," October 2, 1984; Flynn and Gerhardt, *The Silent Brotherhood*, pp. 8, 89, 248, 282.

9. Flynn and Gerhardt, *The Silent Brotherhood*, pp. 119, 140, 144, 206; David Eden Lane, "Statement to the World by the Holy Order of the Bruder Schweigen," *Calling Our Nation*, no. 53 (1987), pp. 11–12. David Lane has also had significant links to the Odinist movement.

10. Robert C. Mansker, "First Blood," *Calling Our Nation*, no. 47 (n.d.), p. 22.

11. Dan Gayman, *Articles of Faith and Doctrine for the Churches of Israel, Diocese of Manasseh, United States of America* (Schell City, Mo.: Church of Israel, 1982), p. 16, emphasis in original; *Watchman* 11 (Winter 1989), pp. 11–12, emphasis in original.

12. *Identity* (Burnaby, British Columbia) 47 (September 1985), back cover.

13. Flynn and Gerhardt, *The Silent Brotherhood*, pp. 160–64, 193–95.

14. Eckard Toy, " 'Promised Land' or Armageddon?: History, Survivalists, and the Aryan Nations in the Pacific Northwest," *Montana: The Magazine of Western History* 36 (Summer 1986): 82.

15. Joel Garreau, *The Nine Nations of North America* (Boston: Houghton Mifflin, 1981), pp. 250–51, 300–301, 310; Callenbach, *Ecotopia*.

16. Aho, *The Politics of Righteousness*, p. 58; *Background Report on Racist and Far-Right Organizing in the Pacific Northwest* (Atlanta: Center for Democratic Renewal, n.d.), p. 4. The *Background Report* incorrectly identifies Robert Miles as an Aryan Nations leader. A photocopy of the Butler letter appears in *Aryan Nations, Far Right Underground Movement* (Atlanta: Center for Democratic Renewal, 1986), p. 8. Robert Miles, "Mountain Free State," *From the Mountain* (July–August 1982), pp. 1–4.

17. Miles, "Mountain Free State," p. 4; "Five States Is All We Ask," *From the Mountain* (March–April 1985), p. 7.

18. Miles, "Mountain Free State," pp. 3–4.

19. "Five States Is All We Ask," pp. 7–8.

20. "Separatists Launch New Nation," *WAR* 5, no. 3 (1986), p. 1.

21. "What We Taught," *From the Mountain* (March–April 1985), p. 5; Miles, "Mountain Free State," pp. 1–2.

22. David Lane, "Migration," *Calling Our Nation*, no. 59 (1989), p. 8; John C. Calhoun [*sic*], "Of Man, God, and War—Thoughts from the Fifth Era," *Inter-Klan Newsletter and Survival Alert*, no. 5 (1984), p. 10.

23. Louis R. Beam, Jr., "Seditious Conspiracy," supplement bound into *Calling Our Nation*, no. 58, pp. 15–16; *Seditionist* 1 (Winter 1988), p. 2.

24. "Being Honest," *From the Mountain* (March–April 1985), p. 9; "Five States Is All We Ask," p. 7.

25. Beam, "Seditious Conspiracy," pp. 19, 21, emphasis in original.

26. "The Out Trek," *From the Mountain* (March–April 1985), p. 8; "Aryan Renaissance," *Calling Our Nation*, no. 53 (1987), pp. 1–2.

27. *New York Times*, February 18, 19, 28, April 8, 1988; "The Trial at Fort Smith," *From the Mountain* (March–April 1988), pp. 1–4.

28. Michael Barkun, "Reflections after Waco: Millennialists and the State," *Christian Century* 110 (June 2–9, 1993): 596–600.

29. *New York Times*, September 1, 1992, July 9, 1993.

Chapter 12

1. An unknown but very small number of American British-Israelites did not follow the transformation to Christian Identity described here, and I know of no data on their social backgrounds. The British-Israel movement in the United Kingdom itself has shrunk dramatically, so that the British-Israel-World Federation now claims only seven hundred members and conspicuously lacks the aristocratic patrons that were once its ornament. Interview with A. E. Gibb, secretary of the British-Israel-World Federation, London, June 1992. The only detailed social background study of Identity believers appears in James A. Aho, *The Politics of Righteousness: Idaho Christian Patriotism* (Seattle: University of Washington Press, 1990), chap. 7. His large but nonrandom sample shows Identity believers to be similar to their non-Identity neighbors, although somewhat better educated. Despite the nonrandom nature of the sample, Aho went to great pains to control for distorting effects, and there is no reason to doubt the validity of his conclusions. Insofar as his observations bear on a comparison with British-Israelism, two comments are in order. First, Idaho, where he conducted his research, is a relatively nonurban state. Second, his data show the conspicuous absence in Identity of the kind of high government officials, ranking military officers, and persons of social prominence who often set the tone of Anglo-Israelism.

2. Roy Wallis, *Salvation and Protest: Studies of Social and Religious Movements* (New York: St. Martin's, 1979), p. 44. The principal formulation is Colin Campbell, "The Cult, the Cultic Milieu and Secularization," *A Sociological Yearbook of Religion in Britain* (London: SCM Press, 1972), 5:119–36.

3. "God's Silent Witnesses," *America's Promise Newsletter* (January 1988), pp. 1–5; "Mysterious Stonehenge," *America's Promise Newsletter* (February 1989), pp. 2–3.

4. Barbara Udvary, "Garlic," *New Harmony Christian Crusade Newsletter*, no. 47 (December 1988), pp. 8–10; "Industrial Waste Sold as Health Food," *Christian Vanguard Newsletter*, no. 175 (November 1988), pp. 9–13; Reginald Bradbury, "U.F.O.'s—Are They a Sign That the End Is Near?," *Christian Vanguard*, no. 26 (December 1973), p. 6.

5. Norman Cohn, *The Pursuit of the Millennium: Revolutionary Millenarians and Mystical Anarchists of the Middle Ages*, rev. ed. (New York: Oxford University Press, 1970), p. 281.

6. Interview with Floyd Cochran, December 9, 1992.

Chapter 13

1. *New York Times*, April 24, August 11, 1995.

2. *The Sunday Times* (London), February 4, 1996; *New York Times*, February 11, 1996; April 24, May 4, 1995; *Orlando Sentinel*, reprinted in *Syracuse Post-Standard*, April 28, 1995; *New York Times*, July 5, 1995.

3. *Witchcraft and the Illuminati* (Zarephath-Horeb, Mo.: Covenant, Sword and Arm of the Lord, 1981), p. 40; Pat Robertson, *The New World Order* (Dallas: Word Publishing, 1991).

4. Jim Keith, *Black Helicopters over America: Strikeforce for the New World Order* (Lilburn, Ga.: IllumiNet Press, 1994); Mark Koernke, *America in Peril*, videotape.

5. Richard Hofstadter, *The Paranoid Style in American Politics* (New York: Knopf, 1965), pp. 35–36; "The 'Genesis' of Revelation's Mark?," *Relevance* (Birmingham, Mich.) 1 (November 23, 1994), pp. 9–10.

6. *Dayton Daily News*, April 23, 1995; *Chicago Tribune*, May 14, 1995; Alex Heard, "The Road to Oklahoma City: Inside the World of the Waco-Obsessed Right," *The New Republic* 212 (May 15, 1995), pp. 15–20; *Arizona Republic*, May 16, 1995.

7. William R. Pabst, *Concentration Camp Plans for U.S. Citizens* (Houston, Tex. [?], 1979), pamphlet; Koernke, *America in Peril*; *New York Times*, April 29, 1996; Keith, *Black Helicopters*, p. 93; "An Urgent Message! You May Not Have a Country After 1995!" (Canton, Mich.: The American Freedom Network, 1995), brochure. The reference to a "Satanic eye" atop a pyramid is an allusion to the Great Seal of the United States, reproduced on the back of the one-dollar bill, and regarded by conspiratorialists as an NWO/Illuminatist emblem.

8. *New York Times*, May 31, June 7, 1993.

9. Ibid., May 28, April 22, 1995.

10. See, for example, *The Spotlight*, May 31, June 7, 1993.

11. *Waco: The Big Lie* (Indianapolis: American Justice Federation, 1994), videotape; *Waco II: The Big Lie Continues* (Indianapolis: American Justice Federation, 1994), videotape; Department of Justice, *Report to the Deputy Attorney General on the Events at Waco, Texas, February 28 to April 19, 1993* (Washington, D.C., 1993), pp. 152, 153; *Armed and Dangerous: Militias Take Aim at the Federal Government* (New York: Anti-Defamation League, 1994), p. 12. The report of UN tank sightings is in Anson Shupe and Jeffrey K. Hadden, "Cops, News Copy, and Public Opinion," in Stuart A. Wright, ed., *Armageddon in Waco: Critical Perspectives on the Branch Davidian Conflict* (Chicago: University of Chicago Press, 1995), p. 197.

12. Heard, "The Road to Oklahoma City."

13. *Criminal Politics*, July 1993, p. 2; William L. Pitts, Jr., "Davidians and Branch Davidians: 1929–1987," in Wright, *Armageddon in Waco*, pp. 33–35.

14. "Waco Remembrance" press release. In addition to antigovernment polemics on the right, events at Waco occasioned considerable opposition in the academic and religious communities as well. See, for example, Dean M. Kelley, "Waco: A Massacre and Its Aftermath," *First Things*, no. 53 (May 1995), pp. 22–37; and Michael Barkun, "Millenarian Groups and Law Enforcement Agencies: The Lessons of Waco," *Terrorism and Political Violence* 6 (1994): 75–95. The quoted inscription appears in Charles Strozier, "Apocalyptic Violence and the Politics of Waco," unpublished paper.

15. *New York Times*, April 21, May 20, 1995; *Taking Aim* (Noxon, Mont.) (December 1994), p. 1.

16. *Taking Aim* (December 1994), pp. 1, 2, 13.

17. Kevin Flynn and Gary Gerhardt, *The Silent Brotherhood: Inside America's Racist Underground* (New York: Free Press, 1989), pp. 260–61.

18. A brief biography of Richard Wayne Snell appears on the inside cover of his privately published book, *The Shadow of Death! (Is There Life after Death?)*. *The Shadow of Death!*, p. 45.

19. *State of Arkansas v. Richard Wayne Snell*, Circuit Court of Sevier County, Arkansas, October 1984 (No. CR-84-24), pp. 1347, 1358–59; Flynn and Gerhardt, *The Silent Brotherhood*, p. 260; *State of Arkansas v. Richard Wayne Snell*, p. 1333.

20. *State of Arkansas v. Richard Wayne Snell*, pp. 1336, 1338; *The Shadow of Death!*, p. ii; *State of Arkansas v. Richard Wayne Snell*, p. 1257; *The Shadow of Death!*, p. ii.

21. *Taking Aim* (March 1995), p. 7, emphasis in original. One of the fullest discussions of the April 19 date appears in Eugene V. Gallagher, "Religion and Politics: The Oklahoma City Bombing," comments at the annual meeting of the American Academy of Religion, Philadelphia, November 18, 1995.

22. Robert C. Masker, "First Blood," *Calling Our Nation*, no. 47 (n.d.), p. 22; "Special Report on the Meeting of Christian Men Held in Estes Park, Colorado, October 23, 24, 25, 1992, Concerning the Killing of Vickie and Samuel Weaver by the United States Government," p. 25, emphasis in original.

23. For an example of bombing conspiracy theories, see *The Spotlight*, October 2, 1995.

24. *Klanwatch Intelligence Report*, no. 79 (August 1995), p. 3; *New York Times*, May 25, 1995; *Newsweek*, February 19, 1996, pp. 29–31.

25. *New York Times*, May 22, 1995; *Tulsa Tribune*, April 2, 1985; *New York Times*, May 22, 1995.

26. Flynn and Gerhardt, *The Silent Brotherhood*, pp. 257, 259; *Tulsa Tribune*, April 2, 1985; *New York Times*, May 25, 1995.

27. *State of Arkansas v. Richard Wayne Snell*, pp. 1246–48; *New York Times*, May 20, 1995.

28. *New York Times*, May 22, 1995.

29. Ibid., July 5, 1995; Andrew MacDonald [William Pierce], *The Turner Diaries*, 2d ed. (Washington, D.C.: National Alliance, 1980), pp. 35–39.

30. *Charleston (W.Va.) Daily Mail*, April 22, 1995.

31. William L. Pierce, "OKC Bombing and America's Future," American Dissident Voices (radio series), aired April 29, 1995.

32. David H. Bennett, *The Party of Fear: From Nativist Movements to the New Right in American History*, 2d ed. (New York: Vintage Books, 1995), p. 447.

33. Michael Kelly, "The Road to Paranoia," *The New Yorker*, June 19, 1995, p. 74. The figure of 100 million presumably refers to troops under UN command.

34. Cheri Seymour, *Committee of the States: Inside the Radical Right* (Mariposa, Calif.: Camden Place Communications, 1991), p. 275.

35. *Syracuse Post-Standard*, May 3, 1995; *New York Times*, November 14, 1994; *Beyond the Bombing: The Militia Movement Grows* (New York: Anti-Defamation League, 1995), p. 1; *Klanwatch Intelligence Report*, no. 78 (June 1995), p. 1; *New York Times*, April 17, 1994; March 27, 1996.

36. *Central Michigan Regional Militia Manual 1-1* (1994), pp. 5–6.

37. *The Spotlight*, August 28, 1995.

38. Hofstadter, *The Paranoid Style*, p. 4.

39. *Field Manual Section 1: Principles Justifying the Arming and Organizing of a Militia* (The Free Militia, 1994), pp. 4, 8, 11; *Central Michigan Regional Militia Manual*, pp. 5, 6; *Washington Post*, May 20, 1995.

40. List of "Recorded Messages from the 1992 Rocky Mountain Rendezvous" (flyer). Bennett, *The Party of Fear*, p. 444; *Klanwatch Intelligence Report*, no. 79 (August 1995), p. 4; *Spokane Spokesman-Review*, October 30, 1994.

41. *Washington Post*, May 18, 1995.

42. *USA Today*, May 16, 1995; *Washington Post*, May 18, 1995.

43. *New York Times*, September 15, 13, October 20, August 12, 16, 1995.

44. Ibid., July 27, 28, 1995. Earlier administrative inquiries are described in Department of Justice, *Report to the Deputy Attorney General on the Events at Waco*, and Department of the Treasury, *Report of the Department of the Treasury on the Bureau of Alcohol, Tobacco, and Firearms Investigation of Vernon Wayne Howell also known as David Koresh* (Washington, D.C.: Government Printing Office, 1993).

45. For scholarly critiques, see Wright, *Armageddon in Waco*, and James D. Tabor and Eugene V. Gallagher, *Why Waco?: Cults and the Battle for Religious Freedom in America* (Berkeley: University of California Press, 1995).

46. Andrew MacDonald [William Pierce], *Hunter* (Hillsboro, W.Va.: National Vanguard Books, 1989), pp. 179, 157.

47. Richard Kelly Hoskins, *Our Nordic Race* (privately published, 1975), pp. 5, 18, 24, 30; idem, *Vigilantes of Christendom: The Story of the Phineas Priesthood* (Lynchburg, Va.: The Virginia Publishing Co., 199), p. 32.

48. Hoskins, *Vigilantes of Christendom*, pp. 434, 435.

49. *Klanwatch Intelligence Report*, no. 70 (December 1993), p. 8.

50. Louis Beam, "Leaderless Resistance," in "Special Report on the Meeting of Christian Men," pp. 20–23.

51. *Central Michigan Regional Militia Manual*, p. 5; *Southern Michigan Regional Militia Manual 4-8* (1995), not paginated.

52. *Taking Aim* 1, no. 8 (1994), pp. 2, 3; *The Spotlight*, September 18, 1995.

53. *Taking Aim* 1, no. 8 (1994), pp. 2, 3; *The Spotlight*, September 18, 1995.

54. *Taking Aim* 2, no. 2 (April 1995), pp. 4, 17, emphasis in original.

55. "Special Report on the Meeting of Christian Men," pp. 1, 24; Hoskins, *Vigilantes of Christendom*, pp. 32–33.

56. James A. Aho, *The Politics of Righteousness: Idaho Christian Patriotism* (Seattle: University of Washington Press, 1990), p. 14; *National Law Journal*, June 26, 1995; *Field Manual Section 1*, p. 44, emphasis in original.

57. *Field Manual Section 1*, p. 31, emphasis in original; *National Law Journal*, June 26, 1995; "United States Christian Posse Association," *Identity* 6 ([1972]), p. 2.

58. *Field Manual Section 1*, p. 54; *Taking Aim* 2, no. 4 (June 1995), p. 2, emphasis in original.

59. *New York Times*, April 17, 1994; March 27, 1996.

60. "Common Law Memorandum, Rodney O. Skurdal vs. de facto corporation state of Montana, Roundup, Montana, October 28, 1994," p. 14. The document also bears the title "Edict," by which it was often referred to in news media accounts. *Washington Post*, April 9, 1996; *New York Times*, April 12, 28, 1996.

61. "Common Law Memorandum," p. 11, emphasis in original.

62. *New York Times*, February 16, 25, March 8, 1996; List of "Recorded Messages from the 1992 Rocky Mountain Rendezvous."

63. Texe Marrs, *Dark Majesty: The Secret Brotherhood and the Magic of a Thousand Points of Light* (Austin, Tex.: Living Truth Publishers, 1992). Broader interest in Robertson's *New World Order* was the result of two articles: Michael Lind, "Rev. Robertson's Grand International Conspiracy Theory," *The New York Review of Books* 42 (February 2, 1995), pp. 21–25, and Michael Lind and Jacob Heilbrun, "On Pat Robertson," *The New York Review of Books* 42 (April 20, 1995), pp. 71–76. For Robertson's disavowals of anti-Semitism, see *New York Times*, March 4, 1995, and "An Open Letter from Christian Coalition," *The Forward* (New York), March 31, 1995. Nesta Webster was an English anti-Semitic writer of the interwar period. Eustace Mullins, a protégé of Ezra Pound, writes prolifically on anti-Semitic and conspiracy topics.

64. Michael Barkun, "Conspiracy Theories as Stigmatized Knowledge: The Basis for a New Age Racism?," paper presented at Harry F. Guggenheim Foundation conference on "Brotherhoods of Race and Nation: The Emergence of a Violent Euro-American Racist Subculture," New Orleans, December 8–11, 1995; Mathew Kalman and John Murray, "New-age Nazism," *New Statesman and Society*, June 23, 1995, pp. 18–20.

Index

tion, 63; and Bertrand Comparet, 63; organizes church, 63; and Gerald L. K. Smith, 63, 64–65; tenth anniversary of ministry, 63–64; and Ku Klux Klan, 64; and Christian Defense League, 66–68; on Second Coming, 106; millennialist views, 106–7; on racial origin of Jews, 129, 142–43; on origin of Adamic race, 183; on satanic paternity of Jews, 183–85
Swift, Mrs. Wesley, 62

Taking Aim, 264
Talmage, James E., 186
Tany, Thomas, 5
Tarim Basin, 158–59, 179, 180, 183
Taylor, John, 13
Thirteenth Tribe, The (Koestler), 144–45
This IS Armageddon (MacKendrick), 88–89
Thomas, Mark, 131
Thompson, Linda, 259, 262–63
Tiemann, Joseph, 211
Totten, Charles A. L., 18–21, 30, 67, 96; career, 18–19; relationship with Edward Hine, 19; millennialist views, 81; philo-Semitism, 123–24; anti-Semitism, 124–25
Townsend, Francis, 96
Tracing Our Ancestors (Haberman), 174
Trochmann, John, 272–73, 275, 282–83, 285–86
Turkey, 81, 83, 124; as Edom, 128–29, 132, 143
Turner, Ralph, 263
Turner, William W., 67
Turner Diaries, The, 115, 225–28, 256; and Christian Identity, 115; nuclear weapons in, 226–27; similarities to Oklahoma City bombing, 270–71
Two Babylons, The (Hislop), 168, 193
Two-seedline theory, 161–62, 167, 175, 191
Two Sticks (Eshelman), 18

Tyler, Victor Morris, 30
Tyner, Paul, 140

Union party, 96
United Israel World Fellowship, 54
United States Christian Posse Association, 207, 221

Vancouver: British-Israelism in, 49–52
Views of the Two Seeds (Parker), 161
Vigilantes of Christendom (Hoskins), 278–80, 283–84

Wallace, George, 226
Warner, James K., 62, 145, 209, 211; and Christian Defense League, 68–70; and David Duke, 210
Watchman of Israel, The, 21, 27
Weaver, Randy, 242, 267
Weber, Timothy, 113
Webster, Nesta, 289, 322 (n. 63)
When? ("Ben Judah"), vii, 51, 98, 133, 140, 175–77, 298 (n. 4); anti-Zionism in, 134
When Gog Attacks, 51, 176
White American Resistance, 210
Wickstrom, James: political activities, 209
Wild, Joseph, 17–18, 19; millennialist views, 81
Wilson, John, 6–12, 17; on racial origin of Jews, 7, 126
Winchell, Alexander, 164
Winrod, Gerald Burton, 62
Witchcraft and the Illuminati, 192–93
Worldwide Church of God, xi, 14, 196

Yale University, 18–19, 67
Young, Brigham, 169
Your Heritage (Comparet), 60
Youth Action, 226

Zevi, Sabbatai, 6
Zionist Occupation Government (ZOG), 111

is in control of *controls; directs; governs; manages.* Risk-takers feel that they are in control of their own destiny. *Risk-takers feel that they control their own destiny.*

is in defiance of *defies.* They are in defiance of my orders. *They defy my orders.* ■ This, too, is in defiance of all expert estimates, including that of the one physician in the Senate, the Republican Bill Frist. *This, too, defies all expert estimates, including that of the one physician in the Senate, the Republican Bill Frist.*

is indicative of *argues; attests to; bespeaks; betokens; indicates; shows; signals; signifies; suggests; testifies to; witnesses.* Current sales figures are indicative of a management problem. *Current sales figures indicate a management problem.*

is in disagreement (about; on; with) *clashes with; conflicts with; contradicts; differs from; disagrees with; quarrels with; varies with.* In the most important and urgent political debates of recent years involving science, a major difficulty has been that scientists of equal distinction and accomplishment have been in disagreement. *In the most important and urgent political debates of recent years involving science, a major difficulty has been that scientists of equal distinction and accomplishment have disagreed.*

is in doubt about (of) *disbelieves; distrusts; doubts; mistrusts; questions.* For anyone who is in doubt about whether ministers are ordinary mortals, Mr. Wangerin makes clear that this is the case. *For anyone who doubts whether ministers are ordinary mortals, Mr. Wangerin makes clear that this is the case.*

is in error *errs.* She was in error. *She erred.*

is in excess of *exceeds.* The size of the droplets produced by the unit is in excess of 8 microns. *The size of the droplets produced by the unit exceeds 8 microns.*

is in existence *exists.* More than 1,000 successful AI applications are in existence today. *More than 1,000 successful AI applications exist today.*

is in favor of *backs; endorses; favors; prefers; supports.* We are in favor of reform, but we don't like the way it is being implemented. *We favor reform, but we don't like the way it is being implemented.*

is in fear for (of) *dreads; fears (for); frets (about; over); stews (about; over);*

worries (about; over). I was in fear for my life. *I feared for my life.*

is influential in (-ing) *affects; influences.* The problem with this generalization is that other factors can be influential in determining how many subordinates a manager has. *The problem with this generalization is that other factors can influence how many subordinates a manager has.*

is -ing delete. What the kids are wanting is to be loved. *What the kids want is to be loved.* ■ We have gained a much better understanding of what providers are seeking from our networks, and we are looking forward to presenting our plan. *We have gained a much better understanding of what providers seek from our networks, and we look forward to presenting our plan.* ■ Today, millions of Americans with disabilities are engaging in productive, gratifying endeavors. *Today, millions of Americans with disabilities engage in productive, gratifying endeavors.* ■ Some are speculating that Apple's new device is a digital music product for its iTunes software, while others think Apple may unveil a PDA, a Web pad — or even a set top box. *Some speculate that Apple's new device is a digital music product for its iTunes software, while others think Apple may unveil a PDA, a Web pad — or even a set top box.*

is in harmony with *agrees with; coheres with; concurs with; conforms to (with); corresponds to (with).*

is injurious to *damages; harms; hurts; impairs; injures; mars; wrongs.*

is in keeping with *agrees with; coheres with; concurs with; conforms to (with); corresponds to (with).* This is in keeping with MicroPro International's focus and marketing. *This conforms to MicroPro International's focus and marketing.*

is in line with *agrees with; coheres with; concurs with; conforms to (with); corresponds to (with).* The figures are in line with recent years, when the number of taxpayers filing early in the season declined each year. *The figures conform with recent years, when the number of taxpayers filing early in the season declined each year.*

is in need of *needs; wants.* Thousands of people are in need of medical attention that private insurance does not offer. *Thousands of people need medical attention that private insurance does not offer.* ■ This section seems to be in need of a good deal of updating. *This section seems to need a good deal of updating.*

is in opposition to *conflicts with; contests; disagrees with; disapproves of; disputes; objects to; opposes; protests; resists.* They are in opposition to the United States. *They oppose the United States.*

is in possession of *has; possesses.* They were in possession of a large quantity of cocaine. *They possessed a large quantity of cocaine.*

is in receipt of *receives.* I am in receipt of your impressive résumé and references. *I received your impressive résumé and references.*

is insistent on *demands on; insists on.* If people are insistent on keeping the Electoral College, why not make it fair? *If people insist on keeping the Electoral College, why not make it fair?*

is in step with *agrees with; coheres with; concurs with; conforms to (with); corresponds to (with).*

is instrumental in (-ing) *aids in; assists in; helps.* Far from being the marginal movement they are perceived as being today, 19th-century evangelicals were instrumental in setting the political and social agenda for the century. *Far from being the marginal movement they are perceived as being today, 19th-century evangelicals helped set the political and social agenda for the century.*

is instrumental in helping *aids in; assists in; helps.* He was instrumental in helping them put together a financial plan. *He helped them put together a financial plan.*

is in support of *backs; endorses; favors; prefers; supports.* I myself am in support of women's rights. *I myself support women's rights.*

is (was) in the habit of (-ing) *will (would).* When I was younger, I was in the habit of reading a book a week. *When I was younger, I would read a book a week.*

is in violation of *desecrates; infringes on; violates.* My job is solely to determine whether conduct is in violation of the federal criminal law. *My job is solely to determine whether conduct violates the federal criminal law.*

is in want of *needs; wants.* I would recommend it to anyone who is in want of a good laugh. *I would recommend it to anyone who wants a good laugh.* ■ But the handing over of the land has not been finalized yet, and the Army is in want of funds to do the construction. *But the hand-*

ing over of the land has not been finalized yet, and the Army needs funds to do the construction. ■ She is an older woman and is in want of a young man. *She is an older woman and wants a young man.*

is it possible for *can.* Is it possible for you to tell us about your relationship with your child? *Can you tell us about your relationship with your child?*

is knowledgeable about (in; of) *comprehends; knows; understands.* We also favor choosing directors who have worked in a company's industry at some point in their careers or are knowledgeable in some collateral industry. *We also favor choosing directors who have worked in a company's industry at some point in their careers or understand some collateral industry.*

island (completely) surrounded by water *island.* White, racist American servicemen had struck again, this time on an island surrounded by water away from all civilization. *White, racist American servicemen had struck again, this time on an island away from all civilization.*

is mindful of (that) *comprehends; knows; realizes; recognizes; sees; understands.* We should be mindful of the benefits of free trade while finding ways to limit it. *We should realize the benefits of free trade while finding ways to limit it.*

is mistrustful about (of) *disbelieves; distrusts; doubts; mistrusts; questions.* The two sides are deeply mistrustful of each other after an estimated 1 million casualties. *The two sides deeply mistrust each other after an estimated 1 million casualties.*

is needful of *needs; wants.* Ball State's quaint little paper, *The Daily News*, is needful of inspiring columnists and diligent reporters. *Ball State's quaint little paper,* The Daily News, *needs inspiring columnists and diligent reporters.* ■ In terms of her physical well-being she is needful of extensive dental treatment. *In terms of her physical well-being she needs extensive dental treatment.*

is of assistance in (-ing) *aids in (-ing); assists in (-ing); helps.* Huge expenditures are required for EFRAT's activities, and every contribution is of assistance in expanding its efforts. *Huge expenditures are required for EFRAT's activities, and every contribution helps expand its efforts.*

is of benefit to *aids; benefits; favors; helps.* He agrees that companies need to take caution when choosing a system, but adds that the technology can be of great benefit to a company. *He agrees that companies need to take caution when choosing a system, but adds that the technology can greatly benefit a company.*

is of concern to *bothers; concerns; disturbs; interests; upsets; worries.* Since these factors vary considerably from one country to another, they are of particular concern to the global company interested in a new foreign market. *Since these factors vary considerably from one country to another, they particularly concern the global company interested in a new foreign market.*

is offensive to *insults; offends.* Halloween represents spiritist forces that are offensive to three of the world's major religions, Judaism, Christianity, and Islam. *Halloween represents spiritist forces that offend three of the world's major religions, Judaism, Christianity, and Islam.*

is of interest to *appeals to; attracts; concerns; excites; interests.* Although it is most helpful when read from the beginning to end, you can start with any section that is of interest to you. *Although it is most helpful when read from the beginning to end, you can start with any section that appeals to you.*

is of the belief (that) *asserts; believes; claims; contends; feels; holds; maintains; says; thinks; to.* The vast majority of physicians are of the belief that Ritalin is a safe drug for children. *To the vast majority of physicians, Ritalin is a safe drug for children.*

is of the opinion (that) *asserts; believes; claims; contends; feels; holds; maintains; says; thinks; to.* I am of the opinion that the Celtics are far better off this year than last. *I believe the Celtics are far better off this year than last.* ■ Management is of the opinion that within three years from the inception of this financing, it will be prepared to undertake an IPO. *Management contends that within three years from the inception of this financing, it will be prepared to undertake an IPO.*

is of the same opinion (as) *agrees (with); concurs (with).* Don't assume the person at the receiving end of your email is of the same opinion as you. *Don't assume the person at the receiving end of your email agrees with you.*

is of the view (that) *asserts; believes; claims; contends; feels; holds; maintains; says; thinks; to.* He is of the view that a person between the ages of 30 and 40 is more susceptible to tuberculosis than a person between 60 and 70. *He maintains that a person between the ages of 30 and 40 is more susceptible to tuberculosis than a person between 60 and 70.*

is one (that; which; who; whom)   delete. A European option is one which can be exercised only at maturity. *A European option can be exercised only at maturity.* ■ This situation is one that ought not to be forgotten. *This situation ought not to be forgotten.* ■ The issue of legal or illegal, documented or undocumented immigrant status is one that is still being argued. *The issue of legal or illegal, documented or undocumented immigrant status is still being argued.* ■ A multitasking system is one that can perform several tasks simultaneously. *A multitasking system can perform several tasks simultaneously.*

is on (a) par (with)   equals. U.S. factory wages are already at least 20 percent below comparable German wages, on a dollar basis, and virtually on a par with Japanese levels. *U.S. factory wages are already at least 20 percent below comparable German wages, on a dollar basis, and virtually equal Japanese levels.*

is opposed to   *conflicts with; contests; disagrees with; disapproves of; disputes; objects to; opposes; protests; resists.* I would not be opposed to doing that. *I would not object to doing that.*

is outrageous to   *outrages.* The idea that Florida can collect taxes on cigarettes made in Virginia and sold in California is outrageous to me. *The idea that Florida can collect taxes on cigarettes made in Virginia and sold in California outrages me.*

is persistent in   *perseveres in; persists in.* Friends must be persistent in helping the griever come out of himself. *Friends must persist in helping the griever come out of himself.*

is pertinent to   *applies to; bears on; concerns; pertains to; regards; relates to.* This online manual was written to gather information that is pertinent to the students enrolled in the degree programs of the Department of Electrical Engineering. *This online manual was written to gather information that pertains to the students enrolled in the degree programs of the Department of Electrical Engineering.*

is predictive of   *forecasts; foretells; predicts; presages; portends.* It offers a classification system that may be predictive of the outcome. *It offers a classification system that may predict the outcome.* ■ It follows then that they can be predictive of a wide variety of behaviors. *It follows then that they can predict a wide variety of behaviors.*

is proof of (that) *confirms; evinces; indicates; proves; reveals; shows; signifies; testifies (to).* Legendary silent film director Cecil B. DeMille didn't much alter the way he made movies after sound came in, and this 1956 biblical drama is proof of that. *Legendary silent film director Cecil B. DeMille didn't much alter the way he made movies after sound came in, and this 1956 biblical drama shows that.*

is prone to *tends to.* Company managers are prone to underestimate loyalty and their employees' need for it. *Company managers tend to underestimate loyalty and their employees' need for it.*

is protective against (of) *defends; guards; insulates; protects; shelters; shields.* A diet high in complex carbohydrates may be protective against the development of chronic diseases like heart disease and cancer. *A diet high in complex carbohydrates may protect against the development of chronic diseases like heart disease and cancer.*

is receptive to *welcomes.* While lawmakers are generally receptive to his ideas, the feeling is not mutual. *While lawmakers generally welcome his ideas, the feeling is not mutual.*

is (a; the) recipient of *receives.* The University of South Florida was the recipient of a $600,000 grant from a Florida bank to endow a professorship in banking and finance. *The University of South Florida received a $600,000 grant from a Florida bank to endow a professorship in banking and finance.*

is reflective of *epitomizes; exemplifies; mirrors; reflects; typifies.* Films receiving Oscar nominations are reflective of the image that the film industry wants to convey of itself. *Films receiving Oscar nominations mirror the image that the film industry wants to convey of itself.* ■ Morbid obesity is reflective of a metabolic endocrine disorder. *Morbid obesity reflects a metabolic endocrine disorder.*

is regretful about (of; that) *regrets.* Now I'm regretful that I didn't work harder this week. *Now I regret I didn't work harder this week.*

is related to *correlates to (with); equates with; relates to.* It is generally assumed that a species-wide tendency to favor one hand over the other is related to the development of brain hemispheres with specialized functions. *It is generally assumed that a species-wide tendency to favor one hand over the other relates to the development of brain hemispheres with specialized functions.*

is relevant to *applies to; bears on; concerns; pertains to; regards; relates to.*

is reliant on (upon) *counts on; depends on; relies on.* South Korean builders are heavily reliant upon the Mideast market. *South Korean builders rely heavily on the Mideast market.*

is reminiscent of *recalls.* The apparatus is reminiscent of some Asian musical performances emphasizing the gestures used to play instruments. *The apparatus recalls some Asian musical performances emphasizing the gestures used to play instruments.*

is representative of *emblemizes; indicates; represents; signifies; stands for; symbolizes; typifies.* For the reader to assume that this is representative of the norm is unfortunate. *For the reader to assume that this represents the norm is unfortunate.*

is required to *has to; must.* Managers are required to be able to perform certain roles. *Managers must be able to perform certain roles.*

is resentful of *resents.* He speaks in metaphors and is resentful of the modern media (which, we can safely assume, ignores him). *He speaks in metaphors and resents the modern media (which, we can safely assume, ignores him).*

is resistant to *contests; disagrees with; disapproves of; disputes; objects to; opposes; protests; resists.* In fact, they are resistant to measuring learning and performance in meaningful terms. *In fact, they resist measuring learning and performance in meaningful terms.*

is respectful of (toward) *respects.* The two skaters are friends and respectful of each other. *The two skaters are friends and respect each other.*

is restrictive in (to) *restricts.* Even before the *Sheppard* decision, law enforcement officers and prosecuting attorneys were restrictive in the release of certain information to the news media. *Even before the* Sheppard *decision, law enforcement officers and prosecuting attorneys restricted the release of certain information to the news media.*

is revealing of *reveals.* Both models are revealing of the dynamics of organizational decision making, and they may be related. *Both models reveal the dynamics of organizational decision making, and they may be related.*

is ruinous to *damages; destroys; harms; hurts; impairs; injures; mars;*

ruins. The closeups are ruinous to the performances of Aprüe Millo as Aida and Dolora Zajic as Amneris. *The closeups ruin the performances of Aprüe Millo as Aida and Dolora Zajic as Amneris.*

is scornful of *despises; disdains; scorns.* Many scientists are scornful of him because of his claims that fluoride causes everything from cancer to AIDS. *Many scientists scorn him because of his claims that fluoride causes everything from cancer to AIDS.*

is similar to (with) *compares to (with); corresponds to (with); equates with; relates to; resembles.* These commands are similar to English sentences, and most of them make sense to the casual reader. *These commands resemble English sentences, and most of them make sense to the casual reader.*

is skeptical about (of; that) *disbelieves; distrusts; doubts; mistrusts; questions.* Immigration officials often are skeptical of businesses' claims that they didn't know a worker was illegal or that they weren't aware of the new immigration law. *Immigration officials often disbelieve businesses' claims that they didn't know a worker was illegal or that they weren't aware of the new immigration law.*

is still to be seen *do not know; is not (now; yet) known; is uncertain; is unclear; is unknown; is unsure.* They priced it like a Mercedes; whether it's engineered like a Mercedes is still to be seen. *They priced it like a Mercedes; whether it's engineered like a Mercedes is not yet known.*

issuance *issue.* Municipal bonds and municipal notes are debt obligations of states, cities, municipalities, and municipal agencies which generally have maturities, at the time of their issuance, of either one year or more or from six months to three years. *Municipal bonds and municipal notes are debt obligations of states, cities, municipalities, and municipal agencies which generally have maturities, at the time of their issue, of either one year or more or from six months to three years.*

is subject to *depends on; hinges on.* Completion of the transactions is subject to a definitive agreement and the approval of both boards. *Completion of the transactions hinges on a definitive agreement and the approval of both boards.*

(a; the) ... issue delete. The question of whether a firm's financing decisions affect its value remains an unresolved issue. *The question of whether a firm's financing decisions affect its value remains unresolved.*

is suggestive of *argues; attests to; bespeaks; betokens; indicates; shows; signals; signifies; suggests; testifies to; witnesses.* Any breast mass that is suggestive of malignancy by mammography or on physical examination should be biopsied. *Any breast mass that suggests malignancy by mammography or on physical examination should be biopsied.*

is suitable to *applies to; bears on; concerns; pertains to; regards; relates to.*

is supportive of *endorses; fosters; nurtures; supports; upholds.* This report is supportive of our findings. *This report supports our findings.* ■ Predictably, many measurement experts are supportive of such tests. *Predictably, many measurement experts support such tests.*

is symbolic (symbolical) of *emblemizes; indicates; represents; signifies; stands for; symbolizes; typifies.* The contrast, stark and dramatic, is symbolic of what has happened across California. *The contrast, stark and dramatic, symbolizes what has happened across California.*

is symptomatic of *indicates; signals; signifies; symptomizes.* The small dip is symptomatic of a pause in the housing market in October, as buyers, sellers, and lenders tried to figure out what was occurring in the financial markets. *The small dip indicates a pause in the housing market in October, as buyers, sellers, and lenders tried to figure out what was occurring in the financial markets.*

is tantamount to *amounts to; duplicates; equals; is; matches; rivals.*

is (a) testament to *affirms; attests to; certifies to; declares; testifies to; verifies.* An excellent credit card rating is a testament to your success in business. *An excellent credit card rating attests to your success in business.*

is (a) testimony to *affirms; attests to; certifies to; declares; testifies to; verifies.* The high level of business and consumer confidence is testimony to the success of this Fed policy. *The high level of business and consumer confidence testifies to the success of this Fed policy.*

is there ... (that; who) *is;* delete. Are there different types of restitution available in your jurisdiction? *Are different types of restitution available in your jurisdiction?*

is trustful of *trusts.* Even when a woman is trustful of her physicians, the gravity of the situation demands that she feel fully confident with the diagnosis before beginning any treatment. *Even when a woman trusts her physicians, the gravity of the situation demands that she* *feel fully confident with the diagnosis before beginning any treatment.*

is typical of *exemplifies; symbolizes; typifies.* This kind of comment is typical of the Democrat's campaign. *This kind of comment exemplifies the Democrat's campaign.*

is under the assumption (that) *assumes; believes; feels; supposes; thinks.* I am under the assumption that the *Globe* is trying to ameliorate the situation. *I assume the* Globe *is trying to ameliorate the situation.*

is under the impression (that) *assumes; believes; feels; supposes; thinks.* It was fine the first few times, but now he's under the impression I am his grandson. *It was fine the first few times, but now he thinks I am his grandson.*

is what delete. While consistency is the mainstay of our program, diversity and change are what keep it exciting. *While consistency is the mainstay of our program, diversity and change keep it exciting.* ■ The person–machine interface is what must be retained if security is not to become a purely mechanical effort. *The person–machine interface must be retained if security is not to become a purely mechanical effort.* ■ Another major group is what Ogbu calls "autonomous minorities." *Another major group Ogbu calls "autonomous minorities."* ■ This type of learning process is what is suggested for this preliminary activity. *This type of learning process is suggested for this preliminary activity.* ■ The daily behavior of good citizens is what holds society together. *The daily behavior of good citizens holds society together.*

is witness to *affirms; attests to; certifies to; declares; testifies to; verifies.* Poet Kahlil Gibran's popularity in America is witness to the presence of an essential moral and artistic quality in his work. *Poet Kahlil Gibran's popularity in America testifies to the presence of an essential moral and artistic quality in his work.*

is (a) witness to *sees; witnesses.* He was a witness to the Chinese government's crackdown on students. *He witnessed the Chinese government's crackdown on students.*

it has been called to (my) attention *(I) have been told; (I) have learned; (I) understand;* delete.

it has come to (my) attention *(I) have been told; (I) have learned; (I) understand;* delete. It has come to our attention that some people are not aware of how to operate the intercom properly. *We have learned that some people are not aware of how to operate the intercom properly.*

it is ... (that; who) *is; -(al)ly;* delete. It is our intent to share ideas, thoughts, and methods with GEM users. *Our intent is to share ideas, thoughts, and methods with GEM users.* ■ It is my feeling that it is a human obligation to create meaning. *My feeling is that it is a human obligation to create meaning.*

it is a fact that delete. Regardless of whether the promiscuous mode operation is legitimate or the work of an intruder, it is a fact that all transmissions are subject to reception by stations other than the intended receiver. *Regardless of whether the promiscuous mode operation is legitimate or the work of an intruder, all transmissions are subject to reception by stations other than the intended receiver.*

it is apparent that *apparently; clearly; evidently; manifestly; obviously; patently; plainly;* delete. It is apparent that management needs to take into account a wide range of variables when devising international product development policies. *Clearly, management needs to take into account a wide range of variables when devising international product development policies.*

it is essential that *must; should.* It is essential that remaining barriers to women's entrepreneurship be eliminated. *Remaining barriers to women's entrepreneurship must be eliminated.*

it is evident that *apparently; clearly; evidently; manifestly; obviously; patently; plainly;* delete. It is evident that service industries are more exposed to protectionism in international markets than are most other industries. *Clearly, service industries are more exposed to protectionism in international markets than are most other industries.*

it is (to be) hoped *I (we) hope; let us hope.* It is to be hoped that your exposé will help prevent this kind of performance by others. *Let's hope that your exposé will help prevent this kind of performance by others.*

it is imperative that *must; should.* It is imperative that managers and researchers try to assess the value of the information before the research is undertaken. *Managers and researchers should try to assess the value of the information before the research is undertaken.*

it is important to ... that delete. It is important to emphasize that the incidence of breast cancer has been rising. *The incidence of breast cancer has been rising.*

it is important to keep in mind *keep in mind; remember;* delete. It is important to keep in mind that these applications address only today's problems. *Keep in mind that these applications address only today's problems.*

it is important to mention (say; state) (that) delete. It is important to mention that a group of auxiliary verbs called modals can also express the disposition and attitude of the speaker. *A group of auxiliary verbs called modals can also express the disposition and attitude of the speaker.*

it is important to note *note;* delete. It is important to note that different stores in a chain may perform differently. *Different stores in a chain may perform differently.*

it is important to realize (recognize) *realize (recognize);* delete. It is important to realize that many Chinese willingly remain in their country despite the violence. *Many Chinese willingly remain in their country despite the violence.*

it is important to remember *keep in mind; remember;* delete. It is important to remember that social security reserves are expected to build to about $12 trillion in the next century. *Remember that social security reserves are expected to build to about $12 trillion in the next century.*

it is important to understand *understand;* delete. It is important to understand that not all pressures are the result of marketplace changes, nor do they necessarily affect the marketing activity. *Not all pressures are the result of marketplace changes, nor do they necessarily affect the marketing activity.*

it is interesting to note *interestingly; note;* delete. It is interesting to note that an early meaning of the Spanish word *algebrista* was bonesetter or reuniter of broken bones. *Interestingly, an early meaning of the Spanish word* algebrista *was bonesetter or reuniter of broken bones.*

it is necessary (for; that; to) *must; need to.* It is necessary for this causality to be realistic for the model to be useful. *This causality must be realistic for the model to be useful.*

it is often the case (circumstance; situation) (that) *frequently; most often; often; sometimes; usually.* In applications, it is often the case that descriptive analyses of the individual trajectories, rates of improvement, etc. are of the greatest substantive value. *In applications, fre-*

quently descriptive analyses of the individual trajectories, rates of improvement, etc. are of the greatest substantive value. ■ As with vanity publishing, it is often the case that the amount you pay for the production of the book hardly ever is returned from the sales. *As with vanity publishing, often the amount you pay for the production of the book hardly ever is returned from the sales.*

it is significant to note *note;* delete. It is significant to note that this land is owned by the city and leased to Harvard. *This land is owned by the city and leased to Harvard.*

it is useful (worthwhile) to mention (say; state) (that) delete. It is useful to state that most of the modernization in steel production has occurred as part of a general shift toward all-electric steelmaking. *Most of the modernization in steel production has occurred as part of a general shift toward all-electric steelmaking.*

it is useful (worthwhile) to note (that) delete. It is worthwhile to note that in this outline the results specified in step III could refer to any of several results. *In this outline the results specified in step III could refer to any of several results.*

it must (should) be mentioned (remarked; said; stated) (that) delete. It should be remarked, however, that for both methods success is largely dependent on devising an appropriate method for representing the problem. *However, for both methods success is largely dependent on devising an appropriate method for representing the problem.*

it must (should) be noted *note;* delete. It should be noted that people with gastrointestinal disorders share a number of traits. *People with gastrointestinal disorders share a number of traits.*

it must (should) be pointed out (that) delete. It should be pointed out that Boston Technical students have recently received notices of acceptance from institutions such as Princeton, Tufts, Boston College, and the University of California at Berkeley. *Boston Technical students have recently received notices of acceptance from institutions such as Princeton, Tufts, Boston College, and the University of California at Berkeley.*

it must (should) be remembered *keep in mind; remember;* delete. It must be remembered that even though this course deals with an easily measurable good, money, you must make personal value judgments concerning how money is best used. *Even though this course* *deals with an easily measurable good, money, you must make personal value judgments concerning how money is best used.*

it must (should) be understood *understand;* delete. It must be understood that we have a very complex, interrelated economy. *We have a very complex, interrelated economy.*

it (just) so happens *by chance; luckily; unluckily.*

I (we) would appreciate it if *please.*

J

joint agreement *agreement*. EarthShell Corporation and DuPont Polyester announced today they have entered into a joint agreement to develop and market additional new forms of environmentally friendly packaging for the food service industry. *EarthShell Corporation and DuPont Polyester announced today they have entered into an agreement to develop and market additional new forms of environmentally friendly packaging for the food service industry.*

joint cooperation *cooperation*.

join together *join*. All of these can be joined together by soldering, brazing, or welding. *All of these can be joined by soldering, brazing, or welding.*

judge as *judge*. For an invention to be judged as novel, there must be no information available in the public domain. *For an invention to be judged novel, there must be no information available in the public domain.* ■ Each subject area was judged as excellent, satisfactory or unsatisfactory. *Each subject area was judged excellent, satisfactory or unsatisfactory.*

just about *about; almost; nearly*.

just as (more; most) importantly *just as (more; most) important*. But perhaps most importantly, they offer trustworthiness. *But perhaps most important, they offer trustworthiness.*

just as (more; most) significantly *just as (more; most) significant*. Most significantly, the product champion must have the drive to get the work done and the decisions made. *Most significant, the product champion must have the drive to get the work done and the decisions made.*

just exactly *exactly; just*. He's just exactly what I'm looking for. *He's just what I'm looking for.*

just recently *just; recently*. We just recently went to England. *We recently went to England.*

just simply *just; simply*.

just the same as *just like; the same as*. The DEL command works just the same as the ERASE command. *The DEL command works just like the ERASE command.*

K

keep in mind *remember;* delete. Keep in mind that few people, if any, match a job perfectly, and few employers look for a perfect fit. *Few people, if any, match a job perfectly, and few employers look for a perfect fit.*

(a; the) key ... in (of; to) *a key to.* Market segmentation is a key aspect to strategic planning at the corporate and business levels. *Market segmentation is a key to strategic planning at the corporate and business levels.* ■ In contrast, individualism was the key ingredient to the rise of Greece. *In contrast, individualism was key to the rise of Greece.* ■ Our continued commitment to quality is a key component of our success. *Our continued commitment to quality is a key to our success.*

kinder (and) gentler *amiable; compassionate; gentle; humane; kind; tender; tolerant.*

kind of delete. I kind of stumbled onto the job. *I stumbled onto the job.*

know for a fact *know.* We know for a fact that this firm is trying to swindle consumers. *We know that this firm is trying to swindle consumers.*

known as *called; named; termed;* delete. The three most common knowledge representations in expert system shells are known as rules, frames, and semantic networks. *The three most common knowledge representations in expert system shells are rules, frames, and semantic networks.*

L

label as *label.* The product is labeled as a cosmetic, not a medication. *The product is labeled a cosmetic, not a medication.*

lackadaisical *idle; languid; lazy; listless.*

lack for *lack.*

lacking in *dis-; il-; im-; in-; ir-; lack; -less(ness); mis-; no; non-; not; un-; want; with no; without.* The defense's case was so often lacking in credibility. *The defense's case was so often incredible.*

(a; the) lack of *dis-; few; il-; im-; in-; ir-; -less(ness); mis-; no; non-; not; scant; un-; with no; without.* This is a result of a lack of cooperation between retailers and financial institutions. *This is a result of noncooperation between retailers and financial institutions.* ■ Many a computer programming project has failed because of a lack of careful problem analysis and poor program design techniques. *Many a computer programming project has failed because of careless problem analysis and poor program design techniques.* ■ Jackson concerns me because of his lack of experience in foreign policy and defense. *Jackson concerns me because of his inexperience in foreign policy and defense.*

(a; the) large (overwhelming; sizable; vast) plurality (of) *a good (great) deal (of); a good (great) many (of); almost all (of); (nine) in (ten) (of); many (of); most (of); much (of); nearly all (of); (43) of (48) (of); (67) percent (of); three-fourths (two-thirds) (of).* Large pluralities feel Mr. Bush would do about as well as Mr. Reagan. *Most feel Mr. Bush would do about as well as Mr. Reagan.*

large-size(d) *large.*

last of all *last.*

later in time *at length; eventually; from now; in time; later; ultimately.* Usually the stock will trade lower later in time. *Usually the stock will trade lower in time.*

later on *later.* I will see you later on. *I will see you later.*

later on down the line (pike; road; way) *at length; eventually; from now; in time; later; ultimately.* Later on down the line, there will have to be a settlement. *In time, there will have to be a settlement.*

latter part of *last half of; late.*

law enforcement officers *authorities; cops; officers; police.*

legitimatize *legitimate; legitimize.* Unattended operation is being legitimatized by the major hardware and software vendors. *Unattended operation is being legitimized by the major hardware and software vendors.*

lend out *lend.*

(a; the) length of delete. While adults typically grew to a length of about 30 feet, the embryos measured only about 1.2 feet from head to tail and fit into 7-inch-long eggs. *While adults typically grew to about 30 feet, the embryos measured only about 1.2 feet from head to tail and fit into 7-inch-long eggs.*

lengthy *long.* Communists must go through a lengthy selection process and ideological training before being granted membership in the party. *Communists must go through a long selection process and ideological training before being granted membership in the party.*

less than (enthusiastic) *dis-; il-; im-; in-; ir-; mis-; non-; un-.* You can refinance with us even if your credit is less than perfect. *You can refinance with us even if your credit is imperfect.* ■ This book reveals the sometimes less-than-elegant design of DOS by walking through the source code. *This book reveals the sometimes inelegant design of DOS by walking through the source code.* ■ The lack of consistent definition and the paucity of carefully designed drug studies of PMS have led to less than satisfactory treatment. *The lack of consistent definition and the paucity of carefully designed drug studies of PMS have led to unsatisfactory treatment.*

(a; the) ... level (of) delete. Each organization must assess its level of willingness to take risks. *Each organization must assess its willingness to take risks.* ■ When a relationship reaches a certain level of intensity, the church should have some way of recognizing that commitment. *When a relationship reaches a certain intensity, the church should have some way of recognizing that commitment.* ■ Random access implies that any piece of information can be read with an equal level of difficulty and delay. *Random access implies that any piece of information can be read with equal difficulty and delay.*

level to the ground *demolish; destroy; level; raze; ruin.* Numerous historical churches and monasteries were leveled to the ground in severe bombardments and attacks. *Numerous historical churches and monasteries were razed in severe bombardments and attacks.*

lift up *lift.*

like ... also (as well) *like.* Like 401(k) plans, 403(b) plans also have various investment alternatives: common stocks, bonds, money-market funds, and so on. *Like 401(k) plans, 403(b) plans have various investment alternatives: common stocks, bonds, money-market funds, and so on.*

like ... and others (and so forth; and so on; and such; and the like; et al.; etc.) *and others (and so forth; and so on; and such; and the like; et al.; etc.); like; such as.* Sheet sizes are specified by letters like Size A, Size B, and so forth. *Sheet sizes are specified by letters like Size A and Size B.* ■ It can be printed on any printer, but it will not have formats such as boldfacing, underlining, and so on. *It can be printed on any printer, but it will not have formats such as boldfacing and underlining.* ■ Prosecutors may support the service style of policing by agreeing not to prosecute law violators who seek psychiatric help or who voluntarily participate in programs like Alcoholics Anonymous, family counseling, drug treatment, and the like. *Prosecutors may support the service style of policing by agreeing not to prosecute law violators who seek psychiatric help or who voluntarily participate in programs like Alcoholics Anonymous, family counseling, and drug treatment.* ■ The hotels where the African-American girls worked were forbidden to join the union and didn't have any benefits like sick leave, vacation, health insurance et cetera. *The hotels where the African-American girls worked were forbidden to join the union and didn't have any benefits like sick leave, vacation, health insurance.*

like ... for example (for instance) *as; for example (for instance); like; such as.* The drug is good for ailments like insomnia for example. *The drug is good for ailments like insomnia.* ■ It is not that fascinating, as it uses a standard approach to computing in XSLT, but its advantage is that it works also with XSLT processors (like, for instance, James Clark's XT) that do not have the "node-set" extension function implemented. *It is not that fascinating, as it uses a standard approach to computing in XSLT, but its advantage is that it works also with XSLT processors (for instance, James Clark's XT) that do not have the "node-set" extension function implemented.*

like-gender individuals (people; persons) *men (women).* The creation of rape crisis centers, centers for battered women, and the like all point to the possibility of women helping like-gender individuals through noncriminal justice channels. *The creation of rape crisis centers, centers for battered women, and the like all point to the possibility of women helping women through noncriminal justice channels.*

limitation *limit.* There is no overall limitation on the percentage of the trust's portfolio securities which may be subject to a hedge position. *There is no overall limit on the percentage of the trust's portfolio securities which may be subject to a hedge position.*

(very) limited *bare; few; little; meager; rare; scant; scanty; scarce; short; slight; small; spare; sparse.* While opportunities for broad-scale consumer advertising may be limited for a while, there are lots of opportunities for commercial communications. *While opportunities for broad-scale consumer advertising may be scarce for a while, there are lots of opportunities for commercial communications.*

(a; the) limited number of *a couple; a few; eight (four); little; meager; not many; one or two (two or three); scant; scanty; (only) so many; some; spare; sparse.* A surgeon can only do a limited number of operations. *A surgeon can only do so many operations.*

(a; the) limited selection (of) *a couple; a few; eight (four); little; meager; not many; one or two (two or three); scant; scanty; (only) so many; some; spare; sparse.*

linkage *link.* Particular attention needs to be given to the linkage among the various strategic levels within and across national markets. *Particular attention needs to be given to the link among the various strategic levels within and across national markets.*

link together *connect; link.* It's natural to link the two of them together. *It's natural to link the two of them.*

liquid refreshment *beer; coffee; drink; juice; milk; soda; tea; water; wine.* Plan your menu, which should include liquid refreshment. *Plan your menu, which should include wine.*

listen in *listen.*

little by little *gradually; slowly.*

little (small) child *child.* How do you tell a little child that his father isn't coming home again? *How do you tell a child that his father isn't coming home again?*

little (small; tiny) iota *iota.* I don't care one little iota less than you do about homelessness in America. *I don't care one iota less than you do about homelessness in America.*

locality *area; city; district; locale; place; point; region; site; spot; state; town; zone.* Today, modern water wells are drilled and in some localities are more than 300 meters deep. *Today, modern water wells are drilled and in some sites are more than 300 meters deep.*

located delete. The school, which is located in an old, poorly cared for building, further added to our misgivings. *The school, which is in an old, poorly cared for building, further added to our misgivings.*

lodge a complaint (with) *complain (to).* He threatened to lodge a complaint with the management if he wasn't reimbursed for his losses. *He threatened to complain to the management if he wasn't reimbursed for his losses.*

logical reason *reason.*

long suit *forte.*

look (observe) to see *check; examine; inspect; look; see.* Look to see where you have been and where you might go next. *Examine where you have been and where you might go next.*

lose out on *lose.*

loudly bellow (holler; howl; roar; scream; shout; shriek; yell) *bellow (holler; howl; roar; scream; shout; shriek; yell).* In the early days of VCRs, movie companies howled loudly at the advent of movie rentals and attempted blocking legislation. *In the early days of VCRs, movie companies howled at the advent of movie rentals and attempted blocking legislation.*

-(al)ly enough *-(al)ly;* delete. Ironically enough, many states have loosened their registration laws in the last decade, but turnout still declines. *Ironically, many states have loosened their registration laws in the last decade, but turnout still declines.*

-(al)ly speaking *-(al)ly;* delete. All four of their parents would be the same, genetically speaking. *All four of their parents would be genetically the same.* ■ Although there may be small differences between the jobs, they are, relatively speaking, inconsequential. *Although there may be small differences between the jobs, they are relatively inconsequential.* ■ Personally speaking, I belonged to the Howdy Doody generation. *I belonged to the Howdy Doody generation.*

M

made of delete. The only data show small vestiges of threads made of cotton. *The only data show small vestiges of cotton threads.*

made to measure *custom; customized; custom-made; tailored; tailor-made.*

made to order *custom; customized; custom-made; tailored; tailor-made.*

made up out of *made of;* delete. To keep the spar caps straight, they are made up out of several layers of spruce. *To keep the spar caps straight, they are made of several layers of spruce.*

magnitude *import; moment; scope; size.* Nothing is unthinkable when you try to solve a problem of this magnitude. *Nothing is unthinkable when you try to solve a problem of this size.*

major delete. If the vice president comes in third, it's a major disaster. *If the vice president comes in third, it's a disaster.* ■ Combining these two world-class companies represents a major milestone for the plastics industry. *Combining these two world-class companies represents a milestone for the plastics industry.* ■ It's going to take a couple of years to shake out, but it won't result in a major calamity. *It's going to take a couple of years to shake out, but it won't result in a calamity.*

(a; the) majority (of) *almost all (of); (nine) in (ten) (of); many (of); more (of); most (of); nearly all (of); (43) of (48) (of); (67) percent (of); three-fourths (two-thirds) (of).* Surveys reveal that the majority of chronic fatigue syndrome victims are between 22 and 45. *Surveys reveal that 60 percent of chronic fatigue syndrome victims are between 22 and 45.*

(a; the) major part (percentage; portion; proportion) (of) *a good (great) deal (of); a good (great) many (of); almost all (of); (nine) in (ten) (of); many (of); more (of); most (of); nearly all (of); (43) of (48) (of); (67) percent (of); three-fourths (two-thirds) (of).* Murdoch could borrow a major portion of the purchase price using Triangle's assets as collateral. *Murdoch could borrow most of the purchase price using Triangle's assets as collateral.*

make ... (a; the) ... (about; for; of; to) delete. Why make that admission to them? *Why admit that to them?* ■ We made an agreement that she would keep the stereo for me. *We agreed that she would keep the* *stereo for me.* ■ The company's management may not see any reason for making a shift from their current approach. *The company's management may not see any reason for shifting from their current approach.* ■ Make an estimate of what the person might find if the process were revamped to operate as well as is conceivable. *Estimate what the person might find if the process were revamped to operate as well as is conceivable.* ■ He must graduate before he can make a design for such a machine. *He must graduate before he can design such a machine.*

make ... acquaintance *meet.* I was very pleased to make your acquaintance. *I was very pleased to meet you.*

make allowance for *allow for; arrange for; consider; prepare for; provide for.* You must make allowance for quilting shrinkage, and there is no way of telling how much that is. *You must allow for quilting shrinkage, and there is no way of telling how much that is.*

make an appearance *appear; arrive; attend; come; show up; visit.* She will make an appearance on *The Simpsons* in fully animated form performing the uplifting song "To Hell And Back." *She will appear on* The Simpsons *in fully animated form performing the uplifting song "To Hell And Back."* ■ Four directors were scheduled to make an appearance, and only one canceled because shooting had begun on his new feature. *Four directors were scheduled to attend, and only one canceled because shooting had begun on his new feature.*

make an attempt (effort; endeavor) *try.* We are going to make an effort to hold prices or even reduce them. *We are going to try to hold prices or even reduce them.*

make available *afford; furnish; provide; supply.* Paralleling a business school course of study, our curriculum makes available a stable, inclusive, and continuing transmittal of practices and perspectives to those working managers who want to continue their education in management. *Paralleling a business school course of study, our curriculum affords a stable, inclusive, and continuing transmittal of practices and perspectives to those working managers who want to continue their education in management.*

make believe *feign; pretend.*

make concession for *allow for; arrange for; consider; prepare for; provide for.*

make contact (with) *call; contact; discover; encounter; find; locate; meet* *(with); phone; reach; speak (to); talk (to); visit; write.* In Sturgis, we made contact with the Sons of Silence. *In Sturgis, we encountered the Sons of Silence.*

make conversation *chat; communicate; converse; speak; talk.* It was easy to make conversation with him. *It was easy to talk with him.*

make (a; the) decision (determination) (about; as to; concerning; of; on; regarding) *conclude; decide; determine; resolve.* I made the decision to keep on good terms with all the candidates. *I decided to keep on good terms with all the candidates.*

make (a; the) determined decision (about; as to; concerning; of; on; regarding) *conclude; decide; determine; resolve.* She made a determined decision to overcome her drug dependency. *She resolved to overcome her drug dependency.*

make (a; the) distinction *distinguish.* For some years, economists have enjoyed making a distinction between "salt water" and "fresh water" approaches to economics. *For some years, economists have enjoyed distinguishing between "salt water" and "fresh water" approaches to economics.*

make false statements *lie.* He did this by using a false Social Security number and making false statements on his application. *He did this by using a false Social Security number and lying on his application.*

(to) make matters worse *what is worse; worse still; worse yet.* Making matters worse, a boom in the herring export market has turned to bust. *Worse yet, a boom in the herring export market has turned to bust.*

make mention of *mention.* You made mention of the fact that S&Ls insure you only up to $100,000. *You mentioned the fact that S&Ls insure you only up to $100,000.*

make provision for *allow for; arrange for; consider; prepare for; provide for.* No family can attempt to establish a budget without making provision for these "unexpected" but forever recurring expenses. *No family can attempt to establish a budget without allowing for these "unexpected" but forever recurring expenses.*

make (a; the) statement saying (stating) *comment; remark; say; state.* I think it's important for us to make a statement saying that this veto should be overridden. *I think it's important for us to state that this veto should be overridden.*

make up (my) mind *decide.* King said he will make up his mind by mid-September on whether to seek the GOP nomination for governor. *King said he will decide by mid-September on whether to seek the GOP nomination for governor.*

make (my) way *driving; proceeding; running; walking.* The vice president is now making his way to the platform. *The vice president is now walking to the platform.*

many and varied *divers; diverse; manifold; multifaceted; multifarious; multifold; multiform; multiple; varied; various.* Robberies tend to fall into one of three categories, but their targets are many and varied. *Robberies tend to fall into one of three categories, but their targets are manifold.*

many hundreds (thousands) *hundreds (thousands).* The abacus shown here has been used in China for many hundreds of years. *The abacus shown here has been used in China for hundreds of years.*

many times over *frequently; often; recurrently; regularly; repeatedly.*

mass exodus *exodus.* The mass exodus to Penturbia is the result of a declining quality of life. *The exodus to Penturbia is the result of a declining quality of life.*

mass extinction *extinction.* A comet striking Earth with the power of 300 million Hiroshima-sized atomic bombs may be the cause of mass extinction 11 million years ago. *A comet striking Earth with the power of 300 million Hiroshima-sized atomic bombs may be the cause of extinction 11 million years ago.*

match exactly *duplicate; match.* To find strings that match your case exactly, enter the appropriate characters in uppercase when specifying the string to be searched for. *To find strings that match your case, enter the appropriate characters in uppercase when specifying the string to be searched for.*

match perfectly *duplicate; match.* The fluctuations of the one variable match perfectly the fluctuations of the other variable. *The fluctuations of the one variable duplicate the fluctuations of the other variable.*

match up *match.*

materialize *develop; evolve; form; happen; occur; result; take place.*

matter-of-course *common; customary; habitual; natural; normal; ordinary; regular; routine; typical; usual.*

matter-of-fact *businesslike; factual; literal; plain; prosaic; straightforward; unfeeling.*

maximal *biggest; greatest; highest; largest; longest; most; top.*

maximize *add to; broaden; enlarge; greaten; increase; raise.*

(a; the) maximum ... of *biggest; greatest; highest; largest; longest; most; top.* It is necessary to get the maximum mileage out of existing and new products as rapidly as possible. *It is necessary to get the most mileage out of existing and new products as rapidly as possible.*

(a; the) maximum amount (of) *biggest; greatest; highest; largest; longest; most; top.*

(a; the) maximum number (of) *biggest; greatest; highest; largest; longest; most; top.* Set up your fields for the maximum number of lines. *Set up your fields for the most lines.*

may or may not *may; may not.* Your assessment of Houston's nascent ascent from the urban graveyard may or may not prove to be on the mark, but your classification of its metropolitan area as the nation's fourth largest was not. *Your assessment of Houston's nascent ascent from the urban graveyard may prove to be on the mark, but your classification of its metropolitan area as the nation's fourth largest was not.*

may (might) perhaps *may (might).* Rome has always had some sort of a Pope, and that ambition and wickedness may perhaps have characterized certain persons high in ecclesiastical affairs. *Rome has always had some sort of a Pope, and that ambition and wickedness may have characterized certain persons high in ecclesiastical affairs.*

may (might) possibly *may (might).* She said Concord Academy might possibly be too difficult. *She said Concord Academy might be too difficult.*

meaningful delete. This slope can represent miles per hour, weight versus length, or a number of other meaningful rates that are important to the analysis of data. *This slope can represent miles per hour, weight versus length, or a number of other rates that are important to the analysis of data.*

meaningless gibberish *gibberish.* Byrne deftly makes everything clear in context, using many words and expressions that would, out of context, seem like meaningless gibberish. *Byrne deftly makes everything clear in context, using many words and expressions that would, out of context, seem like gibberish.*

measured against *against; alongside; beside; compared to (with); -(i)er than; less; less than; more; more than; next to; over; than; to; versus; vis-à-vis.* Retrieving data from disks is slow measured against the speed of processing the records once they are in memory. *Retrieving data from disks is slower than the speed of processing the records once they are in memory.*

measure up to *meet.* Because many teachers expect children from the same family to behave in the same manner, it can be particularly difficult for temperamentally different siblings to measure up to their expectations. *Because many teachers expect children from the same family to behave in the same manner, it can be particularly difficult for temperamentally different siblings to meet their expectations.*

mechanical mechanism *mechanical; mechanism.* The final result was the Pascaline, a polished brass box containing a sophisticated, mechanical calculating mechanism composed of gears. *The final result was the Pascaline, a polished brass box containing a sophisticated calculating mechanism composed of gears.*

meet together *meet.* The shores of the sea meet together. *The shores of the sea meet.* ■ Did the parties ever refuse to meet together? *Did the parties ever refuse to meet?*

memorandum *memo; note.* This memorandum is for informative purposes only. *This memo is for informative purposes only.*

mental ability (capacity) *ability (capacity).*

mental telepathy *telepathy.*

(a; the) -ment of *-ing.* The assignment of retirement assets to a money manager may entail a lengthy process of evaluation by the corporate client. *Assigning retirement assets to a money manager may entail a lengthy process of evaluation by the corporate client.* ■ Meetings do not contribute to the attainment of individual objectives. *Meetings do not contribute to attaining individual objectives.* ■ The treatment of these items as expenses results in lower rents and more available apartments. *Treating these items as expenses results in lower rents and more available apartments.*

merge into one (company) *merge.* The two departments are being merged into one. *The two departments are being merged.*

merge together *merge.* First, create the files to be merged together. *First, create the files to be merged.*

mesh together *mesh.* Gears are toothed wheels that mesh together to transmit force and motion from one gear to the next. *Gears are toothed wheels that mesh to transmit force and motion from one gear to the next.*

metaphorically speaking *as it were; in a sense; in a way; so to speak.*

methodology *method.* When developing estimates of market size, data extrapolation methodologies may be useful. *When developing estimates of market size, data extrapolation methods may be useful.*

metropolis *city.*

(with) might and main *force; power; strength.*

might or might not *might; might not.*

mingle together *mingle.* An invitation-only crowd of some 40 people met at Kate's Mystery Books, though many in the crowd apparently did not want to mingle together. *An invitation-only crowd of some 40 people met at Kate's Mystery Books, though many in the crowd apparently did not want to mingle.*

minimal *brief; least; lowest; minor; not much; scant; short; slight; smallest.* We expect the delay will be minimal. *We expect the delay will be brief.*

(a; the) minimal number (of) *a couple (of); a few (of); a handful (of); fewer than half (of); hardly any (of); (one) in (ten) (of); less than half (of); not many (of); (9) of (48) (of); one or two (two or three) (of); one-third (one-fifteenth) (of); (12) percent (of); scarcely any (of).* Smith said a minimal number of people have irreconcilable differences with the roommate they selected. *Smith said hardly any people have irreconcilable differences with the roommate they selected.*

minimize *decrease; lower; reduce.*

(a; the) minimum (of) *at least; (the) least; little; lowest; minimum; scant; shortest; slightest; smallest; tiniest.* Most oxyacetylene welding is done manually with a minimum of equipment. *Most oxyacetylene welding is done manually with minimum equipment.*

(a; the) minority (of) *a couple (of); a few (of); a handful (of); fewer than half (of); hardly any (of); (one) in (ten) (of); less than half (of); not many (of); (9) of (48) (of); one or two (two or three) (of); one-third (one-fifteenth) (of); (12) percent (of); scarcely any (of).* A minority of those who are comfortable financially are good givers, but some of the country's wealthiest give dramatically large sums. *Few who are comfortable financially are good givers, but some of the country's wealthiest give dramatically large sums.*

minutely detail *detail.* Given a problem, engineers and computer scientists, accustomed to working with mathematical procedures, would write a program — a list of minutely detailed instructions logically guiding the computer step by step through its assigned task. *Given a problem, engineers and computer scientists, accustomed to working with mathematical procedures, would write a program — a list of detailed instructions logically guiding the computer step by step through its assigned task.*

mix and mingle *mingle; mix.*

mix together *mix.* The capability to mix text and graphics together in the same document makes it easy to produce newsletters, instructional materials, and other documents where figures, logos, and/or pictures are needed. *The capability to mix text and graphics in the same document makes it easy to produce newsletters, instructional materials, and other documents where figures, logos, and/or pictures are needed.*

modern, state-of-the-art *modern; state-of-the-art.* Today, with modern, state-of-the-art technologies, breast cancer can be detected at very early stages of development. *Today, with modern technologies, breast cancer can be detected at very early stages of development.*

(a; the) modicum of *few; little; some; tiny; trifle.*

months of age *months.* At 14 months of age, these children showed fear and shyness when taken into a room with strangers. *At 14 months, these children showed fear and shyness when taken into a room with strangers.*

more -(i)er *-(i)er; more.* Watching television is more easier than reading. *Watching television is easier than reading.* ■ Watch "Nightstand," where comedy doesn't get any more better. *Watch "Nightstand," where comedy doesn't get any better.* ■ A reduction in engineering expenses of $100,000 to $150,000 would be appropriate and bring the department to a more healthier expense to sales ratio. *A reduction in engineering expenses of $100,000 to $150,000 would be appropriate and bring the department to a more healthy expense to sales ratio.* ■ I think it's more subtler than that. *I think it's subtler than that.*

more extended (lengthy; prolonged; protracted) *longer.* Even the IRS has been testing itself over a more prolonged period. *Even the IRS has been testing itself over a longer period.*

more improved *improved.*

more inferior *inferior.* These two lobes are separated by a major fissure, identical to that seen on the right side, although often slightly more inferior in location. *These two lobes are separated by a major fissure, identical to that seen on the right side, although often slightly inferior in location.*

more often than not *almost always; commonly; customarily; generally; most often; nearly always; normally; typically; usually.*

(the) more ... of the two *(the) -(i)er; (the) more.* Objectivity is certainly the more difficult of the two to sustain. *Objectivity is certainly the more difficult to sustain.*

more preferable *preferable.* We have never said any one group is more preferable to another. *We have never said any one group is preferable to another.* ■ Reorganization of the health care industry still remains one of the alternatives being considered because structural and procedural changes are often more preferable than basic, radical changes in the philosophy behind such a system. *Reorganization of the health care industry still remains one of the alternatives being considered because structural and procedural changes are often preferable to basic, radical changes in the philosophy behind such a system.*

more superior *superior.* It upsets me to think of her with a man more superior to me. *It upsets me to think of her with a man superior to me.*

more than exceeded (surpassed) *exceeded (surpassed).* From all sides, there is little disagreement that while business more than exceeded its component goals, the schools fell short of theirs. *From all sides, there is little disagreement that while business exceeded its component goals, the schools fell short of theirs.*

most but not all *almost all; (nine) in (ten); many; most; nearly all; (43) of (48); (67) percent; three-fourths (two-thirds).* Most, but not all, accounting programs store the data you enter in a database. *Almost all accounting programs store the data you enter in a database.*

most -(i)est *-(i)est; most.* You missed two of the most simplest questions. *You missed two of the simplest questions.* ■ This is probably the most happiest moment in my life. *This is probably the happiest moment in my life.* ■ That was the most stupidest picture I have ever seen. *That was the stupidest picture I have ever seen.*

most favorite *favorite; most favored.* When I was a kid, this was one of my most favorite jobs. *When I was a kid, this was one of my favorite jobs.*

most important *above all.* Most important, the system that files are designated by should be consistent and understood by everyone. *Above all, the system that files are designated by should be consistent and understood by everyone.* ■ Recent studies have shown that for most investors, retiring comfortably is their most important financial goal. *Recent studies have shown that for most investors, retiring comfortably is their foremost financial goal.* ■ The most important factor in determining the amount of pension plan income you receive is your longevity with one company. *The key factor in determining the amount of pension plan income you receive is your longevity with one company.*

most important *central; chief; critical; crucial; foremost; key; leading; main; major; pivotal; principal; seminal.* The company's most important product, Mechanical Advantage, began shipping in early 1987. *The company's leading product, Mechanical Advantage, began shipping in early 1987.*

most ... one *most.* It's fairly obvious that the third approach will get the best results, but it is also the most difficult one to employ. *It's fairly obvious that the third approach will get the best results, but it is also the most difficult to employ.*

most (of the) time(s) *almost always; commonly; generally; most often; nearly always; normally; typically; usually.*

motion picture *film; movie.*

motivating force *drive; energy; force; impetus; motivation; power.* The primary motivating force behind their behavior is the need to shock others. *The primary motivation behind their behavior is the need to shock others.*

motivation *motive.* There is doubt about the ethical standards of life insurance companies as well as the motivations and practices of the agents selling their products. *There is doubt about the ethical standards of life insurance companies as well as the motives and practices of the agents selling their products.*

move forward *advance; continue; go on; happen; move on; occur; proceed; progress.* We urge all involved to move forward with whatever plans make the most sense for both the city and the college. *We urge all involved to proceed with whatever plans make the most sense for both the city and the college.* ■ It will not be possible move forward with the program without the understanding and support of the general public. *It will not be possible continue with the program without the understanding and support of the general public*

move forward into the future *advance; continue; go on; move on; proceed; progress.* These questions and many others should be pondered and discussed among us as we prepare to move forward into the future. *These questions and many others should be pondered and discussed among us as we prepare to advance.* ■ The open industry format will greatly benefit us as we move forward into the future. *The open industry format will greatly benefit us as we progress.*

muchly *much.*

multiple *many; several.* You are taking in data on multiple levels. *You are taking in data on many levels.*

(a; the) multiplicity of *a good (great) many; countless; endless; infinite; many; millions (of); numberless; numerous; thousands (of); untold.* She suffers from a multiplicity of moods and personalities. *She suffers from many moods and personalities.*

(a; the) multitude of *a good (great) many; countless; endless; infinite; many; millions (of); numberless; numerous; thousands (of); untold.* How do our customers and prospects view us given the multitude of changes in customers' needs and behaviors? *How do our customers and prospects view us given the many changes in customers' needs and behaviors?*

multitudinous *a good (great) many; countless; endless; infinite; many; millions (of); numberless; numerous; thousands (of); untold.*

must necessarily (of necessity) *inevitably; must; necessarily; of necessity; unavoidably.* Texts organized around specific topics must of necessity limit their discussion to the features contained in those programs. *Texts organized around specific topics must limit their discussion to the features contained in those programs.*

mutual agreement (mutually agree) *agreement (agree).* The NATO leaders proclaimed mutual agreement about reducing the missile systems. *The NATO leaders proclaimed agreement about reducing the missile systems.*

mutual ... and (between ... and; both; each other; one another; two) *and (between ... and; both; each other; one another; two).* I think all three news directors in town have a mutual respect for one another. *I think all three news directors in town have a respect for one another.* ■ Understanding exists when both parties involved in the communication mutually agree not only on the information but also on the meaning of the information. *Understanding exists when both parties involved in the communication agree not only on the information but also on the meaning of the information.* ■ You can live with many differences of opinion and personal style if you and your partner have mutual respect for each other's abilities. *You can live with many differences of opinion and personal style if you and your partner have respect for each other's abilities.* ■ It's time to begin the healing process, time to bridge the gap of miscommunication, and time to cultivate an atmosphere of mutual respect between law enforcement and our communities. *It's time to begin the healing process, time to bridge the gap of miscommunication, and time to cultivate an atmosphere of respect between law enforcement and our communities.* ■ The attached document presents the essential elements of a statement of mutual cooperation between supervisors. *The attached document presents the essential elements of a statement of cooperation between supervisors.*

mutual communication *communication.* In this way, mutual communication is established, and some type of agreement becomes much more possible. *In this way, communication is established, and some type of agreement becomes much more possible.*

mutual cooperation *cooperation.*

mutual friendship *friendship.*

mutual understanding *understanding.* Marketing executives and financial managers must strive to develop a mutual understanding of each others' viewpoints. *Marketing executives and financial managers must strive to develop an understanding of each others' viewpoints.*

N

name as *name.* They would more aptly be named as request and execute entry points. *They would more aptly be named request and execute entry points.* ■ The Georgetown senior has been named as one of five finalists for the award. *The Georgetown senior has been named one of five finalists for the award.*

... nature delete. The ashes are a reminder of the transitory nature of life. *The ashes are a reminder of the transitoriness of life.*

neat and tidy *clean; neat; orderly; organized; tidy.*

necessarily have to *have to.* It doesn't necessarily have to be a bad place to go. *It doesn't have to be a bad place to go.*

necessary *needed; needful; pressing; urgent; vital.* The symbol is often in a more simple form when all the specifications are not necessary. *The symbol is often in a more simple form when all the specifications are not needed.*

necessary essential *essential; necessary.* Therefore, we have 10-15 years to take the necessary essential steps to reform the current situation. *Therefore, we have 10-15 years to take the necessary steps to reform the current situation.*

necessary prerequisite *necessary; prerequisite.* Detailed knowledge of the people on the beat is undeniably a necessary prerequisite to achieving economy in the use of police force. *Detailed knowledge of the people on the beat is undeniably a prerequisite to achieving economy in the use of police force.* ■ In most cases, readiness tests emphasize the prerequisites necessary for reading instruction. *In most cases, readiness tests emphasize the prerequisites for reading instruction.*

necessary requirement *necessary; requirement.* Naturally, we are complying with any necessary reporting requirements. *Naturally, we are complying with any reporting requirements.*

necessary requisite *necessary; requisite.* He said he has the "toughness and resolve" to bring government spending under control as a necessary requisite to restoring the public's confidence. *He said he has the "toughness and resolve" to bring government spending under control as a requisite to restoring the public's confidence.*

necessitate *demand; exact; must; need; require.* Your husband's job necessitates a great deal of independence and a lot of latitude in his hours. *Your husband's job demands a great deal of independence and a lot of latitude in his hours.* ■ Divided quotations are actually comma splices that necessitate the writer to insert the correct punctuation between the questions or statements. *Divided quotations are actually comma splices that require the writer to insert the correct punctuation between the questions or statements.*

necessity *need.* The emphasis on technical expertise is being balanced by a necessity for good interpersonal skills. *The emphasis on technical expertise is being balanced by a need for good interpersonal skills.*

needless to say *clearly; naturally; obviously; of course; plainly;* delete.

need not necessarily (of necessity) *need not.* This need not necessarily mean that the regime must fall before it can be studied. *This need not mean that the regime must fall before it can be studied.*

needs hardly be said *clearly; naturally; obviously; of course; plainly;* delete.

need to have *need.* We felt in order to support the nugget we needed to have an overall precious metals plan. *We felt in order to support the nugget we needed an overall precious metals plan.*

negative feelings *anger; annoyance; discomfort; disfavor; dislike; displeasure; disregard; distaste; frustration; hate; hatred; indifference; resentment.* I have nothing but negative feelings for her. *I have nothing but hatred for her.* ■ Why do so many people so often take out their negative feelings on others? *Why do so many people so often take out their frustrations on others?*

neither here nor there *immaterial; inapt; irrelevant; not pertinent.*

neither one *neither.* Neither one of us wanted to admit it. *Neither of us wanted to admit it.*

never at any time *never; not ever; not once.*

never ever *never; not ever; not once.* You never ever make concessions to terrorists. *You never make concessions to terrorists.*

nevertheless *anyhow; even so; still; yet.* There are nagging questions, nevertheless. *Still, there are nagging questions.*

new and improved *improved; new.* The original design goals may not have been much different than to create a new and improved version of an earlier operating system. *The original design goals may not have been much different than to create an improved version of an earlier operating system.*

new and innovative *innovative; new.* The health care industry is marketing many new and innovative products. *The health care industry is marketing many innovative products.*

(brand) new baby *baby.*

new construction *construction.* Both firms predict the vacancy rate will fall, if only because of a lack of new construction. *Both firms predict the vacancy rate will fall, if only because of a lack of construction.*

new creation *creation.*

new departure *departure.* The environmental community is hopeful that he will represent a new departure in environmental protection. *The environmental community is hopeful that he will represent a departure in environmental protection.*

new innovation *innovation.* There is now ample evidence that the United States is lagging behind Japan in new innovations. *There is now ample evidence that the United States is lagging behind Japan in innovations.*

new introduction *introduction.*

new (high) record *record.* This computer, introduced in 1981, set a new record for sales and quickly became the standard around which most other manufacturers designed their machines. *This computer, introduced in 1981, set a record for sales and quickly became the standard around which most other manufacturers designed their machines.*

new recruit *recruit.*

next of all *also; and; as well; besides; further; furthermore; moreover; next; second; still more; too.*

no basis in fact *baseless; groundless; unfounded.*

no better (than) *best*. This last point is perhaps no better illustrated than by the recent acquisition of Applied Data Research by Computer Associates. *This last point is perhaps best illustrated by the recent acquisition of Applied Data Research by Computer Associates.*

no longer in existence *dead; deceased; defunct; departed; extinct*. The American Alumni Search allows you to quickly and easily find the Alumni Web Sites for all 106,000 K-12 schools in America including the 20,000 schools that are no longer in existence. *The American Alumni Search allows you to quickly and easily find the Alumni Web Sites for all 106,000 K-12 schools in America including the 20,000 schools that are defunct.*

no longer with us *dead; fired; gone.*

no matter (what) *despite (what); whatever*. No matter what the period to maturity, they are accepted for payment of taxes due at face or par value. *Whatever the period to maturity, they are accepted for payment of taxes due at face or par value.*

no matter how *despite how; however*. She was determined, no matter how long it took, to find out the truth. *She was determined, however long it took, to find out the truth.*

no matter when *despite when; whenever*. No matter when you use them, voice-mail messages are usually a lot briefer and more efficient than the give-and-take of ordinary conversation. *Despite when you use them, voice-mail messages are usually a lot briefer and more efficient than the give-and-take of ordinary conversation.*

no matter where *despite where; wherever*. From the state's point of view, the collider will be a boon no matter where it is located. *From the state's point of view, the collider will be a boon wherever it is located.*

no matter whether ... (or) *despite whether; whether ... or (not)*. It was unwise to make the purchase and consumption of alcohol illegal no matter whether or not all or some of that purchase and consumption was immoral. *It was unwise to make the purchase and consumption of alcohol illegal whether or not all or some of that purchase and consumption was immoral.*

no matter which *despite which; whichever*. No matter which way I decide, I will be blamed for making the wrong decision. *Whichever way I decide, I will be blamed for making the wrong decision.*

no matter who *despite who; whoever.* It is still a good idea and should be adopted, no matter who wins the presidency. *It is still a good idea and should be adopted, whoever wins the presidency.*

no matter whom *despite whom; whomever.* No matter whom the voters choose, investors will be contemplating the first change of presidents since 1980, with all the questions about future economic policies that implies. *Whomever the voters choose, investors will be contemplating the first change of presidents since 1980, with all the questions about future economic policies that implies.*

no more (and) no less *exactly; just; precisely.*

no more than *but; merely; only.*

nonetheless *anyhow; even so; still; yet.*

noontime *noon.* The meeting on the 29th will be held at noontime in room 901. *The meeting on the 29th will be held at noon in room 901.*

not anything *nothing.* There's not anything wrong with this housing code. *There's nothing wrong with this housing code.*

not anywhere *nowhere.* But this total is not anywhere near the level of demand. *But this total is nowhere near the level of demand.*

not a one *none; no one.*

not ... at any time *never; not ever; not once.* My mother was not in a coma at any time; her last few weeks were the only period of very serious pain. *My mother was never in a coma; her last few weeks were the only period of very serious pain.*

notation *memo; note.* Read the entire chapter carefully and methodically, underlining key points and making marginal notations as you go. *Read the entire chapter carefully and methodically, underlining key points and making marginal notes as you go.*

note how (that) *delete.* Note how in this case, the pathname is not preceded by a slash. *In this case, the pathname is not preceded by a slash.*

(does) not ever *never.* This routine is called only when a known internal command is executed, so it does not ever attempt to mediate command line switches for program calls. *This routine is called only* *when a known internal command is executed, so it never attempts to mediate command line switches for program calls.*

not hardly (scarcely) *hardly (scarcely).*

notice how (that) delete. Notice how the message line indicates how many characters were saved on the disk. *The message line indicates how many characters were saved on the disk.*

notification *notice.*

not in favor of *disagree (with); oppose.*

not in the least *not at all.*

notwithstanding *after all; apart; aside; despite; even with; for all; with all.* These misfortunes notwithstanding, the numbers of gorillas are believed to be growing. *These misfortunes aside, the numbers of gorillas are believed to be growing.*

notwithstanding the fact that *although; but; even though; still; though; yet.* Of what relevance to usage (notwithstanding the fact that the topic is interesting) is an entry on eponyms? *Of what relevance to usage (though the topic is interesting) is an entry on eponyms?* ■ Unless a confession is given freely and rationally, it will be inadmissible notwithstanding the fact that it is reliable. *Unless a confession is given freely and rationally, it will be inadmissible even though it is reliable.*

null and void *invalid; not binding; null; void; worthless.*

number-one *central; chief; foremost; key; leading; main; major.* That slow start-up is often the number-one reason why many financial analysts consider biotechnology companies to be a gamble. *That slow start-up is often the main reason why many financial analysts consider biotechnology companies to be a gamble.*

numerical *numeric.*

numerous *countless; endless; many; untold.* There were numerous women in his life. *There were untold women in his life.*

O

observe *see.*

obtain (a; the) ... (for; of; to) delete. Using the first number less than 3.257 and the first number greater than 3.257, it is possible to obtain an approximation for log 3.257 by using linear interpolation. *Using the first number less than 3.257 and the first number greater than 3.257, it is possible to approximate log 3.257 by using linear interpolation.* ■ In order to obtain an understanding of the antiquity of Clan MacKay, we must first look at Ireland's history, which according to many historians, makes the history of all other countries look infantile by comparison. *In order to understand the antiquity of Clan MacKay, we must first look at Ireland's history, which according to many historians, makes the history of all other countries look infantile by comparison.*

obviate the necessity (need) for (of; to) *obviate (-ing).* Of course, an awareness of this uncertainty doesn't obviate the need to make decisions based on your best guess about what the future holds. *Of course, an awareness of this uncertainty doesn't obviate making decisions based on your best guess about what the future holds.* ■ NAS 4 and its support for Enterprise Java Beans obviates the need for the solution proposed in this chapter. *NAS 4 and its support for Enterprise Java Beans obviates the solution proposed in this chapter.* ■ The Active Directory support obviates the need to register a component locally for use on a remote server. *The Active Directory support obviates registering a component locally for use on a remote server.*

occasionally *at times; now and again; now and then; sometimes.* Getting to the actual command you want to execute occasionally means you must select a series of commands from the displayed submenus. *Getting to the actual command you want to execute sometimes means you must select a series of commands from the displayed submenus.*

occur again *recur.* No resident should place items having any value in these bins without being aware that a theft may occur again. *No resident should place items having any value in these bins without being aware that a theft may recur.*

of (a; the) ... delete. I'd like to ask a question of the senator. *I'd like to ask the senator a question.* ■ The article failed to mention that a two-year-old investigation concluded that any irregularities were minor and of no significance. *The article failed to mention that a two-year-old* *investigation concluded that any irregularities were minor and insignificant.* ■ Both of these options draw the reader's attention to data of importance. *Both of these options draw the reader's attention to important data.*

(a; the) ... of *-ing.* For most American families, this means an analysis of the costs of operating and financing their automobiles. *For most American families, this means analyzing the costs of operating and financing their automobiles.* ■ Even more important is a knowledge of the costs of consumption in terms of the alternative consumption opportunities that are given up because of the particular choices made. *Even more important is knowing the costs of consumption in terms of the alternative consumption opportunities that are given up because of the particular choices made.*

of all delete. A cyclical pattern is the most difficult of all to predict. *A cyclical pattern is the most difficult to predict.*

of (a; the) ... character delete. A license may be revoked if a meter is used in operating any scheme or enterprise of an unlawful character, for nonuse during any consecutive 12 months, or for any failure of the licensee to comply with the regulations governing the use of postage meters. *A license may be revoked if a meter is used in operating any scheme or unlawful enterprise, for nonuse during any consecutive 12 months, or for any failure of the licensee to comply with the regulations governing the use of postage meters.* ■ Sellers of such chemicals also are required to report any sale of a suspicious character to the Drug Enforcement Administration. *Sellers of such chemicals also are required to report any suspicious sale to the Drug Enforcement Administration.*

of (a) different opinion *at odds.*

of ... dimensions (magnitude; proportions; size) delete. It was a success of monumental dimensions. *It was a monumental success.* ■ The mess surrounding our president is a tragedy of substantial proportions. *The mess surrounding our president is a substantial tragedy.* ■ Manny Ramirez hit a homerun of historic proportions. *Manny Ramirez hit a historic homerun.* ■ If He did not return when He said He would, we have a dilemma of huge proportions. *If He did not return when He said He would, we have a huge dilemma.* ■ A storm of monstrous proportions developed in the Atlantic that year and several ships were caught in its fury. *A monstrous storm developed in the Atlantic that year and several ships were caught in its fury.* ■ For those of you who don't know, World War II was an event of immense magnitude in world history. *For those of you who don't know, World War II was an immense event in world history.*

offer (a; the) ... (at; of; to) delete. In this column, we offer a brief look at five organizations that have found methods of reducing the burden. *In this column, we briefly look at five organizations that have found methods of reducing the burden.* ■ This author offers an examination of the research findings on age and performance. *This author examines the research findings on age and performance.*

official business *business.*

off of *from; off.* She lived one block off of campus. *She lived one block off campus.*

of from ... to *from ... to; of ... to.* The semitrailer-tank is intended to transport light petrochemical products with the density of from 0.7 to 0.8 g/cm³, along the roads. *The semitrailer-tank is intended to transport light petrochemical products with the density of 0.7 to 0.8 g/cm³, along the roads.* ■ An ATC has between 30 and 50 participants, and lasts for a duration of from 3 to 5 days. *An ATC has between 30 and 50 participants, and lasts for a duration of 3 to 5 days.*

of (a; the) ... importance (that; to) *important; -(al)ly important;* delete. Information service issues are of vital importance to the telecommunications industry as well as to the general public. *Information service issues are vital to the telecommunications industry as well as to the general public.* ■ Since increased involvement is generally associated with increased management and financial costs, not all foreign markets are of equal importance. *Since increased involvement is generally associated with increased management and financial costs, not all foreign markets are equally important.*

of (a; the) ... nature delete. First-level management deals with day-to-day operations of a repetitive nature. *First-level management deals with repetitive day-to-day operations.* ■ This type of analysis is of recent origin and is primarily of a conceptual rather than analytical nature. *This type of analysis is of recent origin and is primarily conceptual rather than analytical.* ■ It was found that the material in his shoe was of an explosive nature. *It was found that the material in his shoe was explosive.*

of (to) no avail *unsuccessful.*

of one form (kind; sort; type) or another *in some way; some form (kind; sort; type) of; somehow; someway(s);* delete. About 15 percent of all U.S. and Soviet missions involving nuclear reactors have suffered failures of one sort or another. *About 15 percent of all U.S. and Soviet missions involving nuclear reactors have suffered some sort of failure.*

of ... own accord (free will) *gladly; readily; willingly.*

of (a; the) ... persuasion delete. A physician of liberal persuasion agonized over the senator's fall from grace. *A liberal physician agonized over the senator's fall from grace.*

of such *so.* The personal balance sheet is of such simplicity that anyone who can add and subtract can also develop the entries. *The personal balance sheet is so simple that anyone who can add and subtract can also develop the entries.*

oftentimes (offtimes) *often.* Oftentimes, bacteria is present in food when you buy it. *Bacteria is often present in food when you buy it.*

of that (this) kind (sort; type) *like that (this).* For an accident of this kind, you can't help blaming yourself. *For an accident like this, you can't help blaming yourself.*

of that (this) nature *like that (this).* The Boston Juvenile Court deals with cases of this nature. *The Boston Juvenile Court deals with cases like this.*

of that (this) year *(1995);* delete. In July of this year, the three-month Treasury stood at 6.73 percent. *In July, the three-month Treasury stood at 6.73 percent.*

of the (them; these) delete. Each of the binomial random variables tends toward *v. Each binomial random variable tends toward* v.

of the fact that *that;* delete. She was jealous of the fact that I could do these things. *She was jealous that I could do these things.*

of the first magnitude *best; central; chief; finest; foremost; key; leading; main; major; most important; principal; superior.*

of the first (highest) order *best; central; chief; finest; first-class; foremost; great; key; leading; main; major; most important; principal; superior.* She called it a tragedy of the first order. *She called it a major tragedy.*

of the same opinion *at one.*

of (a; the) ... variety delete. Snow of the heavy variety is now falling. *Heavy snow is now falling.*

(a; the) ... of which *whose.* It is one of the few gifts the value of which can be juggled successfully to get greater leverage. *It is one of the few gifts whose value can be juggled successfully to get greater leverage.* ■ Wisdom collected over the course of a lifetime is a wealth the loss of which cannot be borne. *Wisdom collected over the course of a lifetime is a wealth whose loss cannot be borne.*

old adage *adage.* As the old adage says, "Patriotism is the last refuge of a scoundrel." *As the adage says, "Patriotism is the last refuge of a scoundrel."*

old cliché *cliché.* Must you always rely on such old clichés? *Must you always rely on such clichés?*

old maxim *maxim.* Your analysis of that proposal vividly demonstrates an old maxim: For every complex problem, there is an answer that is absolutely obvious, absolutely simple, and absolutely wrong. *Your analysis of that proposal vividly demonstrates a maxim: For every complex problem, there is an answer that is absolutely obvious, absolutely simple, and absolutely wrong.*

old proverb *proverb.* He referred to the old proverb: If I give you a fish, you will eat for a day; if I teach you to fish, you will eat for a lifetime. *He referred to the proverb: If I give you a fish, you will eat for a day; if I teach you to fish, you will eat for a lifetime.*

old relic *relic.* There is a gaiety of line which captures, in black and white, the golden opulence of the magnificent old relic. *There is a gaiety of line which captures, in black and white, the golden opulence of the magnificent relic.*

old saw *saw.* The essence of marginal utility boils down to the old saw that pearls don't cost a lot because men have to dive for them, but rather men dive for them because they command a high price. *The essence of marginal utility boils down to the saw that pearls don't cost a lot because men have to dive for them, but rather men dive for them because they command a high price.*

old saying *saying.* The old saying "a picture is worth a thousand words" appropriately applies to computer graphics. *The saying "a picture is worth a thousand words" appropriately applies to computer graphics.*

on a (the) ... basis *-(al)ly;* delete. The exercises must be done for 20 to 25 minutes on a continuous basis. *The exercises must be done continuously for 20 to 25 minutes.* ■ Every exchange has a clearinghouse that transfers funds from losers to winners on a daily basis. *Every exchange has a clearinghouse that transfers funds daily from losers to winners.* ■ Our sole interest in the report is to be sure that each application is evaluated on a fair basis. *Our sole interest in the report is to be sure that each application is evaluated fairly.* ■ It has been estimated that, on a worldwide basis, banks and credit card companies lose $3 million annually. *It has been estimated that, worldwide, banks and credit card companies lose $3 million annually.* ■ Questions as complex as the ones contained in this collection cannot be graded on a right or wrong basis. *Questions as complex as the ones contained in this collection cannot be graded right or wrong.* ■ We will continue to add features to the site and update information on a frequent basis. *We will continue to add features to the site and update information frequently.*

on account of *after; because of; by; due to; following; for; from; in; out of; owing to; through; with.* There are millions of women in this country who have been discriminated against on account of their sex. *There are millions of women in this country who have been discriminated against because of their sex.*

on account of the fact that *because; considering; for; given; in that; since.* Brown suggests that this might be on account of the fact that it posed little challenge to the homosocial order. *Brown suggests that this might be because it posed little challenge to the homosocial order.*

on a couple of (a few) occasions *a few times; once or twice; twice; two or three times.* On a couple of occasions, the entire system shut down. *Once or twice, the entire system shut down.*

on a (the) ... note *-(al)ly;* delete. On a disconcerting note, 18 percent of the children surveyed said they had been approached to buy or use drugs. *Disconcertingly, 18 percent of the children surveyed said they had been approached to buy or use drugs.* ■ The market began the week on a cautious note. *The market began the week cautiously.*

on a number of (any number of; frequent; many; numerous; several) occasions *frequently; many times; numerous times; often; regularly;*

repeatedly; several times. They have done that on a number of occasions. *They have often done that.*

on a regular basis *bimonthly; biweekly; daily; hourly; monthly; regularly; weekly; yearly;* delete. Does it mean we should all start taking aspirin on a regular basis? *Does it mean we should all start taking aspirin regularly?*

on a (the) ... scale (scope) *-(al)ly;* delete. We can do projects on a much larger scale today. *We can do much larger projects today.*

on a (the) ... scene *-(al)ly;* delete. On the national scene, here's what's happening. *Here's what's happening nationally.*

on a timely basis *by next week (tomorrow); fast; in (within) a day (year); in (on) time; promptly; quickly; rapidly; right away; shortly; soon; speedily; swiftly; timely.* It is important that you pay your premiums on a timely basis. *It is important that you pay your premiums on time.*

on (an; the) average *commonly; customarily; generally; normally; often; ordinarily; typically.*

on ... behalf (of) *for.* Nobody is authorized to speak on my behalf. *Nobody is authorized to speak for me.*

once (and) for all *conclusively; decisively; finally;* delete. Analysts expect their questions about Raytheon's nondefense subsidiaries to be answered once and for all when Phillips' successor makes known his intentions. *Analysts expect their questions about Raytheon's nondefense subsidiaries to be finally answered when Phillips' successor makes known his intentions.*

once in a (great) while *at times; now and again; now and then; on occasion; sometimes.*

on certain (some) occasions *at times; now and again; now and then; occasionally; sometimes.* On some occasions, the treatment may retard progression of the disease. *Sometimes, the treatment may retard progression of the disease.*

once ... then *once.* Once this analysis is done, then special attention may be paid to various short pieces of code that consume the most time. *Once this analysis is done, special attention may be paid to various short pieces of code that consume the most time.* ■ Once you determine what you want to tell people, you then need to figure out what's in it for them. *Once you determine what you want to tell people, you need to figure out what's in it for them.*

on (the) condition (of; that) *as long as; if; provided; so long as.* The Maynard computer maker will offer a generous financial support package to 700 employees on condition that they agree to leave the company. *The Maynard computer maker will offer a generous financial support package to 700 employees provided that they agree to leave the company.*

on -day *-day.* All that the police know is the bank was robbed sometime on Monday morning. *All that the police know is the bank was robbed sometime Monday morning.*

on each (every) occasion *all; always; consistently; constantly; each; each time; for (in) each; for (in) every; every time; invariably; unfailingly;* delete.

one and all *all; everyone.*

one and only *one; only; sole.* Is that the one and only time you have engaged in group counseling? *Is that the only time you have engaged in group counseling?*

one and the same *identical; one; the same.* We do not believe that computers and communications are going to converge and become one and the same business. *We do not believe that computers and communications are going to converge and become the same business.*

on earlier (former; previous; prior) occasions *before; earlier; formerly; previously.* I asked Governor Cuomo for his support, as I have on prior occasions. *I asked Governor Cuomo for his support, as I have before.*

one best (most) *best (most).* Each alternative needs to be evaluated to determine which one best achieves the objective. *Each alternative needs to be evaluated to determine which best achieves the objective.*

one-half (one-third) *half (third).* The data is derived from the first one-third of the observations. *The data is derived from the first third of the observations.*

one-half (seven-eighths) of an inch *one-half (seven-eighths) inch.* Alternate pages are offset from the left margin by an additional one-half of an inch. *Alternate pages are offset from the left margin by an additional one-half inch.*

one more time *again; once more; re-.* If you position the highlight over the first or last choice on the menu and then press the arrow key one more time, the highlight wraps around to the other end of the menu. *If you position the highlight over the first or last choice on the menu and then press the arrow key again, the highlight wraps around to the other end of the menu.*

(the) one of delete. In the United States, such a gesture is merely one of politeness. *In the United States, such a gesture is merely politeness.* ∎ The strategy then shifts from one of consolidation to one of integration. *The strategy then shifts from consolidation to integration.*

one-of-a-kind *matchless; novel; peerless; singular; special; unequaled; unique; unmatched; unrivaled.* "Learn C Now" is a one-of-a-kind course that's designed to make beginning programmers productive quickly. *"Learn C Now" is a unique course that's designed to make beginning programmers productive quickly.*

one single *one; (a) single.* Not one single college president has ever attempted to lay off a single high-paid administrator. *Not one college president has ever attempted to lay off a single high-paid administrator.*

one (two) time(s) *once (twice).* We visited them two times in two days. *We visited them twice in two days.*

(in) one way or another *anyhow; anyway; by some means; however; in any way; in some way; in whatever way; somehow; somehow or another; someway(s).* He seemed deranged in one way or another. *He seemed deranged somehow.*

(in) one way or the other *at all; either way; in the least; in the slightest;* delete. It didn't change my religious beliefs one way or the other. *It didn't change my religious beliefs in the least.*

on (the) grounds that *because; considering; for; given; in that; since.* Democratic leaders oppose the tax cut on grounds that it benefits mainly the rich. *Democratic leaders oppose the tax cut since it benefits mainly the rich.*

on ... grounds *about; -(al)ly; on;* delete. The proposed increase in rapid transit fares may be justified on economic grounds. *The proposed increase in rapid transit fares may be economically justified.*

on its (the) face (of it; of things) *apparently; appear (to); outwardly;*

seem (to); seemingly; superficially. On the face of it, no term fits the Parisian beau monde of the late 18th century better than the one invented 200 years later by Tom Wolfe. *No term seems to fit the Parisian beau monde of the late 18th century better than the one invented 200 years later by Tom Wolfe.*

on its (the) face (of it; of things) ... appear (seem) *appear (seem).* On the face of it, this would appear to be a simple evaluation to make. *This would appear to be a simple evaluation to make.*

on (a; the) ... level *-(al)ly;* delete. On a personal level, I cannot stand how he behaves. *Personally, I cannot stand how he behaves.* ■ I feel it's not possible to have a relationship with a man on a spiritual and emotional level. *I feel it's not possible to have a spiritual and emotional relationship with a man.* ■ In the past year, the media has gotten to know her, at least on a superficial level. *In the past year, the media has gotten to know her, at least superficially.*

on more than one occasion *a few times; frequently; many times; more than once; often; several times.* I've been asked that question on more than one occasion. *I've been asked that question more than once.*

on no consideration *never; not ever; not once.*

on no occasion *never; not ever; not once.*

on (the) one hand ... on the other (hand) delete. Another way of looking at the basic strategic tradeoffs that Bell Operating Companies are facing is to look at the relationship between their competitiveness on one hand and the need to avoid conflict with various players on the other. *Another way of looking at the basic strategic tradeoffs that Bell Operating Companies are facing is to look at the relationship between their competitiveness and the need to avoid conflict with various players.*

on one (two; three) occasion(s) *a few times; once; once or twice; one time; several times; three times; twice; two times.* On only one occasion in the three years of our negotiations were the Angels and Dick unable to come to a satisfactory agreement. *Only once in the three years of our negotiations were the Angels and Dick unable to come to a satisfactory agreement.*

on ... part *among; by; for; from; of; -'s;* delete. To beat them will take a great effort on our part. *To beat them will take a great effort by us.* ■ I think it's foolhardy on your part. *I think it's foolhardy of you.* ■ The shorter work hours logged by women had more to do with their heavy concentration in retail trade and service-oriented industries than a reluctance on their part to work longer hours. *The shorter work hours logged by women had more to do with their heavy concentration in retail trade and service-oriented industries than their reluctance to work longer hours.* ■ It was the first time I felt a real commitment on his part. *It was the first time I felt a real commitment from him.*

on ... terms delete. We are no longer on speaking terms with each other. *We are no longer speaking with each other.*

on that (this) (particular) occasion *at present; at that (this) time; currently; (just; right) now; presently; then; today; (just) yet;* delete.

on the basis of *after; based on; because of; by; due to; following; for; from; in; on; owing to; through; with.* The other guards said the vehicle was a minivan, a fact confirmed on the basis of the tire tracks found at the scene. *The other guards said the vehicle was a minivan, a fact confirmed by the tire tracks found at the scene.* ■ Employees do not act on the basis of what management thinks, or what management thinks they think; they act on their own opinions. *Employees do not act on what management thinks, or what management thinks they think; they act on their own opinions.* ■ Its managers should be selected on the basis of their ability to further the company's goals and maximize its earnings. *Its managers should be selected for their ability to further the company's goals and maximize its earnings.*

on the basis of the fact that *because; considering; for; given; in that; since.* Everybody knew that Beijing was the leader on the basis of the fact that they'd been the runner up in the 1993 vote that gave Sydney the 2000 Games. *Everybody knew that Beijing was the leader given that they'd been the runner up in the 1993 vote that gave Sydney the 2000 Games.* ■ This is justifiable on the basis of the fact that the Bible was produced, like Islam, in the Middle East and thus the two may share common factors. *This is justifiable since the Bible was produced, like Islam, in the Middle East and thus the two may share common factors.*

on the bottom of *below; beneath; under; underneath.*

on the contrary *but; conversely; however; instead; not so; rather; still; whereas; yet.*

on the decline *abating; declining; decreasing; waning.*

on the decrease *abating; declining; decreasing; waning.*

on the increase *booming; flourishing; growing; increasing; rising.* The Department of Revenue recently released a report on the state's economic indicators that showed personal savings are on the increase. *The Department of Revenue recently released a report on the state's economic indicators that showed personal savings are increasing.*

on the inside of *inside.* An undercut could also be a recessed neck on the inside of a cylindrical hole. *An undercut could also be a recessed neck inside a cylindrical hole.*

on (upon) the heels of *(just; right) after; (close) behind; ensuing; following; succeeding.* On the heels of an FBI investigation, a federal grand jury has indicted five people on charges they defrauded ComFed Savings Bank. *Following an FBI investigation, a federal grand jury has indicted five people on charges they defrauded ComFed Savings Bank.*

on the occasion of *if (there were); if ... should; in case (of); should (there); were (there; ... to); when;* delete. The machinists' union has agreements that members of other unions will not do their work on the occasion of a strike. *The machinists' union has agreements that members of other unions will not do their work if there were a strike.*

(something; somewhere) on the order (of) *about; around; close to; more or less; near; nearly; or so; roughly; some;* delete. Typically, the ratio of injury to mortality is something on the order of three or four to one. *Typically, the ratio of injury to mortality is some three or four to one.* ■ I counted something on the order of 50 interruptions for applause. *I counted 50 or so interruptions for applause.* ■ For software whose development time is on the order of two years, there are two possible arrangements. *For software whose development time is around two years, there are two possible arrangements.*

on the order of *akin to; close to; like; resembling; similar to; such as.* What you won't see in Chatham is anything on the order of the commercial changes going on in other Cape towns. *What you won't see in Chatham is anything resembling the commercial changes going on in other Cape towns.* ■ Have you ever been in a situation where you ask friends what they want to do tonight, and their response is something on the order of, "Oh, it doesn't matter, surprise us"? *Have you ever been in a situation where you ask friends what they want to do tonight, and their response is something like, "Oh, it doesn't matter, surprise us"?*

on the other hand *but; by (in) contrast; conversely; however; whereas; yet;* delete. A parallel device, on the other hand, sends or receives information in packets all at once over many data lines. *A parallel device, in contrast, sends or receives information in packets all at once over many data lines.*

on the outside of *outside.* The fan blades are on the outside of the engine like a propeller, and all the air that passes inside the engine goes through the combustion chamber as in the earliest jets. *The fan blades are outside the engine like a propeller, and all the air that passes inside the engine goes through the combustion chamber as in the earliest jets.* ■ Either elemental sulfur is formed outside of the cell or the sulfide is oxidized all the way to sulfate. *Either elemental sulfur is formed outside the cell or the sulfide is oxidized all the way to sulfate.*

on the part of *among; by; for; from; in; of; -'s;* delete. Though deliberate discrimination on the part of the Japanese is often charged, it isn't necessary to prove a discriminatory intent. *Though deliberate discrimination by the Japanese is often charged, it isn't necessary to prove a discriminatory intent.* ■ The effective teaching of language arts requires a commitment to excellence on the part of the classroom teacher. *The effective teaching of language arts requires a commitment to excellence from the classroom teacher.* ■ His apt observations point out the need for greater awareness on the part of the public of the architecture that surrounds them. *His apt observations point out the need for greater public awareness of the architecture that surrounds them.* ■ How has the practice of these concepts on your part affected the way you live, and how has the practice of these concepts on the parts of other people affected the way you perceive the world? *How has your practice of these concepts affected the way you live, and how has other people's practice of these concepts affected the way you perceive the world?*

on the rise *booming; flourishing; growing; increasing; rising.* Interest rates are on the rise in the United States, Europe, and Japan. *Interest rates are rising in the United States, Europe, and Japan.*

on the side of *for; with.* The second factor working on the side of savings is the president and his wife. *The second factor working for savings is the president and his wife.*

on the ... side *among; in; -(al)ly;* delete. How would you assess the progress that she has made on the artistic side? *How would you assess the artistic progress that she has made?* ■ There will be some job losses on the manufacturing side, but some employees will be transferred.

There will be some job losses in manufacturing, but some employees will be transferred. ■ The file we would receive is on the large side — 10,424 lines long. *The file we would receive is large — 10,424 lines long.* ■ Increased competition for programming and talent has increased our costs on the network side significantly. *Increased competition for programming and talent has significantly increased our network costs.*

on the surface (of it; of things) *apparently; appear (to); outwardly; seem (to); seemingly; superficially.*

on the surface (of it; of things) ... appear (seem) *appear (seem).* On the surface, a firm may appear to be sound — its balance sheet contains an impressive amount of current assets. *A firm may appear to be sound — its balance sheet contains an impressive amount of current assets.*

on the surface of *on.*

on the threshold of *about to; approaching; close to; near; nearly; verging on.* We are on the threshold of real educational quality and achievement. *We are verging on real educational quality and achievement.*

on the verge of *about to; approaching; close to; near; nearly; verging on.* Is he or is he not on the verge of producing chemical weapons? *Is he or is he not about to produce chemical weapons?*

on the whole *all told; in all; overall.*

on (upon) the whole *almost all; chiefly; commonly; generally; greatly; in general; largely; mainly; most; mostly; most often; much; nearly all; normally; overall; typically; usually.* On the whole, Boston's registered nurses were more likely to describe themselves as satisfied with their earnings than their counterparts in other cities. *Overall, Boston's registered nurses were more likely to describe themselves as satisfied with their earnings than their counterparts in other cities.*

on (the) top of *atop.* It may not be necessary to develop an emergency plan for flooding if the facility is on the top of a well-drained hill. *It may not be necessary to develop an emergency plan for flooding if the facility is atop a well-drained hill.*

on top of (that; this) *also; and; as well; besides; beyond that (this); even; further; furthermore; moreover; more than that (this); still more; then; too; what is more.* On top of that, interest rates went up to 18 percent or more. *What's more, interest rates went up to 18 percent or more.*

on (the) understanding (of; that) *as long as; if; provided; so long as.*

open to doubt *arguable; debatable; disputable; doubtful; dubious; in doubt; in question; moot; questionable.*

open to question *arguable; debatable; disputable; doubtful; dubious; in doubt; in question; moot; questionable; uncertain; unclear; undecided; unknown; unsettled; unsure.* His clout on Capitol Hill remains open to question. *His clout on Capitol Hill remains in doubt.*

open up *open.* When you use the Note command, a window opens up. *When you use the Note command, a window opens.*

(a; the) ... operation *delete.* With the measurement of quality and quantity, process control is a fairly automatic operation. *With the measurement of quality and quantity, process control is fairly automatic.* ■ While this has been programmed correctly, it is a dangerous operation because a call to the QueueReceiver.receive() method blocks the thread until a message becomes available. *While this has been programmed correctly, it is dangerous because a call to the QueueReceiver.receive() method blocks the thread until a message becomes available.*

operational *active; live; running; working.*

operative *active; at work; effective; in action; in effect; in force; in play; working.*

optimal (optimum) *best.* As organizations begin to move their R&D back and forth to various countries, it will be the responsibility of the company's tax advisors to provide counseling on the optimal tax structure for a variety of arrangements. *As organizations begin to move their R&D back and forth to various countries, it will be the responsibility of the company's tax advisors to provide counseling on the best tax structure for a variety of arrangements.*

or anything *delete.*

or else *or.* Two pathnames must be specified, or else the first letter parameter will be incorrectly interpreted as a pathname. *Two pathnames must be specified, or the first letter parameter will be incorrectly interpreted as a pathname.*

orientate(d) *orient(ed).* I didn't have a family-orientated family. *I did-*

303

n't have a family-oriented family. ■ Our site contains sexual-orientated material and is intended for adults only. *Our site contains sexual-oriented material and is intended for adults only.* ■ A more politically orientated analysis was required to understand OPEC. *A more politically oriented analysis was required to understand OPEC.* ■ Ninety-five percent of Textron's business is defense orientated. *Ninety-five percent of Textron's business is defense oriented.*

oriented delete. Some depressed people become more activity oriented. *Some depressed people become more active.*

original coiner (originally coined) *coiner (coined).* Usually the identity of the original coiner of a new word is lost in the mists of history. *Usually the identity of the coiner of a new word is lost in the mists of history.*

original creator (originally created) *creator (created).* An impressive number of neologisms can be traced to their original creators. *An impressive number of neologisms can be traced to their creators.*

original founder (originally founded) *founder (founded).*

original invention (inventor) *invention (inventor).* The courts determined the patents were invalid on the grounds that Atanasoff was the original inventor. *The courts determined the patents were invalid on the grounds that Atanasoff was the inventor.* ■ This approach to children's radio is not Disney's original invention, according to Children's Broadcasting Corp. *This approach to children's radio is not Disney's invention, according to Children's Broadcasting Corp.*

original source *source.*

origination *origin.*

or something delete.

or thereabouts *or so.*

or whatever delete.

other people (persons) *others.* Elizabeth Taylor, among other people, has written about this topic. *Elizabeth Taylor, among others, has written about this topic.*

other similar *similar.* In addition, the order permits the companies to provide electronic mail, voice messaging, and other similar services. *In addition, the order permits the companies to provide electronic mail, voice messaging, and similar services.*

other than *besides.*

other than ... also (as well) *besides; beyond; other than.*

other than to *but to.*

otherwise *other.* In many competitions, athletic and otherwise, the Finns and Swedes excel. *In many competitions, athletic and other, the Finns and Swedes excel.*

out in *in.* I have several relatives out in the Springfield area. *I have several relatives in the Springfield area.*

out loud *aloud.*

out of *in; of.* Three out of every four parents never visit their child's school. *Three of every four parents never visit their child's school.*

(just) out of curiosity *delete.* Just out of curiosity, is Alexander Haig on the Minnesota ballot? *Is Alexander Haig on the Minnesota ballot?*

out of favor *deprecate; disapprove; disfavor; dislike; disparage.* But he goes on to say, the time to buy them is when they are out of favor. *But he goes on to say, the time to buy them is when they are disfavored.*

out of fear (of; that) ... can (could; may; might; shall; should; will; would) *lest.* No one would be so foolish as to sell one's house out of fear that it might someday burn to the ground. *No one would be so fool-ish as to sell one's house lest it someday burn to the ground.*

out of focus *blurred; indistinct.*

(something) out of the ordinary *curious; different; exceptional; extraor-dinary; irregular; novel; odd; rare; singular; strange; uncommon; unusual.* Will you give me a call if anything out of the ordinary happens? *Will you give me a call if anything curious happens?* ■ Tomorrow's show is going to be something out of the ordinary. *Tomorrow's show is going to be extraordinary.*

out of the question *impossible; inconceivable; undoable; unthinkable.* Returning to college was out of the question, so with nothing to do, she signed up for oil painting lessons. *Returning to college was unthinkable, so with nothing to do, she signed up for oil painting lessons.*

out of the realm of possibility *impossible; inconceivable; undoable; unthinkable.* It is not out of the realm of possibility that Exxon could be facing a billion dollars or more in punitive damages. *It is not impossible that Exxon could be facing a billion dollars or more in punitive damages.*

outside of *outside.* Chase Manhattan and Bank of America are following a similar strategy, with less emphasis on domestic markets outside of the United States. *Chase Manhattan and Bank of America are following a similar strategy, with less emphasis on domestic markets outside the United States.*

over again *again; afresh; anew; once more; over; re-.* They asked me to do it over again. *They asked me to do it over.*

overall look (view) *overview.* The introduction gives the readers an overall view of your business and what you want to achieve. *The introduction gives the readers an overview of your business and what you want to achieve.*

over and above *besides; beyond; more than; over.* Anesthesia doesn't add to the risk over and above that of the surgery itself and the extent of the medical problem the patient already has. *Anesthesia doesn't add to the risk more than that of the surgery itself and the extent of the medical problem the patient already has.*

over and done with *complete; done; ended; finished; over; past.* I just want this to be over and done with. *I just want this to be over.*

over and over (again) *frequently; often; recurrently; regularly; repeatedly.* Professor Sommers refers over and over to a "bag of virtues." *Professor Sommers refers often to a "bag of virtues."*

overly *over-.* We thought he was overly enthusiastic about winning. *We thought he was overenthusiastic about winning.* ■ Many supermarkets throughout the U.S. place overly sexualized magazines, notably *Cosmopolitan* and *Glamour*, in their checkout aisles. *Many supermarkets throughout the U.S. place oversexualized magazines, notably Cosmopolitan and Glamour, in their checkout aisles.*

over the course (duration; length) of *during; for; in; over; throughout; when; while; with.* Over the duration of the project, we expect there will be some disruption due to noise, dirt, and dust. *During the project, we expect there will be some disruption due to noise, dirt, and dust.*

over the fact that *because; for; in that; since; that;* delete. I am concerned over the fact that they made us work so hard. *I am concerned that they made us work so hard.*

over the long haul *at length; eventually; in the end; in time; later; long-term; one day; over the months (years); over time; someday; sometime; ultimately; with time; yet.* Over the long haul, I still believe that housing is a good investment. *I still believe that housing is a good long-term investment.*

over the short haul *at first; at present; before long; currently; directly; for now; in (over) a month (week); initially; next month (year); (just; right) now; presently; quickly; shortly; short-term; soon; straightaway; this month (year); tomorrow;* delete. Industry analysts say they expect the new rules to have little impact, at least over the short haul. *Industry analysts say they expect the new rules to have little impact, at least initially.*

(a; the) overwhelming (vast) consensus (of opinion) *consensus.*

(a; the) overwhelming (vast) preponderance (of) *a good (great) deal (of); a good (great) many (of); almost all (of); (nine) in (ten) (of); many (of); most (of); much (of); nearly all (of); (43) of (48) (of); (67) percent (of); three-fourths (two-thirds) (of);* delete. A recent poll showed that a vast preponderance of city councilors oppose the relocation. *A recent poll showed that almost all city councilors oppose the relocation.*

owing to the fact that *because; considering; for; given; in that; since.* However, owing to the fact that NRDC is a well-thought-of organization, capable of good quality research, we're clearly going to go through their report carefully. *However, since NRDC is a well-thought-of organization, capable of good quality research, we're clearly going to go through their report carefully.* ■ Elementary Afrikaans is quite easy, owing to the fact that the base grammar structure is simple, and words are generally written the way they are pronounced. *Elementary Afrikaans is quite easy, because the base grammar structure is simple, and words are generally written the way they are pronounced.*

P

pack together *pack.* Recent advances have made it possible to pack thousands, even millions, of transistors together on a single silicon chip. *Recent advances have made it possible to pack thousands, even millions, of transistors on a single silicon chip.*

(a) pair of twins *twins.* Such a proximity is literalized in the documentation of the plight of Viet and Duc, a pair of twins joined at the abdomen and sharing a leg. *Such a proximity is literalized in the documentation of the plight of Viet and Duc, twins joined at the abdomen and sharing a leg.*

parameter *boundary; limit.*

par for the course *normal; typical; usual.*

part and parcel *part.* This generalized tendency to place conflicts in the outside world is part and parcel of a well-known mechanism of the mind called projection. *This generalized tendency to place conflicts in the outside world is part of a well-known mechanism of the mind called projection.*

partially *partly.* My difficulty with her is partially due to a clash of personalities. *My difficulty with her is partly due to a clash of personalities.*

particular delete. We would hope that you have already found a new church home that you can serve and that can meet your needs at this particular time in your life. *We would hope that you have already found a new church home that you can serve and that can meet your needs at this time in your life.*

pass away (on) *die.*

passing craze (fad; fancy) *craze (fad; fancy).*

passing phase *phase.*

pass judgment (sentence) on (upon) *judge (sentence).* Passing judgment on one's potential earnings is even more painful than passing judgment on a former colleague. *Judging one's potential earnings is even more painful than judging a former colleague.*

past (previous; prior) accomplishment *accomplishment*. It is startling that he supposes some imagined past accomplishment of his should exempt him from paying rent. *It is startling that he supposes some imagined accomplishment of his should exempt him from paying rent.*

past (previous; prior) achievement *achievement*.

past (previous; prior) experience *experience*. A shortage of workers for jobs requiring little skill is forcing some employers to hire people without considering their references, past experience, or education. *A shortage of workers for jobs requiring little skill is forcing some employers to hire people without considering their references, experience, or education.*

past (previous; prior) history *history*. Even though forecasts deal with the future, past history is not irrelevant. *Even though forecasts deal with the future, history is not irrelevant.*

past (previous; prior) performance *performance*. Normally, one judges the ability to succeed based on past performance. *Normally, one judges the ability to succeed based on performance.*

past (previous; prior) practice *practice*. But in keeping with past practice for such flights, the Pentagon is expected to announce a three-hour launch-window early this week. *But in keeping with practice for such flights, the Pentagon is expected to announce a three-hour launch-window early this week.*

past (previous; prior) precedent *precedent*. Based on past precedent, Mr. Indelicato would likely serve between 12 and 18 months in prison. *Based on precedent, Mr. Indelicato would likely serve between 12 and 18 months in prison.*

past (previous; prior) record *record*. Both the summer's drought and the fire's extent surpassed all previous records in the park. *Both the summer's drought and the fire's extent surpassed all records in the park.*

patchwork quilt *patchquilt; patchwork*. The question then becomes how to organize this patchwork quilt of topics. *The question then becomes how to organize this patchwork of topics.*

pathetical *pathetic*.

pathological *pathologic*. Even though this response is accompanied by redness, warmth, and pain, it is not naturally a pathological process. *Even though this response is accompanied by redness, warmth, and pain, it is not naturally a pathologic process.*

pay attention to *attend to; consider; hearken to; heed; listen to; mind; note; notice; observe; regard; see; tend to; watch; witness.* We need to pay attention to the image we're projecting. *We need to consider the image we're projecting.*

pay a visit to *visit.* Pay a visit to your nearest McDonald's. *Visit your nearest McDonald's.*

pay heed to *attend to; consider; hearken to; heed; listen to; mind; note; notice; observe; regard; see; tend to; watch; witness.* Many Americans have paid heed to the results of research and changed their ways of living remarkably. *Many Americans have heeded the results of research and changed their ways of living remarkably.*

peace and quiet *peace; quiet.* South Korea's four major parties declared a one-month political truce yesterday to assure peace and quiet during this month's Summer Olympics. *South Korea's four major parties declared a one-month political truce yesterday to assure peace during this month's Summer Olympics.*

penetrate into *penetrate.*

per *a.* According to this study, the average executive spends 11 weeks per year reading memos. *According to this study, the average executive spends 11 weeks a year reading memos.*

percentage point (unit) *point (unit).* The U.S. Labor Department reported that the September unemployment rate fell 0.2 percentage points, to 5.4 percent. *The U.S. Labor Department reported that the September unemployment rate fell 0.2 points, to 5.4 percent.*

per each (every) *per.* NYNEX will deliver your message for just ten cents per each message. *NYNEX will deliver your message for just ten cents per message.*

perfect (perfectly) match *duplicate; exact; identical; match; (the) same.* Spreadsheets and television may seem unlikely partners, but if what's going on at the Tulsa, Oklahoma, offices of United Video is anything to go by, they are a perfect match. *Spreadsheets and television may seem unlikely partners, but if what's going on at the Tulsa, Oklahoma, offices of United Video is anything to go by, they are a match.*

perform (a; the) ... of *do;* delete. He performed an extensive analysis of the financing patterns of U.S. corporations. *He extensively analyzed the financing patterns of U.S. corporations.* ■ Then perform a comparison of the two disks. *Then compare the two disks.* ■ If an order is executed, the database performs the "clearing" of the trade within an escrow account. *If an order is executed, the database "clears" the trade within an escrow account.* ■ In the first part of the book, Gray offers strategies for empowering staff, boards, volunteers, and clients to perform an evaluation of their organization. *In the first part of the book, Gray offers strategies for empowering staff, boards, volunteers, and clients to evaluate their organization.* ■ For example, you could perform a study of the EMF/leukemia link with animals. *For example, you could study the EMF/leukemia link with animals.*

perhaps ... may (might) *may (might); perhaps.* Perhaps you may want to reread our introductions and note places where we have traded in our role as guides for one as "tour directors." *You may want to reread our introductions and note places where we have traded in our role as guides for one as "tour directors."*

periodical *periodic.*

(a; the) period (time) of delete. After the shock comes a period of doubt and resignation. *After the shock comes doubt and resignation.*

permit ... to *let.*

(a; the) ... person delete. You do not need to be a gourmet cook or model housecleaner to be a worthwhile person. *You do not need to be a gourmet cook or model housecleaner to be worthwhile.*

personal belief (opinion; point of view; view; viewpoint) *belief (opinion; point of view; view; viewpoint).* My personal opinion is that he should be publicly scolded for his actions. *My opinion is that he should be publicly scolded for his actions.*

personal bias *bias.* Some experts do inject personal bias into the process. *Some experts do inject bias into the process.*

personal charm *charm.*

personal feeling *feeling.* What are your personal feelings about this? *What are your feelings about this?*

personal friend (friendship) *friend (friendship).* She is a personal friend of mine. *She is a friend of mine.*

personal rapport *rapport.* Account managers are advised to develop a personal rapport with their clients. *Account managers are advised to develop a rapport with their clients.*

pertain (pertaining) to *about; as for; as to; concerning; for; in; of; on; over; regarding; to; toward; with.* An assets management system can answer these what-if budget questions pertaining to equipment. *An assets management system can answer these what-if budget questions about equipment.*

pharmacological *pharmacologic.*

phone up *phone.*

physiological *physiologic.* It is believed that anxiety is expressed through physiological processes rather than symbolically through coping mechanisms. *It is believed that anxiety is expressed through physiologic processes rather than symbolically through coping mechanisms.*

pick and choose *choose; cull; pick; select.* Its organization into independent topics that you can pick and choose from allows you to use it in a one-semester course. *Its organization into independent topics that you can pick from allows you to use it in a one-semester course.*

pick up the phone (telephone) and call *call; phone.* Buying or selling ownership in a corporation is simply a matter of picking up the phone and calling a stockbroker, who can, within minutes, buy or sell stock listed on a stock exchange. *Buying or selling ownership in a corporation is simply a matter of calling a stockbroker, who can, within minutes, buy or sell stock listed on a stock exchange.*

place (put) (a) ... (in; into; on; under; upon) delete. In determining the relative quality of municipal securities, many investors place great reliance on the rating provided by the two major rating agencies. *In determining the relative quality of municipal securities, many investors greatly rely on the rating provided by the two major rating agencies.* ■ The Act only covers the actual cost of cleaning up pollution damage, and does not put a limit on compensation claims from third parties. *The Act only covers the actual cost of cleaning up pollution damage, and does not limit compensation claims from third parties.*

place (put) a burden on (upon) *burden; encumber; hamper; hinder; oppress; overtax; strain; tax; weigh down.* The result can be the gradual accumulation of policies and practices that, like a bad diet, overload the organs and place burdens on the members struggling to keep it alive. *The result can be the gradual accumulation of policies and practices that, like a bad diet, overload the organs and burden the members struggling to keep it alive.*

place (put) a premium on (upon) *appreciate; cherish; esteem; favor; highly regard; prefer; prize; rate highly; respect; treasure; value.* Like our staff members, who place a premium on their intellectual and professional independence, our clients made it clear that they consider it essential to be able to work with us without concern about any conflicting interests. *Like our staff members, who prize their intellectual and professional independence, our clients made it clear that they consider it essential to be able to work with us without concern about any conflicting interests.*

place (put) a priority on (upon) *appreciate; cherish; esteem; favor; highly regard; prefer; prize; rate highly; respect; treasure; value.* We need to place a priority on education at all levels. *We need to prize education at all levels.* ■ Look for developers who put a priority on producing the best product for you and your customers. *Look for developers who value producing the best product for you and your customers.* ■ We urge newsroom managers to place a priority on diversity as hiring opportunities present themselves. *We urge newsroom managers to favor diversity as hiring opportunities present themselves.* ■ We will always place a priority on simplifying the learning process and motivating educators. *We will always highly regard simplifying the learning process and motivating educators.*

place (put) a strain on (upon) *burden; encumber; hamper; hinder; oppress; overtax; strain; tax; weigh down.* Hot weather puts a strain on the heart and can lead to exhaustion, heart failure, and stroke. *Hot weather overtaxes the heart and can lead to exhaustion, heart failure, and stroke.*

place (put) a value on (upon) *appreciate; cherish; esteem; prize; respect; treasure; value.*

place (put) credence in *accept; believe; credit.* A physical model of health and illness was emphasized that didn't place credence in the idea that our thinking and health were related. *A physical model of health and illness was emphasized that didn't accept the idea that our thinking and health were related.*

place (put) ... in danger *endanger; imperil; jeopardize.* I would prefer a plan that doesn't put people in danger. *I would prefer a plan that doesn't endanger people.*

place (put) ... in jeopardy *endanger; imperil; jeopardize.* The opposition Liberal Party, two weeks away from a crucial general election, has strengthened its position among voters and placed the U.S.-Canada trade agreement in serious jeopardy. *The opposition Liberal Party, two weeks away from a crucial general election, has strengthened its position among voters and seriously endangered the U.S.-Canada trade agreement.*

place (put) ... in (into) peril *endanger; imperil; jeopardize.* To do otherwise would invite serious trouble and even place our nation in great peril. *To do otherwise would invite serious trouble and even greatly imperil our nation.*

place (put) into question *challenge; contradict; dispute; doubt; question.*

place of business (employment; work) *business; company; firm; job; office; work; workplace.* The defendant indicated that he intended to call two witnesses to testify to having overheard Janice yelling at the defendant at his place of employment, a restaurant where the witnesses also worked. *The defendant indicated that he intended to call two witnesses to testify to having overheard Janice yelling at the defendant at his workplace, a restaurant where the witnesses also worked.*

place (put) restrictions on (upon) *bind; compel; force; obligate; restrict.*

place (put) stress on (upon) *strain; stress.* Fasting places great stress on your body. *Fasting greatly stresses your body.*

place (put) under obligation *bind; compel; force; obligate; restrict.*

plain and simple *clear; obvious; plain; simple.* Associating tobacco with the pastoral joy of watching a baseball game or a golf or tennis tournament is plainly and simply false advertising. *Associating tobacco with the pastoral joy of watching a baseball game or a golf or tennis tournament is clearly false advertising.*

plan ahead *plan.* If people would plan ahead, they wouldn't be confronted by these crisis situations. *If people would plan, they wouldn't be confronted by these crisis situations.*

plan in advance *plan.* Plan carefully in advance so that you know exactly when to start and stop the tape. *Plan carefully so that you know exactly when to start and stop the tape.*

plan of action (attack; battle)   *action; course; direction; intention; method; move; plan; policy; procedure; route; scheme; strategy.* Environmentalists say their failure to agree on a plan of battle raises doubts about whether they are up to the challenge. *Environmentalists say their failure to agree on a strategy raises doubts about whether they are up to the challenge.*

plan out   *plan.* It pays in the long run to plan out your career. *It pays in the long run to plan your career.*

plans and specifications   *plans; specifications.* A contractor entered into a written agreement to construct a building according to plans and specifications prepared by the architect. *A contractor entered into a written agreement to construct a building according to plans prepared by the architect.*

plummet down   *down; plummet.* I can provide a litany of cases where competition has brought prices plummeting down. *I can provide a litany of cases where competition has brought prices plummeting.*

plunge down   *down; plunge.*

(a; the) plurality (of)   *almost all (of); (nine) in (ten) (of); many (of); more (of); most (of); nearly all (of); (43) of (48) (of); (67) percent (of); three-fourths (two-thirds) (of).* The poll also found that 89 percent of Americans would not want to be president, and a plurality would not want their children to be. *The poll also found that 89 percent of Americans would not want to be president, and 60 percent would not want their children to be.*

(3:00) p.m. ... afternoon (evening; night)   *afternoon (evening; night); (3:00) p.m.* It was 2 p.m. in the afternoon before we got to see her. *It was 2 p.m. before we got to see her.*

poetical   *poetic.*

point of departure   *starting point.*

point of view   *attitude; belief; opinion; position; posture; stand; standpoint; vantage; view; viewpoint.* In the United States, there is an increase in sympathy for the Palestinian point of view. *In the United States, there is an increase in sympathy for the Palestinian viewpoint.*

point to the conclusion   *indicate; show; signal; signify; suggest.*

polish up *polish.*

polite euphemism *euphemism.* Even its fans call it "difficult" and "uningratiating," polite euphemisms for off the wall, a very appropriate pun to describe this museum-proof collection of dirt piles, rusted girders and "conceptual" creations. *Even its fans call it "difficult" and "uningratiating," euphemisms for off the wall, a very appropriate pun to describe this museum-proof collection of dirt piles, rusted girders and "conceptual" creations.*

popular consensus *consensus.* The opportunity to conduct a rigorous drug trial can only come early in a drug's life, before a popular consensus develops. *The opportunity to conduct a rigorous drug trial can only come early in a drug's life, before a consensus develops.*

position *job.*

(a; the) ... position *delete.* In the mid-1980s, they began a succession of investments in Telerate, which had a monopoly position in the distribution of quotations on U.S. government securities. *In the mid-1980s, they began a succession of investments in Telerate, which had a monopoly in the distribution of quotations on U.S. government securities.*

positive assurance *assurance.* Through the end of last week, we received positive assurances the vote would go through, which makes this doubly frustrating. *Through the end of last week, we received assurances the vote would go through, which makes this doubly frustrating.*

positive feelings *admiration; affection; attraction; confidence; esteem; faith; favor; fondness; hope; interest; liking; love; regard; respect; tenderness; trust.* I'm anticipating this launch with positive feelings. *I'm anticipating this launch with confidence.* ■ Business executives interviewed have positive feelings toward the United Nations. *Business executives interviewed have regard for the United Nations.*

possess (a; the) ... (about; for; of; on; over) *have; own; delete.* If teachers do not possess a firm understanding of both science content and science curriculum goals, even the best of assessments will not be sufficient to guide their classroom instruction. *If teachers do not firmly understand both science content and science curriculum goals, even the best of assessments will not be sufficient to guide their classroom instruction.*

possibly may (might) *may (might).* Swaggart possibly may decide to start his own church. *Swaggart may decide to start his own church.*

posterior to *after; behind; following; later.*

potentiality *potential.* All these tools have the same power sources, materials, and styling, and most important, each has identical market potentiality. *All these tools have the same power sources, materials, and styling, and most important, each has identical market potential.*

pouring (down) rain *pouring.* It'll probably be pouring down rain at the lake. *It'll probably be pouring at the lake.*

predicate on (upon) *base on.*

predict ahead of time (beforehand; in advance) *predict.* I'm not privy to the secret of how to predict ahead of time who will succeed. *I'm not privy to the secret of how to predict who will succeed.* ■ Since the impedance change may vary with frequency, there is no way of predicting in advance how the modulation percentage will vary across the spectrum. *Since the impedance change may vary with frequency, there is no way of predicting how the modulation percentage will vary across the spectrum.* ■ For some applications, you cannot predict in advance how many connection pools you will need. *For some applications, you cannot predict how many connection pools you will need.*

predict ... future *forecast; foretell; predict.* No one, not the fund manager, not the investor, can predict the future course of financial markets. *No one, not the fund manager, not the investor, can predict the course of financial markets.*

predominant (predominantly) *almost all; chief; chiefly; generally; in general; largely; main; mainly; most; mostly; most often; nearly all.* The social structure of this country is predominantly white. *The social structure of this country is largely white.*

prefer ... as opposed to (instead of; rather than) *prefer ... over; prefer ... to.* Most people in any way connected to tourism speak English and prefer to do so rather than deal with a foreigner's French. *Most people in any way connected to tourism speak English and prefer doing so to dealing with a foreigner's French.* ■ Nurses who prefer listening and comprehension as opposed to verbalization generally experience the most productive and satisfying interactions. *Nurses who prefer listening and comprehension over verbalization generally experience the most productive and satisfying interactions.*

prejudicial opinion *bias; prejudice.* Contrary to the prejudicial opinion of most women libbers, physical attractiveness has been and will always be a definite asset. *Contrary to the prejudice of most women libbers, physical attractiveness has been and will always be a definite asset.*

preliminary draft *draft.* He gave me the preliminary draft of their report to review. *He gave me the draft of their report to review.*

preliminary to *before.* Analysis is crucial preliminary to the construction of such a platform, and at times specific research may be required to identify the right platform. *Analysis is crucial before the construction of such a platform, and at times specific research may be required to identify the right platform.*

premises *building; house; office; store.*

preparation (prepare) ... ahead of time (before; beforehand; in advance) *preparation (prepare) ... for.* We did not prepare these people for this ahead of time. *We did not prepare these people for this.*

prepare (for) ... ahead of time (before; beforehand; in advance) *prepare (for).* Try to anticipate problems and prepare for them in advance. *Try to anticipate problems and prepare for them.*

preplan *plan.* In short programs, much of the cognitive input or preplanning takes place on the trainees' own time, thus keeping the seminar to the shortest possible number of hours. *In short programs, much of the cognitive input or planning takes place on the trainees' own time, thus keeping the seminar to the shortest possible number of hours.*

present (a; the) ... (of; on; to) (*v*) delete. We present a summary of the key trends that are important to monitor in the future. *We summarize the key trends that are important to monitor in the future.* ■ Increased competition, shrinking profit margins, and escalating costs are presenting challenges to management. *Increased competition, shrinking profit margins, and escalating costs are challenging management.*

present everywhere *all over; everywhere; omnipresent; ubiquitous; widespread.* Talk about sex is present everywhere. *Talk about sex is ubiquitous.*

present incumbent *incumbent.*

presently *quickly; shortly; soon.*

presently *(just; right) now; today; (just) yet;* delete. No one is presently available to answer your call. *No one is available just yet to answer your call.*

present with *give.* The disabled people met with James O'Leary, MBTA general manager, and presented him with a list of 19 demands. *The disabled people met with James O'Leary, MBTA general manager, and gave him a list of 19 demands.*

pressurize *pressure.* The Indian government is pressurizing Bangaldesh to create a separate homeland for 23 million Hindus within its borders. *The Indian government is pressuring Bangaldesh to create a separate homeland for 23 million Hindus within its borders.*

pretty delete. It's pretty awesome to think of a single gene abnormality that can accelerate the age for a heart attack by 50 years. *It's awesome to think of a single gene abnormality that can accelerate the age for a heart attack by 50 years.*

preventative *preventive.* The idea of preventative training seems to be a necessity in any educational program. *The idea of preventive training seems to be a necessity in any educational program.*

previous (previously) *ago; before; earlier;* delete. We are no closer to resolution than we were three years previously. *We are no closer to resolution than we were three years ago.*

previous to *before.* Previous to yesterday, there was no reason to sound an alarm. *Before yesterday, there was no reason to sound an alarm.*
■ It was later shown that some of the young men had committed crimes both previous to and after the subway incident. *It was later shown that some of the young men had committed crimes both before and after the subway incident.*

primary (primarily) *almost all; chief; chiefly; largely; main; mainly; most; mostly; most often; nearly all.* The assumption is that foreign customers are primarily interested in product availability. *The assumption is that foreign customers are mainly interested in product availability.*

principal (principally) *almost all; chief; chiefly; largely; main; mainly; most; mostly; most often; nearly all.*

prior approval (consent) *approval (consent).* This Software is licensed only to you, the Licensee, and may not be transferred to anyone without the prior written consent of Microsoft. *This Software is licensed* *only to you, the Licensee, and may not be transferred to anyone without the written consent of Microsoft.*

prioritize   *arrange; list; order; rank; rate.* By prioritizing your objectives, devising your plan, and controlling your expenditures, you should be able to build your net worth over the course of your career. *By ranking your objectives, devising your plan, and controlling your expenditures, you should be able to build your net worth over the course of your career.*

prior to   *before.* Prior to the sixteenth century, unknown quantities were represented by words. *Before the sixteenth century, unknown quantities were represented by words.*

prior to ... first   *before; prior to.* Prior to treating external warts in the anogenital region, it is important to first find and treat internal adjacent condyloma. *Prior to treating external warts in the anogenital region, it is important to find and treat internal adjacent condyloma.*

prior to that (the; this) time (of)   *before; before now (then).* We will not pay for transportation expenses incurred prior to that time. *We will not pay for transportation expenses incurred before then.*

probability   *chance; likelihood; prospect.* Others may be less familiar with the model or unfamiliar with the program, thus increasing the probability of mistakes. *Others may be less familiar with the model or unfamiliar with the program, thus increasing the likelihood of mistakes.*

problematical   *problematic.* Since the U.K. banking industry was both mature and increasingly competitive, the clear differentiation of services was becoming problematical. *Since the U.K. banking industry was both mature and increasingly competitive, the clear differentiation of services was becoming problematic.*

(a; the) ... procedure   *delete.* Autocorrelation analysis is a useful procedure for identifying the existence and shape of a trend. *Autocorrelation analysis is useful for identifying the existence and shape of a trend.*

proceed   *go; move; run; walk.*

(then) ... proceed (to)   *later; next; then; delete.* He took my number, which he proceeded to lose. *He took my number, which he later lost.* ■ When you are ill, you don't read the medical encyclopedia, diagnose your case, and then proceed to doctor yourself. *When you are ill, you don't read the medical encyclopedia, diagnose your case, and then doctor yourself.*

proceed ahead (forward; on; onward) *advance; continue; go on; move on; proceed; progress.* We ran into a brick wall on getting the kind of commitment from a big player that we felt was necessary to proceed ahead. *We ran into a brick wall on getting the kind of commitment from a big player that we felt was necessary to proceed.*

(a; the) ... process delete. It's been a gradual process. *It's been gradual.* ■ The assessment process involves rigorously examining the methods used. *Assessment involves rigorously examining the methods used.* ■ Getting into the honesty business, in short, can be an expensive and arduous process. *Getting into the honesty business, in short, can be expensive and arduous.* ■ Doctors should not dismiss complaints of incontinence as an inevitable part of the aging process. *Doctors should not dismiss complaints of incontinence as an inevitable part of aging.* ■ It is an extremely frustrating process to define a new exception in a low-level class and then have to edit and recompile all the classes that use this class. *It is extremely frustrating to define a new exception in a low-level class and then have to edit and recompile all the classes that use this class.*

procure *get.*

produce (a; the) ... (of; to) delete. The model is an analytic framework that produces estimates of future sales. *The model is an analytic framework that estimates future sales.*

proffer *give; offer.* An interesting response to the pricing dilemma has been proffered by several traditional broker-distributed fund sponsors. *An interesting response to the pricing dilemma has been offered by several traditional broker-distributed fund sponsors.*

profitability (profitableness) *profits.* The strategy for achieving higher profitability was simple: organize our businesses around the customer, not the product. *The strategy for achieving higher profits was simple: organize our businesses around the customer, not the product.*

progress ahead (forward; on; onward) *advance; continue; go on; move on; proceed; progress.*

project out *project.* The movement of endolymph in the cochlea results in displacement of tiny hairs projecting out from specialized sensory cells. *The movement of endolymph in the cochlea results in displacement of tiny hairs projecting from specialized sensory cells.*

protestation *protest.* Despite Solomon's protestation, the five-member board is expected to consider changing its rules, which also prohibit CPAs from taking commissions. *Despite Solomon's protest, the five-member board is expected to consider changing its rules, which also prohibit CPAs from taking commissions.*

protrude out *protrude.*

proven (*v*) *proved.* The exact number of data points has not yet been proven. *The exact number of data points has not yet been proved.*

proven fact *fact; proof.* That's a proven fact. *That's a fact.*

prove of benefit to *benefit.*

provide (a; the) ... (for; of; to) delete. This book provides a review of those techniques. *This book reviews those techniques.* ■ Nurses check with other members of the health team when they are unable to provide answers to questions. *Nurses check with other members of the health team when they are unable to answer questions.* ■ The size of the resulting MSE provides an indication of whether additional information is needed. *The size of the resulting MSE indicates whether additional information is needed.*

provided (providing) (that) *if.* You can use the same filename more than once provided that the files are stored in different directories. *You can use the same filename more than once if the files are stored in different directories.*

provide ... with *give.* It provides us with a starting point for our analysis. *It gives us a starting point for our analysis.*

proximity *closeness; nearness.* Its proximity to the edge of the street and the limits of one's field of vision restrict how much of it one can see. *Its nearness to the edge of the street and the limits of one's field of vision restrict how much of it one can see.*

psychiatrical *psychiatric.*

psychical *psychic.*

psychoanalytical *psychoanalytic.*

psychobiological *psychobiologic.*

psychometrical *psychometric.*

psychopathological *psychopathologic.*

psychophysiological *psychophysiologic.*

purchase *buy.* Why would a sensitive, intelligent woman purchase a handgun? *Why would a sensitive, intelligent woman buy a handgun?*

pure and simple *pure; simple.*

pure (and) unadulterated *pure; simple; unadulterated.* This movie is pure, unadulterated blasphemy. *This movie is pure blasphemy.*

pursuant to *by; following; under.* Licenses issued pursuant to this Article shall be issued for terms not exceeding one year. *Licenses issued under this Article shall be issued for terms not exceeding one year.*

put a halt to *cease; close; complete; conclude; end; finish; halt; settle; stop.* Before things get out of hand again this year, let's try to put a halt to it now. *Before things get out of hand again this year, let's try to halt it now.*

put an end to *cease; close; complete; conclude; end; finish; halt; settle; stop.* In the last century, liberals fought to put an end to the cruel traffic in human flesh known as slavery. *In the last century, liberals fought to end the cruel traffic in human flesh known as slavery.*

(to) put (it) another way *namely; that is; to wit.*

put a stop to *cease; close; complete; conclude; end; finish; halt; settle; stop.* I want you to put a stop to all of this nonsense. *I want you to stop all of this nonsense.*

put ... finger on (upon) *identify.*

put forth *advance; exert; give; offer; present; propose; submit; suggest.* Their employees, free to put forth their best efforts, thrive in this environment. *Their employees, free to give their best efforts, thrive in this environment.*

put forward *advance; give; offer; present; propose; submit; suggest.*

put in alphabetical order *alphabetize.* Suppose we have a list of words that we want to put in alphabetical order. *Suppose we have a list of words that we want to alphabetize.*

put in an appearance *appear; arrive; attend; come; show up; visit.*

put into effect *effect; make; perform; produce.* Quaker Fabrics Corp. said it would put into effect cost-cutting measures that specifically exclude personnel reductions. *Quaker Fabrics Corp. said it would effect cost-cutting measures that specifically exclude personnel reductions.*

put on an act *feign; pretend.*

put together *assemble; build; construct; create; devise; fashion; form; mold; set up; shape.* Thus far, KKR has put together four of the largest leveraged buyouts in history. *Thus far, KKR has fashioned four of the largest leveraged buyouts in history.*

put to sleep *destroy; kill.*

put two and two together *conclude; deduce; draw; infer; reason.*

put up with *abide; bear; endure; stand; suffer; tolerate.*

puzzlement *puzzle.*

Q

qualified expert *expert.*

question mark *enigma; mystery; puzzle; question; unknown.* For scientists trying to forecast how the world will react to the burgeoning burden of greenhouse gases, clouds pose a vexing question mark. *For scientists trying to forecast how the world will react to the burgeoning burden of greenhouse gases, clouds pose a vexing question.*

(a; the) question to answer *question.* The question to answer is what value should be used for the beginning periods in the series. *The question is what value should be used for the beginning periods in the series.*

quickly expedite *expedite.*

quixotical *quixotic.*

R

radiate out *radiate.* Tracks run in concentric circles around the disk, and sectors radiate out from the center in pie-shaped wedges. *Tracks run in concentric circles around the disk, and sectors radiate from the center in pie-shaped wedges.*

raise doubts about (on) *challenge; contradict; dispute; doubt; question.*

raise objections about (on; to) *challenge; complain about; criticize; demur; deprecate; differ in; disagree with; disapprove of; dispute; find fault with; object to; oppose; protest; question; resent.* Government employees raised objections to the bill, saying they were worried about getting jobs after leaving government. *Government employees objected to the bill, saying they were worried about getting jobs after leaving government.*

raise opposition about (on; to) *challenge; complain about; criticize; demur; deprecate; differ in; disagree with; disapprove of; dispute; find fault with; object to; oppose; protest; question; resent.* One longs to get a wider view of the times and the people she presents, particularly the women of the period who were raising strong opposition to male authority. *One longs to get a wider view of the times and the people she presents, particularly the women of the period who were strongly deprecating male authority.*

raise questions about (on) *challenge; contradict; dispute; doubt; question.* Congressional critics have raised questions about the plane's future, particularly as cost estimates have increased. *Congressional critics have questioned the plane's future, particularly as cost estimates have increased.*

raise up *raise.*

range anywhere (somewhere) from ... to *range from ... to.* Estimates of sales growth in the industry this year range anywhere from 12 to 50 percent. *Estimates of sales growth in the industry this year range from 12 to 50 percent.*

range from ... all the way to (all the way up to; up to) *range from ... to.* The cost ranges from $500 up to $10,000. *The cost ranges from $500 to $10,000.*

range from a low of ... to a high of *range from ... to.* The 1987 rates

326

range from a low of 14.8 percent at St. Vincent's Hospital to a high of 35.8 percent at St. Joseph's Hospital. *The 1987 rates range from 14.8 percent at St. Vincent's Hospital to 35.8 percent at St. Joseph's Hospital.*

rant and rave *rant; rave.*

rarely (seldom) ever *rarely (seldom).*

rationale *reason; thinking.* The primary rationale is that it is a necessary condition for an otherwise attractive business deal. *The primary reason is that it is a necessary condition for an otherwise attractive business deal.*

rational reason *reason.* There's no rational reason for astrology to work. *There's no reason for astrology to work.*

raze to the ground *demolish; destroy; level; raze; ruin.* A BBC correspondent saw Serbs raze to the ground another ethnic Albanian village. *A BBC correspondent saw Serbs raze another ethnic Albanian village.*

reach (a; the) ... (of) delete. The dividends question is part of the union's proxy fight with the company that is expected to reach a culmination at next week's annual meeting. *The dividends question is part of the union's proxy fight with the company that is expected to culminate at next week's annual meeting.* ■ We tried to reach an accommodation with both parties. *We tried to accommodate both parties.*

reach (an; the) accord *agree; compromise; concur; decide; resolve; settle.* An attorney representing Eastern said the airline wants to reach an accord with the American Society of Travel Agents. *An attorney representing Eastern said the airline wants to settle with the American Society of Travel Agents.*

reach (an; the) agreement *agree; compromise; concur; decide; resolve; settle.* Both he and Chandler said the two sides had reached a tentative agreement on an educational trust fund demanded by the union. *Both he and Chandler said the two sides had tentatively agreed on an educational trust fund demanded by the union.*

reach (a; the) compromise *agree; compromise; concur; decide; resolve; settle.*

reach (a; the) conclusion *conclude; decide; deduce; determine; infer; judge; reason; resolve; settle.* The Japanese did not reach that conclusion by engaging in abstract reasoning but by observing England's industrial relations. *The Japanese did not deduce that by engaging in abstract reasoning but by observing England's industrial relations.*

reach (a; the) decision (on; upon) *conclude; decide; deduce; determine; infer; judge; reason; resolve; settle.* He said the committee also is weighing the issue of who was responsible for the overstatement and probably will reach a decision within a few weeks. *He said the committee also is weighing the issue of who was responsible for the overstatement and probably will decide within a few weeks.*

reach (a; the) determination (on; upon) *conclude; decide; deduce; determine; infer; judge; reason; resolve; settle.*

reach (an; the) estimate (estimation) (of) *approximate; assess; estimate; evaluate; rate.*

reach (an; the) opinion *conclude; decide; deduce; determine; infer; judge; reason; resolve; settle.*

reach (a; the) resolution (about; on) *agree; conclude; decide; determine; resolve; settle.*

reach (a; the) settlement *agree; conclude; decide; resolve; settle.* One union source said that the Justice Department and the union leadership were not likely to reach an out-of-court settlement before the start of the racketeering trial. *One union source said that the Justice Department and the union leadership were not likely to settle out of court before the start of the racketeering trial.*

reach (an; the) understanding *agree; compromise; concur; decide; resolve; settle.*

re- again *re-.* That film will make addicts want to reexperience taking crack again. *That film will make addicts want to reexperience taking crack.* ■ This week, Wright's amazing life is being revisited again, this time on television. *This week, Wright's amazing life is being revisited, this time on television.*

real (really) delete. We know the governor has really serious budget problems this year. *We know the governor has serious budget problems this year.*

(a; the) real fact *fact; truth.*

real live delete. This is a real live medical problem. *This is a medical problem.*

really (and) truly *actually; indeed; in fact; in faith; in reality; in truth; really; truly;* delete. They really truly did have a very unique product. *They truly did have a very unique product.*

reason being is *reason is.* There are a few reasons to add email forms to your website; the best reason being is so you can get information from your guests to you through email. *There are a few reasons to add email forms to your website; the best reason is so you can get information from your guests to you through email.* ■ The reason being is that most of the teachers are going to the war. *The reason is that most of the teachers are going to the war.*

(the) reason (why) ... is because *because; reason is (that).* The reason the business failed was because it was undercapitalized. *The business failed because it was undercapitalized.* ■ Another reason why the example fails as a good strategic goal is because it violates the rule of accountability. *Another reason the example fails as a good strategic goal is it violates the rule of accountability.*

reason (why) ... is due to (the fact that) *because of; due to; reason is (that).* The reason the flooding is so bad this year is due to torrential rains and soil erosion. *The flooding is so bad this year because of torrential rains and soil erosion.* ■ Part of the reason why we've had a growing economy over the last 2 years nationwide is due to the fact that we raised the minimum wage, which put more money in people's pockets and they went out and spent it. *Part of the reason we've had a growing economy over the last 2 years nationwide is that we raised the minimum wage, which put more money in people's pockets and they went out and spent it.*

reason (why) ... is that *because.* The reason we're so successful is that the projects we work with are good ones and we're good at working with community groups. *We're so successful because the projects we work with are good ones and we're good at working with community groups.*

reason why *reason.* It's one of the reasons why we have so much misconduct, so much scandal, in government. *It's one of the reasons we have so much misconduct, so much scandal, in government.*

rebound back *rebound.* How long do you think it will take for the stock to rebound back to its 52-week high? *How long do you think it will take for the stock to rebound to its 52-week high?*

recall back *recall.* Please drop me a line if you would so I can help you recall back those memories at COM. *Please drop me a line if you would so I can help you recall those memories at COM.*

recede back *recede.* When they flood, the velocity in the overbank water may be very low, and the floodwaters may be weeks in receding back into the channel. *When they flood, the velocity in the overbank water may be very low, and the floodwaters may be weeks in receding into the channel.*

receive back *receive.* People express doubt that they will receive back as much in benefits as they paid in Social Security taxes. *People express doubt that they will receive as much in benefits as they paid in Social Security taxes.*

recite back *recite.* You're not asking them to recite back what you said; you're asking them to tell you what they heard. *You're not asking them to recite what you said; you're asking them to tell you what they heard.*

recoil back *recoil.* When the guard stops, the tube will recoil back to the guard for easy access, instead of the guard searching for the strap and pulling it in. *When the guard stops, the tube will recoil to the guard for easy access, instead of the guard searching for the strap and pulling it in.*

record-breaking (high) *record.* The Cape is burdened with a record-breaking number of houses for sale. *The Cape is burdened with a record number of houses for sale.* ■ As record-breaking temperatures continue to assault the nation, people may find themselves snarling where they used to smile and being grouchy when they used to grin. *As record temperatures continue to assault the nation, people may find themselves snarling where they used to smile and being grouchy when they used to grin.*

record high *record.* Young adults are returning home to live with their parents in record-high numbers. *Young adults are returning home to live with their parents in record numbers.*

record-setting *record.* That should mean a blessed end to record-setting heat and a host of problems that arose from or probably interacted with it. *That should mean a blessed end to record heat and a host of problems that arose from or probably interacted with it.*

record size *record*. It appears we've had a record-size turnout at the polls. *It appears we've had a record turnout at the polls.*

rectify *correct; fix; improve*. Why can't they rectify the conditions at Danvers State Hospital? *Why can't they improve the conditions at Danvers State Hospital?*

recur again (and again) *recur*. The lapse has already been corrected within our systems to insure that the problem will not recur again. *The lapse has already been corrected within our systems to insure that the problem will not recur.*

reduce by (to) half *halve*.

reduce down *reduce*. Reduce the number of paid sick days from 20 down to some lower number. *Reduce the number of paid sick days from 20 to some lower number.*

refer back *refer*. The reader may find it helpful to refer back to this diagram after we have completed our discussion. *The reader may find it helpful to refer to this diagram after we have completed our discussion.*

refer to as *call; name; term*; delete. Unconscious attempts to manage anxiety are referred to as defense mechanisms. *Unconscious attempts to manage anxiety are termed defense mechanisms.*

reflect back *reflect*. Reflecting back on my years at BB&N, I tried to understand why neither the school nor the parents were willing to give this case the publicity it deserved. *Reflecting on my years at BB&N, I tried to understand why neither the school nor the parents were willing to give this case the publicity it deserved.* ■ Because the use of your news server reflects back on your organization, you also want to teach your users good netiquette when it comes to participating in newsgroups. *Because the use of your news server reflects on your organization, you also want to teach your users good netiquette when it comes to participating in newsgroups.*

regard (regarding) *about; as for; as to; for; in; of; on; over; to; toward; with*. New Jersey has no law regarding traffic circles. *New Jersey has no law on traffic circles.*

regard as being *regard as*. Cults usually have some literature that they regard as being holy, with which they back up their beliefs. *Cults usually have some literature that they regard as holy, with which they back up their beliefs.*

regardless of (what) *despite (what); no matter what; whatever.* Regardless of what women may accomplish one on one, the most effective agent for change is the company itself. *No matter what women may accomplish one on one, the most effective agent for change is the company itself.*

regardless of how *despite how; however; no matter how.* All lines and lettering must be absolutely black regardless of how fine the lines may be. *All lines and lettering must be absolutely black despite how fine the lines may be.*

regardless of the fact that *although; but; even though; still; though; yet.* Because the aquarium is a private enterprise — regardless of the fact that it is nonprofit — such a transfer is not supposed to take place. *Because the aquarium is a private enterprise — although it is nonprofit — such a transfer is not supposed to take place.*

regardless of when *despite when; no matter when; whenever.* Both proposals would cover all capital assets regardless of when taxpayers bought them. *Both proposals would cover all capital assets despite when taxpayers bought them.*

regardless of where *despite where; no matter where; wherever.* Visible soft hyphens appear on the screen and print out regardless of where they fall in the document. *Visible soft hyphens appear on the screen and print out wherever they fall in the document.*

regardless of whether ... (or) *despite whether; no matter whether; whether ... or (not).* Men's masculinity, looks, and concern about their appearance were rated the same regardless of whether lunch was a salad and coffee or a five-course extravaganza. *Men's masculinity, looks, and concern about their appearance were rated the same whether lunch was a salad and coffee or a five-course extravaganza.* ■ Regardless of whether the reason is internal or external, it has an important bearing on the market-presence alternatives investigated. *Whether the reason is internal or external, it has an important bearing on the market-presence alternatives investigated.*

regardless of which *despite which; no matter which; whichever.* Regardless of which happens, you can change the result. *Whichever happens, you can change the result.*

regardless of who *despite who; no matter who; whoever.* Regardless of who we may be, we all have the right to economic opportunity. *Whoever we may be, we all have the right to economic opportunity.*

regardless of whom   *despite whom; no matter whom; whomever.* Regardless of whom these books are meant for, I think they should be designed and developed to look and feel more accessible. *Whomever these books are meant for, I think they should be designed and developed to look and feel more accessible.*

regress back   *regress.* Over time, growth stocks tend to regress back to reality, while cheaper stocks tend to move higher on a relative basis. *Over time, growth stocks tend to regress to reality, while cheaper stocks tend to move higher on a relative basis.*

regular -(al)ly   *-(al)ly.* We attend the regular monthly meeting of the BCS. *We attend the monthly meeting of the BCS.*

regular routine   *routine.* Hiring, training, and record-keeping are part of the regular routine for running any business. *Hiring, training, and record-keeping are part of the routine for running any business.*

reiterate   *iterate; repeat.* Baker also reiterated his insistence that Bush would not debate before September 22. *Baker also repeated his insistence that Bush would not debate before September 22.*

reiterate again (and again)   *iterate; reiterate; repeat.*

relate (to)   *say; tell.* One executive related to us that in Chile he had almost single-handedly stopped a strike. *One executive told us that in Chile he had almost single-handedly stopped a strike.*

relate back   *relate.* This involves the activation of cognitive processes in your brain in which you think about the meaning of the words, weigh ideas, correlate new ideas with your experiences, and relate the ideas back to former material. *This involves the activation of cognitive processes in your brain in which you think about the meaning of the words, weigh ideas, correlate new ideas with your experiences, and relate the ideas to former material.*

-related   delete. This division provides telemarketing-related and other direct marketing services for clients in four areas. *This division provides telemarketing and other direct marketing services for clients in four areas.*

relate (relating) to   *about; as for; as to; concerning; for; in; of; on; over; regarding; to; toward; with.* We may add to the basic rental price any taxes or other governmental assessments relating to the use or operation of the postage meter or scale. *We may add to the basic rental price any taxes or other governmental assessments on the use or operation of the postage meter or scale.*

relationship *bond; connection; link; relation; tie.* The photograph had no relationship to any of the elements of the story. *The photograph had no relation to any of the elements of the story.*

relatively *-(i)er; less; more.* Lawyer Dukakis repeatedly has expressed disdain for the merger and acquisition business; oil man Bush seems to harbor relatively few such concerns. *Lawyer Dukakis repeatedly has expressed disdain for the merger and acquisition business; oil man Bush seems to harbor fewer such concerns.*

relatively ... as (when) compared to (with) *compared to (with); -(i)er than (less than; more than).* Housing is relatively inexpensive and affordable when compared to Boston and other higher-priced nearby housing markets. *Housing is inexpensive and affordable compared to Boston and other higher-priced nearby housing markets.*

relatively ... compared (contrasted) to (with) *compared (contrasted) to (with); -(i)er than (less than; more than).* Shrinkage remains relatively low compared to mass retailing standards. *Shrinkage remains low compared to mass retailing standards.* ■ They tend to have a relatively high loss and PDL, and are relatively expensive compared to mechanical switches. *They tend to have a relatively high loss and PDL, and are more expensive than mechanical switches.* ■ In fact, Mathers and Bank still stay in close contact with other cast members, and their lives are relatively stable compared with those of other former child stars. *In fact, Mathers and Bank still stay in close contact with other cast members, and their lives are stable compared with those of other former child stars.* ■ Although the UK is relatively small when compared with the United States, its landscape and people are varied and dramatic; what it lacks in physical size it makes up for in culture, history, etc. *Although the UK is smaller than the United States, its landscape and people are varied and dramatic; what it lacks in physical size it makes up for in culture, history, etc.*

relatively -(i)er than (less than; more than) *-(i)er than (less than; more than).* delete. This country is in relatively better shape than other major industrialized nations. *This country is in better shape than other major industrialized nations.* ■ Its real estate portfolio grew relatively faster than anybody else's. *Its real estate portfolio grew faster than anybody else's.*

relatively ... in comparison (in contrast) to (with) *compared (contrasted) to (with); -(i)er than (less than; more than); in comparison (in contrast) to (with).* Solving the legal problems of partnerships is relatively simple in comparison to solving the problems of other types of ownership. *Solving the legal problems of partnerships is simple compared to solving the problems of other types of ownership.*

relatively ... in relation to *compared (contrasted) to (with); -(i)er than (less than; more than); in relation to.* The price or delivery time on a product may be relatively unimportant in relation to overall quality for your Asian customer. *The price or delivery time on a product may be unimportant in relation to overall quality for your Asian customer.*

relatively ... relative to *compared (contrasted) to (with); -(i)er than (less than; more than); relative to.* These potential limitations for CO2 excretion may be partially offset by the relatively high blood volume in these animals relative to other vertebrates. *These potential limitations for CO2 excretion may be partially offset by the high blood volume in these animals relative to other vertebrates.*

relative to *about; concerning; for; on; regarding.* We want to talk to him relative to his wife's death. *We want to talk to him about his wife's death.*

relative to *against; alongside; beside; compared to (with); -(i)er than; less; less than; more; more than; next to; over; than; to; versus; vis-à-vis.* Relative to other societies, Brazil and the United States place considerable emphasis on youth. *Brazil and the United States place considerably more emphasis on youth than other societies.* ■ Consumers in a good mood may be more likely to interpret information more favorably relative to consumers in a less positive mood, thereby causing more favorable opinions to be formed. *Consumers in a good mood may be more likely to interpret information more favorably than consumers in a less positive mood, thereby causing more favorable opinions to be formed.*

relevancy *relevance.* Define the term *system,* and explain its relevancy to the study of mass communication. *Define the term* system, *and explain its relevance to the study of mass communication.*

relic of the past *relic.* But for most people today, CPM is an all-but-forgotten relic of the past which is just a few years old. *But for most people today, CPM is an all-but-forgotten relic which is just a few years old.*

remainder *remains; rest.* No economic indicators are due for the remainder of the week. *No economic indicators are due for the rest of the week.*

remains to be seen *do not know; is not (now; yet) known; is uncertain; is unclear; is unknown; is unsure.* It remains to be seen if he can sustain a housing partnership. *It's not yet known if he can sustain a housing partnership.*

remand back *remand.* The case was decided and remanded back to the Court of Appeals which remanded it back to the District Court. *The case was decided and remanded to the Court of Appeals which remanded it to the District Court.*

remember again *remember.* Remember again, ten dollars times thirty million is three hundred million dollars. *Remember, ten dollars times thirty million is three hundred million dollars.*

remember back *remember.* One of the easiest ways to understand this operator is to remember back to elementary school mathematics. *One of the easiest ways to understand this operator is to remember elementary school mathematics.*

reminisce about the past *reminisce.* NostalgiaStreet.com's mission is to provide a friendly place where people can reminisce about the past while enjoying today and preparing for tomorrow. *NostalgiaStreet.com's mission is to provide a friendly place where people can reminisce while enjoying today and preparing for tomorrow.*

remit back *remit.* You are required to remit back to the plan any reimbursements made for ineligible expenses. *You are required to remit to the plan any reimbursements made for ineligible expenses.*

remittance *cash; fee; money; pay; payment; wage.*

remunerate *pay.*

remuneration *cash; fee; money; pay; payment; reward; wage.*

render *act; do; give; make.* The biggest question remaining about the use of phenethanolamines is whether the drugs will contaminate meat and render it unsafe for human consumption. *The biggest question remaining about the use of phenethanolamines is whether the drugs will contaminate meat and make it unsafe for human consumption.*

render assistance to *aid; assist; help.* I hereby pledge to render assistance to fellow jugglers. *I hereby pledge to assist fellow jugglers.* ■ If possible, render assistance to victims and attempt to limit further injury and property / equipment damage. *If possible, aid victims and attempt to limit further injury and property/equipment damage.*

reoccur *recur.* This behavior tends to reoccur every year. *This behavior tends to recur every year.* ■ Let us examine briefly each of the specific areas in which test bias is a reocurring concern. *Let us examine briefly each of the specific areas in which test bias is a recurring concern.* ■ Failure to remember is a reocurring theme of consumer behavior. *Failure to remember is a recurring theme of consumer behavior.*

reoccurrence *recurrence.* It is even more important that more be done to protect them from the occurrence and reoccurrence of that which precipitates these disorders: sexual abuse. *It is even more important that more be done to protect them from the occurrence and recurrence of that which precipitates these disorders: sexual abuse.*

repay back *repay.* How can they claim they won when their client has to repay back the money plus interest? *How can they claim they won when their client has to repay the money plus interest?*

repeat again (and again) *repeat.* All of this is based on predictable behaviors that are repeated again and again in rather exact ways. *All of this is based on predictable behaviors that are repeated in rather exact ways.*

repeat back *repeat.* Repeat back the answers you hear so you can make sure you understand them. *Repeat the answers you hear so you can make sure you understand them.* ■ These are very intelligent people, and they are being bombarded with monotonous detail that a parrot could repeat back after a few sessions with it owner. *These are very intelligent people, and they are being bombarded with monotonous detail that a parrot could repeat after a few sessions with it owner.*

repeat occurrence *recurrence.* What should he do so as not to have a repeat occurrence of this? *What should he do so as not to have a recurrence of this?*

repeat over (and over) *repeat.* A loop is a sequence of commands, the last of which refers the program back to the first so that the commands repeat over and over until stopped. *A loop is a sequence of commands, the last of which refers the program back to the first so that the commands repeat until stopped.*

reply back *reply.* I sent her a letter and then waited two weeks for a reply back. *I sent her a letter and then waited two weeks for a reply.*

report back *report*. The Insurance Division will report back to the high court within 30 days on whether to rehabilitate them in some ways or declare them insolvent. *The Insurance Division will report to the high court within 30 days on whether to rehabilitate them in some ways or declare them insolvent.* ■ Most Cobol programs will validate the end user's input and report back any invalid input to the end user. *Most Cobol programs will validate the end user's input and report any invalid input to the end user.*

represents *is*. These numbers represent the washer's inside diameter, outside diameter, and thickness. *These numbers are the washer's inside diameter, outside diameter, and thickness.* ■ We believe that our offer represents a fair price and is in the best interest of Pennwalt's shareholders. *We believe that our offer is a fair price and is in the best interest of Pennwalt's shareholders.*

require *need*.

requirement *need*.

requisite *need*.

reside *dwell; live*. I am now residing in New York City. *I am now living in New York City.*

residence *home; house*.

residual trace *trace*. She is still beautiful despite residual traces of three massive strokes suffered when she was three-months pregnant. *She is still beautiful despite traces of three massive strokes suffered when she was three-months pregnant.*

resiliency *resilience*.

respective (respectively) delete. Microsoft hereby limits the duration of any implied warranty(ies) on the disk or such hardware to the respective periods stated above. *Microsoft hereby limits the duration of any implied warranty(ies) on the disk or such hardware to the periods stated above.*

respond back *respond*. I was disappointed the governor could not have responded back to me personally. *I was disappointed the governor could not have responded to me personally.*

respond in the affirmative *agree; say yes.* We hope he will respond in the affirmative. *We hope he will say yes.*

respond in the negative *decline; disagree; say no.* You will be asked if you want to proceed, and if you respond in the negative, the submission is aborted and the previous submission remains unaltered. *You will be asked if you want to proceed, and if you say no, the submission is aborted and the previous submission remains unaltered.* ■ Members who respond in the negative will not be considered for summer employment but will maintain their relative position on the rotation list. *Members who decline will not be considered for summer employment but will maintain their relative position on the rotation list.*

restore back *restore.* If something happens to the files on the disk that you back up, you can use the backup copies to restore files back onto it. *If something happens to the files on the disk that you back up, you can use the backup copies to restore files onto it.* ■ She was optimistic her loving, green thumb could restore the foliage back to health. *She was optimistic her loving, green thumb could restore the foliage to health.*

rest up *rest.*

resultant (*n*) *effect; result.*

resultant effect *effect; result.* Concern exists over the antiandrogenic activity of cimetidine and its resultant effect on feminization of male rats. *Concern exists over the antiandrogenic activity of cimetidine and its effect on feminization of male rats.*

resume again *resume.*

retain ... position as *remain.* I also will retain my position as the Secretary of Jones Family Farm, Inc. *I also will remain the Secretary of Jones Family Farm, Inc.*

retreat back *retreat.* Having conquered consumer electronics, the Japanese firms are attacking in industrial electronics, and the American firms are once again in the process of retreating back to defense electronics to get those higher returns on investment. *Having conquered consumer electronics, the Japanese firms are attacking in industrial electronics, and the American firms are once again in the process of retreating to defense electronics to get those higher returns on investment.*

return back *return.* In the 1980s, we're returning back to the cultural norm of marriage and family. *In the 1980s, we're returning to the cultural norm of marriage and family.* ■ The handler performs its job and finally executes the IRETD instruction to return back to the calling application. *The handler performs its job and finally executes the IRETD instruction to return to the calling application.*

reuse again *reuse.* If you want to create more than one graph for a model so that you can reuse them again, what must you do? *If you want to create more than one graph for a model so that you can reuse them, what must you do?*

reverse back *reverse.* If you so much as breathe funny, the TICK reverses back to the downside. *If you so much as breathe funny, the TICK reverses to the downside.*

revert back *revert.* Some companies that encounter operational problems during an advanced stage may revert back to a previous stage. *Some companies that encounter operational problems during an advanced stage may revert to a previous stage.* ■ This way, if you ever need to revert back to the original version, you can simply open the original document. *This way, if you ever need to revert to the original version, you can simply open the original document.*

root cause *cause; reason; root; source.* White-collar crimes, not poor economic conditions or deregulation, are the root cause of the S&L crisis. *White-collar crimes, not poor economic conditions or deregulation, are the root of the S&L crisis.*

rough sketch *sketch.* A rough sketch is made to indicate the type of illustration required and the method of reproduction to be used. *A sketch is made to indicate the type of illustration required and the method of reproduction to be used.*

routine procedure *routine.* There is a routine procedure that we follow. *There is a routine that we follow.*

rules and regulations *regulations; rules.* Rules and regulations regarding the use of the library have been posted throughout the building. *Rules regarding the use of the library have been posted throughout the building.*

run of the mill *average; common; everyday; mediocre; ordinary; typical; usual.*

S

sad to relate (say) *sadly.* Sad to relate, some bicyclists have become a menace to pedestrian and motor vehicle traffic. *Sadly, some bicyclists have become a menace to pedestrian and motor vehicle traffic.*

safe haven *haven.*

satirical *satiric.* My neighbor often makes satirical remarks about the fanaticism with which people mow and rake their lawns. *My neighbor often makes satiric remarks about the fanaticism with which people mow and rake their lawns.*

save and except *except; save.* I confirm that I have not engaged in Outside Professional Activities that use university resources save and except as set out on page 2 of this report. *I confirm that I have not engaged in Outside Professional Activities that use university resources except as set out on page 2 of this report.*

say, for example (for instance) *for example (for instance); say.* Say, for example, you use a 12 percent home equity loan to finance $10,000 of an automobile purchase. *Say you use a 12 percent home equity loan to finance $10,000 of an automobile purchase.*

scatter in all (every) direction(s) *scatter.* Do people scatter in all directions when they see you coming? *Do people scatter when they see you coming?*

scream and yell *scream; yell.*

secondarily *second.* Secondarily, we serve the community beyond the Air Force Academy through a variety of programs. *Second, we serve the community beyond the Air Force Academy through a variety of programs.*

secondly *second.* First, be correct in your vocabulary or word choices; secondly, use standard grammar in your speeches. *First, be correct in your vocabulary or word choices; second, use standard grammar in your speeches.*

second of all *second.*

seeing (as; as how; that) *because; considering; for; given; in that; since.* Seeing as how I don't have any stamps, I'm going to deliver this myself. *Since I don't have any stamps, I'm going to deliver this myself.* ■ Seeing that I am feeling better about things than I was last week, I will answer the phone if you call. *Since I am feeling better about things than I was last week, I will answer the phone if you call.* ■ Perhaps this comes as no surprise seeing as how *Playboy* is the bellwether for an industry that sells itself. *Perhaps this comes as no surprise given that* Playboy *is the bellwether for an industry that sells itself.*

seek out *seek.* In most cases, we actively seek out foreign investment. *In most cases, we actively seek foreign investment.*

seesaw back and forth (up and down) *seesaw.* The Hang Seng index seesawed back and forth last week as student demonstrations fueled speculation. *The Hang Seng index seesawed last week as student demonstrations fueled speculation.*

select out *choose; pick out; select.* The other approach, selecting out for doctors' treatment those at particularly high risk, is already well established, but it has limitations. *The other approach, selecting for doctors' treatment those at particularly high risk, is already well established, but it has limitations.*

(my)self *(I; me).* Richard and myself are going to lunch. *Richard and I are going to lunch.* ■ Very large people like yourself can eat tiny amounts of food and not lose an ounce. *Very large people like you can eat tiny amounts of food and not lose an ounce.* ■ Let's hope someone comes along, like myself, to take his place. *Let's hope someone comes along, like me, to take his place.* ■ We feel Mr. Roedler's comments do an injustice to collectors like ourselves who currently pay $1,500 to $2,000 for radios of this type. *We feel Mr. Roedler's comments do an injustice to collectors like us who currently pay $1,500 to $2,000 for radios of this type.* ■ Neither the mayor nor myself desires to comment on the status of the matter. *Neither the mayor nor I desire to comment on the status of the matter.*

selfsame *same.*

seminal fluid *semen.*

(a) sense of delete. Our sense of foreboding grew as the afternoon wore on. *Our foreboding grew as the afternoon wore on.* ■ I felt a sense of helplessness when he beat me. *I felt helpless when he beat me.*

(five; many; several) separate   *(five; many; several); separate.* The report cites 171 separate studies, most of them conducted during the past decade, as references. *The report cites 171 studies, most of them conducted during the past decade, as references.*

separate and apart   *apart; separate.* We agreed that these issues ought to be separate and apart from the treaty. *We agreed that these issues ought to be separate from the treaty.*

separate and autonomous   *autonomous; separate.* As separate and autonomous organizations, we are committed to "bridging education and the world of work" and agree to support and cooperate with each other. *As autonomous organizations, we are committed to "bridging education and the world of work" and agree to support and cooperate with each other.*

separate and discrete   *discrete; separate.* We found that 58 percent of respondent worksites had a separate and discrete unit that supports end-user computing. *We found that 58 percent of respondent worksites had a discrete unit that supports end-user computing.*

separate and distinct   *distinct; separate.* Each of us has four separate and distinct vocabularies: a written, a spoken, a heard, and a visual vocabulary. *Each of us has four distinct vocabularies: a written, a spoken, a heard, and a visual vocabulary.*

separate and independent   *independent; separate.* Uncoupling is complete when the partners have defined themselves and are defined by others as separate and independent of each other. *Uncoupling is complete when the partners have defined themselves and are defined by others as independent of each other.*

separate and individual   *individual; separate.* A Covered Person will be fully insured for benefits under the Policy while taking an airline trip only when the fare has been charged separately and individually to the Basic or Additional Cardmember's enrolled account. *A Covered Person will be fully insured for benefits under the Policy while taking an airline trip only when the fare has been charged separately to the Basic or Additional Cardmember's enrolled account.*

separate apart   *separate.* Within each tetrad, the sister chromosomes begin to separate apart. *Within each tetrad, the sister chromosomes begin to separate.* ■ From Egypt to China to Australia to Alaska, cultures believed that each individual had not one, but two souls, which would permanently separate apart at death unless steps were taken to prevent this division. *From Egypt to China to Australia to Alaska, cultures believed that each individual had not one, but two souls, which would permanently separate at death unless steps were taken to prevent this division.*

separate entity *entity; separate.* The artificial separation of these three dimensions is confusing when they are seen as three separate entities. *The artificial separation of these three dimensions is confusing when they are seen as three entities.*

separate individual *individual; separate.* The children were never seen and treated as separate individuals. *The children were never seen and treated as individuals.*

separate out *separate.* If length permits, we should separate out user input from other functions. *If length permits, we should separate user input from other functions.*

seriously addicted *addicted.* I was never seriously addicted to heroin. *I was never addicted to heroin.*

serve up *serve.* Can I serve you up some quiche? *Can I serve you some quiche?*

seventy-five (75) percent (of) *three-fourths; three-quarters.*

shaken up *shaken.*

share (a; the) common *share.* Group action is possible in your meeting, even when everyone does not share a common understanding of the subject. *Group action is possible in your meeting, even when everyone does not share an understanding of the subject.* ■ Cattell and Galton shared a common interest in the measurement of human capacity. *Cattell and Galton shared an interest in the measurement of human capacity.*

share ... in common (with) *share.* U.S. research on global change shares something in common with the legendary horseman who roamed the hills of Washington Irving's Sleepy Hollow: They both appear to lack heads. *U.S. research on global change shares something with the legendary horseman who roamed the hills of Washington Irving's Sleepy Hollow: They both appear to lack heads.* ■ Our research addresses issues related to corporate strategy, operations and general manage-

ment, and we focus on identifying management initiatives, processes, tools and frameworks that will allow our clients to avoid reinventing the wheel in addressing problems they share in common
with their peers. *Our research addresses issues related to corporate strategy, operations and general management, and we focus on identifying management initiatives, processes, tools and frameworks that will allow our
clients to avoid reinventing the wheel in addressing problems they share
with their peers.*

share together *share.* If there is one commitment that defines him, it
is the commitment that we share together. *If there is one commitment
that defines him, it is the commitment that we share.*

short and sweet *brief; concise; pithy; short; succinct; terse.*

short and to the point *brief; concise; pithy; short; succinct; terse; to the
point.*

should ... then *should.* Should the Department of Public Utilities concur that the blame for these plant outages rests with Boston Edison,
then the company's stockholders — not the customers — must
absorb the costs. *Should the Department of Public Utilities concur that the
blame for these plant outages rests with Boston Edison, the company's stockholders — not the customers — must absorb the costs.*

show (a; the) ... (of; to) delete. Figure 14.3 shows a comparison of
dimensions in millimeters with those in inches. *Figure 14.3 compares
dimensions in millimeters with those in inches.* ■ The respondents preferred to retain but not retrain obsolete older employees and showed
a tendency to withhold promotions from older workers. *The respondents preferred to retain but not retrain obsolete older employees and tended to withhold promotions from older workers.*

shown at (in) *at (in).* Each of the sequences shown at the right is an
arithmetic sequence. *Each of the sequences at the right is an arithmetic
sequence.*

shuttle back and forth between ... and *shuttle between ... and.* He
shuttles back and forth between his home in New Hampshire and his
office in Washington. *He shuttles between his home in New Hampshire
and his office in Washington.* ■ In 1982, Hans Toch described the largely ineffective practice of bus therapy, whereby disturbed inmates are
shuttled back and forth between mental health centers and correctional facilities. *In 1982, Hans Toch described the largely ineffective prac-*

tice of bus therapy, whereby disturbed inmates are shuttled between mental health centers and correctional facilities.

sick and tired *annoyed; disgusted; sick; tired.*

side by side (with) *alongside; among; beside; next to; with.*

significant (substantial) *ample; big; grand; great; heavy; huge; immense; large; many; most; much; vast.* The region began the decade with a significant surplus of power. *The region began the decade with a large surplus of power.*

(a; the) significant (substantial) amount (of) *a good (great) deal (of); a good (great) many (of); almost all (of); considerable; many (of); most (of); much (of); nearly all (of); vast.* This difficulty is a major stumbling block, costing end users significant amounts of time and money. *This difficulty is a major stumbling block, costing end users much time and money.*

(a; the) significant (substantial) degree (of) *a good (great) deal (of); considerable; great; much (of); vast.*

(a; the) significant (substantial) element (of) *a good (great) deal (of); a good (great) many (of); considerable; great; many (of); much (of); vast.*

(a; the) significant (substantial) fraction (of) *a good (great) deal (of); a good (great) many (of); almost all (of); (nine) in (ten) (of); many (of); most (of); much (of); nearly all (of); (43) of (48) (of); (67) percent (of); three-fourths (two-thirds) (of).* A significant fraction of leading U.S. weapons production specialists met last weekend to discuss the proposal, with predictable results. *Six of ten leading U.S. weapons production specialists met last weekend to discuss the proposal, with predictable results.*

significant importance *consequence; importance; significance.* Finally, and of significant importance, he was sensitive to our concerns for minimizing the disruption to our lives inherent to most renovation projects. *Finally, and of significance, he was sensitive to our concerns for minimizing the disruption to our lives inherent to most renovation projects.*
■ The recommendations included herein will respond not only to those stated needs, but also to other significantly important requirements that emerged during the course of our proceedings. *The recommendations included herein will respond not only to those stated needs, but also to other significant requirements that emerged during the course of our proceedings.*

significantly (substantially) *a good (great) deal; amply; far; greatly; largely; mostly; much; vastly.* Two of the 13 had slightly higher earnings; only three did substantially better. *Two of the 13 had slightly higher earnings; only three did far better.*

(a; the) significant (substantial) majority (of) *a good (great) deal (of); a good (great) many (of); almost all (of); (nine) in (ten) (of); many (of); most (of); much (of); nearly all (of); (43) of (48) (of); (67) percent (of); three-fourths (two-thirds) (of).* A substantial majority think certain reforms would improve the present primary system. *Many think certain reforms would improve the present primary system.*

(a; the) significant (substantial) minority (of) *almost half (of); fewer than half (of); (one) in (three) (of); less than half (of); nearly half (of); (20) of (48) (of); one-third (one-fifth) (of); (20) percent (of).* A significant minority of agents said that they would not sell the type of insurance our researchers requested in the amount they wanted to buy. *Eighteen of fifty agents said that they would not sell the type of insurance our researchers requested in the amount they wanted to buy.* ■ A new study indicates a significant minority of critical-care nurses are occasionally committing euthanasia. *A new study indicates one in six critical-care nurses are occasionally committing euthanasia.*

(a; the) significant (substantial) number (of) *a good (great) many (of); almost all (of); countless; dozens (of); hundreds (of); many (of); millions (of); most (of); nearly all (of); numerous; scores (of); six hundred (twelve hundred) (of); thousands (of).* We did this because we received a substantial number of reports that the election was unfair. *We did this because we received hundreds of reports that the election was unfair.*

(a; the) significant (substantial) part (of) *a good (great) deal (of); a good (great) many (of); almost all (of); (nine) in (ten) (of); many (of); most (of); much (of); nearly all (of); (43) of (48) (of); (67) percent (of); three-fourths (two-thirds) (of).* Businessland Inc. says mice represent a substantial part of its computer accessories sales. *Businessland Inc. says mice represent 8 percent of its computer accessories sales.*

(a; the) significant (substantial) percentage (of) *a good (great) deal (of); a good (great) many (of); almost all (of); (nine) in (ten) (of); many (of); most (of); much (of); nearly all (of); (43) of (48) (of); (67) percent (of); three-fourths (two-thirds) (of).* The drug can cause serious kidney damage and other side effects, and a substantial percentage of patients cannot absorb it. *The drug can cause serious kidney damage and other side effects, and many patients cannot absorb it.*

(a; the) significant (substantial) portion (of) *a good (great) deal (of); a good (great) many (of); almost all (of); (nine) in (ten) (of); many (of); most (of); much (of); nearly all (of); (43) of (48) (of); (67) percent (of); three-fourths (two-thirds) (of).* The company said that a significant portion of the cuts will be achieved through early retirement. *The company said that most of the cuts will be achieved through early retirement.*

(a; the) significant (substantial) proportion (of) *a good (great) deal (of); a good (great) many (of); almost all (of); (nine) in (ten) (of); many (of); most (of); much (of); nearly all (of); (43) of (48) (of); (67) percent (of); three-fourths (two-thirds) (of).* West German and British firms also account for a significant proportion of U.S. patents. *West German and British firms also account for many U.S. patents.*

(a; the) significant (substantial) quantity (of) *a good (great) deal (of); a good (great) many (of); almost all (of); dozens (of); hundreds (of); many (of); millions (of); most (of); nearly all (of); scores (of); six hundred (twelve hundred) (of); thousands (of).*

simple (and) fundamental *fundamental; simple.* We welcome the opportunity to present the following two descriptions of barriers and gateways to communication, in the thought that they may help to bring the problem down to earth and show what it means in terms of simple fundamentals. *We welcome the opportunity to present the following two descriptions of barriers and gateways to communication, in the thought that they may help to bring the problem down to earth and show what it means in terms of fundamentals.*

simply and solely *simply; solely.* She was fired simply and solely on account of her sex. *She was fired solely on account of her sex.*

simultaneously *as one; at once; collectively; concurrently; jointly; together.* A collaborative work group is several people working on the same document simultaneously. *A collaborative work group is several people working on the same document at once.*

simultaneously ... at the same time *at the same time; simultaneously.* We can be simultaneously hard like rock, firm, unmoving, and at the same time, soft and gentle, and flowing. *We can be hard like rock, firm, unmoving, and at the same time, soft and gentle, and flowing.* ■ All of these synchronous connections must be serviced by the program simultaneously, at the same time. *All of these synchronous connections must be serviced by the program simultaneously.*

simultaneously ... while *while.* A dissemination system must simultaneously develop the capability of people at several levels through staff development and ongoing support while it works to create a context in schools, districts, and states. *A dissemination system must develop the capability of people at several levels through staff development and ongoing support while it works to create a context in schools, districts, and states.*

simultaneous (simultaneously) with *with.* The selection of the media to be used for advertising campaigns needs to be done simultaneously with the development of message, theme, concepts, and copy. *The selection of the media to be used for advertising campaigns needs to be done with the development of message, theme, concepts, and copy.*

(ever) since that time *since; since then.* Since that time, a lot has changed in my life. *A lot has since changed in my life.*

(ever) since then *since.* Since then several states have passed laws against the misuse of sickle cell screening. *Several states have since passed laws against the misuse of sickle cell screening.*

since ... then *since.* Since the objective of unattended operation is quality, then the primary benefit is consistent, high-quality service. *Since the objective of unattended operation is quality, the primary benefit is consistent, high-quality service.* ■ Since each telephone call is sampled 8,000 times each second, then each time slot must contain a packet of 8 samples, each 8 bits in length. *Since each telephone call is sampled 8,000 times each second, each time slot must contain a packet of 8 samples, each 8 bits in length.*

single best (biggest; fastest; greatest; largest; most) *best (biggest; fastest; greatest; largest; most).* Our single biggest concern is the capacity issue. *Our biggest concern is the capacity issue.* ■ The BSA does give its prestigious annual Harleston Parker Award for the single best new building in the Boston area. *The BSA does give its prestigious annual Harleston Parker Award for the best new building in the Boston area.*

sink down *sink.*

(a; the) -sion (-tion) of (that; to) *-ing.* Determination of consumer's needs requires greater attention. *Determining consumer's needs requires greater attention.* ■ Their subordinates are nonmanagement workers — the group on which management depends for the execution of their plans. *Their subordinates are nonmanagement workers — the group* *on which management depends for executing their plans.* ■ Self-improvement and career planning both begin with an identification of your skills. *Self-improvement and career planning both begin with identifying your skills.* ■ I would suggest that, given the importance of building confidence in these tradesmen-turned-entrepreneurs to the proposal, inclusion of more background on them would be a good idea. *I would suggest that, given the importance of building confidence in these tradesmen-turned-entrepreneurs to the proposal, including more background on them would be a good idea.*

situated   delete. Many of the hospital incinerators are situated in heavily populated areas. *Many of the hospital incinerators are in heavily populated areas.*

(a; the) ... situation   delete. We are in a crisis situation. *We are in a crisis.* ■ If he doesn't do something, it could be an embarrassing situation for him. *If he doesn't do something, it could be embarrassing for him.*

skilled craftsman (craftswoman)   *craftsman (craftswoman).* High wages ensure skilled craftsmen will work on public projects, saving money in the long run on repairing shoddy work. *High wages ensure craftsmen will work on public projects, saving money in the long run on repairing shoddy work.*

skirt around   *skirt.*

slight trace   *trace.*

(a; the) small (tiny) amount (degree; part; percentage; portion; proportion; quantity) (of)   *a couple (of); a few (of); a handful (of); fewer than half (of); hardly any (of); (one) in (ten) (of); less than half (of); not many (of); (9) of (48) (of); one or two (two or three) (of); one-third (one-fifteenth) (of); (12) percent (of); scarcely any (of).* Only a small percentage of the state's bridges will be repaired. *Only one-fourth of the state's bridges will be repaired.*

(a; the) smaller (tinier) amount (degree; part; percentage; portion; proportion; quantity) (of)   *less.* Americans are spending a smaller percentage of their incomes on food than ever before. *Americans are spending less of their incomes on food than ever before.* ■ The result will likely be more work done in a smaller amount of time. *The result will likely be more work done in less time.*

(a; the) smaller (tinier) number (of)   *fewer.* The instructor would back off, slow down, and give students a chance to follow and absorb the development of a smaller number of scientific ideas. *The instructor would back off, slow down, and give students a chance to follow and absorb the development of fewer scientific ideas.*

(a; the) small (tiny) fraction (of) *a couple (of); a few (of); a handful (of); fewer than half (of); hardly any (of); (one) in (ten) (of); less than half (of); not many (of); (9) of (48) (of); one or two (two or three) (of); one-third (one-fifteenth) (of); (12) percent (of); scarcely any (of).* His deputy sold only a small fraction of his stock, not one-third as reported. *His deputy sold only one-twelfth of his stock, not one-third as reported.*

(a; the) small (tiny) minority (of) *a couple (of); a few (of); a handful (of); fewer than half (of); hardly any (of); (one) in (ten) (of); less than half (of); not many (of); (9) of (48) (of); one or two (two or three) (of); one-third (one-fifteenth) (of); (12) percent (of); scarcely any (of).* A small minority may be troubled or are troublemakers. *A few may be troubled or are troublemakers.*

(a; the) small (tiny) number (of) *a couple; a few; eight (four); hardly any; not many; one or two (two or three); scarcely any.* Many observers believe that by the turn of the century only a small number of giant financial supermarkets will cover the range of financial services. *Many observers believe that by the turn of the century only eight giant financial supermarkets will cover the range of financial services.* ■ A relatively small number of the examples in this chapter have a direct engineering application. *Few of the examples in this chapter have a direct engineering application.*

small (tiny) particle *particle.* With the high speeds and small spaces involved, even a small particle can cause the readwrite head to crash. *With the high speeds and small spaces involved, even a particle can cause the readwrite head to crash.*

small (tiny) peccadillo *peccadillo.* But this is only a small peccadillo and we will continue to commit it unabashed. *But this is only a peccadillo and we will continue to commit it unabashed.*

small-size(d) *small.*

so as to *to.* Salespeople often make their estimates low so as to keep their sales quotas down and make them easier to attain. *Salespeople often make their estimates low to keep their sales quotas down and make them easier to attain.*

sociological *sociologic.*

so consequently *consequently; hence; so; then; therefore; thus.*

some but not all *a few; several; some.* Some studies, but not all, found cancerous tumors in rats and mice fed dye chemicals. *Some studies found cancerous tumors in rats and mice fed dye chemicals.*

some day (time) in the future *at length; eventually; in due time; in the end; in time; later; one day; over the months (years); over time; someday; sometime; ultimately; with time; yet.* Some time in the future, the problems could precipitate a crisis — a run on the dollar, a decline in living standards — the price the United States must pay for its profligacy. *Eventually, the problems could precipitate a crisis — a run on the dollar, a decline in living standards — the price the United States must pay for its profligacy.*

somehow or other *in some way; somehow; someway(s).* Somehow or other, people get used to a system, even if it takes a little time. *Somehow, people get used to a system, even if it takes a little time.*

someplace (somewhere) else *elsewhere.* The meeting should run no more than two or three hours and provide obvious benefits for being there instead of somewhere else. *The meeting should run no more than two or three hours and provide obvious benefits for being there instead of elsewhere.*

something like *or so; some.* Pensions and Social Security may provide, on average, something like 60 percent of the household's prior working income. *Pensions and Social Security may provide, on average, some 60 percent of the household's prior working income.*

somewhere along the line (the way) *at some point; at some time.* Somewhere along the way, people got the idea that biotechnology is a magic solution to the food problem. *At some point, people got the idea that biotechnology is a magic solution to the food problem.*

somewhere around (round) *or so; some.*

sooner or later *eventually; ultimately; yet.*

sort of delete. I'm sort of curious to find out what your thoughts are. *I'm curious to find out what your thoughts are.*

so therefore *hence; so; then; therefore; thus.*

speciality *specialty.*

springtime *spring.*

stall for time *stall.*

stand in (marked; sharp) contrast to *clash with; conflict with; contest; contradict; contrast with; differ from; disagree with; dispute; oppose.* That view stands in sharp contrast to those expressed by legislators and state business leaders. *That view sharply differs from those expressed by legislators and state business leaders.*

stand in need of *need; require.* The country stands in need of a strong gesture in support of both science and education. *The country needs a strong gesture in support of both science and education.*

stand in opposition to *conflict with; contest; disagree with; disapprove of; dispute; object to; oppose; protest; resist.*

stand in support of *back; endorse; favor; prefer; support.* With only 8 of the 1,176 voting delegates refusing to stand in support of the election, it appears Lee may have won the mandate he has been seeking. *With only 8 of the 1,176 voting delegates refusing to support the election, it appears Lee may have won the mandate he has been seeking.*

stand in the way of *block; frustrate; hinder; impede; interfere with; obstruct; prevent; thwart.* The public health threat posed by AIDS is so great that we must find ways to overcome social and cultural taboos that stand in the way of improved AIDS prevention. *The public health threat posed by AIDS is so great that we must find ways to overcome social and cultural taboos that thwart improved AIDS prevention.*

start off (out) *start.* Lotus 1-2-3 assumes that you would prefer to start off by typing information into the worksheet. *Lotus 1-2-3 assumes that you would prefer to start by typing information into the worksheet.* ■ She started off by showing a hilarious example of how her parents wrapped her Christmas gifts when she was a child. *She started by showing a hilarious example of how her parents wrapped her Christmas gifts when she was a child.*

(a; the) ... state of *delete.* All cultural dimensions of a society and individuals are in a constant state of flux. *All cultural dimensions of a* *society and individuals are in constant flux.* ■ Although still in its infancy, and in a state of transition, the ASP market has been hopping for the past two years. *Although still in its infancy, and in transition, the ASP market has been hopping for the past two years.*

stereotypical *stereotypic.* These theorists believe women have been taught and conditioned in stereotypical role behavior that predisposes them to the development of agoraphobia. *These theorists believe women have been taught and conditioned in stereotypic role behavior that predisposes them to the development of agoraphobia.*

sticktoitiveness *determination; perseverance; persistence; resolve; tenacity.* Loyalty, empathy, diligence, and sticktoitiveness are highly regarded, whether in a co-worker or a friend. *Loyalty, empathy, diligence, and resolve are highly regarded, whether in a co-worker or a friend.*

still and all *even so; still; yet.*

still continue (endure; last; persevere; persist; prevail; remain; survive) *continue (endure; last; persevere; persist; prevail; remain; survive); still.* The department has set up an internal review process to deal with some of these cases, but problems still persist. *The department has set up an internal review process to deal with some of these cases, but problems persist.* ■ Unfortunately, that attitude still prevails today. *Unfortunately, that attitude prevails today.*

still in existence *current; extant; surviving.*

stoical *stoic.*

straight horizontal (vertical) *horizontal (vertical).*

strange to relate (say) *oddly; strangely.* Strange to say, that interest does not seem to be more than a few hundred years old. *Strangely, that interest does not seem to be more than a few hundred years old.*

strangle to death *strangle.* The ex-wife of South Africa's last apartheid president was stabbed and strangled to death in her luxury beachfront flat. *The ex-wife of South Africa's last apartheid president was stabbed and strangled in her luxury beachfront flat.*

stressed out *stressed.*

strong point (suit) *forte.*

study up *study.*

subject (topic) area (field; matter) *area; field; subject; theme; topic.* Each new title is arranged by subject area. *Each new title is arranged by subject.*

subsequently *after; afterward; later; since (then); then.* He resigned his positions in 1963 and was subsequently jailed. *He resigned his positions in 1963 and was later jailed.* ■ I have subsequently learned the manner in which Mr. Satoh was chosen for the position. *I have since learned the manner in which Mr. Satoh was chosen for the position.*

subsequent to (that; this) *after; afterward; later; since (then); then.* Subsequent to that, I had surgery to remove half of my stomach. *Afterward, I had surgery to remove half of my stomach.*

subsequent to the time (of; that; when) *after; following.* The stock can be transferred any time subsequent to the time that a person actually receives it. *The stock can be transferred any time after a person actually receives it.*

substantiality *substance.* Jackson has exhibited a remarkable degree of substantiality and common sense. *Jackson has exhibited a remarkable degree of substance and common sense.*

substantiate *back up; confirm; prove; support; verify.* Recent studies clearly substantiate the health and economic advantage of car safety seat belts. *Recent studies clearly confirm the health and economic advantage of car safety seat belts.*

substantive *ample; big; grand; great; heavy; huge; immense; large; many; most; much; vast.* The recent improvement in the economic well-being of most nations occurred without substantive change in the physical bulk or weight of gross national product. *The recent improvement in the economic well-being of most nations occurred without much change in the physical bulk or weight of gross national product.*

succumb to (the) illness (injuries) *die.* Shortly after Harold's return, his father succumbed to the illness. *Shortly after Harold's return, his father died.*

such as ... and others (and so forth; and so on; and such; and the like; et al.; etc.; or whatever) *and others (and so forth; and so on; and such; and the like; et al.; etc.; or); like; such as.* In addition to individuals, you may select a topic that informs your audience about groups of people such as skinheads, the Mafia, Aborigines, Motown musicians, and others. *In addition to individuals, you may select a topic that informs your audience about groups of people such as skinheads, the Mafia, Aborigines, and Motown musicians.* ■ You can explore the results of various approaches such as gross margin, markup over cost, and so on. *You can explore the results of various approaches such as gross margin and markup over cost.* ■ Weevils are very destructive pests which can decimate stored whole grain products such as corn, wheat, barley, rice, etc. *Weevils are very destructive pests which can decimate stored whole grain products such as corn, wheat, barley, rice.*

such as ... for example (for instance) *as; for example (for instance); like; such as.* One of the book's main themes is the "fact" that women were responsible for all the important contributions to the advancement of civilization (such as the development of agriculture, for instance), often despite the arrogance and stupidity of men. *One of the book's main themes is the "fact" that women were responsible for all the important contributions to the advancement of civilization (such as the development of agriculture), often despite the arrogance and stupidity of men.* ■ If a substance is not on our chart (such as vanadium, for example), it's not yet considered essential by the National Academy of Sciences. *If a substance is not on our chart (vanadium, for example), it's not yet considered essential by the National Academy of Sciences.* ■ They also don't support other advanced elements of FrontPage Web sites, such as input forms, for example. *They also don't support other advanced elements of FrontPage Web sites, such as input forms.*

such as (your)self *like (you).* It's very rare that we have an opportunity to talk to someone such as yourself. *It's very rare that we have an opportunity to talk to someone like you.*

such is the case *so it is.* Such is the case with an individual who is considered a high potential in a semiconductor firm. *So it is with an individual who is considered a high potential in a semiconductor firm.*

suddenly and without warning *suddenly; without warning.* Survivors said the pier in Butterworth, 180 miles northwest of Kuala Lumpur, collapsed suddenly and without warning yesterday. *Survivors said the pier in Butterworth, 180 miles northwest of Kuala Lumpur, collapsed suddenly yesterday.* ■ Most workers seldom think about the financial consequences of long-term disability and that the disability can occur suddenly and without warning. *Most workers seldom think about the financial consequences of long-term disability and that the disability can* *occur without warning.*

sufficient (sufficiently) *due (duly); enough.* Bright ideas alone are not sufficient. *Bright ideas alone are not enough.* ■ Since responsibility is assigned not to individuals but to the group, members may not devote sufficient time and effort to the task. *Since responsibility is assigned not to individuals but to the group, members may not devote due time and effort to the task.*

(a; the) sufficient amount (of) *due; enough.* It's time we include a sufficient amount of money in the state budget for snow removal. *It's time we include enough money in the state budget for snow removal.*

sufficient (sufficiently) enough *duly; enough; sufficiently.* There may be an economy of scale if the outcome is sufficiently rigorous enough to warrant the state's participation. *There may be an economy of scale if the outcome is sufficiently rigorous to warrant the state's participation.*

(a; the) sufficient number (of) *enough; five (ninety).* If it gains the sufficient number of signatures to qualify, we'll have to watch it even more carefully. *If it gains enough signatures to qualify, we'll have to watch it even more carefully.*

sum (summary) and substance *center; core; crux; essence; gist; heart; pith; substance; sum; summary.* He asked, in summary and substance, whether GAF wanted to have Union Carbide close at a specific price for several days in a row. *He asked, in essence, whether GAF wanted to have Union Carbide close at a specific price for several days in a row.*

summation *sum; total.* The summation of these products is 4320.154. *The sum of these products is 4320.154.*

summertime *summer.* Even in summertime, snow sometimes occurs high up in rain clouds, and the flakes can terminate the arc of a rainbow. *Even in summer, snow sometimes occurs high up in rain clouds, and the flakes can terminate the arc of a rainbow.*

summing up *in brief; in fine; in short; in sum.* Summing up, I feel strongly that my criteria capture the characteristics of firms that are likely to be successful in the Information Age. *In sum, I feel strongly that my criteria capture the characteristics of firms that are likely to be successful in the Information Age.*

sum total *sum; total.* Women have always commanded over half the sum total of human intelligence and creativity. *Women have always commanded over half the total of human intelligence and creativity.*

sum up *add; sum; total.*

superimpose one ... on top of (over) another (the other) *superimpose.* Overlays allow you to superimpose one data range on top of another. *Overlays allow you to superimpose data ranges.*

surrounded on all sides *surrounded.* Cyclones are areas of low pressure that are surrounded on all sides by high pressure. *Cyclones are areas of low pressure that are surrounded by high pressure.*

swallow down *swallow.*

switch over *switch.* School systems in Maryland and California tried to switch over after the 1975 legislation. *School systems in Maryland and California tried to switch after the 1975 legislation.*

sworn affidavit *affidavit.*

symbolical *symbolic.* I think the present change is more symbolical than realistic. *I think the present change is more symbolic than realistic.*

symmetrical *symmetric.* If one of the functions is symmetrical, then reflection is unnecessary. *If one of the functions is symmetric, then reflection is unnecessary.*

symptomatize *symptomize.*

systematic *systemic.*

systematical *systematic; systemic.*

T

tailor-made *custom; tailored.* The event seemed tailor-made to give the vice president the upper hand. *The event seemed tailored to give the vice president the upper hand.*

take account for (of) *allow for; consider; provide for; reckon with; regard; weigh.* But HMO officials say that current reimbursements fail to take account for medical inflation. *But HMO officials say that current reimbursements fail to allow for medical inflation.*

take action (to) *act; delete.* If we are to save the right whales, we will have to take action. *If we are to save the right whales, we will have to act.*

take ... action (on; to) *act -(al)ly; delete.* The operator has to determine the cause of the deviation and then take corrective action. *The operator has to determine the cause of the deviation and then correct it.* ■ He issued a statement calling on the NRC to take immediate action to correct deficiencies identified in the report. *He issued a statement calling on the NRC to act immediately to correct deficiencies identified in the report.*

take advantage of *abuse; cheat; deceive; exploit; ill-treat; mistreat; misuse; use; victimize; wrong.* He took advantage of her good nature. *He exploited her good nature.*

take advantage of *benefit from; gain; profit by; reap.* There are several easy ways to take advantage of Fidelity's expertise in retirement planning. *There are several easy ways to profit by Fidelity's expertise in retirement planning.*

take aim *aim.*

take a ... look (at) *consider; look; regard; view.* We need to examine each, but let's first take a brief look at the foundations of management theory. *We need to examine each, but let's first briefly look at the foundations of management theory.*

take a measure of *approximate; estimate.* The balance sheet yields financial data that can be used in various ratio calculations to take a measure of the company's financial health. *The balance sheet yields financial data that can be used in various ratio calculations to estimate the company's financial health.*

take a stand against (in opposition to) *contest; contradict; contrast with; differ from; disagree with; dispute; oppose; resist.*

take a stand for (in favor of; in support of) *back; endorse; favor; prefer; support.* Delegates at the annual meeting of the American Medical Association took a strong stand in favor of abortion rights this week. *Delegates at the annual meeting of the American Medical Association strongly backed abortion rights this week.*

take a (the) ... view (of) *consider; look; regard; view.* Financial institutions can no longer take a passive view of product development. *Financial institutions can no longer regard product development passively.*

take delivery of (on) *accept; acquire; buy; collect; confiscate; get; obtain; possess; procure; purchase; receive; seize; take.* When you take delivery of the phone it is immediately ready to use. *When you receive the phone it is immediately ready to use.*

take enjoyment in *admire; delight in; enjoy; rejoice in; relish; savor.* Team members take enjoyment in their work and in their interactions with others at work. *Team members enjoy their work and their interactions with others at work.*

take exception to *challenge; complain about; criticize; demur; differ in; disagree with; dispute; find fault with; object to; oppose; protest; question; resent.* I take exception to the statement: "Angiography is not only expensive but also painful and risky." *I disagree with the statement: "Angiography is not only expensive but also painful and risky."*

take (a) hold of *grasp; seize; take.*

take into account *allow for; consider; provide for; reckon with; regard; weigh.* It fails to take into account the impact of the U.S. federal budget deficit on U.S. competitiveness. *It fails to regard the impact of the U.S. federal budget deficit on U.S. competitiveness.*

take into consideration *allow for; consider; provide for; reckon with; regard; weigh.* His prior offenses, even though they were in a different state, can be taken into consideration by the court. *His prior offenses, even though they were in a different state, can be weighed by the court.*

take into custody *arrest; capture; catch; seize.*

take issue (with) *attack; challenge; contradict; demur; differ (with); dis-*

agree (with); dispute; object (to); oppose; question. He also takes issue with the state plan to pay. *He also opposes the state plan to pay.*

take measures (to) *act (to);* delete.

taken by surprise *startled; surprised.* Everyone I talked to today was taken by surprise by his announcement. *Everyone I talked to today was surprised by his announcement.*

take note of *attend to; consider; hearken to; heed; listen to; mind; note; notice; observe; regard; see; tend to; watch; witness.* The United States should take note of the percentage of technical graduates and lawyers in Japan's population. *The United States should note the percentage of technical graduates and lawyers in Japan's population.*

take notice of *attend to; consider; hearken; heed; listen to; mind; note; notice; observe; regard; see; tend to; watch; witness.* Clouds in the extremely dry stratosphere were rarely sighted — mostly because they form near the poles only during winter and early spring, when darkness eclipses the sky and few spectators are around to take notice. *Clouds in the extremely dry stratosphere were rarely sighted — mostly because they form near the poles only during winter and early spring, when darkness eclipses the sky and few spectators are around to watch.*

take offense at *disagree with; dislike; object to; resent.* I take offense at the *Globe*'s editorial ("Scorsese and the stone-casters") and will no longer sit by and watch the Christian-bashing continue. *I resent the Globe's editorial ("Scorsese and the stone-casters") and will no longer sit by and watch the Christian-bashing continue.*

take pity on (upon) *pity; sympathize (with).*

take place *happen; occur.*

take pleasure in *admire; delight in; enjoy; rejoice in; relish (in); savor.*

take possession of *accept; acquire; buy; collect; confiscate; get; obtain; possess; procure; purchase; receive; seize; take.* The airline said that it will take possession of all 43 aircraft scheduled for 2001, the majority of which were delivered to United prior to September 11, 2001. *The airline said that it will accept all 43 aircraft scheduled for 2001, the majority of which were delivered to United prior to September 11, 2001.*

take precedence over *antecede; come before; exceed; forego; go before; outrank; precede; surpass; transcend.* Criminals' rights take precedence over the victims'. *Criminals' rights come before the victims'.* ■ Generic standards take precedence over basic standards while product standards take precedence over generic standards. *Generic standards forego basic standards while product standards forego generic standards.*

take priority over *antecede; come before; forego; go before; precede.* He says that in women's shoes, fashion always takes priority over comfort. *He says that in women's shoes, fashion always precedes comfort.*

take satisfaction in *admire; appreciate; be pleased with; delight in; enjoy; like; rejoice in; relish (in); savor.* Brown alumni can take satisfaction in the contributions their college has made during 175 years both in the sacrifices of war and the arts of peace. *Brown alumni can delight in the contributions their college has made during 175 years both in the sacrifices of war and the arts of peace.* ■ Encourage your child to compare recent achievements with earlier efforts and to take satisfaction in their progress. *Encourage your child to compare recent achievements with earlier efforts and to be pleased with their progress.*

take the position (that) *assert; believe; claim; consider; contend; feel; hold; judge; maintain; regard; say; think; to; view.* He takes the position that, as a meeting leader, you will be more effective if you view yourself "as the servant of the group rather than as its master." *He maintains that, as a meeting leader, you will be more effective if you view yourself "as the servant of the group rather than as its master."*

take the view (that) *assert; believe; claim; consider; contend; feel; hold; judge; maintain; regard; say; think; to; view.*

take the wrong way *misinterpret; misunderstand.*

take to task *admonish; chide; criticize; rebuke; reprimand; reproach; reprove; scold.* He took the project's tenant leaders to task for their selection of an architectural consultant for the remodeling job. *He admonished the project's tenant leaders for their selection of an architectural consultant for the remodeling job.*

take umbrage at (with) *disagree with; dislike; object to; resent.* Some people, such as the NRA, took umbrage with the message of the show. *Some people, such as the NRA, disliked the message of the show.*

take under advisement *consider; contemplate; reflect on; review; think* *about; weigh.* Pillsbury's board is taking the franchisee group's protest under advisement. *Pillsbury's board is reviewing the franchisee group's protest.*

take under consideration *consider; contemplate; reflect on; review; think about; weigh.* About 1 in 50 products is taken under consideration. *About 1 in 50 products is considered.*

tell the difference *discriminate; distinguish; tell apart.* The reality is that science and technology have made it almost impossible to tell the difference between telecommunications and computers. *The reality is that science and technology have made it almost impossible to distinguish between telecommunications and computers.*

temperature *fever.*

temporary reprieve *reprieve.*

temporary stopgap *stopgap.*

(my) tendency is to *(I) tend to.* Our tendency is to get up a little later each morning and go to sleep a little later each night. *We tend to get up a little later each morning and go to sleep a little later each night.*

tense up *tense.*

term as *term.* They term agents whose behavior depends on past history as "hysteretic agents." *They term agents whose behavior depends on past history "hysteretic agents."* ■ In college, you will be primarily dealing with what is termed as expository writing. *In college, you will be primarily dealing with what is termed expository writing.*

terminate *cancel; cease; conclude; end; finish; halt; stop.* Having no plan at all would be better than terminating one. *Having no plan at all would be better than canceling one.*

test out *test.* At this point, you might want to test out our map by trying the following experiment. *At this point, you might want to test our map by trying the following experiment.*

that (this) being the case *consequently; hence; so; then; therefore; thus.* That being the case, the only apparent remedy is for owners of family firms to begin early in earmarking shares of the business for their children. *The only apparent remedy, then, is for owners of family firms to* *begin early in earmarking shares of the business for their children.* ■ That being the case, many financial advisors recommend a technique called "laddering" CDs for those individuals willing to commit their funds for longer periods in order to earn a higher rate of return. *Thus, many financial advisors recommend a technique called "laddering" CDs for those individuals willing to commit their funds for longer periods in order to earn a higher rate of return.*

that (the; this) business of *that (this);* delete. We've got to get over this business of seeing everything in cartoon terms. *We've got to get over seeing everything in cartoon terms.*

that (this) fact *that (this).* The world beyond visual range is a haze of anxiety, and the most sophisticated radar sets in the world do not change that fact. *The world beyond visual range is a haze of anxiety, and the most sophisticated radar sets in the world do not change that.*

that (which) happens (occurs; takes place) when *when.* What about the inevitable disappointment that happens when a child doesn't win a trophy? *What about the inevitable disappointment when a child doesn't win a trophy?*

that is delete. This relates to the cost that is incurred by start-up firms. *This relates to the cost incurred by start-up firms.*

that is (this is; which is) as much as to say (that) *namely; that is; to wit.* That is as much as to say that it is perfectly natural while it is gloriously supernatural. *That is, it is perfectly natural while it is gloriously supernatural.*

that is (which is) to say (that) *namely; that is; to wit.* That is to say, the person named by the testator in his will will normally be appointed by the court, despite lack of great intelligence or experience. *That is, the person named by the testator in his will will normally be appointed by the court, despite lack of great intelligence or experience.*

that (this) kind (sort; type) of stuff (thing) *it; that (this);* delete. If there's a lot of that kind of thing, I will try to figure out whether things will stay depressed forever. *If there's a lot of that, I will try to figure out whether things will stay depressed forever.*

that (this) juncture (moment; period; point; stage) in time *(just; right) now; that (this) time; then.* Not until that moment in time did I understand what being homeless meant. *Not until then did I under-*

stand what being homeless meant.

that (those) of -'s. Toronto's population is close to 3 million, which is slightly larger than that of Boston. *Toronto's population is close to 3 million, which is slightly larger than Boston's.* ■ As the more aggrieved party, the victim's rights must take precedence over those of the perpetrator. *As the more aggrieved party, the victim's rights must take precedence over the perpetrator's.*

that (these; this; those) of delete. Another exercise is that of completing the views when some or all of them have missing lines. *Another exercise is completing the views when some or all of them have missing lines.*

(of) that (these; this; those) delete. For those calculators that do not have a 10x key, the antilogarithm can be found by using the INV or 2nd key. *For calculators that do not have a 10x key, the antilogarithm can be found by using the INV or 2nd key.* ■ Those options with the word patch in their titles are especially complicated. *Options with the word patch in their titles are especially complicated.*

that (this) time around (round) *that (this) time; then (now).* Such an outcome has a far higher probability this time around. *Such an outcome has a far higher probability now.*

the above *that; the; this.* Please call me if you have any questions concerning the above. *Please call me if you have any questions concerning this.*

the above-mentioned *that (those); the; this (these).*

the act of delete. The act of making sketches and writing statements about the problem helps to get the designer off dead center. *Making sketches and writing statements about the problem helps to get the designer off dead center.*

the aforementioned *that (those); the; this (these).* Each of the aforementioned techniques can be used to solve a specific employee problem in the workplace. *Each of these techniques can be used to solve a specific employee problem in the workplace.*

the aforesaid *that (those); the; this (these).*

the age of delete. It predicts a tightening labor market will force the hiring of more people between the ages of 35 and 45. *It predicts a tightening labor market will force the hiring of more people between 35 and 45.*

the area of (the ... area) delete. The main interest for me is the history area. *The main interest for me is history.* ■ These teams should be granted broad functions, with key roles being played by representatives from the engineering, manufacturing, marketing, and finance areas. *These teams should be granted broad functions, with key roles being played by representatives from engineering, manufacturing, marketing, and finance.*

the (this) author (reader; writer) *I; he; her; him; me; she; them; they; us; we;* delete. Every word processing manual the authors have seen assumes you know what a hanging indent, widow, and running header are. *Every word processing manual we have seen assumes you know what a hanging indent, widow, and running header are.* ■ The athletic Springsteen is back in this new tour, judging from the opening night this writer caught at the Meadowlands. *The athletic Springsteen is back in this new tour, judging from the opening night I caught at the Meadowlands.* ■ The author is unaware if any such experiments have been performed. *She is unaware if any such experiments have been performed.* ■ This book is meant to help the reader learn how to program in C. *This book is meant to help you learn how to program in C.* ■ This reader was dismayed by his cynical and narrow view of the public sector. *I was dismayed by his cynical and narrow view of the public sector.*

the better part (of) *almost all; most; nearly all.* Manufacturers Hanover Corp. spent the better part of 175 years reaching the top of American banking alongside the Citicorps and Chase Manhattans. *Manufacturers Hanover Corp. spent most of 175 years reaching the top of American banking alongside the Citicorps and Chase Manhattans.*

the biggest (greatest; highest; largest) amount (degree; extent; number; part; percentage; portion; proportion; quantity) (of) *(the) most.* The concept of calories has been well embedded in the minds of people throughout the largest portion of the twentieth century. *The concept of calories has been well embedded in the minds of people throughout most of the twentieth century.*

the both (of) *both.* I saw the both of them on a talk show today. *I saw both of them on a talk show today.* ■ It is uncomfortable for the both of us. *It is uncomfortable for both of us.*

the (great) bulk (of) *almost all; most; nearly all*. Unfortunately for the startups, though, a few major players have secured the bulk of the orders. *Unfortunately for the startups, though, a few major players have secured most of the orders.*

the case *right; so; true*; delete. I think that's probably the case. *I think that's probably true.* ■ Such companies are often durable goods manufacturers, but this is not always the case. *Such companies are often durable goods manufacturers, but this is not always so.*

the character of delete. He played the character of a picaro. *He played a picaro.*

the city (town) of delete. In the city of Chicago, there are a lot of counseling centers. *In Chicago, there are a lot of counseling centers.*

the color delete. I noticed the predominance of the color green in their costumes. *I noticed the predominance of green in their costumes.*

the ... company delete. In 1986, the Hitachi company displaced General Electric as the firm receiving the most U.S. patents. *In 1986, Hitachi displaced General Electric as the firm receiving the most U.S. patents.*

the concept of delete. The following example illustrates the concept of correlation. *The following example illustrates correlation.*

the condition of delete. British companies do not hesitate to go to the market with a share issue when the condition of the balance sheet warrants it. *British companies do not hesitate to go to the market with a share issue when the balance sheet warrants it.* ■ The condition of his health has deteriorated. *His health has deteriorated.*

the continent of (the ... continent) delete. Despite droughts, floods, wars, and low oil and commodity prices, the African continent as a whole is better off now than a year ago. *Despite droughts, floods, wars, and low oil and commodity prices, Africa as a whole is better off now than a year ago.*

the country of delete. Revelation was first written for Christians living in seven cities in Asia Minor, in what today is the country of Turkey. *Revelation was first written for Christians living in seven cities in Asia Minor, in what today is Turkey.*

the date of delete. This paper illustrated this definition with examples supplemented by Nancy Mew, the speaker on the date of September 26, 2000. *This paper illustrated this definition with examples supplemented by Nancy Mew, the speaker on September 26, 2000.*

the decade (period; period of time; span of time; time; years) between ... and *between ... and; from ... through (to); to.*

the decade (period; period of time; span of time; time; years) (from) ... through (till; to; until) *between ... and; from ... through (to); to.* The United Nations General Assembly recently declared the decade from 1990-2000 to be the International Decade of Natural Disaster Reduction. *The United Nations General Assembly recently declared 1990 to 2000 to be the International Decade of Natural Disaster Reduction.*

the degree of *how much; the;* delete. The closer the value of r to either extreme, the greater the degree of association. *The closer the value of r to either extreme, the greater the association.* ■ I am concerned with the degree of difficulty they're having getting the product out. *I am concerned with how much difficulty they're having getting the product out.*

the degree to which *how; how far; how much; how often.* The GOP's principal concern is the degree to which the law would regulate child-care facilities nationwide. *The GOP's principal concern is how much the law would regulate child-care facilities nationwide.*

the equal (equivalent) of *equal (equivalent) to; like.* The loss of 1 high-value customer was the equivalent of losing the business of 36 small-value customers. *The loss of 1 high-value customer was equivalent to losing the business of 36 small-value customers.*

the existence of delete. The existence of even one extra, undocumented Write statement in a module may change what appears on a user's terminal. *Even one extra, undocumented Write statement in a module may change what appears on a user's terminal.*

the extent of *how much; the;* delete. Most people know something about Social Security, but few know the extent of the monthly benefits they will eventually receive when they retire. *Most people know something about Social Security, but few know the monthly benefits they will eventually receive when they retire.* ■ Despite early campaign rhetoric, the extent of actual change a new treasurer would attempt is of course unknown. *Despite early campaign rhetoric, how much actual change a new treasurer would attempt is of course unknown.*

the extent to which *how; how far; how much; how often.* The extent to which these facilitating and reconciling capabilities are needed, and how they are developed and structured, depends on the company's involvement in exporting or foreign marketing. *How much these facilitating and reconciling capabilities are needed, and how they are developed and structured, depends on the company's involvement in exporting or foreign marketing.* ■ Eastern cannot predict the extent to which its operations and financial results will continue to be affected by the negative public perception generated by the investigations. *Eastern cannot predict how its operations and financial results will continue to be affected by the negative public perception generated by the investigations.*

the fact that *that.* This ignores the fact that increased use of kilowatts has significantly decreased our use of oil. *This ignores that increased use of kilowatts has significantly decreased our use of oil.*

the fact is (that) *actually; indeed; in fact; in faith; in truth; really; truly;* delete. The fact is we have to deal with the public every day. *We have to deal with the public every day.* ■ The fact is that Mrs. Eddy doesn't advocate any kind of a positive thinking or "think good, feel good" philosophy. *Indeed, Mrs. Eddy doesn't advocate any kind of a positive thinking or "think good, feel good" philosophy.*

the (simple) fact of the matter is (that) *actually; indeed; in fact; in faith; in reality; in truth; really; truly;* delete. The fact of the matter is you cannot copyright an idea. *You cannot copyright an idea.*

the fact remains (that) delete. The fact remains we have the overwhelming support of the Christian and Jewish religions. *We have the overwhelming support of the Christian and Jewish religions.*

(what is) the fashion (manner; way) (in which; that) *how.* What do you think about the fashion in which this testing program was introduced into the plant? *What do you think about how this testing program was introduced into the plant?* ■ More important than the sample's size is the manner in which the sample is taken. *More important than the sample's size is how the sample is taken.*

the feeling of delete.

the female (male) gender (sex) *females; males; men; women.* I like talking to the female gender. *I like talking to women.*

the field of delete. This process became known as Boolean algebra and is widely used in the fields of computing and philosophy. *This process became known as Boolean algebra and is widely used in computing and philosophy.*

the foregoing *that (those); the; this (these).* On top of the foregoing, the recent legislation on extending mandatory retirement further heightens the concern about job performance in the later years. *On top of this, the recent legislation on extending mandatory retirement further heightens the concern about job performance in the later years.*

the forenamed *that (those); the; this (these).*

the function of delete. The function of settling disputes requires the exercise of tact and concern for resolution of conflicts. *Settling disputes requires the exercise of tact and concern for resolution of conflicts.*

the heart of the matter *center; core; crux; essence; gist; heart; pith; substance; sum.*

the history of delete. For the first time in the history of this century, the death penalty is extended beyond the borders of a single country, in spite of the laws of other countries. *For the first time in this century, the death penalty is extended beyond the borders of a single country, in spite of the laws of other countries.*

the hows and (the) whys *aims; causes; goals; motives; purposes; reasons.* Our association has attempted to encourage proactive lending in low-income communities by working with the Fed to educate banks about the hows and whys of these investment opportunities. *Our association has attempted to encourage proactive lending in low-income communities by working with the Fed to educate banks about the aims of these investment opportunities.*

the idea of delete. A large number of today's teens have actually thought about the idea of suicide. *A large number of today's teens have actually thought about suicide.*

the interesting thing is (that) *interestingly;* delete. The interesting thing is that he never realized what he had done. *He never realized what he had done.*

the issue of delete. We shall first consider the issue of plotting the historical series we want to analyze. *We shall first consider plotting the historical series we want to analyze.*

theistical *theistic.*

the language of (the ... language) delete. Twelve of his novels have been translated into the Russian language. *Twelve of his novels have been translated into Russian.*

the last time *last.* A fifth bit acts as a flag indicating whether the file has been modified since the last time it was backed up. *A fifth bit acts as a flag indicating whether the file has been modified since it was last backed up.*

the length of time *how long; the time.* The purpose of a network is to show all activities needed to complete a project and to enable the planner to calculate the length of time a project will take from start to finish. *The purpose of a network is to show all activities needed to complete a project and to enable the planner to calculate the time a project will take from start to finish.*

the lion's share *almost all; most; nearly all.*

the long and (the) short *center; core; crux; essence; gist; heart; pith; substance; sum.*

the manifestation of delete. Looking first at managers, one once again sees the manifestation of the tendency toward caution with age. *Looking first at managers, one once again sees the tendency toward caution with age.*

the medium of delete.

the method of delete.

the month of delete. Between the months of July and September, only three more ventured-financed firms went public. *Between July and September, only three more ventured-financed firms went public.*

the more (most) *more (most).* Testing can answer which of these two models is the more appropriate. *Testing can answer which of these two models is more appropriate.*

then and only then *only then; then.* I suggest that then and only then will people such as Mr. Becker realize that there really is no free lunch. *I suggest that only then will people such as Mr. Becker realize that there really is no free lunch.*

then at that (this) juncture (juncture in time; moment; moment in time; period; period of time; point; point in time; stage; stage in time; time) *then.*

the nature of *like;* delete. Disagreement on the viability of standardization strategies also reflects varying interpretations on the nature of the environment facing the international company. *Disagreement on the viability of standardization strategies also reflects varying interpretations of the environment facing the international company.*

the notion of delete. While not necessarily new, the notion of livework developments is seeing a revival. *While not necessarily new, livework developments are seeing a revival.*

then subsequently *then.* Then subsequently he left Digital and started his own business. *Then he left Digital and started his own business.*

theocratical *theocratic.*

the ... of *-'s.* I needed the help of my mother to care for my child. *I needed my mother's help to care for my child.* ■ The task of the analyst is to find the coefficients a and b in Equation 2-2. *The analyst's task is to find the coefficients a and b in Equation 2-2.* ■ The failure to recognize expenses of this type can affect the profitability of a product. *The failure to recognize expenses of this type can affect a product's profitability.*

theological *theologic.*

the one (that) delete. The one that seems to be the most popular is the use of the pull-down Mac menus for function keys. *The most popular seems to be the use of the pull-down Mac menus for function keys.*

the one best *the best.* The emphasis of scientific management was to try to find the one best way by examining the way work was done, the sequence of steps, and the skills of the workers. *The emphasis of scientific management was to try to find the best way by examining the way work was done, the sequence of steps, and the skills of the workers.*

(of) the opposite sex *female; male; man; woman.* He is abandoning his hemline indicator because it tended to offend too many investors of the opposite sex. *He is abandoning his hemline indicator because it tended to offend too many female investors.*

theoretical *theoretic.*

the other way around (round) *the opposite; the reverse.*

the passage of time *time.* Meanwhile, the passage of time has made it increasingly apparent that last year's stock market crash was not the immediate precursor of a corresponding plunge for the economy. *Meanwhile, time has made it increasingly apparent that last year's stock market crash was not the immediate precursor of a corresponding plunge for the economy.*

the practice of delete. Japan shares the United States' concern about the practice of using aid funds for export promotion. *Japan shares the United States' concern about using aid funds for export promotion.*

the presence of delete. Mammography uses an X-ray technique to detect the presence of lesions, such as tumors, within the breast. *Mammography uses an X-ray technique to detect lesions, such as tumors, within the breast.*

(of) the present ... *here; this;* delete. In the present chapter, we introduce capital structure theories. *In this chapter, we introduce capital structure theories.*

the present day *(just; right) now; nowadays; the present; these days; today.* Ever since MIT economist Rudiger Dornbusch first firmly broached the suggestion, the financial world has been absorbed in the resemblance between 1968 and the present day in macroeconomic terms. *Ever since MIT economist Rudiger Dornbusch first firmly broached the suggestion, the financial world has been absorbed in the resemblance between 1968 and today in macroeconomic terms.*

the present-day *nowaday's; the present's; today's.* Discoveries, innovations, surprises, and complexities of the present-day South multiply beyond what it seemed possible for him to cover. *Discoveries, innovations, surprises, and complexities of today's South multiply beyond what it seemed possible for him to cover.*

the principle of delete.

the problem of delete. Of all the approaches that can be taken to address the problem of fraud, the most important may be a demonstrated intolerance for the problem. *Of all the approaches that can be taken to address fraud, the most important may be a demonstrated intolerance for the problem.*

the procedure of   delete. Let's now look at the procedure of how teams are eliminated. *Let's now look at how teams are eliminated.*

the process of   delete. The process of selecting the proper school for your child can be hugely exciting. *Selecting the proper school for your child can be hugely exciting.* ■ For many people, trading in their current car plays an important role in the process of purchasing a new car. *For many people, trading in their current car plays an important role in purchasing a new car.*

the purpose of ... is to   delete. The purpose of this view is to allow you to work on the outline's organization. *This view allows you to work on the outline's organization.*

the question of   delete. Corporate dividend policy deals with the question of how much of the firm's earnings should be paid to its stockholders in cash dividends. *Corporate dividend policy deals with how much of the firm's earnings should be paid to its stockholders in cash dividends.*

therapeutical   *therapeutic.*

thereafter   *later; next; then.*

the reality of   delete. Patients facing an ileostomy, colostomy, or urostomy must come to terms with the reality of the disease. *Patients facing an ileostomy, colostomy, or urostomy must come to terms with the disease.*

the realm of   delete. Brainstorming has broadened its appeal to the business world and has found widespread acceptance in the realm of business meetings. *Brainstorming has broadened its appeal to the business world and has found widespread acceptance in business meetings.*

there exists ... (that; who)   *exists;* delete. This is true for current products where there exists a sales history. *This is true for current products where a sales history exists.* ■ There exist two kinds of photoreceptors in the retina. *Two kinds of photoreceptors exist in the retina.* ■ This means that either party has the right to terminate the relationship, whether or not there exists just cause for doing so. *This means that either party has the right to terminate the relationship, whether or not just cause for doing so exists.* ■ According to Figure 3.4, there exists a set of weights that classifies all of them correctly. *According to Figure 3.4, a set of weights exists that classifies all of them correctly.*

therefore *hence; so; then; thus.* The front view is more descriptive than the top view; therefore, the front view should be dimensioned. *The front view is more descriptive than the top view, so the front view should be dimensioned.*

the region of *of;* delete. The F-layer is the region of primary interest to radio communications. *The F-layer is of primary interest to radio communications.* ■ If you are located in the region of Arkansas, Missouri or Oklahoma you will particularly find "Conscious Connections" a useful resource for events and services. *If you are located in Arkansas, Missouri or Oklahoma you will particularly find "Concious Connections" a useful resource for events and services.*

therein *there.*

there is ... (that; who) *is;* delete. There are fifteen people in the group. *Fifteen people are in the group.* ■ There are millions of people who feel the way you do. *Millions of people feel the way you do.* ■ For every discovery that scientists make about Egyptian antiquity, there are hundreds that remain unsolved. *For every discovery that scientists make about Egyptian antiquity, hundreds remain unsolved.* ■ There's a healthy percentage of public investors who are interested and participate in the market throughout their lives. *A healthy percentage of public investors are interested and participate in the market throughout their lives.*

thereupon *later; next; then.*

the role of delete. The role of research and development is crucial to the future of a nation's economic growth and to the future of an industry and an individual business. *Research and development is crucial to the future of a nation's economic growth and to the future of an industry and an individual business.*

the same (thing) as *equal to; like.* Asserting that the deficit numbers "have no clothes" is not the same thing as saying that all is fine in the nation's economic affairs. *Asserting that the deficit numbers "have no clothes" is not like saying that all is fine in the nation's economic affairs.*

the same exact *just (the); the exact; the same.* These are high-grade municipal bonds, the same exact ones that the banks buy. *These are high-grade municipal bonds, the same ones that the banks buy.*

the same thing *as much; the same.* Looking back, I find I did the same thing. *Looking back, I find I did the same.* ■ Other rivals have discovered the same thing. *Other rivals have discovered as much.*

375

the same way *as; like*. Normally when you make a printout, it looks the same way it does when displayed on the screen. *Normally when you make a printout, it looks as it does when displayed on the screen.*

the scale of delete.

the scope of delete. The scope of the loss of control over one's body can only be understood through a personal experience. *The loss of control over one's body can only be understood through a personal experience.*

the single best (biggest; greatest; largest; most) *the best (biggest; greatest; largest; most).* The single most important issue for women is equal pay for equal work. *The most important issue for women is equal pay for equal work.* ■ Smoking is the single most preventable cause of premature death. *Smoking is the most preventable cause of premature death.* ■ It's probably the single slowest day I've seen in four years. *It's probably the slowest day I've seen in four years.*

the situation (with) *right; so; the case; true*; delete. This is often the situation with inexperienced managers, but it can be remedied with management training. *This is often so with inexperienced managers, but it can be remedied with management training.*

the space of delete. Within the space of a few minutes, he was dead. *Within a few minutes, he was dead.*

the state of delete. The state of Massachusetts is considering a similar law. *Massachusetts is considering a similar law.*

the state of (the ... state) *the*; delete. Consumers were more confident about the state of the economy in December than during the same month last year. *Consumers were more confident about the economy in December than during the same month last year.* ■ Many priests feel celibacy is no greater than the married state. *Many priests feel celibacy is no greater than marriage.*

the sum of *all*; delete.

the time will come when *at length; eventually; in due time; in the end; in time; later; one day; over the months (years); over time; someday; sometime; ultimately; with time; yet.* The time will come when you will appreciate all I've done for you. *One day you will appreciate all I've done for you.*

the topic of delete. He spoke on the topic of probate lawyers and fiduciaries at the recent ABA convention in Toronto. *He spoke on probate lawyers and fiduciaries at the recent ABA convention in Toronto.*

the total (of) *all;* delete.

the totality of *all;* delete. If you look at the totality of votes cast, Jackson is very well off. *If you look at all the votes cast, Jackson is very well off.*

the truth is (that) *actually; indeed; in fact; in faith; in truth; really; truly;* delete.

the truth of the matter is (that) *actually; indeed; in fact; in faith; in reality; in truth; really; truly;* delete. The truth of the matter is that glasnost and communism are incompatible. *In truth, glasnost and communism are incompatible.*

the ... use of *using;* delete. Would the use of these exacerbate the situation? *Would using these exacerbate the situation?* ■ This construction is performed with the use of a compass and a straightedge. *This construction is performed with a compass and a straightedge.*

the way *as.* Look carefully at the results, and try to determine why they behave the way they do. *Look carefully at the results, and try to determine why they behave as they do.*

the whys and (the) wherefores (of) *aim; cause; explanation; goal; grounds; motive; purpose; reason.* We're going to be talking about the whys and the wherefores of his lead. *We're going to be talking about the reasons for his lead.* ■ But for those who'd like to know what to do before hearing all the whys and wherefores, I start with the three main CORBA "developer action items." *But for those who'd like to know what to do before hearing all the reasons, I start with the three main CORBA "developer action items."*

the year (of) delete. Nearly 2,500 years ago, in the year 500 B.C., the first object which could project an image was made in ancient China. *Nearly 2,500 years ago, in 500 B.C., the first object which could project an image was made in ancient China.*

(a; the) ... thing delete. Censorship is a very dangerous thing. *Censorship is very dangerous.* ■ It's a very difficult thing. *It's very difficult.*

thinking in (my) mind *thinking*. What were you thinking in your mind when you bought the two guns and the knife? *What were you thinking when you bought the two guns and the knife?*

think to myself *think*. As they were yelling at me, I thought to myself, "These can't be my parents." *As they were yelling at me, I thought, "These can't be my parents."*

thirdly *third*.

third of all *third*.

this coming *next; this*. This coming Wednesday we are having our town fair. *This Wednesday we are having our town fair.*

those individuals (people; persons) *people (persons); those*. Only those people authorized to have access to information are allowed to see it. *Only people authorized to have access to information are allowed to see it.*

through and through *all through; completely; entirely; thoroughly; throughout; totally; wholly.*

throughout ... entire (whole) *entire (whole); throughout*. He was in trouble throughout his entire life. *He was in trouble his entire life.*

throughout the length and breadth (of) *all through; completely; entirely; thoroughly; throughout; totally; wholly.*

through (throughout) the course (duration; length) of *during; for; in; over; throughout; when; while; with*. This report is our opportunity to share the insights we have gained throughout the course of the study. *This report is our opportunity to share the insights we have gained throughout the study.*

through the medium of *by; from; in; on; over; through; with*. My basic interest is the lucid communication of ideas through the medium of print. *My basic interest is the lucid communication of ideas through print.*

through the use of *by; in; through; with*. Verbal reasoning is the ability to think, comprehend, and communicate effectively through the use of words. *Verbal reasoning is the ability to think, comprehend, and communicate effectively with words.*

through whatever (whichever) manner (means) *despite how; however.* Through whatever manner we meet, this fact has always remained the same. *However we meet, this fact has always remained the same.*

through what (which) means (mechanism) *how.* Through what means can Congress control the actions of a bureaucracy? *How can Congress control the actions of a bureaucracy?*

throw into a rage *enrage.* Thrown into a rage, he attacked the abuser with a knife, and then confessed to the killing without mentioning the woman. *Enraged, he attacked the abuser with a knife, and then confessed to the killing without mentioning the woman.*

throw into doubt *challenge; contradict; dispute; doubt; question.*

throw into jeopardy *endanger; imperil; jeopardize.* The sale was thrown into jeopardy Friday when an FTC request for more information for antitrust appraisal pushed the transaction into 1989. *The sale was jeopardized Friday when an FTC request for more information for antitrust appraisal pushed the transaction into 1989.*

throw into question *challenge; contradict; dispute; doubt; question.*

thusly *thus.* Since this is a policy that can be initiated by the principal, he/she would be the focus of our change campaign, thusly, allowing us to bypass the need to find consensus among the board members. *Since this is a policy that can be initiated by the principal, he/she would be the focus of our change campaign, thus, allowing us to bypass the need to find consensus among the board members.* ■ I have no television at present and thusly have had to get all my news via the web-based media. *I have no television at present and thus have had to get all my news via the web-based media.*

till (until) after *before; till (until).* Do not delete the first code until after you have made the adjustments. *Do not delete the first code until you have made the adjustments.*

till (until) the juncture (juncture in time; moment; moment in time; period; period in time; point; point in time; stage; stage in time; time) (that; when) *till (until).* Until the time that deposit interest rates were set free to seek levels dictated by the financial markets, the thrift business was uncomplicated. *Until deposit interest rates were set free to seek levels dictated by the financial markets, the thrift business was uncomplicated.*

till (until) ... then *till (until)*. Until we realize that all addictive chemical substances are fair game in the war on drugs, then the war cannot be won, much less fought. *Until we realize that all addictive chemical substances are fair game in the war on drugs, the war cannot be won, much less fought.*

till (until) the recent past *till (until) lately; till (until) of late; till (until) recently;* delete. Until the recent past, such courses were taken, often as electives, by advanced undergraduates who already had a certain degree of sophistication. *Until recently, such courses were taken, often as electives, by advanced undergraduates who already had a certain degree of sophistication.*

time after time *frequently; often; recurrently; regularly; repeatedly.* Time after time, the Democrats have turned to the idea of raising taxes. *The Democrats have regularly turned to the idea of raising taxes.*

time and (time) again *frequently; often; recurrently; regularly; repeatedly.* This has been demonstrated time and time again in their subsequent on-the-job experiences. *This has been repeatedly demonstrated in their subsequent on-the-job experiences.*

(a; the) time frame (of) *age; eon; epoch; era; interval; period; time;* delete. Outpacing both, however, were the regional banks, which moved up 29 percent over the same time frame. *Outpacing both, however, were the regional banks, which moved up 29 percent over the same period.* ■ Some automotive assemblers can make every car to order, at a reasonable price and in a reasonable time frame. *Some automotive assemblers can make every car to order, at a reasonable price and in a reasonable time.*

(a; the) time horizon (of) *age; eon; epoch; era; interval; period; time;* delete. Estimates are then made of the values of these factors over an appropriate time horizon. *Estimates are then made of the values of these factors over an appropriate time.*

(a; the) time interval (of) *interval; period; time.* Float is the time interval between the time a check is written and the time it is finally taken from the check writer's account. *Float is the interval between the time a check is written and the time it is finally taken from the check writer's account.*

time of day *time.*

(a; the) time period (of) *age; eon; epoch; era; interval; period; time;*

delete. The Greek material is similar to stone tools from Hungary and Bulgaria dated to about the same time period. *The Greek material is similar to stone tools from Hungary and Bulgaria dated to about the same age.*

(five) times over *(five)fold.* He was able to increase the conviction of drug traffickers five times over. *He was able to increase the conviction of drug traffickers fivefold.*

(a; the) time span (of) *age; eon; epoch; era; interval; period; time;* delete. Over the same time span, the savings rate rose from 4.1 to 5.4 percent. *Over the same period, the savings rate rose from 4.1 to 5.4 percent.*

time was when *formerly; long ago; once.*

tiny (little) bit *bit; fragment; hint; piece; shred; speck; trace.* I think Kroger management is just a tiny bit more relaxed than they were yesterday. *I think Kroger management is just a bit more relaxed than they were yesterday.*

tiny little *little; tiny.*

(in order) to accomplish (achieve) that (this) aim (end; goal; objective) *to that (this) end; toward that (this) end.* To accomplish this goal, two special task forces were established. *To this end, two special task forces were established.* ■ In order to achieve that objective, Congress in 1985 authorized the Peace Corps to double its volunteers to 10,000. *Toward that end, Congress in 1985 authorized the Peace Corps to double its volunteers to 10,000.*

to a certain (limited; some) degree *in a sense; in part; less often; less so; more or less; partially; partly; rather; some; somewhat;* delete. This depends to a limited degree on whether the company follows a global or a national strategy focus. *This partly depends on whether the company follows a global or a national strategy focus.* ■ You can intimidate umpires to a certain degree. *You can intimidate umpires somewhat.*

to a certain (limited; some) extent *in a sense; in part; less so; more or less; partially; partly; rather; some; somewhat;* delete. These are two factors that women can control to some extent. *These are two factors that women can somewhat control.* ■ In Germany, and to some extent in Japan, our products are now priced competitively. *In Germany, and less so in Japan, our products are now priced competitively.*

to a degree *in part; more or less; partially; partly; rather; some; somewhat;*

delete. Any choice would have been controversial to a degree. *Any choice would have been somewhat controversial.*

to a (the) ... degree *-(al)ly;* delete. We have reduced our nuclear weaponry to a significant degree. *We have significantly reduced our nuclear weaponry.* ■ To a surprising degree, we find the outlook hopeful. *We find the outlook surprisingly hopeful.*

to a (the) ... extent *-(al)ly;* delete. It's a change that's already been worked out to a considerable extent at the local level. *It's a change that's already been considerably worked out at the local level.*

to a great (large) degree *almost all; chiefly; commonly; generally; greatly; in general; largely; mainly; most; mostly; most often; much; nearly all; normally; overall; typically; usually; well.* Because the state will pay for the bulk of building and running the school, it will naturally be involved in the project to a large degree. *Because the state will pay for the bulk of building and running the school, it will naturally be much involved in the project.* ■ In Malaysia, imports are controlled to a great degree by a handful of European commission houses. *In Malaysia, imports are mostly controlled by a handful of European commission houses.*

to a greater (larger) degree (extent) *more; more often; more so.* The risks of radiation are understood to a much greater degree than many other risks we take for granted. *The risks of radiation are understood much more than many other risks we take for granted.* ■ Black males suffer from debilitating health problems to a greater degree than males in other ethnic and racial groups. *More black males suffer from debilitating health problems than males in other ethnic and racial groups.*

to a greater or lesser degree (extent) *in part; in some way; more or less; partially; partly; rather; some; somehow; someway(s); somewhat; to some degree (extent); various; variously; varying; varyingly;* delete. When people leave an organization, their departure results in a disruption that affects the remaining people to a greater or lesser degree. *When people leave an organization, their departure results in a disruption that variously affects the remaining people.*

to a great (large) extent *almost all; chiefly; commonly; generally; greatly; in general; largely; mainly; most; mostly; most often; much; nearly all; normally; overall; typically; usually; well.* To a large extent, the success of any business venture depends on planning. *The success of any business venture chiefly depends on planning.*

to a lesser (lower; smaller) degree (extent) *less; less often; less so.* Some have been dramatically affected by this pilgrimage; others to a lesser degree. *Some have been dramatically affected by this pilgrimage; others less so.* ■ It is only in Iowa and, to a lesser extent, in New Hampshire, that candidates meet so many rural Americans. *It is only in Iowa and, less often, in New Hampshire that candidates meet so many rural Americans.*

to all appearances *apparently; appear (to); outwardly; seem (to); seemingly; superficially.*

to all appearances ... appear (seem) *appear (seem).* To all appearances, he seems to be a brilliant career executive. *He seems to be a brilliant career executive.* ■ To all appearances, the market's outlook appears to be very bright as year-end institutional buying is likely to surface in a big way. *The market's outlook appears to be very bright as year-end institutional buying is likely to surface in a big way.*

to all intents and purposes *effectively; essentially; in effect; in essence; practically; virtually.* To all intents and purposes, their revenue possibilities are now extremely limited. *In effect, their revenue possibilities are now extremely limited.* ■ This is to all intents and purposes an inertial force. *This is essentially an inertial force.*

to all practical purposes *effectively; essentially; in effect; in essence; practically; virtually.* As you may recall, the natural regeneration of trees in the Pennypack is, to all practical purposes, nonexistent. *As you may recall, the natural regeneration of trees in the Pennypack is, virtually, nonexistent.*

to a major or minor degree (extent) *in part; in some way; more or less; partially; partly; rather; some; somehow; someway(s); somewhat; to some degree (extent); various; variously; varying; varyingly;* delete. All of us are involved in the writing of the shows to a major or minor degree. *All of us are somehow involved in the writing of the shows.*

to an extent *in part; more or less; partially; partly; rather; some; somewhat;* delete.

to an increasing degree (extent) *increasingly; more and more.*

to a (the) point of *to.* The business is very close to the point of breaking even. *The business is very close to breaking even.*

to a (the) point (stage) that (when; where) *so (that); so far (that); so much (that); so that; to; to when; to where;* delete. It got to the point where I didn't leave the house at all for fear of missing her phone call. *It got so that I didn't leave the house at all for fear of missing her phone call.* ■ Because of the mathematics involved, forecasting intimidates some managers to the point that they accept projections at face value. *Because of the mathematics involved, forecasting so intimidates some managers that they accept projections at face value.* ■ Her Parkinson's disease has progressed to a point where she is now semipsychotic. *Her Parkinson's disease has progressed to where she is now semipsychotic.*

to be *-(al)ly; to;* delete. To be frank, I think their products are inferior to ours. *Frankly, I think their products are inferior to ours.* ■ To be successful, you must work furiously. *To succeed, you must work furiously.* ■ If tobacco were to be declared illegal, I would feel comfortable in predicting a black market in nicotine smuggling. *If tobacco were declared illegal, I would feel comfortable in predicting a black market in nicotine smuggling.*

to begin (start) with *first.* To begin with, I never thought so many people would respond to such an intimate question. *First, I never thought so many people would respond to such an intimate question.*

to be sure *certainly; of course; surely.*

to do delete. Saving money can be difficult to do. *Saving money can be difficult.* ■ I have to decide if I should retrace Sherman's route to the South as I originally planned to do. *I have to decide if I should retrace Sherman's route to the South as I originally planned.*

to find (a) fault in (with) *blame; criticize; fault.*

together as a team (unit) *as a team (unit); together.* Here, in one location, specialists work together as a team to fulfill all aspects of a patient's needs. *Here, in one location, specialists work together to fulfill all aspects of a patient's needs.*

together ... in combination *in combination; together.* They can even be used together in combination. *They can even be used in combination.*

together ... in groups *in groups; together.* Although people around the world live together in groups and create their own cultures, in few cases does the intensity of human interaction approach the level found in prisons. *Although people around the world live in groups and create their own cultures, in few cases does the intensity of human interaction approach the level found in prisons.*

together with *along with; and; as well as; combined with; coupled with; joined with; paired with; with.* Morgan proposed construction of a system of five reservoirs together with substantial channel improvements. *Morgan proposed construction of a system of five reservoirs coupled with substantial channel improvements.*

to make (a; the) ... (about; of; on; with) *to; to -(al)ly.* I need to make a correction about something I said yesterday. *I need to correct something I said yesterday.* ■ I wanted to make a comment on his appearance. *I wanted to comment on his appearance.* ■ We will give the audience a chance to make inquiries about this. *We will give the audience a chance to inquire about this.* ■ I will do everything possible to make a thorough evaluation of your application. *I will do everything possible to thoroughly evaluate your application.* ■ I am eager to make a deal. *I am eager to deal.*

to one degree (extent) or another *in part; in some way; more or less; partially; partly; rather; some; somehow; someway(s); somewhat; to some degree (extent); various; variously; varying; varyingly;* delete. Competition is present in nearly all of our markets to one extent or another. *Competition is present to some extent in nearly all of our markets.*

to such a degree *so; so far; so much; so well; such.* Never have so many crucial issues confronting a president depended to such a degree on science and technology. *Never have so many crucial issues confronting a president depended so much on science and technology.* ■ The writings of Thoreau retain importance and vitality to such a degree that a century later they have had significant influence on the greatest leaders of our time. *The writings of Thoreau retain such importance and vitality that a century later they have had significant influence on the greatest leaders of our time.*

to such an extent *so; so far; so much; so well; such.* He believes Americans are deluged to such an extent with health messages that they exist in a state of heightened health consciousness all the time. *He believes Americans are so deluged with health messages that they exist in a state of heightened health consciousness all the time.* ■ Young Sioux boys literally lived with their favorite horse and came to know it to such an extent that they commonly talked with their animals. *Young*

Sioux boys literally lived with their favorite horse and came to know it so well that they commonly talked with their animals.

to summarize (sum up) *in brief; in fine; in short; in sum.*

to take this opportunity delete. I'd like to take this opportunity to commend these women for their courage in sharing their stories. *I'd like to commend these women for their courage in sharing their stories.* ■ We would like to take this opportunity to update you on the status of our investigation. *We would like to update you on the status of our investigation.*

total (totally) delete. He went totally bankrupt. *He went bankrupt.* ■ This person totally destroyed my career. *This person destroyed my career.* ■ I'm the total antithesis of my mother. *I'm the antithesis of my mother.*

total up *add; sum; total.* When you total up the outside and inside executives, you get an overwhelming preponderance of board members with a managerial mindset. *When you total the outside and inside executives, you get an overwhelming preponderance of board members with a managerial mindset.*

to tell (you) the truth *actually; candidly; frankly; honestly; truthfully;* delete. She was a very sweet, kind woman, but to tell you the truth, a few of us worried about her. *She was a very sweet, kind woman, but frankly a few of us worried about her.*

to that (this) degree (extent) *so; so far; so much; such.* I didn't realize women could lose hair to that extent. *I didn't realize women could lose so much hair.*

(something) to that (the; this) effect (that) *affirming; claiming; conveying; declaring; professing; purporting; saying; suggesting.* A call to its former office in Dallas resulted in a telephone company answer to the effect that "service has been disconnected." *A call to its former office in Dallas resulted in a telephone company answer declaring "service has been disconnected."* ■ He has never met him, and he produced witnesses to that effect. *He has never met him, and he produced witnesses professing that.*

to the contrary *but; conversely; however; instead; no; not so; rather.* To the contrary, we found there's a strong tendency for counties that have high radon levels to have low lung-cancer rates. *Instead, we* *found there's a strong tendency for counties that have high radon levels to have low lung-cancer rates.*

... to the contrary *after all; apart; aside; despite; even with; for all; with all.* Appearances to the contrary, he insists he doesn't plan to run for office. *Despite appearances, he insists he doesn't plan to run for office.*

to the degree (that; to which) *as far as; as much as; so far as; so much as.* To the degree that Divi Hotels can do so, it has purchased distressed properties at discount prices and has then renovated them. *So far as Divi Hotels can do so, it has purchased distressed properties at discount prices and has then renovated them.* ■ Volume markdowns did not occur to the degree they did last year. *Volume markdowns did not occur as much as they did last year.*

to the degree (extent) of *up to.* In the event of either a partial or total loss, the person is self-insured to the extent of one-third of the damage. *In the event of either a partial or total loss, the person is self-insured up to one-third of the damage.*

to the extent (that; to which) *as far as; as much as; so far as; so much as.* To the extent that the distribution of income and wealth goes to the heart of a country's political ethic, the United States has grown unfair. *So far as the distribution of income and wealth goes to the heart of a country's political ethic, the United States has grown unfair.* ■ I help out here and there, but maybe not to the extent that she'd like me to. *I help out here and there, but maybe not as much as she'd like me to.*

to the greatest (largest) degree (extent) *as far as; as much as; so far as; so much as.* Nynex asked the judge to expedite consideration of the request to the greatest extent possible by ordering the DOJ to submit its response within 14 days under special procedures. *Nynex asked the judge to expedite consideration of the request as much as possible by ordering the DOJ to submit its response within 14 days under special procedures.*

to the point *apt; pertinent; relevant.*

to the purpose *apt; pertinent; relevant.*

to the tune of delete. It's the lagniappe that members of Congress collect (to the tune of $9.8 million in 1987) in return for talking to special interest groups with money to spend on them. *It's the lagniappe that members of Congress collect ($9.8 million in 1987) in return for talking to special interest groups with money to spend on them.*

toward the direction of *toward.*

toward the east (north; south; west) *eastward (northward; southward; westward).*

to what degree *how; how far; how much; how often.* Privacy provisions in current law leave ambiguous to what degree such information can be shared. *Privacy provisions in current law leave ambiguous how much such information can be shared.* ■ To what degree are you conscious of the theme as you write? *How conscious of the theme are you as you write?*

to whatever degree (extent) *however; however far; however much; however often.* You can learn to develop your psychic ability to whatever degree you wish. *You can learn to develop your psychic ability however much you wish.* ■ The mentor will assist the company to whatever degree the client wishes. *The mentor will assist the company however the client wishes.*

to what extent *how; how far; how much; how often.* What I would like to know is to what extent this is the result of reduced parental involvement in the child's upbringing. *What I would like to know is how much this is the result of reduced parental involvement in the child's upbringing.* ■ To what extent they carried that admiration, only they know. *How far they carried that admiration, only they know.*

to what length *how far; how much.* Apart from other fascinating aspects of the ménage à trois, we are shown to what lengths some will go to further their objectives. *Apart from other fascinating aspects of the ménage à trois, we are shown how far some will go to further their objectives.*

trace amount *trace.* He found trace amounts of chemicals in unrinsed containers, probably from the glue used to keep felt on the balls. *He found traces of chemicals in unrinsed containers, probably from the glue used to keep felt on the balls.*

trace back *trace.* From dinosaurs to dogs, all land vertebrates trace their ancestry back to the water. *From dinosaurs to dogs, all land vertebrates trace their ancestry to the water.*

track record *record.* He built the company into a fine organization with an excellent track record, until the last three or four years. *He built the company into a fine organization with an excellent record, until the last three or four years.*

tragical *tragic.*

trained expert *expert.*

transvestitism *transvestism.*

trivial details (facts; ideas; information; matters; things) *trivia.* While withholding such seemingly trivial information as the astronauts' in-orbit menus might appear ridiculous, even that might provide some clues as to the timing of the launch. *While withholding such seeming trivia as the astronauts' in-orbit menus might appear ridiculous, even that might provide some clues as to the timing of the launch.*

(a; the) true fact *a fact; factual; the truth; true; truthful.* That's a true fact. *That's a fact.*

true to fact *fact; factual; the truth; true; truthful.*

turn and turn about *by turns.*

twelve midnight *midnight.*

twelve noon *noon.*

twenty-five (25) percent (of) *one-fourth (of); one-quarter (of).*

two twins *twins.* We discovered that the two twins were still listed on our welfare case even after, according to media accounts, the children were already living with other families. *We discovered that the twins were still listed on our welfare case even after, according to media accounts, the children were already living with other families.*

type (of) delete. It was a small, compact type of car. *It was a small, compact car.* ■ It's not a premeditated type of act. *It's not a premeditated act.* ■ Dungeons and Dragons is a very seductive type of game. *Dungeons and Dragons is a very seductive game.* ■ I'm basically a creative type person. *I'm basically a creative person.*

U

unaccustomed to *not used to; unused to.* Adults and children who are unaccustomed to caffeine are more likely to be affected than the habitual consumer. *Adults and children who are not used to caffeine are more likely to be affected than the habitual consumer.*

unbeknown (unbeknownst) *unknown.* Condominium loans were the favored product, but unbeknownst to the bank, the market for condos had already peaked. *Condominium loans were the favored product, but unknown to the bank, the market for condos had already peaked.*

unconfirmed (unfounded; unsubstantiated) rumor *rumor.* The Committee on Standards suspended him for two terms and permanently marred his academic record on the basis of innuendo and unfounded rumor. *The Committee on Standards suspended him for two terms and permanently marred his academic record on the basis of innuendo and rumor.* ■ Wall Street staged an explosive late recovery Thursday after unsubstantiated rumors of an imminent rate cut all but erased a 274-point loss in the Dow Jones industrial average. *Wall Street staged an explosive late recovery Thursday after rumors of an imminent rate cut all but erased a 274-point loss in the Dow Jones industrial average.*

under any circumstances (conditions) *altogether; at all; completely; entirely; ever; fully; never; no matter what; not ever; utterly; whatever; wholly.* I will not see him under any circumstances. *I will not see him at all.*

under certain (some) circumstances (conditions) *at times; every so often; for (in; with) some (of us; people); from time to time; now and again; now and then; occasionally; once in a while; on occasion; some; sometimes; delete.* Why does fiber, which fights constipation, also cause constipation under some circumstances? *Why does fiber, which fights constipation, also at times cause constipation?*

underneath *below; beneath; under.* Here was a perfect chance to demonstrate that the Square had not completely ossified underneath a layer of brick and limestone. *Here was a perfect chance to demonstrate that the Square had not completely ossified beneath a layer of brick and limestone.*

under no circumstances (conditions) *in no way; never; not; not ever; not once.* Under no circumstances is it to be used or considered as an offer to sell, or a solicitation of any offer to buy, any security. *Never is it to be used or considered as an offer to sell, or a solicitation of any offer to buy, any security.*

under obligation *bind; compel; force; obligate; oblige; require; restrict.* The lessee usually has the option to buy the auto at the end of the lease for the assumed residual value but is not under obligation to do so. *The lessee usually has the option to buy the auto at the end of the lease for the assumed residual value but is not obligated to do so.*

under the weather *ill; sick; unwell.*

unfair and inequitable *inequitable; unfair.*

unite into one *unite.*

unite together *unite.*

universal panacea *panacea.*

unless and (or) until *till; unless; until.* Unless or until they know what is happening, they obviously cannot file complaints to trigger an investigation. *Unless they know what is happening, they obviously cannot file complaints to trigger an investigation.*

unless ... then *unless.* Unless we're prepared to say the Japanese are just smarter than we are, then we're looking at motivation and role models and parents encouraging kids to keep their options open. *Unless we're prepared to say the Japanese are just smarter than we are, we're looking at motivation and role models and parents encouraging kids to keep their options open.*

unnecessarily *needlessly.* The Japanese countered that moving part of the wing production would unnecessarily drive up the costs. *The Japanese countered that moving part of the wing production would needlessly drive up the costs.*

unproven *unproved.* In the context of Western medicine, acupuncture is still unproven. *In the context of Western medicine, acupuncture is still unproved.*

unsubstantiated *baseless; groundless; unfounded.*

until and (or) unless *till; unless; until.*

until such point (time) as *until.* Instead of a 50-percent pay raise, they should have a 50-percent pay cut until such time as they rule with honesty, integrity, and compassion. *Instead of a 50-percent pay raise, they should have a 50-percent pay cut until they rule with honesty, integrity, and compassion.* ■ Discussions will continue until such point as I have something to show on paper. *Discussions will continue until I have something to show on paper.*

(an; the) untold number (of) *countless; endless; infinite; millions (of); myriad; numberless; untold.* If state government fails to actively support one of the world's most promising industries, it will be letting an untold number of jobs and revenue dollars slip through its fingers. *If state government fails to actively support one of the world's most promising industries, it will be letting untold jobs and revenue dollars slip through its fingers.*

up in the air *unanswered; uncertain; unclear; undecided; unresolved; unsettled; unsure.* Plans for an interview with Castro himself remain up in the air, according to a CBS News spokesperson. *Plans for an interview with Castro himself remain uncertain, according to a CBS News spokesperson.*

upon *on.* Do you wish something of the sort had happened when the senate was called upon to ratify ABM? *Do you wish something of the sort had happened when the senate was called on to ratify ABM?*

up till (until) *till (until).* I was a model up until the age of 19. *I was a model until the age of 19.* ■ Up until now conflicting standards and problem hardware have kept plug and play from working properly. *Until now conflicting standards and problem hardware have kept plug and play from working properly.*

up till (until) that (this) juncture (juncture in time; moment; moment in time; period; period in time; point; point in time; stage; stage in time; time) *so far; thus far; till (until) now (then); to date; up to now (then); (as) yet.* Up until this point, he hasn't been able to show what he stands for. *Until now, he hasn't been able to show what he stands for.* ■ Up until this time, we have had one personnel director who took care of everybody. *To date, we have had one personnel director who took care of everybody.*

up to a maximum of *up to.* If set to Yes, text wraps around the box (up to a maximum of 20 boxes per page). *If set to Yes, text wraps around the box (up to 20 boxes per page).*

up to and including *through.* Every WordStar Professional command, feature, and function up to and including Release 5 is listed and described in detail. *Every WordStar Professional command, feature, and function through Release 5 is listed and described in detail.*

up to a point *rather; somewhat.*

up to the current (present) (time) *so far; thus far; till now; to date; until now; up to now; (as) yet.*

up to that (this) juncture (juncture in time; moment; moment in time; period; period in time; point; point in time; stage; stage in time; time) *so far; thus far; till now (then); to date; until now (then); up to now (then); (as) yet.* Up to this point, we have discussed these motivation theories relating to the needs of the individual. *Until now, we have discussed these motivation theories relating to the needs of the individual.*

upward(s) of *more than; over.* In 1984, Peru had upwards of 40,000 acres of coca plants; today, it has 600,000 acres. *In 1984, Peru had more than 40,000 acres of coca plants; today, it has 600,000 acres.*

usage *use.* We project that ATM usage will increase to nearly 60 percent by 1995. *We project that ATM use will increase to nearly 60 percent by 1995.* ■ The usage of credit cards to fund small businesses seems to be the method of choice these days. *The use of credit cards to fund small businesses seems to be the method of choice these days.*

usually but not always *almost always; most often; nearly always; often; usually.*

utility *use; usefulness.* This has resulted in the much needed return to utility of our long-idled bridge. *This has resulted in the much needed return to use of our long-idled bridge.*

utilization *use.* Utilization of existing schools in a region could be optimized to reduce variances caused by local population fluctuations. *Use of existing schools in a region could be optimized to reduce variances caused by local population fluctuations.*

utilize *employ; use.* If utilizing the master antenna system is impossible, we will devise a plan for running the cable within the building. *If using the master antenna system is impossible, we will devise a plan for running the cable within the building.*

V

(a) valuable asset *(an) asset; valuable.* The wasting of this valuable national asset, through neglect and privation, makes no sense. *The wasting of this national asset, through neglect and privation, makes no sense.*

vantage point *vantage.* That it should do so is hardly surprising when one considers the unique vantage point from which he is able to view the historical scene. *That it should do so is hardly surprising when one considers the unique vantage from which he is able to view the historical scene.*

various and sundry *assorted; divers; diverse; sundry; varied; various; varying; delete.* There was a huge group of kids there of various and sundry ages. *There was a huge group of kids there of various ages.*

various different *assorted; countless; different; divers; diverse; extensive; many; numerous; scores of; sundry; varied; various; varying.* Couples have various different ways of splitting their money. *Couples have various ways of splitting their money.*

verbalization *speech; talk.*

verbalize *speak; talk; write.* Request that those who call you regularly put their thoughts in writing instead of verbalizing on the phone. *Request that those who call you regularly put their thoughts in writing instead of talking on the phone.*

very *delete.* It's a very tragic story. *It's a tragic story.* ■ The driving conditions are very treacherous. *The driving conditions are treacherous.* ■ I thought her performance was very memorable. *I thought her performance was memorable.* ■ Last year's event was a very huge success. *Last year's event was a huge success.* ■ Moreover, the wind at the peak can be very deadly. *Moreover, the wind at the peak can be deadly.*

very much -ed (-en) *much -ed (-en).* I was very much concerned about that. *I was much concerned about that.* ■ Their efficacy as classroom texts would be very much improved if their pedagogical features were more plentiful. *Their efficacy as classroom texts would be much improved if their pedagogical features were more plentiful.*

vestigial remnant *remnant; vestige.* We Americans have only a vestigial remnant of several basic industries — consumer electronics, photography, toymaking, and office equipment to name a few. *We Americans have only a remnant of several basic industries — consumer electronics, photography, toymaking, and office equipment to name a few.*

viable   delete. Having an affair is not a viable solution. *Having an affair is not a solution.*

violent explosion *explosion.*

(a; the) vital ... in (of; to) *vital in (to).* We have been very pleased with their performance and have found them to be a vital part of our operation. *We have been very pleased with their performance and have found them to be vital to our operation.*

vital necessity *necessity; vital.*

vocalize *express; say; state; tell; voice.*

voice ... (about; for; of; to) delete. They voiced doubt that trees will prove to be a bigger source of hydrocarbons than cars in most cities. *They doubted that trees will prove to be a bigger source of hydrocarbons than cars in most cities.* ∎ He voiced strong support for the international effort to make ISDN the universally accepted worldwide network of the future. *He strongly supported the international effort to make ISDN the universally accepted worldwide network of the future.*

voice concern (about) *agonize (about; over); brood (on; over); dread; fear; fret (about; over); regret; stew (about; over); worry (about; over).* U.S. officials have voiced concern about possible Chinese sales of newly developed short-range M-9 missiles elsewhere in the Middle East. *U.S. officials have worried about possible Chinese sales of newly developed short-range M-9 missiles elsewhere in the Middle East.*

voice opposition to *contest; criticize; disagree with; disapprove of; dispute; object to; oppose; protest.* Congress in 1986 passed the Montgomery Amendment after several governors voiced opposition to the Reagan administration's Central American policy. *Congress in 1986 passed the Montgomery Amendment after several governors objected to the Reagan administration's Central American policy.*

voice skepticism (about) *disbelieve; distrust; doubt; mistrust; question.*

voice sorrow (about) *bemoan; deplore; grieve; lament; moan; mourn; regret.*

W

wage (a; the) ... delete. The report notes that the state has been waging a battle against drugs for several years. *The report notes that the state has been battling against drugs for several years.*

wait around *wait*. The key customers are not going to wait around while those issues get resolved. *The key customers are not going to wait while those issues get resolved.*

want to have *want*. We don't want to have the drug in our formulary unless it has a superior patient care advantage. *We don't want the drug in our formulary unless it has a superior patient care advantage.*

warn in advance *warn*.

(the) way (in which) *how*; delete. This overview should give you a feel for the way these programs work and the way you can use them. *This overview should give you a feel for how these programs work and how you can use them.* ■ That's the way people can reduce their blood pressure. *That's how people can reduce their blood pressure.*

ways and means *means; methods; ways*.

weather conditions *weather*. The adverse weather conditions on Saturday postponed the running of the race until a day later. *The adverse weather on Saturday postponed the running of the race until a day later.*

weld together *weld*. They manufactured their samples by welding together two single-crystal gold films. *They manufactured their samples by welding two single-crystal gold films.*

(all) well and fine (good) *all right; fine; good; great; nice; pleasant; pleasing; welcome; well*. Variety and customization are well and good, but they are low on most consumers' lists of priorities. *Variety and customization are nice, but they are low on most consumers' lists of priorities.*

were it not for *but for; except for*.

what appears (seems) to be *apparent; seeming*. Manchester police also said a bottle of nonprescription pills was found in the room along with what appeared to be a suicide note. *Manchester police also said a* *bottle of nonprescription pills was found in the room along with an apparent suicide note.*

what ... does is. delete. What they do is provide repair and replacement of Sun and HP products. *They provide repair and replacement of Sun and HP products.*

what ... for *why.* What did you do that for? *Why did you do that?*

what ... happens (occurs; results; takes place) is (that) delete. What happens with motherhood is you rarely repeat the problems of your own mother. *With motherhood you rarely repeat the problems of your own mother.* ■ What happens, again and again, is that people with good intentions falter. *Again and again, people with good intentions falter.*

what have you *whatnot.*

what in God's (heaven's) name *whatever; what ever.* What in God's name does it have to do with the subject of business? *Whatever does it have to do with the subject of business?*

what in the world (on earth) *whatever; what ever.* What on earth are you talking about? *Whatever are you talking about?*

what is ... (is that) *-(al)ly;* delete. What we need is a way to go directly to the partition block. *We need a way to go directly to the partition block.* ■ What we hope to do is increase our inventory and decrease our costs. *We hope to increase our inventory and decrease our costs.* ■ What we have described is a typical, hierarchical, central-processor-based, online architecture. *We have described a typical, hierarchical, central-processor-based, online architecture.* ■ What is not so clear or commonly accepted is the scope and nature of these obligations. *Not so clear or commonly accepted is the scope and nature of these obligations.* ■ If a broadband LED signal is sent through a filter, what comes out is only the portion of the LED spectrum that is passed by the filter. *If a broadband LED signal is sent through a filter, only the portion of the LED spectrum that is passed by the filter comes out.* ■ What create static electricity are different potentials. *Different potentials create static electricity.* ■ What is more alarming is that Black women made up less than 25 percent of the city's population. *More alarming is that Black women made up less than 25 percent of the city's population.*

what is called (known as; named; referred to as; termed) delete. Many municipal and rural developments are located within what is referred to as the flood plain. *Many municipal and rural developments are located within the flood plain.*

what is the time frame (time horizon; time period; time span) in which (of) *when.* What was the time frame in which you had your relationship with President Kennedy? *When did you have your relationship with President Kennedy?*

what is the likelihood (probability) (of) *how likely (probable).* What is the likelihood of that? *How likely is that?*

what it is (that; who) *what.* I took it upon myself to research what it was that made this matter such a hot commodity. *I took it upon myself to research what made this matter such a hot commodity.* ■ It's time for us to rethink what it is we are asking of our employees. *It's time for us to rethink what we are asking of our employees.*

what (whatever; which; whichever) one(s) *what (whatever; which; whichever).* Which one would be accomplished better or faster with the help of a computer? *Which would be accomplished better or faster with the help of a computer?* ■ Whichever one you select, it will be an improvement on the one you now have. *Whichever you select, it will be an improvement on the one you now have.*

whatsoever *at all; whatever.* As far as I'm concerned, twins have no ESP ability whatsoever. *As far as I'm concerned, twins have no ESP ability whatever.*

what with *given; since; with.* What with the constant change in today's world, financial plans must be continually updated. *With the constant change in today's world, financial plans must be continually updated.* ■ You might think the MTV generation would be too jaded to notice, what with Mariah Carey's washcloth-size skirts and Janet Jackson also in the buff. *You might think the MTV generation would be too jaded to notice, given Mariah Carey's washcloth-size skirts and Janet Jackson also in the buff.* ■ There's going to have to be a lot of support to get Gore elected what with Bush in there. *There's going to have to be a lot of support to get Gore elected with Bush in there.*

when all is said and done *all in all; all things considered; all told; altogether; in all; on the whole; overall.* When all is said and done, Mr. Marshall emerges as a monster by anyone's standards. *All in all, Mr. Marshall emerges as a monster by anyone's standards.*

when and as *as; when.* Late payments are subject to a late-payment charge of 1.5 percent per month, and the advertisers agree to pay any such late-payment penalty when and as billed by the publisher. *Late payments are subject to a late-payment charge of 1.5 percent per month, and the advertisers agree to pay any such late-payment penalty when billed by the publisher.*

when and (or) if *if; when.* So when and if the discount rate is charged, it could well be interpreted on Wall Street as nothing more than a "catch-up" move. *So if the discount rate is charged, it could well be interpreted on Wall Street as nothing more than a "catch-up" move.*

when and (or) whether *if; when; whether.*

when, as, and if *if; when.*

when compared to (with) *against; alongside; beside; compared to (with); -(i)er than; less; less than; more; more than; next to; over; than; to; versus; vis-à-vis.* There is a 23 percent higher suicide rate of Vietnam veterans when compared to other persons in the same age group. *There is a 23 percent higher suicide rate of Vietnam veterans compared to other persons in the same age group.* ■ IBM is expected to price the line aggressively, when compared to the competition. *IBM is expected to price the line more aggressively than the competition.*

when compared to (with) ... relatively *compared to (with); -(i)er than (less than; more than).* Although the UK is relatively small when compared with the United States, its landscape and people are varied and dramatic; what it lacks in physical size it makes up for in culture, history etc. *Although the UK is small when compared with the United States, its landscape and people are varied and dramatic; what it lacks in physical size it makes up for in culture, history etc.*

when (a; the) ... done (finished; over; through) *after.*

when it (you) comes (gets) right down to it *all in all; all things considered; all told; altogether; in all; on the whole; overall.*

when it comes to *about; as for; as to; concerning; for; in; of; on; over; regarding; respecting; to; toward; when; with;* delete. She's very shy when it comes to performing in front of an audience. *She's very shy about performing in front of an audience.* ■ Employers, employees, and society are often in conflict when it comes to dealing with five key issues facing them today in the workplace. *Employers, employees, and* *society are often in conflict over dealing with five key issues facing them today in the workplace.*

when measured against *against; alongside; beside; compared to (with); -(i)er than; less; less than; more; more than; next to; over; than; to; versus; vis-à-vis.* The size of the Pennwalt takeover offer isn't large when measured against the multibillion-dollar bidding wars that have reshaped 1988 as the year of unprecedented megadeals. *The size of the Pennwalt takeover offer isn't large alongside the multibillion-dollar bidding wars that have reshaped 1988 as the year of unprecedented megadeals.*

whensoever *whenever.*

when ... then *when.* When the detector no longer sounds, then you know you have reached safety. *When the detector no longer sounds, you know you have reached safety.* ■ When the reference count is zero, then the control can destroy itself and free memory for other purposes. *When the reference count is zero, the control can destroy itself and free memory for other purposes.*

whereabouts *where.*

where ... at *where.* We don't really know where we are at. *We don't really know where we are.*

wherefore *why.*

where ... is concerned *about; as for; as to; concerning; for; in; of; on; over; regarding; respecting; to; toward; with;* delete. Bank customers are often less venturesome where their money is concerned. *Bank customers are often less venturesome with their money.* ■ Keep in mind that bigger isn't necessarily better where information is concerned. *Regarding information, keep in mind that bigger isn't necessarily better.* ■ It's beginning to show signs of weakness where demand is concerned, but that's true everywhere. *It's beginning to show signs of weakness in demand, but that's true everywhere.* ■ Most investigators use one of three primary methods where sketching is concerned. *Most investigators use one of three primary methods of sketching.* ■ Geller is notoriously tight-lipped where matters of sex and romance are concerned. *Geller is notoriously tight-lipped about matters of sex and romance.*

wheresoever *wherever.*

where ... to *where.* Where are you going to? *Where are you going?*

whereupon *whereon.*

wherewithal *assets; cash; funds; means; money; supplies.* He added that the Minnesotan also has the wherewithal to shore up finances during bad times. *He added that the Minnesotan also has the cash to shore up finances during bad times.*

whether *if.* A patent can be granted only after the PTO examiners have searched existing patents to determine whether the invention has been previously patented. *A patent can be granted only after the PTO examiners have searched existing patents to determine if the invention has been previously patented.*

whether and (or) when *if; when; whether.*

whether or not *if; whether.* With so many choices, the question is not whether or not to buy a server but what to implement as a server. *With so many choices, the question is not whether to buy a server but what to implement as a server.*

which is delete. There's a certain enzyme which is lacking in their systems. *There's a certain enzyme lacking in their systems.* ■ Tandy Corp., which is probably the largest U.S. distributor of small business systems, also sells personal computers in its stores. *Tandy Corp., probably the largest U.S. distributor of small business systems, also sells personal computers in its stores.* ■ The Moscow Papyrus dealt with solving practical problems which are related to geometry, food preparation, and grain allowance. *The Moscow Papyrus dealt with solving practical problems related to geometry, food preparation, and grain allowance.*

whichsoever *whichever.*

while at the same time *as; at the same time; while.* So the objective of the game within the Administration was to finesse the longer-term implications of SDI while at the same time manipulating the shorter-term impact of the program in such a way as either to advance arms control or to stop it in its tracks. *So the objective of the game within the Administration was to finesse the longer-term implications of SDI while manipulating the shorter-term impact of the program in such a way as either to advance arms control or to stop it in its tracks.* ■ Women's colleges are offering women innovative programs, while at the same time they are opening doors for minorities. *Women's colleges are offering women innovative programs, while they are opening doors for minorities.*

while concurrently *as; while.* Researchers joined development projects for one month and participated in interface design while concurrently interviewing other project participants and employees. *Researchers joined development projects for one month and participated in interface design while interviewing other project participants and employees.* ■ A message can be sent to the driver vectoring her to a repair center, while concurrently a message is sent to the repair center alerting it to the car's arrival. *A message can be sent to the driver vectoring her to a repair center, as a message is sent to the repair center alerting it to the car's arrival.*

while simultaneously *as; while.* While getting signatures, volunteers were simultaneously assessing the degree of support for my candidacy. *While getting signatures, volunteers were assessing the degree of support for my candidacy.* ■ Our aim is to help professional and semi-professional freelance writers promote their work to thousands of publications worldwide, while simultaneously providing editors with a valuable resource for written material. *Our aim is to help professional and semi-professional freelance writers promote their work to thousands of publications worldwide, while providing editors with a valuable resource for written material.*

who in the world (on earth) *who ever.* Who in the world is that? *Who ever is that?*

who is delete. The groups can vary from project associates to laymen who are unfamiliar with the project and its objectives. *The groups can vary from project associates to laymen unfamiliar with the project and its objectives.*

whole (wholly) delete. Never in my whole life have I ever seen such a thing. *Never in my life have I ever seen such a thing.* ■ There's a whole plethora of new technologies emerging. *There's a plethora of new technologies emerging.*

wholly and completely *completely; utterly; wholly.* A member of group C, for example, remains wholly and completely a C. *A member of group C, for example, remains wholly a C.*

whomsoever *whomever.*

whosoever *whoever.*

why in the world (on earth) *why ever.* Why in the world would liberals oppose the idea? *Why would liberals ever oppose the idea?*

(many) widely varying *assorted; broad; countless; different; divers; diverse; extensive; many; numerous; scores of; sundry; varied; various; varying.* If a distributor bases its application programs on the Unix operating system, it can choose among many widely varying computers. *If a distributor bases its application programs on the Unix operating system, it can choose among various computers.*

widow (widower) of the late *widow (widower).*

widow woman *widow.*

window of opportunity *chance; opportunity.* Interviews with government scientists and physicians suggest a critical window of opportunity was missed. *Interviews with government scientists and physicians suggest a critical opportunity was missed.*

wintertime *winter.* In the wintertime, however, the sun's weaker rays generate less heat energy near the Earth's surface. *In the winter, however, the sun's weaker rays generate less heat energy near the Earth's surface.*

-wise delete. He has a lot of sense, businesswise. *He has a lot of business sense.* ■ I don't know that that would be very effective, costwise. *I don't know that that would be very cost effective.* ■ What do you look like, facewise? *What does your face look like?* ■ Make sure it is as close as possible to perfect, spelling and grammar wise, as you are able to make it. *Make sure it is as close as possible to perfect spelling and grammar as you are able to make it.*

with a (the) thought of (to) (-ing) *for (-ing); so as to; to.* We assume that they wish to examine their consumption patterns with a thought to increase their savings rate. *We assume that they wish to examine their consumption patterns so as to increase their savings rate.*

with a (the) view of (to) (-ing) *for (-ing); so as to; to.* All categories of terms have been reviewed and in some areas an entirely new approach has been adopted with a view to making the book more useful for the reader. *All categories of terms have been reviewed and in some areas an entirely new approach has been adopted so as to make the book more useful for the reader.*

with few (rare) exception(s) *almost all; almost every; most; nearly all; nearly every.* With few exceptions, federal and state policies are not aimed at upgrading the technology of existing firms. *Almost all feder-*

al and state policies are not aimed at upgrading the technology of existing firms.

with increasing frequency *increasingly; more and more.* Women are dating younger men with increasing frequency. *More and more women are dating younger men.*

without a (any) question (shadow) of a doubt *certainly; doubtless; no doubt; surely; without (a; any) doubt.*

without basis in fact *baseless; groundless; unfounded.* The imputation was totally without basis in fact, and was in no way a fair comment, and was motivated purely by malice. *The imputation was totally groundless, and was in no way a fair comment, and was motivated purely by malice.*

without (a; any) doubt *certainly; doubtless; no doubt; surely.*

without equal *matchless; novel; peerless; singular; special; unequaled; unique; unmatched; unrivaled.*

without exception *all; always; consistently; constantly; every; everybody; everyone; every time; invariably; unfailingly;* delete. Without exception, consumers should be aware that caveat emptor is an understatement in this field. *Consumers should always be aware that caveat emptor is an understatement in this field.*

without foundation *baseless; groundless; unfounded.* Most allegations of men abusing their children are totally without foundation. *Most allegations of men abusing their children are totally unfounded.*

without number *countless; endless; infinite; millions (of); myriad; numberless; untold.*

without peer *matchless; novel; peerless; singular; special; unequaled; unique; unmatched; unrivaled.* He is the entrepreneur extraordinaire; he is without peer. *He is the entrepreneur extraordinaire; he is peerless.*

without (a) question *certainly; doubtless; no doubt; surely.*

with reference to *about; as for; as to; concerning; for; in; of; on; over; regarding; respecting; to; toward; with;* delete. With reference to the stereo, I think she should have put it in storage. *Concerning the stereo, I think she should have put it in storage.* ■ With reference to your article on the World Bank, the Bank has no plans to issue commodity bonds or to make commodity-indexed loans. *As for your article on the World Bank, the Bank has no plans to issue commodity bonds or to make commodity-indexed loans.*

with regard to *about; as for; as to; concerning; for; in; of; on; over; regarding; respecting; to; toward; with;* delete. The evidence is mixed with regard to the existence of an optimal capital structure. *The evidence is mixed on the existence of an optimal capital structure.* ■ With regard to the first rationalization, how can a manager know how far is too far? *As to the first rationalization, how can a manager know how far is too far?*

with relation to *about; as for; as to; concerning; for; in; of; on; over; regarding; respecting; to; toward; with;* delete. There are conflicting reports with relation to the altitude of the Iranian airliner. *There are conflicting reports about the altitude of the Iranian airliner.*

with respect to *about; as for; as to; concerning; for; in; of; on; over; regarding; respecting; to; toward; with;* delete. Something very interesting was said with respect to gender differences. *Something very interesting was said about gender differences.* ■ Each Licensee hereunder shall have the following rights with respect to the Licensed Software. *Each Licensee hereunder shall have the following rights concerning the Licensed Software.* ■ The floodway within communities that have adopted flood-plain regulations is usually subject to strong restrictions with respect to building. *The floodway within communities that have adopted flood-plain regulations is usually subject to strong building restrictions.*

with the exception of (that) *apart from; aside from; barring; besides; but for; except; except for; excepting; excluding; other than; outside of.* With the exception of their paper, these studies found a link between financial structure and industry class. *Except for their paper, these studies found a link between financial structure and industry class.* ■ Overall, bears and other stuffed animals, with the exception of dinosaurs, are out. *Overall, bears and other stuffed animals, other than dinosaurs, are out.*

with the exclusion of (that) *apart from; aside from; barring; besides; but for; except; except for; excepting; excluding; other than; outside of.*

with the intent of -ing (to) *for (-ing); so as to; to.* The Intra-Arterial Cardiac Support System 8000 is being designed with the intent to expand the use of nonsurgical cardiac support systems by providing significantly greater support to the heart than is possible with clinically available non-surgical systems. *The Intra-Arterial Cardiac*

Support System 8000 is being designed to expand the use of non-surgical cardiac support systems by providing significantly greater support to the heart than is possible with clinically available nonsurgical systems.

with the passage of time *at length; eventually; in due time; in the end; in time; later; one day; over the months (years); over time; someday; sometime; ultimately; with time; yet.* The distinctions that now exist between stationary and mobile communications will disappear with the passage of time. *The distinctions that now exist between stationary and mobile communications will ultimately disappear.* ■ He did not improve with the passage of time. *He did not improve over time.*

with the purpose of -ing *for (-ing); so as to; to.* The writer wrote the article with the purpose of teaching American businesspeople about Japanese gifts. *The writer wrote the article to teach American businesspeople about Japanese gifts.*

with the result (that) *so (that).* All graven images were banned by the new Protestant Church, with the result that only a shadow of the Chapel's Medieval glory remains. *All graven images were banned by the new Protestant Church, so that only a shadow of the Chapel's Medieval glory remains.*

worthy of attention *considerable; newsworthy; noteworthy.* To give the media pride of place reinforces the impression that any event is worthy of attention only to the extent that a cameraman is blocking our view. *To give the media pride of place reinforces the impression that any event is noteworthy only to the extent that a cameraman is blocking our view.*

worthy of blame *blamable; blameworthy.*

worthy of commendation *admirable; commendable; praiseworthy.* The fact that her article presents the Palestinian as well as the Israeli viewpoint is worthy of commendation. *The fact that her article presents the Palestinian as well as the Israeli viewpoint is commendable.*

worthy of (my) consideration *considerable; newsworthy; noteworthy.* As a critical reader and listener, you will be able to recognize ideas that are accurate, logical, and worthy of consideration. *As a critical reader and listener, you will be able to recognize ideas that are accurate, logical, and considerable.*

worthy of gratitude (thanks) *thankworthy.*

worthy of note *considerable; newsworthy; noteworthy; outstanding.* One change worthy of note has been made in the condominium form. *One noteworthy change has been made in the condominium form.*

worthy of praise *admirable; commendable; praiseworthy.*

worthy of trust *honest; trustworthy.*

would appear (guess; hope; imagine; seem; submit; suggest; suspect; think) *appear (guess; hope; imagine; seem; submit; suggest; suspect; think).* I would suspect that the greatest gains would be from teaching the existing users to make even better use of current machines. *I suspect that the greatest gains would be from teaching the existing users to make even better use of current machines.* ■ I would hope that's what he meant. *I hope that's what he meant.* ■ I would submit that a number of shaky S&Ls could be salvaged over the next few years. *I submit that a number of shaky S&Ls could be salvaged over the next few years.*

written communication (correspondence) *correspondence; email; letter; memo; note; report.* Written correspondence is answered within a week, and phone calls are returned within 24 hours. *Letters are answered within a week, and phone calls are returned within 24 hours.*

X Y Z

x-ray photograph *x-ray.*

year in (and) year out *annually; always; ceaselessly; consistently; constantly; endlessly; eternally; everlastingly; every year; forever; invariably; never ending; perpetually; routinely; unfailingly; yearly.* Eighty percent of what retailers are ordering are classic lines whose demand is stable year in and year out. *Eighty percent of what retailers are ordering are classic lines whose demand is always stable.*

years (old) delete. The study began in 1981-82 with a statewide survey of a sample of women 45 to 55 years old. *The study began in 1981-82 with a statewide survey of a sample of women 45 to 55.*

years of age delete. I have committed my life to public service since I was 29 years of age. *I have committed my life to public service since I was 29.*

yell and scream *scream; yell.* My wife and I yell and scream at each other about a lot of things, and we have a very healthy marriage. *My wife and I yell at each other about a lot of things, and we have a very healthy marriage.*

you know? delete.

you know what I mean? delete.

you know what I'm saying? delete.

young child (infant) *child (infant); young.*

zero in on *focus on; pinpoint.* It zeroes in on the problem of how expectations are formed — and changed. *It pinpoints the problem of how expectations are formed — and changed.*

zoological *zoologic.*

zoological garden *zoo.*

About the Author
A Q & A with Robert Hartwell Fiske

Q: How did your interest in the English language start?

A: I think there are a number of reasons for my having developed an, atypical perhaps, interest in the English language. I remember when I went to college, I sought to increase my vocabulary by collecting words I wasn't familiar with; I looked them up and wrote down the definitions, and then studied them. That's how I spent many of my college evenings. My interest in language progressed from there I suppose.

I eventually became fascinated by how people spoke. I studied overseas for a couple of years. When I returned, it was the day after Kent State, and I found myself returning to a very unpleasant New York City. I was in a taxi with some rather loud women, and they were remarking about how a young man had just gotten off a plane from Vietnam, and that he said he had "shot himself a number of gooks." These women took great and gleeful pride in this man's having said this. And that astonished me.

But then, I started hearing things I never had heard before, or never was aware of having heard before, and I was thunderstruck by how inane so many people's conversation was. At that point, I started to write plays. The first play I wrote, called *Subject to Approval* [available at www.vocabula.com/vrebooks.htm], is about a person who fears rejection. And *Speaking of Silence*, as the title suggests, is about ineffective communication, noncommunication. I spent a great deal of time just listening to how people spoke. I took notes. I actually hid around corners and behind doors so as to secretly listen to people talking. That's how I developed some skill in writing honest, truthful dialogue.

Q: Why did you write *The Dictionary of Concise Writing*?

A: I think the impetus for *The Dictionary of Concise Writing* was a former girlfriend of mine telling me that she was "in the process of cleaning the house." I thought, how is that different from simply "cleaning the house"? So I think it was that sentence of hers that just lead me to pay more attention to all the needless words and phrases that people use.

Q What was the inspiration for *The Dimwit's Dictionary*?

A I am not sure what the impetus for this book was. I guess I am disturbed by the insincerity of so many people's speech and writing. So little of it seems genuine. And that's because people rely on ready-made formulas to express themselves, and that is hurtful. So I thought that people who rely on these formulas, on perfunctory statements, cannot be telling us much that is truthful about what they are speaking of or even about themselves. And I find that disturbing. I thought if I could help persuade people to take more care in how they speak and write, and perhaps not rely so much on the glib and imitative phrases (and thoughts) people are wont to use, that we might actually be able to achieve something quite wonderful.

Q Can you describe the process of writing *The Dictionary of Concise Writing* and *The Dimwit's Dictionary*?

A I started compiling examples for *Concise Writing* before I had a computer, before perhaps there were PCs. So I did this all with pen and paper. I read newspapers and magazines and anything I could get my hands on and wrote it down whatever examples I found. Only later did I put it on disk.

I am not so much a writer as I am a compiler. While compiling *The Dimwit's Dictionary*, it occurred to me that there were various kinds of dimwitticisms, plebeian sentiments and moribund metaphors and so on. Some of them are easily recognizable; others, perhaps less so.

Q What was most difficult about writing these dictionaries?

A I never had much trouble doing it. Some people might think, oh my God what a laborious undertaking. I never considered it laborious. That's what an interest in something prevents, or shields you from feeling.

Q Who do you think will buy these books?

A Certainly anyone interested in the English language, writers and editors. Students. People who like dictionaries or dictionarylike books. ESL students might also profit from reading these books or at least having them as a reference.

Q The manifesto on *The Vocabula Review* [www.vocabula.com, a website Fiske operates] mentions the devolution of English language. What do you think the causes of this devolution are?

A Carelessness and mimicry are certainly two good reasons. People don't pay much attention to their own words. I think people pay more attention to other's words than they do their own. By which I mean they will imitate what people say, and perhaps not give a lot of attention to what it is they themselves are saying. I think those are factors. And certainly dictionaries haven't been helpful in many ways. A dictionary (today, more than ever) is largely a compilation of how people use the language, not how the language ought to be used. Many of the entries in a dictionary are suspect or actually promote suspect usages and even spellings.

Q What do you think are the best books about writing? Aside from your own, that is?

A Certainly Fowler's *Modern English Usage* is at the top of my list. Bryan Garner's *A Dictionary of Modern American Usage* is also very well done.

INTERVIEW BY EMILY BOEHM